Praise for *The Lord's Words*

Theobald's monograph is the most detailed and thorough investigation of the sayings tradition behind the discourses of Jesus in John. It is indispensable for any discussion of the historical source value of the fourth gospel and the growth of the Johannine tradition. Fortress Press is to be commended for making this important work available in English.

—**Jörg Frey**, professor of New Testament, University of Zurich

This is a major contribution to Johannine scholarship. Focusing on memorable sayings of Jesus, Michael Theobald shows how they form the core of Johannine discourses. He traces a dynamic process in which sayings like those in the Synoptics and those unique to John were transmitted and shaped by a community. He provides a way to understand the interplay between Synoptic and Johannine traditions that moves beyond older paradigms and illuminates the final form of the text. This volume makes his rich and detailed work accessible to English-language readers. Its insights enrich current discussion of the fourth gospel.

—**Craig Koester**, Asher O. and Carrie Nasby Professor Emeritus of New Testament, Luther Seminary

In this updated and translated version of his work, Theobald invites readers to reconsider John's creativity alongside the Gospel's connections to developing early Christianity. As John is grounded in high Christology and an emphasis on the Paraclete's ongoing hermeneutical endeavors, Theobald argues we should not expect this Gospel to simply restate Jesus's words but to reshape them through Spirit-inspired remembrance. While we may not be able to recover all the twists and turns in this process, Theobald takes readers on a journey that adds texture and connection between John's Gospel and the larger second-century Roman world.

—**Alicia D. Myers**, associate professor of New Testament, Baylor University, and author of *Reading John and 1, 2, 3 John* and *The Theology of the Gospel of John*

THE LORD'S WORDS

THE LORD'S WORDS

THE HERMENEUTICS AND THEOLOGY OF MEMORY IN JOHN'S GOSPEL

MICHAEL THEOBALD

Translated by
JACOB N. CERONE

FORTRESS PRESS
Minneapolis

THE LORD'S WORDS
The Hermeneutics and Theology of Memory in John's Gospel

Copyright © 2025 Fortress Press. All rights reserved. Except for brief quotations in critical articles or reviews, no part of this book may be reproduced in any manner without prior written permission from the publisher. Email copyright@fortresspress.com or write to Permissions, Fortress Press, PO Box 1209, Minneapolis, MN 55440-1209.

30 29 28 27 26 25   1 2 3 4 5 6 7 8 9

Library of Congress Control Number: 2024061917 (print)

Cover design: Kris E. Miller

Print ISBN: 979-8-8898-3235-5
ebook ISBN: 979-8-8898-3236-2

CONTENTS

Foreword   vii

1. The Riddle of the Johannine "Revelation Discourses"   1
   Tasks and Questions

Part I
"Words of the Lord" on the Basis of the Synoptics
(Tradition Criticism)

2. "Words of the Lord" with Synoptic Parallels   39
3. "Words of the Lord" as Metatexts of Synoptic Traditions   113

Part II
Specific Johannine "Words of the Lord"

4. The "I Am" Sayings   151
5. Parables and Similar Metaphors   203
6. Wisdom Sayings   247
7. Sayings of Promise and Consolation   283

Part III
The Johannine "Line of Development"

8. Between an Origin in Jesus and Gnostic Dissolution?   329
   The Tradition-Historical Location of the Johannine Saying

Part IV
The Reception of the "Words of the Lord"
in the Gospel of John

9. The Tradition of the Sayings and Their Transformation
   into Dialogue   355

10. The Evangelist's Interpretations of the Words of the Lord   375
    Theological Principles

11. Hermeneutics of "Remembrance"   389

Bibliography   407
Index of Ancient Sources   421
Index of Contemporary Names   435
Index of Subjects   439

FOREWORD

The sayings of Jesus in the Fourth Gospel continue to fascinate with the power of simple imagery, such as light and water, bread and wine, shepherd, door, and house of the Father. When Johannine Jesus declares "I am the way, the truth, and the life," it reveals the love of the Father to all who wish to hear the love of his Father for a world in need of salvation. His words are compelling. They irresistibly draw in listeners and invite reflection.

For a long time, I have been moved by the question of why the Johannine Jesus speaks so differently than the Jesus of the Synoptics—John's Jesus is enigmatic, as his speech comes from a deep understanding as the "only begotten" Son with his Father. Building on earlier studies, particularly those of the English-speaking world, this book offers a new explanatory model for the genesis for the sayings of the Johannine: They are based on traditional "core words" of the Johannine community, which the Evangelist inherits, develops, and reinterprets in his composition.

Some surprising insights emerge from this study. These "core words" derive from older Jesus-traditions and draw upon motifs from ancient sayings of Jesus to reshape them. In the Johannine Jesus, we witness an astonishingly creative engagement with the memory of Jesus. To remember him several decades after his death does not mean simply to repeat his words or document slavishly. Rather, Jesus is remembered by the Johannine community in such a way that his significance for understanding its own faith journey becomes clear.

Memory bridges this chasm of time, bringing Jesus into the present, demonstrating his enduring truth for the listeners of the Gospel under new historical conditions. For us today, who live in a world that is even more different from that of the Galilean itinerant preacher Jesus of Nazareth, this perhaps represents the most significant theological encouragement of the Gospel. Theology must articulate Jesus's message for contemporary life in a new cultural context and horizon—while also, like John, remaining faithful to the Nazarene.

This book is a new version of my 2002 work *Herrenworte im Johannesevangelium*, which drew a significant amount of attention. This version has been revised in multiple respects: The text is shortened while being simultaneously clarified and further developed. The dialogue with the latest Johannine research, especially English-speaking scholarship, has been brought up to date.

For the publication of the English edition, I have many to thank, especially the colleagues who encouraged, stimulated, and enabled this edition: Paul N. Anderson, Newberg/Oregon; Alan Culpepper, Atlanta/Georgia; and Jörg Frey, Zurich/Switzerland, who established the contact with the editor from Fortress Press, Carey Newman. I thank him and Lisa Eaton for their careful support during the publication of the book.

Jacob Cerone, Erlangen/Germany, has given the book a smooth, readable linguistic form after an initial preliminary translation by Dipl. Theol. Michael Neumaier. Jacob Cerone deserves my special thanks, as do the Association of Dioceses of Germany and the University of the Free State Bloemfontein/South Africa for funding the translation.

Tübingen, Germany, October 2024
Michael Theobald

CHAPTER 1

The Riddle of the Johannine "Revelation Discourses"
Tasks and Questions

IN 1977, F. Hahn wrote, "Unfortunately, we still do not have a convincing historical analysis of the Johannine discourses that would be widely recognized and could be drawn upon."[1] Even today this opinion remains valid. A volume of essays published in 1999 in honor of Adolf Jülicher's great book on parables reads:

> In exegetical work on the Gospel of John, the determination of given traditional material in the area of the discourses is not a task that is tackled very often. In contrast to the exegesis of the Synoptics, one tends to exercise restraint here. This is certainly not least for reasons of the history of research. After all, Rudolf Bultmann's great commentary understood the discourses as literary products. The interpretation of the discourses as literary homilies, as Barnabas Lindars sought to justify with broad impact, also aimed in a different direction than the question of individual traditions. Charles Kingsley Barrett significantly influenced English-speaking research to the effect that it was the task of exegetes to interpret only the present form of the Johannine text.[2]

As a decisive reason for this reticence, J. Becker, who penned these lines, is the representative of the widespread image of John as an individual author: "Those who ... are only able to interpret the unique language of the Johannine writings through the thesis of an individual author are hardly interested in analyzing

---

1. Hahn, "Worte," 61; when he speaks of "traditional-historical analysis" (*traditionsgeschichtliche Analyse*), he does not mean a "motif-historical analysis" (*motivgeschichtliche*) but a tradition-critical investigation of the discourses. To get clear the terminology see p. 10–11.

2. J. Becker, "Die Herde des Hirten und die Reben am Weinstock. Ein Versuch zu Joh 10,1–18 und 15,1–17," in *Die Gleichnisreden Jesu 1899–1999. Beiträge zum Dialog mit Adolf Jülicher*, ed. U. Mell, BZNW 103 (Berlin: de Gruyter, 1999), 149–78.

Johannine texts in terms of tradition."[3] In 2001, R. A. Culpepper published an instructive analysis of the Amen-sayings in the Gospel of John. The result of his analysis was that within the twenty-five sayings in this category there are at least thirteen that the Gospel writer took from the tradition of his community.[4] Seven among these twenty-five could have been authentic sayings of Jesus.[5] At the end of his study he writes:

> Further study of the transformations of these traditional sayings, and FE's (= Fourth Evangelist's) interpretation of them through the discourses in FG (= Fourth Gospel), may eventually help us to understand more clearly the role of traditional sayings in the life of the Johannine Community. Are there other formulas or typical constructions that identify groups of sayings that were important in the development of the Johannine discourses? *Eventually a full analysis of the formation and function of the Johannine sayings material will need to be written.*[6]

Our study addresses this desideratum in exegetical research. We do not have to start from scratch. The following notes on the most recent history of the Johannine "revelation discourses" attempt to show which models and perspectives to follow and which not to (1.1). Against this background, we can focus on the present task and on how to bring it to its realization. Therefore, we search for evidence to make our question plausible at a literary level (1.2). We have to explain the criteria of the tradition-historical method and the possibilities of applying it to the special case of the Gospel of John (1.3). This will provide us with the foundation needed to work on the concrete texts.

1.1 The So-Called "Revelation Discourses" in Twentieth-Century Exegesis

We are especially interested in whether and how Jesus traditions influence each analysis of the Johannine material: Instead of the alternative between viewing

---

3. Becker, "Herde," 177–78.

4. John 1:51; 3:3, 5; 6:27; 6:53; 8:51; 10:1–5; 12:24; 13:16; 13:20; 13:21; 13:38; 16:23–24; 21:28.

5. John 3:3; 10:1–5; 12:24; 13:16; 13:20; 13:38; 21:18.

6. R. A. Culpepper, *The Johannine School: An Evaluation of the Johannine-School Hypothesis Based on an Investigation of the Nature of Ancient Schools*, SBL.DS 26 (Society of Biblical Literature, 1975), 262.

The Riddle of the Johannine "Revelation Discourses"   3

the material as "Jesuanic" or the "invention of the evangelist," is there a middle way? Could the discourses we find in the Gospel of John have originated in the Johannine community? Our sketch will show that this is not often the case.

1.1.1 Research on the "Revelation Discourses" Before Bultmann
Between the "Tübinger Kritik" (F. C. Baur), Source Division, and Apologists

The "Johannine question" of the nineteenth century only focused on the following riddle: From the standpoint of the Synoptics, who wrote this strange Gospel? Was it written by John, the son of Zebedee, a follower of Jesus from the very beginning, as church tradition since Irenaeus of Lyon claims? Or was it an "anonymous" work, composed perhaps in the second century, as the "Tübinger Kritik" led by F. C. Baur (1844) argued? According to this view, the discourses of Jesus are only "poetry." True, they contain great beauty and theological depth, but possess no relationship to the historical Jesus. It is easy to imagine how the research after Baur had to wrestle with this statement: This "spiritual gospel" (Clement of Alexandria)—the foundation of later Christology and all the great councils—is "poetry"!?

In the course of his investigation of the Gospel of John, C. H. Weiße (1838) was the first to suggest a distinction between epic and rhetorical material (Erzählung und Reden). He argued that the core of the rhetorical material were the "notes" of John, the son of Zebedee. This explanation functioned as the dominant model (A. Schweizer [1841], H. Delff [1889/90], and H. H. Wendt [1900]) until it was displaced by the literary critics who attempted to free themselves from theological a prioris (J. Wellhausen/E. Schwarz [1907/1908]). Wellhausen (1908) rejected the hypothesis that the Gospel of John was based on the "notes" of an eyewitness and instead postulated the existence of a *Grundschrift*. He attributed all the material that was viewed to be representative of the "Johannine" perspective to this *Grundschrift*.

While the apologists of this view long made use of the methods of separating sources, others persistently resisted the temptation to divide up the "unsewn body of which it (the Gospel) tells us" and which it itself represents (D. F. Strauß [1860]). If, like B. Weiss (1912), one adhered to the "uniformity" of the book and at the same time wanted to save its historical core, then the method of distinguishing between older material on the one hand and its manifold continuation in the Gospel on the other came about automatically. As a result, B. Weiss attributed some sayings or sayings complexes to Jesus himself. Even later, scholars came to see them as "traditions" without reference to B. Weiss. Theologically, he knew the limits of his hypothesis. He wrote, "I consider it a grave and fatal error that the truth of this teaching (i.e., of John) stands and falls with the testimony of such words, since Jesus could not yet be understood before the completion of his work."[7] From an exegetical point of view, however, his concern was not to completely abandon the Fourth Gospel as a possible source for the reconstruction of the historical Jesus, contrary to the trend of the time.

1.1.2 The "Source for the Revelation Discourses" according to Bultmann

Although R. Bultmann's commentary on John, published in fascicles between 1937 and 1941, represents something like the watershed of twentieth-century research on John, the thesis of a "source of the revelation discourses" developed in it received only a small response. Bultmann did not succeed in establishing a new paradigm for explaining the origins of the Johannine discourses. In short, his thesis contains the following: In addition to the source of the signs and a passion narrative like that found in the Synoptics, the evangelist would also have made use of a discourse source translated from Aramaic or Syriac that would have contained so-called revelation discourses as well as basic components of the prologue. *In terms of form*, this source would have been characterized by a rhythmic sentence structure and parallelisms, especially of an antithetical nature, and *in terms of content*, by the adoption of the gnostic redeemer myth. The evangelist would have edited, commented on, and added to this source throughout, with the intention of reinterpreting the redeemer myth from the perspective of the incarnation (John 1:14).

Today, no one speaks of such an alleged source underlying these discourses. However, H. Koester, a student of Bultmann, has retained his teacher's thesis of the existence of a gnostic source and its anti-gnostic interpretation by the evangelist, but has modified it in significant ways. He does not speak of a "source" but of individual "words of the Lord." We must therefore deal with his theory in more detail in 8.2 below. There is, however, one reason Bultmann's model should not simply be shelved: There is no twentieth-century commentator on the Gospel of John who observed the linguistic grain of Jesus's discourses, e.g., the fault lines between key sayings and their accompanying comments, as carefully as the Marburg exegete. These observations can be found in the

---

7. B. Weiss, Das Johannesevangelium als einheitliches Werk. Geschichtlich erklärt, Berlin 1912, XIII + XIV: "The truth of Christianity is not based on individual words of Jesus that can be established with certainty as authentic, which are always subject to criticism, but on the proof of the spirit and power that the apostolic proclamation has in itself."

notes section of his commentary. Bultmann's study clearly shows the necessity of replacing his *literary-critical* paradigm with a *tradition-critical* paradigm. Despite these critiques, Bultmann's linguistic observations continue to be highly beneficial.

1.1.3 Contributions from English-Speaking Research

The crucial question in the research of the Gospel of John therefore comes as no surprise: What does one think about the Gospel of John and the Synoptics?[8] Did the fourth evangelist know them (or at least one or two of them) or did he write his work *independently of them*? And what about the subsequent redaction of the book, which gave it its final form?

P. Gardner-Smith (1938) was one of the first to argue in a small but substantial and highly influential volume for the independence of the Fourth Gospel from the Synoptics. He postulated that (1) the historical value of John's traditions should be assessed more highly than is generally assumed and (2) John's author could well have been a contemporary of Mark.[9] In a little study on the logion in John 13:16/15:20, he defended these insights against their detractors.[10]

In England, C. H. Dodd's magnum opus, *Historical Tradition in the Fourth Gospel* (1963), offers in its second part ("Part II: The Sayings") a broad analysis of the logia tradition in the Gospel of John for the first time. The scholarly context in which Dodd locates his work is decidedly that of "form history."[11] Thus, he is not concerned with "source criticism" but wants to apply the method that was successfully tested after the First World War, especially by M. Dibelius and R. Bultmann on the Synoptic Gospels, to the Fourth Gospel in order to ascertain the "oral tradition" behind it. The *aim* of his book (as the title suggests) was the expansion of possible sources to reconstruct the life and work of the *historical* Jesus. At the very end of his book, Dodd reveals his expectations for a corresponding analysis of the Johannine

---

8. A research-historical overview (twentieth century) can be found in D. M. Smith, *John among the Gospels: The Relationship in Twentieth-Century Research* (Minneapolis, MN: Fortress, 1992); see also the compilation of essays in A. Denaux, ed., *John and the Synoptics*, BEThL 101 (Leuven, Belgium: Peeters, 1992), who documents the latest change in research.

9. P. Gardner-Smith, *St. John and the Synoptic Gospels* (Cambridge University Press, 1938).

10. P. Gardner-Smith, "St. John's Knowledge of Matthew (Mt 10,24–25; Joh 13,16; 15,20)." *JThS.NS* 4 (1953): 31–35.

11. C. H. Dodd, *Historical Tradition in the Fourth Gospel* (Cambridge University Press, 1963), 8: "The early Church was not such a bookish community as it has been represented."

tradition: "a stereoscopic view of the facts, from more than one angle."[12] In Dodd's opinion, this is the only way to understand the historical complexity of the Jesus phenomenon.

The aim and method of the undertaking determine the *unique nature of its realization*. Two aspects should be mentioned: (1) Since Dodd focuses entirely on the survey of the oral tradition, he does not consider the so-called "logia source" (= Q) to be an intermediate variable in the section "Sayings Common to John and the Synoptics."[13] A renewed examination of the material will have to take a different approach here (see part B in this volume). (2) Dodd can only understand the material gleaned from the Gospel of John as a "pre-Johannine tradition,"[14] that is, as testimony to an early and possibly authentic stratum of Jesus's words. *He does not yet recognize the intermediate size of the Johannine community as a hub of old traditions and a melting pot of new ones.*

In general, one can say with Dodd that "it is clear that he (s.c. the evangelist) had at his disposal a body of traditional sayings, parables, and dialogues, handed down separately or in formal sequences, which were drawn from the same general reservoir as those in the Synoptic Gospels, dealing with the same, or kindred, themes."[15] Of particular importance for him in this context is the so-called Johannine logion of the Synoptics, Matthew 11:27 par. Luke 10:22/John 10:15, because it proves the presence of a "purely Johannine theologumenon" in an old stratum of the synoptic tradition. Conversely, the survival of synoptic forms in the Gospel of John with the inclusion of seemingly Johannine content, as in the case of the saying about the grain of wheat (John 12:24), shows that "there seems [to be] no reason to doubt that in such cases John did find in his tradition a direct starting point for the development of his distinctive theology."[16] *Synoptic and Johannine content overlap!*

---

12. Dodd, *Historical Tradition*, 432. But with the following restriction: "In the ensuing investigation we are not asking, in the first place, whether this or that statement in the Fourth Gospel is likely to be historically correct.... No doubt we must, in the long run, take responsibility for our judgements of historical probability.... The first question we are asking is this: Can we in any measure recover and describe a strain of tradition lying behind the Fourth Gospel, distinctive of it, and independent of other strains of tradition known to us?" (p. 8).

13. Dodd, *Historical Tradition*, 337 n. 1. On p. 6 he declares: "I still believe that the 'two-document hypothesis' did, within its limits, offer a solution which is basically capable of standing against attack."

14. Dodd, *Historical Tradition*, 429.

15. Dodd, *Historical Tradition*, 430.

16. Dodd, *Historical Tradition*, 431.

The Riddle of the Johannine "Revelation Discourses" 7

B. Lindars (1972[17]) followed in the footsteps of his compatriot but focused more intensely on the question of how the evangelist used his traditional sources. Like Dodd, Lindars held on to the hypothesis of the independence of the Fourth Gospel at a time when the trends in scholarship were changing. Also like Dodd, he thought that the "sayings" in John originated from Jesus himself. He did not attribute them to an intermediate stage of development within the Johannine communities. Influenced by R. E. Brown, he understood the Johannine discourses as a kind of homily.[18] Since "sayings traditions" are usually found at the beginning of major discourse compositions but are then surpassed by the evangelist's own remarks up to the climax of his discourses, one might think, according to Lindars, that the evangelist proceeded like many preachers who use "their" word of Scripture as "a jumping-off place for what he really wants to say."[19] But then the real intention of the evangelist would be missed. He did not want to implement his high Christology without clearly marking the connection to the ancient Jesus tradition, even if it was clear that its sayings could only implicitly be the basis of the Johannine perspective.

1.1.4 Contributions from German-Speaking Exegesis

Even though Bultmann marks the "watershed" of the research on the Fourth Gospel in the twentieth century, we should not declare him the patron of the project "the words of the Lord in the Gospel of John." Instead, Martin Dibelius, his comrade-in-arms within the so-called "form history school," has to be seen as more important.

In 1927, shortly after his *Geschichte der urchristlichen Literatur*, Dibelius published a case study on the form-historical investigation of John's discourses entitled "Johannes 15,13. Eine Studie zum Traditionsproblem des

---

17. The year of the publication of his commentary (B. Lindars, *The Gospel of John*, NCeB [Grand Rapids: Eerdmans, 1972])! Even more important are his numerous essays on the tradition of "sayings" in the Gospel of John, almost all of which appeared *after* his commentary was published and are now available in a volume edited and introduced by C. M. Tuckett: B. Lindars, *Essays on John*, ed. C. M. Tuckett, SNTA 17 (Leuven, Belgium: Peeters, 1992).

18. B. Lindars, "Traditions Behind the Fourth Gospel" (1977), in *Essays on John*, ed. C. M. Tuckett, SNTA 17 (Leuven: Peeters, 1992), 87–104, here 89: "I am impressed by his (s.c. the evangelist's) skill in building up his material to a climax, often producing a powerful emotional impact. This seems to me to be the quality of a preacher rather than a writer, and it is for this reason that I favour the homiletic view of the composition of the gospel."

19. B. Lindars, "Discourse and Tradition: The Use of the Sayings of Jesus in the Discourses of the Fourth Gospel" (1981), in *Essays on John*, ed. C. M. Tuckett, SNTA 17 (Leuven: Peeters, 1992), 113–129, here 113–14.

Johannes-Evangeliums," which F. Hahn remarked in 1975 had remained "methodologically as good as unevaluated."[20] In this study, Dibelius demonstrates with exemplary argumentation that John 15:13 contains an older "tradition" of "traditional early Christianity." Two reasons for this are decisive for him: (1) the "intrinsic value" of the saying at the center of the "midrash-like digression" of the overarching theme "you are my friends" (vv. 13–16) and (2) the semantic incongruence between it and the rest of the book in terms of ἀγαπή: "The meaning of the word 'love' in the saying 15:13 . . . is not Johannine, but a more popular, general one; the idea of sacrificial death out of love implied here is not emphasized in the Gospel either elsewhere or here."[21] The following sentences written by Dibelius on the intention he associated with his remarks are groundbreaking (and therefore quoted here at length): This is "not initially directed toward the rediscovery of a word of Jesus, whose original application would be closed to us after all, but toward the separation of *tradition* and *composition* in the Gospel of John. For this task is essentially still unresolved. Literary criticism has proven to be an unsuitable way of understanding the Gospel. This can be said with all certainty today, without misjudging the strong impulses of literary criticism. What we need is something else. We need to answer the question to what extent this evangelist is a mediator of traditional, early Christianity and to what extent it is a representative of new ideas. This newness, which we are used to calling 'Johannine,' is often enough the result of a long spiritual development."[22]

The Baltic scholar K. Kundsin is, as far as I know, the first to systematically treat the central revelation discourses of the Fourth Gospel as *"core sayings"* in his book *Charakter und Ursprung der johanneischen Reden*, published in Riga in 1939.[23] "If the synoptic discourses of Jesus form compositions that can easily be broken down into independent components—prophetic sayings, wisdom sayings, parables, etc.—the Johannine discourses are more like uninterrupted chains of statements that only here and there are condensed into more striking individual

---

20. F. Hahn, "Foreword" to Dibelius, *Geschichte*, 11.

21. M. Dibelius, "Joh 15,13. Eine Studie zum Traditionsproblem des Johannes-Evangeliums" (1927), in *Botschaft und Geschichte I* (Tübingen: Mohr, 1953), 204–20, here 217–18 as well as 206.

22. Dibelius, "Joh 15,13," 217–18.

23. K. Kundsin, *Charakter und Ursprung der johanneischen Reden*, Acta Universitatis Latoiensis I/4 (Riga: Latvijas Universitate, 1939), 193, 195, 209, 268, 279, etc. However, the expression "core sayings" can also be found sporadically even earlier, for example in J. Weiß, *Das Urchristentum*, ed. R. Knopf (Göttingen: Vandenhoeck & Ruprecht, 1917), 616: John often takes "the short themes of his speeches from tradition . . . in order to then artfully wrap his own reflections around these core sayings. To use a metaphor: grains of gold from the words of Jesus are hammered out by the evangelist and used to plate his artistic shrine."

The Riddle of the Johannine "Revelation Discourses"   9

sayings, into simple but at the same time sublime 'core sayings.' In places, of course, individual ῥήματα rise like mountain peaks from the plain, but then the saying slides back down into the lowlands of somewhat monotonous meditative reflection."[24] In this distinction, Kundsin sees the solution to the complex puzzle that the Johannine discourses represent: the distinction between their "original words" or "root words,"[25] which he traces back to authentic revelatory experiences,[26] and their "literary garb and adaptation," which must have taken place years later[27] and may also have come from the pen of someone other than the original recipient of the revelation. He focuses especially on the I am–sayings of the Gospel, Jesus's *ego-eimi* sayings, but also other sayings in which the "I" of Jesus plays an important role. Kundin understands this Johannine material as the authentic expression of revelatory experiences, which in turn were to be understood as experiences of the exalted Christ. Kundin intends to prove a genuine Christian foundation for the Johannine core sayings. According to Kundin, the inner Christian parallels to the Johannine "I sayings"—in particular the *ego eimi* material from Revelation—are the key to solving the fundamental question of the origin of the Johannine I-am-sayings.[28]

Of particular importance for our project is the study by the Dane B. Noack (1954), published in German, which tackles Bultmann. His criticism of the hypothesis of the "revelation discourses source" was far-reaching in that it paved the way for a paradigm shift from "literary criticism" to "traditional criticism" as the method appropriate to the Johannine Jesus discourses.[29] He not only collected a whole series of indications that point to the closeness of these sayings to the oral tradition (for example, observations on the repetition of sayings in the book that are never verbatim), but also offered a rough classification of the Johannine logia into two groups: *logia with synoptic parallels and those without synoptic parallels*. In discussing the former, he was particularly interested in proving that their derivation from a written source could not succeed. Even

---

24. Kundsin, *Charakter*, 195.

25. Kundsin, *Charakter*, 228, 265.

26. Kundsin, *Charakter*, has in mind (see John 18:15–16) a "Jerusalemite who had come into contact with Jesus in the last week of the passion, (as the) main guardian of the author (of the Gospel), or, what seems even more likely, the one who had these memories was the recipient of the words of revelation himself" (285–86).

27. Kundsin, *Charakter*, 283.

28. Kundsin, *Charakter*, 268.

29. B. Noack, *Zur johanneischen Tradition. Beiträge zur Kritik an der literarischen Analyse des vierten Evangeliums*, TheolSkr 3 (Kopenhagen: I kommisjon hos Rosenkilde og Bagger, 1954).

if the fourth evangelist had known one or other Synoptic Gospels, one had to reckon with the survival of oral tradition, since this had by no means come to a standstill through the process of its being written down. With regard to the logia without synoptic parallels, he notes characteristic constructions and stylistic features (antitheses; conditional clauses; participle phrases: "everyone doing..."; correlative clauses: "just as—so also"[30]) and also refers to compositional means used by the evangelist to link them (such as "keyword connections"). However, he does not yet advance to an independent examination of the sayings that would merit the name "tradition criticism."

The most comprehensive attempt to survey "sayings material" in the Gospel of John comes from the pen of J. Becker (1979/1981). In his two-volume commentary, he consistently replaced Bultmann's hypothesis of a "revelation discourse source" with the assumption of a logia tradition of the Johannine community. He was able to identify a total of thirty sayings, some with variants. In the commemorative publication for his sixty-fifth birthday, I systematically presented and appreciated his conception, which he himself never developed independently, and added to it additional reflections.[31]

Above we presented some important studies about our topic. In addition to them, there is a wealth of research literature on the individual groups of sayings: on the Son of Man sayings, the Amen-sayings, the *ego eimi* figurative sayings, the Paraclete sayings, the eschatological logia. We will return to these in due course.

1.1.5 How to Work Methodologically on the Gospel of John? A Plea for a Distinction Between Motif Criticism and Tradition Criticism

Two methodological conclusions need to be drawn from the history of research sketched above that will be important for our subsequent work on the text:

Anyone who insists with good reason that the compositions of the Gospel of John have a diachronic prehistory are often satisfied with evidence that merely indicates the use of traditional motifs to prove the existence of "tradition" (*Überlieferung*). What is going on here is a creeping *confusion of motiv criticism*

---

30. Noack, *Zur johanneischen Tradition*, 47–53.

31. M. Theobald, "'Spruchgut' im Johannesevangelium. Bestandsaufnahme und weiterführende Überlegungen zur Konzeption von J. Becker," in *Das Urchristentum in seiner literarischen Geschichte*, FS J. Becker, ed. U. Mell und U. Müller, BZNW 100 (Berlin: de Gruyter, 1999), 335–67. In the "inventory" listed there (337–46) John 10:1–5 is overlooked; on this, see J. Becker, "Die Herde des Hirten und die Reben am Weinstock. Ein Versuch zu Joh 10,1–18 und 15,1–17," in *Die Gleichnisreden Jesu 1899–1999. Beiträge zum Dialog mit Adolf Jülicher*, ed. U. Mell, BZNW 103 (Berlin: de Gruyter, 1999), 149–78.

and tradition criticism (= Überlieferungskritik). This confusion has consequences for the interpretation of the texts that are difficult to assess. For this reason, the following distinction between the two methodological aspects, which must also be distinguished terminologically, is fundamental to the attempt to shed light on the origin of the texts.[32]

(1) By *"tradition"* (in the sense of *Überlieferung*) we mean an originally independent, self-contained and formed *oral unit* that is now written down in a text and functions as the basis of that text. This can be a narrative connection but also a logion or a saying. Only the latter is under discussion here.

Accordingly, *tradition criticism* (= Überlieferungskritik) develops criteria with the help of which one can recognize and reconstruct a unit in a text that was originally handed down as an oral tradition. This also includes, as an accompanying measure, *form criticism and genre criticism*,[33] both of which remain important and remain a desideratum of research on the Gospel of John and the discourses therein.

The term "tradition" is defined differently when it refers to motifs, characteristic features, and themes in a particular text that link it to other texts, insofar as these also draw on the same reservoir of motifs as the text. *Tradition criticism* in this sense develops criteria that can be used to identify predetermined motifs and distinctive features from different, independent texts.[34] The detection of such elements in a particular text, however, is by no means an indication of the existence of a "tradition" in the sense defined above (= Überlieferung). Conversely, evidence from tradition criticism (= Überlieferungskritik) may subsequently find support from tradition (= motif) criticism arguments.

(2) A plausible tradition (= Überlieferung) must not only be examined in terms of form and genre criticism but its *Sitz im Leben* must also be the subject of investigation. This, however, can only be done deductively: The hypothesis of a "Johannine school" provides the framework. Nevertheless, the question remains as to whether individual traditions do not themselves also reveal indications of their origin and use in the Johannine community.

---

32. Lindars, "Traditions," 103, writes: "It has been necessary to distinguish between the influences upon John's mind, which may embrace a wide spectrum, and the actual traditions, whether oral or written, which he has used in writing the gospels. These traditions include narratives, sayings, and an account of the passion."

33. We understand "*form*" to mean the structure of an *individual text*, and "*genre*" to be the *type of text* realized in it, which can only be ascertained after comparison with other related but independent texts.

34. Helpful here is the *Neuer Wettstein*. - While in German the terms *Tradition* (such as motifs etc.) and *Überlieferung* can be distinguished, this is not possible in English; only the one word *tradition* is available.

1.2 The "Core Sayings" of Jesus in the Sayings and Dialogue Compositions of the Gospel of John

A Survey and Initial Evidence

In the following, the first step is to gather evidence for the existence of a distinctive "words of the Lord" tradition in the Johannine community (1.2). Since such evidence does not yet prove the actual existence of a tradition in an individual case, the next step is to clarify the criteria which, in the sense of the preceding methodological considerations (1.1.5), permit a decision to be made on a tradition criticism basis in each individual text (1.3).

It cannot be denied that the Johannine Jesus speaks a different language in comparison to the Synoptic Jesus. He makes grand speeches with astonishing theological density. Less well-known is the fact that even the fourth evangelist is aware that Jesus's strength was not that of a rhetorician who gave extensive speeches but rather that he was able to form concise sayings that have left a lasting impression on people's memories: words of wisdom, prophetic sayings, metaphors, and parables. In this sense, the following analysis seeks to collect evidence that reveals that the structure of the Johannine compositions is based on smaller units. These *core sayings* are unfolded in these lengthier speeches and may originate from the tradition of the Johannine community. These indications include the treatment of Jesus's words as small *quotable* units (1.2.1); their formal evaluation in *correspondence with words of the Holy Scriptures*, that is, the so-called Old Testament (1.2.2); as well as their role as *programmatic sayings* in the "revelation discourses" (1.2.3). Finally, introductory formulas and the frequently encountered affirmation or authorization formula "Very truly, I tell you" in John should also be acknowledged (1.2.4).

1.2.1 Self-Citations of Jesus and Other Repetitions

Even the *oldest evangelist* demonstrates with his three prophecies of passion (Mark 8:31; 9:31; 10:33–34) that the characteristic variants can make sense both compositionally and in the service of its different illumination in different contexts. But as a rule, "his" Jesus does not repeat himself![35]

Matthew is quite different, offering a wealth of repetitions[36] that cannot only be explained by the more extensive tradition material (*Überlieferungsgut*),

---

35. See, however, the reference in 16:7 to 14:28 in the angel's Easter proclamation: "But go, tell his disciples and Peter that he is going ahead of you to Galilee; there you will see him, *just as he told you* (καθὼς εἶπεν ὑμῖν)." See also Mark 14:72!

36. 3:2//4:17//10:7; 3:7//12:34//23:33; 3:10//7:19; 4:23//9:35//10:1; 5:17//7:12//22:40; 5:18//24:34–35; 5:29–30//18:8–9; 5:32//19:9; 6:10b//26:42; 6:15//18:35; 7:17//12:33; 8:12 //13:42//13:50//22:13//24:51//25:30; 9:13//12:6; 9:27–31//20:29–34; 9:32–34//12:22–24;

The Riddle of the Johannine "Revelation Discourses"   13

especially the numerous overlaps his two major sources (Mark and Q = Sayings Source). Furthermore, his own editorial work should be seen as a reason for the repetitions. Therefore, it would be absurd to ascribe the use of repetitions to Matthew's literary incompetence or his commitment to tradition.[37]

Considering each case, it is interesting to ask why Jesus cites a saying of John the Baptist (Matt 3:2 with 12:34 and Matt 3:10b, 23:33 with 7:19) and why it is even put into the disciple's mouth (see Matt 3:2 with 4:17 and 10:7) or why a saying of Jesus appears two or three times or more often—in front of which audience? (See, e.g., Matt 5:29 with 18:8-9, 5:32 with 19:9, 6:15 with 18:35, 9:13 with 12:6-7, and so on). Thereby, the author shows how, by implanting a logion in different contexts, its range of meaning can be expounded. The redactional method of the Gospel writer gives the impression that he had in mind the Jewish rule that one learns by means of repetition.

In comparison to Matthew, Luke uses a different strategy. Distinct from Matthew, who has catechetical and didactic intentions clearly seen in Jesus's five discourses (Matt 5-7; 10; 13; 18; 23-25), Luke works as a historian. For him, chronological sequence, development, and consistency in the progression of the story of Jesus are important, and he therefore avoids repetition.

The Gospel of John also uses the repetition of logia. Jesus not only repeats himself often[38] but repetitions can be marked explicitly as *citations* of earlier spoken words.[39]

Repetitions by Jesus Himself

These can be divided into two groups: (1) regular *self-citations*, in which the reference to the primary text is clear (category I), and (2) *paraphrasing* or *summing*

9:34//10:25; 10:6//15:24; 10:15//11:24; 10:22a//24:9; 10:22b//24:13; 11:14//17:12; 11:15//13:9//13:43; 12:35//13:52; 13:12//25:29; 14:5//21:46; 16:19//18:18; 17:20//21:21; 20:26//23:11; 21:9//23:39; 21:9//21:15; 24:42//25:13; 26:32//28:7/28:10.

37. U. Luz, *Die Jesusgeschichte des Matthäus* (Neukirchen: Neukirchener Verlag, 1993), 14-15: "The evangelist uses such repetitions to indicate what is important to him or to mark the structure of an entire section. Repetitions are therefore literary intention, not inability."

38. In the narrations about the Baptist, too, there are three repetitions of logia: 1:15b/1:30, 1:29b/1:36b, 1:20, 27/3:28 (here marked explicitly as repetition: "You yourselves testify to me that *I said*, 'I am not the Christ, but I have been sent before him'"). See also Noack, *Tradition*, 136-51.

39. See the brief notes in R. Bultmann, *Das Evangelium des Johannes*, 19th ed. (Göttingen: Vandenhoeck & Ruprecht, 1968), 214 n. 7. See also the more extensive list in in R. Schnackenburg, *Das Johannesevangelium*, HThK.NT IV/1-4 (Freiburg: Herder, 1965-1984), 2:71 n. 1, who states, "The self-quotations of the Johannine Jesus pose similar problems to those of the Scriptures, since they are often not literally attested (cf. especially 6:65; 10:25.36; 11:40)."

up repetitions, in which the references can extend beyond the boundaries of a particular quotation or larger text complexes (category II).

The Gospel contains eight explicit *quotations of Jesus himself* (category I):

Citation	Primary text	Citation formula
(1) 3:7 →	3:3	Do not be astonished that I said to you
(2) 6:65 →	6:44[40]	For this reason I have told you
(3) 8:24 →	8:21	I told you
(4) 13:33 →	7:33–34/8:21	as I said to the Jews so now I say to you
(5) 15:20 →	13:16	Remember the word that I said to you
(6) 16:15b →	16:14b	For this reason I said
(7) 16:19c →	16:16	Are you discussing among yourselves what I meant when I said
(8) 18:8 →	18:5	I said to you that...

Characteristic of this group of texts is the use of a *citation formula* formed from λέγειν, which usually precedes the quotation. Only in no. 4 (13:33) is it inserted into the cited logion. In most cases, a saying is repeated shortly after its first occurrence, but in exceptional cases the distance from the primary text can be considerable (as in nos. 4 and 5). The wording of the saying remains intact in the quotation, but this does not rule out significant variants (see 1 and 2).

The technique of changing the addressee, which is used in 4, is also remarkable: A saying that was originally addressed to the "Jews" (7:33–34; 8:21) gains new meaning because it is later promised to the disciples.

We still have to discuss no. 7 in more intensive detail because in 16:16–19 we find a very artificial repetition to which we will not return in the following chapters. It is significant that this passage revolves almost insistently around an enigmatic saying of Jesus[41] and focuses ever more sharply on a single word from this saying—τὸ μικρόν—more and more. Here, the reader recognizes the saying as the actual riddle that needs to be solved:

---

40. On this verse, see my study: M. Theobald, "Gezogen von Gottes Liebe (Joh 6,44f.). Beobachtungen zur Überlieferung eines johanneischen 'Herrenworts,'" in *Schrift und Tradition*, FS J. Ernst, ed. K. Backhaus and F. G. Untergassmair (Paderborn: Schöningh, 1996), 315–41.

41. This passage not only contains a self-citation of Jesus but is also the only time in the Gospel when the disciples cite a word of their master and discuss it.

The Riddle of the Johannine "Revelation Discourses"

16 "A little while (μίκρον),
and you will no longer see me,
and again a little while (μίκρον)
and you will see me."
17 Then some of his disciples said to one another, "What does he
mean by saying to us (ὃ λέγει ἡμῖν),
'A little while (μίκρον)
and you will no longer see me,
and again a little while (μίκρον),
and you will see me'?
And because (καὶ ὅτι)
'I am going to the Father'?"
18 They said, "What does he mean by this when he says (λέγει),
'a little while (τὸ μίκρον)'?
We do not know
what he is talking about (τί λαλεῖ)."
19 Jesus knew that they wanted to ask him, so he said to them, "Are you
discussing among yourselves what I meant when *I said* (ὅτι εἶπον),
'*a little while* (μίκρον)
and you will no longer see me,
and again *a little while* (μίκρον)
and you will see me'?
20 *Very truly, I say to you* (λέγω ὑμῖν) . . ."

At first, the disciples discuss the saying, because they do not understand it.[42] It is worth noting how artfully the author narrates their perplexity. *Three times* he directs them back to Jesus's words with the phrase "what does he mean by saying to us" (v. 17), whereby the gradient of their speech becomes increasingly precipitous, as it were, to eventually end in speechlessness: While the first time they still quote Jesus's entire saying (v. 17) and the second time they leave it at the repetition of his admittedly central term μίκρον. The third time they completely dispense with mentioning a specific element of the saying. The quotation formula remains empty, so to speak: "We do not understand *what he says (at all)*."

The narrator then reports that Jesus knew what was on the disciples' minds. Jesus cites his own saying, again formulated as a question. Thus, we have the enigmatic μίκρον seven times within the span of these few verses. After this passage, it does not occur again. This is surprising because one might expect it to appear in the Amen-saying in verse 20, whose solution is based on the enigmatic μίκρον. But Jesus does not refer to it anymore and leaves it unresolved. Therefore, the readers' suspense intensifies when reading the following verses.

---

42. They not only cite 16:16 with the phrase "I am going to the Father" but also 16:10 (see 16:5).

In the Gospel, we find five *paraphrased* repetitions or repetitions that summarize earlier explanations by Jesus himself (category II):

Repetition	Primary text	Introductory Phrases
(1) 6:36 →	6:26	but I said to you
(2) 10:36 (10:25) →	5:17–18	because I said
(3) 11:40 →	11:4, 25–26	did I not tell you that …
(4) 14:2–3 →	13:33, 36	I would have told you
(5) 14:28(29) →	14:1ff.	because I told you

As with the texts in category I, the repetitions in category II are marked by introductory formulas: an "I have said" together with an ὅτι-*recitativum* is followed by a short and concise statement. However, these clauses are not quotations, as their wording is not found anywhere else in the context, but rather "meta-reflexive" statements that summarize what was previously said from a new point of view on a higher level of speech. We will demonstrate this with two examples:

In 6:36, the Johannine Jesus said at the beginning of a new sequence of his "bread of life discourse":

"But *I said to you that* (εἶπον ὑμῖν ὅτι)
you have seen me and yet do not believe."

A saying with the same meaning, to which Jesus could be referring here, is not found anywhere before 6:36. Nevertheless, it is obvious that the author wants to remind the reader of the beginning of the "bread of life discourse" in 6:26: "They have seen signs and yet do not believe, as their search for Jesus shows for purely external reasons."[43] In any case, a reference that goes beyond the "bread of life discourse" is unlikely. The "analogous summary" of the opening statement in the "bread of life discourse" with the concise tandem "And you have *seen* me and yet do not *believe*," was probably derived from the crowd's reply in 6:30, in which the word pair already played a role, and it also appears again in 6:46/47. "See and believe" is therefore something of a *Leitmotif* in the discourse.

14:2–3 (no. 4) reads as follows:

2a "In my Father's house there are many dwelling places.
 b If it were not so,
 c would I have told you that (εἶπον ὑμῖν ὅτι)
 d *I go* (πορεύομαι) *to prepare a place for you?*

---

43. Schnackenburg, *Johannesevangelium*, 2:71; see also Bultmann, *Johannes*, 173 n. 4: "The relationship of v. 36 to v. 26 seems to me to be certain."

The Riddle of the Johannine "Revelation Discourses"

3a And if I go and prepare a place for you,
 b I will come again and will take you to myself,
 c so that where I am, there you may be also."

Even if the ὅτι in verse 2c is not unanimously handed down,[44] it cannot simply be disposed of by text-critical means in order to smooth out the text.[45] It cannot be denied, considering the other passages, that we have here a *self-citation formula* that is mostly combined with a ὅτι-*recitativum*.[46]

If the textual tradition is also divided here, as in 11:40 and 13:33, this is because copyists liked to consider a ὅτι-*recitativum* superfluous and therefore deleted it.[47] A causal reading of the ὅτι is thus likewise obsolete. There is no getting around the assumption that the evangelist has Jesus quote himself once again, whereby the "quotation" can actually only be contained in the last cola of verse 2 because of the concatenation of verses 2 and 3:[48] "I am going to prepare a place for you." As in 11:40, the citation is formulated as a question that intends to remind the reader insistently of something.[49] As in 11:40, it is difficult to identify a reference text, so that one is inclined to interpret: "If this were not so [namely that there are many dwellings in my Father's house], then I would not have conveyed this one basic thought to you earlier: I am going to *prepare a place for you*." It does not seem advisable to search for the reference text(s) of this retrospective beyond the first Farewell Discourse, as is done by Bultmann.[50] It is

---

44. It is missing in p⁶⁶ c² Q a e f q and in the Byzantine Majority Text.

45. This is what R. E. Brown, *The Gospel According to John* (vol. 2 AncB 29A, New York: Doubleday, 1970, 619–620) does, who translates: "There are many dwelling places in my Father's house; otherwise I would have warned you. I am going off to prepare a place for you." (617).

46. See 6:36; 6:65; 8:24; 11:40; 13:33; 16:15; 18:8. A ὅτι is missing in 3:7; 14:28; 15:20; and 16:19.

47. See B. M. Metzger, *A Textual Commentary on the Greek New Testament* (Stuttgart: Deutsche Bibelgesellschaft, 1994 [= London: United Bible Socities, 1994]), 243.

48. The statement "I am going to prepare a place for you" is repeated in v. 3.

49. See Bultmann, *Johannes*, 464: The remark "is probably intended to emphasize the certainty of what has been said." J. Frey, *Die johanneische Eschatologie II–III*, WUNT 110 and 117 (Tübingen: Mohr Siebeck, 1998 and 2000), 3:136 (referring to Noack, *Tradition*, 148–49): "It cannot be ruled out that the introduction to the quotation was chosen partly because the phrase it introduces was already known to the community of readers as a traditional word of promise"; cf. 1 John 2:18: καθὼς ἠκούσατε.

50. Because of 14:3 ("so that where I am, you also may be") Bultmann has 12:26(32) and 17:24 in mind (he reorders chapter 17 in the text, namely before 13:31); but according to what has been said above, the resumption can only refer to v. 2fin.

more plausible to think of their introduction in 13:33, like R. Schnackenburg.[51] Verse 36 should be added, for it is only here that we encounter the positive aim that is still missing in 13:33 ("where I am going [ὑπάγω], you cannot come"): "Where I am going [ὑπάγω], you cannot follow me now; *but you will follow afterward* (ἀκολουθήσεις δὲ ὕστερον)." Such a promise of discipleship, which is by no means exclusively addressed to Peter but rather *to everyone* by means of him as the spokesperson for the disciples, presupposes precisely what 14:2 explicitly states: namely that Jesus's departure in death serves to prepare a place for the disciples, a home in heaven, to which they too can arrive on the *path of following Jesus*.[52]

Repetitions of the Words of Jesus in the Mouths of Other People

Not only does Jesus himself repeat his words, they are also constantly echoed in the responses of his "dialogue partners." The following table may illustrate this:

Citation	Primary Text	Quoter	Citation Formula
(1) 6:42 ⟶	6:38a	Jews	How can he now say, "...."
(2) 7:36 ⟶	7:33–34	Jews	what does he mean by saying[53]
(3) 8:22 ⟶	8:21	Jews	because he says
(4) 8:33 ⟶	8:31–32	Jews	how can you say that...
(5) 8:52 ⟶	8:51	Jews	and you, what do you say?[54]
(6) 12:34 ⟶	3:14; 12:23/32	crowd	and just as he said that...
(7) 16:17 ⟶	16:16	disciples	what does he mean what he says to us
(8) 19:21 ⟶	18:37	high priest of the Jews	because this one said that...

---

51. Schnackenburg, *Johannesevangelium*, 3:66: "Another point of reference is difficult to find."

52. What happens here is a highly creative reinterpretation of the old idea of discipleship from Jesus according to the sense of a change of place in faith, which is only made possible after Easter by Jesus's departure to the Father and in whose power they are able to re-found their lives here *on earth* as their actual home and dwelling place *in heaven*.

53. p^{66} *pc* add a ὅτι-*recitativum* that is probably not original.

54. p^{75} and 0124 also read ὅτι.

The Riddle of the Johannine "Revelation Discourses"

It is above all the "Jews" who repeat Jesus's words. This is consistently an expression of their helplessness and lack of understanding. The readers of the Gospel learn from this that only believers can unravel and understand Jesus's enigmatic words.

As a rule, a saying of Jesus is repeated in the immediate vicinity of its first occurrence. This is different in no. 6. Toward the end of Jesus's public ministry in Jerusalem, the crowd in 12:34 recalls a saying of Jesus that he did not say in their presence:

"So the crowd answered him,
'We have heard from the Law that (ἠκούσαμεν ἐκ τοῦ νόμου ὅτι)
the Christ remains forever.
How can you say that (πῶς λέγεις σὺ ὅτι[55])
the Son of Man must (δεῖ) *be lifted up?*
Who is this *Son of Man?*"

The reference to Jesus's previous sayings is twofold: on the one hand, Jesus's saying from 12:23, which opens the scene in 12:20–36 as a whole, is in focus: "The hour has come for *the Son of Man to* be glorified." In addition, 12:34 ties in with verse 32: "And I, when I am *lifted up* from the earth, will draw all people to myself." In this respect, the quotation in the mouth of the people does not exceed the episodic framework. On the other hand, it is significant that δεῖ has no point of reference in the aforementioned sayings of Jesus but reminds us all the more emphatically of the "saying about the brazen serpent" in 3:14–15, the second half of which corresponds verbatim with the quotation from 12:34: "so *the Son of Man must be lifted up.*" So we can say that the narrator has deliberately spanned the arc from Jesus's last public appearance to his first confrontation with a representative of Israel, Nicodemus, and has also made this clear by quoting Jesus's words. This places a special emphasis at the beginning and end of his public activity.

Repetition of Jesus's Sayings by the Narrator

Finally, there are a few places where Jesus's sayings are quoted or recalled by the narrator. The following table again provides an overview:

---

55. This ὅτι is missing in p[75] G D 28.700.1424 *pm* vg.

Citation	Primary Text	Citation Formula
(1) 4:44 ⟶	?	For Jesus himself had testified (ἐμαρτύρησεν) that...
(2) 6:41 ⟶	6:38a	because he said...
(3) 13:11b ⟶	13:10c	that is why he said...
(4) 18:6 ⟶	18:4	when Jesus said to them...
(5) 18:9 ⟶	6:39 (10:28–29; 17:12)	this was to fulfill the word that he had spoken...
(6) 18:32 ⟶	12:(32)33	this was to fulfill the word that Jesus had spoken...
(7) 21:23 ⟶	21:22	yet Jesus did not say to him that... but...

When the narrator repeats the words of Jesus, this formal peculiarity belongs to the broad field of *commentary statements* typical of him:[56] He knows the deeper meaning of Jesus's sayings, repeats them, and thus opens them up to the understanding of his readers (as in no. 3). However, the texts listed also contain some special features that are worth noting.

First of all, no. 1 is striking for two reasons: first, μαρτυρεῖν is no longer encountered in a quotation formula before Jesus's sayings.[57] Second, the quotation communicated does not have its point of reference anywhere in the text preceding 4:44, but *outside it*. In other words, the author does not assume that his readers know this saying of Jesus on the basis of his own Gospel but because of its general familiarity, which is grounded in other sources. These sources could be the Synoptic Gospels or the synoptic tradition, but they do not have to be.[58] The verse and its immediate surroundings read:

> After two days he departed for Galilee.
> (For Jesus himself had testified that
> *a prophet has no honor in his hometown*.)

---

56. See, e.g., C. J. Bjerkelund, *Tauta Egeneto. Die Präzisierungssätze im Johannesevangelium*, WUNT II/40 (Tübingen: Mohr Siebeck, 1987).

57. But see 1:15, 32, 34 and 1:19; 5:33. Μαρτυρεῖν + ὅτι occurs seven times in the Corpus Johanneum: 1:32, 34; 3:28; 4:39; 7:7; 12:17.

58. It should be noted that the saying is also found in POxy I 6 and Gos. Thom. (Log. 31): "A prophet is not approved in his hometown (Gos. Thom.: his village); a physician does not heal those who know him." The proverb is also found in secular literature: Dio Chrysostom 30 (47).6; Philostratus, *Vit. Ap.* 1.354.12; Epictetus, *Diss.* 3.16.11; in the OT: Jer 11: 21; 12:6; cf. 9:38, and also as a general topos in 2 Chr 36:16.

The Riddle of the Johannine "Revelation Discourses"

So when he came to Galilee,
the Galileans welcomed him,
having seen all
that he had done in Jerusalem at the feast.
For they too had gone to the feast (4:43–45).

The fact that the quotation not only points *out of the book*, but is also *relatively isolated* in the immediate context—the rejection of Jesus in his homeland, which can actually only mean Galilee, is only finally revealed in John 6, although 4:48 already casts a dark shadow[59]—explains why this verse, which is difficult to integrate, is repeatedly classified as a "marginal note," "which a reader from the Johannine community wrote in the margin of the text at an early stage and which was then incorporated into the text when John was copied."[60] This question, however, does not need to be decided here.

Also noteworthy are nos. 5 and 6: In both passages, a quotation introduction formula is used that is otherwise only known from quotations from Holy Scripture: "So that the word he spoke might be *fulfilled*." The analogy that emerges here in dealing with the words of Jesus and the words of Scripture is very important. We will, therefore, address this below.

"What does he mean by saying . . . ?" (7:36)

Let us note three insights from the observations made so far:

(1) The astonishingly long list of quotations and explicit repetitions of Jesus's words proves that even the Gospel of John is aware of the stylistically and formally peculiar character of the genuine Jesus tradition, despite the very different manner "his" Jesus speaks compared to that of the Synoptics: This is first and foremost a saying tradition, containing small *quotable* units that invite reflection and repetition and are memorized.

(2) Often enough, the repetition of a saying of Jesus in the form of a quotation (in whosever mouth) has the function of drawing the readers and listeners of the book into the process of reflection on the meaning of Jesus's words. Their formal repetition forces us to think about them. If it is the Jews who repeat a saying of Jesus as a sign of their lack of understanding ("how can he now say . . . ?" [6:42]), then the *enigmatic nature of* Jesus's words, which not everyone can

---

59. Verse 44 acts "almost as a heading . . . which stands over the whole work of Jesus in Galilee," whose ultimate lack of success it anticipates in the form of a "sweeping judgment"; so Blank, *Johannes*, Ia:322.

60. See Becker, *Johannes*, 1:222.

understand, comes to light because of their reaction. Only those readers of the book who already believe are able to grasp their deeper meaning.

(3) It is remarkable how, in the process of quoting or paraphrasing, a saying sometimes gives birth to a new saying, as it were. The generally imprecise way of quoting is by no means a sign of carelessness in dealing with texts, nor is it merely due to the joy of variations, but reveals a creative understanding of tradition: The quotation itself has a status of its own in relation to the original wording of the quotation and thus testifies to a dynamic of deeper and better understanding, which is documented in the *re-statement* of the saying. Reason enough for us to take a closer look at the postulate of an idiosyncratic Johannine "sayings of the Lord" tradition in the individual texts!

1.2.2 Citation of Scripture and "Words of the Lord" The Two Authorities in the Gospel of John

We have already drawn attention to the formal equal treatment of the citation of Old Testament Scripture and "the words of the Lord" above. This equal treatment is not only revealing with regard to the theological status of the "words of the Lord," which are already equated with sayings from the canonical Scriptures, indeed are superior to them, but also confirms once again the presumed Johannine knowledge of them as small quotable units.

Very instructive is the manner of citation which we discussed above. We find it within the canonical Gospels only in the Gospel of John. It can probably be explained by the analogy to the citations of Scripture. This assumption can be based on the two citation formulas in 18:9 and 18:32, which, as the following overview shows, are modeled on the Old Testament fulfillment citations in the second half of the Gospel. The proximity to 12:38 and 15:25 is particularly striking.

Words of the Lord	18:9	*to fulfill the word that he had spoken . . .*
	18:32	*this was to fulfill the word of Jesus that he had said* when he indicated the kind of death he was to die
Words of scripture	12:38	*this was to fulfill the word spoken by the prophet Isaiah*
	13:18	*to fulfill the scripture*
	15:25	*to fulfill the word* that is written in their law . . .
	17:12	*to fulfill the scripture*
	19:24	*to fulfill what the scripture says*
	19:36	*to fulfill the scripture*

The Riddle of the Johannine "Revelation Discourses" 23

Various passages are possible reference texts for 18:9 (6:39; 10:28–29; 17:12). The situation for 18:32, however, is clear: This narrator's commentary unquestionably reminds readers of 12:32–33.

A formally equivalent treatment of Old Testament citations and "words of the Lord" can be discovered elsewhere in the book.[61]

Three texts are then noteworthy in which a saying from Scripture and a saying of Jesus are carefully juxtaposed and are even contradictory to one another. The narrative of the so called "temple cleansing" consists of two parts in the Johannine version (2:14–17/18–22) that, with a reference to Scripture and the so-called temple logion ("Tear down this temple and in three days I will raise it up again"), have two comparable points:

> 2:17: "His disciples <u>remembered</u> (ἐμνήσθησαν),
> that it was written,
> 'Zeal for your house will consume (καταφάγεται) me.'"
> 2:22: "After he was raised from the dead,
> his disciples <u>remembered</u> (ἐμνήσθησαν)
> that he had said this (ὅτι τοῦτο ἔλεγεν);
> and they believed *the scripture* (τῇ γραφῇ)
> and *the word* (τῷ λόγῳ)
> that Jesus had spoken."

Formally speaking, the saying from Scripture (Ps 69:10) and the saying of Jesus stand side by side here as two authorities. According to verse 22, both also appear to be equally important points of reference for the post-Easter faith of the disciples. And yet the saying of Jesus clearly takes priority. For the saying of Scripture as an announcement of Jesus's death only reveals its meaning in the light of Jesus's saying, which speaks of his death and resurrection according to the image of the destruction and rebuilding of the temple. Since this saying presents Jesus himself in incredible Christological fashion as the true temple of God, that is, as the only "place" where God can still be experienced now, in retrospect, in the light of this word, one also recognizes that the "*zeal for God's house*" in the psalm can only be spoken of in a figurative sense as a zeal for God's holiness (cf. also 4:21, 23–24). *The words of Jesus therefore provide the hermeneutical key for the only appropriate understanding of the words of the psalm!*

A fundamental statement about the inner link between the saying of Scripture and saying of Jesus as well as about the referential character can be found in 5:45–47:

> Do not think
> that I will accuse you before the Father;

---

61. See 12:34, 15:20/25.

your accuser is Moses,
on whom you have set your hope.
If you believed Moses,
you would believe me,
for he wrote about me.
But if you do not believe what *he wrote*
how will you believe *what I say*?

The extraordinary dignity of Jesus's words is, of course, not only expressed in the fact that the Johannine community treats them as if they were words of Holy Scripture but in that the Gospel applies to them what otherwise only applies to God's instructions in the Torah: They are to be "heard" (5:24; 12:47),[62] "guarded" (12:47), and "kept" (8:31, 51–52; 14:23–24; 15:20; 17:6)[63] because they have the life in them.

When the Johannine community begins to treat the "words of the Lord" in its Gospel as words of Holy Scripture and even places them above Scripture, this must be seen historically in the light of the process that soon began to emerge in early Christian literature, in the course of which Christian writings were given equal status as the word of God alongside the so-called Old Testament and which ultimately led to the two-part Christian canon. The first stage of this generally complex process certainly includes the citation of the "words of the Lord" as authoritative, which can be clearly observed in the 2 Clement (130–150 CE).[64] The fact that a decisive starting point for the development of Scripture in the New Testament lies in the "words of the Lord" can already be seen in the Gospel of John, which emphasizes the "words of the Lord" as a quotable authority.[65]

---

62. See Exod 33:4, Num 12:6; Ezek 13:2, 16:35, etc.

63. See Exod 12:24, Deut 13:1, Ps 119:17, 57, 101, etc.

64. See 2:4; 3:2; 4:2; 6:1; 8:5; 9:11—see also 1 Tim 5:18, where a citation of Scripture (Deut 25:4) is combined with a "word of the Lord" (Matt 10:10 par. [?]), also 1 Clem 13:1-3.

65. In addition, there is the observation that the Gospel as a whole "through its claim to be a written saying (20:31)" also places itself "close to the circle of writings recognized as sacred" (A. Obermann, Die christologische Erfüllung der Schrift im Johannesevangelium. WUNT 2/83, Tübingen: Mohr Siebeck, 1996, 422, who on p. 420 n. 78 refers to A. Schlatter, *Der Evangelist Johannes. Wie er spricht, denkt und glaubt. Ein Kommentar zum vierten Evangelium* [Stuttgart: Calwer, 1975], 363 on 20:31: "γέγραπται transfers the same idea, which then adheres to the formula when it is used of the Old Testament saying, to the Gospel as well. Its written version gives it timeless validity for the whole community."). But 1:1–5 is also of great importance here, insofar as these verses, in their function as the beginning of the book, constitute the Gospel as a "metatext" to Holy Scripture through their reference to the beginning of the Bible (Gen 1:1ff.), which provides the right key to its interpretation (see M. Theobald, *Die Fleischwerdung*

1.2.3 The Prominent Position of the "Words of the Lord" in the Discourse and Dialogue Compositions of the Gospel of John

Our evidence also includes the observation that the words of Jesus—sayings that rest in themselves in terms of form and content—often have a prominent position in the "revelation discourses." The author treats them like programmatical sayings that depict "his" Jesus and therefore are repeated by him (see 2.1.2) or mark the topic of the following sequences. C. H. Dodd observes this and comments on it concisely: "A dialogue commonly opens with an oracular utterance by Jesus."[66]

Here are some examples that we will develop in more detail in subsequent chapters:

The saying about *entering the kingdom of God* (3:3/5) is Jesus's seemingly unmediated response to the compliments that Nicodemus pays him at night but actually marks the important point at which the perspective of those who are committed believers in Jesus differs from the outwardly permanent position of the benevolent observer such as Nicodemus. Jesus provides different perspectives on this saying and outlines its soteriological core.

The key saying in the great "bread of life discourse" of 6:26–58 is not Psalm 78:24[67] quoted by the crowd in verse 31b but *Jesus's ego-eimi statement* in 6:35. This statement determines the body of the discourse, which is repeatedly directed back to him. This statement determines the body of the discourse. The word "to have faith" (πιστεύειν) 6:29 is also decisive from the opening of the dialogue, which is repeatedly encountered as a leitmotif at the junction points of the discourse (vv. 30, 35, 40, 47, 64, 69) and is also taken up and interpreted by the central first-person *eimi* saying with its metaphor of "coming to Jesus."

The *ego-eimi saying* in 8:12 ("I am the light of the world...") may seem to stand out from its surroundings like a sore thumb, but it subsequently finds a strong echo if one only thinks of the great story of the healing of the man born

---

des Logos. Studien zum Verhältnis des Johannesprologs zum Corpus des Evangeliums und zu 1 Joh., NtA NF 20 [Münster: Aschaffendorf Verlag, 1988], 229).

66. Dodd, *Tradition*, 317–18. See also Lindars, *John*, 48; F. Hahn, "Die Worte vom lebendigen Wasser im Johannesevangelium. Eigenart und Vorgeschichte von Joh 4,10.13f.; 6,35; 7,37–39," in *God's Christ and His People*, FS N.A. Dahl, ed. J. Jervell and W. A. Meeks (Oslo: Universitetsforlaget, 1977), 51–70, here 61ff.; F. Hahn, "Die Hirtenrede in Joh 10," in *Theologia Crucis—signum crucis*, FS E. Dinkler (Tübingen: Mohr, 1979), 185–200, here 191, 198.

67. Against P. Borgen, *Bread from Heaven. An Exegetical Study of the Concept of Manna in the Gospel of John and the Writings of Philo*, NT.S 10 (Leiden: Brill, 1965), who understands 6:31–58 as a homily on this passage of Scripture. For a refutation of this thesis, see M. Theobald, "Schriftzitate im 'Lebensbrot'-Dialog Jesu (Joh 6). Ein Paradigma für den Schriftgebrauch des vierten Evangelisten," in *The Scriptures in the Gospels*, ed. C. M. Tuckett, BETL 131 (Leuven: Peeters 1997), 327–366, here 331–345.

blind in chapter 9 as a narrative "commentary text" on this Christological saying about the light.

The logion of the "*truth that sets you free*" (8:31–32) is at the head of Jesus's offensively sharp confrontation with the Jews who have (apparently) come to believe in him 8:31–59.

The saying about the "*many mansions in my Father's house*" (14:2–3) is the programmatic saying in the first Farewell Discourse in chapter 14 and is interpreted through it.

We could go on. Special mention should also be made of 1:51, Jesus's first Amen-Amen-saying and at the same time his first ever self-revelation in the Gospel. This saying of the Son of Man stands like a thematic statement over the entire work that will keep its promise—to see the heavens open above Jesus—in the narrative of his work and death as a whole.

1.2.4 Introductory Applications and Formulas

Two additional series of observations strengthen the hypothesis of a Johannine tradition of the "words of the Lord" as the core of Jesus's "revelation discourses":

(1) As a rule, the narrator fits the words of Jesus precisely into the communicative situations of his dialogues through his introductory formulas: "Jesus answered and said *to them*" is repeatedly used in the "bread of life discourse."[68] However, there are also examples of him not naming a specific addressee. As a result, the words of Jesus that are thus introduced in a vague manner experience a certain isolation in context: it stands out from its surroundings and gives the impression that Jesus says it over the heads of his dialogue partners within the scene. The purpose of such literary artifice can vary depending on the context.[69] Sometimes it emphasizes the relevance of Jesus's words beyond their fictional embedding in the narrative context and directly affect the book's readership. We present some examples here:

Three sayings in the pericope of the Feast of Booths in Jerusalem (7:10–52), which are Jesus's only remarks in this lengthy passage, stand out from context like islands: 7:28–29, 7:33–34, and 7:37–38. The first two are salutations (7:28:

---

68. See 6:26, 29, 43, but also 32, 35, 61, 70. On the introductory formulas with μαρτυρεῖν see Dibelius, "Studie," 207–208: four times (1:15, 32, 4:44, 13:21) μαρτυρεῖν introduces a saying in the Fourth Gospel, "and each time it is probably a logion that was not first formulated by the evangelist" (208).

69. It must be admitted that there does not always have to be a conscious literary intention. See, e.g., 8:19, 49, 54. The situation is perhaps different in the introductory formulas to passages where Jesus is judged by Pilate (18:34, 36, 37b), which consistently (19:11 is text-critically uncertain) avoid the dative case of the addressee: "Jesus said" is constantly used here and finally: "He did not give him (s.c. Pilate) an answer" (19:9).

"*you* know me, and you know where I am from...."; 7:33; "I will be *with you* a little while longer..."), whereas the third saying ("if *anyone* thirsts...") is deliberately formulated openly, which is then made more precise by the commentator in 7:39 by explicitly applying this saying to those who believe after Easter. The saying's lack of context, which refers to the time of the readers, fits in with the narrator's introduction without an addressee: "On the last day of the festival, the great day, while Jesus was standing there, he cried out (ἔκραξεν λέγων)." The introductions to the two preceding sayings are similarly without addressees.[70] In both cases, their isolation is underlined by a lack of or hostile reaction from the listeners, whether this is because their violence toward him is noted[71] or because they do not even address Jesus with their response, but rather begin to whisper among themselves.[72] Finally, the situational superiority of 7:33–34 is expressed, as already observed above,[73] through the transposition of the saying into other contexts.

Also noteworthy is the only introductory formula to the *collection of verses spanning 12:44b–50*. It gives the impression of an addendum since Jesus's public ministry has already come to an end with 12:36b and is followed only by a longer narrative commentary in 12:37–43. The addendum, which is thus without a context, corresponds to the unaddressed introductory formula in verse 44a: "But Jesus cried out and said...". It signals that Jesus's subsequent words are addressed directly to the readers of the book.

A final example comes from 13:31, 32, the *opening verses of the first Farewell Discourse*. It corresponds to its character as a poetic declaration that introduces the mystery of Jesus's death as his glorification when the evangelist, through his use of the present tense and unnamed addressees ("when he [s.c. Judas] had gone out, *Jesus said*..."), places the saying, as it were, freely in the space that is then occupied by the community that eventual reads this work.

(2) The fact that twenty-five sayings of the Gospel contain the obviously old introductory formula "*Very truly, I tell you*" because it is found in various Synoptic branches of tradition also has significant value for a Johannine "sayings of the Lord" tradition. Some scholars even go so far as to classify all corresponding Johannine sayings as traditions.[74] J. Jeremias also assumes that the

---

70. 7:28: "Then Jesus cried out as he was teaching in the temple..."; 7:33: "Jesus then said...."

71. 7:30: "Then they tried to arrest him...."

72. 7:35: "The Jews said to one another, "Where does this man intend to go that we will not find him? Does he intend to go to the Dispersion among the Greeks and teach the Greeks?"

73. See 14!

74. See Lindars, *John*, 48 and K. Berger, *Die Amen-Worte Jesu. Eine Untersuchung zum Problem der Legitimation in apokalyptischer Rede*, BZNW 39 (Berlin: de Gruyter, 1970).

comparatively high number of these sayings in John is due to the use of the Amen-formula "by prophets who appeared in the name of the exalted Lord."[75] It is probably appropriate to be cautious about making a blanket judgment. Each saying requires a separate critical analysis of the tradition. Nevertheless, the fact that the Gospel makes extensive use of this introductory formula is already significant: The formula, which, as in the Synoptics, is only found in the mouth of Jesus without exception and is therefore—at least in the opinion of the evangelists—a characteristic of Jesus's own authorized speech, can be regarded as a link between the Johannine and Synoptic Christ. In addition, J. Jeremias famously held the view that "Amen" in this introductory formula without response could hardly be explained in any other way than that we are actually dealing with "a linguistic creation of Jesus" because "not a single piece of evidence for this new use of language has been found in the entire literature of Palestinian and Hellenistic Judaism and the early church."[76] The latter is still true, especially since the alleged counterevidence of Hebrew, Aramaic, and Greek provenance provided in recent times has not stood up to scrutiny. If one understands the Amen-sayings in the way Jeremias does, this does not mean "that every single one of Jesus's sixty-two different Amen-sayings is authentic, but the phenomenon itself is."[77] At least one saying of the Markan tradition, the so-called eschatological outlook in Mark 14:25, is seen mostly as authentic. But a number of other sayings can also lay claim to this status. If we want to ascertain the function of the opening formula for the subsequent sayings of Jesus, we can agree with Jeremias on three things[78]:

(a) As a rule, the Amen-sayings contain *discipleship instruction* ("Truly, I tell *you*") of an apocalyptic nature, "whereby the words of salvation and doom are more or less balanced."

(b) According to various indications, the *amen* retains its character as a *formula of affirmation.*[79] "As an expression of affirmation, *amen* was suitable to serve as a substitute for oath formulas, the use of which in everyday speech

---

75. J. Jeremias, Art. Amen, *TRE* II:386–391, 389.

76. J. Jeremias, "Kennzeichen der ipsissima vox Jesu," in *Abba. Studien zur neutestamentlichen Theologie und Zeitgeschichte* (Göttingen: Vandenhoeck & Ruprecht, 1966), 145–52, here 148–49: "While according to established Jewish usage the word *amen* is used to affirm, confirm, and appropriate the words of another, in the tradition of the Jesus logia the word is used *without exception* to introduce and confirm one's own speech."

77. Jeremias, Art. Amen, *TRE* II:389.

78. Jeremias, Art. Amen, *TRE* II:389. The following quotes can be found there.

79. Joachim Jeremias refers, among other things, to the solemn oath in Mark 8:12 as well as "the frequent connection of Amen with the oath-like assurance formula οὐ μή: Mark 9:1, 41; 10:15; 13:30; 14:25; Matt 5:18, 26; 10:23; 18:3; 24:2; Luke 18:17, 29–30; John 8:51; 13:38.

Jesus fought against as an abuse of the divine name according to Matt 5:33–37; 23:16–22."

(c) In the prophetic speech of the Old Testament, the opening formula corresponds to the messenger formula "Thus says the Lord." This is why one can recognize in the Amen formula "an expression of Jesus's authority that avoids the name of God."

In the Gospel of John, the authoritative character of Jesus's discourse, which is based on his authority as the eschatological messenger of God, is probably at the forefront of the use of the Amen formula. However, the Christology of the messenger only determines the Johannine framework of reception. For those sayings that were actually given to the evangelist as a tradition, the model of the messenger cannot be postulated in this way, that is, the theocentricity associated with it cannot be read into them. It is therefore probably necessary to distinguish between the evangelist's understanding of the formula and that of the given tradition.[80] Jeremias's observes that the Johannine doubling of the Amen[81] has a liturgical function and "reveals a formulaic use in the early church tradition."[82] This can possibly be interpreted as an indication of the *Sitz im Leben* of these sayings.[83]

There are at least two reasons that prevent us from declaring the Johannine sayings that open with the Amen formula to be a predetermined tradition without closer examination of each individual case:

(a) It is very likely that the opening phrase "Very truly, I tell you" in John also has a *macro-contextual structuring function*. It can be seen that various Amen-sayings open larger discourses by Jesus: 5:19 (speech about the Son's authority to give life and judge); 6:26 (bread of life discourse); 10:1 (Good Shepherd discourse). But Amen-sayings can also be important for the perception of the internal structures of the discourses. This is the case, for example, with the bread of life discourse (6:26, 32, 47, 53) and the Good Shepherd discourse, in which both halves (the figurative speech in 10:1–6 and

---

80. In case of Christology of God's messenger, see p. 380–383.

81. Also in Num 5:22; Neh 8:6; Pss 41:14; 72:19; 89:53; Ezra 9:47 B (LXX); 1QS 1:20; 2:10, 18; LAB 22:6; 26:5. Further evidence from Jewish prayers, inscriptions, Talmud, but also from magical texts, see J. Jeremias, "Review of Goodenough, *Jewish Symbols*," *ThLZ* 83 (1958): 504.

82. Jeremias, "Kennzeichen," 149–50. See already Noack, *Tradition*, 65–66; Schnackenburg, *Johannesevangelium*, 1:318: "the doubling typical of the Gospel of John ... will derive from liturgical usage."

83. See also above n. 75 on Jeremias's reference above to the role of the early Christian prophets, who would have used the Amen formula to refer to the authority of the exalted Lord, in whose name they proclaimed the saying.

its interpretation in 10:7–18) open with an Amen-saying. Of course, there are also examples of Amen-sayings without a macro-contextual structuring function.[84] As far as the first of these is concerned, it must be assumed that the evangelist formed them or at least placed the opening formula himself as a macro-contextual signal. This is clear, for example, where a saying is so interwoven into its macro-context that the assumption of its independent transmission seems impossible.

(b) The large number of Amen-sayings in the Gospel of John (at least in certain layers or sections of the book) is connected with their affinity to Johannine Christology. Therefore, neither the formation of such sayings nor the independent use of the formula by the evangelist can be ruled out in general. Criteria must be developed that do or do not permit the attribution of an Amen-saying to pre-Johannine tradition. Apart from the criteria of tradition criticism (which are also relevant for other sayings and which we will deal with in the next section), in the case the Amen-sayings we are specifically concerned with the question of whether, in individual cases, there is a correspondence between the Amen-formula and the subsequent saying in terms of form and content, which can be proven to be traditional by comparison with the synoptic Amen-sayings. This should then be regarded as tradition criticism evidence.[85]

1.3 "The Words of the Lord" in a New Way
Tasks and Concrete Implementation of the Project

What is the aim of this book? What do we mean by the "words of the Lord"? How can we carry out the task of "tradition-criticism," (= Überlieferungskritik) that is, what criteria are there to be able to identify given "sayings"?

1.3.1 The Task

The outline of the history of research should already have made it clear that the first aim of this book *cannot* be to provide a Johannine contribution to the so-called *quest of the historical Jesus*. Rather, it is first and foremost about *a better*

---

84. As far as the first of these is concerned, it must be assumed that the evangelist formed them or at least placed the opening formula himself as a macro-contextual signal. This is clear, for example, where a saying is so interwoven into its macro-context that the assumption of its independent transmission seems impossible.

85. An example of this is the combination of the Amen-formula with the promise articulated as a denial in John 8:51, which is also often quoted in the synoptic sayings (see above at n. 79). This points to the fact both elements originally belonged together in the Johannine saying.

The Riddle of the Johannine "Revelation Discourses"   31

understanding of Johannine thought. More specifically, I am looking at the characteristics of the compositions of the Johannine discourses and dialogues. B. Lindars describes it with the image of a "spiral staircase": "John's method of argument is like a spiral staircase, continually returning to its point of entry, but always a stage higher until the top is reached."[86]

Such images are often found in the literature on the Gospel of John. But we want to know more precisely: What methods does he use to compose his discourses (ch. 10)? What is the hermeneutic behind them (ch. 12)?

When we turn to the analysis of the "core sayings" themselves—and this will make up a large part of our task (ch. 3 to 8)—we hope to gain insight into the religious-historical factors that played a role in the development of Christology in the "Johannine school." The Johannine "words of the Lord" are witnesses to this Christology. Of course, this undertaking does not exclude the possibility that we may also gain insights into the connections between the oldest Johannine tradition and the synoptic tradition (cf. ch. 4: John's "Words of the Lord" as *metatexts* to synoptic traditions?) or to recognize points of connection of the Johannine tradition with the historical Jesus. We can also recognize links between the Johannine tradition and the historical Jesus. However, this is not the immediate aim of our investigation.

1.3.2 The Term "The Words of the Lord"

Τὰ λόγα τοῦ θεοῦ or τὰ κυριακὰ λόγια—"words of the Lord": Since the time of Papias of Hierapolis, this has been the common term in early Christian literature for orally transmitted sayings of Jesus or rather sayings that were recorded in the Gospels—but also for the message of Jesus as a whole, for his words and his deeds.[87] However, in the first century, people spoke of the "λόγοι (or ῥήματα) of the Lord" and primarily had in mind the sayings of Jesus.[88] If these were consistently referred to as "words of the *Lord*" (not of Jesus),[89] then this was associated with the conviction of their superior authority. Paul had already introduced a word of Jesus in 1 Corinthians 7:10 (cf. v. 12) with reference to the authority of the "Lord." There was no reference to a possible *post-Easter* origin of a word designated in this way, which would then have to be assumed to have been spoken

---

86. Lindars, *Traditions*, 101.

87. E.g., in Polycarp, *Phil.* 7:1; Papias: Eusebius, *Hist. eccl.* 3.39:1.15–16; Irenaeus, *Haer.* 1.praef.1; 1.8.1; Clement of Alexandria, *Quis div.* 3:1; *Paed.* 2.10; 113.3 (see G. Kittel, Art. λόγιον, *ThWNT* 4:143–145).

88. See J. M. Robinson, "History of Q Research," in *The Critical Edition of Q*, ed. P. Hoffmann and J. S. Kloppenborg (Leuven: Peeters, 2000). XIX–LXXI, here XXV.

89. See Luke 22:61; Acts 11:16, 20:35; 1 Tim 6:3 as well as the other references discussed in 11.1!

(and formed) by an early Christian prophet in the name of the exalted κύριος. It is therefore all the more striking that it does not appear anywhere in the Gospel of John. John 18:32, for example, says: "so that the word of *Jesus* (ὁ λόγος τοῦ Ἰησοῦ) might be fulfilled."[90] Is there a reason for this linguistic finding? We will return to this question at the very end of our study (in 11.1 and 11.2). Although the Gospel of John does not use the term "words of the Lord" anywhere in the work, the idea designated by the phrase is, as we have already seen, omnipresent in the Gospel.

1.3.3 The Criteria of the Method of Tradition Criticism

Only "words of the Lord" that were originally handed down in isolation, not words that served as punchlines in Jesus's stories, will be the subject of discussion here. What criteria do we have for distilling them from the compositions of discourse and dialogue within the Gospel of John? How can we classify these criteria? How should they be weighted?

(1) *Multiple attestation within and outside the New Testament*: A tradition is also attested in other literary works, irrespective of the present context. This criterion should be conclusive, *provided that* the other writing in which the presumed tradition has *no direct* literary reference to the Gospel of John or, conversely, does not refer to that writing. But this is precisely where the difficulties in applying the criterion lie. Three constellations need to be considered:

(a) *John—Synoptics*: It is not the correspondences in wording between John and the Synoptics *as such* that are relevant for establishing a *direct* literary dependence of John on the Synoptics, especially not if they extend to two or even all the Synoptics. However, if there is a significant agreement between John and a Synoptic Gospel, say Matthew, against Mark and Luke, at a point that can obviously be traced back to the redaction of Matthew, then a *literary dependence* of John on Matthew becomes probable. Likewise, in the case of similarities only between John and Mark, the question arises as to whether the oldest evangelist is merely a witness to an old tradition received by him (to which John could also have had access) or whether the wording in question goes back to the editing of Mark. In this case, the scales would also tip in favor of the assumption of a *literary* dependence of John on Mark, et cetera. It is therefore important to distinguish between redaction and transmission in the Synoptics as well, and even, if possible, between the redaction of Q and the sayings received from Q. Given the complexity of the literary relationships and the importance of the oral tradition, it is not easy to prove direct dependence between two writings.

---

90. See also 2:22; 4:44, 50c; 18:32.

The Riddle of the Johannine "Revelation Discourses" 33

(b) *John, the church fathers, and other early Christian writings*: This constellation leads to difficult questions, as have been discussed in the research for some time with diametrically opposed answers. Did Ignatius of Antioch, for example, know the Gospel of John? And if he does not quote it, does he at least allude to it? Or is he an independent witness to traditions that are only *indirectly* related to the book? Up to what point can we expect a living oral tradition? In any case, the bishop of Hierapolis, Papias, who was probably active during the reign of Emperor Hadrian (117–138), is still a witness to its high esteem. In the opinion of many scholars, the sources of tradition had not yet dried up by the middle of the second century, such that we can expect a "still lively coexistence of oral and written tradition"[91] for this period. As far as the establishment of *criteria* by which the question of the use or knowledge of a gospel by later generations can be measured is concerned, T. Nagel notes in principle that:

> the development of a consciously textual and literal reception of the Gospel tradition only took place in the course of the 2nd century CE. If one compares the early Christian literature of the first half of the 2nd century with that of the second half with regard to the echoes of the Gospel tradition to be found in it, a characteristic picture emerges. While a relatively exact use of Scripture can be observed for the second section, particularly in heterodox circles at the beginning of this development, there is hardly any evidence of an exact reproduction of the text in the first half of the 2nd century. Here it is "more appropriate not to speak of quotations at all, but of the transmission of the synoptic material through the reshaping, reformulating, adding and expanding power of the living, Spirit-filled church and its preaching." To explain this finding, one can point with Aland to a lack of "textual awareness" on the part of the authors, especially in the period before the formation of the canon.[92]

Then Nagel develops in detail "categories for the formal description of reception as textual absorption" ("text adoption" and "references to texts"), "categories for the description of reception in terms of content" and, finally, on this basis,

---

91. T. Nagel, *Die Rezeption des Johannesevangeliums im 2. Jahrhundert. Studien zur vorirenäischen Aneignung und Auslegung des vierten Evangeliums in christlicher und christlich-gnostischer Literatur*, Arbeiten zur Bibel und ihrer Geschichte 2 (Leipzig: Evangelische Verlagsanstalt, 2000), 100 on Justin.

92. Nagel, *Rezeption*, 37–38; here the reference to the Aland quote. The whole matter becomes difficult if one takes into account the phenomenon of a "second orality."

"criteria for the probability of the reception of the Gospel of John," which are extremely helpful for concrete work on the text.[93]

(c) *Repetitions in the Gospel of John*: This constellation, which we have studied in detail in 1.2.1 above, does not really belong here, as it does not involve further independent attestations of a tradition but rather repetitions in the same literary corpus. Nevertheless, as we have seen above, this *internal* citation procedure can be understood as an indication of the existence of a tradition.

(2) *Criterion of Independence from a Context or the Sufficiency of a Unit of Transmission*:

- A given unit stands out from its context through its *formal* and *contextual* unity. It is self sufficient, which is the *sine qua non* of its ability to be handed down.
- *In terms of form and style*, it is generally short and concise. Memorability is therefore one of its most prominent features.
- Moreover, it adheres to its own *genre*, which is decisive for its identity.
- This also corresponds to a certain *Sitz im Leben* of the unit.

(3) *Criteria resulting from the relationship between the unit of transmission and the context*:

- There may be *tensions* between the adopted unit and its new context, or perhaps only *incoherences* resulting from the fact that the statement of a given unit has only been partially integrated in the Johannine context.
- Formally and stylistically, the presence of a unit of tradition can be shown at the *seams* of its contextual embedding, possibly by a change of stylistic levels.
- Given the great importance of the Johannine "sociolect" for the Gospel and the difficulty of distinguishing an "idiolect" of the evangelist from it, *stylistic-quantitative* observations are often not very meaningful. However, this cannot be a reason to refrain from the whole undertaking. The identification *of hapax legomena* remains important. For the survey of a Johannine "sociolect," similarities between John and 1–3 John are informative. Purely quantitative surveys of stylistic features say little in themselves, unless one

---

93. Nagel, *Rezeption*, 35–45.

establishes that certain stylistic characteristics are more frequent in the already ascertained saying.[94]

- Insights into the *composition methods* of the Johannine units of discourse and dialogue can support arguments in favor of a postulated unity of tradition that have already been gained elsewhere. B. Lindars's suggestion should be taken up here. Lindars observed that given logia are mostly found at exposed points in the compositions, at their beginning or other central points.[95]

---

94. Helpful for the evaluation of Johannine stylistic characteristics: E. Ruckstuhl and P. Dschulnigg, *Stilkritik und Verfasserfrage im Johannesevangelium. Die johanneischen Sprachmerkmale auf dem Hintergrund des Neuen Testaments und des zeitgenössischen hellenistischen Schrifttums*, NTOA 17 (Göttingen: Vandenhoeck & Ruprecht, 1991).

95. See above on p. 25-26.; see also Dodd, *Tradition*, 317-18.

Part I

"Words of the Lord" on the Basis of the Synoptics (Tradition Criticism)

A CONSENSUS IN the research is that when reading the Gospel of John, you enter an entirely new sphere in comparison to the Synoptics, which *as a whole* are not that of the historical Jesus. Therefore, it is rather surprising that a significant portion of the Johannine "words of the Lord" are based on the other three canonical gospels. As already mentioned in the previous chapter, we will not treat the sayings of Jesus that fundamentally belong to narrative pericopes such as the "Feeding of the Five Thousand," "Jesus Walking on Water," or the passion tradition. We will only focus on such sayings that could represent independent traditions.[1] How important are they in the Fourth Gospel? Did its author (or the redactor[s] of the book) know about the Synoptics or did the sayings originate from oral tradition? Are their origins rooted in the historical Jesus or do we have to assume a transformation of these "words of the Lord" in the synoptic tradition based on the theology of the Johannine community? Do these "words of the Lord" have a particular thematic focus? How do we assess the weight of the segment of the synoptic tradition taken up into the Johannine world in comparison with the subjects which obviously were filtered out of the theological mainstream of the Johannine community in the development of the Gospel?

---

1. C. H. Dodd, *Historical Tradition in the Fourth Gospel* (Cambridge: Cambridge University Press, 1963), presents fourteen of these, including parallels, in his chapter "Sayings common to the Synoptics."

There is a wide range of potential Johannine "words of the Lord" with a connection to the Synoptic Gospels. Therefore, the examination of the material within chapters 2 and 3 will take this into account. First, we will look at "words of the Lord" with synoptic parallels—the criteria that will serve as the basis for this category will be outlined and justified. In chapter 4 we will focus on the Johannine words whose degree of independence is much higher in comparison to their possible synoptic pre-texts. We could speak of these sayings as *meta-texts* to the synoptic tradition. The degree of independence of certain Johannine logia can be so great that their relationship to the synoptic models can be asserted only tentatively and with great reservation, such that we can only speak of common motif clusters. As useful as the distinction of these two categories in chapters 2 and 3 might be, we nevertheless must reckon with slight graduations and fluent transitions.

CHAPTER 2

"Words of the Lord" with Synoptic Parallels

WHAT DO WE mean when we speak of a Johannine "word of the Lord" with synoptic parallels? Three conditions should be met for this classification: (1) it must be a single coherent logion, perhaps combined with others of its kind but independent of its narrative context; (2) the reference to a synoptic parallel should concern its form (structure and genre) and its content, which can appear in a new stylistic way; (3) the semantic similarity of a Johannine logion to a synoptic parallel should be obvious by signals or, if there is stylistic variation, by synonymous relations or affinities of a similar kind (see 2.3).

Of course, there is still room for discretion. We have to deal with creative transformations which can generate independent, "new" logia. Depending on the degree of the transformative work, these logia are more likely to be listed with the group of "meta-texts" (ch. 3). Despite the remarkable transformations, we analyze the logion found in John 3:3, 5 within this chapter because it contains a clear synoptic afterthought. On the other hand, we treat John 3:14–15 in chapter 3 because here we have a new Johannine "creation" that is only based on Mark 8:31. Fulfilling these three conditions is the prerequisite for a tradition-historical relationship between John and the Synoptics, be it direct or indirect dependence.

2.1 Entering God's Kingdom (John 3:3, 5/ Matt 18:3/Mark 10:15 par. Luke 18:17)

For a long time, exegesis assumed that the author takes up an old tradition and reworks it in John 3:3, 5.[1] This assumption doubted again and again with reference to the argument that the fourth evangelist made his statements with knowledge of the Synoptics. How does John 3:3, 5 correlate to the parallels in Matt 18:3 and Mark 10:15 (= Luke 18:17)? Was it the evangelist who transformed the synoptic metaphor of a child into the symbol of birth from above, or do we have to think of other intermediary traditions? What theological

---

1. R. Bultmann, *Das Evangelium des Johannes*, 19th ed. (Göttingen: Vandenhoeck & Ruprecht, 1968), 95 n. 5; Dodd, *Tradition*, 358–59; B. Lindars, "John and the Synoptic Gospels: A Test Case," *NTS* 27.3 (1981): 287–94.

importance does the evangelist attach to the saying? Despite the attention scholars have given John 3 in recent years, a methodologically rigorous demonstration of the tradition of the saying and its interpretation by the evangelist is still a desideratum of exegesis.

2.1.1 The Context of John 3:3, 5

The dialogue with Nicodemus in John 3 is introduced by John 2:23–25. Here we read: "many (in Jerusalem) believed in his name because they saw *the signs that he* (Jesus) *was doing*" (2:23b). This note by the narrator becomes concrete in Nicodemus: "Rabbi, we know that you are a teacher who has come from God; for no one can do these *signs that you do* apart from the presence of God" (3:2). This thread is continued in John 3:3, which represents Jesus's first reply in the three-part dialogue with Nicodemus. Corresponding to John 2:23b and 3:2, John 3:3 is about "*seeing* the kingdom of God."

Where the Nicodemus-dialogue begins and ends within the Gospel of John is still disputed. The difficulty lies in the transition from dialogue to Jesus's monologue. Nicodemus simply disappears unnoticed. Although there are several suggestions for how to structure the text, the one that proposes a caesura between verses 15 and 16 should be preferred for form critical reasons and on the basis of content:

From a *form critical* perspective, it stands out that the third part of the dialogue (like the other two parts) consists of several elements with their own linguistic connections that function like grout within the semantic construction (e.g., keywords and synonyms): a rhetorical opening (v. 10b), an Amen-saying (v. 11), a question which functions as a hinge (v. 12), and two sayings about the Son of Man which are added by the conjunction "and" (v. 13; vv. 14–15.). In contrast to this, 3:16–21 builds a two-part meditation whose first line (3:16–18) is developed out of the traditional soteriological sending-scheme as nucleus. The fact that in verse 16 the Christological title used for Jesus changes—the text no longer uses "Son of Man" as it did in verses 13–15 but "only son" (vv. 16–17, 18)—confirms the presence of a caesura between verses 15 and 16. With regard to content, it is remarkable that both sayings about the Son of Man in verses 13 and 14–15 build the Christological foundation for the preceding dialogue; they represent the counterpart to the two introductory logia in verses 3 and 5.

Therefore, our thesis is that the dialogue with Nicodemus, which seeks to promote the interpretation of the "Words of the Lord" in verses 3/5, ends with verse 15. John 3:16–21 contains commentary at a new reflective level and is connected to the preceding content with γάρ ("namely"). It sets forth the Christology of 3:13–15.

2.1.2 Five Arguments for the Assumption of a "Proverbial Saying" in John 3:3, 5

The prerequisite for the assumption that John 3:3, 5 is based on an old tradition of sayings is the conviction that a direct relation to the Synoptic Gospels (specifically Matt 18:3 and Mark 10:15 [= Luke 18:17]) cannot be demonstrated for our pericope; the differences between the logia in the Synoptic versions are too substantial. Therefore, we cannot plausibly explain the Johannine variations as redactional transformations of these logia. The following five observations speak in favor of the assumption of related *oral* tradition:

(1) The introduction of both sayings with *Very truly, I tell you* hints at an old tradition. This is not, however, a sufficient proof, since the author could have used this phrase by himself (i.e., not reliant on tradition) to mark special and important logia in his Jesus's speeches.

(2) The sayings in verses 3 and 5 are rounded in form and content; one does not need a broader context to understand their meaning (criteria of the *inner and outer sufficiency of the saying*).

(3) What is striking is the linguistic observation that here not a term appears that is atypical for the evangelist and characteristic for an old Jesus tradition—namely the term "reign of God/kingdom of God"[2]—but that this term also appears in a formulaic connection which was constitutive for the genre: the so-called entry-sayings.[3] It is rather unlikely that the evangelist willfully formulated these verses in an archaic style to correspond to this type of saying and by using a common *Leitwort* spoken by Jesus when one considers its prominent relation to the tradition of Matt 18:3 and Mark 10:15 in terms of content.

(4) The fact that there are also independent, parallel traditions (Matt 18:3; possibly also Justin, *1 Apol* 61.4) is another strong argument that an older tradition was used here.

(5) Finally, the weight the author has attributed to the saying within the context of Jesus's dialogue with Nicodemus is remarkable: Jesus refers to it in the version found in verse 3 in a (free) *citation* (v. 7: "Do not be astonished that *I said to you*, 'You must be born from above'"); in verse 8 we also find an *allusion* to a second version in verse 5 ("So it is with *everyone who is born of the Spirit*"). In doing so, he indirectly reveals the quotability and predetermined nature of the saying.

---

2. Dodd, *Tradition*, 360: "an erratic block of 'Synoptic' material in the Fourth Gospel."

3. See Matt 5:20; 7:21; 18:3; Mark 10:15 par. Luke 18:17; Mark 10:23/25 par. Matt 19:23, 24/ Luke 18:24, 25.

2.1.3 A "Word of the Lord"
Doubly Illuminated or Two Variants of the Same Tradition?

In light of the arguments and observations above, it is obvious that John 3:3, 5 represents an older piece of tradition. Now we need to ask whether the two versions represent duplicates in the tradition or—which seems more plausible—if the author doubly redacted a single tradition that had been handed down to him. Two possibilities seem conceivable. Either one version represents the original form of the tradition and the other represents the evangelist's duplication and reworking of that tradition, or both sayings contain traces of the evangelist's redactional work. A synopsis of John 3:3, 5 could make it clearer:

(1)	*Very truly, I tell you,*	*Very truly, I tell you,*
(2)	*If one is not born*	*If one is not born*
	from above,	of water and Spirit,
(3)	*he cannot*	*he cannot*
	see *the kingdom of God*	enter *the kingdom of God.*

The Apodosis of the Saying

Let us start with the apodosis of the saying (line 3) using our questions about tradition-criticism. Its variants can be accounted for unambiguously by the author's intent. Nicodemus begins with the compliment: "Rabbi, we know that you are a teacher who has come from God; for no one can do these signs that you do apart from the presence of God" (3:2). Jesus seems to ignore the compliment and reacts in a surprising way in verse 3. Nevertheless, the evangelist subtly attunes the saying to the present scene: "Very truly, I tell you, no one can see the kingdom of God without being born from above." This is not the first instance we encounter the topic of seeing. In 2:23 the people see the signs Jesus did. Similarly, the complement in 3:2 is also about seeing Jesus's signs. The provision, which the author outlines in 2:24 concerning a faith that is grounded on signs, suggests that in his religious conception this manner of "seeing" has no depth but rather remains at the surface of the miraculous. What is crucial for the evangelist is the kind of "seeing" by faith which recognizes that God's saving actions become a sign in Jesus. This "sight" grasps God's salvific Lordship and recognizes the *present* kingdom in Jesus. This seeing does not stay at the surface of the miraculous but penetrates into their actual symbolic significance. Seeing in this manner is not possible if one remains only an enthusiastic listener (like Nicodemus) and does not participate in Jesus's story and does not allow themselves to be seized in the center of their very being: "Very truly, I tell you, no one can *see* the kingdom of God without being born from above" (v. 3). We can conclude from this that the evangelist editorially inserted the motif of "seeing" in this saying. The original apodosis of this saying can be found in 3:5: "No one can *enter* the kingdom of God." This corresponds to the genre of the entry-sayings.

The Protasis of the Saying

The tradition-critical analysis of the protasis (line 2) is much more difficult because it cannot be reduced to the simple alternative of whether this or that version preserved the original wording of the saying. Let us consider the form in John 3:3, the ambiguous adverb ἄνωθεν, which can mean either "again" or "from above." Thus, it has either a *temporal* or *spatial* meaning. As such, it belongs to what is typical of Johannine language. This means that we cannot claim the ambiguous term "born from above/born a new" as a piece of the older given tradition. Rather we have to assume that the evangelist added the idea of a "birth *from above*" to this saying because of his dualistic terminology with spatial connotations which is present also in other passages (see, e.g., 8:23); In any case, the evangelist's use of ἄνωθεν carries the meaning "from above" and reflects the point of the saying. In favor of this assumption is the fact that the idea of a "*re*birth" is prominent in the early Christian literature[4] but not that of a "birth *from above*." For this reason, we can venture the hypothesis that originally the saying was about "*re*birth" according to the regular early Christian theology of baptism (maybe formulated as ἀνα-γεννᾶσθαι). The evangelist then transformed the term ἀνα-γεννᾶσθαι within his tradition into ἄνωθεν γεννᾶσθαι. In so doing, he created the idea of a "birth *from above*," which we find only in his texts.

The version of the protasis in 3:3 gives us an insight into the prehistory of the logion. This does not mean that the parallel version in 3:5 has to be excluded from analysis. On the contrary, we have to assume that the saying about the "rebirth" contained the indication of a causal reason for it; this is true, for example, of 1 Peter 1:23 and Titus 3:5.[5] The only question is, which of the elements in 3:5, "water" and "spirit," is worthy of consideration or rather if the phrase ἐξ ὕδατος καὶ πνεύματος should be reclaimed as a whole for the given saying. However, if the question is posed in this manner, then another promoted by Bultmann is rejected out of hand.[6] Bultmann takes exception to the fact that the motif of "water" in 3:5 is isolated and is never mentioned in the subsequent dialogue; moreover, as a cipher for baptism, it is not compatible with 3:8 ("the wind blows where

---

4. See 1 Pet 1:3, 23; Titus 3:5; Justin, *1 Apol.* 61.3; 66.1; *Dial.* 138.2; Acts Thom. 132.

5. First Peter 1:3: "He has given us a new birth into a living hope *through the resurrection of Jesus Christ* from the dead"; 1:23: "You have been born anew, not *of perishable but of imperishable seed, through the living and enduring word of God*"; Titus 3:5: "*through the water of rebirth and renewal by the Holy Spirit*."

6. Bultmann, *Johannes*, 98 n. 2.

it chooses . . .") since, as an assertion about God's absolute freedom, it cannot "be quite right that the Spirit is bestowed by a sure means, by the sacrament of baptism."[7] Therefore, like Julius Wellhausen before him, Bultmann concludes that ὕδατος καί should be deleted because it was a later gloss, and he assigns this addition to the category of "ecclesiastical redaction," to which the reference to the Last Supper in 6:51b–58 also belongs.

But it seems that in the Johannine communities there was no dispute about baptism, which they most certainly practiced as a matter of course, and that "whoever wished to inscribe sacramentalism in John 3 would probably have done a more thorough job."[8]

It is also noticeable that the topic of baptism is anchored in the narrative framework of 3:22–23/25–26 (see also 4:1–2). Therefore, it does not seem appropriate to eliminate both words from the text. But since the given saying with its presumed talk of "rebirth" needed a more precise explanation, everything speaks in favor of the conclusion that ἐξ ὕδατος belonged to the older tradition. The singularity of the motif in the immediate context can be explained by the observation that the author cites fully the given saying but does not incorporate the motifs of water and baptism in the subsequent dialogue. Of greater importance to him is the birth of the new human out of God's spirit (see vv. 6 and 8). The method used by the evangelist—that is, commenting on a given saying—gives us reason to assume that the saying led the author to his conviction that rebirth in the Holy Spirit is necessary. In other words: The whole phrase ἐξ ὕδατος καὶ πνεύματος belonged to the older sayings tradition. This assumption is further strengthened by the observation that *both* motifs—the one about the water and the other about the spirit—are also found together in, for example, Titus 3:5, as well as in catechetical sources (see also Gen 1:2).

There is no doubt that the evangelist transformed the Amen formula in 3:3/5* from the plural to the singular and adapted it to the Nicodemus-dialogue (see also 3:11) because this formula appears both in the Synoptics and in the Gospel of John as the second-person plural. The double "Amen" (in distinction to the single in the Synoptics) seems to be a peculiarity of the tradition behind John.[9]

Therefore, the saying handed down in the tradition would have been as follows:

Truly (truly) I say to you,
"If one is not born again of water and the Spirit,
he cannot enter the kingdom of God."

---

7. Wellhausen, *Evangelium*, 17.

8. Becker, *Johannes*, 1:163.

9. See p. 27–30.

2.1.4 What Is the Origin of the Evangelist's Saying?

The saying probably stems from oral tradition. But the postulated tradition cannot be identified with the presumed original of the logion because one would expect the Johannine community to function as transmitter of the words of Jesus. Thus, the community was a filter for the received tradition. A good example of this is the theology of baptism in our saying, which is neither to be considered a part of the oldest *stratum* of the saying, nor did it belong to the evangelist's special interests. It represented what was commonly believed and practiced in the Johannine community.

Our thesis, therefore, is that John 3:3/5* is probably a single saying which had its *Sitz im Leben* in the catechesis of baptism or the baptismal liturgy of the Johannine community.

2.1.5 John 3:3, 5 and Its Synoptic Parallels

Let's take a methodological step back and ask: Did the author of John have Mark and Matthew in mind such that we can categorize John 3:3, 5 as a *relecture* of Mark 10:15 and Matt 18:3? The following synopsis shows that the Johannine formulations have different coherences with the two synoptic versions:

John 3:3.5	Mark 10:15 (= Luke 18:17)	Matt 18:3
Very truly I say to you, "*if one is not* born from above/again (ἄνωθεν)	Truly I say to you, "Whoever does not	Truly I say to you, "*if you do not* change (στραφῆσθε) and become
of water and Spirit he cannot	receive the kingdom of God as a little child, never	as a little child, never
(see) / enter *into the kingdom* of God.	will he enter into it."	will you enter *into the kingdom* of heaven.

There are not many parallels with Mark 10:15. The typical idea in Mark of receiving the kingdom of God like a child has no equivalent in John. Furthermore, the versions differ in their afterword. Here, John corresponds largely with

Matt 18:3.[10] Moreover, there is an analogy between "becoming childlike" and the pre-Johannine idea of "rebirth." So we can state with Eduard Schweizer: "The traditional statement in John 3:5 ... corresponds to Matt 18:3."[11]

Thus, our question as to whether John knew the Synoptics focuses specifically on the Matthean version. We cannot rule out the possibility that John knew Matthew. However, according to Rudolf Schnackenburg, a relationship between John and both of the synoptic versions seems less probable "since the fourth evangelist would have strongly reversed the idea: he would have turned 'becoming (again) like children or like a child' into a direct 'becoming a child,' which he understood very realistically to be a new birth, new creation, or 'begetting from above.' This *how* belongs indissolubly to both figures of the synoptic *logion*, just as, conversely, the Johannine *logion* does not aim at the conversion of man but at God's act toward man."[12] The transformation took place nevertheless, whether in a pre-Johannine context or by the evangelist himself. Therefore, Schnackenburg's argument is not a sufficient explanation. Important, however, is the observation that in the following sections the evangelist ignores the term "from water" because baptism as a sacramental act is not important to him in this context. *Therefore, it is improbable that he was responsible for the baptismal-theological transformation of Matthew 18:3 in John 3:3, 5; he only used it.*

To further substantiate this thesis, we need to take two analytical steps below. The first focuses on Matt 18:3: if this version of the saying is a part of the redaction of Matthew, it would seriously undermine the assumption that John 3:3, 5 is independent of Matthew's Gospel; the argumentation would be different if the first evangelist in Matt 18:3 were to testify to an independent variant of the saying compared to Mark 10:15. The second step of analysis focuses on Mark 10:15: Does the framework of the episode of the blessing of the child belong constitutively to the logion or was this originally a single logion? If the latter is the case, this would support the assumption that Matthew 18:3 is also independent. Let us begin with this question.

---

10. Furthermore, Matt 18:3 is formulated as a form of address, whereas John 3:3, 5 contains a remark formulated in the 3rd sg.; moreover, we find the typical expression "kingdom of *heaven*" in Matthew.

11. Schweizer, *Matthäus*, 235: "The image (of Jesus?) presented there was thus linked to baptism, as we find similarly in 1 Pet 2:1ff, and then understood in the sense of the church's doctrine of baptism as being born of water and the Spirit."

12. Schnackenburg, *Johannes*, 1:381. This argument is directed against a possible generation of the Johannine *logion* from a variation of Matt 18:3 *and* Mark 10:15; but the concept of "becoming like ..." is found only in Matthew.

2.1.6 "Like a child"
Mark 10:15 and Blessing the Children

The "biographical apophtegma" of blessing the children (Mark 10:13–16) is:

13	a	People were bringing little children to him,
	b	in order that he might touch them;
	c	and the disciples spoke sternly to them.
14	a	But when Jesus saw this,
	b	he was indignant
	c	and said to them,
	d	"Let the *little children* come to me;
	e	do not stop them;
	f	for the *kingdom of God* belongs such as these.
15	a	Truly I tell you,
	b	whoever does not receive the *kingdom of God as a little child*
	c	will never enter it."
16	a	And he took them in his arms
	b	and blessed them,
	c	by laying his hands on them.

Verse 14d–f contains the point of this small episode; verse 16 only adds Jesus's corresponding action as a climax: the blessing of the children. In contrast, verse 15 expands on what has been described with a paraenetic intention. "Without it, the narrative seems more closed."[13] Thus, at least since the work of Rudolf Bultmann, the conviction of exegetes seems to be that this verse reproduces "an originally free word of the Lord" that was only subsequently "inserted into the scene."[14] Did Mark, to whom the insertion probably goes back, preserve the "word of the Lord" in its original form? Several observations speak against this:

(1) At first, it is remarkable how precisely the saying is fitted into its new context: the saying about "*receiving* the kingdom" in verse 15b corresponds to "*belonging* to the kingdom" in verses 14–15. In other words: The *promise* of God's kingdom to the children precedes it as an indication of salvation, and is followed by people's *acceptance* of the kingdom with the attitude of children, that is, in their willingness to become little before God and people.

---

13. Gnilka, *Markus*, 2:80.

14. Bultmann, *Geschichte*, 32.

(2) The dovetailing with verse 14 thus explains the fact that verse 15 already speaks of the kingdom of God in its protasis. However, this results in a strange inconsistency in the structure of the sentence: What should actually only be the content of the apodosis, namely entrance into the *kingdom of God*, is already anticipated by the protasis with its talk of accepting the *kingdom*: "One cannot ... well 'accept' something and then 'enter.'"[15] According to B. Lindars, the Markan version is even "almost tautologous."[16] If we compare Mark 10:15 with Matt 18:3 and John 3:3, 5, we get the impression that form and content are still in balance and fit together: The *apodosis* announces in each case the entrance into the kingdom of God, the *protasis* states in advance the condition that must be fulfilled. The suspicion arises that Mark has intervened considerably in the form of the saying when incorporating it into its new context.

(3) The following linguistic observation also points in this direction. The phrase "receive the kingdom of God" (par. Luke 18:17) is unique in the New Testament. It is probably derived from 9:37, the first scene with children in the Gospel, which speaks of "receiving the children" in the name of Jesus.[17] If it is said that such "acceptance" of the children is actually the acceptance of Jesus and thus of the one who sent him (i.e., God), then the phrase "receiving the kingdom of God" in 10:15 is obvious. The conclusion is inescapable: Mark himself formed the original Amen-saying in 10:15. It cannot be claimed for the given tradition.

The analysis of Mark 10:15 according to tradition criticism has a positive and negative result. The positive result: The oldest evangelist has demonstrably put this word of the Lord into the present form. The negative result: The ancient tradition on which it is certainly based cannot be reconstructed on the basis of Mark 10:15 alone. It remains to be seen whether Matthew 18:3 can help here.

2.1.7 Matthew 18:3
A Parallel Tradition to John 3:3/5?*

At first glance, it seems as if Matthew 18:3 is a new redactional version of Mark 10:15[18]: Matthew ignores the saying in his revision of the episode of the blessing of the children (Matt 19:13–15) to use it as a programmatic opening of his

---

15. Schweizer, *Matthäus*, 235.

16. Lindars, "Test Case," 106.

17. See also the speech about "receiving the word (of God)": Luke 8:13; Acts 8:14; 11:1; 17:11; 1 Thess 1:6; 2:13; Jas 1:21.

18. See Bultmann, *Geschichte*, 32: Matt 18:3 "is evidently not based on any particular tradition but is the version of Mark 10:15 formed by Matthew and placed in a different context."

discourse on community in Matthee 18. There, he places it in the context of the other Markan scene involving children (Mark 9:36–37). Here, he uses the second-person plural (instead of the third-person singular in Mark) because the saying is now addressed directly to the disciples who have asked Jesus "who is the greatest in the kingdom of heaven" (Matt 18:1).[19] The transformation of the singular "like a child" into the plural "like children" can be explained by this change. Moreover, it could be argued that Matthew could not have used the Markan phrase "*accept* the kingdom of God" in his community discourse because it is addressed to converted disciples or Christians. So he redacts[20] the saying and transforms it, writing: "Unless you *change* and become like children, you will never enter the kingdom of heaven," thus signaling that the speech that follows is not about one's initial conversion but about the resulting ethical consequences.

At this point, a word on the translation of στραφῆτε is in order. Even if one does not usually recognize a major problem here, there are still four (!) suggested translations to choose from:

(1) στρέφεσθαι is almost universally understood as a synonym of μετανοεῖν and is therefore translated as follows: "If you do not *repent (convert)* and become like children . . . ."[21] The text, however, does not have the verb μετανοεῖν.[22] Furthermore, it is necessary to mention here, in agreement with P. Joüon, whom J. Jeremias followed, that the passive στρέφεσθαι (*not* ἐπιστρέφεσθαι) *cannot be found* in the LXX as a translation of שוב with the meaning "to convert." We find the active στρέφειν with this religious sense only once, in a variant of Jer 34 (41):15 (Codex A). The passive στρέφεσθαι likewise only occurs once in the New

---

19. The answer is not found in v. 3, but in v. 4: "Whoever becomes humble like this child is *the greatest in the kingdom of heaven*." Verse 3 prepares for the answer.

20. U. Luz, *Das Evangelium nach Matthäus I–IV*, EKK I/1-4 (Zürich: Benziger, 1985–2002), 3:11, claims a "strong red(actional) adaptation of our logion by Matthew" (similarly Pryor, "John," 81–84); 3:11 n. 14: "Our verse is formed according to the pattern of the likewise red(actional) 5:20." However, this conclusion from the agreement between the two verses is premature, as it only extends to the common type of saying of a "word of admission," the characteristics of which can be found in 5:20 *and* 18:3. In other words, 18:3 does not have to be based on 5:20. It could have also been independently realized as a type of saying Matthew used editorially in 5:20. Luz himself makes another restriction, 3:11 n. 14: "More difficult is στραφῆτε, which occurs twice in Matthew (always aorist passive), but not, as here, in a metaphorical sense."

21. Among many other translations see, e.g., Luther.

22. Μετανοεῖν in Matt 3:2 (redaction); 4:17; 11:20 (redaction); 11:21; 12:41. In Mark, we only find two references. In Luke, however, Luke nine, plus five in Acts. Additionally, there are two references with μετάνοια: Matt 3:8, 11 (Mark: one; Luke: five; Acts: six). We cannot claim that μετανοεῖν does not belong "to the words preferred by Matthew" (Trilling, *Israel*, 108) if we consider this observation.

Testament, in John 12:40 (translation of Isa 6:10). Furthermore, in koine Greek this meaning is not common according to the lexica.[23] Thus, we can conclude that "στρέφεσθαι here hardly means 'to convert.'"[24]

(2) The translation proposed by P. Joüon and J. Jeremias[25] is based on their interpretation of στραφῆτε + finite verb as a Semitism. Pointing to the linguistic result that in Hebrew/Aramaic שוב/תוב together with a finite verb connected with ו can have the function of an "auxiliary verb" (*verbum relativum*) and can therefore be translated "again...."[26] They translate Matthew 18:3 accordingly as follows: "Unless you become like children *again*, you will not enter the kingdom of heaven."[27] Now it is by no means impossible that this linguistic interpretation that the Matthean text goes back to an earlier Aramaic form of the text is correct (see below!), but there are doubts as to whether the Greek phrase of Matthew 18:3 can also be understood iteratively.[28]

The range of possibilities for translating שוב as a *verbum relativum* in the LXX is interesting. When examining the references, one does not get the impression that a corresponding fixed idiomatic phrase has developed in Greek;[29] the translations are variable and are apparently intended to give the Hebrew שוב a *unique* and *independent* semantic meaning in Greek. A few examples: If repetition should be expressed, the translator could use the adverb πάλιν (= again; see Gen 26:18; 30:31; Jdg 19:7 [A]; Jer 18:4). However, the verb προστίθεσθαι could also serve that purpose (see 2 Kgs 1:11: "the king did it once again [προσέθετο] and sent another captain"; see also 1:13). If the statement refers to God, then

---

23. Furthermore, Bauer-Aland 1539 only lists Sib. Or. 3.625 from early Jewish literature.

24. Jeremias, *Gleichnisse*, 189 n. 2; Jeremias, *Theologie*, 154; according to P. Joüon, "Notes philologiques sur les évanglies", RSR 18 (1928) 347–48

25. More representatives of this translation can be found in Dupont, "Matthieu," 50–51.

26. See Gesenius, *Handwörterbuch*, 811; Jastrow, *Dictionary*, 1649–1650.

27. Jeremias, *Theologie*, 154; see also the *Bible jerusaleme*: "si vous ne retournez à l'état des enfants...."

28. For Dupont, "Matthieu," the most important argument against the assumption of a Semitism in Matt 18:3 is the fact that LXX nowhere uses the simplex στρέψεσθαι for an iterative שוב: "Given the biblical Greek, it is therefore not very appropriate to use the verb שוב or תוב to account for Matt 18:3." (53). This is also the opinion of Luz, *Matthäus*, 3:11 n. 15: The thesis of Jeremias is "almost (!) certainly incorrect"! See also Pryor, "John," 83–84.

29. Indeed the verb ἐπιστρέφειν dominates but with a different syntactic usage: in the active and passive. Furthermore, we find other formulations of the verb (1 Kgs 3:5: ἀναστρέφειν; Deut 24:4: ἐπαναστρέφειν) and entirely different verbs (e.g. 2 Kgs 1:11, 13: προστίθεσται; Deut 23:14: ἐπάγειν).

ἐπιστρέφειν is often chosen, less to express, for example, the *renewal* of his grace toward people than his (repeated) *turn* toward them. In Jerimiah 12:15 (LXX) we find: "And it shall be, after I have driven them out (i.e., the house of Judah), that I will turn back (ἐπιστρέφω) and have mercy on them...."[30] In Psalm 85 (84):7 the worshipper speaks: "O God, will you turn back (ἐπιστρέψας) and revive us, then your people will rejoice in you." Sometimes the LXX reinterprets the *verbum relativum* שוב with the meaning: *conversion* of humans. In the Hebrew version, Isaiah 6:10 originally says: "Make the heart of this people fat..., so that... their heart does not come to understand and they are healed *again*." The LXX changes the subject and translates: "For the heart of this people has become fat (ἐπαχύνθη)..., such that they will not (μήποτε)... turn back (ἐπιστρέψωσιν) and *I* will heal them (ἰάσομαι)."[31] Of course when שוב originally functioned as an auxiliary verb, where the context permits or requires it, it can be understood in its direct, literal sense of "returning," "turning around," or "coming back," et cetera. Then the semantic characteristic of "repetition" is preserved but with a stronger connotation in the *spatial* sense of "*come back.*" Thus, the law for divorce in Deuteronomy 24:4 is about the forbidden "coming back" (ἐπαναστρέψας) of the man to his divorced wife. And Psalm 104 (103):9 is about the boundaries of the waters of the primordial flood set by God so that they "do not come back to cover the earth" (οὐδὲ ἐπιστρέψουσιν καλύψαι τὴν γῆν).[32] If as a *verbum relativum* שוב does not denote the repetition of an act but the restoration of an earlier state,[33] then the LXX expresses this with ἐπιστρέφειν. For example, it is said about king Manasseh in 2 Kings 21:3: "He returned (to a previous state; ἐπέστρεψεν) and rebuilt the high places that his father Hezekiah had destroyed."[34]

If one considers the range of possible Greek translations of שוב as a *verbum relativum*, then one will have to abandon a mechanical rendering of Matthew 18:3 in an iterative sense. It depends on the context what meaning Matthew wanted to give the phrase στραφῆτε καὶ γένησθε ὡς τὰ παιδία. This brings us to the third suggested translation.

---

30. The "turning" of YHWH corresponds to ἐπιστρέφειν, the conversion of man. In addition to Jer 12:15, 17: ἐὰν δὲ μὴ ἐπιστρέψωσιν, see also Mic 7:19.

31. See also Matt 13:14–15; Mark 4:12; Acts 28:26–27.—In Mal 3:18, too, the thought of conversion came into the text by way of the LXX: καὶ ἐπιστραφήσεσθε καὶ ὄψεσθε. The Hebrew text only speaks of a *repeated* seeing: ושבתם וראיתם.

32. See, too, 1 Kgs 3:5, 6, 9.

33. See Wolff, *Hosea*, 37, on Hos 2:11.

34. See also 2 Kgs 24:1 and references in Wolff, *Hosea*, in the previous fn.

(3) It is worth noting the other uses of στρέφειν in Matthew.[35] If he consistently uses the verb in its immediate, spatial sense, then it is not unreasonable to base the interpretation of 18:3 on this, regardless of the fact that the verse speaks metaphorically. Then the translation would be: "Unless you *turn* and become like children, you will not enter into the kingdom of heaven."[36] It would mean a "change of position that leads back to the position of the child," in other words: "What is meant is an attitude opposite of one which would claim greatness for itself."[37]

(4) A fourth and final translation possibility arises if one considers στρέφειν/στρέφεσθαι to mean "transform" or "to be transformed" (a translation of הפך), which is a rendering frequently found in the LXX.[38] A good example is 1 Samuel 10:6 (LXX). There we find a lengthy speech by Samuel to Saul: "Then the Spirit of the Lord will come upon you and you will go into rapture/speak prophetically (προφητεύσεις) with them [i.e., the enraptured crowd at Nabis; v. 5] and *be transformed into another person* (στραφήσῃ εἰς ἄνδρα ἄλλον)." Similarly, Matthew 18:3 is about the transformation into another man. Especially in connection with "becoming like children," this interpretation makes sense and therefore is to be preferred. Thus, the translation would be: "Unless you are *transformed*, that is,[39] become like children, you will by no means enter the kingdom of heaven." Or, "Unless you *change*, that is, become like children, you will by no means enter the kingdom of heaven."[40] The second translation of the passive in the medial sense probably corresponds better to the Matthean context with its ethical-parenetic accent[41] and is therefore preferable to the passive.

The tradition criticism alternative is: Matthew did not incorporate Mark 10:5 in a revised version in his speech about community (ch. 18) but in 18:3

---

35. See Dupont, "Matthieu," 59. We find the verb στρέφω six times in Matthew, twice in the active (5:39; 27:3) and four times in aorist passive (7:6; 9:22; 16:23; 27:3) with the meaning: "to turn around," "to come back."

36. Here Gnilka, *Matthäusevangelium*, 2:120.

37. Gnilka, *Matthäusevangelium*, 2:122.

38. See Dupont, "Matthieu," 53, with examples. "In biblical Greek, the 'reversal' signified by στρέφομαι applies to a change resulting from a profound." Exodus 7:15: "take the staff that has changed into a snake (στραφεῖσαν εἰς ὄφιν) with you!" (YHWH speaking to Moses).

39. Gnilka, *Matthäusevangelium*, 2:122 n.10, rightly recommends interpreting the connecting καί explicatively.

40. Dupont, "Matthieu," 54: "if you do not change ... ," "if you do not transform." He adds, "Certainly, the idea of conversion is very close; but it is not made explicit, as it would be by the use of the compound verb ἐπιστρέφω."

41. See the reflexive ταπεινοῦν ἑαυτόν in the conclusion in 18:4!

"Words of the Lord" with Synoptic Parallels 53

adopted an independent oral tradition older than the redactional version in Mark.[42] This thesis is plausible considering the fact that all other early Christian versions of the logion[43] do not speak like Mark of "receiving God's kingdom" and are closer to the first evangelist than to the second. However, we must prove this:

(1) First, the argument that Matthew incorporates Mark's version into his text has to be defused. As plausible as it sounds, caution is advisable because it is not at all the style of the first evangelist to avoid "doublettes" or "repetitions." On the contrary, "repetitions" of Jesus's words (or of the words of the Baptist) a second or even third time can be found throughout his entire Gospel because, for catechetical reasons, he does not find it cumbersome to repeat important material.[44] That Matthew ignores Mark 10:15 in Matthew 19:13–15, does not mean that he already included the saying in 18:3. The author rather ignores Mark 10:15 in his version of the "blessing of the children" in 19:13–15 because in the catechetical context of the pericope 19:3–20:16[45] only the *children* of the community are important to him. He is not concerned with the general question of how to gain access to the kingdom of God. As a consequence, Matthew 18:3 *could* be a revision of Mark 10:15 but *does not have* to be one.

(2) Important, too, is Pryor's conclusion on Mark 10:15: "If the case for Mark 10:15 being an independent logion is to be believed, then here is further ground for supposing that an isolated saying in various forms existed in the early church."[46]

(3) The consistent form of the logion in Matthew (the *apodosis* announces the entrance into the kingdom of God, the *protasis* names the condition for this), which agrees with John 3:3, 5, speaks unconditionally for its non-editorial character—irrespective of the possibility that the evangelist is partly responsible for its formulation.[47]

---

42. Here I follow Lindars, "Test Case," 106–107.

43. Justin, *1 Apol* 61.4; Clement of Alexandria, *Protr.* 9.82.4; Ps-Clement, *Hom.* 11.26.2; Ps-Clement, *Recog.* 1.69.5; 6.9.2; Hippolytus, *Haer.* 8.10.8; Const. ap. 6.15.5.

44. See already p. 12–13.

45. Topics here are marriage—unmarried persons—children—richness—succession.

46. Pryor, "John," 87.

47. This is obvious if we look at the phrase ἡ βασιλεία τῶν οὐρανῶν.

(4) The relevant message of the protasis in Matthew, namely to *change his life* and *become* like a child, is not offered in Mark 10:15. The first evangelist would have added it to the logion independently. This may well be linguistically possible,[48] but we are skeptical that especially the important topic of "transformation" or "renewal" has an analogy to the Johannine saying about the community and its focus on "rebirth." This speaks in favor of the tradition in Matt 18:3.[49]

(5) Here we must return again to the Aramaism thesis of Joüon and Jeremias, albeit modified in that it cannot stipulate the translation of the *Greek* version in Matthew in advance. It does, however, provide an explanation for the *origin* of the conspicuous combination of both verbs with the assumption of a possible Aramaic assumed original of the logion. There should be no doubt that this logion goes back to Jesus. If one distinguishes between the original Aramaic version of the logion and its Greek rendering handed down in Matthew, then Dupont's seemingly incontestable reference to the fact that in the LXX an iterative שׁוב is never translated with στρέφειν/στρέφεσθαι loses its weight.[50] For who would want to rule out the possibility that Matthew deleted the expected preposition ἐπί in the logion he received because he could not use the idea of reversal or conversion?[51] We do not know how the logion Matthew used was formulated exactly in Greek. But that the conspicuous combination of στρέφεσθαι καί + *verbum finitum* is *caused* by Aramaism is, in this modified form, still an attractive hypothesis and an important argument for the traditional character (*Überlieferungscharakter*) of Matt 18:3.[52]

---

48. See above at n. 35! On γίγνεσθαι (ὡς) see Matt 5:45 (cf. Luke 6:35); 6:16; 10:16; 10:25 (cf. Luke 6:40); 24:44 (Dupont, *Matthieu*, 58–59, with n. 38). We can state that a metaphorical use of στρέφεσθαι is used only here in Matthew.

49. Right here is Pryor, *John*, 87: "The strangeness of στραφῆτε καὶ γένεσθε, which in a number of ways is not Matthean and certainly is not a borrowing from Mark, leads one to suspect that another tradition beside Mark lies behind Matthew's redaction."

50. See above fn. 28! But Isa 6:10fin. in John 12:40 is rendered with στραφῶσιν, contrary to the usual textual form of the LXX (according to the best textual witnesses P$^{66\,75}$ א B D, etc.).

51. In the NT ἐπιστρέφειν (like μετανοεῖν) belongs to the terminology of conversion: Trilling, *Israel*, 108; Bertram, Art. ἐπιστρέφω κτλ. *TDNT* 7: 722–729. Of course in Matthew only in 13:15 (= Isa 6:10); when used according to its actual (spatial) meaning 10:13; 12:44; 24:18.

52. Similarly see Schweizer, *Matthäus*, 235: "The sentence in Matthew (can) be traced back to an even more primitive Aramaic form."

(6) If the logion in Matthew cannot be reconstructed verbatim, then this also has to do with the fact that we cannot rule out the possibility that Matthew transformed a logion originally formulated in the third person into the form of address according to the scenario he created in Matthew 18:1–2.[53] After all, Mark 10:15 *and* John 3:3, 5 attest to the basic form in the third person.

As result of our tradition criticism (*überlieferungskritische*) analysis we can conclude that an independent version of our logion is probably the basis of Matthew 18:3, likely its oldest accessible version. It is remarkable that the Aramaic original shines through its Greek, which may have sounded like this in translation:

Truly, I say to you,
"If you do not become like children again,
you will not enter the kingdom of God."

If one wished to follow the version of Mark and John, then you have to assume following original logion:

Truly, I say to you,
"Whoever does not become like a child again
this one will not enter the kingdom of God."

This reconstruction (in the one or the other form) is supported by the existence of an analogous pre-Johannine version, as we have seen above: What Jesus expressed in a very simple and catchy metaphorical form has been theologized with the help of the idea of "rebirth" and with reference to Christian baptism. While in the context of Matthew 18:1–5 the saying has an ethical-parenetical accent, Jesus probably spoke about becoming like a child without accentuating the aspect of repentance.[54] J. Jeremias, following T. W. Manson, who believed that Matthew 18:3 was related to Jesus's address of God as *Abba*, presented an excellent interpretation of Jesus's saying: "This will indeed be the solution: "'To become a child again' means: to learn to say *Abba* again," "to cast one's full trust in the heavenly Father, to return to the Father's house and into the arms of the Father."[55]

---

53. Trilling, *Israel*, 108: "In v. 3 Matthew interchanges the third person with the second person, thereby inserting the logion into the context of the speech" n. 14: "This happens frequently; see 5:13; 12:33–34.; 23:34ff."

54. See Schweizer, *Matthäus*, 235.

55. Jeremias, *Theologie*, 1:154–55 (with a hint to Manson).

2.1.8 The Genealogical Tree of This Jesus Logion

The results of our analysis allow us to bring together the different versions of the saying in a genealogical tree. We do not know the form of the logion that the oldest evangelist used in Mark 10:15, but we can assume a connection between Mark 10:15* and the "original logion."[56] It is also unclear whether John 3:3/5* is an independent evolution of the saying rooted in the original logion or if it is based on the logion used in Matthew 18:3.[57] The question marks in the tree below signal doubt in instances where the reconstruction is hardly decisive.

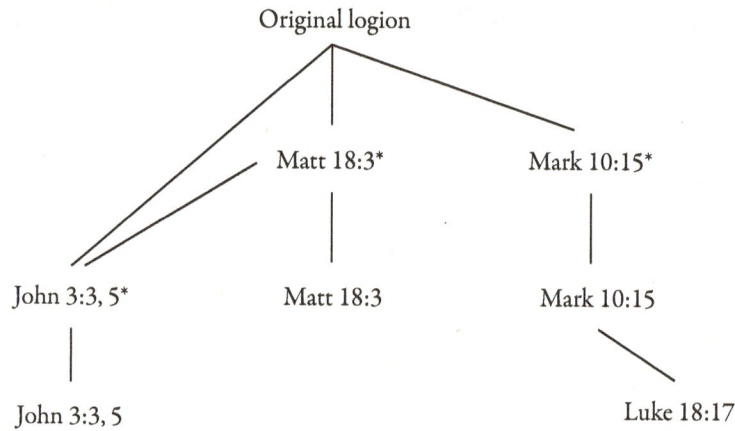

2.1.9 From the Metaphor of a Child to the Symbol of Rebirth
Motif-Critical Observations

What Jesus meant with the vivid metaphor of "becoming like a child"—to learn to address God as "abba," father, in a childish confidence—the members of the Johannine community translated into the archetypical symbol of *"rebirth."* They were guided by the experience of their initiation rite, baptism, in which the conversion demanded by Jesus received a new, socially tangible form when one becomes a member of the community. Different factors were responsible for the process of translation, but overall we have to be aware that this process in its broadest sense took place on the basis of *early Jewish* theology.

---

56. At least, there are congruences between Matt 18:3 and Mark 10:15 concerning the elements ὡς παιδίον/τὰ παιδία of the protasis and εἰσελθεῖν in the apodosis.

57. See here Pryor, "John," 93–94: "It is highly likely that it was the tradition behind Matt 18:3 (and not the Gospel itself) to which John's tradition was either closest, or upon which it perhaps drew."

The first thing to mention here is the idea of a new creation through the eschatological gift of the Spirit, which could be linked above all to Ezekiel 36:24–28. This pericope is so important for understanding John 3:3, 5* because it combines the idea of a new creation, which refers to the gathering of the broken *Israel*, with the motifs of purification through *water* and the *gift of God's Spirit*. It does not speak of the new creation conceptually, but with the help of the metaphor of the "new heart" (v. 26):

This pericope is important for the understanding of John 3:3/5* because it combines the thought of a new creation, referring to the collection of the scattered *Israel*, with the motifs of purgation by *water* and the gift of *God's Spirit*. The prophet doesn't speak of a new creation but with the metaphor of the "new heart" (v. 26):[58]

> [24]Then I will take you from all the nations and gather you from all the countries and bring you into your own land. [25]And I will sprinkle clean *water* on you to cleanse you from all your defilements. [26]And I will give you a new heart and remove the heart of stone from your flesh and give you a heart of flesh. [27]And I will put *my Spirit* within you and make you walk in my statutes and observe my judgments and do them. [28]And you shall dwell in the land that I gave to your fathers, and you shall be my people. And I will be your God.

That this text, like its Old Testament relatives (see Deut 30:1–10; Jer 31:31–34; 32:37–44), continued to live in the early Jewish theology can be seen in Jub. 1:23–25:

> [23]And after this they will return to me in all righteousness and with all their heart and with all their soul. And I will circumcise the foreskin of their heart and the foreskin of the heart of their seed. And I will give them a holy *spirit*. And I will *make* them *clean*, so that they will not turn away from me from this day until eternity. [24]And their souls will cleave to me and to all my commandments. And they will do my commandment. And *I will be their father, and they will be my children.* [25]And they will all be called children of the living God. And all the angels and all the spirits will know them. And they shall know them, that they are *my children*, and *I am their Father* in righteousness and justice, and that I love them.

---

58. Psalm 51 translated the collective idea of Ezek 26 onto the individual: "*Create* for me, o God, a pure heart . . . !" (v. 12).

What is remarkable about this text is the replacement of the covenant formula ("you shall be my people and I will be your God") with the adoption formula: "I will be their father and they will be my children" (see 2 Sam 7:14; Isa 43:6; Jer 31:9 etc.). If we combine this with the idea of the renewal of man by the Spirit of God articulated shortly before, then the idea of a rebirth is not far off.

Helpful for understanding the "translation" of the Jesus-saying into the baptismal-saying of the Johannine congregation is furthermore a reference to the fact "that Judaism already taught that the proselyte at the time of conversion was like 'a child just born,' like one 'newly created.'"[59] This is because the comparison with newborn children is made here in connection with an *initiation*, as in John 3:3, 5*, where, according to our analysis, the comparison with children *in the context of an initiation rite* has also acquired deeper meaning. Of course, the pre-Johannine saying goes beyond a comparison when it speaks of real rebirth, which leads us to a further aspect.

"There is no Hebrew or Aramaic word for rebirth. Palestinian Judaism speaks much more of a new creation (2 Cor 5:17) than of a rebirth."[60] Thus, one would be remiss in not wanting to trace the idea articulated in John 3:3 back to the biblical promise of a spiritually constituted sonship with God and an eschatological new creation through the Spirit. Although this "opens up the horizon of understanding of John 3, it alone is not sufficient to explain the motif of birth 'from above' or 'of water and the Spirit.'"[61] However, a look at the Hellenistic Judaism of the diaspora, as represented by Philo of Alexandria, takes us further.

Here we not only find texts which generally point to the fact that Jews like him used the language of Hellenistic mystery cults to apply it to analogous biblical issues (see Philo *Cher.* 40–50; *Som.* 1.164–165; *Gig.* 54.57; *Spec.* 1.319–323; *Leg.* 3.100). We also know of a text, written by him, which could prove an idea of "rebirth" present in sources about mystery cults already existed.[62]

---

59. J. Jeremias and H. Strathmann, *Die Briefe an Timotheus und Titus. Der Brief an die Hebräer*, NTD 9 (Göttingen: Vandenhoeck & Ruprecht, 1934), 67. See especially a baraita in b. Yebam. 48b: "A proselyte who has converted to Judaism is like a newborn child."

60. K. H. Schelkle, *Die Petrusbriefe. Der Judasbrief*, HThK.NT 13/2, 3rd ed. (Freiburg: Herder, 1970), 29.

61. T. Söding, "Wiedergeburt aus Wasser und Geist. Anmerkungen zur Symbolsprache des Johannesevangeliums am Beispiel des Nikodemusgesprächs," in *Metaphorik und Mythos*, ed. K. Kertelge, QD 126 (Freiburg: Herder, 1990), 168–219, here 187 with n. 65.

62. W. Burkert, *Antike Mysterien. Funktion und Gehalt*, 3rd ed. (München: C. H. Beck, 1991), 29: "It is plausible to think that the center of all initiation must be death and rebirth, that death and new life are thus anticipated in the ritual and that real death is thus turned into a secondary repetition; direct testimonies to this are sparse."

This refers to his interpretation of Exodus 24:16 in *QE* 2.46, which interprets Moses's ascent to the mountain of God as a primal religious experience and in this context states, "the calling above of the prophet is a *second birth* better than the first."[63] Admittedly, the mystery-theological background of a second birth is assured due to the lack of additional signals in the text, but it cannot be ruled out that the idea of a corresponding perception is influenced by initiation rites in mystery cults. In any case, elsewhere Philo portrays Moses quite clearly as a "mystagogue" using the specific terminology (*Somn.* 1.164; *Virt.* 178; *Mos.* 2.71).[64]

For an assessment of John 3:3, 5*, the following results from these few observations: (1) The *concept* of "being born again" cannot be explained solely on the basis of *specifically Jewish* precepts (eschatological new creation from the Spirit of God). The development of this Jesus saying points to a Jewish-Hellenistic milieu, as attested for example by Philo of Alexandria. (2) The symbol of "rebirth" is found in John *in connection with the initiation rite of baptism*, as well as with 1 Peter 1:3, 23, and Titus 3:5 in two other texts that are independent of each other and of John 3, which are also related to baptism. It is therefore reasonable to assume that, in using the motif, the New Testament authors were referring to mystery cults in which it was also used in connection with initiation rites in the broadest sense, or that they were at least reckoning with such cults when they used the motif. Now, in line with W. Burkert's warning, this assumption will not be made "the actual key to the ritual and proclamation of the ancient mysteries,"[65] but it does seem to be the case that with their talk of "rebirth," New Testament texts took up a symbol that they considered to be highly characteristic of contemporary religious wishes and longings. At any rate, this must have been their external perception of the flourishing mystery cults. In articulating the matter this way, in the transformation of the old Jesus saying into the rebirth of man in John 3:3, 5* one can see a piece of *inculturation of faith* within a Hellenistic environment, which is a good testimony to its vitality and will to be understood in new cultural frames.

---

63. Philo, *QE* 46: LCL, Suppl. 2.91 (Marcus). After that the text speaks about "the divine birth" (92).

64. See C. Riedweg, *Mysterienterminologie bei Platon, Philon und Klemens von Alexandrien*, UALG 26 (Berlin: de Gruyter, 1987).

65. Burkert, *Mysterien* 85-86: "There is ... no text that speaks of 'rebirth' as extensively and resoundingly as Paul or the Gospel of John. That the conception of the New Testament is directly dependent on pagan mystery teachings is so far unprovable from a philological-historical point of view; all the less should it be made the actual key to the ritual and proclamation of the older mysteries."

2.1.10 Genre and Intention of the Johannine Congregational Saying

So fare we spoken of John 3:3, 5* as and "entrance saying." From a genre-historical perspective, this has the benefit that the assignment of our logion to the analogous words of the synoptic tradition remains recognizable.

Appropriate to its genre, the saying, which was adapted by the community because of its reference to baptism, articulates the necessary condition of renewal in order to enter God's kingdom. However, it is not water baptism as an *external* rite and external requirement that is the crux of the condition for entry into the kingdom but the rebirth "out of water *and spirit*." The point is that it is *not* man's conversion or his *efforts* that guarantees entrance into the kingdom of God but the *gift* of the new birth from *God's* transformational Spirit. This gift radically precedes all human endeavors.

If we ask who the saying was aimed at or what it intended to achieve with whom and by what means, then it seems plausible to start with its symbolism of "rebirth" and the idea of a radical caesura between the old and new existence of the baptized. Different pragmatic constellations are imaginable.

Read against the background of the conflict-laden process of separation of the Johannine congregation from the synagogue, the saying could have emphasized the need for a socially perceptible line of separation between old and new in the lives of the baptized with regard to the so-called "crypto-Christians" who wanted to remain in the synagogue with their confession of Christ; the idea of "rebirth" would have been the theological symbol for this.[66] If, on the other hand, the saying had more in mind those who, having been baptized, clearly confessed themselves to be members of the Johannine community, then it could have been intended to strengthen their identity in the face of an overpowering synagogue: The certainty that following Jesus, which caused some social disadvantages, was based in God's Spirit which creates anew, had to give them hope and strength to withstand all troubles as born-again individuals. If we think of the *Sitz im Leben* of baptismal catechesis or liturgy, the saying would have set free its pragmatic impulses in this context.

That the "entrance saying" in John 3:3, 5 could be interpreted in other ways can be found in Pseudo-Clement, *Homilies* 13.21.2–3, where the saying is called δόγμα θεοῦ or νόμος, which declares the necessity of baptism for salvation. This "provision" of God is, according to the author of this homily, valid even in case of a "righteous person" (δίκαιος), who could not enter God's kingdom without baptism. Such considerations have to be seen distinct from John 3:3, 5*. We are not dealing with a *sacramental legal*

---

66. For more information see pp. 284–285, 366–368.

"constitution"[67] here but with an "entrance saying" which is intended to provide orientation, consolation, and strength.

2.1.11 Reception and Interpretation of the Saying in John[68]

At first we want to mention observations concerning *form*: to make full use of the richness of the given saying, the evangelist elucidates it *twofold*. In 3:3 he adapted it more to his language, whereas in its repetition the original wording is maintained. In the dialogue between Jesus and Nicodemus the saying functions as the first important remark of the revelator to which he often refers in the following passages. The saying is interpreted by the Nicodemus-dialogue 3:2–15. That Nicodemos reacts with helplessness shows that—according to the author's conviction—opinions about the understanding of the saying differ here.

Concerning *content*, the Christologization of the saying by the evangelist is noteworthy. The saying does not inherently contain any explicit Christological statement. However, the way in which the evangelist has structured Jesus's dialogue with Nicodemus as it progresses indicates that the first fundamental word of Jesus in this dialogue is to be read in the light of 3:13, that is, the beginning of the actual Christological statements of the chapter. The first saying about the Son of Man in 3:13 is the Christological complement to the logion in 3:3, 5. It influenced the redaction of 3:3, 5. Of course, this is not immediately recognizable, but the evangelist has established signals that put the reader on this track.

Speaking of man, he says in in redactional exaggeration, "unless one is born from *above*, he cannot see the kingdom of God" (3:3). He says of Christ: "And no one has ascended to heaven *except the one who descended from heaven*, the Son of Man" (3:13). Thus, there is an analogy between the baptized and Christ: Like Christ came from heaven, the baptized is born from above by water and the Holy Spirit and therefore receives his existence from God. We can assume that the evangelist wrote "from above" in 3:3 with 3:13 in mind.

How can the analogy between the event of the new birth of man out of water and the spirit in verses 3, 5 and the event of Christ's coming be understood according to the author's intention? We could formulate an answer by following B. Lindars: The one aspect supports the understanding of the other. That Jesus is the *preexistent Son of Man* who descended from heaven—and therefore is greater than the eschatological prophet who like Moses is "earthly" (i.e., of human origin)—can be seen according to the evangelist already by the fact that Jesus promises everyone who believes in him a birth *from above*. He

---

67. See J. Becker, *Das Evangelium nach Johannes I–II*, ÖTK 4/1–2 (Gütersloh: Gütersloher Verlagshaus, 1979/1981 [3rd edition 1991]), 1:160, 163–164.

68. See also pp. 114–117, 127–130, 378–379!

sees believers analogically to himself grounded *in God's world*. In my opinion, verse 12 is the hinge verse between the first two passages on the new birth of *man* (3:3–9) and the third on the significance of *Christ* (3:13–15) and demonstrates that there is a progressive logic of the evangelist's instruction on faith or rather targeted guidance of the reader. Here we read, "If I have told you about *earthly* things and you do not believe, how will you believe if I tell you about *heavenly* things?" While Nicodemus and those like him may find it hopeless to progress catechistically from the *earthly* to the *heavenly*, for the listeners and readers of John this is exactly what the evangelist expects of them. In case of the *earthly* things, we have to think of what will happen in the birth from above (described in vv. 3, 5) whereas the *heavenly* things consist of the way and fate of the Son of Man who stems from heaven and will again ascend to heaven.[69]

This analysis of the dialogue shows that the evangelist projected his own Christology, which focuses on the preexistence of the Son of Man, on the logion in 3:3, 5. The dialogue communicates the insight that the analogy between the Son of Man and the believer refers to a similarity with a greater dissimilarity. Verses 13 and 14–15 are dedicated to the Christological *pre* in the sense of a soteriological exclusivity of Christ. So when the author speaks of a birth of the believer *from above*, it is clear that this birth is attainable only because "the Son of Man who descended from heaven" will also "ascend to heaven" (3:13), more specifically, he will be "exalted" (3:14) there. Only in this way does he open a path for man out of the darkness of this world of death into the light of the godly life. Only through faith in the exalted Christ (3:15) does the possibility open up for him to be placed on a new foundation of life by the Spirit of God to a new status of living. In the words of the evangelist this is what it means to be born *from above*.

In the question about "where Christ is from," we can find an analogy between Christ and his community. The same goes for the dimension of "where he is going." However, this keyword is missing (cf. 3:8). Nevertheless, the correspondences between the Son of Man's ascent into heaven—the world of God— and the "entrance" of believers into the "kingdom of God" *made possible by him* are clear enough. Of course, despite all the similarities between these two processes, there is also a greater dissimilarity between them. They do not run parallel to each other, but the believer's "entry" into the kingdom of God is based on the Son of Man's "ascent to heaven." Furthermore, the believer's "entrance

---

69. However, one should not separate the *earthly* and *heavenly* aspects like two parts of a curriculum. Rather, they are two different perspectives of *one* and *the same* "object of faith": What happens in *baptism is grounded* in the heavenly events pertaining to the Son of Man. The transformation of the traditional terminology (earthly—heavenly things) can be seen by the fact that the Fourth Gospel does not purport the idea of heavenly things *in the plural*, i.e., heavenly mysteries in sense of apocalyptical scenarios, rather the *one* secret of the person of Son of Man.

into the kingdom of God" (his kingdom) does not only take place at the end of days but already now in the community of life with the exalted Christ. Verse 15 says this as follows, "so that everyone who believes may have eternal life *in him*." But verse 3, which bears the signature of the evangelist, already expresses this idea: "Seeing the kingdom of God" means nothing other than seeing in Christ, especially in this death (3:13, 14), the beginning of God's reign in life. Thus, the Christologizing of the saying in 3:3, 5 is also linked to its transformation in the sense of present eschatology: it is no longer about a *future* entrance into the kingdom of God, but about the *present* perception of God in Jesus's life and life's work.

Finally, if we ask about the *pragmatic* intention that the evangelist pursued with his interpretation of John's congregational saying in John 2:23–3:15, then we can say the following. Nicodemus is certainly more than just the "supplier of a keyword" for Jesus's contributions to the conversation. However, how his portrait contributes to the dialogue with Jesus is uncertain. We should rule out the thesis that the evangelist understands Nicodemus as a representative of "the Jews," that is, Jesus's opponents in Jerusalem, who first become active in the gospel in 1:19 and then appear on the scene themselves in 2:18–20. Since Nicodemus not only confesses Jesus in 3:2 (admittedly insufficiently in the evangelist's view), but also appears as a representative of the "believers" of 2:23, it would not be wrong to see him as a typical representative of "Jewish Christianity" (also found elsewhere in John), who is still part of the synagogue and from which the evangelist distances himself, particularly in Christological terms. If this hypothesis is correct,[70] then the pragmatics of John 3:1–15 can be broadly defined as follows: first, the evangelist emphasizes what is already laid out in the Johannine congregational logion (cf. 3.1.11), namely that the remembrance of the new birth in baptism contains the knowledge of a profound break with the old existence of man, which also includes parting with the old life in Judaism. Second—and this is the emphasis in John 3:1–15—the evangelist justifies such a dramatic change of existence with *Christology*: To belong to Jesus, who is a stranger in this world, who does not come from it, but as the Son of Man "came down from heaven," also means for those who believe in him to be *strangers in this world* as those born "from above." There is much to suggest that John 3:1–15 wanted to legitimize such a preexistence Christology vis-à-vis Nicodemus as a fictitious representative of a prophetic Christology of "Jewish-Christian" origin that remained entirely within

---

70. See M. Theobald, *Die Fleischwerdung des Logos. Studien zum Verhältnis des Johannesprologs zum Corpus des Evangeliums und zu 1 Joh*, NtA NF 20 (Münster: Aschaffendorf Verlag, 1988), 204–255; see further M. de Jonge, "Nicodemus and Jesus. Some Observations on Misunderstanding and Understanding in the Fourth Gospel," in *Jesus, Stranger from Heaven and Son of God. Jesus Christ and the Christians in Johannine Perspective* (Missoula, MT: Scholars Press, 1977), 29–47.

the Jewish continuum. Read in this way, the testimony of this chapter about Jesus the Son of Man, who towers above all prophets and messianic figures, only gains its full significance against the background of a specific community situation.

2.2 The Answer to Prayer "in the Name of" Jesus (John 14:12–14/Mark 11:24; John 15:7; 16:24/Q11:9–10)

Let us begin with an illustration: A stone falls into water and makes ripples. Jesus threw the stone and the ripples were enormous: two logia stand at the beginning, Q 11:9–10 ("ask and it will be given to you . . .") and Mark 11:24 ("whatever you pray for and ask, believe that you have received it, and it will be given to you"). The beginnings of these ripples can already be seen in Matthew: Beside his tradition based on Mark (in Matt 21:22) and the sayings source (in Matt 7:7–8), the first evangelist presents a third version in Matthew 18:19–20 that reveals his own handiwork. In the Corpus Johanneum the tradition "expands." There are seven references in all the layers of this group of writings: in the Gospel (John 14:13–14), in Jesus's later farewell discourses (John 15:7; 15:16; 16:23–24.; 16:26), and in 1 John (1 John 3:21–22.; 5:14–15). Both of the older traditions influenced the corpus (for Mark see especially John 14:13–14; for the sayings source see John 15:7; 16:24). But that is not all. The letter of James attests to the ripple effect of this saying (Jas 1:5–8; 4:2–3), and it is possible that Ephesians also alludes to it (Eph 3:20). Moreover, we find an astonishing echo of this Q-sequence about asking, searching, and knocking in the noncanonical, early patristic and gnostic literature.[71] How can we explain this phenomenon?

Obviously, Jesus provoked his hearers with his *unconditional* promise to grant the requests of unceasing prayer. The promise evoked hope and constituted belief in the power of prayer but could not avoid disappointment. Was Jesus's promise only applicable and effective for him alone? But already the oldest evangelist subsumed Jesus's prayer under the general statement that is also preserved in the Lord's Prayer in Matthew: "but not what *I* want, rather what *you* want" (Mark 14:36). Furthermore, the frequent repetitions of the saying about granting requests in prayer show that its unconditionality was important: A lot of these passages treat the conditions under which the words of Jesus become true.

In the Johannine community theological reflection on the logion became fruitful in a special way as can be readily seen in the multitude of contexts in which it appears (as we have seen above). The Johannine starting point is certainly John 14:12–14. Therefore, first we will examine these verses and the origins of

---

71. See, e.g., Shephard of Hermas, Similitudes 6.3.6 and Gos. Thom. 94; see also Log. 2.92; POxy 654; Ep. Jas 10.32–34.

this tradition. Then we will shed light on its development in the later layers of the Gospel (John 15-16) and in 1 John. Finally, we will focus on Jesus's position (as concrete as possible) to understand better from this perspective the struggle of the early Christian tradition, especially of the Johannine community.

2.2.1 A Johannine Amen-Saying (John 14:12-14)
Context, Form, and Structure

First, it is necessary to present the text:

12	a	Truly, truly I say to you,
	b	Whoever believes in me, the works,
	b¹	which *I* do,
	b²	*he* also will do (them),
	c	and he will do works greater than these,
	d	for I am going to the Father.
13	a	And whatever he prays for in my name,
	b	I will do *this*,
	c	so the Father will be glorified in the Son;
14	a	if you ask for anything in my name,
	b	*I* will do it.

The context of this saying unit is the first farewell discourse, more precisely its first half (14:1-14), which, following the theme of verses 2-3—the announcement of Jesus's departure and second coming—primarily addresses aspects of his presence among them, which is now coming to an end. However, this part of the saying already leads to the second main part of the speech (14:15-26) which is about the second coming of Jesus at Easter in the form of the Spirit. On the one hand, the unit of speech once again takes up the theme of Jesus's imminent departure (v. 12d); on the other hand, it focuses on the post-Easter period. Nevertheless, the connections of the unit of speech with the preceding context are closer[72] than with the following. This unity therefore can be understood as the end of the first half especially since "believing" is a leitmotif here, whereas in verse 15 "loving" takes on the role of leitmotif.

In terms of *form*, verses 12-14 are an independent, self-contained, consistent unit of speech. It is introduced by the Johannine Amen-formula. Even though

---

72. The connecting keywords are: "works" (vv. 11 and 12) and "believe" (vv. 1:10, 11/12).

the two halves of verses 12 and 13, which are linked by "and," each follow their own syntactic pattern.[73] The intention of their semantic linking is obvious: the four main clauses use the verb "do" throughout, whereby the two leading subjects (he who believes in me—I) result in a paired formation that is revealing for the interpretation of the saying unit:

he will do (12b)
he will do (12d)
I will do (13b)
I will do (14b)

Moreover, both halves are connected by the fact that they make a statement concerning Father and Son which are in a causal or final relationship to the superordinate main clause:

12d: for I am going to the Father
13c: so that the Father might be glorified through the Son

Just as these two statements explain each other, the same also applies to the two halves of the saying as a whole: The specific Johannine part of verse 12 sheds light on the synoptic tradition in verses 13–14. Vice versa, verse 12 is protected against misinterpretation by the synoptic tradition in verse 13. The reader is expected to relate the two halves of the unit of speech to each other in a meaningful way. However, we have already anticipated the forthcoming analysis. For this analysis, it is important to notice that verses 12–14 are an independent unit which has to be interpreted with respect to its inner relationships. According to its *genre*, we have here a Johannine Amen-saying, more precisely a word of promise.

The passage has the following *structure*:

1. *Opening-formula* (12a)
2. *First promise* (12b–d)
2.1 promise doing something for everyone "who believes in me" (12b)
2.2 specification of the promise (12c)
2.3 Christological reason (12d)
3. *Second promise* (13, 14)

---

73. While v. 12 is more general ("whoever believes in me . . .," in v. 13 Jesus speaks directly to his disciples ["you"]). This change of person can be explained on grounds of the tradition (see below the synoptic parallels!).

3.1 promise of grant of prayer (13a.b)
3.2 Christological aim (13c)
3.3 specification of the promise (14)

Syntactically 2.1 (= v. 12b) is complex which is in itself meaningful: The fact that the participial formulated subject of the main clause ("the one who believes in me") is pointedly taken up again by the demonstrative "this one also" after the insertion of the relative clause 12b[74] results in a powerful contrast: "what *I* do, *he also* will do" (12b). This contrast leads to the decisive question of the unit: How do the actions of the disciples relate to the actions of Jesus, that is the one who has been exalted at Easter (12d)?

The complex syntactic form of 2.1 (= v. 12b) means that "faith" and "works"—two keywords which are laden with tradition due to their controversial mutual relationship—are situated side by side in the first colon. That is not a coincidence: The one who *believes* in Jesus will perform *works*!

What is striking about the second half of the unit of speech is the repetition in verse 14 of the promise to answer prayer from verse 13a, b, which consists of a conditional relative clause as the protasis and a corresponding apodosis. To want to eliminate this as a literary-critical duplicate of verse 13a, b[75] would be to misjudge the semantically significant variations of this verse compared to verses 13: the subordinate clause introduced by "if" in verse 14a corresponds to the relative conditional clause in verse 13a, but by adding the personal pronoun *me* two accusatives are dependent on the predicate ("something"—"me"). Furthermore the main clause of verse 14b corresponds to that of verse 13b but instead of the demonstrative pronoun "this" which emphasizes the *issue of* prayer, in verse 14b the use of the personal pronoun "I" (ἐγώ), which corresponds to the *me* in the protasis, emphasizes the *originator* of the works. Verses 13 and 14 accentuate different aspects of the same promise: that it applies to *everything*[76] the Johannine community prays for (v. 13) and it respectively is the *exalted one* ("I") who realizes such promise by his *own* work. We will see below that this shift in emphasis is important for the interpretation of this unit of speech.

---

74. Here we have Johannine stylistic device; see E. Ruckstuhl and P. Dschulnigg, *Stilkritik und Verfasserfrage im Johannesevangelium. Die johanneischen Sprachmerkmale auf dem Hintergrund des Neuen Testaments und des zeitgenössischen hellenistischen Schrifttums*, NTOA 17 (Göttingen: Vandenhoeck & Ruprecht, 1991), 78: "There are also no actual parallels in the Hellenistic literature examined."

75. See Becker, *Johannes*, 2:555. For older representatives of literary critical operations, see R. Schnackenburg, *Das Johannesevangelium*, 4 vols., HThK.NT IV/1–4 (Freiburg: Herder, 1965–1984), 3:83 n. 80.

76. ὅ τι ἄν ... functions as a "general" relative pronoun.

2.2.2 "Ask and it will be given to you!" The Synoptic Parallels to the Johannine Aphorism

The core of the second half of the unit in John 14:13–14 is an old aphorism which we also find in the Synoptics. Here, however, John transforms it in service of its new context. It consists of a conditional relative clause in the protasis and the promise to grant one's prayer in the apodosis. It seems plausible to view this as an aphorism[77] because—as the following overview demonstrates—there is a close relationship between our saying and the synoptic logia and between the Synoptics among themselves. Nevertheless, it seems impossible that John 14:13, 14 is based directly on one of these sources (Mark, Matthew, Luke, or Q). The divergences of the traditions, also between the Synoptics themselves, can be better explained by the assumption of an *oral* aphorism that was adaptable in many ways.[78] The oldest evidence of our tradition can be found in the sayings source Q 11:9–10.[79] This version is identical to Matthew 7:7–8 and Luke 11:9–10, so its originality can be verified by them:[80]

9   a   (And I say to you,)
       b   Ask and it will be given to you,
       c   seek and you will find,
       d   knock and it will be opened to you.
10   a   For everyone who asks, receives,
       b   and whoever seeks, finds,
       c   and to him who knocks, it will be opened.

---

77. See Dodd, *Tradition*, 349 n. 1 ("self-contained aphorisms") and J. D. Crossan, *In Fragments. The Aphorisms of Jesus* (San Fransisco: Harper & Row, 1983), 95–104 (on genre see pp. 3–36). See, too, D. Aune, *Jesus and the Oral Gospel Tradition*, ed. H. Wansbrough (London: T&T Clark, 2004).

78. See especially Dodd, *Tradition*, 349–352, who speaks of the "independent use of traditional material" (352); Crossan, *Fragments*, 103, follows his opinion. Similarly, H. W. Attridge, "'Seeking' and 'Asking' in Q, Thomas and John," in *From Quest to Q* (FS J. M. Robinson), BEThL 146 (Leuven: Peeters, 2000), 211–265, here 297: "Whatever the relationship of John to the Synoptic Gospels generally, there is no evidence here of direct dependence on either Q or its Synoptic offspring."

79. See also Crossan, *Fragments*, 103.

80. Apart from the opening of the saying v. 9a (it is missing in Matt 7:7) and the tense in v. 10c: future tense in Matt 7:8, "it will be opened"; present tense in Luke 11:10 (some witnesses also have the future tense).

Whether or not the opening of the saying in verse 9a originally belongs to the text of Q is disputed because it is missing in Matthew.[81] "Actually, however, the energetic imperative new clause calls for a new sovereign introduction."[82] Moreover, if in the original context of Q the Lord's Prayer in Q 11:2–4 was followed by Q 11:9–10[83] then the introductory addition to the Lord's Prayer would make sense structurally.[84] Furthermore, we can assume that it was an integral part of the originally independent saying in Q 11:9–10,[85] even before it was incorporated by the redactors of Q into the composition of sayings included in the Lord's Prayer. This is indicated by the astonishing finding that a large part of the evidence for our aphorism in the Gospels also has a corresponding introductory formula, although they are otherwise quite different in their formulations.[86] This suggests that the certainty with which Jesus promises to grant one's prayer here is connected with his own authority,[87] which authorizes him to make this

---

81. E.g., J. A. Fitzmyer, *The Gospel According to Luke. Introduction, Translation, and Notes I–II*, AncB 28/28A (New York: Doubleday, 1981 and 1985), 2:913–14 claims that it is part of Q; for a Lukan redaction, see François Bovon, *Luke 2: A Commentary on the Gospel of Luke 9:51–19:27* (Minneapolis, MN: Fortress, 2012), 151; Attridge, "Seeking," 296 n. 7. See also Robinson etc., *Edition*, 214–215.

82. H. Schürmann, *Das Lukasevangelium I–II*, HThK.NT III/1–2.1 (Freiburg: Herder, 1969 and 1993), 2:215.

83. With good arguments J. S. Kloppenborg, *The Formation of Q. Trajectories in Ancient Wisdom Collections* (Philadelphia: Fortress, 1987), 203 and 205–206; Robinson, etc., *Edition*, 210–217.—The parable Luke 11:5–8 (special material [*Sondergut*]) was incorporated into the context of Q by the third evangelist.

84. Q 11:2: "When you pray, say . . . ."—Verse 9: "I say to you . . . ." Also concerning content, Q 11:9ff. refers to the Lord's Prayer in the composition of Q. Schürmann, *Lukasevangelium*, 1:221: "The pair of sayings in 11:9–10, 11ff.—in the context of the Lord's Prayer in 11:2–4— encourages us to dare to pray with the petitions of 11:2–4. It thus accentuates Jesus's prayer in retrospect as a petition."

85. See Schürmann, *Lukasevangelium*, 1:215–216, 219–220: Q 11:9–10, 11ff. is a "pair of sayings" that consist of a "basic statement" 11:9–10 and an "additional saying" 11:11ff. Both of them were "transmitted in isolation" and are understandable "from the preaching situation of Jesus and the congregation" (221); R. A. Piper, "Matthew 7,7-11 par. Luke 11,9-13. Evidence of Design and Argument in the Collection of Jesus' Sayings," in *Logia. Les paroles de Jésus* (FS J. Coppens), BETL 59 (Leuven: Peeters, 1982), 411–418, here 412. Differently Luz, *Matthäus*, 1:383.

86. Apart from Luke 11:9a, see Mark 11:24a: "therefore I say to you" (about that see below); Matt 18:19: "again, truly, I say to you"; John 14:12: "truly, truly, I say to you"; 16:23: "truly, truly, I say to you."

87. Schürmann, *Lukasevangelium*, 1:214, calls Luke 11:9a an "formula of authority."

promise. In this respect, the "Truly, I say to you" formula can be described as an integral part of the saying.

It seems questionable whether this saying itself can be deconstructed in a tradition criticism manner. Methodically, two approaches are conceivable: Either one focuses on the fault lines in the logion itself or confronts it with other manifestations of the tradition of answered prayers. Goldsmith, who wanted to reconstruct Q 11:9a, 10a with reference to Mark 11:24 as an authentic earlier logion (*Urlogion*) about the coming kingdom of God, did the latter.[88] This is not absurd[89] if one also considers the manifold Johannine verses (especially John 16:24, "pray and you will receive") and then see that only in Q 11:9–10 is the petition motif extended by the metaphor of seeking and knocking. But are we forced to trace the different versions of tradition back to *one* original form? Ultimately, such an attempt will remain speculative. Inner fault lines in the logion are also recognizable in the second part[90] of the saying of exhortation, which updates the older saying in light of wisdom theology. An addition is also suspected in verse 10.[91] But even here one wonders whether the linguistic evidence is sufficient to support these hypotheses or whether the well-proportioned form of the saying (two sets of threefold components) testifies to its integrity.

In terms of content, Heinz Schürmann has made the saying[92] understandable as an inner unity from its implicit reference to Jesus's proclamation of the kingdom of God. "To whom it [i.e., the kingdom of God]—in Jesus's words and deeds—has shone forth and come, he will now first ask for it, then also seek it,

---

88. D. Goldsmith, "'Ask, and it will be given...' Toward Writing the History of a Logion," *NTS* 35 (1989): 254–265, here 258–262.

89. See, however, M. Ebner, *Jesus—ein Weisheitslehrer? Synoptische Weisheitslogien im Traditionsprozess*, HBS 15 (Freiburg: Herder, 1998), 309 n. 36.

90. Ebner, *Jesus*, 309 n. 36: "The second word of exhortation, which also stands out formally (no *passivum divinum*), introduces the motif of seeking wisdom (cf. Prov 8:17b; Sir 6:37; 51:26b) and may represent the first actualization [of the saying]." Moreover, v. 9 is an "bedrock." See already H.-J. Klauck, "'Christus, Gottes Kraft und Gottes Weisheit' (1 Kor 1,24). Jüdische Weisheitsüberlieferungen im Neuen Testament," in *Alte Welt und neuer Glaube. Beiträge zur Religionsgeschichte, Forschungsgeschichte und Theologie des Neuen Testaments*, ed. H.-J. Klauck, NTOA 29 (Fribourg: Universitätsverlag, 1994), 251–275, here 256–257.

91. See with some differences P. S. Minear, *Commands of Christ* (Nashville: Abingdon Press, 1972), 117–118; D. R. Catchpole, "Q and 'the Friend at Midnight' (Luke XI. 5–8/9)," *JThS.NS* 34 (1983): 407–424, here 418–419.

92. On the structure, note that the unit of the first three lines is "a prayer request, the second with the assurance of the certainty of answering the motivation for this prayer request" (Schürmann, *Lukasevangelium*, 1:214).

also knock, and in the end it will be opened to him."[93] This interpretation is characterized by the fact that it sees the wisdom-based experiential reference of the saying, which is also discussed in research,[94] transported into the eschatologically unique,[95] in order to derive its persuasive power not from what anyone can confirm on the basis of their life experience, but from the authority of the one who coined this saying.[96] For the definition of its *genre*, this means that it cannot simply be subsumed under the category of "wisdom admonitions,"[97] but rather, like Jesus's Amen-saying, has the characteristics of a prophetic promise of salvation.[98] The imperatives to dare to ask, seek, and knock are to be understood in the light of the unconditional promise to hear.

If we compare the core of the tradition of John 14:13 and 14 with Q 11:9–10, we can detect the similarity of the two sayings in terms of their content (in each case it is about the *assurance* of prayer being granted), in their character as a form of address (second-person plural), and in the verb "praying." However, we should not overlook the differences between them. Apart from the metaphorical expansion of the synoptic saying into a three-line structure, both sayings each follow their own basic syntactic pattern: Q 11:9–10 offers three imperatives, each followed by the indicative of the future tense together with a likewise threefold

---

93. Schürmann, *Lukasevangelium*, 1:216. To all of the three elements—praying, searching, knocking—he shows the specific semantic fields associated with the preaching of God's kingdom: Luke 13:24 ("they will seek to enter"); Luke 12:31 ("seek his basileia"); Matt 13:45 ("seek" in the parable); knocking—open: Luke 13:25; see Matt 25:11; on God's kingdom as gift: Mark 4:11; Luke 12:32; see 22:29–30. "The Trinity becomes unambiguous against the background of Jesus's proclamation of the kingdom of God" (215).

94. See D. Zeller, *Die weisheitlichen Mahnsprüche bei den Synoptikern*, FzB 17 (Würzburg: Echter Verlag, 1977), 127–131; Klauck, "Christus," 256: According to him, the saying is about the "generally human experience that intensive searches and energetic efforts to make oneself noticeable often lead to success, and are in any case preferable to refraining from searching and disruptive maneuvers." But the text speaks in principle ("everyone")! Hence, Schürmann, *Lukasevangelium*, 2:215 writes: "The threefold assurance in v. 10 is certainly not a sentence based on experience, as every supplicant will be able to confirm. It corresponds to the unconditional request in v. 9 that an absolute assurance is given here authoritatively, which contradicts all experience. It still stands in the light of the introductory formula of autority."

95. Schürmann, *Lukasevangelium*, 2:215: "The threefold *passivum divinum* is—as is usually the case—a *passivum eschatologicum*." Different, however, is Zeller, *Mahnsprüche*, 127, who argues that "it will be opened" should be understood "gnomically."

96. See Schürmann, *Lukasevangelium*, 2:215.

97. See Zeller, *Mahnsprüche*, 127–131.

98. See also S. Schulz, *Q—Die Spruchquelle der Evangelisten* (Zürich: Theologischer Verlag, 1972), 162–163.

staggered clause that provides justification; John 14:13 and 14, however, are based on a conditional relative clause with a future tense verb in the main clause. Now these two syntactic patterns are not as far apart as one might initially think.[99] However, *Mark 11:24*—the *second* witness of our tradition of the answer to prayer—is closer to our saying in John 14:13/14 in Greek, because not only do both passages have the same syntactic sentence pattern, they both focus on the subject of supplication.

Here we present the text of Mark 11:24:

a Therefore, I say to you,
b Everything
c for which you pray
d and for which you ask,
e believe
f that you have (already) received it,
g and it will be granted to you.

The verse is the centerpiece of a teaching by Jesus on the subject of *prayer* and *faith* to his disciples in Jerusalem, consisting of three sayings including a "heading" (Mark 11:22–25).[100] Because Mark develops this theme stringently in his small composition, it can be assumed that he has left his own editorial mark on the individual sayings that have come down to him. This can also be seen in Mark 11:24.

First, the introductory formula is noteworthy, which here takes the form of a conclusion: "therefore I say to you." Rudolf Pesch asks us to consider *dia touto = therefore* as a replacement of the original *Amen*.[101] This is quite possible, for one must reckon with its original independence because of the other New Testament parallels to this saying. However, the word "therefore" is a signal of

---

99. See K. Beyer, *Semitische Syntax im Neuen Testament I. Satzlehre*, StUNT 1, 2nd ed. (Göttingen: Vandenhoeck & Ruprecht, 1968), 1:251–255.

100. The unit is separated from the context by the narrator's note in v. 22a: "and Jesus took the floor and spoke to them." The "heading" of v. 22b reads: "Have faith in God!" This is followed by three logia, the first of which about faith moving mountains (par. Matt 21:21) has a parallel in Q (Luke 17:6 par. Matt 17:20) and the third about mutual forgiveness is reminiscent of Matt 6:14, the first evangelist's appendix to the Lord's Prayer.

101. R. Pesch, *Das Markusevangelium II*, HThK.NT 2/2 (Freiburg: Herder, 1977), 203: "to avoid a duplication of v. 23."

its integration into the existing composition, which can be read from the *content* of *three* features of the saying:

(1) The doubling of the two verbs προσεύχεσθε and αἰτεῖσθε is striking. The second has a profane sound (to ask), whereas the first is of a religious nature (to pray). For this reason alone, this verb makes a more reflective impression compared to the second and is therefore probably secondary. Additionally, it prepares the third logion of the group of sayings: "And when you stand *praying* (προσευχόμενοι), forgive, if you have anything against anyone, so that your Father in heaven may also forgive you your trespasses" (v. 25). Mark has thus placed the topic of prayer in two contextual relationships. If we start from the first saying, the faith that moves mountains, then the second saying, that of answered prayer, says, "Prayer is the *expression* of such *faith*, indeed it is in it that it is realized and proven." If we then move on to the third saying, we become familiar with a second important dimension of prayer: its *vertical* orientation toward God requires *horizontal* truthfulness as a basis; those who entrust themselves completely to God in prayer with faith and open themselves to him must also break down all barriers against their fellow human beings in forgiveness. Turning to God and turning to one's neighbor belong inseparably together and are the basis for the weight of prayer.[102]

(2) It is then syntactically striking that Mark prefers the relative clause in verse 24b–d ("everything for which you pray ..."), which is dependent on the object clause in verses 24–25 ("that you have already received *it*") that comes later. The reason for this is probably that the saying began with the conditional relative clause[103] and was followed by the main clause. Mark has retained this structure but overlaid it with his imperative "believe that you have (already) received (it)." The syntactic complexity of the sentence thus reflects its multilayered complexity: It is no longer just about the *performance* of the supplication as such but about the *mode* in which the supplication is to be made, namely in the belief that the supplicant has already obtained what he is asking for.[104] God always already knows what the person needs; the person can trust that God is ahead of him in everything.

Only this theological deepening of the saying with the terminology of faith also guarantees its connection to the first saying: "Have faith in God" (v. 22b), which can move mountains, do not doubt in your heart (v. 23)! "*Therefore*, I also

---

102. See also Matt 5:23–24!

103. See John 14:13, 14; 15:7, 16; 16:23.

104. Matt 6:8b: "For your Father knows what you need *before you even ask him*."

say to you" (v. 24a): Carry out your petitions and prayers in a faith that trusts God for everything, let your prayer become an *expression* of your faith!

(3) The fact that the first two sayings are so closely linked can also be seen by their mutual linguistic similarity:

23:	24:
he believes	believes
what he says will happen,	that you have received,
it will be given to him.	and it will be given to you.

The syntactical function of both parts of the verse is comparable: Whereas in verse 24 the imperative clause *believe* . . . + *and it will be given to you* replaces a *conditional clause*,[105] *believe* in verse 23 builds the frame of a conditional *relative clause*: "Whoever . . . believes that what he says will happen, it will be given to him." The agreement between the two sayings at their climax *and will be given to him / to you* is convincing. It is obvious that Mark wanted to connect both sayings.

Once one has become aware of the linguistic and intellectual interlocking of the sayings in the Markan composition, we can at least take a small step forward in answering the question of what the saying about the answer to prayer given in Mark looked like. Although it cannot be reconstructed verbatim, we can at least say the following: The reflected theological character of the saying in Mark can be attributed to the first evangelist. This means that the saying did not originally use religious terminology, which is otherwise characteristic of Jesus, but spoke simply of "asking" and certainly did not yet attest to the dimension of faith in this saying. If the climax *"and it will / be given"* is also suspect due to its similarity with verse 23,[106] then one can hypothetically postulate the following predetermined form of the saying:

Truly, I say to you,
Everything
you ask for,
you receive it (will receive it).

The proximity of John 14:13/14; 15:7b; 16:23b to this aphorism is evident.

---

105. *"If* you believe that . . . it will be given to you!"

106. Of course Mark could have adapted v. 23 to v. 24, but the *formal* character of the phrase εἶναι + dative in both verses hints at the first evangelist.

Matthew has tightened Mark 11:24 stylistically and deleted the opening formula to avoid a duplication with 21:21b (*"truly I say to you"*).[107] In addition, he offers an application of this aphorism in his congregational discourse in chapter 18, which, like that of Mark, is also characterized by a reflective, this time ecclesiologically oriented reception of Jesus's promise to grant prayer:

> 18:19: Again,
> truly,[108] I say to you,
> If two of you on earth agree about anything pertaining to
>   what they ask,
> it will be done unto them by my Father in
>   heaven.
> 18:20: For where two or three are gathered together in my name,
>   there am I also in their midst.

Let us summarize. Jesus's promise to answer prayer is found in two syntactic forms in the Synoptics: as a conditional imperative clause together with an indicative in the future tense (= Q^{109}) and as a conditional relative clause together with a main clause in the indicative future tense.[110] The independence of the Q-version is demonstrated by its metaphorical filling to form a threefold figuration with a corresponding explanatory sentence.

2.2.3 "Faith" and "Works"
The Johannine Reception of the Aphorism in John 14:12–14

From perspective of Mark 11:22–24, one thinks that John 14:12–14 is a new interpretation of the Markan composition. According to Mark, the believer also performs miracles and works (he moves mountains)—like Jesus who let the fig tree wither by his word of power. The following logion also says that the prayer consists of such faith. However, the following tradition-criticism assumption is closer to the mark: Like Mark, the fourth evangelist has also taken up the well-known aphorism from the *oral* tradition to develop it theologically in the context of his first farewell discourse. This gives us two possible readings: synchronically

---

107. Matt 21:22: "And whatever you ask in prayer, you will receive it."

108. This amen is not clearly proved in the text.

109. See moreover John 16:24b: "Ask and you will receive."

110. Mark 11:24; John 13:13,14; 15:7b; 16:23b.

from verse 12 to verses 13–14 *and* diachronically from the tradition to its reception by John.

(1) The "works" Jesus does[111] will be accomplished by those who "believe" in him, and they will be done after Easter after Jesus has ascended to the Father (12d). That the disciples continue the Master's acts "is also known in the synoptic tradition"[112] and is therefore nothing new in early Christianity. "But v. 12 gives this idea a double, very particular form. The disciples' actions, in which Jesus's actions are continued, are explicitly transferred to the post-Easter era and made dependent on the occurrence of the post-Easter era. Added to this is the quality of the work promised to the disciples: they will do *greater* works than Jesus. These two characteristics are mutually dependent."[113] In what way?

With Christian Dietzfelbinger "one will assume that the disciples will continue Jesus's work in a manner that corresponds to this work, that is, through the word."[114] For a better understanding of John 14:12, reference can be made to the words of commission given to the disciples by the exalted one in John 20:21–23,[115] which also provide a commentary on our verses (perhaps it would be better to formulate it the other way round: John 14:12–14 comments in advance on the Easter pericope):

21 Then Jesus said to them again,
"Peace (be) with you!
As the Father has sent me,
so also I send you."
22 And when he had said this,
he breathed on them
and said to them,
"Receive the Holy Spirit!

---

111. Present tense, not the aorist! Jesus does not look back on the miracles he performed during the time of his public ministry, but also includes his present actions—speaking as a revelator—in the terms of "works." This observation alone is informative for its interpretation.

112. C. Dietzfelbinger, *Der Abschied des Kommenden. Eine Auslegung der johanneischen Abschiedsreden Abschied*, WUNT 95 (Tübingen: Mohr Siebeck, 1996), 46, especially refers to Luke 10:16: "He who listens to you listens to me, and he who does not recognize you does not recognize me." "This logion . . . rests on the principle of so-called substitution: the messenger is as valid as his client, and so his powers are also appropriate to him. In v. 12 this principle is interpreted in a certain direction: the disciple does the work of the Master." Moreover, Dietzfelbinger, *Abschied*, refers to 2 Cor 5:19–20; Rom 14:3; 15:7.

113. Dietzfelbinger, *Abschied*, 47.

114. Dietzfelbinger, *Abschied*, 47.

115. More details in the following section.

23   If you forgive the sins of anyone,
     they are forgiven them;
     if you retain (the sins) of anyone,
     they are retained."

Two things can be inferred from this text with regard to John 14:12: (1) The disciples continue the works of their Master in that, just as he had been sent by his Father for his earthly task, they themselves are now also sent by him as the exalted one to continue his works during the time of his absence on earth. (2) Apart from the fact that this requires the gift of the Spirit and thus the new creation of the disciples ("he breathed on them," see Gen 2:7) as the necessary prerequisite, the words of commission also reveal what the "works" to be done by the disciples as followers of Jesus consist of. They are two-sided, having a salvation side and a judgment side just like the work of Jesus, as John 5:21–22 shows: "For just as the Father raises the dead and *gives them life*, so the Son also *gives life* to those he wills.[116] Neither does the Father judge anyone, but has given all *judgment* to the Son." This is precisely what takes place after Easter in the word of the disciples, which is not "smoke and mirrors" but an *effective* word, that is to say: It creates a new *reality*, whether it is freedom from sin—that is, life—or, if it is rejected in favor of people's adherence to their sins—that is, death.

From these observations, it is now possible to answer the question of the significance of the "*greater* works." Once again, we can trust Dietzfelbinger, "Just as the work of the disciples, which corresponds exactly to the work of Jesus, goes beyond the boundaries of Judaism (this is a decisive element in the Greek pericope 12:20–23), so also it extends in time into an unlimited future. It is therefore not a higher or different quality of the disciple's work that is expressed by the 'greater,' but rather that spatial and temporal limitation, and this takes place with the Easter commission (20:23)."[117]

This outlines the starting point for the evangelist's probable intention behind verses 13 and 14: How did the post-Easter "works" of the disciples relate to the soteriological exclusivity of Christ? The fourth evangelist answers this question by referring to Christ himself as the *originator* of these works: "I will do!" he says in verse 14b, verbally picking up on the keyword "deeds" following verse 12. Verses 13–14 do not explicitly establish the connection between this "do" and the previously mentioned "deeds," and verse 13a with its indefinite relative pronoun ("*whatever* you ask . . .") is also broader than this contextual reference realized by the reader. Nevertheless, here a peculiarity of the textual constitution comes into play that is typical of the Johannine discourses in general. They assign the

---

116. See Jos. Asen. 8.3, 10.

117. Dietzfelbinger, *Abschied*, 48.

reader an active, productive role in their reading in that they do not simply spell everything out but often enough, as here, leave it at the exciting juxtaposition of individual text elements. It is then up to the reader to link them together and solve the puzzle. What is more, verses 13a and 14a is traditional material (*Überlieferungsgut*), so the indefinite character of these statements was predetermined.

If one accepts the challenge of the text to contribute productively to its constitution of meaning, then this leads to the following track: the disciples' post-Easter "works" of proclamation are not their own accomplishment, but are embedded in the congregational performance of prayer; that is, they want to be requested. From a theological point of view, this means that the actual subject of all the disciples' "works of proclamation" is the exalted Christ because he himself answers their prayers ("I will do").

The text does not say to whom the prayer in Jesus's name is addressed after verse 13a; there is a blank space here, which is then filled by verse 14a.[118] But it is questionable whether the information in verse 14a can also be included in verse 13a.[119] Following the preceding colon, "I am going to the Father" (v. 12d), the evangelist was able to dispense with naming the addressee of the prayer of supplication, as every reader knew how to complete it from the prayer tradition with which they were familiar. Its theocentricity seems to be preserved, which the evangelist also hints at by saying that if the exalted one "does" what the congregation asks, it is "so that through the Son the Father may be glorified" (v. 13c).[120] This initially gives the impression that the petition is addressed to the Father, but that the Father leaves it to the Son to answer. However, verse 14 then sharpens the thought such that answering is not only a matter for the Son, but that the petitions are also addressed to him.

The reason for this Christological concentration,[121] which is unique in the early Christian history of prayer, is probably to be found in the overarching idea of the "works" that are indeed the "works" of *Jesus*, but then, in the time of his *absence* after Easter, also the "works" of his disciples, or according to verses 13–14 the "works" of the *exalted* one himself, who "does" them through them

---

118. "If you ask *me* for something in my name."

119. See R. Bultmann, *Das Evangelium des Johannes*, 19th ed. (Göttingen: Vandenhoeck & Ruprecht, 1968), 472 n. 3.

120. On the theocentricity of the farewell speech, see also v. 28: "If you loved me, you would be glad that I am going to the Father because *the Father is greater than I am*."

121. Otherwise, supplication is always addressed to God, and God is also the one who answers prayers. In the synoptic traditions discussed above, this is expressed with the *passivum divinum*. In this respect, John 14:13–14 also stands out from the evidence in John 15–16 and thus proves its special position.

in response to the congregation's prayer. Seen in this light, these "greater works" of the congregation already reveal the new way of the paschal presence of the exalted one, which the second half of the discourse from verse 15 onwards will deal with. This Christological problem of the necessity of Jesus's departure in death for the sake of his new *presence* with his own after Easter has also left its unmistakable mark on the tradition of the answer to prayer received in 14:13–14. Read in a synchronic direction, this has the critical function of protecting verse 12 from misunderstandings in the aftermath: The "works" that Jesus promises his disciples to do for the post-Easter era are ultimately not theirs but *his own "works"* that he does through them.

(2) Now one can also read the Johannine unit of speech diachronically and ask, What does it contribute to the interpretation of the old aphorism? What potential meaning does it reveal?[122] Concerning *form*, it should first be noted that the evangelist has pulled the opening formula of the aphorism forward, thereby signaling that his own commentary and the ancient tradition are to be understood as a unit. Concerning *content*, through his commentary he relates the promise of answered prayer to the time after Easter and thus allows it to be strictly Christological: It applies exclusively because the exalted Christ is present in a new way among his own and remains *effective* in creating salvation through them. Consequently, the promise of answered prayer does not denote a universally valid truth but is strictly bound to the name of Jesus. Now the old aphorism probably already offered an implicit Christology, but its Johannine interpretation clearly defines it as *conditio sine qua non* of granting petitions by referring to Jesus's ascent to the Father and his glorification by the Son.

It is difficult to interpret the formula "*in my name*," which is found only in the Johannine references of the aphorism (14:13, 14; 15:16, 23, 24, 26) and not in the Synoptics (see, however, Matt 18:20 together with 18:19). Perhaps the evangelist already found it in the version of the saying he used.[123] Here it probably denotes the justification for the supplication: "Whatever you ask *by appealing to me.*"[124] Its interpretation in the Johannine context goes further. This is evident from the fact that in verse 14a it also retains its authority alongside "you ask me." Asking the *Father* in the name, that is, with reference to (the earthly) *Jesus*,

---

122. As already mentioned, at the synchronic level, the situation is reversed. Here v. 12 does not interpret vv. 13–14 but v. 13 subsequently clarifies v. 12 and prevents it from being misinterpreted.

123. This could be supported by the fact that the formula is also found in the second and third farewell discourses, if they have not simply reproduced it from 14:13–14.

124. Bultmann, *Johannes*, 203 n. 1.

who encouraged this, makes sense. But what does it mean to ask Jesus (i.e., the exalted one) "in his (Jesus's) name"? We can only make progress here if, with the help of the other references to the "name" in the gospel (especially 1:12; 3:18; 5:43; 10:25; 12:28), we recognize the Christological depth of the formula, which generally refers to the mystery of the unity of Father and Son. If this is the case here,[125] then the formulation means to ask Jesus because of his name: to address him believing that he is the Son and as such lives in inner unity with the Father and carries out his will. This unity of Father and Son is the reason prayer can be addressed to the exalted one. On this basis, we can understand the Christological intensification of the formulation of verse 13a in verse 14a.

The indefinite form ("whatever you ask") of the aphorism was certainly a problem for the early church. The unit of speech in John 14:12–14 preserves the "stumbling block" when it leaves the phrase "whatever" but makes it more concrete: On the one hand, it only allows a prayer of supplication in the "name" of Jesus; on the other, it focuses its object on the "works" that Jesus promises his disciples will accomplish in the post-Easter period. In other words: Not everything possible or any of man's selfish desires can be the object of his supplication before God, but only that which is related to the "works" of proclamation promised to the community in faith.[126] This also gives supplication an ecclesiological dimension. According to John 14:12–14, its primary place is not in the heart of the individual, but in the public sphere of the community.

2.2.4 The Later Johannine Variants of the Logion

The logion occurs four more times in the farewell discourses, in pairs: in John 15:7–8 and 16 in the second discourse and in John 16:23–24 and 26–27 in the third discourse. The first reference resumes John 14:12–14. But for all four texts their proximity to the older synoptic versions is characteristic. The tradition, which the evangelist has confidently subjected to his own interpretation in his farewell discourse, comes through more clearly in the layers of editing. On the one hand, it is quite naturally the Father who hears the petitions addressed to him; on the other hand, we now also encounter the pairs of terms in their exact

---

125. This seems obvious because vv. 12–13 separately mention the relationship between Father and Son.

126. Dietzfelbinger, *Abschied*, 49: The evangelist gave "the indefinite 'whatever you ask' its definiteness . . .: the congregation, far from being powerful to accomplish 'greater works' by itself, is to ask that it might be able to do these works. By asking, it receives the unconditional ability to do what it asks."

synoptic equivalents,[127] as both syntactic patterns are documented.[128] The first two texts read:

(1) John 15:7–8:

7	a	If you remain in me
	b	and my words abide in you,
	c	*whatever you want,*
	d	*ask for it,*
	e	*and it will be done for you.*
8	a	In this my Father is glorified,
	b	that you bear much fruit
	c	and you prove yourselves to be my disciples.

(2) John 15:16:

16	a	You have not chosen me,
	b	but I have chosen you
	c	and appointed you,
	d	that you should go
	e	and bear fruit
	f	and your fruit will remain,
	g	so that
	h	*whatever you ask the Father in my name,*
	g	*he will give it to you.*

"If you abide in me and my words abide in you"! This is how the author begins (1) before he pronounces the promise of Jesus's answer to prayer. Thus, this promise is not made in a vacuum, but is made to those who are already living out of their union with Christ. The ecclesiological dimension of prayer is emphasized even more strongly than in John 14:12–14 in the two related texts (1) and (2). Both texts are about "bearing fruit," with the metaphor standing for the preservation of mutual love, of concrete responsibility for one another in the congregation. In

---

127. (1) "ask"—"give": Q 11:9; (2) "ask"—"receive": Mark 11:24 par. Matt 21:22; (3) "ask"—"it will happen for you," Mark 11:24, see Mark 11:23 par. Matt 21:21.

128. Imperative second person plural + indicative future: John 15:7c, d.; 16:24b; conditional relative + apodosis: John 15:16g, h; 16:23c, d.

both cases, this "fruit" is intended as the object of supplication: "It is not arbitrary and self-centered petitions that are promised to be heard, but the petition of the congregation for the fruit appropriate to it. After all, it asks as the congregation in which Jesus is believed; it therefore asks as a congregation that knows and understands Jesus. Consequently, it asks that it may remain and become what it is and that it may be able to represent what it is in its actions. This is precisely what the congregation needs."[129] With regard to text (2), the recourse to supplication is also suggested here by the leading theme of Jesus's friendship with his disciples in John 15:12–17. For where else is the space in which requests can be made without reservation and can count on an answer than among friends? Epictetus is also aware of prayer as a characteristic of friendship with God.[130]

(3) John 16:23–24:

> 23 a And in that day you will ask me nothing.
> b *Truly, truly, I say to you,*
> c *"Whatever you ask the Father in my name,*
> d *he will grant to you."*
> 24 a Until now you have asked for nothing in my name.
> b *Ask and you will receive,*
> c *that your joy may be full.*

(4) John 16:26–27:

> 26 a *In that day you will ask in my name,*
> b and [with this] I do not say to you,
> c that *I* ask the Father on your behalf;
> 27 a for *he himself, the Father*, loves you,
> b because you have loved me
> c and have believed (πεπιστεύκατε)[131]
> d that I came forth from God.

In these two immediately adjacent units of the third farewell discourse, the promise of answered prayer carries a striking temporal index: "Until now" the disciples have not prayed to God "in the name of Jesus" because they still had

---

129. Dietzfelbinger, *Abschied*, 116.

130. Epictetus, *Diatr.* 2.17, 29.

131. J. Frey, *Die johanneische Eschatologie III*, WUNT 110 (Tübingen: Mohr Siebeck, 1998), 219 n. 203: "Note the two perfect tenses, which (in conjunction with the stative lexeme) denote the *present* faith of the community of disciples, as well as the present tense *he loves you*."

him with them. But "on that day," that is, at Easter[132]—and "that day" will always dawn in the time of the congregation—they will ask in the name of Jesus, and the Father will hear them. Being able to count on this is a sign of the time of salvation and fills believers with joy (16:24c; cf. v. 22), as the Holy Scriptures have already predicted.[133] Here it becomes completely clear "that prayer is the heart of Christian life. In the prayer of believers, the reality of their participation in the life of Jesus—and 'in him' in the life of God—can be experienced concretely, in the joy in God that is given to them in their participation in the joy of the glorified Jesus (cf. 15:11!)."[134]

Although the second unit of speech does not take up the promise of hearing—which the first unit had mentioned twice shortly before in verse 23d and verse 24b—it does take up the announcement that the disciples will ask *in his name* on that day (26a). The author is now solely concerned with the correct understanding of this formula in this new unit of speech. That is why he immediately adds a correction in verse 26b: "I do not say to you that I ask the Father for you; he himself, the Father, loves you." From the perspective of other texts in the New Testament, this statement seems awkward because in those texts the statement of faith that the exalted Christ "intercedes for us" confirms the confession of Christ's mediation in salvation. John 16:26-27, however, does not intend to override this confession but rather to make its own contribution to this understanding, specifically with regard to the name formula. This also seems to have been appropriate in view of the fact that in the religion and philosophy of the time, there was much talk of the mediation of the divine to human beings, of intermediary beings (angels and demons) and intermediaries (such as the Logos). Against this background, the assertion from John 16:26-27 that the paschal Christ does not come *between* God and the disciples, but rather takes them

---

132. See Schnackenburg, *Johannesevangelium*, 3:179: "but the following shows that not only Easter day but the whole time beginning then is intended...." R. E. Brown, *The Gospel According to John*, 2 vols, AncB 29-29A (New York: Doubleday, 1966-1970), 735; another view can be found in Schnelle, *Das Evangelium nach Johannes*, ThKNT 4 (Leipzig: Evangelische Verlagsanstalt, 1998), 251-252. according to which the *parousia* is to be considered from a textual-pragmatic perspective; "On that day there will be no more questions, for the believers will then have finally entered the realm of divine truth, and their prayers will be fulfilled." However, according to v. 26a, "they" also "pray" on that day, which is incompatible with the consummation of time heralded by the *parousia*, and in v. 24a the phrase "until now" marks "the 'historical' context of the speech and the difference between the pre-Easter and the post-Easter period" (Frey, *Eschatologie*, 3:218 n. 201).

133. "Your heart will rejoice" in v. 22 corresponds to Isa 66:14 LXX (καὶ ὄψεσθε, καὶ χαρήσεται ὑμῶν ἡ καρδία) but joy is also otherwise considered a sign of the end times.

134. U. Wilckens, *Das Evangelium nach Johannes*, NTD 4 (Göttingen: Vandenhoeck & Ruprecht, 1998), 255.

into a new *immediacy* to God, gains its own profile: "The Father himself loves you *because you have loved me*," whereby the verb φιλεῖν, "certainly chosen with intentionality," allows the idea of friendship to be associated here.[135] "Jesus's own friendship, which he assures the disciples in 15:15 and thus explains that he has made known to them everything they have heard from the Father, expands for them into a direct friendship with God."[136] So the idea of soteriological fellowship is not abandoned here but gains new contours: Jesus takes his own into his own direct relationship with God. Praying "in his name" therefore means standing before God in openness and freedom because of the revelation of Jesus's sonship with God. This brings the keyword—παρρησία—into view, which has become the leitmotif in the reception of the saying in 1 John in both references:

(5) 1 John 3:21–22:

    21 a Beloved,
          b if the heart does not condemn [us],
          c we have boldness (παρρησίαν) before God,
    22 a and *whatever we ask of him,*
          b *we receive from him,*
          c because we obey his commandments
          d and do what pleases him.

(6) 1 John 5:14–15:

    14 a And this is the boldness (παρρησία),
          b we have in him,
          c that *if we ask anything according to his will,*
          d *he will hear us.*
    15 a And if we know
          b *that he hears us*
          c *in whatever we ask,*
          d we know
          e *that we have (already obtained) the requests,*
          f *that we have asked of him.*

---

135. Schnackenburg, *Johannesevangelium*, 3:184.

136. Schnackenburg, *Johannesevangelium*, 3:184.

In text (5), the unconditional answer to prayer is again embedded in statements that show the way in which supplication belongs at the center of Christian life: On the one hand, it is an expression and concrete experience of παρρησίαν, boldness and trust in God; on the other hand, it arises from a way of life in accordance with God's commandments.[137] According to this, the certainty of receiving what one asks for is based on a prior alignment of one's own life with what is "pleasing to God" (v. 22d), so that one can say: "Where this succeeds, it is obvious that all requests only ever reflect what God wants and are therefore certain to be granted." "What we can still reasonably ask for under this condition is, above all, that we may increasingly succeed in harmonizing with God's will. And this request has the best chance of being heard."[138]

In text (6), which belongs to the secondary postscript of 1 John, we find the clause "according to God's will" in the protasis of the logion as a condition of assurance that the prayer will be granted. It is striking that the unit of speech refers three times to Jesus's promise, emphatically stressing its fulfillment. The reason for this is probably that it "is not written for its own sake, but for the sake of verses 16 and 17. In order to encourage readers to do something as tremendously difficult and questionable as intercession for the sinful brother, John falls back on the certainty of the answer to prayer in all its unconditionality."[139]

2.2.5 Disillusionment Concerning a Saying of Jesus? A Diachronic Sketch

It is highly probable that we can attribute both Q 11:9–10 and Mark 11:24* as the two oldest witnesses to the tradition of answered prayer to *Jesus* himself. If both sayings "with an unlimited and, in their absoluteness, almost bold certainty

---

137. The meaning of the causal clause in v. 22c, d ("because we keep his commandments and do what pleases him") is controversial. H.-J. Klauck, *Der erste Johannesbrief*, EKK 23/1 (Zürich: Benziger, 1991), 222, asks: "Does the causal clause in 22c, d therefore indicate the condition that must be fulfilled for requests to be heard by God?" only to answer this question in the negative. Contrary J. D. Crossan, "Aphorism in Discourse and Narrative," *Semeia* 43 (1988): 121–140, here 133: "I interpret this precisely as a caution against a too ecstatic understanding of the *Ask* sayings in the Gospel.... This version of the *Ask* aphorism insists that any guaranteed response is dependent on fundamental ethical obedience"; see Crossan, *Fragments*, 103, about both texts: "Their cautionary emphasis on ethics ('commandments ... please him ... his will') indicates, however, that they are not earlier and primitive versions of the *ask* theme, but rather the final stage in its development, with the author reacting to specific problems within the Johannine community."

138. Klauck, *1. Johannesbrief*, 222.

139. F. Büchsel, *Die Johannesbriefe*, ThHK 17 (Leipzig: Evangelische Verlagsanstalt, 1933), 86.

of being answered,"[140] then this unmistakably points to his personal conviction of the closeness of God, whom he encourages his disciples to address in prayer as a benevolent Father[141] who is determined to save.

Moreover, the saying about asking, seeking, and knocking reflects the whole dynamic of his message of God's kingdom. Because this has a real place on earth thanks to Jesus's work, it can be *asked for* as God's gift, it can be *sought*, and it can be *found* like a treasure in a field, and at the end we gain *entrance* to its gates. Because the two sayings are therefore not intended to be understood as universally valid religious truths but rather remain bound as promises to the concrete historical constellation of Jesus's proclamation, it is conceivable (even if not conclusively provable) that the "truly, I say to you" formula was an original part of the tradition as an expression of the special authority of Jesus that stands behind the words.

Even if there are Christological implications related to the words about the unconditional certainty that the prayer of supplication will be answered, Jesus was probably also drawing on Jewish tradition. He is probably picking up on the prophetic expectation that in the coming age of salvation, God will answer people before they call out to him (see Isa 65:24). This expectation is now fulfilled in his work with the arrival of the *basileia*.

Whether Jesus with his "absolute certainty of fulfillment ... is unique," as Ulrich Luz believes,[142] does not seem so certain. The opposite view is also held: "In the certainty of the answer to prayer, Jesus is in agreement with the Jewish tradition."[143] What distinguishes him from this tradition is the particular eschatological form of his justification for the closeness of God.

The way in which all later versions of these words work their way through the provocative specification of Jesus provides a counter-test for the assumption of the authenticity of the Jesus statement in Q 11:9–10 / Mark 11:24*. The

---

140. See O. Cullmann, *Das Gebet im Neuen Testament. Zugleich Versuch einer vom Neuen Testament aus zu erteilenden Antwort auf heutige Fragen*, 2nd ed. (Tübingen: Mohr Siebeck, 1997), on Luke 11:9–10 par.; 11:11ff. par.; 18:1ff. Because he does not analyze Mark 11:24 according to redaction criticism, he reclaims the saying as a Jesus saying. Jesus "knows that there are prayers of the disciples that go unanswered. This knowledge prompts him not to leave his promises unconditional, but to tie them to the necessity of faith" (41). This does not seem plausible to me in view of the secondary features in Mark 11:24. Even the paradoxical logia of faith moving mountains or planting a tree in the sea, which claim authenticity in their substance, do not understand this as a necessary subjective condition for the growing of something unheard of but understand them as power.

141. Pesch, *Markusevangelium*, 2:206: "The certainty of faith that Jesus made possible and demanded arises from the revelation of the unconditional love of God the Father."

142. Luz, *Matthäus*, 1:331.

143. Pesch, *Markusevangelium*, 2:206.

Markan redaction profiles *faith* as the necessary attitude of the one who makes the supplication, whereby it understands faith as a firm trust in the power of God that allows "no doubt in one's own heart" (Mark 11:23). Matthew follows this view in 21:22 but elsewhere emphasizes the ecclesiological dimension of supplication: He is assured of being heard when the petitioners are in consensus, not on any arbitrary matter, but on matters that profoundly affect the holiness of the congregation (Matt 18:19). The reason for all certainty is the presence of the exalted one among his own (Matt 18:20). The redactors of Q added Q 11:9–10 to the Lord's Prayer, thereby establishing the inner reference of Jesus's words to the great theme of his proclamation ("Your kingdom come!").

In the Johannine tradition, the saying is embedded in the relational structure of those involved in the revelation event (Father—Son—believers); to ask "in the name of Jesus" therefore does not mean to be concerned about everyday needs but to look to the progress of the Son's revelation in the world. In contrast, the author of James is concerned with practical wisdom in accordance with the theme of his letter, which should be the subject of the supplication, but he also emphasizes the *undivided* and *complete* trust in God that should characterize the supplicant. For his theology, it cannot be valued highly enough that he placed the Jesus logion at the head of his letter and elevated it to the nucleus of a small parenesis. This shows how naturally the wisdom of a God-pleasing way of life is itself a gift of God for him, i.e., anything but so-called "works piety":

James 1:5–8:

5   a   But if any of you lacks wisdom,
      b   *he should ask for it from God,*
      c   who *gives to* all in a simple way
      d   and does not scold (them),
      e   *and it will be given to him.*

6   a   *But he should ask in faith,*
      b   *without the slightest doubt.*
      c   Because whoever doubts,
      d   resembles a wave in the ocean,
      e   which is moved and driven back and forth by the wind.

7   a   For that person does not believe,
      b   that he would receive anything from the Lord:

8   a   a man with a divided soul,
      b   fickle in all his ways.

With Jewish early Christian theology, the author of James also sees very soberly and realistically what stands in the way of man's unconditional and complete trust in God within himself. In accordance with tradition, he ties it in with the term "desire."

James 4:2–3:

2 a If you desire
  b and you do not have,
  c you murder and have envy
  d and still cannot achieve it;
  e you fight and wage wars.
  f *You do not have*
  g *because you do not ask;*
3 a *you ask*
  b *and you do not receive,*
  c *because you ask poorly*
     (namely with the intention):
  d to waste it according to your own desires (cf. v. 1b, 2a).

The author clearly assigns the blame for the failure of supplication to the supplicant himself and thus exonerates God. The desire to always have more, ἐπιθυμία as the fundamental sin of man, also repeatedly spoils people's supplication before God.

Of course, such an unquestioning assignment of responsibility for the failure of the supplication is not the only answer in the New Testament, quite apart from the fact that the judgment about the success or failure of his prayer is often drawn from the person praying. At the heart of the New Testament is certainly what Jesus himself first had to learn in his prayer and what Mark in particular brought to literary expression with his depiction of the Gethsemane and crucifixion scene: the shuddering before the silent riddle about God's will. Does this refute Jesus's own words, "ask and it will be given to you"?

2.3 "If you forgive the sins of any..." (John 20:23; see Matt 16:19b, c; 18:18)

Matthew 16:19b, c par. 18:18 and John 20:23 do not agree in a single word, and yet the Matthean double tradition and the Johannine logion can be traced back to a common "word of the Lord." Did the author of John 20:23 form the saying on the basis of Matthew 18:18[144] or are both versions based on related oral tradition?[145] It is not at all clear—as is usually assumed—that the older version is preserved in Matthew and that John 20:23 is derived from it. The reverse solution is also conceivable.[146] Caution, however, seems appropriate with regard to attempts to precisely reconstruct the presumed original form of the "word of the Lord."[147]

We will address these questions below, beginning with a synoptic comparison of the three versions. The aim is to prove that they agree in substance such that we can assume the presence of a single, original logion.

2.3.1 Synoptic Comparison of the Three Versions

Math 16:19b, c	Matt 18:18	John 20:23
And what you bind on earth, it will be bound in the heavens, and what you loose on earth, it will be loosed in the heavens.	Truly, I say to you, whatever you bind on earth, it will be bound in heaven, and whatever you loose on earth, it will be loosed in heaven.	(a) whichever you retain, they are retained. (b) Whose sins you remit, they have been left behind,

The *differences* between the Johannine and Matthean logion in 16:19b, c and 18:18[148] are immediately obvious: While Matthew speaks of "binding" and

---

144. See, e.g., Haenchen, John, 573.

145. Dodd, *Tradition*, 349, on John 20:23: "We seem driven to postulate an alternative form of tradition regarding the authority committed to the apostles by the lord, akin to, though not identical with, the tradition followed by Matthew, an alternative form which the Fourth Evangelist has independently followed."

146. See Brown, *John*, 2:1041, with support from G. Claudel, "Jean 20,23 et ses parallèles matthéens," *RevSR* 69 (1995) 71–86, 85.

147. G. Vermes, "The Targumic Versions of Genesis 4,3–16," in *Post-Biblical Jewish Studies*, SJLA 8 (Leiden: Brill, 1975), 92–126, postulates that John 20:23 and Matt 16:19; 18:18 are based on a common Aramaic logion in which both play on words—"binding" and "loosing" in Matthew and the Johannine "forgiving" and "retaining"—were still connected with each other. He reconstructs it as follows: "Whatsoever you shall bind and retain on earth, shall be bound and retained in heaven; and whatsoever you shall loose and remit on earth, shall be loosed and remitted in heaven" (124). See also J. A. Emerton, "Binding and Losing—Forgiving and Retaining," *JThS.NS* 13 (1962): 325–331.

148. See R. Metzner, *Das Verständnis der Sünde im Johannesevangelium*, WUNT 122 (Tübingen: Mohr Siebeck, 2000), 266: "On the whole ... the Matthean logia and John 20:23 are quite different, despite their relationship in terms of tradition."

"loosing," the fourth evangelist speaks of "loosing" and "retaining" sins. In Matthew the action with a negative outcome comes first, whereas in John it is the other way round. Matthew's reference to "earth" and "heaven(s)" has no equivalent in John. Whereas Matthew uses a general formulation ("whatever"), John refers to the people whose sins are forgiven or retained. Accordingly, Matthew contains relative clauses with a conditional sense, whereas John 20:23 offers a sequence of two iterative conditional sentences. Are we therefore dealing with two completely different traditions?

Their *similarities* in terms of form and content speak against two different traditions. Matthew and John each offer an antithetical parallelism consisting of two periods, whereby the protasis is always in the active, the apodosis in the passive, namely a *passivum divinum*: An action on the part of man corresponds to an action on the part of God, which affirms and validates that human action! What Matthew explicates with the typical pair "on earth"—"in heaven" is thus already firmly anchored syntactically in all three versions. Additionally, as G. Claudel[149] points out, the passive forms are each in the perfect tense, whereby Matthew 16:19b, c and 18:18 make use of a periphrastic construction. Moreover, John 20:23 and Matthew 18:18 agree in the form of address of the second person plural ("you"), whereas Matt 16:19b, c is addressed to Peter.

In terms of content, the similarities between the logia are not immediately apparent, as their terms "binding" and "loosing" or "forgiving" and "retaining sins" belong to different semantic fields. The Matthean versions are more juridical, whereas the Johannine versions are more religious in nature. Nevertheless, they seem to be compatible with each other under certain conditions, which is remarkable only for John 20:23 and Matthew 18:18, not for Matthew 16:19.

What is certain is that the meaning of "forbid" and "permit" for "binding" and "loosing" is well-documented by numerous Jewish (rabbinic) texts. Here the Greek words δέω and λύω correspond to the Hebrew pair אסר and התיר and to the Aramaic אסר and שרא. "The usual meaning of these rabbinic expressions is equally unquestionable: to *declare forbidden or permitted by doctrinal decision, to impose or* cancel *an obligation*."[150] "For the primary task of the scribes was precisely to declare by their decisions certain interpretations of the Torah concerning *the life* (not: the faith!) of the Jewish people to be binding or not (no longer) binding."[151]

---

149. G. Claudel, "Jean 20,23 et ses parallèles matthéens," *RevSR* 69 (1995): 71–86, here 85.

150. F. Büchsel, Art. δέω, *TDNT* 2: 60–61.

151. M. Limbeck, *Das Gesetz im Alten und Neuen Testament* (Darmstadt: WBG, 1997), 140.

"Words of the Lord" with Synoptic Parallels 91

The controversial question of whether this terminology also has a disciplinary meaning and in what sense is a different matter. The problem is that "the Jewish parallels that point in such a direction are ... sparse."¹⁵² For example, there is obviously only *one example of* the meaning "to impose or dissolve the ban," namely in the Babylonian Talmud, MQ 16a (in a word ascribed to Schemuël [†254).¹⁵³ At least this reference shows that the terminology, also in other contexts for authority and teaching, could be used differently in certain cases. The reference to Josephus, *J. W.* 1.111, cited in Strack-Billerbeck, is not useful because the passage does not attest to a metaphorical understanding of "to loose" and "to bind" but rather speaks only of the authority "to release and put into chains." Nevertheless, in Matthew 18:18, "from the context," the reference "to judicial decisions" immediately suggests itself, with the result that here the word pair "bind" and "loose" has "the sense of 'keep sins' or 'forgive.'"¹⁵⁴

If this is the case,¹⁵⁵ then there is indeed a connection from Matthew 18:18 to John 20:23. What is expressed here as the forgiveness of sins by the disciples (!) in a rather religious play on words is formulated there in the context of the communal rule 18:15–17 in terms of its "binding," juridical aspect. The relationship between John 20:23 and the Matthean saying in Matthew 18:18 therefore seems undeniable.

2.3.2 Teaching, Discipline, Mission/Baptism
The Three Contexts of the Logion

With the last remarks, we have arrived at the question of contextual embedding of the logion. Now we focus on this question and answer it more precisely.

2.3.2.1 Matthew 16:19b, c and 18:18
A Matthean "Repetition"

The two related passages Matthew 16:18 and 18:18 are among the numerous "repetitions" in the Gospel of Matthew which its author used almost as an editorial stylistic device.¹⁵⁶ In most cases, the repetitions offer a complement to the first passage, adding new accents, so that a saying only reveals the fullness of its

---

152. Luz, *Matthäus*, 3:46, see Str-B 1:738–739 (English ed. at pp. 839–841). (See next footnote.)

153. Str-B 1:739 (English ed. at p. 841): "We have not found other passages for אסר with the meaning 'to impose the ban.'"

154. Luz, *Matthäus*, 3:46.

155. Further discussions and arguments in Theobald, *Herrenworte*, pp. 179–181.

156. See above, pp. 12–13.

meaning through its reflection in different contexts. This is probably also the case with Matthew 16:18 and 18:18.

First, it is important that Jesus's words to Peter *precede* those to the disciples. If their circle represents the post-Easter *ecclesia* according to the community discourse in Matthew 18, then it can be said that Matthew 16:18—Jesus's interpretation of Peter's name—names in advance the perspective in which this sequence is to be understood: "and I say to you, 'You are *Peter*, and on this rock I will build my *church*, and the gates of Hades will not prevail against it.'" If, according to these words, Peter has a "unique, foundational function" for the later church, then it is only logical that the first evangelist has Jesus give the word of binding and loosing first to Peter and then to the circle of disciples as a whole. There should be consensus on this; however, the question of how exactly Peter's "unique, founding function" is to be understood and what this means for the understanding of the word about binding and loosening in its respective literary location is controversial.

In Matthew 16:19 the singular saying is connected to verse 19a by an epexegetical "and" (= that is): "I will give you the key of the kingdom of heaven."[157] Because of that we can conclude: *Verse19a and 19b mutually interpret themselves.* This can be seen even on the *structural* level: Both halves of the verse speak about the entrance into the "heavens." Verse 19a uses the metaphor of keys; verse 19b uses a promise of reliability and validity of decisions which, when made on earth, are also binding in the "heavens" (i.e., for God). If we wish to know what decisions this relates to, those pertaining to teaching or to discipline, then it is not only the firmly established rabbinic usage just mentioned that tips the scales toward the assumption of Peter's teaching authority as stated here, it is above all the immediate and wider context of the passage that tips the scales in favor of this interpretation. The only place in the Gospel where the key metaphor of 16:19a is encountered again, namely in 23:13, is revealing: "Woe to you, scribes and Pharisees, hypocrites, you *shut* the kingdom of heaven from men, for you (yourselves) do not go in, nor do you let those who (want to) go in." This saying of woe is, as it were, the counter-text to 16:19. Peter is entitled to the key power that the scribes possess due to their own competence but which they betray through their concrete actions. Obviously, this verse is about the correct interpretation of the law. In terms of understanding Peter's key authority, this means that Peter's task is to "open the kingdom of heaven to people through his authoritative interpretation of the law. He is to interpret the will of God from Jesus in order to lead people along the narrow path at the end of which the narrow gate to the

---

157. Such a deliberate assignment can also be recognized by the fact that both times we have "heavens" in the plural (in 18:18 both times singular).

kingdom of heaven is unlocked (cf. 7:13-14). The keys to heaven are therefore the commandments of Jesus, which Peter proclaims and interprets."[158]

On the other hand, "the general formulation (of v. 19b, c) with 'whatever...' suggests that it should be interpreted as openly as possible and that, for example, the idea of church discipline or the forgiveness of sins should not be fundamentally excluded."[159] This seems plausible because this thought is dominant in 18:18 and both texts correspond to each other according to the redactional technique of "repetition." For it cannot be inferred from 16:19 and 18:18 that Matthew wanted to see the competences carefully divided, with the teaching authority assigned to Peter and the disciplinary authority to the congregational assembly.[160] Such selectivity also does not seem appropriate because doctrinal decisions consistently refer to the *practice of* the law, the observance of which, on the other hand, is monitored by the disciplinary authority. With his compositional arrangement of 16:19 and 18:18, Matthew seems much more concerned with ensuring that the authority that Jesus himself entrusted to the "first" of his disciples (Matt 10:2) now lives on in the congregation and is practiced, as the congregational order of Matthew 18 at least partially reveals. In other words: Peter's power and authority will be exercised by the community after his death. More specifically by the assembly of the community (*ecclesia*), to which the pluralistic formulated saying in 18:18 is addressed. Formulated another way: The performed juridical authority of the community at the moment has its ground in Peter's authority. Going back to the "first" of the apostles, the representative of the discipleship or of the community, is an ecclesiological figure of legitimization, comparable to that used by the Fourth Gospel with its reference to the witness of the "beloved disciple" or by the author of Ephesians with its claim of the authority of Paul, regardless of the peculiarity that Peter (not only according to Matthew, but also according to John 21:15-17 and the Acts of the Apostles) is the "founding figure of the *universal church*," whereas the "beloved disciple" and Paul are not. Peter "does and is exactly what *all* disciples do and are."[161]

If we summarize the discussion, then despite all the difficulties mentioned above with regard to the terminology of "binding" and "loosing" in Matthew

---

158. Luz, *Matthäus*, 3:466.

159. Luz, *Matthäus*, 3:466. "founding figure of the *universal church*."

160. See W. Wiefel, *Das Evangelium nach Matthäus*, ThHK 1 (Leipzig: Evangelische Verlagsanstalt, 1998), 325: "Whereas in the similarly formulated word that followed Peter's promise in 16:19, the teaching authority of the apostle was affirmed with 'binding and loosing,' here this applies to the disciplinary authority of the community." "The difference between teaching and disciplinary authority" should not be "flattened."

161. Luz, *Matthäus*, 3:469.

18:18, it seems to be the simplest solution, and also the one required by the context, to interpret the "binding and loosing saying" as the reason for the earlier assignment of disciplinary competence to the *ecclesia*. "The double logion of binding and loosing in verse 18 ties in well with verses 15–17: Because readers inevitably relate 'binding' and 'loosing' to the community's behavior toward the sinner in verses 15–17, verse 18 is easily understood as an affirmation by the Lord."[162]

2.3.2.2 The Mission and Authorization of the Disciples (John 20:21-23)

The context of John 20:23—the sending and empowerment of the disciples by the exalted Lord on "Easter Sunday" (John 20:19–23)—has already been discussed above in 2.4.3 in relation to 14:12–14.[163] Here, attention should be drawn to the way in which the saying granting authority to forgive sins is integrated into the Easter scene and how it differs once again from Matthew 18:18.

First, it is important to note that John 20:23 *does not refer to* a *postbaptismal* practice of forgiveness of sins by the church; in contrast to Matthew 18:18, the focus is not on settling problematic cases *within the congregation*. Rather, the saying is about the authority given by the exalted Christ to grant people, regardless of their origin, forgiveness of their sins in the first place in the context of (missionary) *preaching*.[164] The point of the saying is not that the disciples are commissioned in their mission to only *communicate* to people in their word of forgiveness what God in heaven has already done for them in his act of forgiveness.[165] Rather, their act of speaking ("forgiveness of sins") itself has

---

162. Luz, *Matthäus*, 3:39.

163. See the text of John 20:21–23 above, p. 76–77.

164. "Ecclesiastical interpretation later brought some questions to this text which are still far removed from it and to which it therefore gives no or only unsatisfactory answers" (Schnackenburg, *Johannesevangelium*, 3:388). Among these he counts: "Is it a question of the redemption of sins through baptism or the remission of sins after baptism? In the first three centuries, the interpretation of baptism dominated. Cyprian even concludes from the passage 'that only the rulers of the church are authorized to baptize and to grant forgiveness of sins' (Ep. 73.7; CSEL III, 783). Later theologians claim with regard to the sacrament of penance that sins committed after baptism are remembered." Schnackenburg himself holds the view that "John 20:23 includes baptism *and* later remission of sins."

165. In this case, the perfect tense of the apodosis in v. 23b "would have to be understood as a *strict* perfect, i.e., the *passive divinum* is premature to the respective ἀφιέναι or κρατεῖν of the disciples"; Weidemann, *Bemerkungen*, 122 n. 4, rightly rejects this syntactically possible interpretation with reference, among other things, to the related logia in Matt 16:19 and 18:18 with their "*futuric* coniugatio periphrastica." This leaves the interpretation of the apodosis as a "future perfect" (BDR § 323), without the envisaged future therefore having to be thought

performative power: When they forgive sins (to whomsoever), the forgiveness of sins is carried out *by God himself.* That in John 20:23 (different from Matt 6:19 and 18:18) the *positive* aspect of the possible double act *comes first,* reaffirms its interpretation in the context of an initial missionary preaching. This also applies to the formal characteristic of the antithesis about "retaining sins," which is not—different from the aorist ἀφῆτε in verse 23a—formulated in present tense (κρατῆτε): "While ἀφιέναι τὰς ἁμαρτίας ["loose sins"] is an action carried out by the disciples, κρατεῖν τὰς ἁμαρτίας ["to retain sins"] by way of contrast, has the character of 'leaving, confirming, fixing an existing state.'"[166] Despite the traditional early Christian linguistic garb, this fits in perfectly with Johannine theology. The saving gift of life happens only through faith in Jesus. Apart from him, man *remains* in the darkness of his death; "born blind" (John 9), Jesus alone brings him "the light of life" (John 8:12); to refuse this in disbelief is the "sin" of man.[167]

The radical way in which the fourth evangelist thinks of the "forgiveness of sins"—namely as the *new birth* of the "man born blind"—is shown by the gesture with which he lets Jesus speak his words, as well as the "headline" that he places before the word of forgiveness: "And when he had said this, *he breathed on [them]* (ἐνεφύσησεν) and said to them, '*Receive Holy Spirit*!' . . ." (v. 22). In the gesture of "breathing on," which alludes to Genesis,[168] the *rebirth* of man takes place.

---

of as strictly eschatological, i.e., also from the point of view of the readers of the Gospel. If the saying is read in the context of the Gospel, this would contradict its present eschatology. Rather, the saying looks to *the* future, which becomes an event *wherever* the word of forgiveness of sins *is* granted by the disciples.

166. M. Zerwick, *Biblical Greek, Illustrated by Examples,* English edition a*dapted from the Fourth Latin edition by J. Smith,* SPIB 114 (Rome: Gregorian & Biblical Press, 1994), § 249: "the writer spontaneously uses the aorist for the notion of forgiving, because it is an act which is posited, but the present for that of retaining, because here we have simply continuing in the same state"; see also Brown, *John,* 2:1023: "The aorist implies an act that in a moment brings forgiveness, whereas the present implies that the state of holding or refusing forgiveness continues."

167. Jesus says to the Pharisees in 9:41, "Your sin remains." The Pharisees claim that they *see* but thereby only suppress the admission of their *blindness,* which is possible only in the presence of Jesus, the true "light of the world" (John 8:12).

168. See Gen 2:7; Wis 15:11 refers to the fact that "he [the idol-forming potter] has not recognized his own sculptor, the one who *breathed into* him an active soul and *breathed into* him the breath of life." In Ezek 37, it is God's breath itself which will breathe on the dead so they come back to life. In this text, the creator or his Spirit is the subject of the breathing on; in 3 Kgs 17 this refers to Elijah as a "man of God." Interesting here is the reminiscence to Genesis: "In 3 Kgs 17:21, the depiction of the resuscitation of the dead is transformed according to the archetype of the resuscitation of Adam: the Mas(ora) reports on how Elijah stretches out three times and calls out to God for the life of the dead man. The LXX renders it ἐνεφύσησε τρίς" (E. Stauffer, Art. ἐμφυσάω, *TDNT* 2:536 n. 2).—Important for the interpretation of John 20:22 is Philo, who not

However, this new creation includes an inner dynamic in accordance with the word of mission that precedes it in verse 21c ("as the Father has sent me, so I am sending you"), which does not allow the disciples renewed by the Spirit to be with *themselves*, but rather empowers them to perform "works,"[169] life-giving "works." This is precisely what the word of authority in verse 23—which interprets the preceding "headline"—attempts to express: "For those whose sins you forgive, they are forgiven them . . .!" The creative power of the Spirit mediated by the exalted one thus invests and exudes itself in the *forgiveness of sins* brought into the world by the disciples, whereby the prefix of verse 23a also says something about the preponderance of salvation in Johannine thought.

How Jesus's words "Receive the Holy Spirit! . . ." are accompanied by a sign—his act of "breathing on" the disciples—we may ultimately assume something similar for their performative word of the forgiveness of sins. Since the connection between the bestowal of the Spirit and the forgiveness of sins with baptism is firmly established in the early congregation,[170] one would not be wrong in assuming that, according to the evangelist, verse 23a, b also has its *Sitz im Leben* in baptism, in which, according to the tradition of the Johannine congregation, the "(re)birth" of the disciples is expressed. The community, the "(re)birth (of man) from water and the Spirit" (John 3:3, 5) takes place.[171] The promise of the forgiveness of sins is therefore not merely a verbal event but is to be thought of as connected with the rite of baptism, even if the fourth evangelist does not specifically explain this background, which he probably takes for granted. "Our text thus reveals itself to be a specifically Johannine contribution to the theological foundation of early Christian baptism in the Easter (and 'Pentecost') event."[172]

2.3.3 From the Right to Be a Messenger to Discipline in the Congregation
Observations on the History of the Tradition of the Logion

I want to propose the following hypothesis concerning the diachronic relation between Matthew 16:19/18:18 and John 20:23: *Originally, there was a single*

---

only cites and comments on Gen 2:7 often (*Opif.* 134f.; *Leg.* 1.31–42; 3.161; *Det.* 80; *Her.* 56; *Som.* 1.34; *Spec.* 4.123), but also understands the gift of God's breath to Adam as soteriological model for the reception of "true life": "God breathed into him the power of true life" (*Leg.* 1.32).

169. On 14:12–14 as proleptical commentary to our passage see above p. 75–80.

170. See Acts 2:38; 10:44–48; 19:5–6.

171. See above at 2.1!

172. Weidemann, *Beobachtungen*, 127.

logion in the environment of the early Christian right to be a messenger. This logion then is transformed in different contexts: in connection with the pre-Matthean 18:15–17:18*, which the first evangelist included in his composition of Matthew 18, in Jesus's speech to Peter in Matthew 16:17–19, and finally in the Easter scene of the fourth evangelist in John 20:19–23, here in a form that comes very close to the original logion. This will be explained below.

2.3.3.1 The Priority of the Plural or Singular Version (Matt 18:18; 16:19)

For some time now, the majority of scholars have voted in favor of the saying addressed to Peter when it comes to the question of which of the two versions of the "binding and loosing saying" should be given priority, but generally do not take John 20:23 into account. Instead, recourse is made to historical considerations that are brought to bear on the texts[173] and based on judgments of taste,[174] combined with the admission that "in terms of style ... a decision [is] not possible."[175] If one wants to arrive at a reasonably plausible solution, one

---

173. R. Bultmann, *Die Geschichte der synoptischen Tradition*, FRLANT 29, 10th ed. (Göttingen: Vandenhoeck & Ruprecht, 1995), 147–148, 150–151: The fact that in Matt 16:19 "Peter is attributed authority in matters of doctrine or discipline" means that "the saying points to the debates of the Palestinian church as its place of origin, even if one does not think, as J. Kreyenbühl does . . . , that it is the response of the early church to Paul's attack in Galatians"; in contrast, Matt 18:18 "is a variant of Matt 16:19, and a later one. The right of legislation is here attributed to the congregation, i.e., practically to its representatives. It will therefore originate from the time of the early church, in which the personal authority of Peter was replaced by an institutional authority of church leaders, i.e., presumably from the time after the persecution by Agrippa, to which the Zebedee James and probably also John fell victim, and through which Peter was expelled from Jerusalem." We must object to this reconstruction because Peter did not exercise authority in Jerusalem alone, but was one of the three "pillars" (Gal 2:9). Thus, it had to undergo modifications, e.g., by J. Gnilka, *Das Matthäusevangelium I–II*, HThK.NT I/1-2, 2nd ed. (Freiburg: Herder, 1988), 2:56: "Bultmann has seen something correct in the sequence from the individual to the college, only one will have to shift the geographical framework from Jerusalem to Syria (Galilean border region). Peter is the authority for the church of this province and is now a great figure of the past."

174. "The plural formulation is more comprehensive, more intensified, and could therefore be secondary" (Gnilka, *Matthäusevangelium*, 2:56).

175. Gnilka, *Matthäusevangelium*, 2:55–56, with reference to the fact (n. 34) that we find the term "whatever" also in 7:12; 23:3 (see also 18:25, 21:22). On the other hand, the plural "in the heavens" (16:19) is editorial due to contextual alignment, whereas 18:18 offers the singular. "The latter is certainly more original," as Gnilka, *Matthäusevangelium*, 2:55, rightly states, because here, in 18:18, "on earth" and "in heaven" correspond to each other on the one hand, and on the other hand the singular "in heaven" stands out conspicuously from the other eight plural occurrences in ch. 18.

is left, in my opinion, with the following three lines of argument, two positive ones and a third that critically questions the alternative:

(1) As far as the *similarities* between John 20:23 and Matthew 18:18 are concerned, it is important to point out that these do not only refer to the plural version common to both logia, but also to their semantic relationship as described above. Under the plausible assumption that John 20:23 *does not* stem from knowledge of the Gospel of Matthew but rather that with John 20:23 and Matthew 18:18, there are two *independent* witnesses for the logion in its plural version, this finding should provide the decisive argument for the assumption of the priority of Matthew 18:18 over 16:19.

(2) G. Claudel rightly states: "On a literary level, I find it difficult to conceive of an independent *logion* addressed to an individual person: even the *logia* in 'you,' such as Matt 18:15–17, have a general scope."[176] An exemplary proof of this thesis will be shown in chapter 3, 3 where we focus on the difference between Mark 9:1 and John 21:22–23. If general statements ("you" or e.g., "everyone who . . .") can disregard concrete contexts, a logion that is addressed to a specific person is at least dependent on a corresponding introduction to the speech, which provides information about who the logion is addressed to (in our case Peter). It is dependent on a scenic frame.[177] Moreover, there is the following observation: "Furthermore, while in Matt 18:18 there is no requirement to change from the singular to the plural, in Matt 16:19 the context requires the singular."[178] In other words: If we can count on a single logion in our tradition, it seems clear that the plural version is the original.

(3) Historical arguments like the hierarchy of authority from an individual (Peter) to a collegium (the three pillars) will be met with skepticism if one recognizes that the literary conception in the Gospel of Matthew (at first Jesus announces Peter, later he gives the same authority to the congregation) is about an *ecclesiological figure of legitimization* that should not be evaluated historically any more than the claim supporting the authority of the Fourth Gospel that the "beloved disciple" "wrote" it (John 21:24). Also, the Gospel of Matthew, written some years after 70 CE, belongs to the Christian generation which had to secure the story of their origins.

If, therefore, the decision on the question of priority is in favor of Matthew 18:18, this does not mean that the saying was given to the first evangelist in the exact linguistic form in which it is now found in Matthew 18:18. If the linguistically

---

176. Claudel, "Jean 20,23," 75.

177. Here one would have to fall back on the completely hypothetical postulate of a *Petrine protophanic narrative*. Then the climax would have to be sought in the logion in Matt 16:19. However, the transmission of Matt 16:19; 18:18; and John 20:23 speaks much more for the existence of an originally isolated *single logion*.

178. Claudel, "Jean 20,23," 75.

balanced opposition "on earth" / "in heaven" belongs to the given saying,[179] this cannot be said of the corresponding generalization "anything"[180] in verse 19.[181] We can therefore expect the following form for the logion processed by Matthew:

(Truly, I say to you,)[182]
Whatever you bind on earth,
will also be bound in heaven;
and whatever you loose on earth,
will be loosed in heaven.

2.3.3.2 John 20:23 as a Climax of the Scene on Easter Sunday (John 20:19–23)

What is of primary interest in the context of our problems with the scene of John 20:19–23 is the question of whether verse 23, like Matthew 16:19 par. 18:18, can actually be claimed as an originally independent logion and, if so, at what stage it then grew into the Johannine scene. Was it original, or was it added to the scene later by the evangelist? There is a consensus among scholars that the author follows the passion and Easter story in 20:19–23, which was his base. It is also possible that the scene originally was its own tradition of Jesus's epiphany on Easter[183] and found its place later as the final scene of the passion and Easter account. Consequently, one would have to reckon with three textual stages for John 20:19–23 (independent tradition—passion narrative—evangelist).

We will see that verse 21 with its missional Christology virtually spells out the matrix that characterizes the word of commission in verse 23. In addition, it concretizes what the sending out of the disciples by the resurrected one consists of. However, the insight into the synchronic connections do not rule out the possibility that verse 23 was originally an independent logion. Especially the

---

179. A proof for this assumption is the secondary adaptation and alignment of the singular "*in heaven*" in Matt 16:19 to the broader context.

180. Verse 19: "If two of you agree on earth about *anything* they ask for, it will be granted to them by my Father in heaven."

181. Claudel, "Jean 20,23," 74: "For the ὁ ἐάν vs. ὅσα ἐάν, the former, more classic maxims with a legal profile in the congregation, seems more primitive."

182. It cannot be ruled out that the Amen formula was part of the given logion, especially as it has a parallel in Matt 16:18a: "and I say to you . . . ."

183. The arguments for this can be found in Bultmann, *Johannes*, 534–535, who points out "that the story in vv. 19–23 is self-contained and—apart from the redaction. Apart from the redactional link in v. 19, it has no connection with the previous one. . . . Neither Mary's message (v. 18) nor the fact that two disciples have already seen the empty tomb (vv. 3–10) are recalled"; likewise J. Becker, *Johannes*, 2:732: "That the apparition legend . . . originally circulated separately in the oral tradition is rightly generally assumed."

comparison with Matthew 16:19 and 18:18 makes this plausible. Therefore, it is the view of quite a few authors that verse 23 has at least the character of a tradition (*Überlieferung*), without therefore having to rule out any involvement of the evangelist in the formulation of the saying. With its two complementary halves, the saying is rounded in itself and does not need a context to be understood.

It is more difficult to answer the ensuing question of the stage at which the saying grew into our scene. Even though its "tradition-criticism" is problematic, the following can be said with some certainty: *The logion of the power to forgive sins in verse 23 was at the origin of the (individual) tradition 20:19–23*; *. Indeed this can be understood as its staging in the sense that it legitimates the disciples' power to forgive sins with the word of the resurrected Christ, naming this as its actual reason for legitimization.* This thesis will be explained in more detail, beginning with an analysis of the final text.

Its very structure is revealing:

          1. Scenic frame (v. 19a–c)
   - time and place (closed doors)

          2. Beginning of action (v. 19d–e)
   - Jesus comes and enters the center

PART A   3. WORDS of Jesus (v. 19f, g)
   - Greeting of peace

          4. GESTURE of Jesus (v. 20b)
   - he shows his hands and side
   - reaction of the disciples with
   - commentary of the narrator (v. 20c, d)

          5. WORDS of Jesus (v. 21)
   - (Renewed) greeting of peace
   - sending statement

PART B   6. GESTURE of Jesus (v. 22b)
   - he breathes on the disciples

          7. WORDS of Jesus (vv. 22c–23d)
   - interpretation of the gesture
   - saying about the forgiving of sins

After the symbolically charged, brief opening of the scene (the frame is not closed after verse 23; the text ends openly!) and the highly significant prelude to the action ("Jesus came and stood in their midst"), the narrative leads directly into Jesus's first word, his greeting of peace.[184] After this the narrative alternates between Jesus's words and gestures:

words (v. 19)—gesture (v. 20)—words (v. 21)—gesture (v. 22b)—words (vv. 22d and 23)

If the words are preceded by an introduction, both gestures are linked to the preceding word by means of the phrase "and after he had said this." A climax can be observed with respect to the words: Jesus's second word takes up the opening greeting of peace once again in order to follow on from the sending. For its part, the sending saying is concretized by the concluding word about the power to forgive sins, which is given an accent by the fact that it is preceded by the imperative "receive the Holy Spirit." This is probably the climax of the whole scene.

If we compare the two accounts of Jesus's gestures, we first notice that the narrator notes a reaction on the part of the disciples when Jesus shows his hands and side, which he also comments on (v. 20c, d: "so the disciples rejoiced because they had seen the Lord"), whereas no comparable reaction on their part is reported to the statement that Jesus "breathed on" the disciples. The narrator's note in verse 20c, d creates a slight caesura between verses 20 and verse 21, which is also emphasized by the resumption of the greeting of peace from verse 19 in verse 21a ("and *again* Jesus spoke to them"). Moreover, the second gesture ("he breathed on them") is interpreted by the immediately following interpretative word ("receive the Holy Spirit!"); the first gesture does not have such an interpretative comment, but the narrator indirectly adds the interpretation of that gesture by means of his note in verse 20c, d ("so the disciples rejoiced *because they had seen the Lord*"). It helps to recognize Jesus![185]

If we take into account the caesura between verse 20 and verse 21 and also consider the inner context of the words about the sending, the transmission of the Spirit, and the transfer of the authority to forgive sins in verses 21–23,[186] then the *structure of the scene is* as follows: Part A (with elements 1–4) recounts the process of his disciples *recognizing* the resurrected Jesus, Part B (with elements 5–7) reports on their *empowerment* for the salvation-mediating mission through the paschal Christ. Part A is oriented toward Part B and has its climax in it.

There are probably three ways to elucidate the *diachrony of the text*; they are only reasonably feasible if they are checked against each other: (1) a comparison

---

184. This is entirely appropriate to the situation, but the evangelist will want to see it interpreted in greater depth in the light of 14:27 as a promise of eschatological salvation.

185. See Luke 24:30–31, 35.

186. The transmission of the Spirit denotes the *inner reason* for the authority to forgive sins. It designates the twofold mode in which the mission takes place.

with the Lukan parallels, (2) an identification of clearly Johannine textual elements, and (3) the determination of the genre matrix of the text in the sense of a survey of what is absolutely necessary for its basic form (*Grundgestalt*). In the interest of our overarching question, we will focus our investigation on verse 21–23.

(1) The Johannine version of the story (part A: John 20:19–20) corresponds to the Lukan parallel (Luke 24:36–40) in its basic structure: *In the evening of Easter day Jesus comes in the midst of the disciples, spoke the greeting of peace, and gives them proof of his identity by showing them his hands and feet.*[187] This basic narrative was continued and redactionally appended on a large scale (!) by both evangelists with their own intentions. The Fourth Gospel writer did not know the Lukan version but only the same tradition with him. It is, however, difficult to say whether John 20:21–23 (= part B) par. Luke 24:41–49 also follow the same original.

For if in part A of the presumed tradition the similarities between Luke and John can be established right down to the formulations and their sequence, the mostly mentioned similarities in part B are rather overlaps in motif with completely different conceptions: εἰς ἄφεσιν ἁμαρτιῶν—"for the forgiveness of sins" (Luke 24:47) corresponds to our logion in John 20:23, ὑμεῖς μάρτυρες τούτων—"you are witnesses to it" (Luke 24:48). John 20:21c, d and the announcement of the coming of the Holy Spirit on Pentecost in Luke 24:49 corresponds with the transmission of the Spirit together with the word of interpretation in John 20:22. What is usually hardly taken into account in a comparison is the finding that Jesus's discourse in Luke 24:44–49 is characterized through and through by Lukan influence which, of course, does not exclude the possibility that in the background of this text there are nevertheless elements of tradition (which can, of course, no longer be determined in detail). In other words, *the three Lukan-Johannine correspondences cannot automatically be claimed given tradition.* We cannot conclude from the promise of the Holy Spirit in Luke 24:49, which builds a bridge between book one and two of the Lukan double work, that John 20:22 was also a given element of the Johannine tradition that could not have stemmed from the evangelist himself. In Luke 24:49 (see Acts 1:8; 2:1–41) we find the typical Lukan *polarity* between Easter and Pentecost. Correspondingly, in John 20:22 we find the specific expression of the Johannine *identification* of exaltation and transmission of the Holy Spirit.[188]

---

187. Τὴν πλευράν = "*the side*" originally stands for τοὺς πόδας = "the feet" (Luke 21:40); the narrative element has its reason in the combination of the Easter tradition with the Joahnnine passion narrative (see John 19:34).

188. On the other hand, the correspondences between the motifs are too unspecific to assume John's knowledge of Luke.

(2) It is also difficult to identify clearly Johannine elements.[189] The mention of the time in verse 19[190]—a doublette to the following "first day of the week"—and the narrative element of the closed doors out of fear of the Jews can surely be attributed to the evangelist. They are only understandable in the context of the whole gospel. But the evangelist used the whole tradition and transformed it for his theological purposes.[191] Decisions about clear redactional additions of the old tradition remain doubtful.

Verse 21c, d ("as the Father has sent me, so also I send you") sounds like John. But we cannot rule out that this verse (together with 13:16, 20) belongs to the traditional elements of the gospel from which the author was inspired for his Christology.[192] The way in which the Spirit is transferred in verse 22b does indeed seem "archaic,"[193] but since the narrative passage of "breathing on" is used here in a very reflective way, alluding to Scripture, the "archaic" impression can also be deceptive and does not necessarily have to be an argument for the antiquity of verse 22.[194] Also the words about authority in verse 23 were used by the evangelist (see below!) even though his terminology[195] shows clearly that there was a model for it; the original form—as the original end of the Easter scene in John 20:19–23* or a free logion which the evangelist added to this scene—can be evaluated after obtaining insight into the inner logic of the narrative.

(3) If part A of the tradition has its climax in part B, the question arises as to which of the three logia (v. 21c, d; v. 22c ["Receive the Holy Spirit!"]; v. 23) necessarily belonged to the given tradition. It is certain, also due to the structure of the other Easter narratives, that to be complete, our scene had to lead to a commissioning of the disciples by the exalted one as its climax[196] (also in

---

189. A careful reflection of the criteria can be found in Brown, *John*, 2:1029.

190. It corresponds to John 14:20: "on that day." John 14:20 interprets the Easter scene in John 20:19–23.

191. We should read v. 19: *"Jesus came"* in light of 14:18; "I come to you" and the greeting of peace in vv. 19.21 in light of 14:27: "Peace I leave with you, my peace I give to you."

192. See Becker, *Johannes*, 2:735–736.

193. Becker, *Johannes*, 2:737.

194. Similary Brown, *John*, 2:1030: "Of the three sayings of Jesus in John XX 21–23, the mention of the giving of the Spirit is the one most intimately related to the Johannine theological dialogue about the purpose of the ascension in (20,)17, and so Vs.22 may very well represent the evangelist's expansion of the primitive appearance narrative." More arguments for this option in Dodd, *Tradition*, 144 n. 1.

195. Dodd, *Tradition*, 348: "The expression ἀφιέναι ἁμαρτίας [= *"forgive sins"*] and κρατεῖν [= *"retain them"*] are never found in the Fourth Gospel, apart from this one place."

196. See Matt 28:19; Mark 16:15; Luke 24:47.

comparison with the structure of the other Easter narratives). It is also certain that verse 23 could have been handed down as an independent logion, but not verse 22c, which, together with the gesture of breathing on the disciples, prefigures the final logion of verse 23. Verse 21c, d also does not represent an independent logion but requires a subsequent concretization because it does not say *what* the mission consists *of;* only verse 23 does this.

Conversely, verse 23 does not need either the words about sending to be connected to the narrative, nor the scenic gesture of breathing on together with its interpretation ("receive the Holy Spirit!").

Be that as it may, the narration runs up to the saying about the authority to forgive sins which is indispensable for the scene because both sayings depend necessarily on it. It is unlikely that all three sayings are originally part of the old tradition because this "trinity" points to a process of growth and the original tradition is more likely to have *one* climax, either with verses 21c, d and 23 or verses 22 and 23. This also brings us to the tradition-criticism alternative, which is the only serious option for solving the diachronic problem:

Solution A (vv. 22–23 = tradition; v. 21 = evangelist)[197] has the advantage of a clear literary critical distinction. For since the second greeting of peace in verse 21b is in any case suspect,[198] the evangelist would then have used its insertion to place his missionary idea in a separate speech element in the original. For an appraisal of verse 23, this means that the evangelist would have used the missionary idea of verse 21c, d to indicate in advance the framework in which he wanted the word about the power to forgive to be understood. The prefixing of the *positive* statement about the forgiveness of sins and the subordination of the *negative* fits in with this: the messengers of the exalted Christ promise people the forgiveness of sins. If they are rejected, then from their point of view the consequence is that those who reject the word of Christ remain in their sins, but the messengers can only confirm this state of calamity ("... which you retain [the sins], [they] are retained").

Solution B (vv. 21c, d + 23 = tradition; v. 22 = evangelist)[199] seems more complicated. In this case, the evangelist's specifically new contribution would not be the idea about mission but the pneumatologic foundation of the authority to forgive sins in verse 22. The evangelist would make clear that the forgiveness of sins (analogous to 3:3, 5 etc.) is an eschatological *new creation* and therefore the fruit of the Holy Spirit, which in turn arises from the death and exaltation of Jesus. The fact that the evangelist names the *Father* as the giver of the Paraclete

---

197. Exemplarily in Schnackenburg, *Johannesevangelium*, 3:381–382.

198. The first greeting of peace (v. 19) is given; to have three parts the evangelist adds v. 21 and v. 26.

199. Exemplarily in Brown, *John*, 2:1029–1031.

in his farewell discourse, but here it is the *exalted* one who "breathes" the Spirit, does not, as is sometimes claimed,[200] argue against the origin of verse 22 from the evangelist's pen. This is because both statements are situated on different levels: 14:16, 26 are reflexive theological *explanations*; 20:22 is a narrative text to which belong the figurative sayings in 7:38 ("rivers of living water will flow from within *him* [i.e., *Christ*]"[201]), and in 1:32 ("it is he who will baptize with the Holy Spirit"). The reflexive statements in 14:16, 26 which emphasize the *theocentricity* of the Christ event, are also linked back to Christology.[202] There are no real *linguistic* objections to the evangelist's authorship of the material.[203] On the contrary the macro-contextual references in which 20:22 is embedded are remarkable: Together with 1:33, the first pneuma passage of the Gospel, 20:22 builds a large-scale *inclusio*; 7:39 ("but he said this about the Spirit, which those who believed in him were to *receive*") finds its fulfillment in 20:22: "*receive the Holy Spirit*!" Seen in this light, verse 22 is neccessary for the evangelist's whole composition of the gospel. If he had not found this verse in his original—which we do not want to decide here—he would have had to formulate it himself.

Let us summarize: (1) John 20:23 is originally an independent logion. (2) In the tradition of an Easter appearance of Jesus to his disciples, this logion was given a Christological framework: The missionaries' authority to forgive sins is based on the authority of the resurrected Christ *who* endowed his disciples with this authority. (3) By the passion and Easter narrative, this scene came into the Gospel where its author used it in service of his own Christology and pneumatology.

2.3.3.3 The Development of the Logion

Summary

Contrary to popular opinion, there is much to suggest that not Matthew 18:18 (16:19) but John 20:23 represents the older version of the logion. We have demonstrated that John 20:23 represents the older version. First, the missionary context of John 20:23* is more original than the ecclesiological context of Matthew 18:18 (16:19). Second—this aspect is connected with the first—the matrix of the Johannine logion, the right to be a messenger, might be older than the

---

200. See Becker, *Johannes*, 2:737.

201. See the commentary on 7:39: "Now he said this about the *Spirit*, which believers in him were to receive..." See ch. 6, 2.

202. 14:16: "And *I will ask the Father* and he will give you another Paraclete"; 14:26: "the Holy Spirit, whom the Father will send *in my name*."

203. Schnackenburg, *Johannes*, 3:385.

inner-ecclesiastical juridical connotation found in Matthew.[204] Here we have the solution to why there is a different order of positive and negative terms in the two versions: The priority of the *positive* aspect (John) corresponds to the missionary context (see above!); the priority of the *negative* aspect corresponds to the inner-ecclesiastical practice of banning in the Jewish-Christian community of Matthew because it necessarily requires the priority of an actually dangerous measure of exclusion, whereas the positive side (different from the Johannine version) can be understood as the *abolition* of the negative state, and therefore *has to* be secondary. The Jewish character of the terminology of Matthew 18:18 and 16:19 is a strong indication that this juridical version originated in the Jewish-Christian context of the Matthean community.

The origin of the Johannine version in the right to be a messenger could make the parallel of the sending speech of Q 10:5–6 clear and more reasonable:

Whichever house you go to,
first say:
"Peace be to this house!"
And if there is a son of peace there,
your peace shall come upon him;
but if not,
your peace shall return to you.

Here, *peace* (εἰρήνη) means the universal gospel of the disciples who have been sent out, similar to the forgiveness of sins in the Johannine saying. Like there, so also here the message of peace comes first. The rejection of this peace means that the messengers take the peace with them and leave those who closed their doors to them in a state of discord, of calamity, as is also the case in the Johannine logion. However, according to its terminology of forgiving or retaining sins, this is more reflective than the very primitive speech of peace that "returns" to the messengers if the message is refused.[205] This is probably why we are not dealing with a Jesus logion in John 20:23*.

---

204. Brown, *John*, 2:1041: "In many ways the Johannine formula is more kerygmatic and preserves more of the original import of the saying than does the juridic formula used in Matthew." Coulot, "Jean 20,23," 85, highlights the different "worlds" of the First and Fourth Gospel: "the Christian scribal world for the so-called pre-Matthean, and the Christian Baptist world for the so-called Johannine," with the consequence that "a certain anteriority" has to be attributed to the Johannine logion.

205. G. Theissen and A. Merz, *Der historische Jesus. Ein Lehrbuch* (Göttingen: Vandenhoeck & Ruprecht, 1996), 380: Afterward, the disciples bring "a magical 'aura of peace' into the houses, which protects the house in the final judgment and already now, as the power of the imminent reign of God, permeates the house and its inhabitants with salvation."

In conclusion, the history of the logion's tradition can be illustrated as follows:

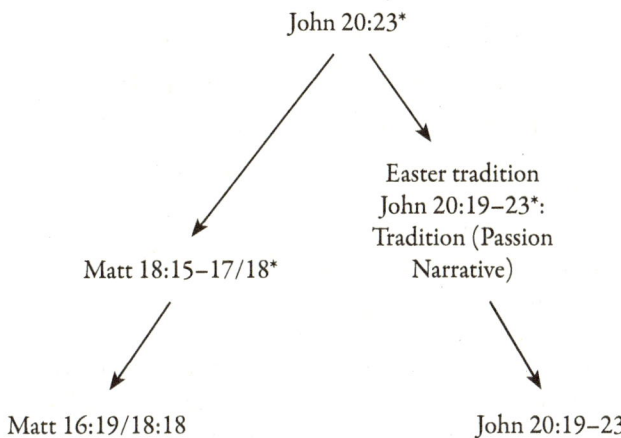

We should refrain from reconstructing an original form of the logion, as we do not know to what extent the fourth evangelist actually intervened in the form of John 20:23. In any case, it is clear that the original "word of the Lord" was not a "commissioned word of the risen one," but only became one in the course of its scenic realization in John 20:19–23.

Concerning the Matthean tradition, we must seriously reckon with the possibility that the first evangelist received the binding and loosening word of Matthew 18:18* in combination with the congregational rule of 18:15–17. In any case, the endeavor behind that rule to establish a reliable congregational order describes precisely the milieu in which one can imagine the juridical metamorphosis of the old logion in the service of a theonomic justification of the establishment of law by the congregation. The Amen-saying in verse 18 and the inclusion of the community rules in a speech of Jesus in Matthew's version strengthens the Christological anchoring and standardization of that rule.[206] So also the Johannine tradition attempts to justify *Christologically* the authority of the disciples (the exercise of which even binds God [!]), namely by recourse to the words of the *exalted* Jesus. Let us not forget, too, that already in 14:12–14, with

---

206. The Christological normativity of the law in Matthew also has a *limiting* function—Jesus as the authentic and final interpreter of the Torah or of God's will highlights "justice, mercy, and faith" (Matt 23:23) as center of the law, according to God's words: "I desire mercy and not sacrifice" (Hos 6:6: Matt 9:13; 12:7). In Matt 18 this can be seen in the addition of the logion about the never ending desire for reconciliation (Matt 18:21–22): "Then Peter came and said to him, 'Lord, if another member of the church sins against me, how often should I forgive? As many as seven times?' Jesus said to him, 'Not seven times, but, I tell you, seventy-seven times.'"

its provocative speech about "greater works" of the disciples, the author prepares the ground for understanding 20:23.²⁰⁷

2.4 From Jesus's Messengers to the Community of the Baptized
The Synoptic Logia in the Gospel of John as a Reminder of the Beginning

Finally, let us put the results of the above analyses together to form a mosaic! In doing so, we gain remarkable insights into the roots of the Fourth Gospel in the history of tradition and their significance for its theology:

(1) There is no evidence that the evangelist drew his synoptic logia from one of the Synoptic Gospels. Maybe the redactor of the book knew the speech about sending in Matthew (this could be implied in John 15:20-21).²⁰⁸ But the idea that the redactor would have taken the opportunity somewhere in the book to add synoptic traditions, because their absence was already perceived as a deficiency per se, is an assumption that can hardly be proven. T. K. Heckel claimed this for John 21. According to his view, the author of this chapter intentionally used the motifs of fishing (see Luke 5:4-11) and of Peter as a shepherd in sense of Christ's deputy (see Matt 16:17-19). He connected the Gospel of John to the Synoptic Gospels.²⁰⁹ As debatable as a reference from John 21 to Luke 5 is, a specific option in favor of a coexistence of the Gospel of John *and the* Synoptics is difficult to establish from the text.²¹⁰

(2) C. H. Dodd had already noticed a certain proximity of the Johannine logia to the first evangelist. This is indeed the case with John 3:3/5 (cf. Matt 18:3); John 13:16, 20 (cf. Matt 10:24-25, 40); John 12:25 (cf. Matt 10:39) and John 20:23 (cf. Matt 16:18; 18:18). However, there are also points of contact with the Markan logia tradition (cf. John 12:26a, b with Mark 8:34 [ἀκολουθείτω μου] and John 14:13-14 with Mark 11:24), and these would certainly have been more striking if Mark had not edited the logia he received so heavily (cf. above on Mark 9:37; 10:15; 11:24). Here a tradition-criticism analysis is helpful: *What seems like a special correspondence with Matthew proves on closer inspection to be related*

---

207. See p. 76-78.

208. See Theobald, *Herrenworte* 97-152, esp. 145-146.

209. T. H. Heckel, *Vom Evangelium des Markus zum viergestaltigen Evangelium*, WUNT 120 (Tübingen: Mohr Siebeck, 1999), 158-192.

210. The derivation of John 21:15-19 from Matt 16:17-19 seems particularly problematic to me, since there are no linguistic similarities at all in the decisive motifs.

"Words of the Lord" with Synoptic Parallels 109

to traditions received by the first evangelist—Q-sayings whose wording we find similar to Matthew (e.g., 14:24–25) or special Jewish-Christian traditions that have found their way into Matthew (see Matt 18:3 and 18:18). Points of contact with Mark arise above all where the oldest evangelist has parallel traditions to Q (cf. for example Mark 8:34–35; 9:37). In other words: *The Synoptic logia received by John do not come from the Synoptics but are parallel traditions on level with the pre-gospel material.* These are Q and pre-Markan as well as pre-Matthean traditions. The result is that if we want to avoid making rash connections between Johannine logia and the synoptic tradition, we have to assume a Johannine interlayer. In other words: *The Johannine community must be regarded as a tradent of ancient logia. The Johannine community must be taken seriously as the bearer of ancient logia, from which the evangelist received his material. Here it also received its pre-Johannine character, as can be seen in certain peculiarities of the phraseology.*

(3) It is noteworthy that the critical inquiry into the traditions could at least make their origin from the historical Jesus plausible for some logia. For example, John 3:3/5; 13:16; 13:20; and 14:13–14 are probably based on *authentic words of Jesus*, whereas this is less likely for 12:24 and 20:23.[211] Which segments of Jesus's preaching are in focus?

On the one hand, there is the logion in John 3:3, 5, which is based on a saying such as Matt 18:3, a keyword of Jesus's proclamation: to become like a child before God means to call him Abba as the first step on the way to his kingdom! On the other hand, there are sayings (also 12:25 and 20:23) that belong to the topic of sending, that is speak to the right to be messenger (13:20; 20:23), to make them aware of the messengers' fate with Jesus (13:16), to make clear the importance of their efforts (12:25), and to grant them unshakeable trust in the God who accompanies them in prayer (14:13–14/Mark 11:24).

(4) It is noteworthy that some of these words achieved their far-reaching effect through the *sayings source*, whose bearers saw themselves as the end-time messengers and missionaries of Jesus, sent out to Israel. Q 10:16 (see John 13:20) had a prominent position at the end of the speech in Q 10 concerning selection and sending,[212] whereas Q 6:40 (disciples—master) was part of Jesus's programmatic speech that opened the main part of the sayings source. The saying about the answer to prayer, Q 11:9–10, followed directly after the messenger speech from the sayings source in the context of the sequence Q 11:2–4, 9–10, 11–13, which is dedicated to the topic of "prayer." Because of the correlation of the Johannine logia to this prominent Q-saying, can we conclude that the sayings source was known by the Johannine community? The following two aspects speak against this: the aphorism on prayer received in John 14:13–14 is

---

211. See below pp. 221–222 and 142–143.

212. See Robinson, et al., *Edition* 158–189.

closer to Mark 11:24 than to the sayings from Q. The words about the power of Jesus's messengers to forgive sins in John 20:23 also correspond structurally to the instruction from the messenger's speech in the logia source Q 10:5-6. However, there they have no parallel *in terms of content* but rather touch on the Jewish-Christian tradition of the Matthew community. All in all, the Johannine community probably did not gain access to the sending traditions via Q, but through other oral channels.[213]

(5) The legacy that connects the Johannine community with the beginnings of the Jesus movement is therefore the tradition of the sending of Jesus's messengers. The fact that this is not simply a reminder of the origins of a now settled community is demonstrated by the references in the letters of John to the still vibrant missionary messenger system, now perhaps partly transformed into a network of lively exchange between the Johannine communities. What was not passed on of the traditions of the messengers were its specific content about the Jesus like the announcement of God's kingdom (Luke 10:11 par. Matt 10:7), the bestowal of authority to fight against demons (Mark 6:7; Matt 10:8), and healing the sick in general (Matt 10:8, Luke 10:9; see Mark 6:13). Exorcisms generally are dismissed in the Johannine tradition.[214] Instead we find the authority of Jesus's messengers to forgive or retain sins (John 20:23), which means a religious subordination of Jesus's contract.

The high tradition-historical importance of the old model about messengers in the Fourth Gospel is found in the book's Christology. It does not seem to be a coincidence that the second main part of the work, John 13–20, inherits synoptic content especially at the beginning and at the end, namely in 13:16, 20 and 20:23 (20:21-23). This is the climax of Johannine Christology related to the messengers. Obviously, the author made the verses which frame chapters 13–20, compatible with each other: 13:20 ("whoever receives one whom I send receives me . . .") corresponds with 20:21 about the authority to forgive sins: "as the Father sent me, so also I send you." John 13:20 looks forward ("*I will send*"); this promise is fulfilled at Easter according to 20:21. So, we can say: *In his Christology, the evangelist follows the old Jesus tradition. The synoptic logia are signs of remembering the beginning.*

---

213. This result could be proved by a comparison of Q 7:1-10 and John 4:46-54, and Q 10:22 with Johannine parallels (see Theobald, *Logion*, 165-189).

214. On the missing exorcisms in the Gospel of John see, e.g., R. A. Piper, "Satan, Demons and the Absence of Exorcisms in the Fourth Gospel," in *Christology, Controversy and Community: New Testament Essays in Honour of David R. Catchpole*, ed. D. Horrell and C. M. Tuckett, SuppNovT (Leiden: Brill, 2000), 253-278, here 253-278, 264-265: "The language of demon possession is not in the fourth gospel related to matters of magical healing; but to rivalry. It is reserved for demonising one's opponents."

(6) The Johannine community is a filter of old logia before the evangelist or secondary redactor used them. A Johannine sociolect emerges. In 3:3, 5 the metaphor to become children is replaced by the symbol of rebirth. Thereby, the whole Johannine corpus is steered in a specific direction. The *Sitz im Leben* of the saying is baptism, which is the common sacrament of initiation practiced in the community. Similarly important in this context is 12:26*: "and where I am, there my servant will be also." Behind this is a deepened understanding of salvation and life that has grown out of dealing with the question of death.[215] Transformations of this kind, which we can also follow more closely in the next chapter, show the independent theological path of the Johannine community.

---

215. See the German version of this book, *Herrenworte*, 127–129.

CHAPTER 3

"Words of the Lord" as Metatexts of Synoptic Traditions

IN HIS PAPER "Tradition und Interpretation im Spruchgut des Johannesevangeliums," Rudolf Schnackenburg recognizes an intermediate group alongside the "synoptic logia in the Gospel of John" on the one hand and the "Johannine logia without reference to synoptic tradition" on the other, which he titles: "Johannine logia with reference to synoptic tradition." On these logia, he writes, "This group consists of sayings that are so strongly Johannine in character that their formation must be ascribed to the evangelist, but which on the other hand, according to their structure, choice of words, and similarity of meaning, reveal a connection with synoptic logia in terms of the history of tradition."[1] For Schnackenburg the Johannine community plays no role as an independent bearer of traditions. Therefore, he only has two options: They are either synoptic logia or Johannine logia, that is, logia formed by the evangelist. This dichotomy seems inadequate. Schnackenburg does not reckon with the creativity of the community in the continuation of tradition. He only wants to reduce this creativity to the synoptic tradition as if the evangelist only took his synoptic logia directly from Mark, Matthew, and Luke. However, if we take seriously the evidence collected in the previous chapter that the Johannine "words of the Lord" with synoptic parallels reveal the presence of an *intermediate layer* that involves the Johannine community, then one would have to *be open* to the possibility that even sayings with references to synoptic material but containing highly Johannine characteristics are creations of the Johannine community. Of course, tradition-criticism arguments must be provided for such an assumption. The following examples present three different cases: The third text, *John 21:22-23*, is the clearest, insofar as it *explicitly* mentions a word of the Lord circulating in the community. In *John 12:28*, it was clearly the evangelist who created a logion of Jesus with reference to an old Jesus tradition—the Lord's Prayer. First, we look at *John 3:14-15*, a saying that is often attributed to the evangelist, but was probably already circulating in his community. We see here that the evangelist is not the solitary thinker he is often thought to be. Rather, he could strongly rely on the traditions of his community.

---

1. R. Schnackenburg, "Tradition und Interpretation im Spruchgut des Johannesevangeliums" (1980), in *Johannesevangelium*, HThK.NT IV/1-4 (Freiburg: Herder, 1984), 4:72-89, here 78.

114   The Lord's Words

Before we begin, I must open with some words about terminology: The term *metatext* denotes a Johannine text that was developed in conversation with the synoptic tradition as its *basic text*. To be able to claim a Johannine text or tradition as a metatext to a synoptic basic text, it is not sufficient to merely establish a correspondence—for example, with only *one* motif. Rather, what is required for proof is correspondence in a cluster of motifs (that means two or more motifs) or an identical motif combined with a characteristic motif and/or proof that the common motif was not widespread but points to a specific basic text. Only an overview of all the material makes it possible to assess the type and manner of the transformations carried out in the Gospel of John.

3.1 The Serpent of Brass (John 3:14–15; see Mark 8:31)

It is probable that John 3:14–15 stems from the tradition of the Johannine community. The evangelist uses it to conclude his Jesus-Nicodemus dialogue and takes it up again at Jesus's last public appearance in Jerusalem (12:34). In this way, it frames Jesus's public ministry in Israel, to which chapters 2 to 12 of his work are dedicated. The logion does not have a synoptic parallel. However, it is so close to the Son of Man–saying in Mark 8:31 that it can be claimed as the basic text for the Johannine tradition.

3.1.1 The Context of John 3:14–15
Initial Composition-Critical Observations

Between verses 15 and 16 there is a caesura. Here, the dialogue between Jesus and Nicodemus changes to a monologue closer to the kerygmatic teaching in 3:16–21. The saying about the Son of Man in verses 14–15 closes the dialogue, or more precisely the third part of the dialogue (3:10–15). It leads into the following sequence:

 10   a   *Jesus answered and said to him,*
      b   You are a teacher of Israel
      c   and do not understand this?
 11   a   *Very truly I tell you,*
      b   what we know,
      c   we proclaim,
      d   and what we have seen,
      e   we testify to,
      f   but you do not accept our testimony.

12 a When I have told you of earthly things
    b and you do not believe,
    c how,
    d when I tell you of heavenly things,
    c will you believe?
13 a *And* no one has ascended to heaven,
    b except for the who descended from heaven,
    c the Son of Man.
14 a *And* just as Moses lifted up the serpent in the wilderness,
    b so also must the Son of man be exalted,
15   so that everyone who believes may have eternal life in him.

The individual building blocks of this piece of speech are rebuke (v. 10), the Amen-saying (v. 11), a hinge verse (v. 12), and two Son of Man–sayings (v. 13/14–15). The hinge verse leads from the instruction on baptism in the first and second part of the dialogue to the Christological climax in verses 13–15. Each of these building blocks obeys its own play on language: The Amen-saying makes use of testimonial terminology, the hinge verse processes catechetical topoi, the first Son of Man–saying draws on the ascent-descent scheme, and the second on the early Christian model of exaltation. Each of these plays on language (*Sprachspiele*) has its own merit, which is particularly true of the two Son of Man–sayings. Nevertheless, the author considered these plays on language to be compatible with each other and interlocked them to form a whole. Here are the following observations:

(1) Starting from the rebuke in verse 10, the two subsequent elements in verses 11 and 12 each lead to a remark of *resignation*: "you do not understand?"—"but you do not accept our testimony"—"how will you believe?" Only the Christological climax in verses 14–15, in which the semantic isotope "recognize/accept/believe" is continued, offers a *positive* statement of purpose in its final sentence "so that everyone who believes may have eternal life in him."

(2) According to the amen word in verse 11, authentic testimony is based on "knowledge" from experience ("what we have seen"). With this, the saying not only ties in with verse 3 but also opens the way for verse 12. For if verse 11 applies, will Nicodemus, who already did not believe the "earthly," be able to believe the "heavenly," which is intrinsically beyond human experience?

At the same time, verse 11 also seems to provide the basis for verse 13. The fact that authentic testimony requires knowledge authenticated by *experience* also applies exclusively to Jesus with regard to the proclamation of "heavenly things," for he alone is "from heaven," as the first Son of Man–saying claims. However, verse 13 does not explicitly speak of a *proclamation* of "heavenly things" as the goal of the Son of Man's descent. Thus, it is possible that the expectation of gaining knowledge about the "heavenly things" mentioned verses 11–12 is modified in verses 14–15.

(3) Verses 12 and 13 are interlinked by the common keywords "*heavenly things*"/"*heaven*." However, because verses 14–15 do not communicate any "heavenly things," a gap remains. This means that the descent of the Son of Man from heaven cannot be about the revelation of "heavenly things" or mysteries in the plural but only about the *one* heavenly reality of salvation in the singular. This is revealed in the second saying of the Son of Man: "*eternal life.*"[2]

Moreover, verse 13 is linked to verse 12 by a coordinating "and/also." We can therefore expect an *additional* argument to support the doubts expressed in verse 12 about the ability of Nicodemus or the group he represents to believe: "How are they to attain to faith in the 'heavenly things' if the 'earthly' are beyond them?" (see v. 12). Verse 13 continues, "*Nor has any man* yet ascended into heaven" to behold the heavenly mysteries, which are closed to man per se. However, the latter part of the previous sentence is not explicitly stated, and so the polemic against presumed claims to gain insight into the heavenly mysteries through "ascension into heaven," that is, ecstasy or rapture or any other means, which is always suspected here, remains rather subliminal (see also John 1:18a; 5:37b; 6:46a). Rather, verse 13 (like later 6:46b) transforms the thought Christologically by highlighting the Son of Man's descent from heaven as a necessary condition of his later ascension (v. 13b, c).

(4) Just as the first Son of Man–saying in verse 13 is added to verse 12, so too the second Son of Man–saying is added in verses 14–15 with a coordinating conjunction ("*and*") and a the keyword ("*the Son of Man*"). Semantically, the transition is made with the help of the two compatible phrases "ascend into heaven" and "(be) exalted into heaven." The intention to link the two Son of Man–sayings is therefore obvious, despite the difference between their two linguistic games ("ascend"—"be exalted"). Verse 13 denotes the *interpretative framework* for the subsequent second Son of Man–saying and therefore has a superordinate status:

(a) Verse 13 is formulated actively, whereas verses 14–15 are formulated passively. However the passive voice of verse 14b is to be interpreted—as an expression of suffering at the hands of men or a reference to God's activity—verse 13 makes it clear in advance that the Son of Man does not relinquish his own sovereignty in dying: *He ascends into heaven.*

(b) Verse 13 is *more comprehensive* than verses 14–15 in that it deals with both descent *and* ascent, whereas verses 14–15 only deal with the "ascent." Additionally, verse 13 begins *generally* ("no one . . ."), whereas verses 14–15 only contain the events surrounding the Son of Man. The fundamental nature established in verse 13 (no ascent to heaven without a previous descent!) helps

---

2. This transforms a *cognitive* model of revelation (proclamation of "heavenly things") into a *personal* model of sharing in life.

to interpret the ascension event around the Son of Man, which is appropriately referred to in verse 14 as "exaltation."

(c) From the perspective of time, verse 13 also prepares the second saying. It has a *prospective* view on the elevation of Jesus and corresponds to the standpoint of the speaker, the *earthly* Jesus.[3] Verse 13 fits into this perspective when it mentions the "descent" of the Son of Man but does not say anything about his coming "ascension."[4] This is mentioned in verse 14 in the speech about ascension.

(d) Verse 13 provides a Christological definition, and verses 14–15 climax in soteriology ("so that everyone who believes may have eternal life in him"). Obviously, the first sentence cannot stand on its own; it is linked to the second and ensures its proper interpretation.

Let us summarize: The fabric of 3:10–15 is tightly woven. Nevertheless, different sayings, each with their own linguistic game and differing genre, stand out from one another. This leads to the question of whether this material also contains predetermined units of tradition—logia that the evangelist found and incorporated into the composition of his dialogue.[5] This is indeed the case with the Son of Man–saying in 3:14–15, which will be explained in more detail below.

---

3. The post-Easter retrospective in the following kerygmatic teaching in 3:16–21 stands out from this: v. 16, "the Father has given the only Son"; v. 17, "he has sent him" (by which not merely his "descent" in v. 13 is meant, but also his mission as a whole, which culminates in his death); v. 19, "the light has come into the world"; v. 19, "people loved the darkness more than the light" (like 1:11, this already summarizes people's reaction to Jesus's work).

4. With its expected addition, the elliptical statement in v. 13 reads, "no one has ascended (ἀναβέβηκεν) into heaven, except the one who descended, the Son of Man; he will ascend into heaven." The addition suggested by J.-A. Bühner, *Der Gesandte und sein Weg im 4. Evangelium. Die kultur- und religionsgeschichtlichen Grundlagen der johanneischen Sendungschristologie sowie ihre traditionsgeschichtliche Entwicklung*, WUNT II/2 (Tübingen: Mohr Siebeck, 1977), 380–381 is absurd. He says, "John wants to say that the other *anabatiker* never came out of the realm of the earthly; only Jesus was really in heaven, which can be recognized by the fact that he descended as the Son of Man." When and in what form was Jesus already in heaven? Bühner answers this question: during his "vocational vision . . . the *anabatiker* was transformed into a heavenly one and returns to earth as such" (382; similar to K. Berger, *Die Auferstehung des Propheten und die Erhöhung des Menschensohnes. Traditionsgeschichtliche Untersuchungen zur Deutung des Geschickes Jesu in frühchristlichen Texten*, StUNT 13 [Göttingen: Vandenhoeck & Ruprecht, 1976], 414 n. II). Verse 13 should therefore be supplemented, "no one has ascended . . . unless the one who descended, the Son of Man, has ascended to heaven [at his calling]." Here, the role of v. 13 as an interpretative instruction for vv. 14–15 is completely misguided.—The perfect ἀναβέβηκεν fits into the temporal perspective of v. 13. It looks back at the supposed *anabatiker* of the past (especially Moses [?], cf. below . . .) and states that none of them actually reached heaven. If a perfect "usually denotes an achieved state of the present" (HvS § 200, "an event of the past continues to have an effect in the present [resultative aspect of the perfect tense]"), then it could also be used of Jesus, who ascended to heaven with lasting success. Of course, it should be noted that v. 13 does not say this explicitly, so as not to destroy the prospective perspective of vv. 14–15.

5. This was suspected in exegetical studies long ago. See, e.g. B. Lindars, *The Gospel of John*, NCeB (Grand Rapids: Eerdmans, 1972), 155, at v. 11: "The use of the truly formula is a sign that this

3.1.2 Tradition-Critical Arguments

The following observations may be regarded as indications of tradition:

(1) The Son of Man-saying stands out from its context. John 3:13 is an anticipated commentary by the evangelist.
(2) The logion stands on its own and is understandable without any connection to the context.
(3) Genre criticism shows that the saying also adheres to its own genre (see below).
(4) The specific typology that characterizes the saying is otherwise foreign to the fourth evangelist.[6]
(5) In terms of motifs, the saying takes up an old, early Christian tradition with its speech of the exaltation of Jesus.[7]
(6) The saying is based on a synoptic logion (Mark 8:31, see below).
(7) Concerning style, nothing speaks against the tradition hypothesis. Rather, the saying might be a typical example of the Johannine sociolect which also influenced the individual style of the evangelist.
(8) The evangelist comes back to the saying once again in a characteristic quotation in 12:34.

3.1.3 John 3:14–15 as "Eschatological Correlative" *The Genre of the Saying*

"Comparative sentences" are "a common stylistic device in the old Bible."[8] The following proverbs from the so-called sayings source are particularly close to our logion:

---

is a verse which John has taken over almost verbatim from the tradition of words of Jesus, as in verse 3. It is the appeal to special revelation, characteristic of prophets and religious pioneers, which always meets with some opposition"; H. Koester, *Ancient Christian Gospels. Their History and Development* (London: SCM Press, 1990), 259, on vv. 13/14–15, 16: "traditional material."

6. He refers to Moses either polemically (John 6:32), downgrades him in comparison to Jesus (1:17), or claims him as a direct witness for Christ. Apart from 3:14–15, nowhere is it claimed that the reality of Israel's history testified to by Moses has independent weight and points to the event of salvation in Christ in the last days.

7. See Phil 2:9; Acts 2:33; 5:31; Heb 7:26. In John, the "exaltation" is otherwise only mentioned in 8:28 and 12:32/34, whereby the last two passages refer back to 3:14–15.—The situation is different with the reference to the story of the copper serpent in Num 21:4–9. It is found nowhere else in the NT, but is present in other parts of early Christian literature, such as Barn. 12:5–7; Justin Martyr, *1 Apol.* 60; *Dial.* 91.4; 94.1–5; 112.1–3, which leads Bultmann, *Johannes*, 109 n. 1, to the assumption: "The typological use of Num 21:8–9 was probably given to the evangelist by the Christian tradition."

8. A. Vögtle, Die "Gretchenfrage" des Menschensohnproblems. Bilanz und Perspektive, QD 152 (Freiburg: Herder, 1994), 152.

Luke 11:30 (par. Matt 12:40):
"*As* Jonah became a sign to the Ninevites,
so also will *the Son of Man* be [a sign] to this generation."

Luke 17:24 (par. Matt 24:27):
"For *as* the lightning, when it flares up, from one end of the heaven to the other,
so also will *the Son of Man* be in his day."

Luke 17:26–27 (par. Matt 24:37–39):
"And *as* it was in the days of Noah,
so also it will be in the days of *the Son of Man*:
They ate, drank, married, and got married—
until the day Noah entered the ark;
then the flood came and destroyed them all."

Luke 17:28–32:
"Just *as* it was in the days of Lot:
They ate, drank, bought, sold, planted, built—
but on the day Lot left Sodom,
it rained fire and brimstone from the sky
and destroyed them all.
It will be *exactly the same* on the day,
on which *the Son of Man* will be revealed."

Not only the *form* ("as A ..., so also B ..."), but also *the content of* these sayings are reminiscent of John 3:14–15. In three of them, the *future of the Son of Man* is confronted with an event from *past* biblical history (Noah, Lot, Jonah).[9] This also can be seen in John 3:14–15 (Moses in the desert—the Son of Man). But the epilogue of the Johannine saying does not contain a real future. However, the epilogue of John's saying does not contain a genuine future tense, but looks ahead from the point of view of the earthly Jesus to his *paschal* exaltation. Luke 17:24 differs from the other three sayings in that the comparison for the future appearance of the Son of Man is not drawn from the *history of* the Bible, but from the observation of *nature* in the manner of wisdom. As John 3:14–15 shows, the formal pattern of the typologically oriented comparison was able to develop its own type of saying. If in Luke 17:26–27 and 17:28–32 this is present in an extended form, whereby in each case the comparison is placed within the horizon of a "word of judgment," the comparison in John 3:14–15 is similarly embedded

---

9. On the Jonah saying, see Vögtle, *Gretchenfrage*, 148–163: "In my opinion, the Q saying in Luke 11:30 means from its origin ... that 'this generation' will see the Son of Man as miraculously saved from death, namely at the parousia." (163).

in an addressee-related context through the final soteriological sentence at the end, which forms the climax of the saying.

R. A. Edwards was the first to point out that the words of the Son of Man belong together due to their genre. He erroneously assumed that the genre "eschatological correlative" which he postulated was a creation of the group behind the sayings source with its *Sitz im Leben* in the liturgy of the Lord's Supper.[10] M. Sato interpreted the texts in terms of genre history as examples of a "prophetization" of the "originally popular-wisdom micro-genre" of *comparison that* had already taken place in the Old Testament.[11] He refers to texts in which the comparisons "no longer come from the world of creation, but from the history of Israel" or the biblical primeval period, meaning that "the typological correspondence in the history of God's salvation (or calamity) comes to the fore."[12] Isaiah 54:9 is a characteristic example of this:

"As in the days of Noah, this is for me:
As I swore
that the waters of Noah should no longer flood the earth,
so also I swear
not to be angry with you any longer,
to rebuke you no more."[13]

The Johannine saying thus draws on a type of saying that has developed in prophetic and apocalyptic literature[14] and which obviously owes its existence to a Christological interest in the Scriptures of Israel. The *necessity* (δεῖ) of the exaltation of the Son of Man is substantiated by reference to a *typos* of the Old Testament that prefigures the Easter event.

---

10. R. A. Edwards, "The Eschatological Correlative as a Gattung in the New Testament," *ZNW* 60 (1969): 9–20.

11. M. Sato, *Q und Prophetie. Studien zur Gattungs- und Traditionsgeschichte der Quelle Q*, WUNT II/29 (Tübingen: Mohr Siebeck, 1988), 278–287. Prov 11:22: "*Like* a golden ring on a pig's snout, *so also is* a beautiful woman without common sense." "Prophetization" refers to "the concrete situating" of a comparison "in a particular phase of history" (see Jer 5:27) or its embedding, for example, in the framework of a "proof of guilt" (e.g., Jer 3:20; 6:7 etc.) or a prophetic "announcement" (e.g., Amos 3:12; Ezek 34:12); Sato, *Q*, 280. On the whole, see also Westermann, Vergleiche, esp. 104–105. C. Westermann, *Vergleiche und Gleichnisse im Alten und Neuen Testament* (CThM.BW 14), Stuttgart, 1984.

12. Sato, *Q*, 281.

13. C. Westermann, *Das Buch Jesaja. Kap. 40–66*, ATD 19, 2nd ed. (Göttingen: Vandenhoeck & Ruprecht, 1970), 218. See also, e.g., Ezek 20:36; Jer 50:40; or Jos 1:5.

14. See, e.g., 4 Esdras 6:6; 13:52.

3.1.4 John 3:14–15 as a Metatext to Mark 8:31

Mark 8:31 reads:

a "And he began to teach them,
b *It is necessary (δεῖ) for the Son of Man to suffer*
c and be rejected by the elders, the chief priests, and the scribes
d and be killed
e and rise again after three days."

Mark 8:31 is the *basic text* for John 3:14–15*. This can be seen in the following *similarities*: (1) in the signal word δεῖ + infinitive in connection with the subject "the Son of Man,"[15] (2) in the common reference of both sayings about the death and resurrection of Jesus, and (3) in their reference to Scripture which is used to prove the divine necessity (δεῖ) of Jesus's life, death, and resurrection.

The *differences* between Mark 8:31 and John 3:14–15* are within this common framework: What the synoptic logion unfolds from a historical perspective as a succession of suffering, rejection, death, and resurrection, the Johannine logion brings together in the one event of "being exalted." The saying in Mark verifies the divine δεῖ by allusions to biblical tradition of the suffering of a righteous one;[16] the Johannine logion refers to the tradition of Numbers 21:4–9 and also alludes to Isaiah 52:13. Scriptural reflection required the genre of the "eschatological correlative."

If one sums up these observations, on the basis of the similarities between Mark 8:31 and John 3:14–15* the historical connection between the two sayings about the Son of Man should be clear.[17] But how are the differences between them to be interpreted? Is John 3:14–15* based on the *text* of Mark or are the two sayings *indirectly connected* via a common pre- or original form of the logion? The latter is probably the better solution, since it lets us explain the scriptural-theological ramification of the logion in the inclusion of the *passio-iusti* tradition in Mark on the one hand and in that of Numbers 21:4–9 in the Johannine community on the other. The original logion, with its divine necessity (δεῖ), which is only asserted but not yet proven by scriptural reflection, would then have repeatedly invited us to fill this gap with concrete references to Scripture. The prerequisite for this hypothesis is the well-founded assumption that the

---

15. This δεῖ is missing in the parallels at Mark 9:31; 10:33–34.

16. See especially Ps 34(33):20; 118(117):22; Ps 34 (33):20.

17. See also John 20:9 ("for they did not yet know the Scripture, *that he must rise from the dead* [δεῖ]").

three prophecies of suffering and resurrection in Mark[18] go back to an original form, which the oldest evangelist took up and elevated to the central theme of the middle section of his book in three variations, editing them in each instance.[19]

It is disputed which of the three prophecies of the passion and resurrection is closest to the original form, either the short form 9:31b ("the Son of Man is given into the hands of men"), or rather 14:41,[20] or maybe 8:31.[21] P. Hoffmann has argued convincingly that the old tradition should be sought in its first occurrence in 8:31, and that it probably originally read like this:

"The Son of Man must suffer much
and be killed
and rise again after three days."[22]

John 3:14–15* supports this assumption, since δεῖ is only found in Mark 8:31, but not in the other two versions of the prophecy of suffering and resurrection. Mark has specified the general idea of the historical-theological (apocalyptic) necessity of the death and resurrection of the Son of Man through the idea of scriptural fulfillment,[23] which is shown by the addition of "be rejected by..." to the logion, an allusion to Psalm 118 (117):22 (see also Mark 12:10–11).[24] If we transfer this to John 3:14–15, we can conclude that the development there was analogous.

---

18. Mark 8:31; 9:31; 10:33–34; moreover see 14:21, 41.

19. In addition to the representatives of this assumption listed in the notes below, see also E. Lohmeyer, *Das Evangelium des Markus*, KEK, 17th ed. (Göttingen: Vandenhoeck & Ruprecht, 1967), 164–165, who reckons with an apocalyptic core sentence that spoke of the necessity of suffering (see Dan 2:28: ἃ δεῖ γενέσαι ἐπ' ἐσχάτων τῶν, Rev 1:1) ("the Son of Man must suffer much and be rejected") and was then enriched with further motifs.

20. See, e.g., F. Hahn, *Christologische Hoheitstitel. Ihre Geschichte im frühen Christentum*, FRLANT 83, 5th ed. (Göttingen: Vandenhoeck & Ruprecht, 1995), 46–53.

21. See, e.g., Vögtle, *Gretchenfrage*, 167–168.

22. P. Hoffmann, "Mk 8,31. Zur Herkunft und markinischen Rezeption einer alten Überlieferung," in *Orientierung an Jesus. Zur Theologie der Synoptiker* (FS J. Schmid), ed. P. Hoffmann, in collaboration with J. Schmid (Freiburg et al.: Herder, 1973), 170–204, here 287–295. His arguments are: (1) the uniform formulation in contrast to 9:31; 10:33–34 ("an A.c.I. construction is dependent on δεῖ"), (2) the constancy of the four elements of the *killing, Son of Man, resurrection, after three days* in all three texts, (3) outside of this series of sayings, Mark does not prefer this terminology (287 with n. 27).

23. Hoffmann, "Herkunft," 290: δεῖ, an "initially ambiguous expression that can be understood both in an apocalyptic, end-time sense and in the narrower sense of scriptural necessity."

24. Hoffmann, "Herkunft," 289: "14:21 and 14:41 (cf. 14:49) also emphasize the scriptural truth of the handing over of the Son of Man. The suspicion is therefore justified that not only

This results in the following family tree for the logion:

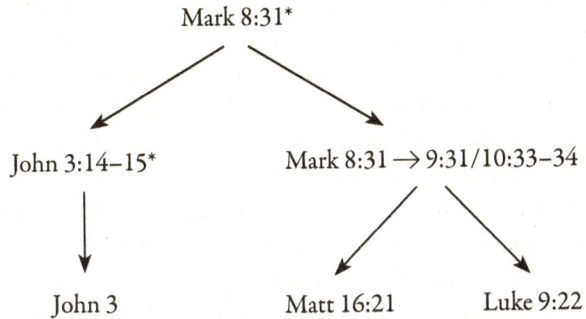

3.1.5 Alienation
Old Themes in New Perspective

The central motif of the logion is that of the "exaltation" of the Son of Man. Alongside this is the biblical image of the serpent in the wilderness (Num 21:4–9), which has incorporated the Christological play on language of "exaltation," which is also of biblical origin (Isa 52:13). In this way, both motifs are interlinked, as corresponds to the "eschatological correlative."

(1) From the point of view of the history of tradition, the saying about the Easter *"exaltation"* or *enthronement of Jesus* is very old. It is not only found in the pre-Pauline Hymn in Phil 2:9[25] but also in the kerygmatic formulae on which Luke based his speeches to Peter (Acts 2:33; 5:31).[26] The author of Hebrews is also familiar with the play on language (Heb 7:26).[27] It is characterized by three things: first, its theocentric structure (it was *God who* exalted Jesus *to himself* [above all the heavens or to his right hand]); second, its Christological content (Jesus was saved by God from death and thus rehabilitated by him); and third, its cosmic-soteriological finality (Jesus's exaltation or enthronement means his

---

the naming of the instances, but also the mention of the (scriptural) rejection goes back to Mark himself."

25. Phil 2:9: "Therefore God also *exalted* him and bestowed on him a name that is above every (other) name."

26. Acts 2:33: "so he was *exalted* to the right hand of God"; "to the right hand of God" alludes to Ps 110:1.—Acts 5:31: "God has *exalted him* to his right hand as leader and savior."

27. Heb 7:26: "he became higher than the heavens." See also 1:3: "he sat down at the right hand of the exalted [God] *in the heights*"; here, too, the idea of exaltation is linked to an allusion to Ps 110:1.

representation of God to the world). Against this background, the reception of the play on language in the Johannine logion can only be seen as its alienation. Although it retains the theocentricity, it no longer understands the exaltation of Jesus as God's act of salvation only *following* his death but rather allows it to begin with his death on the cross. In addition, it transforms Jesus's originally intended act of exaltation into his function of conveying "eternal life" to those who believe.

The precise relationship between cross and exaltation is disputed. An exclusive identification of both does not seem to be in view in the Johannine logion. This logion does not seem to have an exclusive identification of both in mind.[28] The fact that it wants to be understood as a continuation of the synoptic announcement of Jesus's death *and* resurrection speaks against this. Additionally, the motif of "exaltation" is traditionally endowed with the paschal element, which must have resonated for the first recipients. For this reason, his intention is accentuated differently.

The logion is concerned with proving the necessity (δεῖ) of Jesus's *cross on his way to Easter glory*. To this end, it uses the Old Testament story of the serpent in the desert as a *typos*.[29] This *typos* shows that the giving of life to believers through the Son of Man necessarily presupposes his "exaltation" on the cross. As offensive as it is, according to God's counsel, Jesus's paschal journey already *began* on the cross. It is not the identity of *exaltation* and the event of the cross but the theological necessity of the *cross* that is the aim of the logion.

(2) The decisive point of comparison between the Old Testament *typos* and the Christ event is the idea of "exaltation": The verb, which comes from the Christological Easter tradition (cf. above),[30] is projected back into the Old Testament image in the logion, where it denotes the process of attaching the copper serpent to a pole from the basic text in Numbers 21:4-9. "Not the 'objects' of 'exaltation,' the serpent and Jesus, but those two acts of 'exaltation'" themselves are placed in relation to each other here.[31] The salvific consequences of the two

---

28. See Schnelle, *Johannes*, 74-75, who defines "the cross as a place of exaltation and glorification" (Schnelle, *Johannes*, 74 n. 83). "As in John 8:28; 12:32, here too ὑψοῦν means the crucifixion of Jesus" (74). Similarly, Wilckens, *Johannes*, 71-72, who, however, rightly adds, "The traditional statement of exaltation thus loses neither its content nor its own weight." Rightly J. Frey, "'Wie Mose die Schlange in der Wüste erhöht hat . . .'. Zur frühjüdischen Deutung der 'ehernen Schlange' und ihrer christologischen Rezeption in Johannes 3,14f," in *Schriftauslegung im antiken Judentum und im Urchristentum*, ed. M. Hengel and H. Löhr, WUNT 73 (Tübingen: Mohr Siebeck, 1994), 153-205, here 186: "the Johannine ὑψοῦσθαι (is) not simply equal to σταυροῦσθαι, but at the same time carries the traditional sense of exaltation to dominion."

29. See Frey, "Mose," 184.

30. Older linguistic attempts to derive the verb as a term for "to crucify" (= to pull up) from the Aramaic or from the targumim to Num 21, which wanted the copper serpent in Num 21:8-9 to be placed in an "elevated place" (cf. Frey, "Mose," 186-187), should be rejected.

31. Frey, "Mose," 183.

acts of exaltation also correspond to each other and denote the reception of life.[32] The situation is different when it comes to the question of whether the reference to the lifted-up serpent is to be considered or associated as a counterpart to "faith" in John 3:15. This is possible if the reference to Numbers 21:8 is also taken into account.[33] However, two observations merit caution. First, the absolute "believe" is directed toward the event of Jesus's "being lifted up" as a whole, that is, it also has its Easter dimension in mind.[34] Second, the cross is not mentioned as a possible typological counterpart to the "pole/standard."[35] This reinforces the previously mentioned assumption that the logion links the idea of "being exalted" to the crucifixion of Jesus but does not let it coincide with the Easter enthronement event to which it refers.

The story of the copper serpent (Num 21) had a rich history of interpretation and reception in early Judaism.[36] One characteristic tendency in the treatment of Numbers 21:4–9 is *the theocentric effort to emphasize God's power of salvation and life and its uniqueness.*

This tendency is already laid out in the *basic narrative* with its confession of the sole salvific efficacy of YHWH and his word. "The narrator of Num 21 no longer wants to recognize any inherent power of the image; for him, the salvation of the Israelites takes place quite naturally through the mercy of YHWH and on the basis of obedience to his instruction to look at the means of salvation he has commanded."[37] The danger of this cult image is evident by the fact it was later worshipped in Jerusalem. According to 2 Kings 18:4, King Hezekiah ordered it to be destroyed.[38] But this danger is no longer present in

---

32. See v. 15 with Num 21:8: "Everyone who is bitten and looks at it (the copper serpent) *will live* (ζήσεται)."

33. Schnackenburg, *Johannesevangelium*, 1:408, remains skeptical: "Rabbis and Jewish mystics have speculated about this 'looking up'; John does not."

34. Wis 16:7 is also not the external process of looking at the serpent. Rather the inner "turning" or "conversion" to God is the decisive moment.

35. The Epistle of Barnabas is different in that it expressly says of the serpent that it is "hung on a tree" (12:7), but "looking" to the cross does not play a role for him either, nor for Justin, *Dial.* 91.4; 94.2–3; 112.1–2.

36. See H. Maneschg, *Die Erzählung von der ehernen Schlange (Num 21,4–9) in der Auslegung der frühen jüdischen Literatur. Eine traditionsgeschichtliche Studie*, EHS.T 23/157 (Frankfurt: Peter Lang, 1981); Frey, "Mose," 154–177; M. Morgen, "Le fils de l'homme élève en vue de la vie eternelle (Jn 3,14–15 éclairé par diverses traditions juives)," *RevSR* 68 (1994): 5–17

37. Frey, "Mose," 158.

38. "It was he who abolished the high places, smashed the pillars, cut down the Asherah, and smashed the bronze serpent that Moses had made, for until those days the Israelites offered incense to it, and it was called Nehushtan."

the text of Numbers, for Numbers conceals the name of the cult image and exposes it to "*damnatio memoriae.*"[39]

The interpretation of the Numbers narrative in *Wisdom 16:5–14* goes a decisive step further. It omits the "brazen serpent" altogether and instead speaks of a "sign of salvation" that was intended to remind the Israelites in the desert of the law of God. Moreover, it is made clear that "whoever turned to [him] was not saved for the sake of what he saw, but for *your sake*, who are the Savior of all (τὸν πάντων σωτῆρα)" (Wis 16:7).[40] What the author takes offense at is "that Num 21:9 could be understood as if the sight of the serpent as such would already bring about healing. And he opposes such a magical understanding." Thus he holds "a theological college for his readers,"[41] in order to then state quite fundamentally in verses 12–13, "For neither herb nor plaster healed them, but your word, Lord, which heals all things. For you have power over life and death, and you lead down to the gates of Hades and back up again."

The tendency is similar in m. Roš Haš 3:8, where Number 21:8, together with Exodus 17:11,[42] provides biblical evidence that complete Torah obedience depends on the orientation of the heart toward God. Thus the Mishnah comments on Numbers 21:8 with the words: "Was it the serpent that kills or makes alive? Rather: Whenever the Israelites looked up and submitted their hearts to their Father in heaven, they were healed; if not, they perished."[43] The parallel tradition in the Mekhilta of R. Ishmael to Exodus 17:11, which adds to the two examples from Exodus 17 and Numbers 21 a third example of the same nature, namely the story of the blood on the doorpost (Exod 12), presents the theological conclusion drawn from these texts in the following form: When Moses raised his hands (Exod 17:11) or sets up the serpent (Num 21), "then the Israelites looked to him [Moses] and *believed* in the one who had given Moses the command to do so."[44] In R. Simeon's view, the conclusion from all three examples is the same: "Whenever the Israelites did the will of the place [= God] and *believed in* what the place [= God] had instructed Moses to do."[45] Characteristic of these texts is the *intention* to ward off a magical understanding of the image of the serpent, to *deny the mediating variables* (such as the blood on the

---

39. Frey, "Mose," 158.

40. Translated according to D. Georgi, Die Weisheit Salomos, in: JSHRZ III/4, 458.

41. H. Hübner, Die Weisheit Salomons 192.

42. "As long as Moses held up his hand, Israel was stronger; but as often as he let down his hand, Amalek was stronger."

43. m. Roš Haš. 3:8.

44. Mek. Exod. 17:11.

45. Mek. R. Sim. Exod. 17:11.

doorpost or the action of Moses raising his hands) any *saving power* in order to establish the *uniqueness of* God as the Lord over life and death.

Against this background, John 3:14-15 gains a profile. Like Wisdom 16:6-7 and the Mishnah, the Johannine logion is also focused on Numbers 21:8-9. Like the early Jewish interpretations, John 3:14-15 also deepens the saving point of view toward the holistic act of faith. Like those interpretations, John 3:14-15 is ultimately also based on a theocentric view of the act of salvation. But it is precisely at this point that the unmistakable profile of the Johannine logion can be seen. Instead of withdrawing the mediating dimensions of God's act of salvation, as in the early Jewish testimonies, it places the accent precisely on the mediator when it says that "*in him*," the Son of Man, the believer receives a share in "eternal life." Christology has appropriated the biblical tradition[46] and given it a new shape—a remarkable process indeed!

3.1.6 The Interpretation of the Logion in the Context of John 3

The Son of Man in 3:14-15 definitively concludes the Jesus-Nicodemus dialogue, and at the same time becomes the impetus for the following kerygmatic teaching in 3:16-21. It thus has a twofold editorial relationship: On the one hand, it receives light from the preceding verses, especially verse 13, and on the other hand, it experiences a subsequent interpretation in the teaching that follows.

(1) If we first ask about 3:13 as an interpretative instruction for 3:14-15, then the following insights emerge: Verse 13 makes it clear in advance that the Son of Man does not relinquish his own sovereignty in dying: "*He ascends into heaven.*" At the same time, verse 13 with its play on language not only visualizes the specifically Johannine "dualism" of heaven and earth, above and below, but above all makes it clear that the conceptual framework associated with this is a function of the Christological statement that is actually intended: Apart from the "Son of Man" and his way, the infinite gulf between earth and heaven, death

---

46. Whether this had a point of reference in early Judaism can at least be asked in view of Philo's allegorical reading of Num 21:8. In Leg. 2.81, Philo writes, "'And whomsoever the one serpent bites, if he looks upon the brazen serpent shall live:' in which Moses speaks truly, for if the mind that has been bitten by pleasure, that is by the serpent which was sent to Eve, shall have strength to behold the beauty of temperance, that is to say, the serpent made by Moses in a manner affecting the soul, and to behold God himself through the medium of the serpent (διὰ τούτου τὸν θεὸν αὐτόν), it shall live. Only let it see and contemplate it intellectually" (trans. C. D. Yonge). As far as this allegorizing interpretation of Scripture (cf. also *Agr.* 97.109) is removed from John 3:14-15, the strengthening of the mediating greatness is structurally comparable, especially if, as H. Odeberg claims in *The Fourth Gospel: Interpreted in Its Relation to Contemporaneous Religious Currents in Palestine and the Hellenistic—Oriental World* (Amsterdam: Almquist & Wiksell, 1929), 105, for Philo the serpent of Moses is a symbol of the *Logos* itself.

and life cannot be bridged.[47] For 3:14–15 this means that ἀνάβασις (= "ascension") is the leading category for the interpretation of "being raised." The actual and deeper meaning of the event of the cross is the Son of Man's ascent into heaven, which has soteriological relevance. The ἀνάβασις of the Son of Man has made the salvific breach in the wall of heaven, which now enables the believer to attain life "in him" (i.e., the Son of Man). In other words, verse 13 realizes the type of a *way Christology*.[48] The text emphasizes that the possibility of ἀνάβασις presupposes a prior κατάβασις (= descent), that is, the exaltation of the Son of Man cannot be conceived without his heavenly future (= preexistence). Thus, this verse is not determined by a concept of atonement theology but rather a model that works with the semantics on the surface and at a deeper dimension: Behind the surface of the cross lies its actual depth, *Jesus's* liberating *way to the Father*, which finally opens the heavens and thus offers the prospect of life, and which can only be understood as his salvific return to him.

The interpretation of 3:3, 5 developed in chapter 3, according to which the evangelist sees an analogy between Jesus and his own community, shows that such a way-Christology in verse 13 (14–15) is actually soteriological: just as Jesus came entirely *from God's world* and returned to it in order to clear the way to heaven for those who believe, so they too receive a share in the divine life because of their new birth *from above*—from the Spirit—through Jesus. In this respect, the assumption made at the beginning is confirmed, that 3:13, 14–15 definitively conclude the Jesus-Nicodemus dialogue by placing it on its actual Christological foundation.

(2) The kerygmatic teaching in 3:16–21 is connected to the previous text with a substantiating or explicating "for," which signals that the saying about the Son of Man in 3:14–15, the climax of the preceding dialogue, is now expounded further.

The kerygmatic teaching is doubly "interlinked" with verses 13–15. On the one hand, it takes up the *soteriological* statement of the goal of the Son of Man in verses 14–15; on the other hand, it continues the specifically *Christological* discourse of the "descent" of the Son of Man by transposing it into the discourse of his gift or mission. The accent of the continuation lies on a specification of the soteriological goal, which verse 16c, d takes up literally.

John 3:16–21 contributes in two ways to the interpretation of the saying about the Son of Man in verses 14–15. First, it explicates the soteriological statement of purpose in verse 15 by deliberately excluding its opposite: God does not

---

47. See 3:6: The boundaries of σάρξ (= earthly existence) are unbridgeable from a human perspective!

48. This is also found in Luke and Hebrews. See Luke 24:26; Acts 2:31, 33–34; 3:15; Heb 2:10; 13:20, etc.

want man to perish but to have eternal life. The actual goal of God's salvific initiative is not the judgment of the world (i.e., its damnation) but its salvation. "It is therefore about an *explicit and clear prevalence of the intention of salvation in God's loving action on the cosmos, about a priority of salvation over disaster.*"[49]

Second, the text reacts to the fact, which in a missionary historical perspective is undeniable, that the majority of people (v. 19) did *not* believe in Christ's message *despite* God's definite will to save and love. In view of this situation, the instructional piece (*Lehrstück*) uses a kind of strategy of exoneration concerning God himself and his salvational initiative. This strategy is used in two ways. Verses 16–18 explain that whoever believes in the Son, *will not* be judged. Whoever does *not* believe has already brought judgment upon himself because he did not believe in the name of the only Son of God (see v. 18). In other words, God does not cut people off from life but individuals do this themselves when they do not. Verses 19–21 go further by explaining the—from the community's perspective—incomprehensible. How is it that people say no to the message of Christ? It is intended to remove the sting of scandal and ultimately serve to strengthen the identity of the community of faith itself. The text continues to use the terminology of judgment but cleverly combines it with the metaphor of light: Judgment uncovers that is hidden,[50] brings it to light, and makes it irrefutable. Because of this, people also shy away from the light since they do not wish to see their "bad deeds" uncovered. For this reason they do not come to Christ and the light does not shine on them. The text therefore works not only with the category of faith but also with the ethical category of "works." It does so only to make people's "no" to Christ comprehensible with reference to their "work," which is always already determined by evil and does not wish to be exposed by the light. The asymmetry of the corresponding formulations shows that the evangelist is not interested in asserting an ethical predisposition of man to faith.[51] Above all, however, we must not lose sight of the overarching aim of the text to establish the *unambiguity* of "God's will to save and love" (Blank) unequivocally and in all clarity despite the fact that people (see v. 19) reject Christ. This is helpful for

---

49. J. Blank, *Das Evangelium nach Johannes*, GSL.NT 4/1–2 (Düsseldorf: Evangelische Verlagsanstalt, 1977 and 1981), 1a:259: "This is to say that, according to the clear statement of the Johannine text, 'salvation' and 'disaster' of man are not equally weighted alternatives, but that salvation clearly takes precedence. According to our text, there is the clear will of God for salvation and love; there is no divine 'will to do harm' alongside it, i.e., no divine predestination to eternal destruction."

50. ἐλέγχειν in v. 20c = "to bring to light, expose, set forth" (*BDAG* s.v.). The verb fits the light metaphor as well as theme of judgment.

51. While the negative side speaks of "doing evil" and "evil works," the positive side speaks of "doing the truth" and that the works of those who come to the light are "wrought *in God*."

the interpretation of the soteriological aim of the saying about the Son of Man verses 14–15.

The intention behind 3:16–21 is probably the following: In the scenic opening to the Jesus-Nicodemus dialogue of 2:23–25, the text says that although "many" believed in Jesus's name when "they saw the signs he did," Jesus nevertheless *did not* confide in them, *did not* reveal himself to them, because he "recognized" them and saw through the manner of their faith. They only saw him as prophetic-messianic man but did not see the Son of Man who descended from heaven. This corresponds to the observation that the following dialogue does not bring Jesus and Nicodemus together. On the contrary, in the form of the misunderstandings on the part of the "teacher of Israel," it shows the deep rifts between Jesus, the *heavenly* revealer, and the *"earthly"* thinking of Nicodemus. Thus, this section affirms the Christological faith of the readers of the dialogue within the Johannine community. The question that arises more and more clearly when reading 2:23–3:15, however, is: Why does Jesus close himself off to Nicodemus and the "many" others whose faith is only deficient or does not reach Jesus at all? Does it really correspond to God's intention that only a few believe in Jesus and that the vast majority deny him? John 3:16–21 answers these kinds of questions. Our thesis is that this text counters false conclusions that the reader could draw from 2:23–3:15 at a new level of reflection when it elaborates the "preponderance of salvation," the clear "prevalence of the intention of salvation in God's loving action on the cosmos." At the same time, these verses show to what extent it is not God's fault that "people loved darkness rather than light" (v. 19). In this respect, 3:16–21 represents a continuation of the basic text of 2:23–3:15, and this is a process that can also be observed elsewhere in the Gospel.[52] The subject of the continuation of 3:16–21, however, is the correct interpretation of the soteriological purpose of the Son of Man's words in 3:14–15: *"So that everyone who believes may have eternal life."*

3.2 The Plea to Glorify the Name of God (John 12:28a; see Matt 6:9b par. Luke 11:2c)

"Father, glorify your name!" (John 12:28a).—It is very likely that this request of the Johannine Jesus is based on Luke 11:2c par. Matt 6:9b.[53] Although it is only

---

52. See J. Zumstein, *Kreative Erinnerung. Relecture und Auslegung im Johannesevangelium* (Zürich: TVZ Theologischer Verlag, 1999).

53. E. Lohmeyer, *Das Vater-unser*, 2nd ed. (Göttingen: Vandenhoeck & Ruprecht, 1947), 45: John 12:28a is "the Johannine form of the first petition of the Lord's Prayer." References to the Lord's prayer are also recognized by Brown, *John*, 1:476; X. Léon-Dufour, *Lecture de l'Évangile selon Jean I–IV* (Paris: Seuil, 1987–1996), 2:471; Lindars, *John*, 431; "Discourse and Tradition:

"Words of the Lord" as Metatexts of Synoptic Traditions   131

a small synoptic fragment that the evangelist has clothed in his own language, this statement is linked to the further assumption that the "Lord's Prayer" *as a whole* was known to both the evangelist and his congregation: This snippet allows us to draw a conclusion about the whole, especially since it is not just any petition, but the opening of the Lord's Prayer, the transformation of which we can follow here.

3.2.1 John 12:28a as a Transformation of the Opening of the Lord's Prayer

The following synopsis illustrates the close connection between John 12:28a and the tradition of the "Lord's Prayer":

Luke 11:2c	Father,	hallowed be your name (ἁγιασθήτω)!
Matt 6:9b	Our Father, who is in the heavens,	hallowed be your name!
Did. 8:2	Our Father, who is in heaven,	hallowed be your name!
John 12:28a	Father,	*glorify* (δόξασον) *your name!*

Of course, John 12:28a is formulated in Johannine language—"glorification" (δοξάζειν) is the author's preferred word (twenty-three times)—but, beside the common structure (form of address + plea), the following two observations ensure a reference to the Lord's prayer:

(a) As often as δοξάζειν occurs in the Gospel, nowhere else is it connected with the noun "name"; also the opening of the "high priestly prayer" in 17:1, which ties in with 12:23b, 28a, asks for the glorification of the *Son*, not of the name.

(b) On the surface, the two imperatives ἁγιασθήτω and δόξασον differ from one another but semantically are very close. E. Lohmeyer already stated: "'To be sanctified' is by and large synonymous with 'to be glorified,'"[54] and referred

---

The Use of the Sayings of Jesus in the Discourses of the Fourth Gospel" (1981), in *Essays on John*, ed. C. M. Tuckett, SNTA 17 (Leuven: Peeters, 1992), 113–129, here 118.

54. Lohmeyer, *Vater-unser*, 45; The synagogal *Kaddish* is also noteworthy, the original form of which goes back to the time of Jesus and is known to offer the closest parallel to the Lord's Prayer: "*Glorified and sanctified* be his great name in the world, which he created according to his will. May his kingship reign in your lifetime and in your days and in the lifetime of the whole house of Israel with haste and speed. And then say: Amen" (see J. Jeremias, "Das Vater Unser im Lichte der neueren Forschung," in *Abba. Studien zur neutestamentlichen Theologie und Zeitgeschichte* [Göttingen: Vandenhoeck & Ruprecht, 1966], 152–171, here 164). In contrast to the majority

to Leviticus 10:3; Isaiah 5:16b; Ezekiel 28:22 (cf. also 29:43; 38:23); Tobit 8:5 and Sirach 36:4, among other passages. The majority of these references speak of *God* sanctifying or glorifying his name, but there is also the other line that leads from the Old Testament (Exod 20:7; Lev 22:32; Isa 29:23) into the world of Jewish prayers, according to which *people* are the subject of the sanctification of the name.[55] How can we understand the plea in light of this? If we take the commentary of the Fourth Gospel as a guide, the answer is clear. If God himself is to glorify—magnify—his name, then ἁγιασθήτω is a *passivum divinum*. At least that is how the author of John 12:28a understood the request. "The sanctification of his name is therefore God's own work. This is ... expressed in the Lord's Prayer by the passive formulation."[56] If, however, contrary to this broad tradition of interpretation, the wording does require "an 'open' interpretation," as is occasionally suggested if the petition should come "close to a self-invitation" such as "Let us sanctify the name of God,"[57] then one would have to say that the fourth evangelist would have transformed this "openness" into a statement about God's sovereignty: God may glorify his name himself and of his own accord. It is clear how closely John 12:28a is semantically based on the first "Lord's Prayer." The formulation in John wants to be understood as a transformation of this plea. A look at the context can confirm this.

3.2.2 Jesus's "Hellenic Discourse" (John 12:23, 27–32) Against the Backdrop of the Gethsemane Scene

Whether the passion narrative given to the fourth evangelist and received by him also contained a Gethsemane scene related to the Synoptic Gospels is still disputed. However, evidence suggests that the first part of Jesus's "Hellenic Discourse" (John 12:23, 27–32) retains elements of Jesus's prayer from this scene

---

of the OT sources cited above, in which the name to be sanctified is the object, here it is the subject, connected with an hithpael which comes close to the passive ἁγιασθήτω of the "Lord's Prayer" (see the doxology Dan 2:20, a possible root of the Kaddish; see D. Telsner, *The Kaddish. Its History and Significance* [Jerusalem: Tal Orot Institute, 1995]).

55. Luz, *Matthäus*, 1:343, with references.

56. See E. Schweizer, *Das Evangelium nach Matthäus*, NTD 2, 13th ed. (Göttingen: Vandenhoeck & Ruprecht, 1973), 94, on Matt 6:9b.

57. Schweizer, *Matthäus*, 343. This seems to me to be ruled out because of the parallelism of the first two "you" petitions, the second of which undoubtedly implores God himself, the Father, to enforce his reign, the coming of his kingdom. Furthermore, it is not a self-invitation ("*Let us...*"), rather the intention is *universal*, as can be seen from the renunciation of all limitations in the first part of the prayer (in contrast to the Kaddish).

"Words of the Lord" as Metatexts of Synoptic Traditions   133

and transposes them to the heights of the Johannine Christology. This may be illustrated by the following synopsis:

Mark 14	John 12
41: "*The hour has come,* Behold, *the Son of Man* is delivered into the hands of sin."	23: "*The hour has come,* that *the Son of Man* may be glorified."
34: "And he said to them, '*My soul* is saddened to the point of death...'"	27: "Now *my soul* is shaken.
35–36: "And he... prayed, that if it were possible, may *the hour* pass him by.	
"And he *said*, 'Abba, *Father*, everything is possible for you. Let this cup pass me by; *but* not what I want,	And what can I *say*? *Father*, save me from this *hour*? (cf. John 18:11c) *But* that is why I have come to this hour.
but what you want.'" 37–38: "And he said to Peter, '... Watch and pray that you do not fall into temptation.'"	28: Father, glorify your name!"

The last lines of this synopsis are interesting for our question. Obviously, the Markan Jesus also finds words at the turn of his prayer that are reminiscent of the "Lord's Prayer" or allude to it specifically.[58] *It becomes tangible and vivid in this scene as a criterion of authentic prayer.* It is no coincidence that Jesus puts aside his fear of death, including his request for salvation from it *for God's sake*, with the words of the third petition of the prayer (in the form handed down in Matthew and the Didachist). If the version of the Gethsemane scene preserved in Mark is based on the "Lord's Prayer," then it cannot be ruled out that the fourth evangelist was also inspired to reformulate the opening of the "Lord's Prayer" in

---

58. This applies to Mark 14:36 fin, but also 14:38a!

12:28a by the Gethsemane episode handed down to him but not reproduced by him in the scene.[59] Of course, this cannot be said with certainty.

3.2.3 The Meaning of the Johannine Transformation

The *situation* (i.e., setting) of the speech is decisive: The hour of the glorification of the Son of Man has come (12:23), and Jesus enters it consciously. At first glance, it seems to be the hour of his emotional shock (12:27a) in the face of death, a shock that he overcomes by praying, "Father, glorify your name!" This request can be paraphrased as follows: "Father[,] glorify your name by making the Son carry out the 'work' of revealing your name to the utmost (through death on the cross)."[60] Until now, when the Gospel has spoken of the "name of the Father" (John 5:43; 10:25b; cf. 12:13b), the phrase was used in a rather formulaic way to refer to the Father as the principal and sovereign in Jesus's mission of salvation ("in the name of my Father . . ."). Now the traditional "Our Father" petition offers the opportunity to go into greater depth: The ὄνομα of the Father does not mean the Father per se but "precisely *the Father, in so far as he* reveals *himself*";[61] "God's 'name' stands for his essence, his holiness, his inviolable will, but also for his mercy and love; for the address to the Father has defining power precisely here."[62] Seen in this light, the plea to the Father to glorify his name in the hour that has dawned has an openness and breadth which, in the glorification of Jesus, now also includes "all" (v. 32) those whom Jesus will draw to himself when he is exalted. Accordingly, verse 32 certainly represents the soteriological dimension of the δοξάζειν of verse 28.[63]

What is striking about the subsequent "voice from heaven"—the answer to Jesus's prayer—is that the object of the twofold δοξάζειν is omitted: "I have glorified and will glorify again" (12:28c). The meaning of this blank cannot be

---

59. See Dodd, *Tradition*, 80: "A comparison of John XII 27–9 with relevant passages in other New Testament writings makes it probable in the highest degree that John had a distinct form of tradition about the prayer, and reasonably probable that it was part of the Passion tradition as it reached him."

60. F. G. Untergaßmair, *Im Namen Jesu. Der Namensbegriff im Johannesevangelium. Eine exegetisch-religionsgeschichtliche Studie zu den johanneischen Namensaussagen*, FzB 13 (Stuttgart et al.: Verlag Katholisches Bibelwerk, 1973), 97.

61. Untergaßmair, *Im Namen Jesu*, 97.

62. Schnackenburg, *Johannesevangelium*, 2:486.

63. Verse 28 (δοξάζειν) and the concluding logion of the speech section in v. 32 with its speech of "exaltation" are related to each other in terms of structure and content.

"an intended ambiguity" with regard to the *object* of glorification,[64] but with its natural addition from the preceding prayer, that is, from τὸ ὄνομα, only the focusing of the *predicate itself*, namely with regard to the two temporal determinations connected with its repetition, which form a coherent whole. However, due to the presupposed situation, the following future tense should be provided with a special accent. Accordingly, the answer of the heavenly voice can be paraphrased as follows: "I *have already* glorified (my name in the mission and revelatory work of Jesus) and *will* therefore glorify (it even more) again in the hour of his death as the hour of his exaltation."[65] What follows from this interpretation of Jesus's request—together with the answer given to it—for the understanding of the opening of the Lord's Prayer from the perspective of John 12:28? Three things should be noted.

(1) On the one hand, the evangelist concentrates the plea for the glorification of God's name entirely on the *Christological* event. This petition does not reach out to the coming of God's reign, the full form of which is yet to come, but finds its fulfillment in the *death and exaltation of Jesus*, in the completion of his work of salvation as given to him by the Father.

(2) Seen in this way, the actual and primary person praying this prayer (like the "Lord's Prayer" in general) is Jesus himself in the face of his death, and his prayer has already been answered—in his glorification on the cross. The eschaton *has already* become present, the second characteristic of the evangelist's reception of the "Lord's Prayer."

(3) Jesus does not pray in solitude, in distress for his own soul, which is shaken, but performs his prayer precisely by transcending himself in view of the glorification of the name of *God*, who wants the salvation of mankind. Seen in this light, his prayer is profoundly *soteriologically* oriented. The third thing to note is that Jesus asks for the glorification of God's name, insofar as in its glorification God becomes the Father of all believers. In the first farewell discourse (John 14:13–14), Jesus tells them that the believers themselves are also empowered to pray in the name of Jesus and are assured that their prayer will be fulfilled. Significantly, it says there—possibly also in recollection of our scene: "And whatever you ask in my name I will do so *that the Father may be glorified through the Son*."

---

64. See Bultmann, *Johannes*, 329: "Even if grammatically ἐδόξασα and δοξάσω are to be added to τὸ ὄνομά μου as object, an intended ambiguity arises as a result of the omission of the object: by making his ὄνομα known, God at the same time makes the revealer known."

65. Schnackenburg, *Johannesevangelium*, 2:486.

3.2.4 Outlook
The Lord's Prayer in the Johannine Communities

Of course, John 12:28a does not reveal the form in which the fourth evangelist knew the "Lord's Prayer." The "Father" (πάτηρ) address, which corresponds to Luke 11:2c, is therefore not conclusive because, if "Our Father" (πάτηρ ἡμῶν) was the address known to the evangelist, he could have changed it into a πάτηρ for the sake of Christological narrow-mindedness. A look at John 17 leads further, as this chapter alludes several times to the "Lord's Prayer," in a form close to Matthew and the Didache. To call the "high priestly prayer" a "midrash" to the "Lord's Prayer,"[66] however, certainly goes too far and leads to exaggerated interpretations. Nevertheless, some references are beyond doubt:[67] The request for protection from evil in 17:15 clearly echoes the conclusion of the "Lord's Prayer" in Matthew 6:13; the requests for the protection of the disciples in the "name" of God, which Jesus revealed to them (17:6, 11b, 26), are reminiscent of Matthew 6:9b.[68] On the other hand, there are also profound differences between the world of the "Lord's Prayer" and that of the Johannine prayer. Whereas the "Lord's Prayer" implores the final coming of the kingdom of God in its full form, Jesus's concept of the βασιλεία hardly plays a role in John. In John 3 it has been replaced by the specifically Johannine concept of "(eternal) life," and in John 17 the term "eternal life" appears instead in verses 2–3. We have already drawn attention to a second, more fundamental difference in John 12:28a: the "Lord's Prayer" is "the prayer that Jesus gave to his disciples as their prayer to the Father. In contrast, John 17 is the exclusive prayer of Jesus as the Son to his Father. Does the evangelist want this difference to be understood in such a way that this prayer of Jesus at the beginning of his "going to the Father" is the origin and center of all prayer for the Christians of the post-Easter community? After all, God can only be called Father because he is originally the Father of Jesus—in Jesus's name (14:13–14; 15:16; 16:23–24, 26)."[69] Wilckens answers this question in the affirmative and concludes with the thesis: "John 17

---

66. See W. M. O. Walker, "The Lord's Prayer in Matthew and in John," *NTS* 28 (1982): 237–257, here 238: "the High Priestly Prayer represents a type of 'midrash' on the Mattean version of the Lord's Prayer."

67. See Brown, *John*, 2:747; Dodd, *Tradition*, 333–334; B. Standaert, "Crying 'Abba' and Saying 'Our Father.' An Intertextual Approach of the Dominical Prayer," in *Intertextuality in Biblical Writings* (FS B. van Iersel), ed. S Draisma (Kampen: Peeters, 1989), 141–158, here 154: "The traditional requests of the Lord's Prayer are not entirely unknown to John. He plays with them and reinterprets them in his own fashion, not without depth."

68. Dodd, *Tradition*, 333, is right in seeing 17:11 as parallel to Matt 6:9: Πάτερ ... ἁγιασθήτω τὸ ὄνομά σου.—John 17:11: Πάτερ ἅγιε τήρησον αὐτοὺς ἐν τῷ ὀνόματί σου.

69. Wilckens, *Johannes*, 269.

can thus be understood as the Christological foundation of all the prayers of the community, which in turn needs the help of the Spirit, who mediates all petitions to the Father (Rom 8:15–16, 26–27; Acts 4:25; Rev 22:17)."[70]

How can we interpret the references of John 17 to the Lord's Prayer in view of the differences between the two prayers? In my opinion, the thesis that Jesus's high priestly prayer is the "origin and center of all Christian prayer" (Wilckens), that it also has a criteriological function in the question of the true prayer of the Christian, offers the key to the correct relationship to the "Lord's Prayer." The prayer was certainly known in the Johannine communities. For John 17 it functions as a "reference text" that suggests it enjoyed special esteem as a prayer inherited from Jesus. To simply push it aside would have been a difficult undertaking. On the other hand, it is obvious that for the Gospel in its final form, the authoritative prayer of Jesus is the "high priestly prayer," which thus has a function that could no longer be granted to the "Lord's Prayer" with its orientation toward the soteriological central symbol of Jesus's proclamation, the "kingdom of God." The relationship of John 17 in particular to the "Lord's Prayer" can perhaps be defined as follows:

The "high priestly prayer" does not *subordinate* itself as a midrash to the authoritative authority of the "Lord's Prayer" but conversely begins with it as the basic text and then advances beyond it. According to its author, this prayer authentically expresses the intention of Jesus in the face of his death—in retrospect of the "work" he accomplished as well as in anticipation of the life of the church. The close connection between the prayer and the completion of the work of salvation in Jesus's death means that this death itself is now seen as the completion of prayer, to the point that Jesus is not only portrayed as praying to the Father in death but that this death, as the beginning of his exaltation to God, also appears as the *answer to* his prayer.

C. H. Dodd points to another trace of the Lord's Prayer in the Gospel of John:[71]

John 6:32c: *"My Father* (ὁ πατήρ μου) *gives* (δίδωσιν) you *the bread* (τὸν ἄρτον)
from heaven, the true [bread].''

Mt 6:11: "Our *bread* (τὸν ἄρτον), which is necessary (τὸν ἐπιούσιον), *give* (δός)
us today (σήμερον).''

---

70. Wilckens, *Johannes*, 269.

71. Dodd, *Tradition*, 333: Such passages [e.g., John 6:33; 17:11, 15] seem to presuppose a homiletical treatment of the several petitions of the prayer: . . . the Father in heaven to whom they pray for ἄρτος ἐπιούσιος answers the prayer by the gift of ἄρτος ἀληθινός." See also B. Lindars, "Traditions Behind the Fourth Gospel" (1977), in *Essays on John*, ed. C. M. Tuckett, SNTA 17 (Leuven: Peeters, 1992), 87–104, here 97; Lindars, *Use*, 118.

The petition of the people following John 6:32–33 is perhaps closer to the petition for *bread* in the "Lord's Prayer," which reads:

"Lord, always (πάντοτε)[72] *give us* (δὸς ἡμῖν) this *bread* (τὸν ἄρτον τοῦτον)!" (v. 34).

Of course, in the opinion of the evangelist, this request for a perpetual material supply of manna from heaven, stretching out toward messianic abundance, is a profound misunderstanding of what Jesus really wants to say in his bread of life discourse. He does not promise them daily bread, but that "whoever comes *to him will* hunger no more" (6:35); only faith in him, who is "the bread of life," satisfies the need for life.

So it is probably not wrong to assume that in the dialogue in John 6:34–35 an understanding of the petition for bread that takes it literally is disavowed as superficial. Its true meaning refers to Christ as the "bread of life," which man now really needs as the only thing necessary for salvation. The Christological interpretation of the petition for bread, which was common practice at the time of the church fathers and medieval exegesis,[73] is established already in the Fourth Gospel. It reveals a way of dealing with the "Lord's Prayer" that is also evident in John 12:28a and John 17: The "Lord's Prayer" is subjected to a radical Christological interpretation that is tantamount to *destroying* its original meaning.

3.3 "If I wish that he remains until I come...?" (John 21:22–23; cf. Mark 9:1)

What did the resurrected Jesus really say and what did he not say? John 21:20–24, the last paragraph of the editorial supplemental chapter of John 21, offers the rare case in the Gospel that the exact wording of what Jesus said is important in order prevent serious misunderstandings of his intention.[74] His words about the "beloved disciple" in verse 22 have (and this is special in John!) a peculiar interpretation behind it. The redactor has ambitions to revise it. However, it remains unclear what his intention was with his revisions. Of course, we cannot expect a similar parallel to Jesus's words about the beloved

---

72. The plea for bread in the Lord's Prayer also inherits a determination of time, σήμερον (Matt 6:11) or rather τὸ καθ' ἡμέραν (Luke 11:3).

73. See Luz, *Matthäus*, 1:345 (alongside the eucharistic interpretation); W. Foerster, Art. ἐπιούσιος, *TDNT* 2:595–597 (the spiritual understanding of the bread petition "widespread in the early church" led, e.g., in the Greek text of the Acts Thomas to the "omission of the whole bread petition" [ch. 144]).

74. See above pp. 12–22: "Self-Citations of Jesus and Other Repetitions"!

"Words of the Lord" as Metatexts of Synoptic Traditions   139

disciple in the Synoptic Gospels. Nevertheless, we find a logion in Mark 9:1 parr. Matthew 16:28; Luke 9:27 that could be a *basic saying* for the concrete personalized Johannine logion (3.3.3). At first, we want to consider the text itself in its synchronic structure.

3.3.1 Composition and Structure of John 21:20–24

A 20 Peter, who turned around,
       sees the disciple,
       whom Jesus loved,
       following,
       the one who also rested at his breast during the meal
       and had said,
       "Lord, who will betray you?"

B I 21 When Peter saw him,
        he says to Jesus,
        "But Lord, this one, what (is wrong with him)?"

     22 Jesus said to him,
         "If I want him to remain
         until I come,
         what is it to you?
         Follow me!"

B II 23 Then this word spread among the brothers,
         "That disciple will not die."
         But Jesus had not told him [i.e., Peter],
         "He will not die,"[75]
         but rather,
         "If I want him to remain (θέλω μένειν),
         what is it to you?"

C   24 This is the disciple,
         who bears witness to these things
         and who writes this,
         and we know
         his testimony is true!

---

75. D and both old Latin texts e r¹ read: οὐκ ἀποθνῄσκεις (= you will not die). Thus, here the words are directed toward the beloved disciple himself, but see also n. 75.

After an exposition of the scene (= A) the situation is described: Peter sees the "beloved disciple," who is briefly depicted.[76] The main part of the scene consists of a short dialogue between Peter and Jesus about the "beloved disciple" which is a single verbal exchange (= B I). After that, the evangelist reports at a meta-level about its later echo in the Johannine community (= "the brothers"). The narrator corrects this echo without saying clearly what Jesus meant with his riddle (= B II). Verse 24 gives us the solution which is still coded and entrusted to the reader for their own understanding (see below). Then one can consider whether this verse (= C) should be—against the common view within scholarship—declared to be the end of the scene in John 20:19–23.[77]

3.3.2 John 21:22
A Falsified "Word of the Lord"?

Obviously, John 20:20–23, 24 reflects a "word of the Lord" about the "beloved disciple," which, according to the text itself, was circulating in the Johannine communities. It was understood to mean that this disciple would not die after a promise by the (resurrected) Jesus. If the redactor corrects this understanding by referring to the exact wording of that saying in the sense that Jesus did not speak of the disciple "not dying," but of him "remaining" (μένειν), then the background to this correction must be postulated as the death of the disciple, which has occurred in the meantime and which had falsified the "word of the Lord," at least in the understanding that the community has been familiar with up to now.[78] It is conceivable (if not probable) that the death of the disciple, which the text itself does not address, triggered a shock in the Johannine communities. This, however, is not the issue here. The *personal* fate of that disciple or the mourning over his departure is not what moves our text. Nor is it the irritation in the congregation in the face of a possible falsification of a "word of the Lord" that the editor wants to eliminate. The text certainly does not support the assumption that the death of that disciple *before* the expected parousia triggered a crisis in futuristic eschatology in general: The author leaves the eschatological horizon of the near future, which was obviously linked to the "word of the Lord" ("until I come"), untouched. At least he does not make any corrections at this point. His interest lies elsewhere, namely in securing the authority of this gospel by recourse to the

---

76. See M. Theobald, "Der Jünger, den Jesus liebte. Das narrative Konzept der johanneischen Redaktion," in *Geschichte—Tradition—Reflexion III* (FS M. Hengel), ed. H. Cancik, H. Lichtenberger, and P. Schäfer (Tübingen: Mohr Siebeck, 1996), 219–255, here 225–226.

77. As a rule, v. 24 is usually interpreted together with v. 25 as the second ending of the book.

78. See Brown, *John*, 2:1118–1120.

"beloved disciple": "If I want him to *remain* (μένειν) until I come"—says the resurrected Jesus himself!—"What is that to you?" Although the author does not explicitly resolve this "enigmatic word" of "remaining" in what follows, he gives an unmistakable hint to the readers and listeners of the book at the conclusion of verse 24: "This is the disciple who bears witness to this [i.e., the book] and who has written it." The present *participle* "who bears witness" (μαρτυρῶν), which is conspicuous alongside the aorist "who has written this" (γράψας)—moreover, it comes first!—contains the answer: In the testimony of his book, the "beloved disciple" survives. "The word of his remaining" is "fulfilled."[79] *Indeed this gospel is the way he remains present in the community "until he comes," which is actually intended by the exalted one himself (!).*

Is this indeed, as the author suggests, the *original* meaning of that "word of the Lord"? But then *no one* in the congregation would have realized its meaning—apart from the editors of the book in whose name the author writes. Everyone would have been biased by the opinion that Jesus had actually announced the *physical* survival of that disciple until the day of his parousia. How strange! Historically speaking, it probably happened the other way around. If he, the author, or the publishers of the book were the only ones who stood up for what they claimed to be the original wording of the "word of the Lord," then they were likely also the ones who gave it the deeper meaning or gave it the linguistic form in the first place (μένειν). Conversely, the interpretation of the "word" (v. 23a) common in the community would have been close to the original intention of the logion about the "beloved disciple." This means that the substance of the "word" reaches back to an earlier phase of the communities' history (before the evangelist). This period was still characterized by the (early Christian) expectation of the near future parousia. Its tradition was attached to that "disciple" for the reason that he had long outlived other eye-witnesses. This is why he was said to have not only been an eyewitness of the earthly Jesus, but also to have played an important role in the founding of the Johannine community. Therefore, it was said about him that he would not die or rather the Lord would give him life "until he comes." This perspective receives support in the synoptic logion in Mark 9:1 par. Matthew 16:28; Luke 9:27.

3.3.3 Is John 21:22 an Adaptation of Mark 9:1 par.?

Mark 9:1 reads:

"Truly, I say to you,
There are some among those standing here

---

79. Schnackenburg, *Johannesevangelium*, 3:445; cf. C. K. Barrett, *Das Evangelium nach Johannes*, KEK.S (Göttingen: Vandenhoeck & Ruprecht, 1990), 558.

who will not taste death
until (ἕως ἄν), arriving in the kingdom of God in power,
(ἐληλυθυῖαν) they have seen."

Matthew reshapes the concluding temporal clause Christologically (Matt 16:28: "until they see *the Son of Man* coming in *his* kingdom"); Luke deletes the reference to the *coming* of the kingdom and instead only speaks of his "seeing."[80] Of all the various logia mentioned as possible points of reference for John 21:22, most likely Mark 9:1 par. Matthew 16:28 is worthy of consideration, because this logion alone offers the combination of motifs that can also be postulated for John 21:22*:[81] (1) The promise that some of the present generation[82] (John 21: a special witness) will survive—that is, will not die—because (2) they will witness the full dawn of the kingdom of God or the coming of the Son of Man in their lifetimes. This was probably a "word of the Lord" that had already been given to Mark.[83] Its historical authenticity is disputed.[84] Linguistic similarities with John 21:22 can be noted: (1) the temporal conjunction ἔρχεσθαι in the respective epilogue; (2) the verb ἔρχεσθαι ("to come"). The variants concern the motif of "not dying," but this is not surprising.

The origin of the logion about the beloved disciple within the Johannine community can be imagined as follows: Because its founder, still a "disciple of the Lord," outlived other well-known contemporary witnesses of Jesus, a prophecy presumably made by Jesus such as the one found in Mark 9:1 was remembered and applied to him: "*He* will not die until the Lord comes!"[85] The community was still feeding on the expectation of an imminent end and now believed that

---

80. It is possible that he even removes the reference to the temporal proximity of the kingdom in order to speak only of a "seeing" of the kingdom that is already possible now.

81. Mark 9:1 par. Matt 16:28 / Luke 9:27; Mark 13:30 par. Matt 24:34 / Luke 21:32; Mark 14:62 par. Matt 26:64 / Luke 22:69; Matt 10:23b; 1 Thess 4:15. See Brown, *John*, 2:1118.

82. See Mark 13:30: "Truly, I say to you, *this generation* will not pass away until all these things (μέχρις οὗ) take place." In contrast to Mark 9:1 and John 21:22, however, this "appointed word" does not refer to *individuals* who will experience the coming of the Lord, but looks generally at the generation now living.

83. Bultmann, *Geschichte*, 128.

84. Luz, *Matthäus*, 2:488: The word "is nowadays usually denied to Jesus and assigned to the early church, similar to [Matt] 10:23 and 24:34 = Mark 13:30. However, such a derivation must accept the question of whether it does not attempt to circumvent the fact that Jesus was mistaken in his prophecy in a modern historical-critical way. So, was it the desire to exonerate Jesus, who was the father of the idea, from an error? . . . We will honestly have to leave the question open."

85. Brown, *John*, 2:1118: "The saying about the Beloved Disciple may represent a specification of a type of general saying found in the Synoptic Gospels, predicting that the coming of the

they would be able to experience the coming of the Lord in communion with the one who had once brought the saving word of Jesus as a missionary to their own community. Thus a *synoptic* logion became the root on which a *new* saying grew: an expression of the highest esteem for the founder of the Johannine community! Although the saying seemed to be falsified by his imminent death, it was then reinterpreted by the editors of the book who were responsible for John 21. Now it reveals its true meaning: That disciple "remains" with his congregation in the form of the gospel, which is authorized by his eyewitness account—that is what the resurrected Lord himself wanted!

3.4 Door, Way, and Shepherd. Additional Johannine Metatexts?

Three different constellations emerge from our analysis:

(1) John 3:14–15*, a *Son of Man–saying* from the Johannine circle that the evangelist took up and used, is a metatext to Mark 8:31*, a post-Easter Son of Man passage from the synoptic tradition that deals with the fate of the suffering of the Son of Man but also speaks of his resurrection. Despite the shift in genre (John 3:14–15 adheres to scheme of the "eschatological correlative"), the reference to the basic text is clear due to similarities in motifs and structure. We have here two kinds of transformation: *consolidation* and *explication*. The death and resurrection of the Son of Man are interpreted as his exaltation. Their necessity is explicated theologically through the addition of a biblical *typos*.

(2) Behind John 21:22, a saying from a layer of redaction (= R), there is a logion from the Johannine circle best understood as a transformation of a (possibly Jesus) logion of an apostle. If the basic logion in Mark 9:1* ("There are some of those standing here who will not taste death . . .") spoke of several disciples who were to experience the full dawn of God's reign during their lifetime, then the Johannine circle limits this expectation to its founder, probably an eyewitness of Jesus's work. The basic word thus mutated into a logion that became the starting point of a personal legend. The redactor ultimately reinterprets the logion (see the reference to "remaining"!) and claims that his is the only correct understanding of the saying. However, this should not be taken at face value. It is not likely that the saying circulated with the wording found in the redaction. Otherwise, its widespread misunderstanding (according to the opinion of the redactor) would not have been conceivable. Therefore, the transformational process consisted of two steps: First, a (Jesus?) logion was restricted to the founder of the Johannine community. Then it was reinterpreted in such

---

Son of Man would take place before the generation of Jesus' disciples had died out." See also Lindars, *John*, 639.

a way that its original meaning, determined by the so-called expectation of the near future, was critically *destroyed* in favor of a symbolic understanding. The "abiding" refers to the disciple's abiding in *his* story.

(3) Finally, the transformations of the *Lord's Prayer* (or some of its statements) found in John 12:28a should also be mentioned *critically*. It is very likely that the "Lord's Prayer" was known in the Johannine communities. We cannot say what role it played here. If it functions as a reference or basic text in the Gospel, then this is due to its authority as Jesus's prayer. However, this authority did not prevent either the evangelist or the redactor from translating the prayer into their own imaginative world. There is no evidence that it has been replaced by another, new prayer in the community. However, the great "high priestly prayer" of Jesus in John 17 is a literary text that is read out in the congregation and now exercises the standard function for all Christian prayer which the Lord's Prayer had elsewhere.

Consolidation, explication, outdoing, and *criticism* are the categories that characterize the range of transformation processes synoptic traditions undergo in the Johannine communities. The specifically Johannine "words of the Lord," which will be the subject of our investigation in Part C, can also be subsumed under these categories. For example, John 10:9 ("I am *the door*; if anyone *enters* through me, he will be saved") is based on the saying in Q 13:24*: "Enter *through the* narrow *door*, for many will seek *to enter* and few will find it."[86] Christology and, in its function, a new understanding of time are the driving forces of transformation here.

So far, we have only focused on the phenomenon of the transformation of a *certain* pretext by a Johannine metatext. The parable of the shepherd in John 10:1–5* will offer the special case in which a parable from the Johannine circle does not perpetuate a single Jesus pretext (e.g., Q 15:4, 7). Instead, it stands in the history of the impact of a specific *group of* metaphors originating from *Jesus*, namely those drawn from the milieu of the shepherds. Jesus's own parable of the lost and found sheep could have had a formative and genre-forming effect as the initial spark for further traditions. A prerequisite for the assumption of such a continuum in *the history of effects* is the observation that the image of the shepherd was by no means commonplace in the religious metaphors of *early Judaism*, given the widespread reserve toward this profession.[87]

The postulated continuum to which John 10:1–5* and also John 10:11–12 belong concerns motifs and genre (parable). The parable of the bridegroom and his friend in John 3:29 could be added to this category as well. It has a parallel

---

86. See Theobald, *Herrenworte im Johannesevangelium*, pp. 300–303.

87. Theobald, *Herrenworte im Johannesevangelium*, pp. 375–379.

in Mark 2:19–20 par. Matthew 9:15 (see also Matt 25:1–12, 2 Cor 11:2, Eph 5). In contrast, there are loose threads between the way-motif in John 14:6* and the Christian self-designation "followers of the Way" (Acts 9:2 etc.) or between the imagery of the grain of wheat (John 12:24) and that of the mustard seed.[88] In these cases, one cannot go beyond more or less plausible assumptions. What is decisive are the innovations that consistently characterize the Johannine transformations.

3.5 John and the Synoptics from the Perspective of the Sayings Tradition

The following four insights are drawn from the analyses in chapters 2 and 3:

(1) Obviously, synoptic logia lived on in the Johannine communities (independently of their attestation in the Synoptic Gospels). There, they were creatively commented on and further developed. In the process, some of them also acquired their own "Johannine" linguistic style before they were written down by the evangelist or the editors of the Gospel of John. This intermediate layer shines through in John. It proves how much the evangelist owes to his community. He should not be stylized as the solitary theological thinker that many still regard him to be.

(2) A strong synoptic root of the Gospel of John are its sayings, which revolve around the *right of the messenger*. They are not only of great significance in terms of content, as they prefigure the evangelist's missionary Christology. They are also sociologically instructive insofar as they reveal something about the beginnings of the Johannine community. Similar to the group behind the sayings source, the Johannine community probably originated from a movement of Jewish-Christian itinerant missionaries who spread the message of Jesus in the synagogues—probably in the Palestinian-Syrian border region.[89]

(3) Many synoptic traditions did not reach the Johannine communities or were filtered out of their own tradition. Here are two examples:

The central symbol of Jesus's message, preaching the "*kingdom of God*," was familiar to the community according to John 3:3, 5. But it only is found occasionally in connection to the phrase "enter into the kingdom of God." Connections in which "the kingdom of God" is the subject ("your kingdom come!" or

---

88. See p. 221–222.

89. See M. Theobald, Das Johannesevangelium und Q. Wie groß ist ihre gemeinsame Schnittmenge und wie erklärt sie sich?, in: D.A. Smith/G. Harb/C. Heil (Hg.), Built on Rock or Sand? Q Studies: Retrospects, Introspects and Prospects, Biblical Tools and Studies 34, Leuven 2018, 467–495, here 491.

"the kingdom of God has arrived" [Luke 11:20] or "has drawn near" [Mark 1:15]), which are typical of Jesus's eschatological-dynamic understanding of the *basileia*, have not left any traces in the Johannine tradition. There are also no parables about the kingdom of God. The central soteriological term of the Johannine tradition, which replaces Jesus's concept of the *basileia*, is "eternal life." We have already encountered it in John 12:25, but it is also present elsewhere.[90]

A second example is the *Johannine sayings about the Son of Man*. There are nine in total.[91] Of these, only two, perhaps three, can claim to belong to the Johannine logia tradition before the evangelist or alongside the evangelist: 3:14–15; 6:53;[92] and possibly 8:28.

If we take the classical classification of the synoptic sayings about the Son of Man as a yardstick (sayings about the future Son of Man; sayings about the suffering and resurrected Son of Man; sayings about the Son of Man in his earthly existence), then the following is noticeable in connection with the Johannine sayings:

(1) Group A (sayings about the future Son of Man) is totally missing in the Gospel of John (despite the redactional addition 5:[27c.]28–29[93]).

(2) Group B (sayings about the suffering and resurrected Son of Man) is represented by John 3:14–15, a saying to which we can add 8:28 ("if you exalt the Son of Man…"); 12:23 and 13:31–32 (the two words about the glorification of the Son of Man). All four sayings are focused on the death of Jesus and its paschal interpretation, as is also the case for the synoptic sayings of the suffering and resurrected Son of Man.

(3) The remaining Johannine sayings about the Son of Man have specific characteristics that cannot be found in any of the synoptic sayings: 6:53 is a eucharistic saying and 3:13 and 6:62 combine the speech about the Son of Man with the ascent-descent-model.[94]

Conclusion: Despite the very peculiar contour of the Johannine words of the Son of Man,[95] they are rooted in the synoptic tradition. This becomes especially clear in 3:14–15. The authority to judge (actually a privilege of God) attributed to Jesus by the evangelist is also connected with the title Son of Man, as in

---

90. In 3:14f.; 4:35f.; 5:24; 12:25; only ζωή in 6:35; 6:53; 7:37f.; 8:12.

91. 1:51, 3:13, 3:14–15 (see 12:34), 6:27, 6:53, 6:62, 8:28, 12:23, 13:31–32; more over see 5:27b, 9:35.

92. Similarly Lindars, *John*, 267–268; Lindars, "Use," 119.

93. See p. 204–206.

94. See p. 378–380.

95. The descent/ascension scheme is characteristic of them. The earthly presence of Jesus thus appears as the epiphany of the preexistent Son of Man. The idea of preexistence is foreign to the synoptic sayings.

9:35–38/39 (cf. also 5:27b). It follows from this that a knowledge of faith concerning the *future* soteriological role of the Son of Man, Jesus, which is articulated in the synoptic sayings about the coming Son of Man, survived in the Johannine communities but was transformed decisively.

(4) The Johannine tradition of sayings has its own distinct character. One reason for that is the "filtering out" of important synoptic themes or rather a lack of acquaintance with them. Even if the segments in which the Johannine and synoptic tradition of sayings overlap are not too large, they do exist and should not be underestimated. John 3:3, 5, for example, is also significant because this logion in its Johannine form documents the naturalness with which the initiating sacrament of baptism was practiced in it. If we add John 6:53, we can extend this assessment to the celebration of the Eucharist. The Johannine Christians cannot have lived so completely separate from other early Christian communities!

Part II

Specific Johannine "Words of the Lord"

THE FOLLOWING CHAPTERS deal with texts that have no direct parallels in the Synoptic Gospels. We group them according to the *genres* of the traditions they presumably contain: "I am" figurative words (ch. 4), parables and other figurative words (ch. 5), words of wisdom (ch. 6), and words of promise and consolation (ch. 7). The so-called paraclete sayings (14:15–17; 14:25–26; 15:26–27; 16:7–11; 16:12–15) are omitted.[1] Although they deal with synoptic motifs, they are not predetermined sayings that would have been received in the book. It is difficult to speak of a uniform genre for the so-called *Amen-sayings*. They are words of promise and consolation (5:24; 5:25; 8:51; 8:52; 12:24–26; 14:12–14) and not only words of promise (3:3/5; 6:53; 13:16; 13:20). The same applies to the Son of Man–sayings.[2]

---

1. See in detail at M. Theobald, Ein Gott oder "zwei Götter im Himmel"? Zum Wandel der johanneischen "Parakletsprüche" 123–146.

2. We have already discussed 3:14–15 in the previous chapter.

CHAPTER 4

The "I Am" Sayings

TWO OF THE figurative "I am" sayings are presented here: the bread of life saying (6:35) and the saying about the *Way* (14:6).[1] The fact that the absolute "I am" of 6:20 ("I am [it]. Do not be afraid!") immediately precedes the first figurative saying in 6:35 is of great significance for these sayings as a whole: Jesus, who appears in the darkness of the sea with his words "I am," uses a phrase "with which God often introduces himself in the Old Testament."[2] This indicates the background against which the following figurative words should be understood. In chapter 5, which is devoted to the Johannine parables, one of the "I am" sayings has developed into a figurative *speech*: the parable of the vine (15:1-8).[3]

4.1 The Bread of Life Saying (John 6:35)

John 6:35 is the "core saying" of John's bread of life discourse. There is much to suggest that it was part of the tradition the evangelist inherited (4.1.2). It may have had its *Sitz im Leben* in the congregation's celebration of the Eucharist, from which the evangelist took it for his composition (4.1.4). We begin with an analysis of the context.

4.1.1 Against the Separation of Gift and Giver
The Context of John 6:35

In recent decades, scholars have been puzzling over the structure of the Johannine bread of life discourse. The influential thesis of P. Borgen that the bread of life discourse (6:32-58) should be understood as a Christian midrash or a

---

1. On the saying about light (8:12) and the door (10:9), see Theobald, *Herrenworte*, 259-304. John 11:25-26 goes back to the evangelist.

2. C. Dietzfelbinger, *Das Evangelium nach Johannes I-II*, ZBK.NT 4/1-2 (Zürich: Benzinger, 2001), 1:149: "Christ presents himself in the same way as Yahweh in the Old Testament. He presents himself as Yahweh appearing (cf. 18:5-6)."

3. On the parable of the good shepherd (10:11-13), see Theobald, *Herrenworte*, 380-393.

homily on the quotation of Scripture in verse 31[4] has been refuted in more recent scholarship.[5] John 6 is a type of text that is specifically Christian: *a dramatized interpretation of Jesus's words*.

The structure of the dialogue about the bread of life is not easy to ascertain. It is likely that rhetorical aspects were also incorporated into the internal organization of the six components of the dialogue (without 6:51d–58). Thus, the *prooemium* of the speech can be seen in verses 25–29, its *main part* in verses 30–51c, and its *conclusion* or *peroratio* in verses 60–65.[6] The main part is divided into two subsections: the basic part verses 30–35, including the "core saying" verse 35 and its interpretation in verses 36–51c, which at its end leads back to the overarching predication of the "core saying" (v. 48: "I am the bread of life").[7] It thus becomes clear that the saying about the bread of life in verse 35 forms the inner and outer bracket of the entire main part of the composition.

The author probably had this word in mind from the very beginning as the aim of the composition. For our critical examination of the tradition, it is instructive to observe how the author prepares the saying in verses 30ff and at the same time to ask whether this saying protrudes beyond the surroundings from which it grows. The text of 6:30–35 reads:

30 So they said to him,
   "What sign are you going to give us then
   so that we may see it and believe you?
   What work are you performing?
31 Our ancestors ate the manna in the wilderness,
   as it is written,
   'He gave them bread from heaven to eat'" (Ps 78:24b).
32 Then Jesus said to them,
   "Very truly I tell you,
   it was not Moses who gave you the bread from heaven to eat,
   but it is my Father who gives you bread from heaven,
   the true (bread).

---

4. P. Borgen, *Bread from Heaven: An Exegetical Study of the Concept of Manna in the Gospel of John and the Writings of Philo*, NT.S 10 (Leiden: Brill, 1965).

5. See M. Theobald, "Schriftzitate im 'Lebensbrot'-Dialog Jesu (Joh 6). Ein Paradigma für den Schriftgebrauch des vierten Evangelisten," *The Scriptures in the Gospels*, ed. C. M. Tuckett, BETL 131 (Leuven: Peeters 1997), 327–366, here 331–340.

6. This structure of the speech alone, which leaves no room for 6:51d–58, is a strong argument for the idea that the explicitly eucharisitic passage bears the character of a literary addendum.

7. Verses 47–51 serve to interpret the Christological "head clause" of v. 35, while vv. 36–40/41–46 revolve around the keywords "come to Jesus" and "believe" from the soteriological "secondary clause" of v. 35c–f.

33 For the bread of God is that which comes down from heaven
and gives life to the world."[8]
34 They said to him,
"Lord, give us this bread always!"
35 Jesus said to them,
"I am the bread of life.
Whoever comes to me will never be hungry,
and whoever believes in me will never be thirsty."

After Jesus has confronted his listeners with his claim to *them* in the *prooemium*,[9] they turn the tables in verse 30 and ask what *he* is doing and how *he* legitimizes his claim.[10] To this end, they recall Israel's time in the wilderness, when their fathers had enough to eat according to the Scripture: "He gave them bread from heaven to eat" (Ps 78:24b). They are thinking of Moses, who was able to prove his authority by this sign. It seems difficult to imagine that the audience who had just witnessed Jesus's miraculous feeding now ask again for a sign to prove his legitimacy. Have they forgotten what they have just experienced? This tension is probably resolved when the following is considered: If the miraculous feeding was only an isolated event for them, now that they remember Israel's time in the wilderness, they are concerned with more than just an *isolated* sign of legitimacy. In accordance with the early Jewish expectation assumed here, according to which the manna miracle would be repeated in the last days,[11] the evangelist portrays them as people who make their faith in Jesus dependent on whether the messianic era dawns *permanently* with him, whether the golden age is here or not. Accordingly, in verse 34, the evangelist has them pose a question borne of pure ignorance: "Lord, give us this bread *always*!" Behind this is a messianic understanding of salvation that remains attached to the earthly phenomenological sphere and confuses true life with paradise on earth.

In contrast, Jesus's recitation of the scriptural saying in verses 32–33 shows that its wording cannot be properly understood by referring to a meal with *physical* food. That manna was not "bread *from heaven*." It says in 6:49 that "your ancestors ate it in the wilderness and they died." The "true" bread from heaven, however, gives

---

8. Or: "For the bread of God is *that which* comes down from heaven." The wording is deliberately ambiguous in Greek.

9. Verse 27: "Do not obtain for yourselves the food which perishes, but the food which endures to eternal life"; v. 29: "This is the work of God, that you believe in him whom he has sent."

10. Verse 30 specifically takes up the keywords from vv. 27–28 in order to relate them to *Jesus*: "do," "work," "to work."

11. See especially 2 Bar. 29:8: "It will come about at that time that man's treasures will come down again from on high, and they will feed on them in those years, because they are the ones who have come to the end of time."

"life" and salvation in the full sense. Therefore, only the Father can "give" it; Moses "*did not* give" it (v. 32). Important for the continuation of the conversation is the fact that the justification of verse 32 in verse 33 can be understood in a material or personal sense.[12] According to verse 34, Jesus's interlocutors understand the sentence to be objective and therefore believe that the bread Jesus is talking about is heavenly food that guarantees physical life at all times, that is, that it is the foundation of paradise on earth. In doing so, they misunderstand Jesus and tear the gift and the giver apart. Only the saying about bread in verse 35 resolves the ambivalences of verses 34–35 by *identifying the bread with Jesus*. It follows from this that if one reads the saying about bread in light of the whole dialogue in verses 30–34, then only its threefold personal pronoun can be the focus:

"*I* am the bread of life.
Whoever comes to *me* will never be hungry,
and whoever believes in *me* will never be thirsty."

In other words: "*I* am the bread of life (and you should not look for it anywhere else)!" "Whoever comes to *me* (and does not seek bread *apart from* me), *his* hunger and thirst will be satisfied." But can the full meaning of the saying be confined to *this* reading? What does it look like if we read the saying on its own? Its predication "bread of life" only seems to emerge seamlessly from the verses that lead up to it. Although it takes up the keyword "bread" from verses 32–33 and links it with that of "life" from verse 33, the predication is unlikely to have arisen ad hoc from this combination but would have had its own origin in the history of tradition. It would have been linked to the independent I am–saying. This thesis needs to be proven from tradition-criticism.

4.1.2 Observations from Tradition-Criticism

Did the evangelist really compose a saying like 6:35 himself? Of course, we cannot eliminate this assumption. But there are several observations that plausibly show that it is a saying that belonged to the tradition of the Johannine community:

(1) The saying is complete by itself and does not require context to be understood.

(2) There is no further mention of thirst elsewhere in John 6. Although 6:35 offers a link to John 4:10, 13–14, and 7:37–39, the statement appears to be foreign to the context of John 6 because the discourse is exclusively oriented toward the saying about bread in 6:35. This can be explained by the fact that the saying was an independent entity.

---

12. See above at n. 8!

(3) According to R. Bultmann, the I am-sayings are "recognition formulas" in which the "I" is the predicate of the statement. They answer the question, *Who* or *what* is expected? However, this is only a partial aspect that is determined by the context. In the case of 6:35, it arises when the saying is read in conjunction with verses 30–34. According to its formal-syntactic structure, the saying highlights different aspects: It emphasizes that Jesus is the "*bread of life*," which means that whoever comes to him and believes him will *never be thirsty or hungry*. This inner contradiction speaks for the original independent tradition that the evangelist has retooled for the present context.

(4) Future support can be found from motif-critical observations: "Bread of life" is not attested (apart from Joseph and Aseneth) in the common early Jewish texts about manna. Thus, an extrapolation from the preceding interpretation of Psalm 78:24 is unlikely. "The connection of ἔρχεσθαι (= to come) with the idea of discipleship and the parallelization of the idea of discipleship with 'faith in me'" is "such a typical early Christian process that no genuinely Johannine, i.e., editorial, presuppositions need to be claimed for it."[13]

Hunger and thirst, bread and water/wine belong together in early Judaism: See Isaiah 55:1–3; Proverbs 9:5 ("Come, eat of my bread and drink of the wine I have mixed!"); Sirach 15:3 ("She [s.c. Wisdom] feeds him with the bread of wisdom, and with the water of understanding she waters him"); 24:21; 51:24; see also 2 Baruch 29:5–6: "Also the earth will yield its fruit ten thousandfold. On one vine there will be a thousand branches, and one branch will bear a thousand grapes, and one cluster a thousand berries, and one berry will yield a basket of wine. And those who suffered hunger shall rejoice." The *leading function of the bread metaphor* in the title of the saying and the simultaneous inclusion of the corresponding metaphor of thirst is easily explained if the saying had its *Sitz im Leben* in the *celebration of the Eucharist* (more on this in a moment).

4.1.3 The Form, Genre, and *Sitz im Leben* of the Saying

Thus, the saying's original form was like what we read in John 6:35:

6:35   b   I am the *bread of life*.
       c   Whoever comes to me (literally: the coming one to me),
       d   will *certainly no longer go hungry,*
       e   and whoever believes in me (literally: the believing one in me),
       f   will *never thirst again.*

---

13. F. Hahn, Die Worte vom lebendigen Wasser im Johannesevangelium, 51–70, here 61f.; cf. Mt 11:28; 18:6.

The saying has two parts, a "head clause" (v. 35b) and its development in two syntactically parallel sentences with a futuristic sense (v. 35c–f). The two participles, which each represent a relative clause, can be placed in their own cola, as done above, in order to visually emphasize the genre-characteristic element of the "invitation":

A. Self-introduction formula with a word picture (35b)
B. Soteriological consequence (35c–f):
   1. Invitation with a promise (35c, d)
   2. Invitation with a promise (35e, f)

In contrast to 7:37,[14] the two invitations here do not have an independent syntactic status but are integrated into the two promise clauses in the form of substantival participles. They unfold the Christological predication of the head clause "the bread of life" in soteriological terms. The promised quenching of hunger and thirst forever concretizes exactly what "life" means in the head clause. As stated above, the focus is not on the *egō* of the speaker, but on *what* he means for those who believe in him. Nor does the saying offer any *instructions* to come to Jesus and believe in him, but rather wants to be understood as a promise for those who have already come to him. As a word of revelation, the saying primarily has a *cognitive* claim. It clarifies the extent to which all hope of salvation is based on a correct understanding of Christ.

For a long time, the reference of the metaphor of no longer hungering and thirsting to *faith* was reason enough to speak against the presence of *eucharistic* associations, but recently there has been an increase in voices that do not see a mutually exclusive contradiction in the two.[15] However, if the reference to the quenching of all hunger for life in faith in Jesus was also intended to recall the eucharistic meal, at which the Lord himself is the host, without this being at the forefront of the statement, then we can go one step further and ask whether the eucharistic celebration itself was not the original *Sitz im Leben* of the saying. This seems plausible, especially as the predication "bread of life" also points in this direction.

---

14. John 7:37c, d: "If anyone is thirsty, let him come to me!"

15. F. Hahn, "Die Worte vom lebendigen Wasser im Johannesevangelium. Eigenart und Vorgeschichte von Joh 4,10.13f.; 6,35; 7,37–39," in *God's Christ and His People*, FS N.A. Dahl, ed. J. Jervell and W. A. Meeks (Oslo: Universitetsforlaget, 1977), 51–70, here 61: "John 6:35b, c (probably) as well as Rev 22:17b were directly related to the Lord's Supper, which in the present bread of life discourse is only in the background of the argumentation"; see also E. Schüssler Fiorenza, "The Quest for the Johannine School. The Apocalypse and the Fourth Gospel," *NTS* 23 (1977): 402–427, here 417.

4.1.4 "There is here one greater than wisdom!"
The Motif in Context

What early Jewish Scripture confesses about wisdom, that all who come to her will be satiated at her table,[16] applies to our saying about Jesus here. If the Gospel of John refers directly to Sirach 24:21,[17] then the message would also be: "There is something greater than wisdom here!" (see Matt 12:6, 41–42). There, in Sirach 24:19–21, we read:

> Come to me, you who desire me,
> and eat your fill of my fruits.
> For the memory of me is sweeter than honey,[18]
> and the possession of me sweeter than the honeycomb.
> Those who eat of me *will hunger for more*,
> and those who of drink me *will thirst for more*.

If one never gets enough of the wisdom that Sirach 24:21 identifies with the Torah, which is meant positively, then John 6:35 would recognize a limitation in this if his assertion that Jesus means the *final* quenching of all hunger and thirst for life were to be understood as a surpassing of Sirach 24:21. Of course, this cannot be said with certainty. Incidentally, Isaiah 49:10 also promises no more hunger and thirst, namely in the end times.

Of great interest is the finding that there are no parallels to the predication "bread of life" in early Jewish literature apart from Joseph and Aseneth. This Jewish-Hellenistic conversion novel, which was probably written in Egypt in the first century CE, offers several examples of this,[19] in a stereotypical form that is only slightly modified in individual passages and which, in conjunction with John 6:35, 48, suggests that we are dealing with a coined phrase.

The Joseph and Aseneth novella promotes conversion to Judaism. The question of marriage between Jews and pagans is in the background of its propaganda for faith in the true God and the Jewish way of life, which requires a separation from the idolatry and the "impurity" of the pagan lifestyle. This is why Joseph refuses when Aseneth, the Egyptian priest's daughter (see Gen 41:45), wants to

---

16. See Prov 9:2, 5; Sir 15:3.

17. Dietzfelbinger, *Johannes*, 1:160: "It looks as if the Johannine text not only wanted to contrast Jesus with manna, but also with wisdom: It is not she, but Jesus who satisfies."

18. This, Philo, *Fug.* 138 says about the manna which tastes like honey cake (Exod 16:31), adopts every taste, and serves as food for the angels in heaven (Wis 16:20; Ps 78:24–25).

19. 8:5, 9; 15:5; 16:16; 19:5; 21:21. Translation from the NRSV.

greet him with a kiss in her parents' house and then says to her in Joseph and Aseneth 8:5:

> It is not fitting for a man who worships God,
> who blesses the living God (with) his mouth
> and eats the blessed bread (of) life
> and drinks the blessed cup (of) immortality
> and anoints himself (with) blessed ointment (of) incorruption
> (to) kiss a strange woman,
> who blesses dead and mute images (of idols with) her mouth
> and eats from their table bread (of) strangulation
> and drinks from her cup of libation the cup (of) ambush
> and anoints herself (with) the oil (of) destruction.

But when Joseph sees the grief he is causing Aseneth with his words, he is moved with compassion and prays for her (8:9):

> Lord, the God of my father Israel,
> the highest, strongest one of Jacob,
> who gave life to all *things)
> and called from the darkness into the light ...
> you, Lord, bless this virgin,
> and renew her (with) your spirit,
> and reshape her (with) your hand of the hidden ones,
> and revive her (with) your life,
> and she will eat the *bread of your life* [...]
> and drink the cup of your blessing,
> and add her to your nation,
> whom you chose before all (things) were
> and she will live in your eternal life for eternity.

Aseneth is then seized with remorse over her initial contempt for Joseph and fasts for seven days until the archangel Michael comes to her and encourages her (Jos. As. 15:5). On Joseph's next visit, she finally tells him that she has thrown away all her idols (19:5):

> A man came to me from heaven today
> and gave me *bread (of) life*, and I ate,
> and the cup (of) blessing, and I drank,[20]

---

20. In the psalm of Aseneth at Jos. As. 21:21 this refers to Joseph: "and he [s.c. Joseph] gave me the bread (of) life to eat ... and cup (of) wisdom to drink."

and he said to me,
"I have given you (as) a bride to Joseph today,
and he (himself) will be your bridegroom for eternity."

However, the novella does not tell us that Aseneth actually ate bread and drank from a cup of blessing during her encounter with the archangel. Rather, it is about a miraculous honeycomb that Aseneth finds in her pantry at the behest of the archangel, "large and white as snow and full of honey. And that honey was like dew from heaven, and its fragrance like the breath of life" (16:8). Aseneth explains this as follows, "Lord, I (myself) did not have a honeycomb in my storehouse, but you (yourself) spoke and it became. Did it not even come out of your mouth, for its fragrance is like the breath of your mouth?" (16:11). Then the angel says: "Blessed are you (yourself), Aseneth, for the unspeakable mysteries of the Most High have been revealed to you, and blessed are all who join themselves to the Lord God in repentance, for they will eat of this honeycomb, for this honeycomb is the *spirit of life* . . . *and everyone who eats of it will not die for eternity*" (16:14).[21] Then the angel himself eats of this heavenly food, gives "what is left" to Aseneth, and says: "'Eat,' and she ate" (16:15). The angel then interprets the communion as follows: "Behold, you ate the *bread (of) life* and drank the cup (of) immortality and anointed yourself with the ointment (of) incorruption" (16:16).

Obviously, eating the honeycomb is to be identified with the repeatedly announced participation in the meal. If that meal does not refer to the special rite of a honey communion, then "conversely, one must probably take the honey manna as a narrative exegesis of blessed bread, cup, and ointment."[22] The manna story thus becomes an *interpretation* of Jewish meal practices, insofar as it takes place under the blessing of God according to the praises spoken over the food and drink and thereby conveys this to the participants in the meal. They eat the "bread of life," the food of the angels, which people can also partake of, such that "whoever eats of it will not die for ever" (16:14).

If, strictly speaking, the association with manna is linked to the honeycomb motif, then the question arises as to the triple or dual formula "bread of life"—"cup of immortality" (—"ointment of incorruption"), which is to be interpreted through the motif of manna-honey. Is the term "bread of *life*" already included in the association with manna?[23] This is possible, but it cannot be proven beyond doubt due to a lack of clear textual signals. However, the fact that the triad of bread, (wine) cup, and oil stands for the Jewish meal that conveys God's blessing and is moreover given the epithets "life," "immortality," and "incorruption"

---

21. See John 6:50–51.

22. Burchard, *JSHRZ* II/4 605.

23. See R. Schnackenburg, "Das Brot des Lebens (Joh 6)," in *Das Johannesevangelium*, HThK. NT IV/4 (Freiburg: Herder, 1984), 119–131, here 129.

indicates that the reference here is not merely to a general Jewish lifestyle as opposed to pagan impurity,[24] nor the daily Jewish meal,[25] but rather a Jewish "cult meal," "be it the Passover meal of the diaspora, a domestic Sabbath meal, a meal in the synagogue, or a special feast on the occasion of conversion to Judaism, as J. Jeremias appealingly assumes."[26] The decisive factor is that the coined phrase "bread of life" had its *Sitz im Leben* in Jewish banqueting practice, without it being possible for us to narrow down this background further.[27]

What follows from this finding for the tradition-critical assessment of John 6:35*? It must be assumed that there is no direct relationship of dependence either between John and Joseph and Aseneth or specifically between John 6:35* and Joseph and Aseneth. But then "the close motif-historical and terminological convergences can be explained by the fact that both writings draw on a Hellenistic-Jewish tradition that regarded the manna as supranatural life-creating food"[28] or that the coined phrase "bread of life" was known from the context of cultic meal traditions. The latter would confirm the assumption that John 6:35* originally had its *Sitz im Leben* in the celebration of the Eucharist.[29]

4.1.5 "And they had only one loaf of bread with them" (Mark 8:14)
A Synoptic Point of Reference for the Johannine Saying?

"And they forgot to take bread with them, and except for *one* loaf they had nothing with them on the boat" (Mark 8:14).—With this note, the oldest evangelist opens

---

24. This thesis of Schnackenburg, "Brot."

25. See Burchard, *JSHRZ*, II/4, 605.

26. H.-J. Klauck, *Herrenmahl und hellenistischer Kult. Eine religionsgeschichtliche Untersuchung zum ersten Korintherbrief*, NTA.NF 15, 2nd ed. (Münster: Aschendorff, 1986), 196.

27. Nevertheless, it is noticeable that the present tense formulations of the first text, Jos. As. 8:5, have repetitive events in mind (see Burchard, The Importance of Joseph and Aseneth, 111), so it is less likely that they are limited to a single banquet on the occasion of the conversion to Judaism. Sänger, Antikes Judentum und die Mysterien, 174–187, 195, attempts to support his thesis of a proselyte reception banquet by analogy with the initiation of the mysteries in 16:16.

28. B. Kollmann, *Ursprung und Gestalten der frühChristlichen Mahlfeier*, GTA 43 (Göttingen: Vandenhoeck & Ruprecht, 1990), 116 (with reference also to 1 Cor 10:3–4; Did. 10:3), taking into account the context of John 6. With regard to the manna background, one must be more cautious if one (1) looks only at John 6:35 and (2) considers the manna implications of the phrase "bread of life" in Joseph and Aseneth to be uncertain.

29. See also H. Klein, "Vorgeschichte und Verständnis der johanneischen Ich-bin-Worte," *KuD* 33 (1987): 120–136, here 132: "In the background of the words 'I am the bread of life,' as can be seen from the parallel of Joseph and Aseneth, there is probably the conversion together with baptism and the Lord's Supper."

a scene that, according to the almost unanimous opinion of scholars, goes back to his own editorial work: Mark 8:14–21. It serves as a subsequent interpretation of the two preceding feeding narratives Mark 6:35–44 and 8:1–9.

The meaning of the scenic opening of verse 14 is unclear. Is it merely to say, "If five loaves were enough for more than five thousand or four loaves for four thousand at the two feedings of the crowd, one loaf must be enough for twelve?"[30] But is the following conversation really only about relieving the disciples or the readers of their worries about everyday sustenance? The number of baskets necessary to collect the leftover pieces, namely twelve or seven, points in a different direction. But then it is obvious to ask for a deeper meaning in verse 14b as well.[31] "The mention of the 'one loaf in the boat' seems to be unpretentious and only has a meaning that opens the following conversation in the context of the 'situational statement' of verse 14. But more is probably said here. This 'one bread' is to be interpreted symbolically as referring to Jesus himself."[32] *He* is the bread of life, which is the actual meaning of the feeding narratives.

Is there a connection between John 6:35 and Mark 8:14? One might be tempted to assume so in view of the other references between John 6 and Mark 6–8.[33] But caution is necessary. Mark 8:14, a verse composed by the oldest evangelist himself, has nothing at all in common formally with the I am–saying in John 6:35* and only shows, if its Christological reading is correct, that a corresponding deepening of the feeding stories was obvious. The fourth evangelist also followed this path, albeit in a much more pronounced and pointed way, whereby he was able to use the logion of John 6:35* as a crystallization point for his speech. A reference back to Mark 8:14 cannot be established.

4.1.6 John 6:35 as the "Core Logion" of the Bread of Life Discourse

The fact that we are dealing with the "core logion" of the bread of life discourse in John 6:35 is already evident from the fact that it takes up the epiphany formula of the preceding story of Jesus walking on water (ἐγώ εἰμι—"I am [he]," [v. 20]) and continues it in terms of content. Seen in this light, it represents the decisive bridge that supports the composition of John 6, which consists of the two semeia in John 6:1–15/16–21 and the subsequent discourse on bread. The evangelist interprets

---

30. D. Lührmann, *Das Markusevangelium*, HNT 3 (Tübingen: Mohr, 1987), 138.

31. This is also because in vv. 16–17 it says twice explicitly that they had *no* bread with them at all, which subsequently encourages the reader to think about the "*unique* loaf" that they did have with them according to v. 14.

32. K. Kertelge, *Die Wunder Jesu im Markusevangelium*, StANT 23 (München: Kösel, 1970), 172.

33. See Brown, *John*, 1:238–239.

this "core saying" in the corpus of his bread of life discourse, commenting on its parts in reverse order: He begins in verses 36–40/41–46 with the "soteriological explication" in verses 35c–f and concludes in verses 47–51c with the self-predication in verse 35b. The formal consequence of this is that the phrase ἐγώ εἰμι (three times in total: vv. 35, 48, 51!) now *frames* the "core saying" together with the commentary. The scriptural word in verse 31c (= Ps 78:24) and the manna narrative in Exodus 16 form the backdrop to this commentary, which admittedly only appears explicitly in a single passage, namely in verse 43, but is also likely to be in the background of the leitmotif of "descending *from heaven*" (see vv. 33, 38a, 41c, 50a, 51a). This confirms the assumption that it is actually about verse 35 as the "core logion" of the speech: the word from Scripture in verse 31c only has a flanking or supporting function. The "commentary" on John 6:35 revolves around the following three points:

(1) What does it mean when the I am–saying is formulated as an invitation: "whoever *comes* to me . . ." or "whoever *believes* in me . . ."?

An answer to this question is found in the two sequences verses 36–40/41–46 of which the first is framed by the double motif "*seeing and believing in him*" (inclusio: vv. 36/40) and the second picks up the motif of "*to come to Jesus*" (vv. 44a, 45c). Coming to Jesus or believing in him is only possible for those who are *drawn* by the Father (v. 44) or: "All *that the Father gives me* will come to me" (v. 37). Overcoming the offense of faith (see vv. 41-42) is not a question of man's strength or daring; rather, this succeeds solely because and insofar as the Father himself ensures that man is "drawn" beyond all doubt into the divine realm of life through the power of his love.[34] What sounds like an appeal to the decision of those who are still undecided or the perseverance of those who have already made up their minds in faith in the I am–saying, the commentary vv. 44-45 deepens "grace-theologically." His interest is not *generally* directed toward the election and predestination of people through God's salvific counsel but takes as its concrete starting point the problem that there are certain people who "see and yet *do not* believe" (v. 36), "Jews who grumble" (v. 41) or take offense at the fact that in this Jesus, "son of Joseph, whose father and mother" they know, God's Son himself "is said to have descended from heaven" (v. 42). In other words, the "grace-theological" commentary on verses 35c–f is in the perspective of the so-called Israel problem which it wishes to reappraise.

(2) It is possible that the motif of the *supranatural* "bread of life" is also part of the manna tradition. In any case, together with the revelatory formula of the divine "*I am*," it testifies to the supreme claim of the one who claims to be the "I am," and probably also presupposes a confession of his preexistence. In taking up

---

34. For an analysis of the history of motifs, see M. Theobald, "Gezogen von Gottes Liebe (Joh 6,44f.). Beobachtungen zur Überlieferung eines johanneischen 'Herrenworts,'" in *Schrift und Tradition*, FS J. Ernst, ed. K. Backhaus and F. G. Untergassmair (Paderborn: Schöningh, 1996), 315–341.

the logion in a context that is about an argument between Jesus and the "Jews," it is remarkable that the evangelist attaches importance to an interpretation of the divine "I am" which does not violate monotheistic confessions. This is why he formulates the following immediately after the "core logion" in verse 38: "For I did not come down from heaven to do *my* will, but the will *of him who sent me.*" Furthermore, he intersperses the speech with specific references to Jesus's role as the one sent by the Father (vv. 29c, 39a, 44b).

(3) The self-predication, including the figurative word in verse 35b, is interpreted in the final part of the body of the discourse at verses 47–51c. The specifically *Christological* statement that the evangelist connects with the self-predication, namely that Jesus, as the "bread of life," has his actual home in heaven with God the Father, is of course heard everywhere from verse 32 onward. The commentary on the I am–saying in verses 47–51c emphasizes anew its *soteriological* aspect: From verse 47 on, the focus is on the fact that those who believe in Jesus "have *eternal life.*" This is why it is also said that Jesus is "the bread of *life,*" in contrast to the manna that the ancestors ate in the desert and nevertheless *died* (v. 48).

Both perspectives belong together: the *Christological* and the *soteriological.* The latter grounds the former and is its unavoidable consequence. Verses 50–51 at the end of the corpus say this with total clarity: "This is the bread *that came down from heaven* [= Christological statement of origin], so that one may eat of it and *not die* [= soteriological goal]. I am the *living* bread that came *down from heaven* [= Christological statement of origin]. If anyone eats of this bread, *he will live forever* [= soteriological goal]."

4.2 The Light of the World Saying (John 8:12)

John 8:12 is the decisive junction of all Johannine texts about light and darkness. Even if the saying seems to have a life of its own, unconnected to the context, it is nevertheless the prelude to a number of other sayings about light, all of which refer to it in some way (9:4–5; 11:9–10; 12:35–36; 12:46). If it was given to the evangelist, as there is some evidence to suggest it was (see 4.2.1), then it would have been the source for the other sayings from which they drew.

4.2.1 The Tradition-Critical Isolation of the Saying

In his commentary, Bultmann postulated an originally coherent discourse on light as part of a revelation source that the evangelist had broken down into its individual components. The fragments of that source were scattered across the Gospel, but can be easily found since as they were barely integrated into their new environment.[35] However, this hypothesis has been met with little approval.

---

35. Bultmann, *Johannes*, 237. His "light discourse" includes 8:12; 12:44–50; 8:21–29; 12:34–36.

What is actually striking about 8:12—the isolation of the saying in its immediate context—can be explained much more simply and plausibly within the framework of a model of *tradition-criticism*: We do not need to postulate the existence of a written source, for an oral tradition is sufficient. J. Becker has succinctly outlined the important aspects for such an oral source: "The formal rounding, the typical form, the linguistic garb ('light of life' only here in John) and the factual independence from the context lead to the thesis that there is sayings material in 8:12."[36] It can be added that the saying with the motif of succession (ἀκολουθέω—περιπατεῖν) ties in with old synoptic tradition,[37] which is a sign of its corresponding rootedness in the history of tradition. U. Schnelle's observation on chapter 8 as a whole also deserves interest: "A word of revelation forms the starting point for the following scenes, which are mostly structured by the sequence 'words of Jesus—misunderstanding of the Jews—explanation of Jesus.'"[38] If, according to our analyses, 7:33-34; 7:37; 8:21; 8:31-32; 8:51 are predetermined logia, each of which is at the top of the structural scheme identified by Schnelle, then the same applies to 8:12.[39]

4.2.2 Form, Pragmatics, and the Genre of the Saying

The saying includes the introduction to his speech:

8:12   a   Again,[40] Jesus spoke to them,[41] saying,
         b   I am *the light of the world*.
         c   Whoever follows me
         d   will never walk in darkness
         e   but will have *the light of life*.

---

36. Becker, *Johannes*, 1:339-340.

37. See also Klein, "Vorgeschichte," 128: "While the other two (s.c. logia: 6:35; 11:25) fit completely into Johannine thought and expression, the same cannot be said of the word of light. For the evangelist uses the verb 'follow' in the technical sense extremely rarely. In the two passages (12:35-36, 46) where he connects 'believe' with 'light,' he speaks very differently."

38. U. Schnelle, "Die Abschiedsreden im Johannesevangelium," *ZNW* 80 (1989): 64-79, here 154.

39. It is also possible that Gos. Thom. 77 may also be taken as an independent witness for our logion. Admittedly, it is present here in a strongly gnosticized form and is also combined with other traditions: "Jesus said: / I am the light, the one who is above all. / I am the All, / (and) the All has come forth from me, / and the All has come to me. / Split a (piece of) wood, I am there. / Pick up the stone and you will find me there."

40. The reference is to Jesus's last spoken, solemn word of revelation in 7:37-38.

41. Probably the crowd to whom Jesus last spoke in 7:28-29, 33-34, 37-38.

The "I Am" Sayings

The saying is comprised of two parts, a head clause and a subordinate clause. Both are linked by the *inclusio* of "light of the world" and "light of life" in verse 12b/e. If one wants to divide the saying into semantic parts, the required division into 1 + 3 colas is plausible: Not only does verse 12c–e contain *three* verbs, but the separately written participle "the one who follows me" which replaces a relative clause, also represents a separate element of the saying that can be isolated *in terms of genre*, as the following diagram illustrates:

A. *Self-introduction formula with a word picture* (12b)
B. Soteriological consequence (12c–e)
   1. *Invitation* (12c)
   2. *Promise* (12d, e)
      2.1 Negative
      2.2 Positive

Three observations come to mind with this scheme, also in comparison with other first-person "I am" slogans:

(1) The element "invitation" has no independent syntactic status but is integrated into the promise clause in the form of a substantival participle (as in 6:35). Its statements are focused.

(2) This assumption is confirmed by the fact that the promise clause is worded twice, once negatively and once positively. This distinguishes it from 6:35, 10:9, and 14:6.

(3) The already mentioned *inclusio* around the saying, "light of the world" / "light of life" (12e), shows that the focus of the statement in the main clause is *not* on the subject ἐγώ = *I*, but on the *predication* "the light of the world," as this is explicated in the subordinate clause in verse 12c–e: the fact that Jesus is "the light of the world" means that the one who follows this light may also have the *certainty of receiving life and light*.

With regard to the *pragmatics of* the saying, these three observations allow us to draw the following conclusion: The saying is not intended as an instruction for *action*—verse 12c is not a call to discipleship!—and it should certainly not be read as a warning ("follow me, otherwise you will remain in darkness!"). Rather, his intention is to show listeners the fullness of salvation that has appeared in Christ and to give them the *certainty* that their discipleship also includes participation in the saving light of life. Whether the saying is directed at those who already believe, whom it strengthens in their certainty of faith, or at those who are willing to believe, to whom it wishes to show the saving perspective of their possible discipleship of Christ in a missionary and promotional way, is not yet certain. The focus of the saying is a promise, the special feature of which is that it arises from the head clause and draws its persuasive power from it.

As far as the *genre of* the saying is concerned, we have become accustomed (as with the other sayings) to calling it an I am–saying simply because of its initial words. According to our analysis so far, it moves (quite analogously to 6:35) into the vicinity of the *words of promise* to be dealt with in chapter 8. However, this characterization of the content is not satisfactory, because the specific feature of the saying—the connection between the *soteriological* perspective and the emphatically thematized *Christological* foundation—is not yet expressed. Characteristic of the saying is what is otherwise also true of the Johannine tradition. It is characterized by its *cognitive* coloring, its claim to ground the faith of Christians in a deeper *knowledge*, namely Christological knowledge, in a word of revelation. This occurs here by linking the promise back to the superscript "I am the light of the world," which names the *ground of being* for the perspective opened up in the subordinate clause.

If one reads the traditional saying on its own, then the emphasis should be on "light of the world." If we consider the context of chapters 7–8, new aspects emerge. Although the evangelist does not *explicitly* formulate the assertion of soteriological exclusivity in Christ here in opposition to the law or the temple, for example, the setting of the sequence of events in Jerusalem at the Feast of Tabernacles (Jesus does not make his claim anywhere, but in the temple!) suggests such an opposition: "*I* am the light of the world" would then have to be emphasized: "Do not seek this light anywhere, not even in your temple worship, but exclusively with me!"[42] If the evangelist wanted to direct us to such a Christological coding of other religious experiences of light through his quotation of 8:12, especially in the temple scene of chapters 7–8, then he must have reckoned with the corresponding knowledge of the Jewishly enculturated listener about the semantic richness of associations of the speech of the "light of the world." Although this is an archetypal, universal symbol that is understandable across cultures, it has a special form in early Jewish literature and history, as will be recalled below.

4.2.3 The Motif and Its Context

(1) "It is a fundamental religious experience of mankind that the divine is light and manifests itself in light."[43] In the Old Testament and early Judaism, the metaphor of light is also often enough applied to God and, what is of particular

---

42. During the nightly celebrations of the Feast of Tabernacles, the temple was illuminated by large candlesticks in the women's courtyard; m. Sukkah 5:3: "There was no courtyard in Jerusalem that did not reflect the light of the place of creation."

43. W. Beierwaltes, *Lux Intelligibilis. Untersuchung zur Lichtmetaphysik der Griechen* (München: Uni-Druck, 1957), 13.

The "I Am" Sayings

interest to us here in view of John 8:12*, to entities that *convey* God to man, such as the Torah, the Logos, Wisdom, the Messiah, or the temple. This is briefly documented below.

"For with you is the source of *life*, in your *light* we see the light," Psalm 36:10 says. "To see the light of God, to walk in his light [Isa 2:5; Ps 4:7; 89:16], is actually to live properly."[44] "Send your *light* and your *truth* to guide me; let them lead me to your holy mountain and to your dwelling place," prays the pious person in Psalm 43:3. God is the source and origin of light, but as these two testimonies reveal, it only shines indirectly and is mediated: In the sanctuary or in God's care for the righteous, which accompanies him to the sanctuary.

According to the early Jewish view, *God's word and instruction* above all reveal his light: "Your word is a lamp to my feet, a light to my paths" (Ps 119:105). And Proverbs 6:23 explains, "For the commandment is a lamp and the teaching is a light, and the reproofs of discipline are the way of life."

Here the ethical power of God's word is combined with its soteriological perspective in the service of the orientation of life; both are incorporated in the light-metaphor. It occurs often in statements about the Torah,[45] sometimes it is even equated with life. Testament of Levi 19:1 says: "And now, my children, you have heard everything. Choose for yourselves *the light* or the darkness, *the law of the Lord* or the works of Beliar!" And in Testament of Levi 14:3-4, the progenitor complains about his sons and descendants, "The heavens are purer than the earth; and you, the light-bringers of Israel,[46] (are) like the sun and the moon. What shall all nations do if you are darkened by wickedness? And you will bring a curse on our generation, for whom *the light of the law* was given to enlighten every man. This you will do away with by teaching him commandments contrary to the laws of God." The universal significance of the Torah for "all peoples" and "every human being," which is impressively expressed here, is also clear from the depiction of the Israelites' wilderness journey in Wisdom 18:3-4: "Instead of that darkness, you gave your people a flaming pillar of fire as a guide on an unknown path, as a friendly sun on their glorious journey. Those, on the other hand [s.c. the Egyptians], deserved to be deprived of light and imprisoned in darkness, because they once enclosed and imprisoned your sons, through whom *the imperishable light of*

---

44. F.-L. Hossfeld and E. Zenger, *Die Psalmen I. Psalm 1-50*, NEB 29 (Würzburg: Echter, 1993), 228. The preacher experiences God's closeness "in the temple area" (ibid.).

45. See Sir 32:16; 50:29 LXX; 2 Bar. 17:4; 18:1-2; 59:2; 77:16; 4 Es 4:20; LAB 11:1; 19:6; 23:10.

46. Or "Heavenly lights of Israel." For the textual variants see Jonge, The Testaments of the Twelve Patriarchs, 41.

the law was to be given to the world."⁴⁷ "A proper equation of light and Torah may (also) be found in 1QS 11:3 ('For from the fountain of His knowledge He opens His light') and 11:5 ('From His righteousness Born [streams] His law [as] light into my heart')."⁴⁸ R. Yehudah explains succinctly with reference to Proverbs 6:23: *"Light,* that is the Torah!"⁴⁹

If the Torah is light for the nations, then this also applies to *Israel,* the steward of the Torah.⁵⁰ The collective interpretation of the Servant Songs in Isaiah could have promoted such a statement, as they refer to the Servant as the "light of the nations" in Isaiah 42:6 and 49:6. This self-image of Israel is also reflected in Romans 2:17-19,⁵¹ and in Matthew 5:14 ("You are the light of the world") the first evangelist claimed it for the congregation of the Messiah Jesus, insofar as it is prepared to follow his radical interpretation of the Torah in its "works."

The image of the Son of Man, as depicted in 1 Enoch 48:4, stands in the gradient of an individual interpretation of Isaiah's Servant Songs: "And he will be a rod for the righteous, so that they may lean on him and not fall, and he will be the *light of the nations* and the hope of those who have sorrow in their hearts."⁵² The priestly Messiah of T. Levi 18 is also clothed in metaphors about

---

47. The same concept is present in Philo: "The law does not tolerate injustice any more than sunlight tolerates darkness. God, however, is the archetypal pattern of the laws, the sun of the sun, the source of light of the sensually perceptible (sun) that can only be grasped in thought, who guides visible rays from invisible sources to the perceptible" (*Spec. Laws* 1.279).

48. O. Böcher, *Der johanneische Dualismus im Zusammenhang des nachbiblischen Judentums* (Gütersloh: Mohn, 1965), 104, who also refers to 1QS 3:3, 20; 4:2: "As the light of the world... the Torah—alongside the temple—is also referred to by the *rabbis*: b. B. Bat. 4a (Murder of the rabbis according to Prov 6:23 as extinguishing the light of the world)." The text reads: "You have extinguished the *light of the world, as it says: for the* commandment *is a lamp and the law is a light* (Prov 6:23), go and deal now with the light of the world, as it says: *and all nations will flock to it* (Isa 2:2)" (Goldschmidt VIII 10).

49. b. Meg. 16b. Moreover, see b. Ḥag. 76c; b. Ket. 111b; b. Soṭ. 21a; Gen. Rab. 3:5; Mek. Exod. 13:18; Exod. Rab. 36:3; SNum 6:25; Deut. Rab. 4:4; 7:3. This also explains why in Jewish sacred art "only the candlestick and no other cult object was suitable to become the symbol of Judaism in general" (K. H. Rengstorf, "Zu den Fresken in der jüdischen Katakombe der Villa Torlonia in Rom," *ZNW* 31 [1932]: 33-60, here 57).

50. "Midrash Lamentations 1:3 (85A): As the oil brings light to the world, so Israel is the light for the world (אורה לעולם); see Isa 60:3: 'Nations will come to your light.'" (Str-B 1:237 [Eng. 1:264]).

51. Rom 2:17-19: "If you call yourself a Jew and rely on the law... and trust yourself to be a guide for the blind, a light for those in darkness (φῶς τῶν ἐν σκότει)...."

52. Uhlig, *JSHRZ* V/6 590.

The "I Am" Sayings

light: "He will shine like the sun on the earth, and he will take away all darkness from under heaven, and there will be peace in all the earth" (18:3).[53]

Of particular importance for the Christology of the Johannine communities are the light metaphors about wisdom and logos. The light metaphors on *wisdom* and the *Logos* are of particular importance for the Christology of the Johannine communities. We should mention Wisdom 7:26, according to which wisdom is "a reflection of the eternal light and a flawless mirror of God's activity and an image of his goodness."[54] Similar statements about wisdom can also be found in Philo, who also includes the divine Logos in his "metaphysics of light."[55]

Sayings about light in all its shades plays an enormous role in Philo's oeuvre. It is both *hermeneutical* (light = understanding) and *soteriological* (salvation = ascension to light) metaphor. The two are closely tied together whereby the soteriological perspective gives the central question of how the human *nous* can enter the heavenly, life-giving sphere of the divine light from the transient sphere of earthly life.

For Philo, God is absolutely transcendent,[56] but his "representations" λόγος, δύναμις ποιητική, and δύναμις βασιλική and the other (subordinate) δυνάμεις, the angels and messengers of God in Holy Scripture,[57] enter into a relationship with the world. Philo can describe their share of divinity in the image of a stream of light that emanates from God, the source of all light, flows into them and becomes ever weaker in the material world.[58]

---

53. For the comparison of Messiah and light in Tan. Exod., see D. Aune, *Revelation I-III*, WBC 52A-C (Dallas: Thomas Nelson, 1997-1998), 3:1167, 1170.

54. Aristobulus Fr. 5 refers to Gen 1:3 ("And God said: Let there be light! And there was light") to wisdom: "The same (statement) could also be applied to wisdom, for all light comes from it. Followers of the Peripatetic school have also said that (wisdom) has the task of a torch: whoever follows it constantly... will be unshakeable throughout his life. But even more clearly and better, one of our ancestors, Solomon, said that she was there before heaven and earth; this agrees with what was said before" (Walter, *JSHRZ* III/2 276). Aristobulus thus thinks of the preexistent wisdom in the light of wisdom in the footsteps of Prov 8:22-31. See also Philo, *Opif.* 30ff.

55. See E. R. Goodenough, *By Light, Light: The Mystic Gospel of Hellenistic Judaism* (New Haven, CT: Yale, 1935), passim.

56. "The highest possibility of transcendence in Plato was the idea of the good, Resp., VI, 509b. The negative attributes of light are an indication of enhanced transcendence in Philo, ἀσώματον in Conf. Ling., 61, ἀγένητον, Ebr., 208, ἀόρατον, Op. Mund., 31" (Conzelmann, "φῶς," *TDNT* 9, 331).

57. E. R. Goodenough, *Light*, 37: "The Logos and the Powers are modes or aspects of God's nature as well as of His activity."

58. "God is the source of the purest radiance, Mut. Nom., 6. This sounds emanationist, esp. as Philo can say in Platonic fashion that God is light, Som., I, 75; He is the sun of the sun. But the emanationist concept is qualified by the assertion that God is not the archetype of all other

God, that is, the light, can only be recognized through himself (*qua* an act of grace), not through man's own ability. The *principle* applies: *The same can only be recognized and seen by the same.*[59] Therefore, God can only be seen through God, as Philo explains this with a "parable" (εἴκων):

> Surely, we see our visible sun through nothing other than the sun? Likewise the stars through nothing but the stars? And is not light only seen through light? In the same way, God is his own light and is seen through himself alone, without anyone else helping or being able to help in the pure knowledge of his existence ... Only those people who gain the idea of God through God, *the idea of light through light*, arrive at the truth. (*Praem.* 45–46).

In detail, Philo develops this axiom in a variety of ways, scripturally oriented, unsystematic, and highly multifaceted. Three further aspects of his use of the metaphor of light should be added here: (a) Paradigmatically, Philo presents Abraham's *conversion* as an *ascent to the light*: "After Abraham had grown in this faith and had been a Chaldean (star worshipper) for a long time, he opened the eye of his soul as if from deep sleep ... and began to see pure light instead of deep darkness; he followed this light ... and perceived what he had not seen before, a ruler and leader of the world who rules over it and governs his own work in a salutary way" (*Abr.* 70).[60] Ascent as a soteriological process, often enough marked in its character of grace,[61] plays a paramount role in Philo. - (b) "As soon as the divine light shines forth, the human light perishes."[62] Encounters with the divine light therefore often enough bear traits of *ecstasy*, especially in the

---

light but is before every other archetype, Som., I, 75, and also by the doctrine of the δυνάμεις; the divine forces shine forth, not God Himself" (Conzelmann, "φῶς" *TDNT* 9, 330).

59. Philo, *Spec. Laws* 1.339: "But of the philosophical senses, through which (we) are granted to live well, the sense of sight sees light, the most beautiful thing among the existing things, but *with the help of light* it sees everything else." See, too, *Spec. Laws* 1.42 (see below); on the old Greek roots of this principle see Conzelmann, "φῶς" *TDNT* 9, moreover B. E. Gärtner, "The Pauline and Johannine Idea of 'to Know God' against the Hellenistic Background. The Greek Philosophical Principle 'Like by Like' in Paul and John," *NTS* 14 (1967/68): 209-231, here 210-215.

60. See also *Opif.* 69–71 for the depiction of the ascent of the human spirit into the divine spheres (following Plato's Phaedrus), where at the end, when the nous has reached the highest peak of the purely spiritual, it says: "When he is now eager to look, pure and unclouded rays of full light pour over him in streams, so that the spiritual eye is dazzled by their brilliance" (*Opif.* 70).

61. See D. Zeller, *Charis bei Philon und Paulus*, SBS 142 (Stuttgart: Katholisches Bibelwerk, 1990), 33–128.

62. *Her.* 264.

The "I Am" Sayings

case of extraordinary people such as the prophets. Philo shows this in a detailed interpretation of Genesis 15:12, where the LXX reads: "Toward *sunset, a feeling of being outside himself* (ἔκστασις) fell on Abraham."[63] - (c) As already indicated, the encounter with the divine light takes place through the mediation of the Logos in particular as the manifestation of God's creative-organizing reason. This can be nicely illustrated by an allegorical interpretation of Genesis 28:11 that Philo adopted from his predecessors, whom he follows: "He [s.c. Jacob] came to a place (τόπος); for the sun was going down," according to the basic biblical text. "Some assumed that *the sun* here symbolically means sensuality and spirit—the reasons for knowledge usually assumed in ourselves—but the *place* means the divine Logos, and interpreted the passage in this way: The virtuous met the divine Logos when the mortal and human light went down. For as long as the spirit firmly grasps the spiritual and sensuality the sensual and believes itself to be circling on high, the divine Logos stands far away; but as soon as both have admitted their impotence and, as it were sinking, have disappeared, the right Logos immediately comes greeting us, the support of a virtuous soul that gives itself up, but awaits the [Logos] approaching invisibly from outside" (*Somn.* 1.118–119). Philo also sees the Logos elsewhere as a manifestation of the divine light.[64]

Let us break off the overview of biblical and early Jewish metaphorical texts about light! From what has become clear so far, John 8:12* appears to be at the intersection of different currents. Light falls on our saying both from the individually interpreted servant songs ("light of the nations") and from the soteriological understanding of the Torah as well as from the figures of wisdom and the logos in Philo. Can this network of relationships be narrowed down even further?

(2) In addition to the exclusive Christological use of the light metaphor, the trademark of John 8:12* is the *light-darkness dualism* associated with it. It also has a rich history in early Jewish literature that can hardly be reduced to a common denominator.

The Testaments of the Twelve Patriarchs and the Qumran writings such as 1QS should be mentioned in particular. In the Testaments of the Twelve Patriarchs, the antithetical use of the metaphor of light and darkness primarily has an ethical orientation: Those who walk in the way of the law choose the light, those who do the works of Beliar fall into darkness (T. Levi 19:1). The contrast between light and darkness is occasionally intensified eschatologically, for example in

---

63. *Her.* 249–267; 265: "Mortal things cannot dwell together with immortal things. Therefore, the *downfall of reason* and the *darkness* surrounding it brought about an ecstasy (ἔκστασις) and God-born rapture (μανία)."

64. See *Opif.* 31; *Leg.* 3.171: "What would be more brilliant or radiant than the divine Logos (θείου λόγου), since only by sharing in him can the other beings also banish the fog and darkness in their longing to share in the light of the soul (φωτὸς κοινωνῆσαι ψυχικοῦ)?"; *Somn.* 1.75.

the outlook of the Testament of Joseph, where it says: "And he will bring you to the promises of your fathers. But carry my bones with you, for when the bones are brought there, the Lord will be with you *in light*, and Beliar will be with the Egyptians in *darkness*" (T. Jos. 20.1–2). In Qumran, the light-darkness dualism takes on a special form through its obvious reference to the community: Even if truth and injustice are generally attributed to the "source of light" or the "source of darkness" (1QS 3:19) and the front between the two can also run through man himself,[65] there is no doubt that with the "sons of light" (1QS 1:9; 3:13, 24–25), who "walk in the ways of light" (1QS 3:20), refers to the Essene community of the pious, whereas those outside, those who are distant from the community, are called "sons of darkness" (1QS 1:10). Such an ecclesiological "reckoning" of the light-darkness dualism then also has an eschatological component, as the antithetical images of 1QS 4:6–8 (8: abundance of peace "in eternal light") and 4:11–14 (13: "perdition of darkness") in particular show.[66]

John 8:12* exacerbates the early Jewish dualism, which in his case is "worldview-based," but is primarily a function of the overarching Christological statement of exclusivity: if in Christ alone, as the manifestation of God (ἐγώ εἰμι), the saving light of life dawns on the world, then, apart from the epiphany of Christ, *only* darkness reigns in it, death devouring everything in the end.[67] If salvation does not arise from the world itself but only comes to it from outside, from *God*, then for the matrix of the saying this means that it is formed more according to analogies of *wisdom, Logos concepts*, or the Torah given *by God* to Israel than the model of *human* light bearers such as the servant of God. This assumption is confirmed by the following terminological observations.

(3) Only a few parallels can be found in early Jewish biblical literature for the phrase "light of life."[68] The syntagma "light of the world," which is usually derived from Isaiah 42:7 and 49:6, is better placed. But there the role assigned to the Servant of God of being the "light of the *nations*" surpasses his mission to

---

65. See 1QS 3:20fin–21. In the background is the problem that even the righteous continue to sin, although they are under the rule of the Prince of Light.

66. See also 1 En. 108:12, 14: "And I will bring out into the bright light those who have loved my holy name. . . . And they will see how those who were born in darkness will be led into darkness, while the righteous will shine."

67. In principle, the Johannine statement is the same as in 4 Esdras 14:20: "For the world lies in darkness, and its inhabitants are without light." However, the reasoning that follows in v. 21 ("because your law has been burned up, no one knows what has been done by you, nor what deeds are to be done") shows that the focus here is not fundamentally on the "nature" of the world but on the current situation after the destruction of Jerusalem.

68. Ps 56:14; Job 33:30; 1QS 3:6–7 ("for by the Spirit of God's true counsel a man's ways are atoned for, all his sins, so that he may see the *light of life*"); Midr. Ps. (= Midr. The.) 56:4.

Israel, thus introducing a distinction that is not implied in the cosmic-universal formula "light of the *world*." Furthermore, the closest New Testament parallel, namely Matthew 5:14 ("You are *the light of the world*"), a sentence probably composed by the first evangelist himself,[69] which, contrary to the opinion of some scholars, is not connected with the Johannine saying. Contrary to the opinion of some scholars, it has *no* historical connection with the Johannine saying but merely coincides with it in the formulaic syntagma "light of the world." But this is instructive enough: Matthew calls the Christian community the "light of the world" because he expects "good works" (Matt 5:16) from it in accordance with Jesus's more stringent interpretation of the Torah (i.e., Torah piety under the sign of Jesus's instruction to love one's enemies); this indicates that he connected the syntagma "light of the world" with the Torah, as is also seen in Testament of Leviticus 14:4 and Wisdom 18:4 (see above).[70] This should be a clear indication that the predication "light of the world" in John 8:12* also comes from Jewish Torahology.

4.2.4 The Message and Intention of the Saying

A lot has already been said about both in the course of the preceding remarks. Three things should be added:

(1) Is the saying conceived as the word of the *exalted* Christ or of the *earthly* Jesus?[71] The transformation of the model of discipleship that originally adhered to the earthly Jesus into an expression for the realization of faith that includes "the entire way of life"[72] points in the first direction: The saying proclaims the word of the exalted Christ, and the soteriological exclusivity stated here applies to him.

(2) It is worth dwelling a little on the *temporal relationships* of the secondary sentences 8:12d, e*.[73] It seems remarkable that they are not unambiguous. οὐ μή with conjunction aorist in 12d and the future tense in 12e are two sides of the same coin and thus are used in the same sense: If the formulation with οὐ μή, which is often encountered in the Gospel, represents "the strongest negation

---

69. See Luz, *Matthäus*, 1:219–220.

70. Similarly, Böcher, *Dualismus*, 104: "due to the context (Matt 5:16: good works; Matt 5:17ff.: Torah sharpening), Matt 5:14 proves to be less a transfer of a title of honor of Jesus [s.c. John 8:12] to his disciples than a continuation of Jewish mission consciousness and Jewish Torah piety."

71. An answer to this question also has consequences for the other first-person "I am" sayings.

72. Bultmann, *Johannes*, 261 n. 1, on the περιπατεῖν of the saying.

73. The following also applies *mutatis mutandis* to 6:35, since the same temporal relationships are present here (cf. above p. 251 with n. 36).

of a statement about the future,"[74] the indicative future ("it is the only Greek indicative form in which the *temporal stage,* but not the aspect, is expressed"[75]) conveys the assurance that "the one who follows *will have* the light of life." The sentence enters a temporal state of uncertainty when one considers the point of view from which it is formulated. Can it be said that the envisaged future begins when the listener follows Jesus?[76] Or, *Whoever follows me has life before him; he will never again* (or: *certainly not*) *walk in darkness*? It seems to me that no matter how one interprets the sentence, the aspect of a real (salvific) future is constitutively part of its statement, without the emphasis being on it in the sense of an explicitly futuristic eschatology. Rather, the saying is primarily concerned with conveying the *certainty* to the addressees that life is resolved (already now or in its full form when death is overcome) in the fulfillment of their following of Christ (and only in it). In other words: If one wanted to interpret the saying in the sense of a pointed present-eschatological statement, then this could probably be justified from the overall context of the Gospel; in the saying itself, however, the aspect of time remains at least in limbo, unless the future is clearly co-thematized in 12e.[77] The observations made show that the specific Johannine concept of a present eschatology derives from Christology as it can be grasped in sayings such as John 8:12*. For if it is true that the only light of life truly worthy of this name appeared eschatologically in Jesus, then it is not far from this exclusive soteriological thesis to the insight that the time of the real possession of that life is not important, but rather that the light of life is *already* dawning on the believer *now*, namely in his encounter with the exalted, present Christ. The *evangelist's present eschatology is fed not insignificantly by important Christological sayings given by the congregation*, as the I am–sayings in particular prove.

(3) There is much to suggest that the saying is directed more at those who already believe than that it has a missionary, promotional intention. For those who are following Christ and are perhaps challenged by competing offers of salvation from their environment, it attempts to convey certainty about their own path. If the saying (as well as the other I am–sayings) has its *Sitz im Leben* in the worshipping assembly of the Johannine congregations, then this would confirm its presumed objective.

---

74. HvS § 247a. See John 4:14; 6:35; 8:51, 52; 10:28; 11:26; 13:8. The οὐ μή with conj. aor. occurs also in the synoptic logia: see Matt 5:20; 18:3; Mark 9:1; Luke 13:35; 21:18.

75. HvS § 202.

76. But then, instead of the present participle ὁ ἀκολουθῶν, an aorist participle would be expected.

77. Also, the use of the syntagm "light of life" in the few biblical-early Jewish references (see above) also points in this direction.

4.2.5 The Saying about Light
Continuation of a Synoptic Tradition?

Recent research has attempted to use various ways of relating the Johannine saying about light to synoptic words of Jesus, above all to Matthew 5:14–16.[78] However, no saying can be identified to which John 8:12* could have been linked. It is more reasonable to assume that the saying about light generally draws on the Jesus tradition. The motif of "discipleship,"[79] which no longer plays a prominent role in the Johannine tradition, points in this direction. Two texts that are closely related to John 8:12* in terms of *motifs* are noteworthy, without it being possible to say that John 8:12* presupposes them or follows on directly from them. But they show that the identification of Jesus with the light, as explicitly offered in John 8:12*, is in line with synoptic tradition.

The first text, Matthew 4:15–16, 17 contains a quotation from Isaiah 8:23–9:1, which leads to the climax: "The people sitting in darkness saw a great light (φῶς μέγα), and to those sitting in the land and shadow of death light has dawned (φῶς ἀνέτειλεν αὐτοῖς)."[80] This is followed by the sentence: "From then on Jesus began to preach and say, 'Repent, for the kingdom of heaven is at hand'" (Matt 4:17). With this sequence of texts, how else can we understand the prophecy by Jesus about light shining on those in darkness other than as a magnificent image of the person of Jesus himself and his salvific message of the kingdom of God that he came to deliver?[81]

The second text is the figurative word of the lamp in the version of Mark 4:21.[82] Only the oldest evangelist begins with the formulation: "Is a lamp brought

---

78. This is contradicted by the fact that Matt 5:14 goes back to the editorial work of the first evangelist and not to an ancient tradition.

79. To speak about "faith" is much more important in John. "Following" in a technical sense mostly appears in older traditions: John 1:37–38, 40, 43; 10:4, 5; 12:26; 13:36–37; see also 21:19, 22.

80. On the textual form of the quotation in Matt, see Luz, *Matthäus*, 1:169: Because the predicate ἀνέτειλεν does not correspond to the Hebrew text and also not to the Septuagint (λάμψει), he asks whether a reminder of Num 24:17 is implied. If so, the wording of the quotation presumably presupposes a messianic interpretation of Isa 8:23–24 and a Christian interpretation at that, since the passage was not interpreted messianically in Judaism." In Judaism, Isa 9:1 referred to enlightenment through the Torah: Str-B 1:162 [Eng. 1:181]; 4:961.

81. Conzelmann, "φῶς," *TDNT* 9:335: "The question whether light symbolises the person or the teaching of the Messiah misses the relation between the two in Mt. and the position of the quotation in context. The light symbolism should not be restricted to the person; the teaching is included"; also Luz, *Matthäus*, 1:172.

82. The logion exists in a double tradition. In addition to Mark 4:31 par. Matt 5:15; Luke 8:16, see also Luke 11:33.

(ἔρχεται) in to be put under the bushel?" It is very likely that this opening comes from Mark, as the personalization here, as in the following saying in Mark 4:22, suggests a Christological understanding.[83] The metaphor of the lamp—originally a pure parable of Jesus for the assertiveness and revelatory quality of the *basileia* proclaimed by him—has been traced back by Mark to its Christological basis: Jesus is the light, the lamp that has "come"[84] to be revealed; it corresponds to his nature as light when he steps out of concealment as the "Son of God" into the publicity of his worldwide proclamation in the Gospel (see Mark 13:10; 14:9).

Against the background of these observations, the result of 4.2.3 is that the syntagma "light of the world"—the hallmark of our logion—comes from early Jewish Torahology. This assumption also offers the best explanation for the indirect reference between John 8:12* and Matthew 5:14a.

4.2.6 The Saying about Light as Seen by the Evangelist

We do not need to go into the leitmotif of John 8:12* in John 9:4-5; 11:9-10; and 12:35-36, 46 here.[85] The story of Jesus, the "light of the world," healing the man born blind comments on our logion with great literary vividness. In all these texts, the encounter with the *exalted* Christ, as expressed in John 8:12*, is linked back to the historically unique *kairos* of the appearance of the *earthly* Jesus: *"As long as I am in the world*, I am the light of the world" (9:5). *"Only for a little while longer is the light with you.* So walk *while you have the light*, so that the darkness does not overtake you . . . *While you have the light*, believe in the light, so that you may become sons of light!" (12:35-36). Concerning Jesus's encounter with the Jewish crowd, the evangelist is saying that there is a *kairos* of decision that is definite; this also applies to the hearers of the Gospel in the post-Easter period!

The verses that immediately follow John 8:12 (i.e., 8:13-20) are noteworthy. Two views are in opposition to one another. The first emphasizes the independence and isolation of the logion in its context, which can go so far as to claim that it is interchangeable. According to this view, what is important is not *what* the evangelist has Jesus say but only *that* Jesus speaks revelatory words.[86] The second position recognizes that in 8:13-20 not a single significant lexeme from

---

83. See H.-J. Klauck, *Allegorie und Allegorese in synoptischen Gleichnistexten*, NTA.NF 13 (Münster: Aschendorff, 1978), 234, 236.

84. See ἔρχεσθαι in Mark 1:7, 9, 14, 24, 39; 2:17; 10:45; 11:9!

85. Theobald, *Fleischwerdung*, 305-321; O. Schwankl, "Die Metaphorik von Licht und Finsternis im johanneischen Schrifttum," in *Metaphorik und Mythos im Neuen Testament*, ed. K. Kertelge, QD 126 (Freiburg: Herder, 1990), 135-167.

86. See Becker, *Johannes*, 1:339: "John 8:12 can be replaced in the composition by any other word of revelation, e.g., by 7:37-38 with which it shares a completely analogous kind of function."

The "I Am" Sayings

8:12 is taken up again but draws attention to the highly sublime way in which the logion is integrated into its context. The verses that follow say:

> 13 Then the Pharisees said to him,
> "You are testifying *on your own behalf;*
> your testimony is not valid."
> 14 Jesus answered and said to them,
> "Even if I testify *on my own behalf,*
> my testimony is valid
> because *I know*
> where I have come from
> and where I am going,
> but you do not know
> where I come from
> or where I am going.
> 15 You judge by human standards;
> I judge no one.
> 16 Yet even if I do judge,
> my judgment is valid;
> for it is not I alone who judge
> but I and the Father who sent me."

What the evangelist stages in this dialogue, which continues up to 8:19, is the insight that Jesus's testimony can be nothing other than *self-testimony*. It does not speak of earthly, perceivable facts but is a testimony about his divine origin: "The subject is not a generally accessible objective fact but is Jesus as the messenger of God. To put it another way: God's self-testimony in Jesus. This testimony is dependent on self-evidence, which also explains the choice of the metaphor of light in verse 12, for light is also self-evident."[87]

This connection has probably been correctly observed. Just as light and darkness confront each other in the logion, so also in the following dialogue "knowledge" and "ignorance" (vv. 14, 19), "truth" (vv. 13–14, 16:) and falsehood in an earthly judgment (= σάρξ [v. 15]). Jesus's testimony is true. It is not diffuse

---

87. K. Wengst, *Das Johannesevangelium I–II*, ThK.NT 4.1–2 (Stuttgart: Kohlhammer, 2000–2001), 314, with reference to Barrett, *Johannes*, 343, according to whom the metaphor of v. 12 "fits its context perfectly, since the light can do nothing other than bear witness to itself, because it is authenticated by its source."

but has the form of knowledge (v. 14). It is full of inner clarity and *light*. The fact that it *can* only be *self-testimony* due to its specific subject matter, and that it therefore cannot be measured by standards and criteria and tested for a truth that lies *outside* itself, corresponds to the Greek principle of knowledge of like through like.[88] This can be deepened with the help of a text by Philo that has not yet been taken into account in commentary on John 8:12:

> Though we cannot attain to a distinct conception of the *truly living* God, we still ought not to renounce the task of investigating his character, because even if we fail to make the discovery, the very search itself is intrinsically useful and an object of deserved ambition; since no one ever blames the eyes of the body because they are unable to look upon the sun itself, and therefore shrink from the brilliancy which is poured upon them from its beams, and therefore look down upon the earth, shrinking from the extreme brilliancy of the rays of the sun. Which that interpreter of the divine word, Moses, the man most beloved by God, having a regard to, besought God and said, "*Show me thyself*" (Exod 33:13)—all but urging him, and crying out in loud and distinct words—"that thou hast a real being and existence (τοῦ μὲν εἶναί καὶ ὑπάρχειν) the whole world is my teacher, assuring me of the fact and instructing me as a son might of the existence of his father, or the work of the existence of the workman. But, though I am very desirous to know what thou art *as to thy essence* (κατὰν τὴν οὐσίαν), I can find no one who is able to explain to me anything relating to this branch of learning in any part of the universe whatever. (42) On which account, I beg and entreat of thee to receive the supplication of a man who is thy suppliant and devoted to God's service, and desirous to serve thee alone; *for as the light is not known by the agency of anything else, but is itself its own manifestation, so also thou must alone be able to manifest thyself.* For which reason I hope to receive pardon, if, from want of any one to teach me, I am so bold as to flee to thee, desiring to receive instruction from thyself." (Philo, *Spec. Laws* 1.40–42)[89]

---

88. See above p. 170 and n. 59.

89. Translation by C. D. Young. The continuation of this text is also interesting: After God denied Moses his request on the grounds that "the understanding of my nature is ... denied not only to man, but also to the whole heaven and the universe. *Therefore know thyself* (γνῶθι δὴ σαυτόν)" (44), Moses rephrases his request to at least let him see "the glory that surrounds him," by which he means the δυνάμεις at his side (45). In the end (46–50) it becomes clear that Moses—in accordance with the Delphic maxim—can only see the divine δυνάμεις through his own reason, purified of all sensuality, admittedly not themselves, but only the countless wax impressions that they leave behind in the world—visible "not to the physical eye, but only to the

This text shows two things very well: (1) how obvious it must have been for the fourth evangelist to connect the saying about light with a reflection on the necessity of its *self-evidence*, which made it impossible for the Revelator to be witnessed by others, and (2) that the metaphor of light expresses the *divinity* of the Revelator by itself. This prompted the evangelist to define the relationship of the Revelator to God precisely. He does this with commentary in the scene found in 8:13-19, more precisely in the second part of that scene (vv. 16c-19). There, he defines the relationship of the Revelator to God as that of the *Son* to his *Father who sent him*. It can be seen that the dramatic embedding of the saying about light has certainly triggered a deep thoughtfulness with regard to its theological revelatory content.[90]

4.3 The Way of Life Saying (John 14:6)

The way of life saying in John 14:6 arises from the stream of the first farewell discourse like a rock.[91] This indicates that the saying originally existed as an independent logion in its own right.[92] The way in which the evangelist leads over to it and prepares for it in the transitionary verses in 4-5 following verses 2-3 already confirms this assumption.

4.3.1 The Introduction of the Way of Life Saying

Technically, the evangelist creates the transition by anticipating the keyword of the saying in verse 6, namely the "way" (ὁδός), in verse 4. *After* verse 6 and *before* the "transition" in verses 4-5, one searches in vain for the keyword in the farewell discourses. However, the idea present in it is already implicit in the logion in

---

untiring eye of the spirit" (49). Even according to John, God's nature is not revealed directly, but only through Christ, not to the physical eye, but only to faith, which sees more deeply.

90. It is debatable whether the recourse to the logion in John 8:12* was also prompted by the context, i.e., the setting of the Feast of Tabernacles. The symbolism of water and light is known to have played an important role. Not only are numerous water offerings made, which are drawn from the Pool of Siloam (see John 9:7, also pp. 270-271 on 7:37-38), the women's forecourt of the temple is also illuminated at night for the festival. The traditional character of John 8:12 does not argue against an association of this kind, since the *choice of* the saying (not just its wording) may have been determined by such an association. Schnackenburg, *Johannesevangelium*, 2:240, for example, argues for a connection between 8:12 and the overarching scene.

91. See Becker, *Johannes*, 2:552: "Alongside 3:16, 14:6 is rightly regarded as a compact statement of John's Christianity."

92. Becker, *Johannes*, 2:552; Lindars, *John*, 472-473: "we should look for a specific saying in the underlying tradition"; see below in 4.3.5.

verses 2–3, which speaks of Jesus's "going" and "coming again." Another "device" is added to the use of keywords: "Something that has yet to be clarified—Jesus's whereabouts and his way—is asserted as something that has already been clarified [in v. 4]. The objection provoked by this opens up the clarifying dialogue."[93] As is often the case in the Gospel, a disciple's misunderstanding serves here as a "literary device to enable further explication."[94]

In terms of content, the saying is introduced through the deliberate use of a semantic blank space that creates ambiguity: "Wherever I go, you know *the way*" (v. 4). The narrative does not clarify what type of path this is. In the context of the preceding clause ("where I am going"), it seems to refer to the path *Jesus* intends to take in death to his Father's "house." At any rate, this is how Thomas understands Jesus's provocative assertion when he replies in helplessness: "Lord, we do not know where you are going; how can we know the way?" (v. 5). But is this passage really about the way which *Jesus* wants to go? Or does the absolute usage of ὁδός in verse 4, which does not allow an explicit interpretation in this sense, rather prepare the perspective offered in verse 6 where the way of the *faithful* to the Father is the topic? Above all, however, Thomas seems to make a differentiation in his answer between the path and the one who walks on it (i.e., Jesus). This may have been deliberately staged by the evangelist in order to be able to proclaim Jesus himself all the more effectively as the way par excellence in verse 6. The absolute use of ὁδός in Jesus's assertion in verse 4 also points to this.

The disciples' lack of understanding is provoked by verse 4, but it cannot be overlooked that it is also foreshadowed by the *metaphorical-spatial language* of verses 2–3. For when it says "I am going to prepare a place for you . . . , I will come again and take you to myself," this could be understood to mean a distinction must be made between the path to the heavenly dwellings (which in Jesus's case would have to be imagined as an exaltation or rapture to God) and the one who "goes" on it. This is also because the path for Jesus's disciples should ultimately be the same, with the difference that Jesus, as the "heavenly quartermaster,"[95] has gone before him and his disciples will follow him some time later. Thus, the narrative already prepares for the disciples' lack of understanding which comes in verse 5. On the other hand, the illumination of verses 2–3 offered does not correspond to the interpretation the evangelist suggests. The way motif is not emphasized here at all. The accent is rather on the believers' right to dwell in the heavenly dwellings Jesus provides for them. His "going" to heaven is only the necessary prerequisite for this. In this respect, verses 2–3 already assert an

---

93. Dietzfelbinger, *Abschied*, 35, with reference to the technical parallel 3:3–8.

94. Becker, *John*, 2:551.

95. Blank, *Johannes*, 2:75.

absolute Christological advantage but do not yet do so by means of the way metaphor.⁹⁶

Verse 6 is different, and this is already indicated by the semantic independence of this saying. In order to lead us to it, the evangelist takes up the idea of the way implied in verse 2 in the "bridge dialogue" in verses 4–5, but then thoroughly pushes it aside in verse 6. The spatial element is interpreted personally here.⁹⁷ The path of believers to God therefore does not include, as one might initially think following verses 2–3, their (future) relocation with Jesus to the heavenly dwellings at his parousia. No, Jesus *himself* is the path. This means nothing other than the fact that access to God is *already* opened and realized for believers through *him*. The accent in verse 6, read in the style of verses 4–5, is placed here, that is, on a proper understanding of the person of Jesus. The "I" is the focus.⁹⁸ However, as the formal and semantic analysis of this passage shows, the saying itself goes beyond its integration into this new context.

4.3.2 Observations on the Form and Semantic Profile of the Saying

The fact that the logion actually has its own status in relation to the context is shown by observations on its form, which is rounded in itself.

14:6 a Jesus said to him (sc. Thomas):
      b I am the way, and the truth, and the life.
      c no one comes to the Father
      d except through me.

---

96. Michaelis, "ὁδός," *TDNT* 5, 78, is correct: "As Jesus is not ranged alongside His disciples in 14:2, as the μοναί are for them, not also for Him, so in 14:3 His going into the house of God is not parallel to theirs." In 14:3, too, "the focus is not on the similarity of walking, but only on being together at the same destination."

97. Dietzfelbinger, *Abschied*, 38: "The question in v. 5 was about the way Jesus must travel to the heavenly dwellings. Verse 6 not only omits any explanation about the Father's house. The spatial concept of the way is also replaced by the person of Jesus, and instead of the Father's house, to which Jesus sets out according to vv. 2–3, the reference is to the Father himself. But he does not dwell in a fixed place, even if it is in heaven. Rather, he is accessible through Jesus and only through Jesus."

98. "*I* am the way!" Therefore, do not look for the way somewhere else, for example in a future rapture to God, in which case I would only be the companion. But I am not! For I will not become superfluous once you have traveled the path. I *myself* am the way, and in me lies the goal.

Syntactically, the saying has two halves, a *positive* explanation consisting of a first-person "I am" introduction and three predicate nominatives, as well as a *negatively* worded explication with a concessive clause ("unless by me"). The syntactic independence of the concluding statement necessitates the presence of *three* colas (14:6b, c, d). Stylistically, the saying is characterized by the *inclusio* ("I" [ἐγώ]—ἐμοῦ ["me"])[99] and a *chiasmus*: I – way / come – me. This allows us to read it as a sequence of the following *four* parts:

A   I am

B   the way...;

B'   no one comes to the Father,

A'   except through me.

What B says in the figurative saying about "the way," B' formulates verbally; at the same time, B' communicates that the "way" meant in B is access to the *Father*. That B' is connected directly with B by the two nouns "truth" and "life" reveals the special status of this word pair alongside the keyword "the way." If the phrase ἡ ἀλήθεια καὶ ἡ ζωή also stands out from this figurative saying due to its degree of abstraction, it is also irrelevant to the *structure* of the saying. De la Potterie therefore rightly speaks of their character as being "secondary to the theme expressed in ὁδός; they are simply a commentary on it."[100]

Does this analysis reveal anything about the *semantic profile* of the saying? The focus is on ἡ ὁδός = "the way," that is, Jesus's self-predication. It denotes a unique soteriological dignity, namely that Jesus opens up access to the heavenly world for people. The resumption of the self-predication in B' (the way to the Father = God) confirms this.[101] The explanatory phrase then focuses back on δι' ἐμοῦ: Jesus presents himself as the only true way to the Father (= God), in contrast to all possible (self-proclaimed) healers. However, this semantic potential

---

99. I. de la Potterie, "Je suis la Voie, la Vérité et la Vie (Jn 14,6)," *NRTh* 88 (1966): 907–942, here 916, draws attention to this, although he defines the chiasmus noted above differently with regard to its middle members: "The verse indicates twice what Jesus is for his own people: at the beginning, as an image (ἐγώ εἰμι ἡ ὁδός), at the end, by means of a preposition (δι' ἐμοῦ)." It is true that in the Christological use of the preposition διά, its "original local sense" (Oepke, "διά" *TDNT* 2:67) may also "shine through" under its instrumental sense (as in John 10:9; Rom 5:2; Eph 2:18; Heb 7:25); but if one wants to discover a chiasmus in the logion, then it is more obvious to establish its middle members in the explicitly *local* phrases ὁδός and ἔρχεται πρός

100. De la Potterie, "Voie," 916 (emphasis mine).

101. It is possible that, on the part of the addressees/hearers, the saying ties in with a familiar theological use of the figurative saying about the "way." On the motif-critical analysis of the saying see below!

is not used in the following context (for example, in such a way that competing agents of salvation are explicitly named). It is also noteworthy that the claim it makes is *universal*: "*No one* comes to the Father except through me."[102] In other words, the saying is not primarily about the *disciples*, as the context would suggest, but goes beyond this to proclaim the absolute salvific significance of Jesus for *every* human being.

4.3.3 Tradition-Criticism Arguments

The last observations already show that in John 14:6 we are dealing with an originally independent "*word of the Lord*" from the Johannine community tradition. Overall, the following arguments speak in favor of this hypothesis:

(1) Despite its contextual integration, the saying betrays a relative isolation that is an indication of its original independence:

(a) *Formally*, the saying is not designed as an answer to a question. Its affirmative form does not indicate that it was composed from the outset for a dialogically structured text. In comparison, verse 7 with its use of the second person plural immediately directs us back to the conversational situation that determines the framework.

(b) *In terms of content*, the relative isolation of the saying in context is noticeable in different ways:

- Its *fundamental nature*, which transcends the conversation with the disciples, attracts attention. Dietzfelbinger speaks of the "element of exclusivity" in the I am–saying, which has "only an incidental function" in the context, while the saying, "taken in isolation, has the exclusivity of Jesus at its center. This confirms that verse 6 was available to the evangelist and that he took it over unchanged into his train of thought, into which it fits with only part of its content."[103]
- The idea of Christological exclusivity is verbalized in the saying with the help of the absolute *metaphor about the way*. Even if the narrative attempts to integrate it with verses 2–3 with keyword connections ὁδός (= way) and ἔρχεσθαι (= walk), it has its own status thanks to its personal intensification in verse 6 compared to the unpronounced use of the motif in the overarching spatial conceptual framework of verses 2–3.

---

102. Michaelis, "ὁδός," *TDNT* 5, 80: "Nor is the validity of 6b verbally restricted to the circle of the disciples who are addressed just before and just after; we find, not οὐδεὶς ἐξ ὑμῶν, but οὐδείς (cf. Mt. 11:27)."

103. Dietzfelbinger, *Abschied*, 38.

- According to verses 2–3, which speak of the soteriological necessity of Jesus's imminent *departure* as the heavenly "quartermaster," Jesus is only "the way" to God because of his *death*. According to the present tense statement in verse 6, however, he *is fundamentally* so, apparently without any temporal condition. John 14:6 therefore does not contain a statement about the necessity of Jesus's death, as the context would suggest, but one about the salvific function of his *person* as such, although the post-Easter perspective, for which Jesus's death is already a prerequisite, is probably implied.

(c) The relative isolation of the saying in the context is also shown by the continuation of the farewell discourse. The connection of verse 7 to the "I am" saying is revealing:

6 c No one comes to the Father (πρὸς τὸν πατέρα),
   d except through me (εἰ ... δι ἐμοῦ).
7 a If you know me (εἰ ... μέ),
   b you will know my Father also (τὸν πατέρα μου);
   c From now on you do know him
   d and have seen him.

Obviously, verse 7 is connected to the second half of the "I am" saying through a chiasm:[104] the concessive clause "except through me" corresponds to the conditional clause "if you know me," the metaphorical phrase "comes to the Father" corresponds to the conceptual "you will know my Father also." Verse 7 not only applies the saying to the conversational situation of the farewell discourse ("you"), it also reintroduces the temporal component with respect to the fictitious situation of the hour of farewell.[105] Above all, the evangelist's commentary on the "I am" saying, which begins with verse 7, translates its figurative language into *conceptual-theological* diction: reaching the Father through Jesus means nothing other than that the recognition of the Father happens in the recognition of Jesus. "The idea of the way, which was dissolved in the personal in verse 6, is now completely abandoned; it no longer appears in the corpus of the saying."[106]

---

104. Schnackenburg, *Johannes*, 3:75: "Verse 7 can be understood as the positive turn of what is said in v. 6b [= c, d]: No one comes to the Father except through Jesus; but through him one really comes to the Father."

105. "You *will* recognize," "*already now* (ἀπ' ἄρτι) you recognize him, you *have* seen him."

106. Dietzfelbinger, *Abschied*, 38. Spatial ideas, which dominated from v. 2 onward, now recede altogether or are compressed into the one local preposition ἐν = *in*, which is the condensed expression for the deeply personal togetherness of Father and Son (vv. 10–11, 13).

In short: the relationship between verse 6 and the following verses can best be described as a sequence of (given) pretext which is followed by commentary that deepens the meaning of what has been said.

(2) The saying rests in itself. *Formally*, it is well-rounded; *in terms of content*, too, it urges readers to understood on its own terms (see b above).

(3) In terms of word frequency, it is remarkable that ὁδός (= way), apart from 14:4–6 (3 times), does not occur elsewhere in the Gospel or in 1–3 John, with the exception of John 1:23. There, the figurative word refers to the Baptist as a forerunner and is accompanied by a quotation of Isa 40:3. The construction *negation* + εἰ μή is often found in the Johannine sayings tradition,[107] and the absolute ὁ πατήρ (= the Father)[108] as well as the metaphorical ἔρχεσθαι (= walking) are also found there. Therefore, there is nothing to support J. Beutler's thesis that, apart from the traditional motif of the way, verse 6 as a whole is attributable to the redaction of the evangelist.[109]

The question remains as to whether the "I am" saying as a whole goes back to tradition or whether the evangelist redacted it. Only the triad "the way, and the truth, and the life" is up for discussion.

Dietzfelbinger is of the opinion that in the present context of the farewell address, the evangelist finds "no use" for the keywords "truth" and "life." "The context forces him to concentrate on 'way.'" When asked why verse 6 nevertheless contains the other two predicates, he answers: "Because the figurative word with its three predicates already existed before our text was written. This means, however, that it comes from a tradition that was available to the evangelist. He adopted it unchanged but only evaluated it in part."[110] The following considerations point in a different direction:

(1) The fact that the *terms* "truth" and "life" are no longer used in the first farewell discourse is only partly correct. After all, 14:17 speaks of the "Spirit of *truth*," which the world cannot "*know*"; "but you *know* him." Moreover, the *subject* to which the terms refer is omnipresent: This can already be seen in the verbs γινώσκειν ("to recognize") and ὁρᾶν / θεωρεῖν ("to see") on the one hand and ζῆν ("to live") on the other. If ζῆν is connected to the third main concept of 14:6 ("life") via the identical word stem, the common semantic range ("truth"—"knowledge"/perception) forms the bridge for the second main

---

107. See 3:3, 5; 5:19; 6:44.

108. Significantly, the commentary in v. 7 speaks of "*my* father."

109. J. Beutler, *Habt keine Angst. Die erste Abschiedsrede (Joh 14)*, SBS 116 (Stuttgart: Katholisches Bibelwerk, 1984), 41–44, traces the way motif back to Ps 43 (v. 3), which he classifies together with Ps 42 as formative for the first Farewell Discourse.

110. Dietzfelbinger, *Abschied*, 37–38.

concept.¹¹¹ It is even possible to establish the sequence of the themes in the farewell discourse that corresponds to the sequence of the two terms in the "I am" saying: If verses 7–11 are about the recognition of the Father in the recognition of Jesus, that is, about the *"truth"* of God in Jesus,¹¹² verses 18ff. focus on the *life* opened up by the renewed Easter "coming" of Jesus to his own: "In a little while the world will no longer see me; because *I live you also will live*" (v. 19). However, this can be understood as a commentary on the overarching "I am" saying ("I am . . . *life*"). With its two terms "truth" and "life," it thus announces the following sections: 14:7ff. and 18ff.

(2) W. Michaelis stated rightly: "Even if δι' ἐμοῦ is to be taken only instr. (though cf. → 80), this expression in connection with ἔρχεται is so strongly orientated to the figure of the way that there is no place for a corresponding reference to ἀλήθεια and ζωή."¹¹³ This underlines the special position of that pair: It stands out from the figurative word "way" due to its degree of abstraction. The Johannine "I am" sayings are almost exclusively characterized by figurative speech. The relationship with 10:9 is particularly significant here. One would therefore think that the "secondary character" of which de la Potterie spoke with regard to ἀλήθεια and ζωή should also be evaluated in terms of tradition-criticism.

(3) Of course, such a hypothesis must also provide reasons why the evangelist expanded an original "I am the way" saying to include the two concepts about truth and life. In my opinion, this is possible. In its original form, the saying would not have adequately represented the evangelist's Christological concept. If Jesus is the way and no one comes to the Father except through him, this would indeed express the soteriological exclusivity of Jesus but could also have been understood to mean that Jesus as the *way* is not also the *goal*. Once the goal—the Father—has been reached, he himself would become *superfluous*. The addition of "truth" and "life," which interpret the superordinate figurative saying, excludes precisely this possibility.¹¹⁴ Jesus is not the way *to* truth and life, which we leave behind the closer we come to divine reality. He *is* already *the* truth and *the* life at the same time, and therefore belongs permanently in its revelation. Moreover,

---

111. See 1:14 ("we have *seen* his glory, . . . full of grace and *truth*"); 1:17–18 ("grace and *truth* came through Jesus Christ. No one has ever *seen* God . . ."); 8:32 ("you will *know* the *truth*"); 14:17 ("this is the Spirit of *truth* . . . the world neither *sees* him nor *knows* him . . .").

112. "Knowing" and "seeing" are in close proximity in vv. 7, 9, 17, 19/20!

113. Michaelis, "ὁδός," *TDNT* 5, 81 n. 134.

114. Michaelis, "ὁδός," *TDNT* 5, 82, who, however, emphasizes the *realization of* the eschatological concept outlined in 14:2–3: "One may thus assume that it is this use of the *explanatory concepts* ἀλήθεια *and* ζωή *in 14:6 which brings about the redirection to the present* which is so prominent in 14:7ff. . . . But He is already the way, for even now He gives truth and life. *No one either then or now comes to the Father except by Him*" (emphasis mine).

as shown above, the "I am" saying with its two terms "truth" and "life" now points ahead to what the first farewell discourse will unfold. Therefore, there were certainly important reasons that led the evangelist to expand the original saying into the triad "the way, and the truth, and the life."

In short, in John 14:6 the evangelist takes up an already existing saying from his community tradition. In its presumed original form, it would have read:

I am the way.
No one comes to the Father
except through me.

4.3.4 "We will move along the royal road!" (Philo, *Deus* 145) Critical Observations on the ὁδός Motif

It is no exaggeration to say that the Way is an archetypal symbol, omnipresent in the most diverse cultures and religions of the world.[115] It is also widespread in antiquity: in Greek philosophy[116] and in oriental religiosity, in Egypt,[117] in the Old Testament and early Judaism, and finally in the late antique religion of Gnosticism. The latter was long favored as the background of John 14:6.[118] In the meantime, however, this paradigm of interpretation has faded and seems to have given way to the growing realization that early Hellenistic Judaism is the background for our saying.[119] This is where the melting pot is to be found, which on the one hand is essentially fed by the surviving linguistic traditions of the Old Testament but on the other has also incorporated diverse ideas from the

---

115. On its significance in Buddhism, Taoism, and Islam, see K. Waaijman, "Der Weg— Grundmotiv der Spiritualität," in *Arbeitsgemeinschaft Theologie der Spiritualität (AGTS), "Lasst euch vom Geist erfüllen!" (Eph 5,18). Beiträge zur Theologie der Spiritualität*. Theologie der Spiritualität 4 (Münster: LIT, 2001), 31–57, here 36–40.

116. Michaelis, "ὁδός," *TDNT* 5:42–46.

117. M. P. Zehnder, *Wegmetaphorik im Alten Testament. Eine semantische Untersuchung der alttestamentlichen und altorientalischen Weg-Lexeme mit besonderer Berücksichtigung ihrer metaphorischen Verwendung*, BZNW 268 (Berlin: de Gruyter, 1999), 208–292, esp. 259ff.

118. A link to the gnostic idea of the Revelator who paves the *way for* his followers into the world of light was proposed above all by Bultmann, *Johannes*, 466–468.

119. De la Potterie, "Voie," 917–926, and Brown, *John*, 2:628–29, with references to early Jewish wisdom texts. However, it is striking that *Philo* has so far been completely ignored in the interpretation of 14:6; Schnackenburg, *Johannes*, 3:74–75, and Brown, *John*, do not even mention him. In my opinion, this is connected with the influential judgment of Michaelis, "ὁδός," *TDNT* 5, 82: "The corresponding phrases in Philo (→ 60; 61) are even further removed from the content of the Johannine declaration (cf. also → n. 59)."

Hellenistic environment and has also become one of the very important sources for the emerging Gnosticism at its edges. The Gospel of John also participates in this "Hellenistic Judaism." As far as the way motif is concerned, the study of it may be regarded as a prime "history of religions" example from which a lot can be learned about the environment from which the Fourth Gospel grew.[120]

(1) For the *Old Testament*, M. P. Zehnder wrote a comprehensive survey of the way metaphors.[121] According to him, the way metaphors play "a central role" in particular in the Prophets, the Psalms, and the Wisdom literature. He identifies two focal points: the religious or moral realm ("way of life")—and the realm of the "way of life or the way of going."[122]

For both fields, one example among many others is the opening of the Psalms: "Happy are those who do not follow the advice of the wicked, or take the path that sinners tread, or sit in the seat of scoffers; but their delight is in the law of the Lord, and on his law they meditate day and night.... for the Lord watches over the way of the righteous, but the way of the wicked will perish" (Ps 1:1-2, 6). As Psalm 1 shows by way of example, in the Old Testament only that way of life is qualified as good which corresponds to God's instruction or his wisdom. The Old Testament ethos is then placed strictly within the framework of a covenantal relationship and from here gains its typical character of calling for a response. But the texts also see the "way of life" of the pious in strict connection to God, "Teach me your way, O Lord, and lead me on a level path because of my enemies" (Ps 27:11). And: "The human mind plans the way, but the Lord directs the steps" (Prov 16:9). According to Zehnder, without direct parallels in the environment of the Old Testament, "the comprehensive interpretation of the whole existence of the individual is as a 'way,' namely as a way under the personal co-walking of YHWH."[123] The same applies to the extension of this pattern to the history of the whole people, "a process that can only be observed in Israel."[124] Finally, it is noteworthy that the way lexemes in the Old Testament, in contrast to Egypt in particular, "do not apply to the area beyond the boundary of death"; this only reflects "the striking phenomenon" that "the Old Testament is largely insensitive to the sometimes broadly developed ideas of the afterlife of its environment."[125]

---

120. General literature: Michaelis, "ὁδός," *TDNT* 5:42-65.

121. Zehnder, *Wegmetaphorik*, 473-613.

122. Zehnder, *Wegmetaphorik*, 609.

123. Zehnder, *Wegmetaphorik*, 611.

124. Zehnder, *Wegmetaphorik*, 611.

125. Zehnder, *Wegmetaphorik*, 611-612.

The "I Am" Sayings

All in all, the "ways of God" in the Old Testament keep the hearers of his instructions in their own path through life. They do not draw them away from earthly reality but, on the contrary, introduce them to it. "That there are ways that lead to God or to heaven" is a view that is sought in vain in the Old Testament,[126] but it can be found in Philo of Alexandria, as will be shown below.

(2) A comparison of John 14:6* with *Philo* is instructive for a history of religions "localization" of the logion because the Alexandrian theologian and philosopher also knows a soteriological transcendence of man from the earth into the heavenly sphere of salvation, which he often describes figuratively as the *way*. In this context, he also speaks of mediators of salvation who help people make this transition.[127] Two aspects are important when dealing with the way-motif in Philo: First, it is not an unspecific motif within others but a basic symbol of Philo's oeuvre. It concentrates his ideology, his conception of man, and his soteriology.[128] This requires us to expand a little. Philo is regarded as an excellent representative of a Hellenistic diaspora Judaism if only because of his extremely extensive work that has come down to us. But it cannot be overlooked that he is in many ways only a witness to the Judaism that produced him. This is important for a comparison with John insofar as one cannot claim that the fourth evangelist knew his writings. If there are connections to Philo—and this applies in particular to the evangelist's wisdom Christology or the sapiential matrix it presupposes—then they are mediated via Hellenistic Judaism, which can be regarded as an indirect bridge between the Fourth Gospel and Philo. As with the latter, a distinction would also have to be made between the Alexandrian philosopher's traditions and their specifically Philonic reception and interpretation. However, this cannot be done here, which is why in the following, we will make recourse to the still helpful study by B. L. Mack, who (like H. F. Weiss before him) attempted to understand the religious philosopher against the background of late Jewish wisdom mythology. Also, his "typology of wisdom"[129] can provide us with heuristic categories.

---

126. See Michaelis, "ὁδός," *TDNT* 5, 56, on the LXX: "Only once in 4 Macc. 14:5, and thus on the very margin of the LXX, do we find an expression reminiscent of the usage of Philo, namely, ὥσπερ ἐπ' ἀθανασίας ὁδὸν τρέχοντες."

127. On these intermediary figures of salvation, especially the Logos and Wisdom, and on their mutual relationship in Philo, see B. L. Mack, *Logos und Sophia. Untersuchungen zur Weisheitstheologie im hellenistischen Judentum*, StUNT 10 (Göttingen: Vandenhoeck & Ruprecht, 1973), 13: "As intermediary beings between God and the world, they originated from God, are in turn mediators of creation, embody the transcendent world in themselves, and are regarded as the source, path, and goal of salvation."

128. Philo's treatise *De migratione Abrahami* is characteristic. On the migration of Abraham, which is permeated by the motif of the way, see *Migr.* 143, 146, 171, 173–174, etc.

129. Mack, *Logos*, 21–33.

Mack divides the discourse about the kinds of wisdom into three types. Following H. Conzelmann,[130] he divides wisdom into the *hidden*, the *near*, and the *disappearance* of wisdom. According to the first group of images, the mythical figure of wisdom is a "greatness of the beyond, which has its own place and its own path." Man searches for it till the ends of the earth without being able to acquire it of his own accord.[131] According to the second group of images, wisdom reigns as God's creation in cosmos,[132] appears on earth and lives among humans,[133] calls them and offers to be a *guide for their ways*.[134] The specific Jewish adaptation of this thought is the conviction that wisdom came to humans in the form of the Torah.[135] The third group of images is similar to the first. It is about the disappearance of wisdom.[136] According to the apocalyptic timeline, this will happen at the end of days, when human injustice prevails. All three types of wisdom are characterized by the basic post-exilic experience of a distant God which first lent urgency to the question of his mediation, be it through Torah, wisdom, or through the temple. Only now did the conditions arise that made it possible to speak of a "salvific path" upward.[137]

Philo developed his *ascension or way soteriology* within the framework of his Middle Platonic ideology with a very specific anthropological intention with constant reference to Scripture and with philosophical interest. For him, it was (roughly simplified) clear that the sensually perceptible world, the κόσμος

---

130. H. Conzelmann, "Paulus und die Weisheit," *NTS* 12 (1965/66): 231–244, here 236 n. 5.

131. See Job 28; Sir 1:1–4, 6, 8; Bar 3:15ff.; Wis 9:13–18 etc.

132. See Prov 8:22ff.; Sir 24:3–7.

133. See Bar 3:38.

134. Prov 3:17; 4:11; 8:20, 32; Sir 4:17; 6:26; Wis 7:12; 9:11, 18; 10:4, 10.

135. Sir 24:23–34; Bar 3:38/4:1.

136. See 1 En. 42:1–3; 4 Esdras 5:9–10; 2 Bar. 48:36.

137. For Mack, the book of Wisdom is particularly important here because it reveals Philo's intellectual environment: "It is also not unimportant for the idea of the way through and out of the world, which is known to be fundamental for Philo, that the beginnings of the reinterpretation of the 'way of wisdom' can already be found in the book of Wisdom. The path now has a goal, namely dominion (Wis 6:20 et al.), and leads across a border. (See Wis 10:18; 19:8, where the Red Sea is regarded as a boundary and as an expression of the need beyond which the saved experience the miracles of the new change). The path can also be symbolized by the example of Enoch's rapture (Wis 4:11ff.). If we now compare the cycle of wisdom being nearby in Sir 24:5–6 with the salvation of the righteous from the fall (Wis 10:1) or from prison (Wis 10:13–14; cf. 16:13, 'to the gates of the underworld and up'), we see that the idea of the upward direction of the path is already in the background. If the goal is transferred to the afterlife, then the 'wonderful journey' of the exodus way (Wis 19:5) can be understood cosmically and aligned with the idea of exaltation (to rulership)" (Mack, *Logos*, 107).

αἰσθητός, is a world of imperfection and transience, only a shadow of the actual, spiritual world, the κόσμος νοητός. This world of God's ideas, true being, which eludes the sensual world, can only be seen by the human νοῦς ("reason"), but for this he needs divine help, which is also sufficiently given to him in the form of guides. Man cannot exceed the limit of the κόσμος αἰσθητός toward the κόσμος νοητός by himself or by his own strength. The guides who pave the way to salvation, that is, to the vision of God (ὅρασις θεοῦ), in which he shows himself graciously to man, are numerous: God himself,[138] the Logos, wisdom, Moses as hierophant,[139] as well as the patriarchs: Abraham, Isaac, Jacob-Israel. Here the Torah, with whose interpretation Philo is concerned, leads to an extraordinarily rich, multilayered, and by no means always contradiction-free production of meaning. According to Philo, this inconsistency only confirms the fullness of meaning that God has put into it. This picture of Philo's soteriology, which is only hinted at with a few strokes, may now gain a little color in the following by means of exemplary texts on the metaphor of the way in Philo.

Deus 142–143 (trans. Yonge)
All flesh corrupted the perfect *way*[140] of the everlasting and incorruptible being which conducts to God.

And know that *this way is wisdom.*
For the mind being guided by wisdom,[141]
while the road is straight and level and easy, proceeds along it to the end;
and the end of this road is the *knowledge* and *understanding of God.*[142]

Despite its specific anthropology, which cannot be found in the Fourth Gospel, the text comes close to John 14:6* with respect to its *structure*. Philo identifies the way of knowledge of God with wisdom; John 14:6* identifies it with Christ. Particularly noteworthy is the soteriological διά (= through), which also appears in the following passage from *Quod deus sit immutabilis.*

---

138. See Philo, *Decal.* 29.114: "since they use God as their guide in their ascents."

139. See *Conf.* 95: "It is proper to the servants of the existing... to raise themselves in thought to the ethereal height (ἀναβαίνειν), after they have placed *Moses*, the type of the God-loving generation, at their head as a *guide* (ἡγεμόνα τῆς ὁδός)."

140. See John 14:6: "No one comes to the Father."

141. See John 14:6: "through me."

142. See John 14:7: "If you know me, you will know my Father also."

Deus 159–161 (trans. Yonge)
Let us then, without any delay, attempt
to proceed by the *royal road*,
since we think fit to pass by all earthly things;
and the royal road
is that of which there is not private individual in the world who is master,
but he alone who is also the only true king.
And *this (way)* is, as I said a little while ago
wisdom,
by which alone (διά) suppliant souls can find a way of escaping
to the uncreated God;
for it is natural
that one who goes without any hindrance along (διά) the royal road,
will never feel weariness before he meets with the king.
But, then, those who have come near to him *recognise* his blessedness
and their own deficiency.

As elsewhere, Philo also understands what we read here in Numbers 20:17 about the "king's road" through Edom as a reference to the royal road of wisdom.[143] As we learn from *Deus* 161, the knowledge of God to which this path leads implies, as an anthropological counterpart, the insight into one's own human *nothingness*, a specifically Philonic idea that the Alexandrian drew from the Greek tradition.

What is said of wisdom in *Deus* 161, Philo can also say of God's Logos:

Post. 102 [trans. Yonge, modified]
This royal road,
which we have stated to be true and genuine philosophy,
the law calls the word and reason [θεοῦ ῆμα καὶ λόγον] of God;.
for it is written,
"Thou shalt not turn aside from the word
which I command thee this day,
to the right hand nor to the left," [Deut 28:14)
so that[144] it is shown most manifestly,
that the word of God is identical with the royal road.

---

143. See also Philo, *Post.* 101; *Gig.* 64; *Deus* 144ff., 180; *Migr.* 146; Spec. Laws 4.168.

144. The exegetical reason: The Torah speaks of not deviating "neither to the right nor to the left" both in the royal road (Num 20:17) and in the word of God (Deut 28:14).

The "I Am" Sayings

In the next quote, the Logos is personalized and presented as a guide:[145]

> *Migr.* 174 [trans. Yonge)
> for until... he [sc. Abraham) is made perfect
> he uses divine Logos as the guide of his path [ἡγεμόνι τῆς ὁδοῦ),
> for that is the sacred oracle of scripture:
> "Behold, I send my angel before thy face
> that he may keep thee in the road,
> so as to lead thee into the land which I have prepared for thee.
> ... for my name is in him [s.c. my messenger]" (Exod 23:20–21).[146]

Finally, two texts will be presented that show how the worldview about the "above" and "below" is linked to the way metaphor. Here, the mystery of ascension that is fulfilled in a vision of God obtains a cosmic color.[147] This is the deeper interpretation of God's word to Lot in Gen 19:17 ("Flee for your life; do not look back or stop anywhere in the Plain; flee to the hills, or else you will be consumed!") in:

> *Quaestiones et solutiones in Genesin* 4.46:[148]
> When the mind begins to take the higher road (τὴν ἀνωτέραν ὁδόν), it becomes better and progresses, leaving behind earth-bound and low things.... [The mind], becoming light, is elevated to higher things, and looking around observes what is in the air and the ether and the whole heaven together.... This *ascent* is more figuratively called "mountain," but its true name is *"wisdom"* (σοφία), for the soul (ψυχή) which is truly a lover of wisdom (φιλοσοφία) desired a vision of higher and more exalted things, by being in ethereal regions.

According to the following text (see also *Post.* 31), it is *virtue* that inherits the role of guide and accompanies the "upward movement of thoughts":

> *Her.* 241 (trans. Yonge)
> For virtue (ἀρετή) has derived its name not only from the word choice (αἵρεσις), but also from the fact of its being lifted up (ἄρσις), for it is lifted up (αἴρεται) and borne on high because it always loves heavenly

---

145. Moreover, see *Somn.* 1.71; on God: *Somn.* 1.179; *Det.* 114; *QE* 2.40.

146. See John 17:6, 11–12!

147. See also *Det.* 114–118; *Post.* 31.136; *Conf.* 95–96.

148. Text of LCL Suppl. I 321f. Mind the associations with Plato!

things; but wickedness (κακία) is so called from its tendency to go downwards (κάτω), and also because it compels those who practise it to fall down to the bottom (καταπίπτειν).

Although the way to the Father in John 14:6* is not described as *anabasis* of the faithful, in other passages we find a similar model.[149] On the other hand, the *anabasis* model in John is found pointedly in the metaphor of Christ as "guide" who is also identified with the way in John 14:6*. This brings us to our *conclusion*.

(3) The "words of the Lord" in John 14:6* can be understood against the background of a development that has led from the idea of a hidden or vanished wisdom to the idea of "heavenly" wisdom that is inaccessible to man by his own efforts because the more distant wisdom is from man, the more important the way to it becomes for him.[150] It is not possible to establish a direct link between the logion and Philo. The *differences* between the respective conceptions are too great to accomplish this: the gnoseological soteriology of Philo stands in contrast to the soteriology of faith of our logion.[151] "The bridging of the radical distance between God and man by the Philonic model" "leads to a de-secularization of man." The Christian-Johannine model presupposes "the incarnation of God."[152] But the *structural similarities* between the two conceptions are striking. Even if it initially appears as if the majority of mediators in Philo is contrasted with the single mediator in John, this majority is "virtual" and variable because it is not related to historical figures. It corresponds to the exegetical possibilities of the text as interpreted by Philo.

---

149. John 6:44: "No one can come to me unless drawn by the Father"; see also Philo, *Her.* 70, which speaks of the soul being "led by the true Being and *drawn up* to him, while the *truth* goes before it." (Note the personification of *truth*, which is presented here as a guide!) Comprehensive comparative material can be found in Theobald, "Gezogen," 323–334.

150. The historical situation reconstructed by Mack, *Logos*, for the emergence of wisdom speculation (crisis of exile; loss of immediacy in the experience of God; question of the relationship between God and man) corresponds in some respects to the situation addressed by the evangelist in the first farewell discourse: the crisis of discipleship based on Jesus's departure in death and his resulting absence.

151. According to the fourth evangelist, "coming to the Father" presupposes faith in him (cf. John 14:1); indeed, according to John 14:1, "coming to the Father" already takes place in such faith. On the other hand, the evangelist—and this is typical of him—can also deepen faith gnoseologically: See John 4:42; 6:69.

152. See G. Sellin, "Gotteserkenntnis und Gotteserfahrung bei Philo von Alexandrien," in *Monotheismus und Christologie. Zur Gottesfrage im hellenistischen Judentum und im UrChristentum*, ed. H.-J. Klauck, QD 138 (Freiburg et al.: Herder, 1992), 17–40, here 39. However, only the prologue in the Gospel of John articulates the "incarnation." But even the ἐγώ εἰμι ... of our logion naturally presupposes the reference to the *earthly* Jesus, albeit in his identity with the exalted one.

The "I Am" Sayings

On the other hand, the idea of the uniqueness of the mediating figure is certainly present in the majority of the mediating figures and, as *Deus* 159–161 showed, is sometimes also realized. Seen in this light, even the idea of Christological exclusivity has its origins in early Jewish wisdom theology—the matrix common to Philo and John. The same applies to the idea that the way or ways of wisdom lead to *life*,[153] which cannot be thought of in any other way than as a gift from God.

4.3.5 Are There Inner-Christian Connections of the Saying about the Way?

From time to time, scholars have considered whether there are inner-Christian connections with the saying about the way. Three suggestions have been made. The most far-reaching is that of B. Lindars. He assumes that John 14:6 continues a synoptic saying, similar to that of Matthew 7:13–14, if not this saying itself.[154] However, this assumption remains difficult. There is only the bridge of the ὁδός motif as such between the ethically sharpened two-way teaching of Matthew and John 14:6. The *second* suggestion[155] refers to the προσαγωγή motif, which is widely used in Romans 5:2; Ephesians 2:13, 18; 3:12; Hebrews 7:25; 10:19–21; and 1 Peter 2:4; 3:18. Jesus opened "access" to God, his Father, for people through his death and exaltation. Admittedly, this motif has cultic connotations in all these passages. However, it draws attention to the significance of the Christology of the way in early Christianity, in the context of which John 14:6* can also be seen. The *third* suggestion[156] is reminiscent of the self-designation of the congregation as a group of "followers of the Way" (9:2; cf. 19:9, 23; 22:4; 24:14, 22) preserved in Acts, which is one of the oldest Christian self-designations and also has a parallel in the Qumran sect, which also called itself "the Way" (1QS 9:18–19; CD 2:6; see also 1QS 3:9–10, 9:9).[157] "The term probably had an ethical as well as a soteriological meaning: the disciples saw themselves as obliged to follow the 'way of righteousness' (Matt 21:32), i.e., to walk according to the end-time will of God proclaimed by Jesus, and at the same time as being set on

---

153. See Prov 3:17; 8:32, 34; Sir 6:26. M. Scott, *Sophia and the Johannine Jesus*, JSNTS 71 (Sheffield: Sheffield Academic, 1992), 127.

154. Lindars, *John*, 473.

155. See Barrett, *Johannes*, 448.

156. See again Barrett, *Johannes*, 448; moreover Lindars, *John*, 472; Brown, *John*, 2.628–629.

157. Brown, *John*, 2.629, with reference to 1QS 8,12–16, assumes that the self-designation as the "way" is derived from Isa 40:3, as does Lindars, *John*, 472.

a new path of salvation through Jesus ([Acts] 16:17; Heb 10:20; John 14:6)."[158] R. Brown's theory that the logion in John 14:6* should be understood in light of an *impact-historical* context as a self-designation of the Christian community does not seem implausible, even if it is not possible to prove such an assumption beyond doubt.

4.3.6 John 14:6* and the Reception of the Saying by the Evangelist

Alongside the logion in John 14:2–3,[159] John 14:6 is the second the evangelist integrates into the main part of his first farewell discourse (14:1–29). Three things are significant in this reception process:

(1) In the independently transmitted "I am" saying, the accent of the first line is on the predication of Christ as the *way*. The concluding colon in verse 6d ("except *through me*") emphasizes the Christological exclusivity of this predication. If Christ is proclaimed here as the *only* access to the Father, this suggests the implicit negation of other claims to salvation. What is in mind here? Due to the special *Jewish* characteristic of the way metaphor shown above, probably the Torah.[160] However, the evangelist *does not* pick up on this trace in the context of his farewell discourse to the disciples, instead establishing a different emphasis: He is concerned, as the "bridge" verses between verses 2–3 and 6 show, with the *identity of* Christ as the way, which is why the main clause is now to be read as *"I am the way."* The evangelist is concerned with rejecting the assumption that the way into life, as an object of hope (or other spiritual or religious experience), is yet again more or different than the encounter with the living Jesus in his word. *No!* says the evangelist. Jesus and "the way" are so *identical* that the encounter with the present Christ in faith already means walking on the way opened up by him. This is *not* a way we leave behind us in order to reach our goal, but a way that brings the goal within reach on its horizon from the very first steps we

---

158. J. Roloff, *Die Apostelgeschichte*, NTD 5 (Göttingen: Vandenhoeck & Ruprecht, 1981), 148; Heb 10:20 calls the "entrance" into the heavenly sanctuary created by virtue of the blood of Jesus a "new and living way"; E. Grässer, *An die Hebräer III*, EKK XVII/3 (Zürich: Benzinger, 1997), 15: "The NT unique connection ὁδὸς ζῶσα ... has its closest parallel in John 14:6"; his continuation is misleading: "Here as there, gnostic speculations about the way contribute to understanding."

159. See Theobald, *Herrenworte*, 506–521.

160. The absolute use of the way metaphor in Qumram (see above!) is also oriented toward the Torah, i.e., its interpretation by the teacher of justice. Something similar applies to Philo, because for him it is the Torah that documents the wisdom of God, but above all the lawgiver Moses with his exemplary experience of God.

take upon it. But this is where the metaphor of the path reaches the limits of its expressive power.

(2) This also indicates the reason the evangelist *comments* on the figurative saying about the way with the help of the two abstract terms "truth" and "life." The independently transmitted saying *without* these two terms could certainly be understood in the sense of a goal-oriented, future-oriented eschatology: to come to the Father through Jesus will be fulfilled in the eschaton, either in death, or at Christ's parousia. The evangelist's comment on the saying however is different. Now it becomes clear that Jesus is not only the way but also the goal because he contains life within himself. De la Potterie[161] sketched the history of interpretation of our Christological key phrase beginning in the patristic period. He has shown the following two alternative models of interpretation: Either the way (and the truth) were understood as quantities that lead to eternal, future life in heaven (or also to the truth as the Logos of God in heaven), or the two abstracts were understood as an explanation of what the predication of Jesus as the way contains. The latter probably corresponds best to the style of the text and the critical editorial view of the saying advocated here: Jesus is the way to the Father *insofar as* the truth—the reality of God—is revealed in him, becomes epiphanous, or rather makes present the life that is the content of this divine reality. Therefore, in agreement with R. Brown, the καί (= and) between the first and second nouns can therefore be interpreted epexegetically:[162] the way, *that is*, the truth and the life.

(3) As explained above, the two Christological predications—Jesus the *truth* and Jesus the *life*—are interpreted in the following verses. In doing so, the evangelist establishes new emphases. Thus, as an explication of ἀλήθεια (= truth), verses 7–11 ensure that the epiphany of truth in Jesus does not involve the indistinction of divine reality and its bearer, revelation, and Revelator, but is bound to the personal togetherness of Father and Son. At the same time, they "locate" the knowledge of this truth by showing that it is reflected in the words and works of Jesus: insofar as Jesus speaks the words of the one who sent him or does his works, the Father is "in him" and the reality of him becomes obvious in Jesus. Verses 18ff. then explicate the predication of Jesus as ζωή (= life). He is life because he demonstrates it at "Easter" and at the same time gives it to others as a gift: "I live and you will live!" (v. 19d, e). Even now it is clear that it is his words that are the pledge of his love or the love of his Father. If believers hold on to them, they can be certain of life (14:21, 23–24).

In itself, the saying about the way in John 14:6* does not need a temporal framework. Without a further explanation, it is probably conceived of as the

---

161. De la Potterie, "Voie."

162. Brown, *John*, 2:621.

word of the exalted Christ, whose identity with the earthly is presupposed. Its interpretation in the context of the farewell discourse shows that its validity is only put into effect at "Easter."

4.4 The "I am" Sayings
Signals of a Johannine High Christology

The confession of Jesus as the preexistent "Son of God" will have led to the so-called Johannine schism: the group from which the Johannine communities emerged had been forced to separate from their Jewish mother community, as their confession of Jesus as the only "Son" who came from God himself had given rise to the serious suspicion of "ditheism," which was punished as a gross violation of biblical monotheism (see 5:18; 10:33, 36; 19:7) with expulsion from the synagogue (see 9:22, 34; 12:42). Jesus's followers, who saw in him merely a human being, the "son of Joseph" whose parents are known (1:45; 6:41–42), but whom God appointed as the eschatological "prophet" (6:14; 7:40, 52) or "Messiah" of Israel (1:49; 7:31, 41–42; 12:13) and confirmed as such in his resurrection, could, at least in this phase of "Jewish-Christian" history and perhaps under local conditions, the details of which elude us, remain in the synagogue.[163] The evangelist's Gospel is a reaction to this schism, the theological consequences of which should not be underestimated. It seems helpful to recall these key data of John research when it comes to appreciating the "I am" imagery as a whole as a tradition of the Johannine community. For with their ἐγώ εἰμι sayings,[164] which can be derived from the Old Testament formula of revelation, they are prominent witnesses of Johannine high Christology. They grant us insight into the background of the schism. In general, they present Jesus as the eschatological epiphany of God for the salvation of those who believe in him, and in such an exclusive way that the explosive charge is laid with regard to early Jewish concepts of covenant, Torah, and election.

---

163. See M. Theobald, Das Johannesevangelium—Zeugnis eines synagogalen "JudenChristentums"? in Sänger D./Mell U. (Hgg.), Paulus und Johannes. Exegetische Studien zur paulinischen und theologischen Theologie und Literatur. Publikation der Referate (FS Becker), (WUNT 198), Tübingen 2006, 107–158.

164. C. H. Dodd, *The Interpretation of the Fourth Gospel* (Cambridge: Cambridge University Press, 1953; reprint 1963), 93–96; Brown, *John*, 1:535–538; and finally P. Harner, *The "I Am" of the Fourth Gospel: A Study in Johannine Usage and Thought* (Philadelphia: Fortress, 1970); D. M. Ball, *"I Am" in John's Gospel. Literary Function, Background and Theological Implications*, JSNT.S 124 (Sheffield: Sheffield Academic Press, 1996); C. H. Williams, *I Am He: The Interpretation of "Ani hû" in Jewish and Early Christian Literature*, WUNT 2/113 (Tübingen: Mohr Siebeck, 2000).

The "I Am" Sayings

Let us summarize the most important results of the above analyses from this perspective.[165]

(1) From a *formal* point of view, 6:35 and 8:12, on the one hand, and 10:9 and 14:6, on the other, belong together. While the sayings in the first pair each contain an implicit element of invitation (in the form of a participle), the sayings of the second pair are characterized by a focused διά (= through) that only occurs in them. The latter is related to the images of door and path, to which the preposition διά corresponds with its local nuance.

(2) The difference of the *semantic* focus in the two pairs in connected to the first aspect. John 6:35 and 8:12 focus on the metaphor (bread—light), the meaning of which is made explicit by the promise that follows (no longer having to suffer hunger and thirst or no longer having to walk in darkness). The emphasis of the statement is on what Jesus means positively for those who believe in him. In 10:9 and 14:6, things look different due to the concrete content of the chosen images: If they communicate that only "through Jesus" does a door to the heavenly world open or only "through him" does the way to the Father pave the way, then the soteriological exclusivity of Jesus is explicitly marked and the emphasis of the sayings shifts from the element of promise to an implicitly polemical statement. This seeks to achieve the self-assurance of the addressees in such a way that it excludes all other possible agents of salvation without naming them. Through this process of exclusion, the focus of the sayings shifts to their first link: "*I* am the way," "*I* am the door"—and no one else.

This type of polemic, which comes to the fore in the second pair of sayings in 10:9 and 14:6, also determines the choice of imagery in the other sayings. In the predication "light of the world," the origin of the phrase in Jewish Torahology is plausible: John 8:12 stands implicitly against a soteriological interpretation. John 6:35 goes beyond wisdom topoi overall, such that the saying bears the connotation: "There is more here than wisdom!" Whatever the Jewish tradition had to offer in terms of predicates about salvation are gathered together in the consideration of the mystery that the person of Jesus himself represents in a unique way.

(3) Not only does the ἐγώ εἰμι originate from biblical tradition, the images in the logia are also of Jewish provenance. In particular, we have to think of Hellenistic Judaism outside Palestine, as represented by Philo ("way," "light," etc.) or Joseph and Aseneth ("bread of life"). Also noteworthy are the various connections with the synoptic tradition (ideas of discipleship in 8:12; the motif of the door in Luke 13:24).

(4) A monocausal history of religions derivation of the *"I am" sayings*, which consists of a self-conception of the speaker together with a soteriological explication derived from this, does not seem possible. Since E. Norden, it has

---

165. On the saying about the door in 10:9 not analyzed here, see Theobald, *Herrenworte*, 277–304.

been clear that this type of speech, which can be defined more precisely with the help of the Revelation of John,[166] was not born out of the spirit of classical Greek antiquity but has its origins in the haze of "Semitic-Oriental" religious discourse.[167] If the ἐγώ εἰμι saying was originally a divine formula, it was later also transferred to other representatives, the kings, and is also found in the mouths of other people[168]—for example in the pseudo-prophets of Celsus, to whom E. Norden drew attention.[169] However, in agreement with Kundsin we must insist on the fact that the type of speech, as revealed by John and Revelation, stands out through its concise form and strict soteriological orientation from many of the "parallels" provided by the history of religions research: "in the Oriental texts an almost unrestricted accumulation of names of dignity, enumeration of the great deeds of the god or ruler—in the Gospel of John usually only a short depiction of the god or ruler—which, however, in its simple brevity appears all the more monumental and each time exclusively dominates the respective thought."[170] It may be assumed that the form of John's "I am" sayings, as aptly described by Kundsin, is in line with specific content: They are grown out of the soil of the early Jewish, biblical faith in God that urges concentration. They give expression to the conviction that the God of Israel has revealed himself unsurpassably in Jesus, has become epiphanic in him, and will henceforth realize his will of salvation exclusively through him. *The concise form of the sayings corresponds to the Christological narrowness of their content.*

(5) All four sayings are characterized by a basic *cognitive* style. It is not a matter of the promise of life as such, of strengthening through paraenetic assurance, but of *reassurance* in the faith in Christ through the words of Jesus himself. This reassurance takes place in such a way that soteriological consequences are

---

166. See Theobald, *Herrenworte*, 322–329.

167. E. Norden, *Agnostos Theos. Untersuchungen zur Formengeschichte religiöser Rede*, 4th ed. (Stuttgart: WBG, 1956), 177–201.

168. E. Schweizer, *Ego Eimi. Die religionsgeschichtliche Herkunft und theologische Bedeutung der johanneischen Bildreden. Zugleich ein Beitrag zur Quellenfrage des vierten Evangeliums*, FRLANT 56, 2nd ed. (Göttingen: Vandenhoeck & Ruprecht, 1965), 10, summarizing Norden's analysis.

169. Norden, *Theos*, 188–189; according to Origen, *Cels*, 7.8–9, Celsus claims to have heard these pseudoprophets themselves say: "*I am God* (ἐγώ ὁ θεός εἰμι) or the Son of God or the divine spirit. *I have come* (ἥκω δέ): for the end of the world has already come and you, you humans, are at an end because of your transgressions. *But I will save you*, and you will see me ascend again with heavenly power." The reference to Odes Sol 33:11b, 12, an excerpt from a longer speech, is also worth noting; see Norden, *Theos*, 190: "*I am your judge* [s.c. Wisdom?]. And those who have put me on will not be oppressed, but shall possess immortality in the new eon" (Lattke, FC XIX 191).

170. K. Kundsin, *Charakter und Ursprung der johanneischen Reden*, Acta Universitatis Latoiensis I/4 (Riga: Latvijas Universitate, 1939), 218; on pp. 291–293, he refers to the Cymaean Isis-Aretalogy, among others, for comparison.

The "I Am" Sayings

drawn from the Christological predications, or these are presented as being founded in the confession of Christ. This is of the utmost importance for the Christological foundation of the present-eschatological concept of life that as such is not yet formulated in the "I am" sayings[171] but is then developed by the evangelist. The basic cognitive trait of the sayings can also be seen in the highly reflective reception of the figurative words, as this implicitly reveals an assignment of the Jewish institutions of salvation, above all the Torah, to Jesus.

(6) The *Sitz im Leben* of the sayings is very likely the liturgical assembly of the congregation. What we thought we recognized more clearly in the saying about the bread can be extended to all the other "I am" sayings examined, especially since we have parallels with the corresponding words of Revelation that are significant in terms of form history and which in turn support this assumption.[172] In concrete terms, this means that these sayings were uttered in the worship service by prophets within the congregation who spoke them in the name of the exalted Christ as his own assurance to the community. This assurance was intended to reassure them of his saving presence with them. The subject of these sayings is the *exalted* Christ, not the *earthly* Jesus, as in the sayings that bear the temporal framework of Jesus's life (e.g., 7:33-34).[173] It is not the exalted one who leaves aside his earthly life but Jesus himself, as he remains salvifically present to his congregation as a result of his exaltation to God.

(7) The four first-person "I am" sayings (as well as the two more extensive parables in 10:11-12 and 15:1-2, 5-6 which are introduced by "I am") do not show any traces of a *Christology* of Jesus as a messenger. The reference to Jesus, who was sent by God, belongs to the evangelist's theological usage of the sayings. This is significant for the meaning of the sayings insofar as this differentiation opens up the scope that allows ἐγώ εἰμι to be interpreted not as a genuine form of the self-presentation of a messenger but as an echo of the Old Testament revelatory formula.[174] This also corresponds to the position of John 6:20 observed at the beginning of this chapter: It is an interpretative key for all subsequent figurative, first-person "I am" sayings.

---

171. See paradigmatically above at pp. 173-174.

172. There is an *indirect* historical connection between the first-person "I am" sayings in Revelation (1:8; 1:17-18; 2:23; 21:6; 22:13; 22:16) and those in the Gospel. This is not mediated by specific sayings that are common to both literary works but by the form of speech of the first-person "I am" sayings as such. This was at home in the liturgy of the congregation, whereby, according to Revelation, we can count on "prophets" who uttered such sayings in the worship service. For evidence, see Theobald, *Herrenworte*, 322-329.

173. See ch. 6, 2.

174. See Theobald, "Spruchgut," 364-366.

CHAPTER 5

Parables and Similar Metaphors

AS MANY MONOGRAPHS as there are on the "I am" sayings of the Fourth Gospel, research has rarely devoted itself to the other metaphorical texts of the Johannine tradition in comprehensive studies. The major chapter on the topic is "Parabolic Forms" from C. H. Dodd's work *Historical Tradition in the Fourth Gospel*. There, Dodd examines seven passages from the Gospel that (a) deviate from the usual type of Johannine metaphorical speech, (b) are close in form and content to synoptic traditions (without having a textual basis there), and (c) are "genuinely parabolic, and not allegorical."[1] Dodd's conclusion is, "It appears... in the highest degree probable that at any rate for parts of the teaching of Jesus John drew independently upon the common and primitive tradition, and he has preserved valuable elements in that tradition which the Synoptic evangelists have neglected."[2] We will examine this thesis below.

There is nothing equal to Dodd's study. As a rule, one deals with individual texts, but even then the question of tradition criticism is usually sidelined. Despite the general-sounding title, Kaipuram's work does not provide an overall picture.[3] Recently, J. Becker published a study on John 10 and 15 that is of great interest.[4]

---

1. Dodd, *Tradition*, 366-387, here 386. The seven texts (in the order in which Dodd examines them) are: 12:24; 16:21; 11:9-10; 8:35; 10:1-5; 3:29; 5:19-20a (in n. 2 on p. 386; an elaboration of the thesis in C. H. Dodd, "A Hidden Parable in the Fourth Gospel," in *More New Testament Studies* [Manchester: Manchester University Press, 1968], 30-40).

2. Dodd, *Tradition*, 387. Similar is the rather popular book by A. M. Hunter, *The Gospel according to John* (London: Cambridge University Press, 1968), 78-89, who lists and comments on twelve Johannine parables, all of which he attributes to Jesus or the Baptist (3:29): 3:8; 4:35-38; 5:19-20a; 8:35; 10:1-5; 11:9-10; 12:24; 12:35-36; 14:2-3; 15:1-2; 16:21.

3. S. Kaipuram, *Paroimiai in the Fourth Gospel and the Johannine Parables of Jesus' Self-Revelation* (Rome, 1993), briefly discusses the parables 3:8; 3:29; 5:19-20a; 8:35; 10:1-5.11b-13; 11:9f.; 12:24; 15:1-17 and 16:21, but then devotes himself only to 12:24, which he uses as a Johannine model (p. 66).

4. J. Becker, "Die Herde des Hirten und die Reben am Weinstock. Ein Versuch zu Joh 10,1-18 und 15,1-17," in *Die Gleichnisreden Jesu 1899-1999. Beiträge zum Dialog mit Adolf Jülicher*, ed. U. Mell, BZNW 103 (Berlin: de Gruyter, 1999), 149-178. See also J. Frey, R. Zimmermann, and J. G. van der Watt, eds., *Imagery in the Gospel of John: Terms, Forms, Themes, and Theology of Johannine Figurative Language*, WUNT 200 (Tübingen: Mohr Siebeck, 2006).

In the following, we will focus on five parabolic traditions that are of a very different nature and perhaps for this very reason can satisfy the claim of a representative selection: two parables in the narrower sense (John 5:19–20; 10:1–5), a short metaphor (John 12:24), and the two elaborate "I am" speeches (John 10:11–13 and 15:1–8). We will examine these texts in the order in which they occur in the Gospel.

5.1 In the Father's Workshop (John 5:19b–20c)

Jesus's discourse in John 5:19–30 begins with the *parable of the son who is apprenticed to his father* (C. H. Dodd). This discourse does not stand on its own but, following 5:17, aims to reveal the deeper meaning of the healing of the paralytic on the Sabbath narrated earlier. The climax of this story is Jesus's words to the paralytic, "*Stand up* (ἔγειρε), take your mat and walk" (v. 8).[5] Following on from this, the evangelist reflects in 5:19–30 on Jesus's word *that brings* life, as is shown above all by the resumption of the keyword ἐγείρειν in 5:21. Jesus's encouragement of the paralytic at the pool of Bethesda in Jerusalem now appears as a signal for "greater things" (v. 20), namely for the work that happens wherever a person is awakened from death to true life through Jesus's call. "Very truly, I tell you, anyone who hears my word and believes him who sent me has eternal life, and does not come under judgment, but has passed from death to life" (5:24). It is not without reason that this very word is at the center of the composition in 5:19–30, the structure of which we will turn to first below.

5.1.1 John 5:19–30
A Well Thought Out Composition

Frey offers a synopsis of different structures of these verses.[6] We will not consider verses 28–29 in the following since they go back to a rereading of the text by the editors and therefore do not belong to the original composition of the speech. Incidentally, they do not fit in with it from a *structural* point of view either, as the following diagram aims to show.[7]

---

5. Note that the introductory words of v. 8 ("Jesus *says* to him") and v. 6 ("*says* to him, 'Do you want to be made well?'") are the *only* ones in ch. 5 in the present tense. This points to the *current* meaning of Jesus's word of healing, which is also given as a *call to life* at the moment the book is read.

6. Frey, *Eschatologie*, 2:472–473 and at 477–478 for his own attempt.

7. For the justification of this (old) thesis, see most recently Dietzfelbinger, *Abschied*, 97–105 (on p. 104, he speaks of the "unsuccessful integration of 5:28–29 into the context"). See also

A		C	
(1) vv. 19–20:	Amen-saying	(1) v. 25:	Amen-saying
(2) v. 21:	1. explanation (life) "just as—so also"; "for"	(2) v. 26:	1. explanation (life) "as—so also" "for"
(3) v. 22:	2. explanation (judgment) "also not"; "for"	(3) v. 27:	2. explanation (judgment) "and"
(4) v. 23:	aim "so that" (honoring the son by the people)	(4) v. 30:	aim "seeking" (ζητεῖν) (Jesus's search for the Father)
B v. 24: Amen-saying			

The delimitation of the unit in 5:19–30 is straightforward: It is introduced by the introductory formula "Jesus said to them" in verse 19a and is rounded off by the *inclusio* in verse 19c/verse 30a.[8] Additionally, verse 31 begins a thematically different piece that follows the literary genre of the legal dispute.[9]

Internally, the composition is held together and structured by the three Amen-sayings. The central position of verse 24 (= B) is also clearly emphasized in that only here in the text (and in the final word of v. 30) does Jesus speak in his own name ("I"), whereas the two framing pieces (= A/C) deal with him as the "Son (of God)" and "Son of Man." In addition, the participial formula of sending, which occurs three times, has a rhythmic function: at the end of A (v. 23), in the center of B (v. 24), and at the end of C (v. 30).

The grain of the text is clear: If the central Amen-saying of verse 24 stands on its own, the other two are each followed by commentary with a concluding climax. Their independent status is syntactically marked by an explicative γάρ ("indeed," "for"; vv. 21, 22, 26)[10] or a sequential οὐδέν ("*and* also not"; v. 22)

Zumstein, *Johannesevangelium*, 220: "In our opinion, it is illusory to deny a tension, but it is to be prescribed in the dynamics of the reflection of the Johannine school.... In v. 29, the Johannine school... undertakes a relecture of v. 25 and reintroduces the futuristic-apocalyptic dimension of eschatology"; the "identifying mark" for the relecture is v. 28: "Do not be surprised!"

8. "The Son can do nothing on his own."—I can do nothing on my own." The observation that in v. 30, as in v. 19, it is in the *present tense*, "as I *hear*, I judge" (otherwise always the aorist as found in 3:32; 8:26, 40; 15:15) also fits the *inclusio*.

9. Becker, *Johannes*, 1:298–300.

10. The character of vv. 21 and 26 as *commentary* is already signaled by the *explicative* γάρ.

or καί ("and"; v. 27) and can also be recognized by slight dividing lines.[11] The commentary is introduced by a ὥσπερ—οὕτως sentence (just as—so then) (vv. 21/26). In both instances, their sequence is structured by the keywords "life" and "judgment,"[12] although there are specific accents: Since verses 21–22 are about Jesus giving *life* and executing judgment (so that all may honor him as the Son . . .), the *soteriological* perspective is in the foreground here. In comparison, the *second* series of commentary statements in verses 26–27 following verse 25 takes a step back and focuses on the *Christological* perspective, insofar as it addresses the condition of the possibility of Jesus's salvific action.[13] The Father has given the Son "to have life *in himself*," and he has given him the "*authority*" to "exercise judgment, for he is the Son of Man."[14] The respective endings of the two framing sections, verse 23 and verse 30, get to the heart of the matter. While verse 23 explains that everything depends on whether or not the *Son* is honored, because to miss him would also miss the Father—that is, the reason for salvation, verse 30 defines the decisive Christological principle: Jesus himself is fundamentally guided by the will of the one who sent him. Therefore, what he does is also called righteous.[15]

This brief overview of the structure of the text shows that the composition with its slogans (amen sayings), commentary, and summarizing conclusions has a profile that is anything but one-dimensional. The design is aimed at directing readers who reckon with the different levels of the text. The question therefore arises as to whether this result should not also be evaluated diachronically—that is, whether the slogans are based on Johannine tradition. This is explored below for John 5:19–20.

---

11. Thus, the logion in v. 25 speaks of the "Son of God," whereupon the commentary in v. 26 immediately returns to the terminology "the Son"—"the Father," which also predominates elsewhere in the unity.

12. Obviously, this pair of themes also dominates the central Amen saying of v. 24.

13. The tenses chosen in vv. 21–22 and vv. 26–27 correspond to this: if the soteriological statements in vv. 21–22 are formulated in the present or perfect tense, i.e., they look (from the perspective of the Gospel) at the *present* saving action of the Son, the evangelist has chosen the aorist in vv. 26b and 27a in order to express the Christological *precondition* of that saving action—the unique action of God on his Son in the past.

14. The soteriological-anthropological intensification of vv. 28–29—the future resurrection of the dead and their fate according to their earthly way of life—leads away from the Christological perspective, which again determines v. 30. This confirms the supplementary hypothesis.

15. The justice meant here is not the *iustitia distributiva* of the impartial judge but is measured in a manner similar to the Old Testament by Jesus's inner agreement with the will of his Father.

5.1.2 John 5:19b-20c
A Predetermined Parable?

That this piece of text owes its origin to Johannine tradition has been a hypothesis for some time. P. Gaechter and C. H. Dodd developed it independently of each other in 1962/63.[16] Both claim that the text of verses 19b–20c was originally a parable. This assumption has been met with approval[17] but has also been rejected[18] or developed further in other directions.[19] In any case, there are good arguments for the assumption that the verses are based on tradition. What are they?

(1) The first argument arises from the observation of *tensions* between the context and the presumed tradition. J. Blank has precisely identified the crucial point: "One difficulty," he writes, "seems to arise from verse 20b [= 20d]: how can the Father, if he always already 'shows *everything*' to the Son, show him even '*greater*' works'?"[20] The answer he gives to the question is more of a theological nature.[21] In my opinion, it fails because the schematics of his categories "ontological-one"[22]/ eschatological-historical overtax the tension in verses 19b–20c and verse 20d, e. In contrast, R. Bultmann's literary-critical approach, which assigns verses 19b–20c to his "revelation discourse source," while declaring verse 20d, e to be "an addition of the evangelist to the source ... that once again

---

16. P. Gaechter, "Zur Form von Joh 5,19–30," in *Neutestamentliche Aufsätze*, FS J. Schmid, ed. J. Blinzler, O. Kuss, and F. Mußner (Regensburg: Pustet, 1963), 65–68, here 67–68; Dodd, "Parable," 30–40; *Tradition*, 386 n. 2.

17. Brown, *John*, 1:218: "vss. 19–20a bear all the marks of Johannine theological insight; yet one must not be tempted to evaluate these verses as pure formulations of the evangelist"; Hunter, *John*, 80–81; Lindars, *John*, 221; R. F. Collins, "Proverbial Sayings in St. John's Gospel," in *These Things Have Been Written: Studies on the Fourth Gospel*, LThPM 2 (Leuven: Peeters, 1990), 128–150, here 143–145; P. W. Ensor, *Jesus and His "Works": The Johannine Sayings in Historical Perspective*, WUNT 2/85 (Tübingen: Mohr Siebeck, 1996), 195–226.

18. E.g., Schnackenburg, *Johannesevangelium*, 2:129.

19. See, e.g., Becker, *Johannes*, 2:286–288. See also Frey, *Eschatologie*, 3:36 n. 37; 346–347.

20. J. Blank, *Krisis. Untersuchungen zur johanneischen Christologie und Eschatologie* (Freiburg: Lambertus-Verlag, 1964), 118 (emphasis mine).

21. Blank, *Krisis*, 119: "Verse 20d, e marks ... the *transition* from *Christology* to *eschatology*, from the foundational, personal ontological statement to the statements that now explicitly deal with eschatological events."

22. Blank, *Krisis*, 113.

gives the discourse the reference to verses 1–18" to be closer to the text.[23] For in fact the demonstrative τούτων refers beyond the πάντα of verse 20b and verse 17 to the healing of the paralytic and is therefore a signal for the embedding of the speech in the context that takes place in verse 20d, e. Such a reference from verse 20d *including* verse 19 (and vv. 17–18) to the miracle narrative is also striking because the related formulations of 1:50c (μείζω τούτων) and 14:12c (μείζονα τούτων) have their point of comparison in the *immediately* preceding statement.

Now verse 20d, e following verse 20a–c makes perfect sense. The evangelist relates the given parable in verse 19 to the *earthly* work of Jesus and places the preview of Easter or the post-Easter works of Jesus in verse 20d, e alongside it. This interpretation is supported by the expectation of the readers built up by 5:2–18, according to which Jesus's speech in 5:17ff, which unfolds his dictum in 5:17 ("My Father is still working, and I also am working"), justifies his *present* actions in terms of their inner legitimacy. Jesus does this at the beginning of his speech in verses 19b–20. Therefore, in the ποιεῖν discussed here, he initially has nothing else in mind than his work on the Sabbath just recounted and, beyond that, his earthly salvific activity as a whole. But then, as indicated by the hinge verse in verse 20d, e, he directs his gaze to the future, in which his work will gain a new, higher quality. Even if it cannot be ruled out that the evangelist himself formed the opening verse of the speech in verses 19b–20c, the juxtaposition of πάντα δείκνυσιν αὐτῷ and μείζονα τούτων δείξει αὐτῷ, which he uses meaningfully, indicates that he took up a given saying in verses 19b–20c to integrate it in verse 20d, e into his overall concept. The terminology used here ("greater works"), which seems abstract compared to the figurative language of the tradition, reveals his handywork.[24] The decisive factor is whether the Amen-saying itself hints at its transmission.

(2) This is the case when we think of the two *present tenses* "see" (v. 19c) and "show" (v. 20b). The fact that Jesus is dependent on his Father, who sent him, in what he says and does is a topos that occurs throughout the Gospel. The fact that the messenger is always "being taught" by the Father who sends him, however, always *precedes* the performance of the mission[25] and refers to the status of the *preexistence* of the one sent. For this reason, the perfect and not the aorist tense is used exclusively: "He testifies to what he *has seen*[26] and *heard*[27]" (3:32).[28] The

---

23. Bultmann, *Johannes*, 189 n. 2.

24. John 1:50c; 14:12c.

25. John 8:28.

26. John 6:46; 8:38 as well as 1:18!

27. John 8:26, 40; 15:15!

28. John 12:49: "For I have not spoken on my own, but the Father who sent me has himself *given me a commandment* about what to say and what to speak."

fact that 5:19b–20c is the only text in Gospel that deviates from this,[29] when it is noticed at all, has received different explanations. R. Bultmann, who sees "no difference" between the two forms of language,[30] recognizes the myth of the *preexistent* divine entity in the background.[31] J. Blank and R. Schnackenburg, however, interpret the phrases in the present tense ontologically, aiming at the *earthly* status of the incarnate Logos.[32] J. Becker refers to the *postexistence of* the exalted one,[33] but reserves this interpretation for the tradition he postulates, the style of which the evangelist projected back into the life of the earthly Jesus. The text is best understood as referring neither to the preexistence nor to the postexistence of the revelator but to his *earthly* activity, which the evangelist also believes is meant here. If we take the present tense forms "see" and "show" seriously, we cannot avoid their *metaphorical* meaning that makes verses 19b–20c a parable overall. The *special role of* the piece thus becomes obvious. Of course, the evangelist could have formulated it; but it remains striking that in the Gospel the Son's being instructed by the Father (his "hearing" and "learning" from him) is always thematized in terms of his *preexistence with him*, even if this first phase of the heavenly empowerment of the messenger, which precedes the phase of the earthly execution of his mission, is *never* mythically depicted. The messenger's acts of "listening" and "hearing" in his preexistent communion with the Father is intended literally, not metaphorically.

(3) From a *stylistic* point of view, there are hardly any deviations from the evangelist's other use of language in 5:19–20. It is only noteworthy that the love of the Father for the Son is mentioned several times in the Gospel (3:35; 10:17; 15:9;

---

29. John 5:30b is also formulated in present tense for the sake of the framework of 5:19.

30. Bultmann, *Johannes*, 190.

31. "What was once meant in real terms in the myth has become an image for the evangelist—and already for his source: the changing expressions, that the Son does or speaks what he has seen or heard from the Father, indiscriminately express that he is *the revealer in whom God himself acts and speaks*" (Bultmann, *Johannes*, 190).

32. Blank, *Krisis*, 114–115; Schnackenburg, *Johannesevangelium*, 2:130.

33. Becker, Johannes, 2:283–284: Becker, *Johannes*, 2:283–284: "For the Son can only observe the Father in his work in heaven (vv. 19, 20a have the present tense!). Thus, the common heavenly place creates the possibility of the functional unity of Father and Son with regard to their work in the world. Then the exaltation is the time of the appointment, and the present tense is always the description of the status of the dignity of the exalted Son." The prerequisite for this interpretation is the assumption that, in addition to vv. 19b–20c, vv. 21–23b also belong to the tradition. "In terms of genre," these "can be seen as descriptive praise based on the Christology of exaltation" (284–285). However, elements of praise are completely absent from the text. See M. Theobald, "'Spruchgut' im Johannesevangelium. Bestandsaufnahme und weiterführende Überlegungen zur Konzeption von J. Becker," in *Das UrChristentum in seiner literarischen Geschichte*, FS J. Becker, ed. U. Mell and U. Müller, BZNW 100 (Berlin: de Gruyter, 1999), 335–367 here 339 and 362–363.

17:24, 26), always using the verb ἀγαπᾶν except here where φιλεῖν is used. Perhaps we can "conclude from this that the evangelist wanted to emphasize personal love. The two Greek verbs alternate in John for a reason."[34] Here, Ensor sees this as a hint at the presence of traditional material,[35] but the more affectionate connotation present with φιλεῖν (Schnackenburg) fits well with the metaphorical development of the Father-Son relationship. What the Son learns in the presence of his Father is accompanied by the Father's loving gaze. In this respect, the choice of the verb is a marker for the metaphorical character of these verses.

(4) The evangelist gladly circles back to his "words of the Lord" in a theologically reflective manner.[36] He only takes up 5:19 almost literally in an *inclusio* with 5:30. But the saying still has a clear effect later on, in 8:28,[37] 9:33,[38] and 15:15. In this context, it is important to note that 5:19–20 is the *first* passage of the Gospel that Jesus (in the sense of the later developed Christology of the envoy[39]) radically points away from himself and directs attention to the Father as the decisive actor in his mission. In this respect, 5:19–20 fulfills something like the function of a fundamental referential saying that is developed in what follows, especially in Jesus's Jerusalem disputes with "the Jews." P. W. Ensor rightly remarks, "the dominant motif used for Jesus's life and ministry in the Fourth Gospel is [...] 'the revealer envoy model' [...]. Jn. 5,19f. represents a break from this dominant motif since it pictures Jesus as having some kind of experience of the Father in the present as a guide for his own actions."[40]

5.1.3 Form, Genre, and Intention of the Tradition

John 5:19b–20c represents a self-contained, sufficient unit:

>   19 b   *Very truly I tell you,*
>   c   I. the Son can do (ποιεῖν) nothing on his own,
>   d   but (ἐὰν μή) (he does) only what he sees the Father doing (ποιοῦντα).

---

34. Schnackenburg, *Johannes*, 2:131 with n. 2; Spicq, "Agapè," *TLNT* 3:219–245.

35. Also *Ensor, Jesus*, 214 (under c).

36. See above at pp. 47–48!

37. "*I do nothing on my own*, but I speak these things as the Father instructed me"; see also 7:17–18, 28; 12:49; 14:10.

38. "If this man were not from God, *he could do nothing.*"

39. The fact that Jesus is sent by God has already been established in 3:17, 34; 4:34, without, however, unfolding it in the manner of clarifying oppositions.

40. Ensor, *Jesus*, 214–215.

Parables and Similar Metaphors

      e   II. For whatever that one does (ποιεῖ),
      f   the Son does (ποεῖ) likewise (ὁμοίως).[41]
20 a   III. The Father loves the Son
     b   and shows him all
     c   that he himself is doing (ποιεῖ).

Apart from the introductory Amen formula, the saying comprises *three pairs* of lines, whereby the second line of the third unit is split once again due to the concluding relative clause. The first and second sequences form an antithesis: What verse 19c, d states negatively, verse 19e, f explicates positively. Finally, verse 20 states the reason (the Father's love for the Son) for the pupil-teacher relationship articulated above and summarizes it (in v. 20b, c). The fact that the third sequence represents the climax of the saying is also made clear by the following scheme:

I.   Son   –   Father
II.   Father –   Son
III.   Father

According to these relations, I and II are arranged as a chiasm. Sequence III, whose continuous subject is the Father, stands out from pairs I and II. The fact that the Father *shows* the Son everything he himself does corresponds to the second line of I, which says the Son *sees* the Father at work.[42] All lines of the saying contain the prominent keyword ποιεῖν, which, apart from the first line, is always placed at the end of the line. This is hardly a coincidence since the verb signals exactly what the saying is about: the intimate bond between the Son and the Father in *action*.

In terms of *genre*, the saying is a *metaphor* or a *parable in the narrower sense*[43] that does not, however, recognize a division into figurative and factual halves. Recent theories of parables claim that figurative stories can show punctually metaphorical concentration without becoming allegories. Therefore, it is superfluous and against the natural understanding of the text to postulate for this isolated parable a generic understanding of the nouns "Son" and "Father," which occur with a definite article, to reserve its explicit Christological understanding

---

41. ὁμοίως denotes the same quality of action.

42. The words about the acts of the *Son* in v. 19c correspond to the words about the acts of the *Father* in v. 19d.

43. On the terminology, see Bultmann, *Geschichte*, 181. The continuous present tense in vv. 19b–c speaks against identifying its genre as a *parable*. Dodd, "Parable," 39–40, points to Matt 5:15 and Luke 8:16 as formal parallels to John 5:19c, d.

("*the* Son"/"*the* Father") only for the evangelist. Rather, the latter will already apply to the figurative saying, indeed will be at its origin, whereby it is characteristic that it translates the Christological language game "the Son"—"the Father" given to it into a sequence of images without allegorizing the individual elements.[44] Much more, the figurative saying with its little "story" is concerned with a certain point. Its point is that the Son lives in personal communion with the Father; he learns in his workshop by watching him. This is why he could never have accomplished what he actually "does" without his example—namely doing the same as his Father.[45] The dominance of the keyword ποιεῖν could indicate that the figurative word thematizes Jesus's relationship to God in the orientation of his *miraculous activity*. Thus, R. Riesner not without reason draws attention to the following parable in the Jerusalem Talmud in the context of our tradition as well as in view of Matthew 11:27/Luke 10:22:

> A parable of a master carpenter,
> who had a tool
> which he handed over to his son
> when he took his place.
> God also gave the Israelites the knowledge
> to do miracles[46] (y. Roš Haš 57b).

The *pragmatic intention* of the tradition of John 5:19b–20c seems to have pursued *cognitive* rather than paraenetic interests.[47] It was obviously concerned with presenting a proper understanding of the confession of Jesus as the "Son of God," bearing in mind the metaphorical quality of this Christological designation.[48] Perhaps the tradition had its *Sitz im Leben* in the confrontation with the

---

44. Thus "seeing" Jesus cannot be limited to a mystical vision of the "Father" by the "Son."

45. Gaechter, "Form," 67: "In the ancient Orient, as even today as far as China, the son prefers to follow his father's profession. Thus, the physician passes on his art to his son [b. Qid. 82ab], the art of showbread baking is passed on in the Garmo family, the preparation of incense in that of Abbotina [Yoma 3:11]; Jesus himself practiced the craft of his father Joseph (Mark 6:3; Matt 13:55). This is the historical background of the parable." See also Mark 1:19–20. For further illustrative material, see Dodd, "Parable," 32–39. See also Stegemann, Sozialgeschichte, 38, on the economic enterprises of the ancient Mediterranean: "Small businesses undoubtedly predominated, which as family businesses may have employed one or two wage laborers or slaves."

46. R. Riesner, *Jesus als Lehrer. Eine Untersuchung zum Ursprung der Evangelien-Überlieferung*, WUNT II/7 (Tübingen: Mohr Siebeck, 1981; 2nd ed. 1984), 221.

47. At least it is noticeable that the addressees of the figurative saying are not explicitly mentioned. Verse 20d, e ("and he will show him greater works than these, *so that you will not be astonished*") is due to the editing by the evangelist.

48. See *Theobald*, "Sohn Gottes" 185–207.

Parables and Similar Metaphors 213

synagogue. Against the suspicion of a deification of Jesus that was dangerous for biblical monotheism, it would then have presented Jesus's subordination to his Father as a condition for the possibility of his sovereign action with reference to the Son's rightful place in the "family hierarchy." This made it attractive to the evangelist, who used it for exactly the same purpose.

5.1.4 A Parable of Jesus?

One is surprised at the confidence with which some scholars claim John 5:19b–20c for the historical Jesus without much ado. Thus C. H. Dodd recognizes in our figurative word a memory of Jesus's youth, "when he learned his trade in the family workshop at Nazareth."[49] R. Riesner says under the heading "Joseph as Teacher": "The paternal instruction that Jesus received from Joseph in his profession and the Holy Scriptures is also reflected in two genuine Jesus logia," whereby in addition to our saying he also has Matthew 11:27 par. Luke 10:22.[50] P. Gaechter seems to be more cautious when he points out "that John removed all the color from the parable, so that only its framework remained, as when one has stripped the leaves from a bush; so it corresponds to the sayings of Jesus in John."[51] Thus, the Johannine tradition only contained the extract of the original Jesus parable, not the parable itself. But can we really trust the evangelist not only to have preserved a dry, lifeless compact saying from an originally lively and colorful but now lost Jesus parable, but even to have produced it himself? What is not considered in all these discussions are the following two aspects:

(1) If a given tradition of sayings can be made plausible in the Johannine text, this does not automatically determine whether it is also a saying of *Jesus*. We must reckon with the creativity of the Johannine community. (2) The attempt to interpret the terms "Son" and "Father" generically is already dictated by the assumption of the "historicity" of the word, insofar as Jesus is probably credited with a *veiled* use of the term "Son" in the parable, but not with the undisguised use of an absolute "*the* Son" with regard to himself.[52] It is more likely, however, that our figurative word already *presupposes* this absolute use and therefore belongs in the context of logia such as Matthew 11:27 par. Luke 10:22; Mark

---

49. Dodd, "Parable," 40; also Hunter, *John*, 80–81.

50. Riesner, "Jesus," 220.

51. Gaechter, "Form," 67.

52. Thus J. Jeremias, *Neutestamentliche Theologie I. Die Verkündigung Jesu*, 3rd ed. (Gütersloh: Gütersloher Verlag, 1973), 63–65, who says of Matt 11:27 par. Luke 10:22: this logion also contains only "a very general proposition of experience": "only Father and Son really know each other."

13:32 par. Matthew 24:36,[53] the historicity of which is debated and can probably be ruled out.[54]

The fact that John 5:19b-20c belongs to *the context* of Matthew 11:27 par. Luke 10:22[55] does not mean that there is also a *historical* connection with this logion. Such a connection is rather unlikely for the following reasons:[56]

(a) The linguistic differences between the Johannine logion of the synoptic tradition and the linguistic conventions of the Fourth Gospel are unmistakable.[57]

(b) A motif reference of our logion to the saying in Q 10:22 can at most be established via its first sentence *"all things have been handed over to me by my Father,"*[58] if one places John 5:20b, c *"he shows him all that he himself is doing"* to one side and also takes into account the "resumption" of John 5:19-20 in John 3:35b *"and he has placed all things in his hands"* (cf. Dan 1:2 Θ). But caution is advisable. If John 5:20b, c offers a metaphorical statement drawn from everyday imagery, Q 10:22a is theologically charged and has its "closest formal, but probably also substantive analogy in Matt 28:18."[59] "The title Son of Man is not mentioned here. In terms of content, however, the statement about handing over of all power corresponds to the apocalyptic Son of Man

---

53. The absolute usage of "the Son" is found in the New Testament. Apart from the Johannine writings, it is only found in 1 Cor 15:28; Matt 28:19 (Trinitarian baptismal formula) and Heb 1:8.

54. On Matt 11:27/Luke 10:22, see most recently Luz, *Matthäus*, 2:200: "The evidence for a Semitic linguistic background is not unambiguous. Mainly for reasons of content, most authors generally assume a community formation here: Jesus hardly spoke of the 'Son,' nor of the reciprocal and exclusive knowledge of the Father."

55. On the relation of this Q-saying to the Fourth Gospel, see J. D. G. Dunn, *Jesus and the Spirit: A Study of the Religious and Charismatic Experience of Jesus and the First Christians as Reflected in the New Testament* (London: Eerdmans, 1975), 27-34; Tuckett, Gospel, 286-287; Theobald, Das sog. "johanneische Logion" 165-189.

56. Against Lindars, *John*, 221: "Perhaps the *same* parable of Jesus lies at the basis of Matt 11:27; Luke 10:22." Critically Ensor, *Jesus*, 205.

57. Jeremias, *Theologie*, 65: "The fact that ἐπιγινώσκειν (according to Matthew) and ἀποκαλύπτειν are un-Johannean vocabulary and that παραδιδόναι is never said of God in John speaks against the existence of a logion of Johannine character" (Robinson/Hoffmann/Kloppenborg, Edition 192-193, but claims Luke's use is connected to Q 10:22a). But then Jeremias continues: "Conversely, it is easy to imagine that in Matt 11:27 par. once the absolutely used ὁ υἱός is understood titularly, it could give important impulses to Johannine Christology with its statements about knowledge. We may therefore have before us one of the logia of Jesus from which Johannine theology grew. Without approaches in the synoptic tradition, its origin would remain a complete mystery" (65).

58. See Ensor, *Jesus*, 207 n. 45.

59. P. Hoffmann, *Studien zur Theologie der Logienquelle*, NTA.NF 8, 3rd ed. (Münster: Aschendorff, 1982), 118 with n. 81 (Lit.).

Parables and Similar Metaphors

statements."[60] "This transfer of power, however, is not described as a future process, as would correspond to the apocalyptic tradition and, in Q, to the discourse on the future coming of the Son of Man. Rather, the aorist παρεδόθη, similar to Matt 28:18 (ἐδόθη), emphasizes the fact that the transfer of power has (already) taken place."[61] Now John 5:22 also offers a statement reminiscent of this Son of Man Christology, which Nestle-Aland (from 24th ed.) also confirms with its reference in the margin to 1 Enoch 69:27[62] "The Father has *handed over all judgment* to the Son (= Son of Man) (δέδωκεν)." The δέδωκεν can be compared with παρεδόθη from Q 10:22a and ἐδόθη μοι (πᾶσα ἐξουσία...) from Matthew 28:18. It is taken up twice more following John 5:22, namely in verse 26 and verse 27, where verse 27fin. explicitly states: "He (s.c. the Son) is the *Son of Man*." Decisive for this explanation is the traditional motif of judgment/rule—life—Son of Man, whose futuristic-eschatological reference the evangelist has transformed here into his present-eschatological conception. It is precisely this eschatological aspect that is missing in John 5:19b–20c, however, which is why it is not permissible to establish any kind of connection between the Johannine parable and Q 10:22.

(c) It is rather unlikely that Q 10:22 as a whole was originally a unified and self-contained logion. On the one hand, P. Hoffmann has shown that we are probably dealing here with a "word of commentary" in Q 10:21[63] that never existed independently. On the other hand, it has not been proven that the saying also forms a unit *in itself*. Stylistically, its individual lines are strangely disparate. "In its form, the first line is best characterized as a self-portrayal of Jesus..., while the remaining lines speak in the third person in a doctrinal way about the relationship between Father and Son and about the revelatory activity of the Son."[64] U. Luz confirms this insight[65] and adds his own argument:

---

60. Hoffmann, *Studien*, 121, refering to Dan 7:14, but also 1 En. 46:3; 51:3; 52:4; 69:27.

61. Hoffmann, *Studien*, 121.

62. "And he (s.c. the Son of Man) sat down on the throne of his glory, *and the sum of judgment was given to him, the Son of Man*." (JSHRZ V/6 630).

63. P. Hoffmann, "QR und der Menschensohn. Eine vorläufige Skizze," in *Tradition und Situation* (Münster: Aschendorff, 1955), 243–278 here 262: "In my opinion, the first saying (see Matt 11:25–26/Luke 10:21), which may have been handed down independently, could certainly be situated in the life of Jesus... The second saying (see Matt 11:27/Luke 10:22), which was hardly originally handed down in isolation, is to be understood as an interpretation of the first statement under the assumption of Jesus's identity with the coming bearer of God's sovereignty." Similarly, Luz, *Matthäus*, 2:211: Matt 11:27 – "commentary on vv. 25–26."

64. Hoffmann, *Studien*, 118–119.

65. Luz, *Matthäus*, 2:200: "Verse 27 is a peculiar logion that has its closest parallels in the Gospel of John. Formally, it is peculiar because between v. 27a and b there is a transition from the 1st to the 3rd person."

"Accordingly, there are no parallels to the *whole* logion in the Gospel of John."[66] While he, like many other commentators, refers to passages such as John 3:35; 13:3, but also 5:26; 10:29,[67] for Matt 11:27b he notes: "John 10:14–15 was naturally regarded as related to the saying 'I know my own and my own know me, just as the Father knows me and I know the Father.'"[68] This observation, read from a tradition-criticism perspective, means that Q 10:22 unites two different elements: First, the idea (possibly already originally solidified as a saying) of the reciprocal knowledge of Father and Son, in which "to whom the Son wills to reveal it" is included. Second, the implicit Son of Man statement "all things have been handed over to me by my Father" that serves as a "bridge" to the preceding original logion Q 10:21. This "bridge" was first formed by the Q redactor in order to ensure the connection of his "commentary" (beyond the keyword connection of ἀποκαλύπτειν in vv. 25/27) to the original saying.[69] For the relationship between the so-called Johannine logion in the Synoptics to the Fourth Gospel, it follows that differentiations must be made: John 10:14–15 may well be a late stage in the development of the idea of the reciprocal knowledge of Father and Son attested in Q 10:22b;[70] although John 3:35; 13:3; or 5:26, on the other hand are reminiscent of Q 10:22a, they rather have to be seen as an echo of a popular topos. *John 5:20, however, has nothing to do with the "Johannine" logion of Q.*

---

66. Luz, *Matthäus*, 2:200.

67. Luz, *Matthäus*, 2:210 n. 92.

68. Luz, *Matthäus*, 2:212. See also Hoffmann, *Studien*, 124–125.

69. In the original saying, Jesus probably joined with all those to whom the revelation of God applies (the insight into the end of the reign of the demons [cf. Luke 10:18] or the arrival or nearness of the reign of God?), under the self-designation of the "immature" (νήπιοι) (Jesus himself does not count himself among the "wise men" [σοφοί] of Israel!); in contrast, the "commentary" pursues a Christologization of this revelation that apparently comes to the νήπιοι (including Jesus) without distinction. On the one hand, its content is now understood in a strictly theocentric way (it is about the knowledge of the "*Father*"! This link denotes the climax of the commentary), on the other hand, participation in this knowledge is bound to the *mediation of the "Son,"* to whom the authority was given (the πάντα of Q 10:22a is thus focused on this, as is aptly recognized by Luz, *Matthäus*, 2:211).

70. G. Schneider, "Auf Gott bezogenes 'mein Vater' und 'euer Vater' in den Jesus-Worten der Evangelien. Zugleich ein Beitrag zum Problem Johannes und die Synoptiker," in *The Four Gospels*, FS F. Neirynck, ed. C. M. Tuckett and A. Vanasegbroeck, BEThL 100, vol. 3. (Leuven: Peeters, 1992), 1751–1781 here 1777, speaks of a "more distant dependency." For Q 10:22 this means that the historical background of the Father-Son terminology must be answered *independently* of the Son of Man Christology implied in the first half of the logion. It is to be sought rather in *wisdom* contexts; see Luz, *Matthäus*, 2:209 (lit.), 212–213; Hoffmann, *Studien*, 125: "Q offers an early starting point for the later Johannine development" (see also pp. 134–135). Ibid. n. 102 with literature on John—Q!

Let us summarize: The figurative word in John 5:19b–20c does *not* have its origin in a saying of Jesus. There are two arguments in support of this conclusion:

(1) The figurative saying already presupposes the use of an absolute "the Son"—"the Father"; however, this pair of terms documents an advanced post-Easter stage of Christology.

(2) The *Sitz im Leben* of the figurative saying could have been the confrontation of the congregation with specifically Jewish attacks against the emerging Christology. The moment of *subordination of* the "Son" to the "Father" (see 1 Cor 15:28; cf. v. 24; Mark 13:32), which is inherent in Son-Father relationship would then—translated into a parable—ward off the false impression that Christology could betray biblical-early Jewish monotheism. Rather, monotheism remains the natural framework of Christology according to the character of John 5:19b–20c.

5.1.5 The Reception of the Parable by the Evangelist

As is often the case in the Gospel, here too the traditional logion—a parable in the narrower sense—marks the starting point of Jesus's discourse. The evangelist probably used the parable because it fit with the theme of Jesus's miracles (keyword ποιεῖν) and its family metaphor (Father-Son) seemed ideally suited to answer the main accusation of the contemporary synagogue against the Johannine followers of Jesus, namely that they were not being faithful to biblical monotheism with their high Christology and the assertion of Jesus's preexistence. For how can Christians be accused of blasphemy (cf. 5:17 with 10:33, 36; 19:7) if their confession of Jesus as the only Son of God does not violate the sovereignty of the Father? A metaphorical text is especially suitable as an argumentative answer that makes us aware of the implications of the confession of the Son of God. This answer does not amount to mitigating the high Christological claim but it does shield that claim from misunderstandings. These culminate in the insinuation of ditheism, according to which Christ is claimed to be of equal origin with the "one and only God."[71] However, the following text excludes this misunderstanding with all desirable clarity when it formulates: "He (God) has *given* all judgment (δέδωκεν) to the Son" (v. 22) or "as the Father has life in himself, so also he has *granted* (ἔδωκεν) the Son to have life in himself" (v. 26). In other words, the Son does not possess the authority over life of his own accord but has *received* it from the Father. Seen in this way, there is an *asymmetry* between the Father and Son: What the Father always possesses in himself (i.e., life) the Son has in himself

---

71. The immediate context of 5:44 shows that this predication of God is of course also valid for the Johannine community. "How can you believe if you accept honor from one another but do not seek the honor that comes from the one God?"

solely because the Father has *given* it to him. For Johannine Christology, this is the conceptual version of what the parable of the Father *showing* his Son a craft has depicted vividly. But what is the actual trade the Father has at his disposal and which he teaches his Son?

The two *commentaries* on the parable in verses 21 and 22 provide insight: These are the divine privileges of imparting life or raising the dead as well as the authority to judge, both of which in themselves belong exclusively to God; but he has *transferred* them to his Son. If one realizes the traditional layering of the verses, then one also understands the differences between the first and second commentary sayings: The first in verse 21 is connected to the parable via the editorial connector in verse 20d, e, and repeats the structure of the image with the phrase "just as—so also." The Son sees the Father at work and learns from him. It must logically follow that *both* Father and Son accomplish the work of raising the dead. The second commentary in verse 22 is more pointed: Now we are no longer just talking about the parallel work of both but about the fact that the Father has *transferred* the power to judge—the negative flip side of the power to impart life—entirely (πᾶσαν) to the Son. He is therefore conceived as the only fully valid representative of God in this world. This representation, which constitutes his actual equality with God, is understood soteriologically: It consists in the authority to give life. The commentary statements in verses 26, 27 then deepen this *Christologically* to the effect that this soteriological authority has its *ontic* basis in the status of the Son, to whom the Father has *given the power to have life in himself*. How do these remarks on the divine representation of the Son, which was bestowed on him by the Father, relate to what the parable in verses 19–20 has already explained about the Father's and Son's work?

The decisive signal is obviously the hinge in verse 20d, e, which brings the commentary and the parable into the right relationship to one another: *"And he* [s.c. the Father] *will show him* [the Son] *greater works than these, so that you will be astonished."* The signal instructs the listeners to relate the parable retrospectively to Jesus's wonderful healing activity, which he does not carry out by his own authority but because he has learned it from the Father. But there is something even greater than this that the hinge verse wants to say: These are the works of the true impartation of life to people who are condemned to death, not simply the healing of their physical infirmities but the impartation of "eternal life" to them that is already happening in faith (5:24). But what does the one have to do with the other? The evangelist can probably be understood to mean that Jesus's miraculous deeds of healing, in this case "raising up" the man who had been paralyzed for thirty-eight years, should be read as a *sign of* what Jesus's actual soteriological ability is. He imparts "eternal life" to the ailing man. The evangelist is attempting to communicate that it is only when one reads the "miracles" as

Parables and Similar Metaphors

signals according to this sense that one has understood their actual intention, their function of pointing to something greater.

5.2 The Dying Kernel of Wheat (John 12:24)

John 12:24 is one of the most beautiful of the Johannine "words of the Lord," which has left a particularly lasting impression on the religious memory of Christianity.[72] Given the archetypal power of his image, this is not surprising.[73] It gives belief in resurrection an inner plausibility and expresses the deep longing that it may also be the same in the face of human death as can be observed in nature.

The saying belongs to a group of three sayings (vv. 24+25+26part.) that the redactor of the Gospel pasted into the "Hellenic Discourse" (John 12:23/27-36) later.[74] He probably found this group of sayings together with its authoritative introduction "Very truly, I tell you" in the tradition of his community. As far as the prehistory of the saying about the kernel of wheat in particular is concerned, two possibilities are conceivable: Either the saying was originally an independent Johannine "word of the Lord"[75] that was combined secondarily with the Synoptic pair in 12:25 + 26* to form a single sequence, or else this saying was first used in the Johannine community as a special prelude to the paired saying before the whole sequence was incorporated into the "Hellenic Discourse" by the redactor. Whether the text allows a decision to be made in this regard at all, and if so, in what sense, can only be determined after it has been analyzed.

5.2.1 Shape, Form, Genre, and Intent of the Saying

What did the saying about the "grain of wheat" look like when the editor found it together with the other two sayings? Did he make any changes to it when he entered the sequence into the Gospel? The following observation is interesting: the phrase "fallen into the earth" (πέσων εἰς τὴν γῆν) verse 24b² corresponds to

---

72. Dietzfelbinger, *Johannes*, 1:390, recalls that Dostoyevsky placed this saying as a slogan at the beginning of his novel *The Brothers Karamazov*. "In doing so, he turned it into an anthropological concept without cutting off the Christological root: the man who gives himself for others is the fruitful man."

73. Think of its widespread use in the history of religion in antiquity (cf. 5.2.3 below)!

74. See above at pp. 101-103. See Theobald, Das Evangelium nach Johannes 794f.

75. Dodd, *Tradition*, 369. Linguistically it is remarkable: "die" (ἀποθνῄσκειν) occurs twenty-six times in John, but apart from 12:24 *never* in a saying of Jesus; three times others (Caiaphas) use it of Jesus's death (11:50-51; 18:14), three times the narrator uses it in marginal notes (12:33; 18:32; 19:7). For the evangelist, the word is therefore not a typical term for Jesus's death.

the word of exaltation in verse 32 toward the end of the "Hellenic discourse": "and when I am lifted up *from the earth* (ἐκ τῆς γῆς), I will draw all to myself." It looks as if the reader is already being set on a certain track in verse 24 by the emphasis of a single image: The falling of the grain of wheat "to the earth" or "into it" is to be understood as an allusion to the descent of the Son of Man into the lowlands of the earth, which then corresponds to his ascent or exaltation from the earth (see Eph 4:9–10). If the reference to the "dying" of the grain of wheat is a usable metaphor that, in order to be understandable, does not need to be explained by the πέσων εἰς τὴν γῆν,[76] then one can consider whether this adverbial addition is not due to the intention of the author to anchor the group of sayings in their context.[77] Without it, the saying has a well-proportioned form that corresponds exactly to the two other sayings in the sequence, each with four lines. We therefore hypothetically assume the following form of the saying:

If the kernel of wheat does not ... die,
it remains alone;
but if it dies,
it bears much fruit.

The saying bears the marks of *antithetical parallelism* consisting of two syntactically identical conditional phrases. It is a general statement: Without "dying," a grain of wheat will never be able to bear fruit. Is this a "proverbial statement"?[78] What is the nature of this "figurative saying"?[79]

(1) Even if "to die" is a common metaphor for a grain of wheat sinking into the ground, the word choice was probably determined by the view of *Jesus's death*.

(2) Surprising is the opposition of the saying "remain *alone*" and "bear *rich fruit*." If one looks at the first element, it does not seem to be the fate of the grain *itself* (e.g., "if it does not die, *it rots*"), but its unproductivity: It remains *alone*![80] In other words, if it dies, then it bears much fruit in the sense that it *multiplies*. Such a resolution of the metaphor results in its Christological interpretation: Jesus "must die so that he can find followers, a congregation."[81] The fruit that the dying grain of wheat bears is its soteriological productivity! If this reading

---

76. See only 1 Cor 15:36, "Fool! What you sow does not come to life *unless it dies*."

77. At the same time, this is a signal that v. 24 is to be read *Christologically* following v. 23.

78. P. von Gemünden, *Vegetationsmetaphorik im Neuen Testament und seiner Umwelt. Eine Bildfelduntersuchung*, NTOA 18 (Freiburg et al.: Herder, 1993), 205.

79. Bultmann, *Johannes*, 324; Brown, *John*, 1:471.

80. See Brown, *John*, 1:471–472.

81. Von Gemünden, *Vegetationsmetaphorik*, 205.

is correct, then the genre definition of the saying as a "wise saying" falls short. The *matter itself*, the conviction of the soteriological necessity of *Jesus's* death, has found its way into the image. We are not talking about just any grain of wheat but about the true grain of wheat, Jesus; the definite article is not meant generically but individually.

If one agrees with the two preceding observations, then one will take the "figurative saying" seriously in its Christological focus: As already observed with the other Johannine parables and "figurative sayings," the Johannine tradition as a whole seems to be characterized by a Christological appropriation of the parabolic. *On the other hand*, the continuation of the saying sequence with verse 25 shows that verse 24 must also be understood in a broader, namely paradigmatic or better prototypical sense. What can be read from the way of Jesus—that death is the birth of new life—also applies as a "law of life" for his followers: "when the grain of wheat dies, it bears much fruit."[82] Consequently, we can assume a (semantic and generic) *multilayered nature* of the "figurative saying" in verse 24: On the one hand, it is Christologically centered; on the other hand, it is the "basic saying" for verses 25–26 also in the sense that it standardizes the way for the followers of Jesus.

5.2.2 The Figurative Saying and the Synoptic Form History (*Formgeschichte*)

In his study of this figurative saying, C. H. Dodd emphasized its universally valid character, "Here we have a description of a certain natural phenomenon, a phenomenon so constantly recurrent that it can be stated in the form of an 'observed invariable sequence' (which is what is popularly called a 'law of nature'): 'If A occurs, then B occurs.'"[83] According to Dodd, the same structure can also be found in the synoptic figurative sayings that also consist of a conditional "if" clause + a generally valid apodosis. Matthew 5:13: "*If* . . . the salt has lost its taste . . . . It is no longer good for anything." Mark 3:24: "*If* a kingdom is divided against itself, that kingdom cannot stand." John 12:24 is particularly close in formal terms to the antithetical metaphor of Matthew 6:22–23: "So, *if* your eye is healthy, your whole body will be full of light; but *if* your eye is unhealthy, your whole body will be full of darkness." If the interpretation of such figurative words in the synoptic tradition is usually done through their framing, then in John 12:24 the following saying in John 12:25 takes over.

But it is not only in terms of *genre* and *form that* the phrase "grain of wheat" moves along Synoptic lines. C. H. Dodd also places its *imagery* there with

---

82. In this case, the metaphor of the "rich fruit" would stand for "eternal life" (see 12:25).

83. Dodd, *Tradition*, 366. on the following, see pp. 366–369.

reference to the related parable of the mustard seed.[84] However, it is precisely the image of the grain of wheat that indicates the special status of the logion with its spread even in *non-Jewish* religious contexts of the Hellenistic environment.

5.2.3 "Die and become!" The Archetypical Character of Symbol of the Grain of Wheat

"The death of the seed was a common topos in antiquity."[85] Rabbinic Judaism— to name only the most important—uses the image of the grain of wheat that is placed in the earth in order to germinate in the context of the discourse on the burial and resurrection of man.[86]

H. Braun cites two examples from the pagan Greek world: *Epict. diss.* IV 8.35–40[87] and Plutarch, Fragment 104 of Εἰς τὰ Ἡσιόδου Ἔργα.[88] The ancient Hellenistic foundation on which the symbol of the grain of wheat rests becomes clearer if we take into account the mystery cults[89] about which a broad textual

---

84. Dodd, *Tradition*, 367–368: "If John speaks of a κόκκος σίτου, the Synoptics speak of a κόκκος σινάπεως, and the Johannine πεσὼν εἰς τὴν γῆν may be regarded as only one more way of describing the phenomenon of sowing for which Mark has ὅταν σπαρῇ ἐπὶ τῆς γῆς. . . ." The clause αὐτὸς μόνος μένει would have a "distinctively Johannine ring."

85. Von Gemünden, *Vegetationsmetaphorik*, 206: "In the background is the ancient idea that the seed perishes before it grows anew." See also H. Braun, "Das 'Stirb und Werde' in der Antike und im Neuen Testament," in idem, *Gesammelte Studien zum Neuen Testament und seiner Umwelt*, 3rd edition (Tübingen: Mohr Siebeck, 1971), 136–158, here 140–141.

86. See b. Sanh 90b: "Queen Cleopatra said to R. Meir: I know that the dead will rise, for it is said (see Ps 72:16): *They shall spring forth out of the city as the plants out of the earth*; but shall they rise naked, or with the garments [= bodies]? He replied to her: 'This is to be inferred from the lesser to the more important from a grain of wheat: if a grain of wheat that is buried naked comes forth clothed in many garments, how much more the pious who are buried in their garments'"; see also b. Ketub. 111b; b. Ta'an. 4a; y. Ketub. 12:2; Rab. Eccl. 5:10 § 1; Pique R. El. 33. On this, see V. Farina, *Die Leiblichkeit der Auferstandenen. Ein Beitrag zur Analyse des paulinischen Gedankenganges in 1Kor 15,35–58* (Würzburg: Fenske, 1971), 53–66.

87. The "burying of the seed" here is an image for the person practicing philosophy, who must hide until his store of education is large enough to mature to perfection.

88. The seed is hidden in the earth where it rots and gives up its strength to the earth before *one* grain (ἐξ ἑνός) can become a *multitude* of grains (πλῆθος)! Fragment 104 (in LCL XV 212ff.) is about the agrarian process of sowing as such and its right timing, and is not a metaphorical statement.

89. See H.-J. Klauck, *Die religiöse Umwelt des Urchristentums I. Stadt- und Hausreligion, Mysterienkulte, Volksglaube* (Stuttgart: Kohlhammer, 1995), 1:77–128; Burkert, *Mysterien*; M. Giebel, *Das Geheimnis der Mysterien. Antike Kulte in Griechenland, Rom und Ägypten* (Zürich et al.: Patmos, 1990).

Parables and Similar Metaphors 223

evidence is lacking. The topos "die and become!" namely, of death leading to life, plays a central role in almost all such cults in connection with the vegetation cycle: A hero or goddess dies, enters the underworld, and is resurrected from there or proves to be fruitful in another way. In this context, ears of wheat can be found in images of the various cults as symbols of the newly gained life-creating fertility,[90] particularly frequently in the cult of Demeter-Kore in Eleusis,[91] in the cult of Cybele in Phrygia and later in Rome,[92] with Isis and Osiris in Egypt, but also in images of the slain bull of Mithras.[93] Plutarch's remarks on "Isis and Osiris" provide interesting material on the symbol of the grain of wheat in mystery cults:

Plutarch provides the cult myth of Isis and Osiris with clear echoes of the myth of Demeter of Eleusis; we learn that Osiris, who ruled over Egypt, was credited with the introduction of agriculture, among other things (§ 13). A basic feature of his account is that he deals with the myths of the gods in an enlightened and critical manner, distinguishing between the mythical idea and the truth actually meant by it. Thus, he opposes various identifications (e.g., of celestial bodies with gods or of processes from the agrarian cycle of nature with events of the Osiris myth); he rejects, for example, the idea that Osiris is buried when the seed is hidden under the earth and comes to life again and appears as soon as germination begins (§ 65). In this context, Plutarch mentions that Persephone is described by Cleanthes as "the breath blowing and dying through the crops" and that another poet called the cutting of the ears of corn a cutting of the limbs of Demeter (§ 66; also §§ 69–70). In contrast to such superstitious ideas, he emphasizes that the ancients did not regard the crops and their seeds as gods but as "gifts of the gods." At the time of sowing, the seed was laid down in the earth for future perfection, as at a funeral (§ 70). Only later would people in their ignorance have transferred the conditions of the crops to the gods and equated the emergence and disappearance of food with the emergence and disappearance

---

90. See Giebel, *Geheimnis*, with many pictures at, e.g., 19, 134, 159.

91. Giebel, *Geheimnis*, 45: "The initiates recognize the ear of corn as the image of life emerging anew from the womb of the earth; it points . . . to transformation, to a passage through death," p. 19 (pond relief of Eleusis, ca. 430 BCE: the king's son Triptolemos receives the first ears of corn from Demeter); Burkert, *Mysterien*, pic. 4 (Lovatelli-urn: Demeter with ears of corn in her hair); ibid. 68.

92. According to the church father Hippolytus, Attis was called "the fresh-cut ear of corn" by the Phrygians (*haer.* 5.8). Giebel, *Geheimnis*, 134 (fig.: Attis of Ostia with Phrygian cap and the crescent moon, in which ears of grain are inserted). On the equation of Attis with the cut ear of grain, see Burkert, *Mysterien*, 69.

93. Burkert, *Mysterien*, pic. 11: Mithras relief in Neuenheim: Mithras kills the bull, the tail turns into ears of corn.

of the gods, which Plutarch considers to be godlessness: It is ridiculous, he says, to plead plaintively for the crops to come forth again and complete themselves so that they might be consumed and mourned over again. The text not only shows in an exemplary manner how the mythical ideas of the various countries intermingled with Hellenism but also illustrates the link between cult myths and actions and agricultural and seasonal processes. The idea of the grain of wheat buried in the earth, which returns to life with the resulting plant, plays an important role here.

The difference between the cyclical time conception of myth and the Christian-Jewish appreciation of history has repeatedly been pointed out against an understanding of John 12:24 within the horizon of the conceptual world of the mystery cults: If myth claims timeless validity in accordance with the periodically repeating natural processes, a saying such as John 12:24 is based on the uniqueness of the event of Jesus's death and resurrection.[94] As accurately as this difference is marked, it remains true that Jesus's death and resurrection have *a prototypical* character for all those who unite with him in faith, that is, they find their *own path* mapped out in the way of Jesus. Such a structure of uniformity between the fate of Jesus and that of his followers corresponds to the myth and the cultic acts associated with it; here, too, the initiates can perceive the secret of their own path in the fate of the cult hero. So if one interprets the choice of the significant symbolism of the grain of wheat in John 12:24, which extends beyond the related semantic range of in the Synoptics, with all due caution in the light of the Hellenistic mystery cults, then one can state the implicit intention of the saying: what people hope to gain from their initiation into the mysteries in terms of the power to endure the mystery of their death[95] is fulfilled in their participation in the fate of the dying grain of wheat (i.e., Jesus). It is possible that those who formed the saying about the grain of wheat had in mind the attractiveness of following Jesus in the context of the contemporary mystery religions and wanted to express this by choosing this specific symbolism. This does not mean that they leveled out the profound differences between the two religious worlds. An inconspicuous but not unimportant observation may support this: "The emphasis on the *necessity* of dying [. . .] is new and specifically Christian

---

94. Kaipuram, *Paroimiai*, 52: "While in the so-called mystery religions a myth is historicized, in John we have history as the starting point. The Johannine logion symbolizes a divine intervention in history. The essential fatalism involved in the cycle of nature has given way to a free choice.... The death of Jesus ... is a free choice."

95. W. Burkert, *Homo Necans. Interpretationen altgriechischer Opferriten und Mythen*, 2nd ed. (Berlin: de Gruyter, 1997), 292: "That the path to death leads to life is the hope of the mystic."

against the background of the ancient use of metaphors."⁹⁶ Behind this is the knowledge of *Jesus's death*, that is, the belief that all salvation—the gift of "rich fruit"—depends on God's own involvement in history, as demonstrated by Jesus's death.

5.2.4 John 12:24 as a Basic Saying in the Sequence in 12:24–26d

Viewed *diachronically*, the saying about the grain of wheat in verse 24 in the Johannine community is secondary to the synoptic pair of sayings in verses 25/26. Viewed *synchronically*, it represents the basic saying in this constellation, which is interpreted in the following sayings, now both as words of commentary. This concerns two points. First, verses 25–26, especially verse 26a–d, explain what it means that the grain of wheat, when it dies, no longer remains *alone* but bears much fruit: It gets followers (v. 26b), and where Jesus is, there will also be his servant, in life (v. 26c, d). This presupposes a *Christological* reading of the saying about the grain of wheat. On the other hand, verse 25 takes up the saying about the grain of wheat in such a way that it understands it as an expression of a "law of life" that applies to Jesus and his followers: "Whoever loves his life will lose it, and whoever hates his life in this world will keep it in eternal life." Seen in this light, the saying about the grain of wheat that only becomes fruitful when it dies illustrates a *universal* law whose anthropological truth is rooted in the mystery of Christ. In view of our initial question as to whether verse 24 was originally an independent Johannine saying or whether it was a basic saying on its own or was created as a basic saying specifically for the sequence verses 24–26d is not easy to decide. On the one hand, its opposition "remain *alone*"—"bear *much* fruit" in its specific soteriological sense seems to have been designed for explication and could therefore have been specifically designed as a prelude to verses 25–26. On the other hand, it is quite possible (if not probable) that the rounded saying originally existed as a single saying, as its opposition μόνος— πολύς, which was part of the semantic field,⁹⁷ is also understandable on its own.

---

96. Von Gemünden, *Vegetationsmetaphorik*, 206–207; Braun, "Stirb," 145: "This underlining is the *Christianum* in the utilization of the topos of the seed"; cf. 1 Cor 15:36b.

97. It therefore does not have to be interpreted in the specifically soteriological sense, which it *also* has according to the commentary of vv. 25–26 (*one* Christ—*many* followers); according to Plutarch (see n. 296 above), it was part of the semantic range (see also 1 Clem 24:5); Braun, "Stirb," 142: "this trait, apparently often belonging to the topos." See also *Ep. Jac.* 8:16–23 ("For the word is like a grain of wheat. When someone sowed it, he put his faith in it. When it grew, he loved it, because he saw *many* grains instead of *one*. And when he had accomplished the work, he

The fact that it was then open to different interpretations does not argue against the assumption of its original independence, as we have a figurative saying before us that is inherently ambiguous.

The redactors use the sequence that was in the service of the Johannine congregation. Here, the trio of sayings, including the preceding Amen formula (served to proclaim life!), was probably placed in its current position in the Gospel because the motif of the "rich fruit" of the dying grain of wheat seemed highly appropriate as a frame for the scene: Jesus's death brings "rich fruit" because salvation arises from it not only for the Jews but also for the Greeks (v. 20), for Israel *and* the nations, as it says in verse 32: "And I, when I am lifted up from the earth, will draw *all* people to myself!" Of course, this only happens after Easter, in the mission of the community, which is why in this scene there is still no direct contact between the Greek pilgrims to the temple who want to see Jesus and Jesus himself.

5.3 The Vine (John 15:1–8)

For some time now, it has been assumed that 15:1–8 is based on the tradition of a discourse about a grapevine,[98] but it has not yet been possible to present a reconstruction that is conclusive. The results of the few attempts diverge,[99] and the criteria are also not clear.[100] It is therefore not surprising that many commentators, in their interpretation of the text, dispense with critical hypotheses of transmission altogether and believe that they can explain it in purely synchronic terms. The text reveals, however, veins and inner layers that make it seem advisable not to understand it one-dimensionally as a continuous

---

was delivered, having prepared food..."): D. Kirchner, "Brief des Jakobus," in *Neutestamentliche Apokryphen in deutscher Übersetzung*, vol. 1: *Evangelien*, ed. W. Schneemelcher (Tübingen: Mohr Siebeck, 1999], 234–244, here 241.

98. See Bultmann, *Johannes*, 406–415; Becker, "Abschiedsreden," 73 (and n. 43); Becker, *Johannes*, 2:575–577; Schnackenburg, *Johannesevangelium*, 3:123; Schnelle, "Abschiedsreden," 73; moreover, see Brown, *John*, 2:583, 668; Painter, Tradition 55; R. Bauckham, "Rediscovering a Lost Parable of Jesus," *NTS* 33 (1987): 84–101, here 96–97.

99. According to the authors mentioned, the source or the given tradition comprises the following verses: Bultmann, *Johannes*: vv. 1–2, 4a, b, 5a–e, 6a–c; Schnackenburg, *Johannesevangelium*: vv. 1–2, 6; Becker, *Johannes*: vv. 1–2, 5, 8; Schnelle, *Johannes*: vv. 1–2, 4c–6; Dietzfelbinger, "Abschied," 124: vv. 5a–e. See also Dietzfelbinger, "Abschied," 114: "Verse 5 contains the actual I-am-saying.... The question comes to a head: Did the I-am-saying originally have a life of its own and is its present location the result of a literary process?"

100. Schnackenburg, *Johannesevangelium*, suspects "an older form, more in narrative form." Becker distinguishes pieces of "prose" (vv. 3–4, 6–7) from the remaining verses, which have "a bound form and a self-contained meaning"; modified in Becker, "Herde," 170–177.

meditation on Christ as the vine but as the result of the interweaving of a given *figurative speech* with the *commentary* of the redactor. If, therefore, a new reconstruction of the genesis of the text is attempted in the following, then this is justified solely by the fact that it claims to be able to better explain the present text with its special features. The necessity of such an attempt arises from the fact that there are always voices suggesting that verse 3 should be excluded from the text as a later gloss because this verse cannot be integrated into it in a single line and without a break.[101] The question arises, however, as to whether this accurate observation is not better placed within the framework of a model of transmission criticism. This will be examined below.

5.3.1 Context and Form
First Synchronic Observations

John 15:1–8 belongs to the so-called second "farewell discourse" 15:1–16:4a, which goes back to the redaction of the Gospel. We assume this well-founded hypothesis[102] in the following analysis. The text reads:

A. 1   a   I am (ἐγώ εἰμι) the true vine,
       b   and my Father is the vinegrower.
   2   a   He removes every branch in men that bears no fruit.
       b   Every branch that bears fruit he prunes
       c   to make it bear more fruit.

   3   a   You have already been cleansed by the word
       b   that I have spoken to you.

   4   a   Abide in me
       b   as I in you.
       c   Just as the branch cannot bear fruit by itself
       d   unless it abides in the vine,
       e   neither can you
       f   unless you abide in me.

---

101. See Brown, *John*, 2:676–677.

102. See Brown, *John*, 2:582–588; Schnackenburg, *Johannesevangelium*, 3:101–103; Zumstein, Das Johannesevangelium 552f.

B. 5 a   I am (ἐγώ εἰμι) the vine,
     b   you are the branches.
     c   Those who abide in me
     d   and I in them
     e   bear much fruit,
     f   because apart from me you can do nothing.

   6 a   Whoever does not abide in me
     b   is thrown away like a branch
     c   and withers;
     d   such branches (αὐτά) are gathered
     e   thrown into the fire
     f   and burned.
   7 a   If you abide in me,
     b   and my words abide in you,
     c   whatever you wish
     d   ask for it,
     e   and it will be done for you.
   8 a   My Father is glorified by this,
     b   that you bear much fruit
     c   and become my disciples.

C. 9 a   As the Father has loved me,
     b   so I have loved you.
     c   Abide (μείνατε) in my love.
  10 a   If you keep my commandments,
     b   you will abide (μενεῖτε) in my love,
     c   just as I have kept my Father's commandments
     d   and abide (μένω) in his love.

D. 11 a   I have said these things to you
     b   so that my joy may be in you
     c   and that your joy may be complete.

Although the actual figurative speech ends with verse 8, the subsequent sequence in verses 9–11 should be added to this first fundamental section of the second farewell speech for two reasons. First, the keyword "remain" (μένειν), which is so characteristic of verses 1–8, also occurs here.[103] After that, it no longer plays a role, but appears again in verse 16, albeit with a new reference. On the other hand, verse 11 offers a meta-reflexive concluding formula that, in retrospect, combines the two preceding sections, the figurative speech in verses 1–8 and its appendix in verses 9–11, into a single unit. This results in the following structure for 15:1–11. First, there is the figurative speech with its dominant admonition to remain in the vine, that is, to remain in Christ (v. 4a). The appendix in verses 9–10 (= C) translates this admonition into the specifically Johannine language of love: "Remain in my love!" (v. 9c) The closing formula verse 11 (= D) rounds off the first section.

The image speech itself comprises two parts: verses 1–4 / 5–8 (= A/B). These are each headed by the "I am" formula or a two-part predication determined by it (I—the Father; I—you). This is followed in both cases by a pair of statements that contrast a *positive* statement with a *negative* one: in verses 2a/b to the branches that bear no fruit or do bear fruit, in verses 5c–f/6 to those who remain in Christ or do not remain in him. In addition to this parallelism between the two halves (vv. 1–2/5–6), they each offer further special features:

The second half follows on from the contrast of verses 5c–f/6 ("Those who abide in me . . ."—"Whoever does not abide in me . . .") with verses 7–8 yet another positive variant ("If you abide in me, and my words abide in you . . ."), so that a triad on the theme of "abiding" now emerges, which is also identified linguistically by a similar form of the opening cola:

v. 5c: Those who abide in me
v. 6a: Whoever does not abide in me
v. 7a: If you abide in me

The first half of the figurative speech in verses 1–4 has two peculiarities: On the one hand, it adds *commentary* to verse 2 *ad vocem* καθαίειν with verse 3 ("You have already been cleansed [καθαροί] . . ."); on the other hand, with verse 4a, b it offers an *imperative* ("Abide in me as I in you"), which not only anticipates verse 5c, d, but is also already reinforced (as the second half of the text then likewise practices again) by a *negative* statement of contrast (v. 4c–f): "*Abide* in me"—"Just as the branch *cannot* bear fruit by itself *unless* it abides in the vine, neither *can* you *unless* you *abide* in me."

Accordingly, the figurative speech as a whole—which sets it apart from the following "appendix" in verses 9–11—is characterized by the multiple alternation of contrasting statements, resulting in the following rhythm:

---

103. It occurs 7 times in vv. 1–8, and 3 times in the appendix to the figurative speech in vv. 9–11.

2a   negative (general statement)
2b, c positive (general statement)

4a, b positive (imperative clause : YOU)
4c–f   negative (comparison: YOU)

5c–e   positive (general participial clause)
6   negative (indefinite conditional clause)
7.8   positive (conditional imperative clause: YOU)

As the provisional classifications of the individual sentences in parentheses show, the regular alternation of contrasts is combined with a striking change of linguistic levels: Addressee-related sentences ("you") in the form of imperatives, for example (vv. 4a, 7d), alternate with general statements (vv. 2, 5c–6). This leads to the observation of the stylistic multidimensionality of the text in general. In addition to the figurative speech (see below), which is by no means one-dimensional in itself, or rather, interlocked with it, there are further speech acts that can be distinguished from one another: paraenesis (v. 4a, b; v. 7), commentary (v. 3), and Christological principle (vv. 5–6). Such complexity gives rise to a critical examination of the tradition, whereby an account of the criteria must be given.

5.3.2 A Tradition-Criticism Review

The search for "pure forms" as the guiding principle of the critical inquiry into tradition has often been criticized, and rightly so. However, the following is not about purity of form but about the internal consistency of the postulated tradition in terms of form and content. Before that, of course, a reason must be given as to why it makes sense to take the tradition-criticism path in the first place. This can be found, as indicated at the beginning, in verse 3, which can best be understood as commentary on verse 2, with the consequence that verses 1–2 represent tradition, but verse 3 is an addition by the redactor. This is developed below.

(1) There is a *tension* between verses 2 and 3. "While v. 2 speaks of a *purification process* to which the vines are subjected and which, if it goes well, leads to bearing fruit, v. 3 speaks of a *state* of purity that has already been achieved."[104] Dietzfelbinger even asks the question, "Does not v. 3 virtually embrace the

---

104. Dietzfelbinger, *Abschied*, 112.

Parables and Similar Metaphors 231

purification of the community of disciples by the *Father* (v. 2)?"[105] Verse 3 is a commentary (*ad vocem* καθαίρειν) on verse 2: "Purification" is more than just the result of a process; it is already given to believers (in baptism[106]). The keyword "purification" is not taken up again in the following, but that of "words" in verse 7b is: The verse makes it clear that the abiding of Christ in believers is mediated by the *abiding of his words in them*. While verse 3 looks at the previous gift of purification (in baptism), verse 7b goes beyond this with the admonition to abide *permanently*.[107]

(2) The commentary sentence in verse 3 ties in with 13:10 ("you are clean"). This brings another moment into play: There is a layer in the figurative speech that is understandable on its own, and textual elements that interweave the figurative speech with the wider context, in particular with that of the first farewell discourse.[108] It goes without saying that these elements do not belong to the original tradition. In addition to verse 3a (cf. 13:10) and verse 5f,[109] verses 7–8 should be mentioned here, where the prayer tradition from 14:13–14 is taken up,[110] but other threads also come together (with v. 7b; cf. 14:10 ["words"], 23; with v. 8c; cf. 13:35b). The fact that verses 7–8 simultaneously apply the figurative speech to the addressees ("you") confirms the assumption that we are dealing here with the commentary layer of the redaction.

(3) A distinction must be made between the *figurative speech* and its (paraenetic) *application to the addressees* of Jesus's speech.[111] This applies not only to the

---

105. Dietzfelbinger, *Abschied*, 112.

106. Schnackenburg, *Johannesevangelium*, 3:111: "If a 'purifying' power is attributed to the word of Jesus here, this is probably compatible with the 'word' theology of the Gospel of John (see 5:24; 6:63; 8:31, 51; 14:23; 17:17), but it is nevertheless singular and striking. One can assume a connection with the early Christian theology of baptism (see Eph 5:26; Heb 10:22; 1 Pet 1:23; John 1:18)."

107. Bultmann, *Johannes*, 412: "There is no abiding in him ... without bearing fruit, but also no bearing fruit without abiding in him. ... What is required is already given."

108. A. Dettwiler, *Die Gegenwart des Erhöhten. Eine exegetische Studie zu den johanneischen Abschiedsreden (Joh 13,31–16,33) unter besonderer Berücksichtigung ihres Relecture-Characters*, FRLANT 169 (Göttingen: Vandenhoeck & Ruprecht, 1995), 60–100: John 15:1–17 is to be understood as a "relecture of John 13:1–17; 13:34–35."

109. See 5:19, 30; 9:33: Just as Jesus can do nothing without God, so, according to 15:5–6, the disciples can do nothing without Jesus.

110. The reference is ensured by the fact that the theme of the glorification of the Father is also given there: compare 15:8a with 14:13c! See p. 80–81. above!

111. Becker, "Herde," 172: "Metaphorical and direct forms of speech alternate several times."

admonitory imperative in verse 4a, b (cf. also v. 7c, d), which moreover formulates the point of the entire text in the sense of the redaction (cf. its resumption in 15:9c: "abide in my love"), but also to the subsequent comparative clause verse 4c–f, which in its second half explicitly refers to the addressees ("neither can *you* unless you abide in me") and serves to justify the preceding imperative. If figurative speech and paraenesis are to be kept fundamentally apart, then this also corresponds to the shepherd's discourse in John 10, which offers figurative speech without paraenesis.

(4) That verse 4c–f belongs to the commentary layer of the redaction is also shown by a further indication. In the predications in 15:1a, b/5a, b, which open the two halves of the text, we have absolute *metaphorical language* that is characterized by the fact that (a) it dispenses with comparisons, and instead takes the image for the "thing," and (b) in 15:1a it claims the image exclusively for Christ. In contrast to this, verse 4 offers an explicit *comparison* that *juxtaposes the image and subject half* in a "just as"—"so also" construction. If the postulated tradition is to be consistent in itself, only one of the two types of figurative speech can be claimed for it.[112]

Verse 6 also seems problematic from this point of view. Its syntactic form is already conspicuous. Five verbs, coordinated with "and," form two groups (2 + 3): two verbs in the singular aorist, three in the present tense, two of which are in the plural (συνάγουσιν/βάλλουσιν). The first pair ("[he] is thrown away ... and withers") refers in the singular to the one who does not remain in Christ; the group of three looks at the unfruitful vines that are gathered, thrown into the fire, and burned, whereby the change to the plural (*"they* are gathered ...") is conditioned by the image of gathering.

The group of three also deepens the metaphor of the vine: "Gathering," "throwing into the fire," and "burning" refer to divine judgment, for which the fire stands as a usual metaphor.[113] Bultmann therefore thought that this group of three was an extension of the original, which originally only contained the first pair. This has a certain probability and can be supported by looking at the form of the given tradition. If Bultmann's hypothesis is correct, the explicit comparison ὡς τὸ κλῆμα could also be attributed to the redaction, which thus prepares the transition to its small judgment appendix ("one gathers them [s.c. the *vines*]").

---

112. Correctly Becker, "Herde," 176: "Only in vv. 4, 6 does one come across comparisons (and then again in vv. 9, 10), which in each case justify the paraenetic goal, but are to be distinguished from the figure of speech of the allegory." Von Gemünden, *Vegetationsmetaphorik*, 157, also describes the comparisons in vv. 4, 6 as "untypical of the genre."

113. Dietzfelbinger, *Abschied*, 123, speaks of "apocalyptic language of judgment"; see in more detail Brown, *John*, 2:662, 678–679. The metaphor of fire is also occasionally found in biblical vine texts; see Ezek 15:4, 6–7; 19:12.

5.3.3 Structure, Form, and Semantic Structures of the Figurative Speech

The traditional imagery of the vine has a well-formed shape, as the following diagram illustrates:

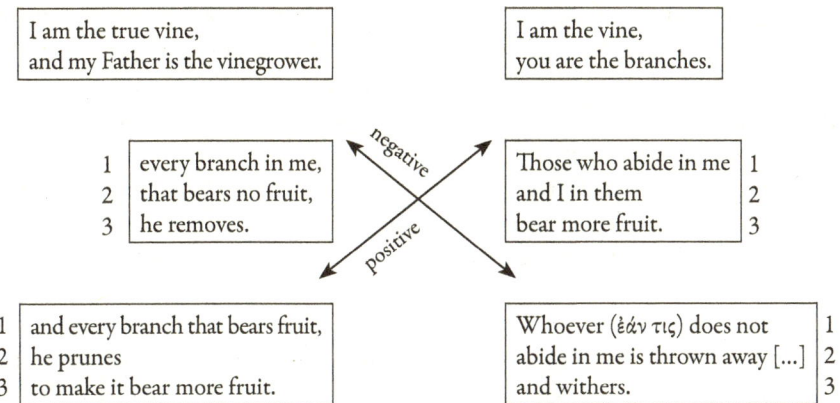

The anaphora in verses 1/5 divide the figurative speech into two "stanzas" (vv. 1–2/5a–e, 6a–c). Each is preceded by two predications in the identificatory first person style, followed by a negative and a positive conditional statement. The condition is syntactically expressed three times by a participle (μὴ φέρον καρπόν; τὸ καρπὸν φέρον; ὁ μένων ἐν ἐμοί), once by an ἐάν-phrase ("whoever"). The two "stanzas" are therefore constructed in the same way.

It is noticeable that the negative and positive statements are chiastically intertwined, which results in an inner interlocking of the two halves of the figurative speech. The third colon of the first positive statement ("that it [the vine] may bear *more fruit*") is taken up almost literally in the corresponding colon of the second positive statement that follows ("whoever abides in me . . . , this [is the one who] bears *rich fruit*").

The exact formal correspondence of the two halves of the figurative speech also supports the assumption expressed above following R. Bultmann that verse 6d–f is a commentary addition by the redactors.

Both predications at the head of the respective "verse" contain the keyword "vine," which is accompanied by an additional element within the semantic field in a second line. While in verse 5 the *whole* (the "vine") is accompanied by its *parts* ("the branches"), in verse 1 the focus goes beyond the whole to name the *superordinate* entity (the "vintner"). The second line determines the perspective of the subsequent "verse": The first is *theocentric* (it is the vinedresser who works on his vine and cares for it), the second is *ecclesiologically* oriented (i.e., it looks at the "branches," or the believers). The following observation shows that the climax of the figurative speech has been reached: If the first pair of contrasts in verse 2 remains entirely on the metaphorical level when it speaks of the "branches" that are either cut off or cleansed, the second pair of contrasts offers the decisive *interpretative* element: "whoever *abides* in me" or "does not *abide* in me." If one asks about the pragmatics of the tradition (see below), then this interpretative element contains the answer. Incidentally, the metaphor of the first "verse" persists in the second, when it does not say: "whoever abides in me is *like* a branch that bears fruit," but rather: "this one bears fruit" and "whoever does not abide in me is *thrown away* and [...] withers."[114]

One stylistic peculiarity, which is a sign of the careful composition of the tradition, should be pointed out (in addition to the *anaphora* already mentioned): the stylistic device of *paronomasia* in verse 2a, b (*airei* [αἴρει]/ *kath-airei* [καθ-αίρει]).

Overall, the analysis of the surviving piece in the manner of a cross confirms the reconstruction presented.[115] The figurative speech identified proves to be well-rounded and consistent in form and content. The following structure of the piece suggests itself:

A. 1. *vine and vinegrower*

  (double predication)

  2. The care of the *winegrower* for his vine

   2.1. he cuts out branches that do not bear fruit

   (negative part)

   2.2. he cleans branches with fruit that they bear more fruit

   (positive part)

B. 1. *vine and branches*

  (double predication)

  2. the future of the *branches*

   2.1. those who remain bear rich fruit

   (positive part?)

   2.2. those who do not stay will die

   (negative part)

---

114. This supports the assumption that "like a branch" (ὡς τὸ κλῆμα) is a secondary insertion.

115. Schnelle, "Abschiedsreden," 73 n. 43, still refers to Johannine hapaxlegomena.

Excursus
The Imagery of the Vine and the Classic "I am" Sayings of the Gospel

The classic "I am" words in John include 6:35; 8:12; 10:9*; and 14:6.[116] They all follow the standard form that J.-A. Bühner has defined as follows: "I am + predicate + participial or causal legal proposition that applies the predicate to the salvation of believers."[117] John 10 and 15 stand out from this, where "metaphor fields" are present, "which are interpreted partly Christologically, partly ecclesiologically and (so only John 15) partly theologically."[118] "Unique is (also) the way in which the vine is linked with the branches, the person of Christ with the disciples in 15:5. In this way, an element that otherwise belongs to the second part (s.c. of the "I am" saying) is brought into the first."[119]

Nevertheless, formal references can be recognized between John 15:1-2, 5-6* and the standard form that concern the second half of the figurative speech.[120] Here too, the "I am" predication in verses 5c-e is followed by a "participial legal clause" that applies the predication to the salvation of believers. If in the classical words the second part can take the form of synthetic (6:35; cf. 11:25-26) or antithetical parallelism (8:12), the same can also be observed in our saying, insofar as a warning is added to the positive sentence in verse 5c-e with verse 6a-c; admittedly, from a formal-syntactical point of view, this has greater independence in comparison to 8:12c, d.

Two things follow from these observations: (1) The vine figurative speech is to be understood as a further development of the classical form of the "I am" sayings. (2) The "I am" sayings represent a living tradition that could be adapted in many ways.

5.3.4 Christ, the Vine: The Origin, *Sitz im Leben*, and Aim of the Metaphor

(1) "In terms of the history of religions, there is a consensus that the Old Testament-early Jewish culture is the special area to which the

---

116. For more information, see ch. 4!

117. Bühner, *Gesandte*, 166.

118. Becker, "Herde," 173.

119. Dietzfelbinger, *Abschied*, 122.

120. See Dietzfelbinger, *Abschied*, 114; Becker, *Herde*, 173: The original form in John 15:5 is "roughly imitated."

Johannine statements belong."¹²¹ With the related pictorial elements of *vine—vinedresser—branches—bearing fruit—purification of the vines*, the tradition draws on a "conventionalized metaphor field"¹²² that has its origins in the Old Testament and found its development in early Jewish literature: Israel is God's vine, planted by himself. ¹²³ God expects it to bear fruit, the lack of which the prophets in particular denounce.¹²⁴ Therefore, Israel has to await judgment. But also its reintegration can be illustrated by the image of the vine or rather vineyard.¹²⁵

The two features that structurally characterize the reception of the metaphorical field are prefigured in the biblical, early Jewish tradition: the *individual* and *corporate* meaning of the vine. This stands for Christ but at the same time also encompasses those who believe in him, who have their life in him.¹²⁶ On the one hand, the history of the image field maintains that it is not individuals from the people of Israel, but the people as a whole, who represent the vine of God;¹²⁷ accordingly, in John 15 the image stands for the community. On the other hand, the image is also used in the Old Testament, albeit sporadically, to refer to the Davidic king as the representative of Israel¹²⁸ or, in early

---

121. Becker, "Herde," 174 n. 36; see, also, von Gemünden, *Vegetationsmetaphorik*, 164–168.

122. Becker, "Herde," 174. According to him, it is a "self-evident cultural asset," i.e., a "knowledge" "that the narrator and the recipient possess together."

123. Hos 10:1: "Israel is a luxuriant vine that yields its fruit."; Jer 2:21: "Yet I planted you as a choice vine, from the purest stock . . ."; Ps 80:9–12, 15–16. On the neighboring image of the vineyard, which also plays a role here, see especially Isa 5:1–7.

124. See, for example, Hos 10:1–8; Jer 2:21; Ezek 15. "The seat in life (s.c. of biblical figurative speech) is mostly the prophetic threatening speech that admonishes one to bear fruit, i.e., to be faithful to the Torah, or interprets the historical catastrophes as judgment and as a consequence of a lack of fruit" (Niemand, Spuren 20).

125. See, e.g., Isa 27:2–6.

126. As true as it is that "within the Old Testament Jewish vineyard metaphor and in all other potential comparative texts to John 15:1–10 . . . there are no statements of immanence" (Scholtissek, In ihm 280), it is also true that the creative linking of the two lines of meaning, the corporate as well as the individualizing one, has *opened* the semantic field for the statements of immanence.

127. Among the early Jewish literature, see LAB 12:8–9; 18:10–11; 23:12; 28:4; 30:4; 39:7. For literature, see Str-B 2:563–564 (ET 2:648–649).

128. See Ezek 17:6–8; 19:10–14. See also Ps 80 (79):15–16 can be understood, "if one takes the text as it stands, as an identification of the vine with the Son (MT) or the Son of Man (LXX),

Jewish literature, to the Messiah;[129] in Sirach 24:17 it is also used in relation to wisdom.[130] This can be understood as a prefiguration of the Christological version of the metaphor.

The Johannine tradition has interwoven the traditional imagery with *statements of immanence* (vv. 5c, d, 6a), which according to John 6:56 have an independent history. The question is whether there is a reason they were associated with the vine metaphor. Another distinctive element is the reference to "bearing fruit," which was "also used in community parables independently of 15:1–7."[131] In the composition of John 15, it moves to the center of the received image field (vv. 2b, c/5e).[132]

(2) Much thought has been given to the idea that the vine discourse represents a possible reference to the *Eucharist*.[133] Schnackenburg has made an important suggestion that has not yet been considered by scholars:[134]

> "A one-sided eucharistic interpretation is not recommended." Rather, a distinction should be made between the older, predetermined form of the grapevine discourse and reception by the redactors which has been tailored and tuned to the congregation, with the consequence that "we would then have to assume two *Sitze im Leben*, as it were." If the given "Christian *mashal*" (= vv. 1–2, 6) had a "polemical-aggressive character,"[135] it would—"placed in the context of Jesus's speeches for his own" and understood "as an address to the congregation with a paraenetic orientation"—have gained "a special sound and a new meaning for the congregation's celebration of the Eucharist (cf. above

---

who can be equated with the Messiah" (von Gemünden, *Vegetationsmetaphorik*, 167 [with older lit.]); see also v. 18.

129. See 2 Bar. 36–40; 39:7: "... then the dominion of my anointed one will be revealed. It will be like the spring and the *vine*."

130. She says of herself: "I produced beautiful shoots like a vine, and my blossoms became a fruit full of splendor and riches" (JSHRZ III/5 565).

131. Becker, "Herde," 174; von Gemünden, *Vegetationsmetaphorik*, 168 et al.

132. See J. G. van der Watt, "'Metaphorik' in Joh 15,1–8," *BZ.NF* 38 (1994): 67–80, here 78–79.

133. See Schnackenburg, *Johannesevangelium*, 3:122–123.

134. Schnackenburg, *Johannesevangelium*, 3:123.

135. Schnackenburg has the dispute with the synagogue in mind: "In exegesis we noticed certain accents that point to a defense: the attribute ἀληθινός, the cutting off (αἴρει) of fruitless branches, the cutting and burning of dry, dead branches" (*Johannesevangelium*, 3:122).

all vv. 4–5, 9–10)." The model of a distinction between tradition and redaction that guides this hypothesis deserves attention, but leads to different results if the scope of the tradition is defined differently. According to our reconstruction, the tradition does not reveal a "polemical-aggressive character" to the *outside world*. Moreover, the figurative elements of "cutting off fruitless branches" and "cutting out and burning dry, dead branches," which Schnackenburg uses for this purpose, point *inwards*. Thus, a reversal of Schnackenburg's hypothesis is recommended in the following sense: *the tradition of John 15:1–2, 5–6* has its Sitz im Leben in the eucharistic celebration of the Johannine community. In 15:1–17, however, the redaction that receives it goes beyond this when it seeks to determine the nature of ecclesial communion in general, standing at the end of tradition but on its foundation.*

When considering the question of whether John 15:1-8 or the tradition used here originally had anything to do with the Eucharist, it must first be considered whether the widespread rejection of a presumed eucharistic reference does not set the standard too high when it says, for example, "that the speech does not consider the vine in terms of its *fruit*, in terms of the *wine* it gives, but only as the tree with its tendrils, which are infused by it with vitality."[136] According to Didache 9:2, the image of the vine could also be used in the context of early Christian meal celebrations, for example in the prayer of blessing over the eucharistic cup. The text reads:

1a Concerning the *Eucharist*,
b   give thanks as follows:
2a First, regarding the *cup*:
b   We thank you, our Father
    for the holy vine of David, your servant,
c   which you have revealed to us through Jesus, your servant.
d   To you be the glory forever."
(Did. 9:1–2)

The interpretation of this prayer is not unanimous. It is probably based on a Jewish blessing of the cup at the meal, which can be found in 2b and was Christianized in 2c. M. Dibelius also interprets the original 2a, b as evidence of a *Hellenistic* Judaism that had already spiritualized the Jewish blessing of the cup.

---

136. Bultmann, *Johannes*, 407 (emphasis mine).

Parables and Similar Metaphors

The expression "holy vine of David" does not refer to the existing Israel, but to the "promised salvation"; "it must be assumed that the expression is already a fixed symbolic saying." "The Christianization of prayer took place in the simplest way through the relative clause: Jesus has made this salvation known."[137]

U. Wilckens offers a different interpretation.[138] He thinks the saying, in "great proximity to the corresponding Jewish meal blessing" with its direct reference to Israel, is "unmistakable," and therefore interprets the Christianizing addition ecclesiologically: "What is Christian is that Israel as 'the holy vine of David' has been 'revealed' through Jesus; what is meant here is therefore probably the church as the people of God 'brought together' into unity through Jesus," for which Wilckens can likewise refer to the analogous saying about the bread, this time to its second part in the Didache (Did. 9:4[139]).[140] It is not necessary to decide here which interpretation is correct.

The use of the traditional motif of the "vine" thus offers a first indication of the eucharistic background of the tradition. With the Christological/ecclesiological dual form present here (the vine represents Christ and the community at the same time), it is also *structurally related* to the eucharistic interpretation of the "body" metaphor in Paul, who in 1 Cor 10:16–17 likewise refers both to Christ (σῶμα τοῦ Χριστοῦ) and to the community (ἓν σῶμα οἱ πολλοί ἐσμεν)

The formula of "abiding in him" (vv. 5c, d, 6a) offers an additional clue. In the Gospel of John, this only occurs here and in 6:56,[141] that is, in the explicitly eucharistic part of the bread discourse. Should the reciprocal immanence formula in its application to believers and Christ in the Johannine school really have a eucharistic background? If the reciprocal immanence formula in its application to believers and Christ in the Johannine school actually has a eucharistic

---

137. M. Dibelius, "Die Mahl-Gebete der Didache," *ZNW* 37 (1938): 32–41, here 35.

138. Wilckens, *Johannes*, 242.

139. "As this (the bread) was scattered on the mountains and has become *one* loaf, so shall your congregation be gathered from the ends of the earth into your kingdom!"

140. Wilckens, *Johannes*, 242. "If one could assume that these prayers were familiar to the Johannine community from their worship service, then John 15 would have to be understood as a theologically deepening interpretation according to which 'the *true* vine' is Jesus and his disciples, the church, branches of this vine." Moreover, in the blessing of the bread, thanks is given "for the *life*" that "you have revealed to us through Jesus, your servant," just as eternal life is the central gift of salvation in John 6 (6:31ff., 53–58): "In both discourses, the Eucharist is interpreted, in John 6 with regard to the bread, in John 15 with regard to the cup."

141. "Those who eat my flesh and drink my blood abide in me and I in them."

background (or root), then this would explain well its connection with the metaphor of the "vine" in the tradition 15:1–2, 5–6*.

But this is not the only reference to the Eucharist; the redactional context of 15:1–17, in which the tradition was included as a base text, also points in this direction. The reception of the synoptic tradition of the answer to prayer twice in 15:7c–e and 15:16g–h, that is, pointedly at the end of each unit, is particularly noteworthy here. In the Johannine context, this word is not addressed to individuals in order to encourage them to pray for their personal intentions, but has the *congregation* and its *liturgical* prayer in mind, which is promised to be answered "in the name of Jesus." The Eucharist therefore comes into serious consideration as a background to experience for John 15, without the speech as a whole having to be interpreted thematically as eucharistic speech, as must be the case for John 6:51c–58

(3) If the above thesis on the *Sitz im Leben* of the tradition is correct, then the following can be said about its *purpose* and *pragmatics*: On the one hand, this revelatory saying of the exalted Christ makes it clear that believers have to *decide* to *partake in the* (eucharistically mediated) communion of the vine *of life* or be *cut off from the powers of life* outside of it. However, the second half of the saying goes beyond the aspect of decision: Only those who *remain*, he says, bear fruit, thereby insisting that the eucharistic union with Christ should *last* and that believers should remain *faithful* to the community.

If we take note of the consistent orientation of the revelation toward the (eucharistic) community, then the assumption that the reference to the "*true* vine" is to be understood as a polemic against Israel and the synagogue and characterizes the entire text in this sense also loses plausibility. Without denying the intention behind this phrase, which is to set the reality of the true and actual "vine" (i.e., Christ) apart from Israel, one would not go so far as to subordinate the internal ecclesiological signals to this intention. Rather, these take precedence and determine the pragmatics of the tradition in a positive way: the participants in the Eucharist are to be strengthened in their *faithfulness to the community*, for which the opening of the saying in verse 1a provides a supporting argument: Christ is the "*true* vine"; outside him one seeks the hoped-for blessings in vain, for nothing else in this world can lay claim to that designation.

5.3.5 The Saying of the Vine as the Base Text of John 15:1–16:4e

Two reasons could have been decisive for the reception of the tradition in 15:1–2, 5–6*. First, with verse 5c, d it provides the keyword that is of interest to the

Parables and Similar Metaphors 241

redactors: μένειν = *to remain*. On the other hand, the figurative saying with eucharistic connotations lent itself to them because, following the first farewell discourse that was dedicated to the question of the necessity of *Jesus's departure in death*, they now intend to focus on the *post-Easter* reality of the community. The imagery of the vine as a *base text* was ideally suited to this. It is also conceivable that the redactors were aware of the traditional (synoptic) place of the Eucharist in the context of Jesus's farewell meal. There are two sides to the reception process, one structural and one concerning content and pragmatism

(1) From a *structural* point of view, the tradition-criticism hypothesis first helps to clarify the question of the delimitation of the text, which has always been considered difficult in research: Does the "vine discourse" end with verse 8 or with verse 11? Insight into the diachrony of the text supports the assumption of a caesura only after verse 11. Why? Although the actual tradition ends with verse 8, together with the redactors' "comments" woven into it, the actual commentary is only provided by the following in verses 9–11. The vine discourse becomes the base text of the entire composition in 15:1–16:4e because it lays the foundation for the two following sections. If 15:12–17 defines the *nature of the community* with a view to the mutual *love* that reigns within it, 15:18–27 speaks of *the world's hatred* of the community. The *distinction* between the two entities, the community and the world, is already established in the image of the vine. The sphere of life of the vine and the sphere of death and judgment are irreconcilably opposed here. John 16:1–4e then forms the conclusion of the entire composition, as can be seen in the diagram below:

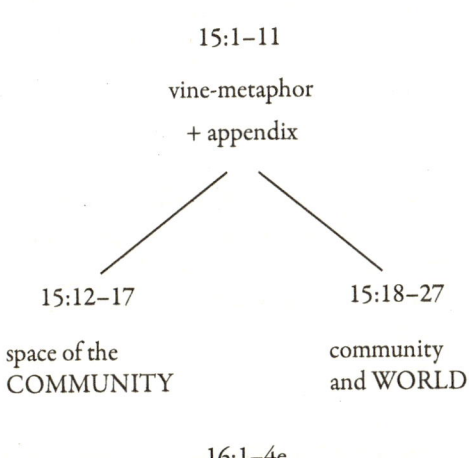

15:1–11

vine-metaphor

+ appendix

15:12–17   15:18–27

space of the   community
COMMUNITY   and WORLD

16:1–4e

conclusion

(2) As far as the *content-related pragmatic* side of the reception of the preexisting tradition is concerned, four features should be mentioned:

(a) In the very first half of the figurative speech, the speaker, anticipating verse 5c, d, has inserted the *imperative* that is decisive for him: "*Remain* in me, as I in you!" (v. 4a, b). For him, it probably has a comprehensive ecclesiological meaning, that is, he is thinking of the unity of the Johannine congregations, which has suffered lasting damage as a result of the schism documented in 1 John.[142] It is quite possible that this trauma is behind John 15, but it cannot be conclusively proven. In any case, the imperative determines the pragmatics of the text throughout.

In 15:9–10 the redactors translate it into the form: "Remain in my *love!*" (9c, 10b). According to verses 9b, 12c, 13, Jesus's love was expressed in *giving of his life for his friends*. This is what is meant when it says in verse 9b (cf. 12c) in the *aorist*: "(also) I have loved you (ἠγάπησα)"! In other words: in these passages, the editors tie the present-oriented, post-Easter perspective of the grapevine discourse back to the decisive salvific event in the life of the *earthly* Jesus: his death. This is the source of motivation and strength for brotherly love and the love of friends in the ecclesial community. The paraenetic logic in verses 9–10 is that if the disciples keep Jesus's instructions, they will remain in his love. If verses 12–17 interpret these instructions from the one instruction of Jesus to "love one another" as he loved them, then this means that abiding in Jesus is bound to result in love for one another; whoever breaks off this love breaks off Jesus's faithfulness.

(b) Beyond the descriptive image of the vine, the redactor states in the manner of a dogmatic sentence in verses 5–6: "*without me you can do nothing*" (cf. also v. 4c–f). Whether this statement of principle had a concrete reason can at least be questioned. According to the testimony of 1 John, there certainly seems to have been a spiritual enthusiasm among the opponents of this letter which, in the opinion of the author of 1 John, needed to be tied back to the faith in Christ as its critical norm.

(c) If the assignment of verses 6d–f to the redactors is correct, then they would have used an apocalyptic metaphor to signal the deadly seriousness of apostasy from the community, i.e., from the habitat of the vine. Such a linguistic process also corresponds to other common Johannine practices (e.g., 1 John 2:18).

---

142. See F. F. Segovia, "The Theology and Provenance of John 15:1–17," *JBL* 101 (1982): 115–128, here 120–122.

(d) Verses 7–8 belong to the references of the vine saying in the first farewell discourse. The synoptic tradition of the unconditional promise of the answer to prayer, which was already to be read in 14:13–14, is given a new interpretation that is not formulated but is nevertheless suggested to the reader by the connection of the two independent statements in verses 7 and 8. It is precisely their (seemingly unmediated) juxtaposition[143] that serves to produce new meaning which the reader must perceive. The reader combines the two statements and then understands: The answer to prayer that Jesus promises the community (!) from the Father serves to glorify the Father. This is demonstrated by the fact that the community bears abundant fruit and thus proves itself to be a disciple of Jesus. In other words: Mutual love—the highest expression of fruitfulness—grows in a climate of prayer. "Whatever you want, ask for it . . . !" As openly as this is formulated in the tradition of Jesus, it receives its orientation from the fact that the prerequisite for congregational prayer is faithfulness to the words of Jesus (vv. 7a, 6), but its fulfillment consists in nothing other than the ongoing creativity of the congregation to practice mutual love.

5.4 On the Christological Transformation of the Figurative Language in the Johannine Community

(1) The parables and figurative sayings examined here represent only a sample of the material contained in the Fourth Gospel. Overall, one is surprised at how often metaphorical language is used in this book over and above the actual "I am" imagery. It is creation in its elementary realities such as light and darkness, day and night, water and storm, growth and harvest, but also human reality with its basic sensitivities such as birth and birth pains, bride and bridegroom, bread and vine, shepherd and worker, which all make their contribution to making the mystery of faith in Christ vivid. Only a part of this is traditional material from the Johannine community. Some of it was created by the evangelist (or the editor). The following table is intended to give an impression of the variety and dispersion of parabolic forms of speech in the true sense:[144]

---

143. They are linked by their common reference to the second person plural; the traditional disciple motif (v. 8) also takes up the reference to "abiding" in Christ.

144. Texts such as 7:37–38 ("living water") or 14:2–3 ("dwellings of my Father"), in which the metaphors and images are not constitutive of the genre, are not taken into account here.

No.	Text	Genre	Metaphor Field	Tradition
1	3:8	parable	wind	x[145]
2	3:29	parable	bridegroom/friend[146]	x (?)
3	4:35–36	metaphorical speech	harvest[147]	x
4	4:37b	sentence	harvest	x
5	5:19–20	parable	father/son	x
6	5:35	metaphorical speech	lamp/light	
7	8:35	metaphor	slave/son	
8	9:4	sentence	day/night, work	x
9	10:3–5	parable	shepherd/sheep	x
10	10:11–12	parable/"I am"	shepherd/day laborer	x
11	11:9–10	sentence	day/night	x
12	12:24	metaphor	wheat kernel	x
13	12:35–36	metaphorical speech	light/darkness	
14	15:1–2/5–6	"I am" metaphor	vine	x
15	16:21–22	parable	birth	

(2) With regard to the genres used, it is striking that the Fourth Gospel does not know or has not received *parables* or *parable narratives* at all, as they are typical for Jesus.[148] Instead, it shows a pronounced preference for *parables in the narrower sense*, whose peculiarity is to use recognized facts or typical or regular processes from nature or human behavior to illustrate or argumentatively and rhetorically convey certain facts. This occurs in the Fourth Gospel with astonishing breadth, whereby the metaphor fields often overlap with those of the synoptic tradition, without there being identical traditions; it is the same agrarian world that connects the synoptic and Johannine tradition with each

---

145. Dodd, *Tradition*, 364–365, treats the parable in the chapter "Sayings common to the Synoptics"; he compares it with Mark 4:27: "Any sort of dependence of one on the other is excluded, but are they not so deeply akin that we could believe them to have come, not only from the same common deposit of tradition, but originally from the same mind?"

146. Dodd, *Tradition*, 386: "There is little that might betray the hand of the evangelist, and the parable, set as it is in a passage which appears to contain many traditional elements, seems to bear a genuinely traditional stamp."

147. See Mark 4:3–8, 26–29; Luke 10:2 par. Matt 9:37f–38; Rev 14:14–20! —Dodd, *Tradition*, 393; R. Cameron, *Sayings Traditions in the Apocryphon of James*, HThS 34 (Philadelphia: Augsburg Fortress, 1984), 53 n. 33; Theobald, "Die Ernte ist da!" 81–108.

148. See Matt 18:23–35; 20:1–16; 22:2–14 par. Luke 14:16–24; Luke 10:25–37; 15:11–32, etc.

Parables and Similar Metaphors 245

other. If it remains difficult to explain such similarities by tracing them back to the historical Jesus, then the only alternative is to regard the Johannine traditions as continuations of the synoptic traditions, whereby these were subjected to a creative reorganization. Apart from the fact that the *genre* of parables influenced by Jesus in the narrower sense survives, this kind of updating of the metaphorical fields remains within narrow limits.[149] It would therefore be wrong to conclude from such findings that there is a stream of continuity between the synoptic and Johannine traditions.

(3) Even if the genre of parables in the narrower sense lives on in John, it is stripped of its original reference to the βασιλεία τοῦ θεοῦ (*kingdom of God*). This is hardly surprising, since Jesus's typical orientation toward the kingdom of God as the central symbol of his proclamation and ministry has been transformed in various ways in the Gospel of John. Instead of the βασιλεία τοῦ θεοῦ (cf. 3:3/5), the focus is now primarily on "eternal life," and the theocentricity of Jesus's proclamation has had to give way to a Christological narrowing of the saying about of God. This may also be the reason there was a transmission barrier against Jesus's parables with their theocentric figures (father, king, etc.), which all reflect God's behavior toward people in their own way.[150]

(4) The Johannine parables and figurative sayings certainly show a certain *thematic breadth*. Parables and figurative sayings certainly do. John 3:8 contains a parable that serves to bring to linguistic expression the reality of the new existence of the faithful, which is beyond comprehension. John 3:29 and 5:35 revolve around the figure of the Baptist and his relationship to Jesus; 4:35–36 is an expression of a certain, namely eschatologically compressed understanding of time; and 9:4 and 11:9–10 are aphorisms which, in the knowledge of the irretrievable *kairos*, provide arguments for man's commitment to faith, which cannot now be postponed. Despite this diversity of themes, the majority of the parabolic texts and traditions in the Gospel of John are Christologically centered: Jesus, the bridegroom, the Son, the only shepherd, the grain of wheat, the true vine. This impression is reinforced if we include the other figurative words—that is, the "I am" sayings.

---

149. Theobald, *Johannine Dominical Sayings as Metatexts of Synoptic Sayings of Jesus*, 383–405.

150. Think of the kind father of the prodigal son and the son who stayed at home (Luke 15) but also of the vineyard owner in Matt 20, the king in Matt 18, or the rich man in Luke 14 who organizes a feast. As much as these narratives certainly have Christological implications, their basic structure is eschatologically theocentric.

CHAPTER 6

Wisdom Sayings

WHEN WE SPEAK of Jesus as a teacher of wisdom, we usually think of the fact that, like the Jewish teachers of wisdom, he formed aphorisms and wise admonitions that are to be understood as a reflection of experience in dealing with everyday reality: "Those who are well have no need of a physician, but those who are sick" (Mark 2:17b). "The wedding guests cannot fast while the bridegroom is with them, can they?" (Mark 2:19b.c). "For there is nothing hidden, except to be disclosed" (Mark 4:22a).—"Lists of Jesus's words of wisdom compiled in research have reached numbers of well over a hundred."[1] It is remarkable that the Gospel of John pays little attention to this side of Jesus's preaching, portraying him not as an expert in the art of living wisely, but as a teacher who imparts knowledge *from the beyond* as a revelator: "The one who comes from above is above all; the one who is of the earth belongs to the earth and speaks about earthly things. The one who comes from heaven is above all...." (3:31–32).

This brings us to another, very different type of wisdom saying also found in the Synoptic tradition, but which also testifies to its continuation and continued existence in the Gospel of John: "Come to me, all you that are weary and are carrying heavy burdens, and I will give you rest. For my yoke is easy, and my burden is light" (Matt 11:28–30). "Therefore also the Wisdom of God said, 'I will send them prophets and apostles, some of whom they will kill and persecute'" (Luke 11:49 par. Matt 23:34). "Nevertheless, wisdom is vindicated by all her children" (Luke 7:35 par. Matt 11:19d). In these and other words attributed to Jesus, personified Wisdom is in the background: Jesus refers to her, or *his* work is associated with *her* work to the point that he is *identified* with her. Because personified Wisdom is of heavenly origin, it also proclaims heavenly things, and it is not far from the Johannine conception. The fact that this idea was not created by the evangelist freehand but is rather based on a specific logia tradition will be shown in the following with two examples: the saying about the futile search (John 7:33–34) and Jesus's invitation to drink of the water of life (John 7:37–38).

6.1 Searching in Vain (John 7:33–34; cf. 8:21; 13:33)

The logion of the futile search appears three times in the Gospel, twice in a speech of Jesus addressed to the "Jews" or "Pharisees" (7:33–34; 8:21) and once in a saying to his disciples at the beginning of his first Farewell Discourse (13:33). In addition,

---

1. Klauck, "Christus," 258 (literature).

there are parallels in motifs in other places, without it being possible to speak of resumptions of the logion (12:35; 14:19, 28; 16:10, 16–17); only in 16:16–17 is it worth considering whether the author of these verses, which come from the subsequent Farewell Discourse, did not have the logion in 7:33–34 in mind as a whole.

Whether we are dealing with variations of one and the same saying in the three different versions of the logion does not seem certain. As J. Becker points out, "Perhaps we should not even ask about 'the' original form of the saying, but should allow for a certain wealth of variants, as can be observed elsewhere in the history of the Johannine tradition. History of tradition can also be observed elsewhere. But 7:33–34 makes a firm and not fragmented impression with a good structure."[2]

What is certain is that for the *evangelist* it is one and the same saying. He explicitly has his Jesus return to the earlier occasions in 13:33, the last occurrence of the saying, "and as I said to the Jews . . . so now I say to you." What Jesus said as a word of judgment to the "Jews" or the "Pharisees" at the Feast of Tabernacles also makes sense in the situation of his Farewell Discourse—in a new way—with regard to his "disciples."

6.1.1 Theme with Variations
Tradition-Criticism Observations

The following synopsis will help us to answer these questions:

	Logion (7:33–34)	First Variant (8:21)	Second Variant (13:33)
1			Little children,
2	I will be with you a little while longer		I am with you only a little longer.
3	and then I am going to him who sent me.	I am going	
4	You will search for me	and you will search for me	You will search for me;
5	but [you] will not find [me];	and will die in your sin.	
6			and (as I said to the Jews,)
7	and where I am,	Where I am going,	"Where I am going,
8	(there) you cannot come.	(there) you cannot come.	(there) you cannot come"
9			(o now I say [it] to you.)

---

2. Becker, *Johannes*, 1:321; Koester, *Gospels*, 259, 119–120, considers 7:33–34 to be a traditional saying because of the parallels in Gos. Thom. 38 and Ep. James 2:23–27; see also Cameron, *Traditions*, 47 n. 9.

Wisdom Sayings

In lines 4 and 8, the three versions correspond verbatim.[3] What is the difference between them?

The temporal statement "I will be with you a little while longer" (line 2) is missing in 8:21. This is probably due to the specific structure of the saying in the version found in 8:21, which has to do with the transformation of line 5. Whereas in 7:34 it says, "but you will not find (me)," the metaphor of this announcement is interpreted theologically in 8:21, "and you will die in your sin." Not being able to find Jesus, being eternally separated from him, therefore means "*dying* in your own sin." The fact that the emphasis in 8:21 rests on this idea is confirmed by the subsequent conversation in that Jesus returns to this line of the logion twice more: "I told you that you would die in your sins, for *you will die in your sins* unless you believe that I am (ἐγώ εἰμι) he" (v. 24). In addition, immediately following the logion, the evangelist has the "Jews" take up the topic of dying, who, in their lack of understanding, do not refer to themselves, as Jesus meant, but to *him*: Ironically, they, who intend to kill him, ask themselves whether he wants to kill himself (v. 22)! If it is therefore clear that line 5 in 8:21 carries a special accent, then the restructuring of the logion as a whole also fits in with this: if the logion in 7:33–34 comprises *three* double lines,[4] then they have been restructured in 8:21 into a three-line structure and a (remaining) two-line structure:

(1a)	*I am going*
(1b)	and you will search for me
(1c)	and you will die in your sins.
(2a)	Where *I am going*,
(2b)	(there) you cannot come.

The first three lines of this saying clearly form a climax that culminates in the announcement of death; the evangelist was only able to achieve this climactic increase in the three lines, which can also be recognized by their increasing length, by dispensing with the temporal statement "I will be with you a little while longer." He emphasizes the new structure of the saying by aligning the first colon of the following two-line structure ("and where I *am*") with the first colon of the three-line structure ("where *I am going*") in deviation from 7:34. The fact that the saying is now organized *in two parts*, in contrast to 7:33–34, is also reflected in the subsequent conversation, insofar as the evangelist first has the Jews take up the couplet in verse 22 ("for he says, 'Where I am going, you

---

3. Solid underlining mark the words in which the three versions agree; dashed lines mark the similarities between only two versions.

4. See below at 6.1.2!

cannot come'") and then has Jesus quote the climax of the preceding couplet in verse 24. The differences between 8:21 and 7:33–34 can therefore be explained as deliberate *editorial* changes made by the evangelist to the first version of 7:33–34 for contextual reasons. This means that not only the temporal announcement "I will be with you a little while longer" would have belonged to the presumed original logion, but also the concrete metaphorical version of line 5 "you will not find (me)" would be preferable to the theological version and must be claimed for the original version of the logion. A look at 13:33 will confirm this result.

The prefix "little children" has a signaling character in 13:33. It corresponds to the change of addressees as well as to the framework of the Farewell Discourse, in the opening of which our logion is now transplanted. From the structural point of view, 13:33 is closer to 7:33–34 than to 8:21 because the tripartite structure of the saying from 7:33–34 is preserved in 13:33:

(1) Little children,
I am with you only a little longer.
(2) You will look for me
(3) and (as I said to the Jews,)
"Where I am going
(there) you cannot come"
(so also I say [it] to you now.)

While the third double line from 7:33–34 is taken up in its entirety, the evangelist has only taken up the first line of the first two double lines from 7:33–34 in 13:33. This reinforces the emphasis on the end of the logion. This is because the reference back to the earlier occasions on which Jesus spoke the saying frames the final part of the logion (3) and therefore only refers to it. This corresponds to the fact that Peter returns to this in the subsequent dialogue: "Then Simon Peter says to him, 'Lord, *where are you going*? Jesus answers him, '*Where I am going, you cannot follow me now,* but you will follow me later'" (v. 36).[5] While Jesus had announced to the Jews that if they sought him, they would not find him or would die in their sins, the evangelist now modifies this announcement in 13:33–38 according to the context of the disciples in that, on the one hand, he deletes the announcement "you will not find me" without replacement because it does not apply to the disciples,[6] and, on the other hand, he speaks of a "*later*"

---

5. If now instead of "come"—according to the given logion—it says "follow," then this is connected with the synoptic tradition, which is processed in 13:36–38.

6. On the subject of finding Jesus, see 1:41 ("*we have found the Messiah*"), 45 ("*we have found* him about whom Moses in the law and also the prophets wrote, Jesus son of Joseph from Nazareth");

Wisdom Sayings

(v. 36), that is, a paschal following of Jesus, in which it will then be realized what 13:33 actually denies according to its immediate wording: "Where I am going, you *cannot* come!" If, therefore, the evangelist receives the logion in 13:33 *against its wording* by stating that this statement can only apply "now" (v. 33 end), that is, at the time of Jesus's departure, but "later" would no longer apply to the post-Easter faith of his disciples, then this clearly shows that the reception of the logion in the context of the disciples' conversation is *secondary*, while its insertion into Jesus's confrontation with the Jews corresponds to its genuine content. We will see that it was originally an "urgent admonition" or a "riddle" that only later took on the function of a comforting *parting word* from Jesus to his disciples. Based on the synoptic comparison of the three versions, we can thus formulate an initial result that is critical of the tradition:

Since 8:21 and 13:33 are recognizable as new *redactional* versions of the logion in 7:33–34, it is unlikely that these versions are *independent* variants of the tradition. Rather, it can be assumed that the original form of the saying is preserved in 7:33–34, which was then adapted to new contexts in 8:21 and 13:33. This is also supported by the fact that the theme of "seeking and finding," as motif criticism will show, originally formed a pair that belonged together, which was dissolved in the other two versions in favor of a particular theological accentuation.

6.1.2 The Form and Style of the Logion 7:33–34

The terminology of the messenger is part of the evangelist's phraseology. So, it cannot be ruled out that the destination of Jesus's departure ("I am going *to the one who sent me*") goes back to him. In any case, this formula has a mysterious character in the present context: Although the *listener to* the Gospel knows that Jesus is referring to God, who has commissioned him for his mission, it conceals the meaning of his speech from Jesus's *interlocutors* in the narrative, who are puzzled as to where he is going. The "Jews" remain caught up in the misunderstanding and speculate that Jesus intends to "go into the diaspora of the Greeks" (v. 35). It is therefore possible, if not probable, that the evangelist added the terminology of the messenger to the logion in order to emphasize the enigmatic character of the saying at the narrative level. We do not know exactly what the saying originally meant. Perhaps we should add: "I am going *to the Father*";[7] but perhaps the saying, in accordance with its open ending ("*where I am you cannot come*"), already had a blank space here, so that its enigmatic

---

on the subject of "seeking," see 20:15!

7. See 16:10, 17; it should also be noted that "go" (ὑπάγειν) in connection with the preposition "to/toward" (πρός) occurs five times in the John (7:33; 13:3; 16:5, 10, 17).

character was inherent from the very beginning. The following original wording of the logion can be assumed:

(1a) I will be with you a little while longer
(1b) and then I am going.

(2a) You will look for me,
(2b) but will not find [me].

(3a) And where I am going,
(3b) (there) you cannot come.

The saying consists of three parallelisms: synthetic (1a/b), antithetical (2a/b), and another synthetic parallelism (3a/b). If Jesus speaks of himself in the first (he is the subject of 1a and 1b), in the second he looks at his contacts (they are the subject of 2a and 2b). In the third parallelism, he himself is again the subject (3a), combined with a statement that concludes by looking at the interlocutors once again (3b). The third double line thus summarizes the first two: If the announcement of Jesus's imminent departure (1a/b) leads into 3a, 3b sums up the futility of the search for him threatened in the second double line and caused by Jesus's departure: "[there] you cannot come."

Stylistically, the concrete language of the logion, which makes use of spatial concepts, is striking: Jesus is still *with* the people, then he *leaves*; people will *look for* him but will not *find* him because the place where he is then will be unreachable for those looking for him. There is also the temporal factor: Jesus's presence with people is temporary. The hour is coming when he will be withdrawn from them. Temporary presence and closeness on the one hand, unbridgeable distance and absence on the other: in this dialectic, which appeals to the listener's imagination, the Christological meaning of the saying is expressed!

Three observations speak in favor of the hypothesis of a preexistent "saying of the Lord." (1) Formally, the logion is rounded and independent. (2) It is attested three times in the Gospel. (3) In each subsequent conversation, the logion is explicitly quoted and interpreted in essential passages, whereby the evangelist implicitly recognizes his reverence for the authority of the tradition of this "saying of the Lord."

6.1.3 Searching and Not Finding
The Motif of Recognition in the Logion

It is no coincidence that the threat *"you will seek me, but you will not find me"* is at the center of the logion. It lends it a special touch because it evokes biblical associations or can be understood as a topos of the early Jewish wisdom myth. This leads to the thesis that Jesus is speaking here *in persona sapientiae*, or to put it another way: God's wisdom has appeared bodily on earth in him.[8]

(1) The first text that is repeatedly referred to in the interpretation of John 7:33–34 in this sense is the speech of Lady Wisdom to the fools in *Proverbs 1:20–33*, because John 7:34 seems to allude directly to Proverbs 1:28.[9] And indeed, the Johannine saying is very close to this saying of Wisdom. After Lady Wisdom has publicly complained that the fools have not listened to her advice, she says to them:

I also will laugh at your calamity;
I will mock when panic strikes you,
when panic strikes you like a storm,
and your calamity comes like a whirlwind,
when distress and anguish come upon you.
(Prov 1:26–27).

Wisdom then switches from *addressing* the fools (in the second person) to speaking *about them* (in the third person):

Then they will call upon me, but I will not answer;
they will seek me diligently, but will not find me
(Prov 1:28).

John 7:34 could allude to this verse if the motif of the futile search (for wisdom) articulated here had not long since become topical. A whole series of texts point to this, including Hos 5:6, 15; Amos 8:11–12 or 4 Esdras 5:10. In an apocalyptic description of the events at the end of days, it says:

Friends shall conquer one another;
then shall *wisdom* hide itself
and wisdom will *withdraw into its chamber,*
and it shall be sought by many but shall not be found,
and unrighteousness and unrestraint shall increase *on the earth.*
One country shall ask its neighbor,
"Has righteousness, or anyone who does right, passed through you?"
And it will answer, "no."

---

8. Brown, *John*, 1:318, on 7:25–36 as a whole: "The theme of Jesus as divine Wisdom is very strong here and underlies many of the statements."

9. Thus, among others, Brown, *John*, 1:318; but a reference only to this passage is questionable in view of the many parallels.

At that time
people shall hope but not obtain;
they shall labor, but their ways shall not prosper
(4 Esdras 5:9–12 NRSV).

In contrast to Proverbs 1:20–33, the withdrawal of wisdom now clearly takes on cosmic-dualistic dimensions. If Wisdom leaves behind "*on earth*" only "unrighteousness and lack of discipline," which are unavoidable without her organizing power, it is clear that the place of her enforced concealment can only be *heaven*. A wisdom myth emerges here that is alluded to in various early Jewish texts[10] and which can be most clearly grasped in *1 Enoch 42,* which was probably a secondary addition to the Ethiopian Book of Enoch:

1   *Wisdom found* no place where she could live,
    she had a home in the heavens.
2   *Wisdom* went forth to dwell among the children of men,
    and she could not *find* a dwelling place;
    wisdom returned to her place
    and took her seat among the angels.
3   And *iniquity* came out of their chambers:
    those who did not seek her, found her and she lived among them,
    like the rain in the desert and like the dew on the thirsty land.

Here there is clear mention of a futile descent of heavenly Wisdom from heaven and her resigned return. The keywords "seek" and "find" also occur again, albeit in a peculiar refraction in contrast to the previous texts: "Wisdom *found* no place" (v. 1; see also v. 2),[11] but "injustice," the antagonist of Wisdom, did not need to make any effort at all to be accepted by people: "Those she did not *seek*, she *found*" (v. 3). Although they did not have to look for her, they found their way to her of their own accord.[12]

(2) The *positive* version of the motif "*seek and find*" is also found in the Old Testament and early Jewish literature. It is possible that the motif of the unsuccessful search is a deliberate challenge to the expectation expressed in such

---

10. See 4 Esdras 14:16–17; 2 Bar, 39:6; 48:33–36.

11. See also 1 En. 94:5: "I know that sinners seduce men to make wisdom evil, *so that no place will be found for it*, and no temptation will abate."

12. See also Job 28:12–13, 20; Bar. 3:15–38.

texts that the human search for wisdom and happiness must always be granted its success by God.

For the positive version of the motif, three texts from the time of the exile should first be mentioned, starting with Deuteronomy 4:29:

> From there [scattered among the nations] you will *seek* the Lord your God, and *you will find* him if you search after him with all your heart and soul. When you are in need, all these words will *find* you. In later days you will return to the Lord your God and listen to his voice. (NRSV modified).[13]

Here, Israel's bad experiences in exile are taken as an opportunity to preach repentance toward God and hope in his saving intervention. If Israel really takes the main commandment of love (Deut 6:5) seriously, or in the words of Deuteronomy 4:29, if they "seek after him with all their *heart and with all their soul*," then their search for God will also be successful: The one who seeks God with his whole being will find him!

The letter of Jeremiah to the exiles in Babylon (Jer 29:1–23), to which the following verses also belong, is equally confident:

> For surely I know the plans I have for you
> says the Lord,
> plans for your welfare and not for your harm,
> to give you a future with hope.
> Then when you call upon me
> and come and pray to me,
> I will hear you.
> *When you search for me you will find me;*
> *if you seek me with all your heart,*
> *I will let you find me*, says the Lord
> (Jer 29:11–14a).

In this text, the metaphor of seeking and finding is linked to the theme of prayer (v. 12): "calling out" to YHWH, "going" to him, and "praying" to him—such a search achieves its goal!

The third text, *Isa 55:6*, opens the epilogue of the Deutero-Isa 55:6–11:

> *Seek* the Lord while he may be *found*,
> call upon him while he is near!

---

13. See Jub. 1:15: "And I will bring them back from all the nations. And *they shall seek me, that I may be found of them, when they shall seek me* with all their heart and with all their soul."

A second group of texts offers the positive motif of "seeking and finding" in wisdom-like tones.

Thus, in *Proverbs 8:17* personified Wisdom says about herself:

I love those who love me,
and *those who seek me diligently find me*
(οἱ δὲ ἐμὲ ζητοῦντες εὑρήσουσιν).

And in 8:35–36 she announces:

For whoever *finds* me *finds life*
and obtains the favor from the Lord;
but those who miss me injure themselves;
all who hate me love *death*.[14]

Sirach 6:27 offers our word pair concisely in an imperative:

Ask and research,
seek and find,
and when you get hold of her [s.c. Wisdom],
do not let go of her.[15]

(3) Finally, the same wisdom tradition also contains Jesus's admonition in Matthew 7:7–11/Luke 11:9–13 (= Q) (*"seek and you will find"*), which will be briefly discussed (cf. 6.1.6). As the reference to "seeking and finding" is not only found in early Jewish biblical literature but also in secular Greek literature,[16] it can be assumed that this is a widespread proverb ("Seek and you will find!"; cf. Matt 7:8), which is conceivably open in its applicability.

As far as John 7:33–34 is concerned, the logion does not tie in with this broad tradition of proverbs, but clearly with the wisdom-apocalyptic tradition, according to which "seeking and not finding" wisdom is connected with its withdrawal from the world of human folly.[17] This can also be seen from the fact that John 7:34 does not speak generally of "seeking," but precisely of *"seeking of me,"* as wisdom does in the previously mentioned traditions.

---

14. See also Prov 2:4–6 or Wis 6:12–14, 16a.

15. Thus the Hebrew text. See also Sir 51:13–14, 18, 20, 25–27.

16. E.g., Epictetus, *Diatr.* 1.28.20; 4.1.51, where the request "seek and you will find" is addressed to the fictitious interlocutor in order to encourage him toward philosophical reflection.

17. Different is Bultmann, *Johannes*, 232 n. 1 and 233 n. 1, who brings "the gnosis" into play with the reference to Mandaean texts.

6.1.4 Further Motifs in the Logion

The motif of the "little while" (μικρόν) originates from prophetic speeches of judgment, in which it has the dual function of threat and promise: Judgment or salvation will befall man "shortly."

The oldest evidence is probably *Hosea 1:4*, the interpretation of the name of one of the prophet's children: "Then the Lord said to him, 'Name him Jezreel; for *in a little while* I will punish the house of Jehu for the blood of Jezreel, and I will put an end to the kingdom of the house of Israel." *Jeremiah 51:33* contains a word of judgment on Babylon: "For thus says the Lord of hosts, the God of Israel: 'Daughter Babylon is like a threshing floor at the time when it is trodden; *yet a little while* and the time of her harvest will come." The shaking of the entire world of nations announced in *Haggai 2:6–7* brings salvation for Jerusalem and its temple in its wake: "For thus says the Lord of hosts: Once again, *in a little while*, I will shake the heavens and the earth and the sea and the dry land; and I will shake all the nations, so that the treasure of all nations shall come, and I will fill this house with splendor, says the Lord of hosts." In *Psalm 37:10*, the motif appears in the context of a wisdom teaching psalm: "Yet a little while, and the wicked will be no more; though you look diligently for their place, they will not be there."

The book of Isaiah offers three instances in which the phrase announces the nearness of the Lord's salvation of Israel. *Isaiah 10:24–25*: "Therefore thus says the Lord God of hosts: O my people, who live in Zion, do not be afraid of the Assyrians when they beat you with a rod and lift up their staff against you as the Egyptians did. For *in a very little while* my indignation will come to an end, and my anger will be directed to their destruction." *Isaiah 26:20–21*: "Come, my people, enter your chambers, and shut your doors behind you; hide yourselves for *a little while* until the wrath is past. For the Lord comes out from his place to punish the inhabitants of the earth for their iniquity." *Isaiah 29:17*: "Shall not Lebanon *in a very little while* become a fruitful field, and the fruitful field be regarded as a forest? On that day the deaf shall hear the words of a scroll, and out of their gloom and darkness the eyes of the blind shall see."

The fact that the LXX renders the Hebrew עוד מעט almost consistently with μικρόν confirms the reference to the Johannine "little while." "μικρόν as an eschatological term is the time of decision and hope. This sense of τὸ μικρόν is also found in the 'Fourth Gospel.'"[18] While in our saying it refers to the time remaining for man to *decide* for or against Jesus's departure, in 14:19 and 16:16–17, 19 it marks the "little while" until Jesus's return at Easter. Thus, in these

---

18. H. Leroy, *Rätsel und Missverständnis. Ein Beitrag zur Formgeschichte des Johannesevangeliums*, BBB 30 (Bonn: Hanstein, 1968), 58.

passages it is rather a stimulant of *hope that reaches* out for a time that will be completely filled with Jesus's saving presence.

6.1.5 Genre and Intention of the Saying

Both are not easy to identify. The saying shimmers, which of course has to do with the fact that we do not know its original *Sitz im Leben*. If we look at its specific motifs, we could speak of a *wisdom-Christological saying*. However, its pragmatic intention is decisive for a more precise definition of the saying's genre. There are two possibilities: Either it is an "*urgent* exhortation"[19] that, in view of the limited amount of time still available, demands a certain action that is only possible within it, or we have a *riddle* before us whose primary intention is to lead its addressees to reflect more deeply on the mystery of Jesus.

The following observation speaks in favor of the second possibility: The saying is silent on the crucial question of where Jesus wants to "go" shortly and what this "going" entails.[20] It speaks in a veiled manner about Jesus's death in order to point to the mystery of faith given with it. It leads us to interpret it in the light of Jewish wisdom as Jesus's progress to the Father. At the same time, he implicitly makes the listeners understand that, due to the abyss that has opened up between Jesus and humanity in death, one can only reach Jesus if he, as the exalted one, overcomes this abyss *of his own accord*.

6.1.6 John 7:33–34: A Metatext to a Synoptic Transmission or a Genuine Wisdom-Christological Saying?

John 7:33–34 is probably a saying that only arose after Easter in the Johannine communities. The reflection on Jesus's death as an approach to God, triggered by the transposition of basic wisdom motifs to Jesus, points in this direction. But then the question arises as to whether there were at least points of reference in the synoptic tradition for the formation of this saying. Three solutions are conceivable.

The first concerns the above-mentioned exhortation by Jesus to trusting supplication (Matt 7:7–8 / Luke 11:9–10 [= Q]):

> Ask, and it will be given to you,
> *search, and you will find;*
> knock, and the door will be opened of you.

---

19. K. Berger, *Formgeschichte des Neuen Testaments* (Heidelberg: Quelle & Meyer, 1984), 271: "In John 7:33–34, (–36) as well as in Luke 13:35; Matt 23:39, the announcement of the departure has the role of an urgent warning to use the short time until then."

20. Even if the reference to Jesus's commissioner ("he who sent me") was originally part of the saying, it would not say *who* this commissioner actually is.

Wisdom Sayings

> For everyone who asks receives,
> and *everyone who searches finds*,
> and for everyone who knocks, the door will be opened.

There are good reasons to assume that this saying of Jesus also continued to have an effect in the Johannine tradition, as John 14:13–14, 15:16, and 16:23–24 indicate.[21] But, in these passages, only the first link of the series of three "Ask and it will be given to you!" has left its mark, whereas the other two, with their metaphor of "searching" and "knocking," have not. One could now, however, construct a connection between 7:34 and the second link from Jesus's saying "search and you will find."[22] This would mean that Jesus's unlimited promise, according to which *every* search is also granted success (*"everyone* who asks ..."), would have been consciously limited by our saying: There is a missed opportunity, a time when the search comes to nothing! We shy away, however, from tying such a thread between the Johannine and synoptic traditions for two reasons: First, the literal echoes of Jesus's saying are too vague, and second, the content of the two sayings is far apart. If Jesus's saying is about a prayerful search directed toward *God* that only *he* can also help accomplish, then "seeking and not finding" in 7:34 refers to *Jesus*. However, this Christological reference is explained by the predetermined identification of Jesus with Sophia, which is why the assumption that our saying was generated, as it were, from Jesus's prayer cannot be plausible.

The findings are equally negative in the attempt to establish a relationship between John 7:33–34 and *Mark 14:21*, the only synoptic logion in which ὑπάγειν occurs as an expression of Jesus's death, admittedly not in the full Johannine sense. The logion reads:

> For the Son of Man *goes*
> as it is written of him,
> but woe to that one
> by whom the Son of Man is betrayed!
> It would have been better for that one
> not to have been born.

In itself, the isolated occurrence of "go" (ὑπάγειν) in this "woe and warning saying,"[23] which was probably given to the oldest evangelist, could lead to the assumption that the logion was known in the Johannine community and

---

21. See above 68–72.

22. See Lindars, *John*, 296: "John may even be playing on the wellknown promise of Jesus: 'Seek, and you will find' (Mt 7:7)." The evangelist himself has developed the Q-saying further in his own sense!

23. Gnilka, *Markus*, 2:238.

provided the impetus for the formation of the saying in 7:33–34. The logion was known in the Johannine community and provided the impetus for the formation of the saying in 7:33–34, in which the now ambiguously used "go" (ὑπάγειν) represents the core of an in-depth reflection on the death of Jesus.[24] But on the (by no means certain) assumption that Mark 14:21 is indeed a predetermined saying of the tradition, one wonders why the second part of the saying, 14:21b, on which its emphasis rests, was not included in the Johannine tradition. ὑπάγειν alone cannot support the hypothesis of a historical connection between John 7:33–34 and Mark 14:21, especially since the reference to Jesus's "going" (ὑπάγειν) in the sense of his withdrawal from this world into the world of God is probably motivated by the corresponding feature of the wisdom myth.

R. E. Brown and most recently H. Attridge draw attention to a third possibility, namely *Luke 17:22*:[25] "The days are coming when you will long to see one of the days of the Son of Man, and you will not see it."[26] Structurally, the proximity to John 7:33–34 is certainly remarkable,[27] but there are no keyword references. Also, Luke 17:22 belongs to the sayings of the Son of Man, whereas John 7:33–34 belongs to the wisdom sayings.

So it remains the same: John 7:33–34 is a genuinely wisdom-Christological saying that arose after Easter in the Johannine tradition. However, there is no concrete point of reference for it in any saying of Jesus. Rather, it testifies to the type of wisdom sayings attested in Q and in Matthew where Jesus and Sophia are placed in a close but differing relationship to one another. The connection with the synoptic tradition is therefore only mediated by the survival of a specific *genre* of Jesus's words that we can also find later, as in the Gospel of Thomas,[28] but not only there.

6.1.7 The Riddle in the Threefold Refraction of the Gospel

How did the *evangelist* receive and interpret the saying given to him in his book? That it is of great importance to him is demonstrated not only by the fact that

---

24. Lindars, *John*, 295: "The Words fulfil the same function as the Passion predictions in the Synoptic Gospels."

25. Brown, *John*, 1:314: "There is a certain similarity in theme to Luke XVII 22"; cautiously Attridge, "Seeking," 298: "a loose parallel."

26. With this, see Matt 13:17 (par. Luke 10:24): "Many prophets and righteous people longed to see what you see, but did not see it."

27. The "wanting to see"—"not seeing" corresponds to the "seeking"—"not finding"; also, the "longing" in Luke 17:22 does not look backward to the past life of Jesus but forward to the coming of the Son of Man.

28. See Gos. Thom. 38: "Jesus said, 'Often you have desired to hear these words, these that I say to you, and you have no one else to hear them from him. The days will come when *you will* seek *me* (and) will *not find me*." On this see Theobald, *Herrenworte*, 445–448.

Wisdom Sayings

he presents it *three times*, but also by the observation that in *7:33–36* he assigns it the role of Jesus's *first public* statement about his imminent death.[29] In the same scenic setting—the wide-ranging narrative of Jesus's visit to Jerusalem on the occasion of the Feast of Tabernacles (7:2–8:59)—he then presents it a second time in 8:21 to the same audience as in 7:33–36, that is, before the Jews, and in a discussion (*8:21–30*) that also deals with Jesus's imminent departure, his exaltation (8:28). The third text, *13:31–38*, is the prooemium to the first Farewell Discourse Jesus delivers among the circle of his closest confidants. The deliberate threefold placement of the saying is therefore guided by the intention of announcing the passion and Easter events in advance and making them comprehensible as the actual climax of Jesus's entire ministry.[30] The listener can already see that this requires in-depth reflection from the fact that in all three texts, people's reaction to Jesus's enigmatic saying evidences their lack of comprehension. This applies not only to the "Jews" (chs. 7–8), but also to Peter (ch. 13), who, like the other disciples (and listeners of the Gospel!), must first be gradually introduced to the mystery of Jesus's death.

(1) 7:33–36:
This passage belongs to the scene "in the middle" of the Feast of Tabernacles (7:14), which consists of three episodes, the two outer ones of which correspond thematically:

Episode 1 (7:[14,] 25–29):   The *"whence"* of Jesus
Episode 2 (7:30–32):   Reactions to Jesus's words[31]
Episode 3 (7:33–36):   The *"whither"* of Jesus

The evangelist has clarified the reference of the third episode to the first by inserting the phrase "to him who sent me" into the saying given to him, as assumed above. This makes it clear to the reader that Jesus's journey to the Father is his return to *the* place from which he came. If our saying was originally only about Jesus's future, the evangelist has thus superimposed the *Christological scheme of "whence" and "whither,"* which is important to him, on it—only in a hint in its wording, but all the more clearly in its contextual integration. A further contextual interweaving of the saying results from the fact that its motif of "seeking" in the connection "they sought to kill him" also occurs in the first and second episode, in each case prominently at their beginning (7:25, 30). Thus

---

29. Lindars, *John*, 279: Verses 33–36, "the first intimation of the Passion in public teaching."

30. See similarly Jesus's three announcements of suffering and resurrection in Mark!

31. These are centered around the message in v. 31 that many of the people are moved by the question of whether the Messiah, when he comes, will really perform more signs or miracles than Jesus. The two negative messages that people wanted to "arrest" Jesus (vv. 30/32) frame this note.

7:34 gains a deeper meaning for the reader who comes from here: the Jews who are now *seeking* to kill him will, if they are successful, want to *seek* him in another sense, but then it will be too late: he will be taken away from them for good!

The evangelist has inserted the saying into a "*dialogue of revelation*," more precisely into an "*interrupted dialogue* in which the enigmatic word remains unresolved and the listeners remain in a state of incomprehension."[32] Admittedly, the "dialogue" is limited to Jesus's saying and a single perplexed reaction from the Jews, whereby the evangelist increases the mutual strangeness of the two "dialogue partners" even more by not allowing Jesus to speak his weighty word explicitly to the "Jews" present and also only "to himself" (v. 35), that is, only *to each other*. There is no mention of those present opening up to one another or approaching one another in conversation. However, this also has the effect that Jesus speaks his words external to the scene, so to speak, that is to an imaginary audience, just as the questioning repetition of his words by the "Jews" in verse 36 "rhetorically functions as an invitation to the readers to reflect on the true meaning of Jesus's announcement and to understand his words more deeply."[33]

The listeners and readers of the Gospel are also involved when they see *how* the "Jews" of the narrative react to the announcement of Jesus's departure: "Where (ποῦ) will he go that we shall not find him? Will he go into the diaspora among the Greeks and teach the Greeks?" (v. 35). Apart from the fact that with this question the evangelist caricatures the unsuspecting Jews in their thinking as being completely attached to this world, it also contains "a prophetic meaning in its depth: it has been fulfilled for him and his Hellenistic readers, not by Jesus himself, but by the Christian missionaries."[34]

In this way, the evangelist reveals a layer of meaning in the given Jesus saying that he will return to several times later in his book: Jesus's death is not a desolate end but rather a passage, a beginning, and an ascent. It opens up a fundamentally new perspective. Life has been opened up to all who believe through Jesus's return home to the Father, not only to the Jews but also to the Greeks.

(2) 8:21–30:
When the evangelist takes up our saying again in verse 21, he interprets it first through the new form he now gives it and second through the subsequent "dialogue" in which he has Jesus refer to it several times. In addition, our saying also receives light from the wider context, both from 8:12 and from 8:31–36.

---

32. Berger, *Formgeschichte*, 254.

33. J. Frey, "Heiden—Griechen—Gotteskinder," in *Die Heiden. Juden, Christen und das Problem des Fremden*, ed. R. Feldmeier and M. Heckel, WUNT 70 (Tübingen: Mohr Siebeck, 1994), 228–268, here 252.

34. Schnackenburg, *Johannesevangelium*, 2:209.

Wisdom Sayings

The formal and substantive reorganization of the saying has already been mentioned above. The most striking change is the transformation of the metaphorically descriptive threat "you will not find me" into its conceptual frame "you will die in your sin." Rejecting Jesus, the incarnation of divine wisdom, is "sin" per se, not being able to find him means death, whereby it would be superficial to think of physical death; "the threat lies in the fact that for such people who are 'in sin' there is then no longer any hope of life, of eternal life with God. . . . The non-believer faces *death in all its destructive power*."[35]

The question then arises: For whom is it the case that missing him means experiencing such immeasurable misfortune but finding him is the epitome of bliss? Who is it that says "I" (ἐγώ) so majestically in the saying itself? The following conversation in 8:22–30, as well as in chapter 8 as a whole, provides an answer to this question.

Both "interlocutors"—the "Jews" and Jesus—explicitly return to the saying in 8:22–30 and quote parts of it. In addition, the evangelist rounds off the section in verse 28 with a saying from Jesus that corresponds exactly to the opening saying: "The composition began with the theme of continuation and it now ends by means of the keyword of the exalted one."[36] With this *inclusio* the first point of the Johannine interpretation is mentioned: the interpretation of the death of Jesus.

(a) "*I am going*": Jesus's sovereignty, even in his death, could not be expressed more impressively. Even if it is the people who will take him out of the way—which is why it says in verse 28, "if you *lift up* the Son of Man," that is, bring him to the cross (cf. 12:32–33)—his inner freedom and determination to accept his fate in the service of glorifying God (cf. 12:27–28) are unaffected. *Jesus's death as an act of his freedom* is the theme the evangelist asks his listeners to reflect upon in the "dialogue" in 8:21–30.

(b) The ἐγώ that Jesus speaks in his saying is also an expression of his freedom and sovereignty. It is the "I" of the giver of light and life, who already said of himself in 8:12: "*I am* (ἐγώ εἰμι) the light of the world." In our dialogue, this "I" is heard throughout (vv. 22, 23, 24, 26, 28, 29) in order to experience its extreme culmination in the absolute "I am" of verses 24 and 28 in a targeted inclusion of the Old Testament revelation formula.[37] "The Jews should"—says the evangelist in our text—"place themselves on the side of God, accept his testimony, and

---

35. Schnackenburg, *Johannesevangelium*, 2:250 (emphasis mine).

36. Becker, *Johannes*, 1:349: "Ring composition based on theme."

37. Brown, *John*, XX. In the background of v. 28 are passages such as Isa 41:4; 43:10; 45:18, 20 etc. Isaiah 43:10–11: "so that you may know and believe me and understand that I am (LXX: ἐγώ εἰμι) . . . I am God, and before me no god was formed"; thus also Schnackenburg, *Johannesevangelium*, 2:253–254; Bultmann, *Johannes*, 265–266.

believe that God speaks his 'I am' *in Jesus*. Then they too would gain a share in God's eschatological salvation."[38] The significance of Jesus's ἐγώ for chapter 8 as a whole can be seen from the fact that it also brings the chapter to a striking close in correspondence with the word of light in 8:12: "Before Abraham was, I am" (8:58).

(c) Being separated from this "I" of the divine giver of life means dying and death. The evangelist interprets this in the "dialogue" in such a way that he contrasts Jesus's origin from the world of God with the mortal corruption of the lower, this-worldly world with dualistic sharpness: "You are *from below*, I am *from above*; you are *of this world*, I am *not of this world*. I have told you that you would die in your sins, for you will die in your sins unless you believe that I am he."

(3) 13:31-38

It goes without saying that the evangelist had to delete the threat "you will not find me!" when he included the logion in the prooemium of his first Farewell Discourse. Of course, the disciples will find Jesus again in faith: *at Easter*. But the problem the evangelist is now concerned with presenting with clarify is: Why is Jesus's departure in death necessary? Why such a painful separation if a new finding of him in faith is promised later? *Is it even possible to attribute meaning to Jesus's death?*

The first Farewell Discourse attempts an answer to this question; however, this is already prepared by our saying and the immediately following conversation between Jesus and Peter (13:36-38) that serves to interpret the saying. In 13:33, that is, directly after the opening sentence in 13:31-32 created by the evangelist, the saying itself has the function of *programmatically* announcing the imminent separation, Jesus's farewell to his "children" (13:33). The emphasis here is on the insurmountability of this separation *on the part of the disciples* ("where I am going, *you* cannot come"), and that Jesus tells them this "*now*" (cf. 13:19; 14:29). Included in this is the possibility that this situation will change *later*, namely when Jesus, as one who has been exalted to the Father, will *of his own accord* remove the separation from his disciples. The conversation between Peter and Jesus then leads us to understand the necessity of the Christological "lead": Jesus responded to the disciple's question "Where are you going?" which is posed "with the intention of following Jesus to where he is going,"[39] with a rejection *and* a promise that "relegates Peter to waiting for the time being":[40] "Where I am going, you cannot follow me *now*; but you will follow *afterward*" (v. 36b). According to this, the purpose of Jesus's "advance" is to *enable* the disciple to

---

38. Schnackenburg, *Johannesevangelium*, 2:254 (emphasis mine), rightly points out that "the claim to the OT predication of God" for Jesus "does not detach him from the idea of revelation." "An ontological approach that sees in this process nothing other than an equalization of Jesus with God misses the right perspective."

39. Bultmann, *Johannes*, 459.

40. Bultmann, *Johannes*, 460.

follow him later—14:2–31 will explain how. Even if there is a tradition of Peter's martyrdom in the background of the promise in verse 36b, this is certainly not primarily meant with the later possible succession. According to the finding that "Peter [must] be understood here as a representative of the disciples,"[41] discipleship, which will only be possible later, namely after Easter, should also refer to the path that will give *everyone who* believes an encounter with the exalted Jesus. R. *Bultmann* got it right when he said that this discipleship has "only become a possibility because of Jesus's victory over the world; it is therefore possible only in faith in the revealer, in whose ὑπάγειν the victory over the world is accomplished"; this discipleship is "discipleship into the δόξα" of Jesus. If, on the other hand, Peter confuses this discipleship with his, as he thinks, *immediately* demanded commitment to protect Jesus from the enemies lying in wait for him,[42] then he (like every disciple!) must be proven wrong by Jesus: It is not the heroism of action, which is not far off anyway, but faith alone as a gift of Jesus, who comes to meet man and draws him to himself (14:2–3), that is capable of cutting the saving path from the darkness of this world to the light of God.

Anyone who continues to meditate on the first Farewell Discourse will notice that our saying has also left its mark in chapter 14.[43] However, we need not pursue this any further in the following.

6.2 Quenching of the Thirst for Life (John 7:37–38 par. Rev 22:17)

Unlike the logion in John 7:33–34 examined above, Jesus's saying in 7:37–38 has no parallel in the Gospel. The saying does have multiple correspondences in motifs to other passages in the book, which together form a veritable network of metaphors on the subject of *thirst and water*.[44] On the other hand, Revelation 22:17e, f offers an astonishing parallel, which moreover belongs in terms of motifs (as is the case with John 7:37–38) to a corresponding network of metaphors in

---

41. Bultmann, *Johannes*, 460 n. 4.

42. "Lord, why can't I follow you *now*? I want to lay down my life for you!" This is commented on in John 18:10–11!

43. Peter's question "where are you going?" is also found in Thomas's mouth in 14:5: "We do not know *where you are going*" (14:4). The end of 14:3 recalls lines 7–8 of the saying: "So that where I am, there you may be also." The announcement of time from line 2 of the logion is reversed in 14:9: "Have I been with you all this time!" With regard to the promised paraclete, there are no longer any time restrictions: He will "be with you forever" (14:16). The announcement of the "short while" is then taken up and continued with great emphasis in 14:19. The motif of "going away" plays the role of a "leitmotif": 14:2, 12fin, 28.

44. E.g., 4:7, 9–15; 6:35d (see 4.1 above), but also 2:7; 3:5; 5:7; 13:5; 19:34. On the interconnectedness of the first group of texts see Hahn, "Worte," 52–54.

this book.[45] In contrast to John 7:37–38, however, this is not a *saying from Jesus*, but an invitation issued in the name of the *author of* the book. It is obvious that Revelation 22:17e, f is of decisive importance for the analysis of John 7:37–38. We begin with a synchronic analysis of John 7:37–39.

6.2.1 Text and Context
On the Last Day of the Feast of Tabernacles

John 7:37–39 is part of the *last* scene of the dramatic narrative of the Feast of Tabernacles in John 7, which comprises three smaller episodes: Jesus's appearance with his word of revelation (7:37–39), a discussion among the people about his messiahship (7:40–44), and a debate about him in the high council (7:45–52). The time indication at the beginning: *"on the last day of the great feast"* (7:37a), which marks the scenic opening, is probably not unimportant for understanding Jesus's subsequent words of revelation. Why does the evangelist have Jesus speak this word precisely at the climax of the Sukkot feast? Did this festive setting affect the form of his words or is it merely an external backdrop?

The text of the first episode reads:

37	a	On the last day of the festival, while Jesus was standing there
	b	he cried out,
	c	"Let anyone who is thirsty
	d	come to me
	e	(38a) and *let the one who believes in me* drink,
38	b	As the scripture has said,
	c	'Out of the believer's heart shall flow (ῥεύσουσιν) streams of living water.'"
39	a	Now he said this about the Spirit,
	b	which they should receive,
	c	*those who had come to believe in him;*
	d	for as yet there was no Spirit,
	e	because Jesus was not yet glorified.

First we must clarify the referent of the personal pronoun αὐτοῦ in the scriptural quotation verse 38c. Does it refer to the "inner being" *of Jesus* or to *the one who believes in him*?[46] Probably to Jesus. Because the quotation from Scripture is

---

45. See Rev 7:16–17; 21:6; 22:1.

46. John 4:14 could speak in favor of a reference to the believer.

Wisdom Sayings

intended to *substantiate* the preceding words of Jesus. However, it can only do this if it offers an exact correspondence to Jesus's overarching statement, which is only the case with the Christological interpretation: Jesus's thirst for life can be quenched because—as the Scripture says—rivers of living water flow from within *him*. The reference to 19:34 should also be noted: There, too, Jesus is the spring from which living water flows. "And if water is a symbol for the Spirit, then 20:22 also belongs here, according to which the Spirit takes its source from Jesus (15:26)."[47] The commentary by the evangelist himself suggests that these texts should be referred to when he speaks of the future Easter glorification.

The *structure of* the verses is simple: After the opening *introduction* with the time and characterization of Jesus's speech as a solemn, inspired proclamation (vv. 37a–b), the *saying of Jesus* follows in verses 37c–38, which is finally *commented on* by the evangelist in verse 39. The semantic and syntactic correspondences between the saying and the commentary are remarkable: (1) the general "*whoever believes in me*" in verse 38a is taken up again in the plural "*those who have come to believe in him*" in verse 39c. The transformation of the present participle into that of the aorist is not accidental, as it corresponds to the statement of the commentary, according to which those who have already come to believe in Jesus—in the narrative world of the book this can only be his disciples[48] will also "receive the Spirit" at Easter. This two-phase nature, which only makes sense on the level of the disciples' journey from their initial faith to their Easter endowment with the Spirit (20:22) as narrated in the book, may ultimately also explain the seemingly "incoherent" form of the invitation in verses 37e, 38a: "and let him who believes in me drink."[49] The fact that the metaphor "drink" here does not simply stand for "believe," but rather that "drinking" presupposes "believing," can only be understood by those who also take note of the commentary in verse 39, according to which "drinking" actually only takes place when the Spirit is received. (2) A second correspondence between the saying and the commentary concerns the future tense ῥεύσουσιν in the quotation, which either refers to the present of the earthly Jesus as a whole from the position of Scripture as a testimony given before time or looks to a future beyond our scene. Only the commentary provides clarity here: The scriptural word is a paschal promise, the ῥεύσουσιν looks ahead to Jesus's death, when water will emerge from his side as

---

47. Dietzfelbinger, Johannes, 1:226.

48. See 2:11c.

49. According to G. Bienaimé, "L'annonce des fleuves d'eau vive en Jean 7,37–39," *RTL* 21 (1990): 281–310, 417–454, here 303, the phrase πινέτω ὁ πιστεύων εἰς ἐμέ lacks "internal coherence." "He who believes already drinks; the *pinetô* imperative, understood as an invitation addressed to the believer, loses its relevance." Similarly M. J. J. Menken, *Old Testament Quotations in the Fourth Gospel. Studies in Textual Form* (Kampen: Pharos, 1996), 190–191, who speaks of a "tautology," because the figurative word "drink" already denotes "faith" (see 6:35, 40, 47, etc.). However, neither of them consider a reference to v. 39!

a result of the thrust of the spear. These correspondences are not insignificant for answering the tradition-criticism question.

6.2.2 Tradition-Criticism Observations

The fact *that* John 7:37c–38 is based on tradition is easy to justify; what is difficult and perhaps almost impossible to clarify conclusively, however, is the question of what exactly the form of the logion received here by the evangelist originally looked like.

There are four reasons for seeing this saying as based upon a preexisting tradition: (1) the logion (8:12 comparable) is hardly connected to the context. The subsequent discussions among the people do not refer to it in terms of content. (2) As far as can be said on the basis of its original form, which can only be determined hypothetically, the logion rests in itself in terms of form and content and does not require its present context. (3) The text itself suggests a critical view of tradition through its (synchronic) layering: Jesus's own words are followed by the evangelist's commentary which adds a new level of reflection. (4) The logion has a surprisingly precise parallel in Revelation 22:17e, f, which, since John and Revelation were written independently of each other, can only be conclusively explained by the assumption of a common tradition. The following synopsis illustrates the similarities and differences between the two texts:

	Rev 22:17e, f	John 7:37f. + 39
1	and those who thirst	if someone is thirsty,
2	let them come,	let him come to me
3	whoever desires,	
4	receive the water of life	and the one who believes in me drank it,
5	free.	
6		as the scripture says,
7		Streams from the inner being
8		will flow with living water.[50]
9		Now he said this about the Spirit,
10		which they should receive those who had come to believe in him ...

The similarities to be noted *between* the two sayings are twofold: In lines 1–4 they extend to the *structure* and *semantic field* of both versions, in lines 6–10 (= John 7:38b, c, 39) only motifs or lexemes are affected that correspond to Revelation

---

50. With lines 7–8; see also Rev 22:1.

Wisdom Sayings

22:17 (line 4). Only the similarities to be mentioned in the first place allow us to postulate a common tradition:

The two versions are each opened by a general conditional clause, either in the form of a participle (Revelation) or in the form of an ἐάν τις subordinate clause (John); both are syntactically equivalent. Moreover, the verb "to drink" (διψᾶν) is identical. *Two* imperatives of the third person singular follow, the first pair of which is identical (ἐρχέσθω), the second consists of synonyms: to *drink* (πίνειν) and to receive *water* (λαμβάνειν ὕδωρ).[51] The given saying may therefore have initially taken the following form:

If someone is thirsty,
let him come...
and drink (?)...

The similarities of the second kind lead to the question of whether other elements can be claimed for the original beyond this basic element. The agreement in the verb "to receive, to take" (λαμβάνειν) (lines 4/10) seems to be of little significance here, as it occurs very frequently in both works and, like the corresponding verb "to give" (διδόναι) elsewhere, appears in the present thematic context, so to speak, by itself;[52] "the Spirit... receives" also occurs in John 14:17 and 20:22. Conversely, the phrase "whosoever will receive..." in connection with δωρεάν (= for free), which the author of Revelation himself introduced into the saying as an allusion to Isa 55:1, could also go back to it. Seen in this light, the agreement between the two versions in this verb does not say much.

The situation is different with the motif "water of life" (ὕδωρ ζωῆς) and "living water" (ὕδωρ ζῶν), two phrases that, according to John 6:48/51, have the same meaning. The similarity in this striking motif, which is also found in other places in both works,[53] cannot be coincidental. Does this lead to the conclusion that even the original author promised the drinking of the "water of life" to those who accept his invitation to come? If so, the scriptural quotation in John 7:38c and its introduction would go back to the evangelist's editorial work, while the simple version of Revelation 22:17e, f would be close to the original. The evangelist would also have found such a simple form of

---

51. In addition, drinking is always meant in the present tense, also in Rev 22:17: "The spring that will flow in the future time of salvation (21:6) is already flowing and gives life-giving water."

52. λαμβάνειν 23 times in Revelation, 46 times in John; διδόναι—λαμβάνειν in Rev 2:17, 28; 10:8/9, in John in 1:12, 16–17; 3:27; 6:11; 7:22–23; 13:26; 14:16–17; 17:8; 21:13; διδόναι in texts with water metaphor: Joh 4:10, 14 (2 times); Rev 21:6.

53. John 4:10: ὕδωρ ζῶν; in Revelation always the other form ὕδωρ ζωῆς, e.g., in the singular in 21:6 and 22:1, in the plural in 7:17!

the saying in his community tradition and would have taken the motif of the "water of life" contained in it as an occasion for his own scriptural reflection in verse 38c.

(1) In contrast to Revelation 22:17e, f., the Johannine version of the saying is explicitly *Christological*, as is shown by the "to me" in line 2, which exceeds the simple "come" in Revelation. The subsequent "(the one who believes) in me" continues this tendency. Now one would not want to assume that this "to me" (πρός με) goes back to the evangelist's editorial work, rather it can be seen as an indication that the saying, before the evangelist included it in his book, had already received its imprint in the tradition of the Johannine community. Such a Christologization of older, traditional material is quite typical. We will see that the analysis of Revelation 22:17e, f confirms this assumption, at least to the extent that the original saying certainly did not contain the phrase πρός με.

(2) As already indicated above, the imperative "let him who believes in me drink" (πινέτω ὁ πιστεύων εἰς ἐμέ) is problematic. The interlocking with the evangelist's commentary in verse 39a–c suggests that it was he who wrote ὁ πιστεύων εἰς ἐμέ into the saying itself in preparation for his own interpretation: "Let *him who believes in me* drink," Jesus said at the Feast of Tabernacles in Jerusalem, meaning: Whoever believes in me and follows me can expect the life-giving Spirit in view of my imminent "glorification" in death. This assumption is confirmed by the fact that (a) the pair "come to me"—"believe in me" is also found in 6:35, which the evangelist may have used here in 7:37–38, and (b) the linking of "let him drink [it]" (πινέτω) with "let him come to me" (ἐρχέσθω πρός με), as the textual and interpretive history shows with overwhelming clarity, is the more "natural" reading. In other words, the difficulties with the delimitation of the text only arose because the evangelist added a further definition of the subject to the two imperatives "come and drink," namely "the one who believes in me," in addition to "if anyone thirsts."

(3) This decides whether the *quotation from Scripture, including the introductory formula*, belongs to the original statement. The following reasons speak in favor of assigning the quotation of Scripture together with the introductory formula to the evangelist.

(a) Given all that we know about the development of logia in terms of form history, it would be unusual to pass on a saying with a scriptural meta-reflection. The latter is much more a sign of a literary adaptation of an oral tradition, in this case an independent saying of wisdom that in itself has sufficient authority.

(b) The independent parallel in Revelation 22:17e, f shows that the saying originally had no scriptural evidence to support it.

(c) There is no passage in the Old Testament that corresponds to the saying claimed as Scripture in verse 38c. The author of verse 38c probably had the whole range of Old Testament motifs in mind that played a role in the early

Jewish tradition of Sukkot,[54] especially in the interpretation of the ceremonial offering of water from the pool of Shiloh, which was practiced every day early in the morning during this festival week: the memory of the water-giving rock in the desert,[55] which merged with the rock on which the temple is built during the celebration of the feast, but also the expectation of a salvation-giving spring in the temple of the end times, when Jerusalem would be gloriously renewed.[56] As the evangelist has now explicitly linked the logion in his scenic introduction of verse 37a with the "last day, the great day, of the (Tabernacles) feast," on which the priests went around the altar seven times with the offering of water,[57] it could only have been him who introduced the scripturally informed meta-reflection in verse 38b, c into the text. The fact that it takes the form of an explicit scriptural recourse underlines the specific reclamation of the biblical traditions for Jesus, which were usually associated with Sukkot in early Judaism.

Even if, as a result of the scenic embedding of the logion, the scriptural saying associates the Old Testament motif context connected with Sukkot as a whole, it can be assumed analogous to the other scriptural quotations in the Fourth Gospel that the author also has a specific textual reference in mind here. It is probably a *mixed quotation*, the combination of two LXX texts, whereby the influence of the Hebrew text is possible.[58] The basis of the quotation was provided by verses 16 and 20 about the water-giving rock in the desert from Psalm 78 (77), which the evangelist had already quoted in John 6:31 when discussing the subject of the gift of manna in the desert (Ps 78 [77]:24):

16 he made *water* come out of the rock
 and let *the waters* flow down *like rivers*.
20 for he struck the rock and *the waters flowed*.

Apart from Psalm 105 (104):41,[59] the three terms used in John 7:38 ("streams"/"rivers" [ποταμοί], "water" [ὕδωρ], and "flowing"/"flowing" [ῥέω])

---

54. G. W. MacRae, "The Meaning and Evolution of the Feast of Tabernacles," *CBQ* 22 (1960): 251–276.

55. Exod 17:6; Num 20:7–11; Ps 78:15–16, 20.

56. Ezek 47:1–12; Zech 13:1; 14:8; Joel 4:18; Ps 46:5.

57. See m. Suk 4:5: "On each day one circles the altar once.... But on this day [s.c. the seventh] one circles the altar seven times." It is very likely that the evangelist is referring to this seventh day, not the eighth, which was regarded as a separate feast: see most recently Wengst, *Johannesevangelium*, 290–291.

58. Menken, *Old Testament*, 194–202.

59. Ps 105 (104):41: "He opened the rock so that *waters flowed out, rivers* poured into waterless regions."

are only used together here in the Old Testament.⁶⁰ ἐκ τῆς κοιλίας αὐτοῦ (= from within) would be the transformation of the biblical ἐκ πέτρας (= from the rock) in accordance with the macro-context of the Gospel (see 19:34),⁶¹ which could have been inspired by the allegorical identification of the water-giving rock with Christ, also attested by Paul.⁶² This reconstruction seems plausible.

The second text that most likely had an impact on verse 38 is Zechariah 14:8a, "and on that day *living water* will come *out of* Jerusalem." The phrase "living water" also occurs elsewhere in the Old Testament (Song 4:15; Jer 2:13⁶³), but here in a context that harmonizes perfectly with John 7:37-39. Zechariah 14:8 is also related to the Feast of Tabernacles, for immediately following it, 14:16 says, "Then all who survive of the nations that have come against Jerusalem shall go up year after year to worship the King, the Lord of hosts, and to keep the *festival of booths*." As the parallels in Ezekiel 47:1-12 and Joel 4:18 show, Zechariah 14:8 can only refer to the eschatologically renewed temple, from which the "living water" will spring forth. In t. Sukkah 3:8, Zechariah 14:8 is used to interpret the rite of giving water at the Sukkot festival.

(4) There is no doubt that the commentary sentence in verse 39 goes back to the evangelist. To relate the *drinking of* water to the reception of the Spirit is quite unusual from a biblical-early Jewish perspective and is therefore an independent creative achievement of our author. Moreover, if he makes the Easter glorification of *Jesus* (*passivum divinum*: ἐδοξάσθη) a prerequisite for the reception of the Spirit, then this corresponds exactly to the paraclete

---

60. In addition to the three terms mentioned, see also the preposition ἐκ = from (the rock / from within it). See also Isa 48:21, another passage on the rock in the desert "and *when they thirst*, he will lead them through the desert, bring them *water from* a rock; the rock will be split open and *water will spring forth*, and my people will be *watered*."

61. The detour proposed by Menken, *Old Testament*, 200-201, via Ps 114:8 ("who turns the rock into a flood of water and the pebbles into a spring [= מעין] of water")—the consonants also could be read like this: מעין (aramaic = *inside*)—seems too complicated and is unnecesary.

62. See 1 Cor 10:4: "But the rock is Christ."—Even if v. 38 goes back to the evangelist in its concrete formulation, he nevertheless made use of congregational scriptural scholarship, as this parallel shows.

63. See also 1QH 8:7 ("and its rootstock has free access to the water of life"); 1QH 8:16 ("But you, my God, have put in my mouth [something] like early rain for all [the thirsty] and a spring of living water that does not deceive . . ."); CD 19:33-34 ("all men who . . . have fallen away again and strayed from the fountain of living water [= Torah; see 3:16; 6:6]). Aune, *Revelation*, 3:1176 (see also 1129), still draws attention to 11Q18 = 11QNJ frg. 24. In addition, see Jos. Asen. 14:12 Odes 11:6, 7 (Syr. text); 30:1.

sayings of the first Farewell Discourse, according to which it is the *Father* who "gives" or "will send" the Spirit (14:16, 26). The fact that, according to the scriptural quotation, he will "spring forth from within *Jesus*" is not a contradiction, as this is a figurative statement whose intention is also preserved in the theocentric statements in 14:16, 26. The Father will "give" the Spirit through the intercession of his Son, that is, because of his own intercession in death for his own.

The result of the critical analysis of 7:37-39 is that the evangelist probably had a saying from his community tradition that not only contained the words, "If *anyone thirsts, let him come to me and drink,*" but also—recognizable by the similarity between John 7:38 and Revelation 22:17e, f—a statement that contained the motif of "living water" or "water of life." It is no longer possible to say what this statement was. One could think of a promise in the following form, "*I will give him the water of life*";[64] such a formulation would then be echoed in John 4:10, 14. But this is nothing more than a conjecture. The motif of the "water of life" gave the evangelist the impetus to link the saying with the scene of the Feast of Tabernacles and to draw on Zechariah 14:6, embedded in Psalm 78 (77):16, 20, for his scriptural proof.

6.2.3 An Invitation to Thirsty People
The Shape, Genre, and Sitz im Leben *of the Saying*

Before drawing further conclusions from a comparison of Revelation 22:17 and John 7:37-38, we need to take a closer look at the version and context of the saying in Revelation. Here we encounter the saying in a small "staging," a dialogue in several stages between the exalted Christ and his church:

16   a   It is *I, Jesus,* who sent my angel to you,
      b   to you[65] with this[66] testimony for the churches.
      c   *I am* the root and the descendant of David,
      d   the bright morning start.

---

64. See Rev 21:6.

65. Who these "you" are is disputed. Probably the group of prophets mentioned in 22:6, 9, who are distinguished here from the communities; τὸ πνεῦμα v. 17a then means the Spirit working in them.

66. "This" does not refer to the following saying of Jesus (v. 16c), but as in 22:20 (see v. 18) to the *whole* book that is now coming to an end.

17 a *The Spirit* and *the bride*[67] say,
    b   Come.
    c And let everyone who hears say,
    d   Come.
    e And let everone who is thirsty come.
    f Let anyone who wishes take the water of life as a gift.

Obviously, this little dialogue has its point of contact in the congregation's worship gathering. Here the call resounds, "Come (Lord Jesus)!"—probably from the mouth of prophets—and "whoever hears it" (17c) takes it up and joins in, "Come (Lord Jesus)!" (17d). The keyword "come" is followed by the saying in verse 17e, f, which uses this motif in a new sense: Everyone who thirsts, that is, who eagerly awaits the *coming of* Jesus, should *come and join in*. There is, however, ambiguity as to where they are to go.

If it is true that the saying is not intended to be a missionary advertisement to all but rather an invitation to the congregation already gathered, then it is not far-fetched to assume that this invitation originally had participation in the eucharistic celebration in mind, thus understanding the call to come as participation in the common table. For the fact that we are dealing with tradition in 22:17e, f is proven not only by the parallel in John 7:37–38 but also by the observation already made several times that elements of the liturgy are preserved in 22:6–21: "The conclusion of the Apocalypse" is "pervaded" by "echoes of the eucharistic liturgy," as G. Bornkamm noted long ago.[68] In support of this idea, he interpreted verse 17e, f, to the "Come, Lord Jesus" = Maranatha in verses 17b, d, and 20 in light of the wedding motif ("bride"), "which according to 19:9 includes the idea of the messianic banquet," as well as to the self-predication in verse 16, "I am the root and the lineage of David," which could possibly be placed alongside "the phrase in the prayer for the Lord's Supper in Did. 9:2."[69] The promise of the messianic banquet in Revelation 2:7

---

67. The bride—like "the angel of the church" in (chs. 2–3)—is probably intended as a heavenly antitype of the earthly church, which becomes present in the church through the Spirit speaking in the prophets (τὸ πνεῦμα). The other Christians in the church assembly only come into view with their call in v. 17, d. This explains well the *staggering of* the expressions of worship in v. 17.

68. G. Bornkamm, "Das Anathema in der urChristlichen Abendmahlsliturgie," in *Das Ende des Gesetzes. Paulusstudien. Gesammelte Aufsätze I*, BevTh 16, 5th ed. (München: Kaiser, 1966), 123–132 here 126–127. The reference of v. 17 to the Eucharist is widely accepted; see Aune, Revelation, 3:1228.

69. Did. 9:2: "We thank you, our Father, for the holy vine *of David, your servant*."

and the motif of the hidden manna in 2:17 (cf. John 6:48-51) also have an "echo of the Eucharist," which ultimately also applies to the words of Rev 3:20–21 ("Listen! I am standing at the door, knocking...") formulated in reference to the image of the messianic banquet.[70]

In favor of the assumption that our saying in 22:17e, f has its *Sitz im Leben* in the eucharistic celebration of the congregation, Didache 10:6 can also be cited as a revealing parallel. Here, too, we have a piece of communion liturgy that can be broken down into the call from the liturgist and answer from the congregation as follows:[71]

Liturgist:	Let grace come and let this world pass away!
Congregation:	Hosanna to the God of David!
Liturgist:	If someone is holy,
	let him come;
	if someone is not holy,
	let him repent!
	Maranatha.
Congregation:	Amen.

Didache 10:6 originally belonged to an opening "entrance liturgy."[72] The correspondence in the call "Maranatha" is also remarkable (see Rev 22:17b, d, 20). The assumption is confirmed that Revelation 22:17e, f* also *originally* belonged to the Eucharist, where the saying—comparable with Didache 10:6—had the function of an invitation to participate in the eucharistic meal.

It is possible, but by no means certain, that the author of Revelation adopted the liturgical invitation from the tradition of his congregations unchanged. In its present form, Isaiah 55:1–3 has rubbed off on the saying, which points to the author of Revelation:[73]

> Ho, *everyone who thirsts, come to the waters*;
> and you that have no money, come
> buy and eat![74]

---

70. Bornkamm, "Anathema," 127.

71. H. Lietzmann, *Messe und Herrenmahl. Eine Studie zur Geschichte der Liturgie*, AKG 8, 3rd edition (Berlin: de Gruyter, 195), 230–238.

72. For proof, see Theobald, Zulassungsbedingungen 111–139.

73. See Rev 22:6, where reference is also made to Isa 55:1.

74. This line is missing in the LXX, in 1QIsa^{a} and the Syriac translation.

Come, buy wine and milk *without money and without price.*
Why do you spend your money for that which is not bread,
and your labor for that which does not satisfy?
Listen carefully to me, and eat what is good,
and delight yourselves in rich food!
Incline your ear, and come to me;
listen, so that you may live.

Not only the participle at the beginning of the saying in Revelation 22:17e, f ("everyone who thirsts"), but above all the keyword "without price"[75] at its end proves the explicit reference to Isaiah 55:1–3: as in a focal point this keyword collects what Isa 55:1 is to be read. If it was the author of Revelation who projected Isaiah 55:1 onto the "invitation," then this does not mean, of course, that he himself did not have Isaiah 55:1 as part of his matrix *from the very beginning.* If this were true, then one would have to assume that the context (i.e., Isa 55:1–3) was also present—in a eucharistic interpretation that could suggest two statements in particular from the biblical model: the rejection of bread that does not truly satisfy (v. 2) and the promise that whoever eats of the "good" will "live" (v. 3).

We can draw the following conclusions about the genre and the *Sitz im Leben* of our saying from the observations made so far: (1) Originally it was a eucharistic "invitation" that was possibly part of an "opening liturgy." (2) It was only in the Johannine tradition that the invitation, which was often spoken by a liturgist, become a "word of the Lord" that can be read in the saying itself by its Christologization, "If anyone thirsts, let him come *to me* . . . !" (3) Just as the fourth evangelist explicitly placed the saying within the horizon of Scripture in verse 38, the author of Revelation also interspersed the invitation with allusions to Isaiah 55:1. It is possible, however, that this biblical text lent the saying its matrix from the very beginning.

6.2.4 The Religious-Historical Background of the Saying

When determining the history of religions background of John 7:37–39, reference is generally made to wisdom, apocalypticism, and gnosis, but tradition-criticism analysis now allows us to obtain more precise information. Possibly generated on the basis of a specific biblical text (Isa 55:1–3) that in turn already possessed wisdom-related coloring, the genre and motifs place our saying alongside the *invitations of personified wisdom* to come to her,[76] to enjoy

---

75. See Rom 3:24!

76. Prov 9:5; Sir 24:19; Sir 51:23; Isa 55:1.

Wisdom Sayings

being at her table (Prov 9:5–6;[77] Sir 51:23–26), or to enjoy or drink oneself (Sir 24:19–21[78]). If these invitations from the mouth of Wisdom always come in the second person plural, then John 7:37d/Revelation 22:17e stands out through the use of the imperative of the third person singular. This difference confirms that we are not originally dealing with an invitation to the participants of the eucharistic banquet by Jesus himself as personified Wisdom, but with an invitation issued by a third party, namely a liturgist. On the other hand, the proximity of the motifs to the invitations of Wisdom shows how easily this liturgical call could be transformed into a saying of Jesus himself, as in the Johannine tradition. Matthew 11:28[79] and Ode of Solomon 30 prove how in the early Christian tradition the element of wisdom could continue to live on in completely different garb:

Ode 30.[80]
An invitation to the thirsty.

1 Fill ye waters for yourselves from the living fountain, of the Lord, for it is opened to you:
2 And come all ye thirsty and take the draught[81]; and rest by the fountain of the Lord.[82]
3 For fair it is and pure and gives rest to the soul, Much ore pleasant are its waters than honey;
4 And the honeycomb of bees is not to be compared with it.[83]
5 For it flows forth from the lips of the Lord and from the heart of the Lord is its name.
6 And it came infinitely and invisibly: and until it was set in the midst they did not know it:
7 Blessed are they who have drunk therefrom and have found rest thereby.
   Hallelujah.

---

77. Sir 9:5: "Come, eat of my *bread* and drink the *wine* I have mixed for you!"

78. Sir 24:21: "who eat me" / "who drink me."

79. Matt 11:28: "Come to me, all you that are weary and are carrying heavy burdens, and I will give you rest."

80. James H. Charlesworth, editor, *The Old Testament Pseudepigrapha*, 2 vols (New York: Doubleday, 1983) 2:762.

81. See Isa 55:1!

82. See Ps 23:2b: "he leads me beside *still* waters."

83. See Ps 19:11; 119:103; Sir 24:20.

Excursus
The Other Sayings of the Water of Life in Revelation (Rev 7:16–17; 21:6; 22:1)

Can the results of the tradition-criticism analysis so far be corroborated by the other water of life texts in Revelation? There is a total of three in which the motif of the water of life has still penetrated:

7:16–17:

They will hunger no more
and thirst no more
the sun will not strike them, nor any scorching heat;[84]
for the Lamb at the center of the throne will be their shepherd
and he will guide them to *springs of water of life*,
and God will wipe away every tear from their eyes.

21:(5a,) 6e:

And the one who was seated on the throne said . . .
I will give water as a gift[85] *from the spring of the water of life.*[86]

22,1a:

Then the angel showed me the *river of the water of life*,[87]
bright as crystal,
flowing from the throne of God and of the Lamb . . .

A closer examination of these texts leads to the following conclusions:
(1) There is no indication that the three texts interlinked by their motifs contain independent *traditions*, as we may assume with good reason in the case of 22:17e, f. All three are based on biblical texts, whereby the degree of

---

84. Isa 49:10: "They shall not hunger or thirst, neither scorching wind nor sun shall strike them down, for he who has pity on them will lead them, and by springs of water will guide them (LXX: διὰ πηγῶν ὑδάτων)."

85. See Isa 55:1, see previous.

86. Jer 2:13: "For my people have committed two evils: they have forsaken me, *the fountain of living water*, and dug out cisterns for themselves, cracked cisterns that can hold no water."

87. See Gen 2:10 LXX: "A river flows out of Eden to water the garden paradise." See Ezek 47:1–12.

reference varies greatly between melted-down quotation (7:16–17) and allusion (21:6; 22:1). The *promise* in 21:6 also reveals that it is to be understood as a corresponding counterpart to the *invitation* to the thirsty in 22:17: What God will "give" to the thirsty *himself* in the new creation (21:2, 5) in an immediacy that leaves all cultic mediations behind (21:6), they can already "receive" in the space of the congregation, in "coming" to the Eucharist—"for free" (22:17).

(2) The apocalyptic John probably took the motif of the "water of life" of 22:17e, f, a tradition within his community. This is indicated by the observation that he adds the keyword "life" in 7:17 to his biblical *Vorlage* Isa 49:10—for the sake of linking the texts—and that he himself redacted 21:6 in correspondence with 22:17e, f.[88] It also seems important to note that, in contrast to 22:17e, f, the other three texts are all linked to the *throne motif*, a fundamental element of the author's conception of the book, and, at the same time, in contrast to 22:17e, f, are provided with the idea of a *spring* from which the water of life gushes forth. The motif of the throne and that of the spring belong closely together: It is God and his Lamb, seated on the throne, who lead to the springs of the water of life (7:17) or, more precisely, designate the *place* where the "water of life" will gush forth in the form of a strong, crystal-clear stream (22:1). In other words: God and the Lamb are *themselves* the source of all water of life! From these observations we can conclude that it was the author of Revelation who integrated the simple liturgical "invitation" in 22:17e, f into the reference network of his images of the "throne" of God and the source. The reverse assumption, that this "invitation" only arose through the subtraction of those images, has nothing to do with it.

(3) In the beginning, therefore, there was a tradition according to which the "water of life" could *already* be received in the congregation. This was probably illustrated by the fact that the eucharistic celebration—drinking from the common cup and eating from the common bread—was understood as participation in the divine stream of life. It is then significant for the apocalyptic John that he took this originally *present-tense* motif of the water of life further in *futuristic-eschatological terms by incorporating* it into his visions of a completed future of salvation. This also opened up the field for associations with biblical texts that contain the motifs of water and thirst in an eschatological sense.[89]

---

88. The formulation with δώσω = *I give* is often found in the victorious sayings of chs. 2–3 (2:7, 17; 3:21). It is not without reason that 21:7 is immediately followed by a victor's saying. Schüssler Fiorenza, "Quest," 418, who wants to recognize the presence of an old Johannine tradition in 21:6, is different.

89. Kollmann, *Ursprung*, 116: "The satisfying of hunger and thirst is identified by numerous texts as a constitutive topos of eschatological expectation" (with reference to Isa 49:10; 55:1; 2 Bar. 29:6; Sib. 3.753–754; Matt 5:6).

Conclusion: Neither the correspondence between John 7:37-38 and Revelation 22:17e, f, which is to be evaluated in terms of tradition-criticism, allows the hypothesis that Revelation and John belong to one and the same school (M. Hengel), nor the assumption that the author of Revelation received the Johannine school tradition (E. Schüssler Fiorenza), and certainly not the hypothesis that Revelation is to be understood as the end point of an *inner-Johannine* re-eschatologization (J.-W. Taeger), nor the reverse hypothesis, according to which both writings were based on Jewish-apocalyptic "tradition," which in Revelation underwent a "gradual Christianization," but in John, "under the influence of the wisdom tradition," a transformation into "statements about the present salvation" (F. Hahn). The result in our specific case, which corresponds exactly to the history of the tradition of the I-am sayings (see the excursus after 4.4.6), is much more modest: John and Revelation meet in a community tradition with a *Sitz im Leben* in the Eucharist, which was originally by no means specifically Johannine (Did. 10:6),[90] but then underwent a Christologization in the Johannine community in order to finally enter the evangelist's context of the Easter "glorification" of Jesus. The Revelation of John, on the other hand, *eschatologized* the eucharistic "invitation" in many ways; that it only gradually moved from a theocentricity (see 21:6) to a Christologization (7:16-17; 22:1) of the motif (F. Hahn) is not discernible.

6.2.5 The "Glorified" Jesus as the Source of the Water of Life
The Evangelist's Reception of the Saying

The evangelist was guided by two interests in interpreting the Johannine sayings about the community:

(1) The setting of the Feast of Tabernacles as a framework for Jesus's appearance in the temple on the one hand and the transfer of scriptural passages that early Judaism usually claims for Sukkot to Jesus on the other show that the evangelist understands the soteriological claim associated with Jesus exclusively and absolutely. Even if the negation of the temple as a place of salvation where the pilgrims experience God's gracious attention not only at Sukkot is nowhere directly expressed in the text of the surrounding chapters, the renunciation of any

---

90. Also considered by Schüssler Fiorenza, "Quest," 417, but then rejected in favor of the priority of Rev 21:6 (see above): "The similarity in wording between Apoc XX.17; John VII.37 and Did. X.6 (conditional sentence or participle [Apoc XXII.17] followed by ἐρχέσθω), as well as the possible Eucharistic context of John VI.35, suggests much more that the image was taken over by the Apoc and the 4 G from the Eucharistic liturgy and does not represent the product of a common school tradition."

reference to the temple cult as such is clear enough. There is an obvious vacuum here, which is filled solely by Jesus's teachings in the temple. The evangelist transfers the expectations previously directed at the Jerusalem temple as the place of God's presence of salvation exclusively to Jesus.[91]

(2) What was originally the saying of a liturgist that was transformed within the Johannine community into a "word of the Lord," the evangelist finally put into the mouth of the earthly Jesus because he was convinced that as the "Son of God" he is exclusively the source of eternal life. But since the metaphor of the saying ("to drink") is soteriological, he linked the saying in the commentary in verse 39 back to the Easter glorification of Jesus. As the first part of his commentary in verse 39a shows, he related the "streams of living water" to the Spirit and accordingly interpreted Jesus's invitation in light of its actual intention as a paschal promise of the Spirit being released for believers in Jesus's death. He would not have given any thought to the soteriological content of a pre-paschal faith in the discipleship of the earthly Jesus. His focus on Jesus the crucified one is rather directed toward the *Trinitarian presence of God* in his death. The *crucified one*, as the one exalted to *God* and glorified by *him*, becomes the source of the life-giving *Spirit* due to this theocentrically oriented event. The fact that the metaphor of water or drinking has sacramental undertones in the present context cannot be proven, but it cannot be ruled out either.

6.3 Jesus
Wisdom Personified

That the Johannine preexistence Christology possesses a *wisdom-theological matrix* is an insight that has been a topic of research for some time, but its full significance for a possible integration of the variety of very different Christological aspects and language games of the Gospel into a comprehensive concept has probably not yet been fully realized. This makes it all the more important, as a first step, to demonstrate in this chapter that there was indeed a very independent and creative continuation of a type of wisdom sayings in the Johannine community that can already be found in the synoptic tradition and has now found a form in the Johannine community where the identification of personified wisdom with Jesus is already taken for granted (John 7:33–34). Beyond the Johannine community, this type of wisdom saying lived on in the apocryphal gospel literature of the second century.

---

91. The point of view that Aune, *Revelation*, 3:1229, mentions with regard to Rev 22:17 is also noteworthy: "In rabbinic literature water is a frequent metaphor for the Torah."

The insight into the genuinely liturgical origin of the saying in John 7:37-38 is remarkable, for wisdom-Christological testimonies have come down to us from this area everywhere. One thinks of the hymn in Colossians 1:15-20, as well as of the Johannine about Christ in the prologue of John 1. The paramount importance of the logion in 7:33-34 for the Christology of the Gospel is shown by the fact that the evangelist takes it up three times and is also influenced by it in his terminology. Thus, the thesis of the wisdom theological *matrix* of the Johannine Christology now also its *genetic* foundation: The evangelist did not freely create the framework of his Christology out of his own inspiration; he was able to rely on the traditions of his community.

CHAPTER 7

Sayings of Promise and Consolation

AFTER THE CHRISTOLOGICAL words of wisdom in chapter 6, we now turn to a final group of logia at the end of the study that are again compiled more from the point of view of content than form: These are *words of promise and comfort* that Jesus addresses to his disciples or those who already believe ("you": 8:31-32; 14:2-3), as well as a logion that is given in general ("if anyone"), but also has (potential or actual) members of the congregation in mind (8:51 par. 52).[1] There are no direct synoptic parallels to any of these words. Whether there are generic-historical bridges must be examined in each individual case.

7.1 "The truth will set you free!" (John 8:31b, c, 32)

The logion John 8:31-32 no longer has any direct echo in the gospel;[2] however, it triggers an exchange of words between Jesus and Jews who have become believers, who take up its last line once again in the form of a *quotation*. John 8:31-36 has already been questioned on various occasions in terms of tradition criticism. In addition to verses 31-32, the figurative word in verse 35 has also attracted the attention of scholars.

7.1.1 The Context
An Exchange of Words Between Jesus and the "Jews who had become believers" (John 8:31-36)

John 8:31-32 opens the third dialogue scene of verses 31-36(38) in chapter 8, the events of which take place in the Jerusalem temple. The exact delimitation of our scene is controversial and raises problems. The easiest question to clarify is whether verse 30 belongs to this scene as is the view of the *Nestle-Aland*[27] or to the previous scene as attested in the *GNT*[4]. The latter is probably in line with

---

1. See Dodd, *Tradition*, 406-420: "Predictions": "(1) predictions of Christ's return after death"; "(2) forecasts of the future destiny of his followers" (407). However, he is concerned with themes and motifs, not with the transmission of words.

2. Noteworthy, however, is 2 John 1, where the Christians are called οἱ ἐγνωκότες τὴν ἀλήθειαν ("who know the truth").

the text because verse 30³ is a typical concluding note that records the people's reaction to Jesus's words. In contrast, verse 31 begins anew in order to situate Jesus's subsequent statement: "*Then (οὖν) Jesus said to the Jews who had believed in him*." Both the macro-syntactic signal οὖν and the renewed qualification of the listeners as "believing Jews" instead of a simple pronominal "to them" confirm the assumption of a caesura between verses 30 and 31.

This apostrophizing of Jesus's addressees in verse 31, however, poses the actual structural problem of chapter 8. There is no scenic signal from the narrator to the effect that the audience would change as the chapter progresses, although it seems hardly comprehensible that Jesus should have spoken the accusation "you seek to kill me," which dominates his speech from verse 37 onwards, to people who were said to have come to believe in him shortly before.[4] Thus, one usually resorts to the (probably unavoidable) makeshift solution of assuming a gradual change of Jesus's addressee in the middle of the speech section in verses 34–38, that is, in verse 37, which is not marked as such by the narrator but which suggests itself due to the new thematic orientation of Jesus's words. According to this interpretation, while in verses 31–36 Jesus speaks to Jews who have believed him but are obviously rejected by him, from verse 37 onwards he increasingly addresses the "Jews," who have been regarded as his actual opponents since the beginning of the book: representatives of an authority that wants to kill him.[5] The real question that arises from this attempt at classification is how it is possible for the evangelist to judge "believing" Jewish Christians and "Jews" hostile to Jesus, holders of official power, in the same way, and even to include the former without any reservations or scruples in the united front that is forming against Jesus and is deadly to him. Only when we have gained some clarity at this point does the strangely smooth transition from one segment to the other become understandable, whereby we must assume that the evangelist deliberately opted for this type of literary design instead of a clear, unambiguous caesura.

But who are the addressees to whom the evangelist has Jesus say the logion in John 8:31–32? Most likely "Jewish Christians" in the evangelist's circle, that is, not listeners of the *historical* Jesus who would have initially placed their trust in him only to then side with his opponents! How the portrait of the "Jews who came to faith" is transparent with regard to the leaders of the contemporary

---

3. "As he was saying these these things, many came to believe in him."

4. Wengst, *Johannesevangelium*, 1:309, following H. Thyen, translates the perfect participle πεπιστευκότας in v. 31 *past perfect plusquamperfektisch* ("einige aus der Partei der Pharisäer, die gläubig geworden waren"). "Then it would not be those who had come to faith mentioned in v. 30 who would be in view, but others, namely apostates" (ibid. 326). But this seems to be ruled out.

5. See 1:19; 2:18, 20; 5:10, 12, 15–18, etc.

synagogue, whose fierce resistance to their preaching of Jesus the Johannine Christians must have painfully experienced, is clear. C. H. Dodd deserves credit for having substantiated this for the first time following a remark by A. Loisy.[6] The desideratum, however, remains to specify the profile of those "Jewish Christians" whom the evangelist treats not as heterodox *Christians* but as belonging to the hostile "*Jews*," that is, the *synagogue*.[7] The following remarks comment on this:

(1) C. H. Dodd writes on John 8:31–58: "It appears to reflect controversies between Gentile and Jewish Christians *in the* Church."[8] Does not the speech of "Jewish *Christians*" on a meta-level here not encourage a false perception of the phenomenon meant by it? Does it not insinuate a juxtaposition of synagogue and church (with "Jewish Christians" in their midst) that did not exist in reality? After all, 12:42–43 knows of many leaders *in the* synagogues who had come to believe in Jesus without feeling compelled to leave them (for whatever reason).[9]

(2) If C. H. Dodd locates the "Jewish Christians" of John 8:30–31, to whose relationship with the Galatian false teachers he refers, only in general terms in the congregation of the first century, then L. Schenke connects them specifically with the history of the Johannine community and sees in them the "schismatics" of 1 John 2:18–19 "who left the high confession of Jesus and defected to the opponents."[10] Elsewhere, he defines their position as a belief in the "resurrection" of Jesus in the sense of his "appointment ... to the messiahship of the future," according to which they would have represented "a much

---

6. C. H. Dodd, "Behind a Johannine Dialogue," in *More New Testament Studies* (Manchester: Manchester University Press, 1968), 41–57, here 41ff. Among other things, he refers to Acts, where the *perfect participle* of πιστεύειν occurs in the same context: Acts 15:5 ("some of the party of the Pharisees who had become believers"); 21:20 ("you see, brother, how many thousands among the Jews have become believers"). "It would appear, then, that the meaning conveyed by the phrase, οἱ πεπιστευκότες Ἰουδαῖοι, to readers in the Greek-speaking Church in the latter part of the first century, was 'Jewish converts to Christianity,' or, as we say, 'Jewish Christians'" (43). See also Acts 10:45 (οἱ ἐκ περιτομῆς πιστοί); 11:17.

7. See now comprehensively *Theobald, Das Johannesevangelium—Zeugnis eines synagogalen "JudenChristentums"?* 107–158.

8. Dodd, *Tradition*, 330 (emphasis mine).

9. The account given in 12:42–43 ("Nevertheless many, even of the authorities believed in him [Jesus]. But because of the Pharisees they did not confess it, *for they loved human glory more than the glory that comes from God*") betrays rather interest-driven polemics and must not be taken at face value.

10. L. Schenke, *Johannes. Kommentar* (Düsseldorf: Patmos, 1998), 175. Wengst, *Johannesevangelium*, 1:326, also points to "apostasy."

more modest" Christology than the evangelist's lofty one.[11] It should be noted, however, that the evangelist does not mention any *apostasy* of those "Jews" from their faith, any turning away from him, following 8:30, 31,[12] which is also not the case in the comparable passages such as 2:23–24; 7:31; 12:42–43.[13] This speaks against the assumption that the evangelist saw former members of his own community in those "Jews who had come to faith."[14]

(3) John 8:30–31 and the parallels just mentioned in 2:23–24; 7:31; 12:42–43 all refer to *Jerusalem*. It is there that people—*many*, as it says each time—have come to believe in Jesus. The evangelist is obviously aware of the specific Jewish Christianity that had its spiritual suburb in Jerusalem until the Jewish war and felt that it belonged to the synagogues there. Thus, in all these passages he probably has those messianic Jesus-Jews in mind, not only those from Jerusalem but also those who remained true to their faith elsewhere after their flight from the city. However, according to him, measured against the high preexistence Christology of their own group, they only represent a very deficient Jesus-ology; they probably believed in Jesus as the messianic prophet, who was also confirmed as such by God in his Easter exaltation, but not in him as the only Son, who came from God, his Father, and from him possesses his divine nature. Not only the fact that those messianic Jesus-Jews remained in the synagogue alliance, but also their limited Jesus-ology in the sense of the evangelist, which misses the essence of the Son, must have been reason enough for him to incorporate their narrative counterpart of 8:30–31 into the united front of the "Jews" hostile to Jesus without much ado. Conversely, the sharpness with which he attacks them in 8:39c–47 as "sons of devils" will also stem from the polemic

---

11. L. Schenke, *Das Johannesevangelium. Einführung—Text—dramatische Gestalt* (Stuttgart: Kohlhammer, 1992), 65–66: "It is indeed striking that after Jesus's words in 8:28–29, in which the exaltation is mentioned as the reason for recognizing and acknowledging the person of Jesus, many of those addressed believed in Jesus (8:30).... So the schismatic disciples held on to the resurrection of Jesus, but did not draw any conclusions from it about the man Jesus and his work," i.e., they did not make up their minds to confess his pre-existence.

12. In my opinion, this is not because, according to the evangelist, it was not an authentic faith or even a first step in such a direction, but a pseudo-faith that did not deserve to be called a πιστεύειν.

13. John 2:23–24: "*many* believed in his name because they saw the signs that he was doing. But Jesus on his part would not entrust himself to them . . ."; 7:31: "Yet *many* in the crowd believed in him and were saying, 'When the Messiah comes, will he do more signs than this man has done?'"; 10:42: "And *many* believed in him there"; 11:45: "*Many* of the Jews therefore, who had come with Mary and had seen what Jesus did, believed in him"; 12:42–43: "*Many*, even of the authorities, believed in him."

14. It is more likely to have been the other way around: The Johannine Christ-believers will have separated themselves from the "Jewish-Christian" movement for the sake of their high Christology or will have been expelled from the synagogue, in which those messianic Jesus-Jews were still at home because of alleged ditheism.

Sayings of Promise and Consolation

against those messianic Jesus-Jews, although it should not be overlooked that the recourse to the "διάβολος" in 8:44 is not a random whim but an expression of the Satanology that is also important for the Gospel in other respects.[15]

The sequence of our text reads as follows:

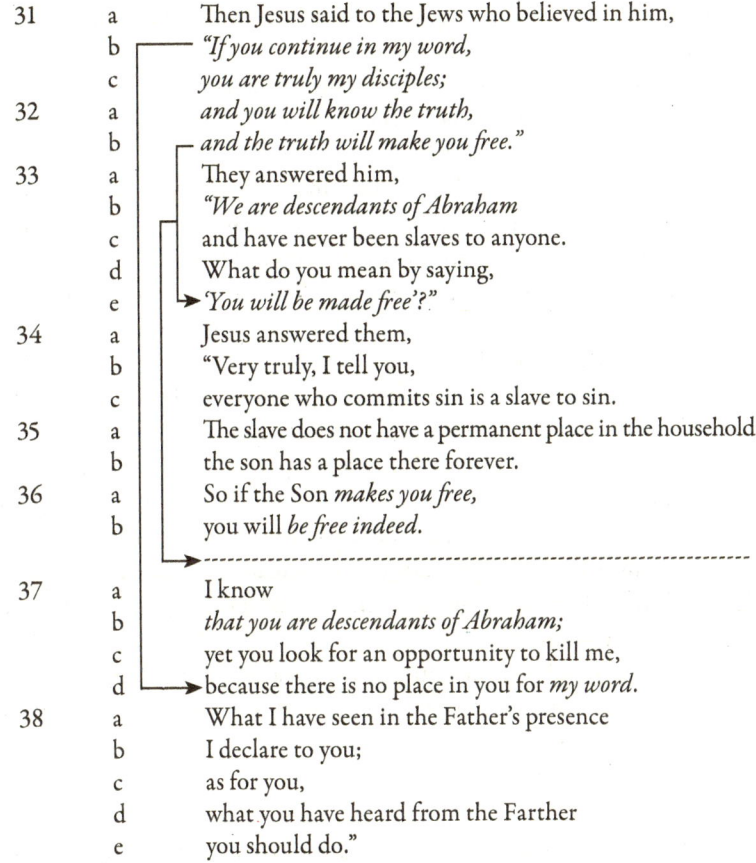

31	a	Then Jesus said to the Jews who believed in him,
	b	*"If you continue in my word,*
	c	*you are truly my disciples;*
32	a	*and you will know the truth,*
	b	*and the truth will make you free."*
33	a	They answered him,
	b	*"We are descendants of Abraham*
	c	*and have never been slaves to anyone.*
	d	*What do you mean by saying,*
	e	*'You will be made free'?"*
34	a	Jesus answered them,
	b	"Very truly, I tell you,
	c	everyone who commits sin is a slave to sin.
35	a	The slave does not have a permanent place in the household;
	b	the son has a place there forever.
36	a	So if the Son *makes you free,*
	b	you will *be free indeed.*
37	a	I know
	b	*that you are descendants of Abraham;*
	c	yet you look for an opportunity to kill me,
	d	because there is no place in you for *my word.*
38	a	What I have seen in the Father's presence
	b	I declare to you;
	c	as for you,
	d	what you have heard from the Farther
	e	you should do."

Verses 37–38 is the link between the sequence of verses 31–36 and verses 39–47. This can easily be seen from the transition from one semantic field to the other: If our sequence is about the dialectic of *freedom* and *bondage*, verses 39–47 are about the true "fatherhood" of Jesus's opponents, as they undoubtedly betray themselves in their efforts to kill him.[16] The basis of the exchange of words in

---

15. See 6:70–71; 12:31; 13:2; 14:30. All passages have to do with the death of Jesus through the figure of Judas Iscariot. This also applies to 8:40, 44, where the devil is regarded as a "murderer of men from the beginning."

16. The riddle posed by the "hinge verse" in v. 38 is only solved in v. 44. It corresponds to the new use of v. 39 when the Jews first put forward their antithesis: *"Abraham is our father"*; it corresponds to the use in v. 33b: *"We are the descendants of Abraham."*

verses 31–36, however, is the "word of the Lord" in verses 31b–32 that provided the impetus for the dispute about freedom and bondage.

7.1.2 "Tradition Criticism" Observations

Following H. Leroy,[17] J. Becker above all has claimed that John 8:31b–32 is a logion given to the evangelist.[18] His arguments are as follows:

(1) "The four-part saying of Jesus" is "rounded in itself."

(2) "Freedom" is "otherwise not a theme [anymore] in the Johannine writings. (8:33–36 is dependent on it.)"[19]

(3) "The original intention of Jesus's words in verses 31b–32" goes in a different direction than the context suggests: "The character of his promise is intended to motivate us to obey the imperative to remain in Jesus's word." In contrast, the context assigns it the function of exposing pseudo-faith. This can be further explored with regard to the above comments on the addressees of the logion: because the evangelist does not even consider them to be people in whom the saying of Jesus would have gained space (even if only initially), it should not actually say of them: "if you *continue* in my word. . . ." Rather, only the formulation that the evangelist himself uses in verse 37d, thus tacitly correcting verse 31b, would apply: "for my word has no place with you." In other words, a change of addressee has taken place in the integration of the logion into its literary context: It is no longer beginners in the faith who are its addressees but only believers in appearance, who in reality are unbelievers.

The following additional arguments in favor of the acceptance of the given sayings have yet to be added:

(1) The language game of the logion—the speaking of "disciples" (= Christians) who go to the school of the sayings of Jesus to recognize and learn the truth there—draws on early Christian tradition.[20]

---

17. Leroy, *Rätsel*, 68–72 in connection with 49–50.

18. Becker, *Johannes*, 1:354–355. But see also H. Koester, "Gnostic Sayings and Controversy Traditions in John 8,12–59," in *Nag Hammadi, Gnosticism and Early Christianity*, ed. C. W. Hedrick and R. Hodgson (Peabody: Hendrickson, 1986), 97–110, here 104–105; *Gospels*, 262; Bultmann, *Johannes*, 332 n. 4, counts the saying among his source of the "revelatory speeches."

19. Added to this is Leroy's observation, *Rätsel*, 69: "Only at this point is ἡ ἀλήθεια the subject of an act in the Fourth Gospel."

20. According to R. Bultmann, "γινώσκω," *TDNT* 1:689–714, here 713, "the traditional use of γινώσκειν (τὴν ἀλήθειαν)" originally refers to "conversion to Christianity" (in the Corpus Johanneum 2 John 1; see also 1 John 2:13–14 21; 5:20; other early Christian references ibid. 705). According to Becker, *Johannes*, 1:356, it is "no coincidence . . . that a comparably comprehensive use of the word [ἀλήθεια] is found precisely in the third generation of early Christianity: truth is the actual content of the Christian message (Eph 1:13; Col 1:5–6; 1 Tim 2:4; 2 Tim 2:15, 25; 3:7; Heb 10:26; Jas 1:18; 2 John 1)." On μαθητής = Christians, see Acts 6:1–2 7; 9:1, 10, 19, 25–26, 38; 11:26, 29 etc.; John 13:35; 15:8 (both passages = R); Ignatius, *Magn.* 9:1. With μένειν ἐν τῷ λόγῳ ("abide in my word"), see 2 Macc 8:1 ("abide in Judaism"); Acts 11:23 ("abide in the

Sayings of Promise and Consolation

(2) The logion is *interpreted* in the following exchange. Not only do the "Jews who have believed" quote its last line again (in v. 33d, e) and confront it with *their* understanding of freedom, Jesus himself also takes up this line once more in his reply in order to refer to himself as the Son:

```
                           ┌── 31 c   you are truly my disciples.
   36  So if the Son           32 b   and the truth
       makes you free,                will make you free.
       you will be free indeed. ──┘
```

The gradient of the scene thus runs from the *core saying* in verses 31b, 32 to its *interpretation* in verses 33–36.[21] This view of things does more justice to the course of the text than its exactly opposite description by B. Lindars, who, following J. Jeremias[22] and C. H. Dodd,[23] identifies *verse 35* as the core logion *to which* the preceding verses 31–34 and *from which* all subsequent verses up to and including verse 58 were shaped by the evangelist.[24] The reason why Lindars

---

Lord"); 13:33 ("abide in the grace of the Lord"); 1 Tim 2:15 ("abide in the faith"); 2 Tim 3:14; in the Corpus Johanneum: John 15:4ff; 1 John 4:16; 2 John 9—The expression "my word" is also found in Synoptic logia, according to H. Schürmann, "Die Sprache des Christus. Sprachliche Beobachtungen an den synoptischen Herrenworten," in *Traditionsgeschichtliche Untersuchungen zu den synoptischen Evangelien, Beiträge*, KBANT (Düsseldorf: Patmos, 1968), 83–108, here 89 with n. 53; Mark 8:38 par.; 13:31 par.; Matt 7:24 par. Luke 6:47 (Q); Luke 24:44.

21. The role of vv. 31b, 32 as the "core saying" is confirmed by the fact that it remains the point of reference: with v. 31b cf. v. 37d, and the motif "my word" still occurs in vv. 43, 51, 52. "Truth" remains the leitmotif in ch. 8: see vv. 44, 45, 46.

22. According to J. Jeremias, *Die Gleichnisse Jesu*, 8th ed. (Göttingen: Vandenhoeck & Ruprecht, 1970), 85, 211, John 8:35 is an authentic figurative saying of Jesus with a non-allegorical character (εἰς τὸν αἰῶνα does not mean "eternal," but "always"), which expresses "the security of his disciples in God's hand"; "they have, says the figurative word . . . forever the right to be children of God."

23. Likewise Dodd, *Tradition*, 379–382, admittedly without naming J. Jeremias, but instead Bultmann (*Johannes*, 337: "Verse 35 seems to have originally been a figurative word"). Dodd's argument is that the figurative saying fits poorly into its Christological environment. In favor of its origin in Jesus, Dodd invokes the numerous related synoptic texts in which servant (e.g., Luke 12:47–48) and son (e.g., Matt 21:28–31) appear as narrative figures, as well as the likewise popular means of contrasting figures.

24. Lindars commented on our text a total of three times, in the commentary *John* (1971), in "Discourse" (1981), 120–125, and in "Slave and Son in John 8:31–36" (1984), in *Essays on John*, ed. C. M. Tuckett, SNTA 17 (Leuven: Peeters, 1992), 167–182. While he unreservedly agreed with Dodd in the commentary, in 1981 he postulated the following wording for the figurative word of Jesus: ὁ δοῦλος οὐκ ἐλεύθερός ἐστιν ἐν τῇ οἰκίᾳ. ὁ υἱὸς ἐλεύθερός ἐστιν ("Discourse," 122). In this way, he wanted to emphasize his thesis that this parabolic saying is "the nucleus of the whole argument" (*John*, 325), insofar as the evangelist would have preferred the otherwise completely

assigns such weight to verse 35 in particular is due to the preceding Amen formula in verse 34, which is also intended to indicate the traditional character of the following saying or its "nucleus" in verse 35 (analogous to 8:51). However, the fact that the evangelist has provided the small unit of Jesus's speech in verses 34–36 with the Amen formula is not due to the presumed traditional nature of verse 35, but to the fact that verses 34–36 offer an authoritative *Christological* interpretation of the core logion.[25] According to this, ἡ ἀλήθεια stands for ὁ υἱός, so the truth that liberates people is the Son himself in person. In other words, verses 34–36 are *subordinate* to the key statement in verses 31b–32, irrespective of the possibility that verse 35 could reflect a traditional sentence, certainly not a Jesus aphorism, as Jeremias, Dodd, and Lindars believe, but rather a simple "social sentence of experience"[26] that served the evangelist to make the liberation intended in the core logion plausible as a process that can only take place through the Son of the house.[27] *It therefore remains the case that the internal structure of the exchange of words in verses 31–36 clearly indicates that the evangelist was concerned with the interpretation of a clearly defined logion that was therefore probably given to him.*

7.1.3 Form, Style, and Genre of the Saying

The traditional statement is as follows:

1 If you continue in my word,
2 you are in truth (ἀλητῶς) my disciples,
3 and you will know the truth (τὴν ἀλήθειαν),
4 and the truth (ἡ ἀλήθεια) will make you free.

Syntactically this quatrain represents a conditional period that obeys the type of a "special prospective case": the "protasis specifically denotes something future

---

unusual terminology of "freedom" from v. 35 to v. 32. He justifies the basic character of v. 35 for the subsequent conversations up to and including v. 58 (!) as follows, "One of the values of the saying ... is that the contrast between slave and son makes a splendid basis for his (s.c. John's) central position, in which sonship to the devil is contrasted with Jesus's sonship to God" ("Discourse," 124). This argument is not convincing, and the reclamation of the terminology of freedom for the allegedly figurative saying of Jesus also seems arbitrary.

25. As an analogy to this, see for example the Amen-saying in John 6:32 as an authoritative Christological interpretation of the scriptural word in 6:31!

26. Rightly Becker, *Johannes*, 1:357.

27. Likewise, v. 34c already contains a theological principle that is firmly established in the form of a sentence (see below).

that can or must be reckoned with,"[28] here the abiding of those addressed in the word of Jesus. Under this condition, they are not only promised true discipleship but also given the prospect of what this holds in store for them in the future: *They will recognize the truth, and the truth will set them free*. Recognition and liberation in the process of recognition are therefore dynamic processes that begin in the present but will accompany discipleship in the future. Thus, the apodosis changes from the present tense of line 2 to the two futures of lines 3 and 4.

Stylistically the inner coherence of the saying is reflected in the *concatenatio* of its lines: Thus, the last line ties in with the last word of line 3 (ἡ ἀλήθεια), which in turn is already echoed in the adverb of line 2 (ἀληθῶς). Semantically, the coherence of the saying is based on the uniformity of its idea: Christians are "disciples" (μαθηταί) who go to the school of the "word" of Jesus; if they do not slacken in this, they not only gain "knowledge," this "knowledge" also changes their lives. Obviously, the latter is the climax of the saying, an assumption that is confirmed by the twofold resumption of line 4 (*"and the truth will make you free"*) in the subsequent exchange of words, namely in contradiction (v. 33) and affirmative clarification (v. 36).

With regard to the *genre* of the saying, two observations are revealing:

(1) Structurally, John 8:31b, c is close to the two sayings in Q 14:26–27 (see Luke 14:26–27 / Matt 10:37–38):

> 26 If one does not hate his own father and mother,
> *he cannot be my disciple*;
> and if one does not hate son and daughter,
> *he cannot be my disciple*.
> 27 Whoever does not take up his cross and follow me,
> *cannot be my disciple*.[29]

Both sayings define what a "disciple" is; they do this by naming the *conditio sine qua non* of true discipleship in a preceding conditional clause or a relative clause. The same thing happens in John 8:31b, c, with the difference that the Q sayings formulate it negatively ("if not . . ."), the Johannine logion positively.

The synoptic tradition does not contain any further definitions on the subject of *disciples*.[30] But, it is noteworthy that Paul knows sentences that, in a

---

28. HvS § 280c under b); protasis: ἐάν + conj., apodosis: mostly future tense.

29. Hoffmann/Heil, Die Spruchquelle Q, 96f.

30. Only Q 6:40 is comparable (see Matt 10:24–25): "The disciple (μαθητής) is not above the teacher; it is enough for the disciple that he becomes like his teacher" (Hoffmann/Heil, Spruchquelle 42f.). These are the only logia of the Jesus tradition in which the term μαθητής occurs!

structurally comparable way, say what a "Christian" is, albeit without using the term "μαθητής":

Rom 8:9:
"Anyone who does not have the Spirt of Christ
does not belong to him."[31]

(2) The two Q sayings are formulated in the third person in the manner of aphorisms, but John 8:31b, c offers a salutation: "If you abide in my word, *[then] you are truly my disciples.*" The Johannine logion does not define discipleship; it is a personal promise. Thus, despite its structural relationship, it follows a different type of saying than Q 14:26–27.

John 8:31b–32 is a *word of promise* with a slightly cautionary undertone;[32] it "belongs in the general initial instruction of the community."[33] Here he wanted to motivate those who had just begun in their faith to remain faithful, which is why the promise in lines 2–3 forms its climax.

The promise has grown up on the basis of the early Christian idea of discipleship. Although it is not possible to establish a specific reference of our logion to Q 14:26–27, it belongs to the wider context of synoptic sayings about the followers of Jesus. This root can be easily identified in verse 31b, c; the continuation of the logion then builds on this, giving it its individual character.

7.1.4 Freedom Through Gnosis? The Religious-Historical Horizon of the Saying

(1) Bultmann understood the promise of our saying, according to which freedom arises from the knowledge of truth, still against the backdrop of "his" gnostic myth of revelation: "The one sent is the liberator."[34] It is true that "truth" and "freedom" here do not mean rational knowledge and the spiritual freedom resulting from it, but a religious reality as it results from

---

31. See Rom 8:14: "*For all who are led by the Spirit of God are children of God.*" See also 1 Cor 8:3; Gal 6:3.

32. Bultmann, *Johannes*, 332: The word is a "promise"; Becker, *Johannes*, 1:355: "It addresses a warning with a promise to newly won members to the community."

33. Becker, *Johannes*, 1:355. Leroy, *Rätsel*, 71, also sees the saying as "referring to the area of catechesis." "The teaching is presented to the newcomers in fixed terms" (ἀλήθεια, λόγος, ἐλευθερία).

34. Bultmann, *Johannes*, 333 n. 4: "In fact, in Gnosticism the earthly world is regarded as a dungeon, the bodily existence as a *captivity* of souls.... The messenger is the liberator" (with many proofs).

Sayings of Promise and Consolation 293

the claim of Jesus's word. On the other hand, the saying lacks any gnostic coloring, which is why its religious-historical classification by Bultmann is probably invalid.[35]

(2) According to C. H. Dodd, verse 32 presupposes an axiom of Hellenistic popular philosophy, "a Stoic commonplace":[36] μόνος ὁ σοφὸς ἐλεύθερος—only the sage is free.[37] The fact that this axiom is also found in Hellenistic Judaism—although only very rarely, apart from the oeuvre of Philo of Alexandria—is certainly remarkable in view of John 8:31b–32*. However, one cannot and will not deny the profound transformation of the axiom that it would have undergone in our logion, if it is part of its "background."[38] After all, "the Stoic doctrine of freedom understands freedom to mean the disposition of man over the alien existence threatening him in the manner of conscious and willful mastery of the soul,"[39] that is, by means of self-knowledge or rational insight into one's own existence,[40] whereas freedom according to our logion *does not* become available to man on the path of self-knowledge, but is *given* to him through the knowledge of the truth hidden in the word of Jesus.

(3) Of interest for our logion is possibly the question of whether the idea of Jesus's saying granting freedom has a counterpart in Hellenistic Judaism, whereby the *Torah* could be thought of as a *freedom-creating habitat*. Such an idea may well have an echo in Judaism,[41] but linguistically it rarely found expression. There

---

35. Even Koester, "Sayings," 104, seems reluctant to follow C. H. Dodd on v. 32b.

36. Dodd, "Dialogue," 48 n. 3.

37. Cicero, *Paradoxa Stoicorum* 33: *Solum sapientem liberum, et omnem stultum servum*. That this is indeed an axiom can easily be seen from the collection of texts in the *Neuen Wettstein*, I/2 430–441, which offers a wealth of evidence from very different works: e.g., Plutarch, *Cato Minor* 67.2: "Finally they discussed the so-called 'Stoic paradoxes,' in which it is said that only the good man is free, but all the bad are slaves"; or Epictetus, *Diss.* 2.1.22: one must believe the philosophers "who say that only those who have studied philosophy are free men."

38. Dodd, "Dialogue," 48 n. 3: "That Christian 'liberty' is not the same thing as Stoic 'liberty' goes without saying."

39. H. Schlier, "ἐλεύθερος," *TDNT* 2: 487–502.

40. Schlier, "ἐλεύθερος," 494: "This knowledge must consider in what spheres we may or may not exercise free dominion. It sees from experience that external things, body, possessions, family etc., are not at our disposal ... on the other hand, it sees that what is inward ... the soul, is completely under our control." *It is* the space from which we can free ourselves from the oppressive "ideas" about the world and our existence.

41. See S. Vollenweider, *Freiheit als neue Schöpfung. Eine Untersuchung zur Eleutheria bei Paulus und in seiner Umwelt*, FRLANT 147 (Göttingen: Vandenhoeck & Ruprecht, 1989), 160–169 ("Freiheit unter dem Gesetz"), there also on the few rabbinical references. Noteworthy is the saying of R. Yehoshua b. Levi (b. 'Avot. 6:2b): "And it (the Scripture) says: 'And the tablets were

are various reasons for this. First, it should be remembered that "there is no conceptual formulation of the phenomenon of freedom in the *Old Testament*."[42] The few references to the semantic field in the LXX, especially in its late, partly deuterocanonical writings, are dominated by the sociological understanding (e.g., liberation of slaves).[43] Even such Hellenistically influenced writings as Aristeas, Wisdom, and Joseph and Aseneth are not familiar with *eleutheria*. Josephus, however, speaks of it with unique emphasis: "The *freedom of Israel* is virtually the leitmotif of his historical work, in which both the promise (as in the *Antiquities*) and the doom (as in the *Jewish War*) of freedom are thematized. He also ascribes to the freedom fighters in Masada the Platonic *noetic* freedom of the soul coming to itself in death."[44] Philo of Alexandria naturally also maintains a connection to the philosophical discussion of freedom, especially of Stoic provenance. The few references to him that specifically address the *law* as the source of freedom should be seen in this context.

The early treatise *Quod Omnis Probus Liber sit*, 45–47 is still entirely on a philosophical level, speaks of the unwritten law of nature as the actual source of freedom, and critically recalls this against the written laws (e.g., Athenian and Spartan); there is no mention of the Mosetora in this context:

> Just as those states which are governed oligarchically or tyrannically are in slavery, since they have cruel and harsh masters in their conquerors and oppressors, while those states which have *laws* that provide for them and govern them are *free*, so it is with men. Those who are ruled by anger or lust or any other affect, or even by deceitful wickedness, are entirely slaves, while those who *lead a life in accordance with the law are free* (ὅσοι δὲ μετὰ νόμου ζῶσιν). But the infallible law is upright reason (ὁ ὀρθὸς λόγος).[45]

In contrast to the Cynic criticism of the written laws and the Stoic shift from concrete legislation to the All-Nomos, Philo now locates the divine law

---

the work of God, and the writing was the writing of God engraved on the tablets' (Ex 32:16). Do not read: 'engraved' (חרות), but 'freedom' (חרות). For there is no one free for you except the one who is engaged in the study of the Torah."

42. Vollenweider, *Freiheit*, 123 "Although Israel is well aware of the differentiation of society into free and slave, it never explicitly analogized salvation from Egyptian bondage to the *liberation of slaves*: redeemed Israel is not a 'freedman' (חפשי). Only *early Judaism*, influenced by Hellenism, interpreted paradigmatized 'redemption' as an act of divine *liberation*" (with evidence).

43. Vollenweider, *Freiheit*, 123–124. But see Prov 25:10a: "Favor and friendship make free."

44. Vollenweider, *Freiheit*, 133. See also pp. 133–138.

45. The latter is reminiscent of Chrysippus (cf. Arnim, *SVF* III 360). On the Stoic concept of freedom as service under the law: Vollenweider, *Freiheit*, 82–85.

Sayings of Promise and Consolation 295

unconditionally in the Mosaic law. Thus, he can also brand the apostasy from the Torah as a loss of freedom: "one can perceive how those who have fallen away from our *laws* become licentious, shameless, unjust... who would sell their *freedom for* food, for wine, for delicacies, for a beautiful figure" (*Virt.* 182).[46] *"Freedom and law go hand in hand."*[47] Of course, Judaism fundamentally understands this freedom as obedience to the law, and only as such does it remain freedom.

Also noteworthy in this context is the reference to the *"perfect law of liberty"* in James 1:25 (cf. also 2:12).[48] This phrase probably means "the law perfected by Jesus" (Matt 5:17!), whereby τέλειος (= perfect) is "added with regard to the 'imperfect' law of the Old Covenant."[49] The author of James could thus have "taken up the Hellenistic distinction between the true nomos, which is associated with freedom, and the legal nomos, which operates with fear and coercion and which Hellenistic Judaism also occasionally refers to"[50] and used for his own understanding of the nomos in light of Jesus's message.

(4) Can one understand the Johannine logion as a counterproposal to the understanding of the Torah just outlined as a living space that opens up freedom, so that what is otherwise true of the Torah would be claimed here for

---

46. It is about apostates who no longer observe the Jewish dietary and marriage laws and thus renounce Judaism.

47. Vollenweider, *Freiheit*, 128. Also noteworthy is *Moses* 2.50–51, according to which Moses in his legislation addresses the Jews not as slaves but as free men, which is why he gives "advice and exhortations rather than commands" and endeavors more "to instruct than to compel."

48. In view of John 8:31b–32, the context of Jas 1:25 is also of interest: "But be doers of the *word*, and not merely hearers.... But those who look into the perfect law, the *law of liberty*, and *persevere*, being not hearers who forget but doers who act—they will be blessed in their doing (Jas 1:22–25). "Word" and "law of liberty" are synonymous here. What is meant is a norm of action, specifically the Torah's commandment of love (Jas 2:8). As in John 8:31b, in James it is also about *remaining with the word*, which James understands ethically and John theologically in terms of revelation; in addition, both attribute a liberating dimension to this word or the law. "For James, the 'freedom' of the νόμος τέλειος, as the context shows, consists *in the liberation from all selfishness that is realized in the loving devotion to one's neighbor*. But then it must be admitted that James represents an idea of freedom for which certain parallels can also be found in Stoic literature and in late [= early] Judaism, such as when Seneca says: *deo parere libertas est* [*De vita beata* 15.7] or Philo: ὅσοι δὲ μετὰ νόμου ζῶσιν, ἐλεύθεροι [see above]" (Mußner, Jakobusbrief 108). James 1:22–25 and John 8:31b–32 are similar in their admonitory, paraenetic intention (μένειν), but differ in their respective execution.

49. Mußner, Jakobusbrief, 109, as does Vollenweider, *Freiheit*, 185: "The 'dark meaning' of the formulation (R. Bultmann, *Theologie des Neuen Testaments*, ed. O. Merk. 7th ed. [Tübingen: Mohr, 1977], 514) can be illuminated if the perfection of the Christian law was originally contrasted with the imperfection of the old law, the Mosaic cultic law...." However, this phrase, which Vollenweider considers traditional, is not "used polemically" in James (185, n. 394).

50. Vollenweider, *Freiheit*, 185.

the word of Jesus? We will probably have to exercise restraint in this respect for two reasons: First, because of the source. Apart from Philo, the idea of the Torah as the source of freedom is not so firmly established in early Judaism that John 8:32 could be immediately identified as its Christological usurpation. On the other hand, it will also have to be taken into account that there was already a pronounced discussion of *eleutheria* in the Pauline circle before John, and that John 8:31b-32* can be understood as a continuation of this. The more recent discussion on the topic of "John and Paul," which is particularly important in view of the controversy about the sonship of Abraham in John 8, which is reminiscent of Galatians 3, has in my opinion strengthened the assumption that the Fourth Gospel does not draw directly from Paul and his literary legacy, but rather had recourse to traditions from the apostle's environment. In the case of Paul, too, it will be necessary to distinguish between traditions and his own theological approach to them. Sayings such as 2 Corinthians 3:17b: "... *where the Spirit of the Lord is, there is freedom*" or Romans 8:14: "*For all who are led by the Spirit of God are children of God*" will not necessarily have come from the apostle but may have been common property of the Hellenistic Christians, whereby it is reasonable to assume that the congregation in Antioch, which for the first time in the young history of Christianity programmatically advocated the coexistence of Jews and gentiles, is their actual home. Other sayings and core statements can also be added to these, all of which in their own way testify to a "consciousness of freedom" that undoubtedly had pneumatic-eschatological traits.[51] The fact that in this context there was also the terminological mention of ἐλευθερία, as in the slogan in 2 Corinthians 3:17b, does not seem to be unimportant as a background for John 8:31b-32*.

In short, if we ask about the "history of religions" roots of our logion, then, in addition to the Stoic axiom according to which wisdom leads to freedom, we cannot ignore the "in-house" Christian experiential background for the experience of freedom in John 8:32. However, noteworthy transformations can also be seen here: "Freedom" is no longer used pneumatically in the Johannine logion as a sign of the dawning of the end-time spirit in the congregations but is much more soberly linked to the knowledge of the truth of revelation in the word of Jesus. It is, so to speak, the school of his word that his disciples must attend that imparts the knowledge of the "freedom" given through him. But what kind of "freedom" does our logion have in view?

---

51. See especially Gal 3:28: "There is no longer Jew or Greek, there is no longer slave or free, there is no longer neither male and female; for all of you are one in Christ Jesus."

7.1.5 Logos—Aletheia—Eleutheria
The Point of the Triad in John 8:31b–32*

As we have seen, lines 1–3 contain the *basis of* the logion, which can also be identified in terms of tradition: a call to faithfulness to the word of Jesus and the promise that this word is not just any word, but contains the "truth," that is, the revelation of God's reality. The final line of the logion, its climax, says that becoming aware of this "truth" means salvation, the transformation of those to whom this happens: *"and the truth will make you free."* What does the word "freedom" mean, which is not defined, but rather leaves the listener to ponder at the end of the logion?

Here, liberation stands for salvation. Far from any political ideological content the word has in Josephus, for example, in the Johannine logion it is aimed at the *fundamental question* of man himself: the meaning of existence in the world's house of the dead. If one considers the neighboring Johannine logion in John 8:52*,[52] then we can say that freedom here means freedom from death, not protection from having to die. Rather, freedom is based on the insight into the saving "truth" of God and therefore means being able to look one's own death calmly in the eye. The power of death is no longer able to obscure a person's view in the face of Jesus's word, which radically reveals reality. Does not the logion pick up on a longing that contemporaries also associated with the keyword of freedom?

7.1.6 "So if the Son sets you free . . ." The Evangelist's Reception of the Saying

The *Jewish Christians* who consider themselves to be a part of the synagogue are the addressees to whom the evangelist now says that Jesus's words in his composition in 8:30—36 were originally intended for beginners in the faith. It will therefore also be *their* self-understanding that is expressed in the listeners' protest against Jesus's suggestion that only the knowledge of *his* word would liberate them to true freedom; admittedly not exclusively their self-understanding, as they are only part of the synagogue, but nevertheless characteristic enough for the position that they are likely to have pointedly represented to other believers in Jesus.[53] In this respect, it could very well be that verse 33b–e allows a historically

---

52. See below at 7.2!

53. Paul's "Jewish-Christian" opponents in Galatia will also have vehemently referred to Abraham.

reliable view of "Jewish Christianity" at the time of the evangelist, as he perceived it: *"We are descendants of Abraham and have never been slaves to anyone. What do you mean by saying, 'You will be made free'?"*

The sonship of Abraham, to which Jesus's listeners refer with these words, has two sides. According to their understanding, they absolutely belong together: the ethical-genealogical (*"we are the descendants of Abraham"*[54]) and the spiritual-religious (*"we have never been slaves* [δεδουλεύκαμεν] *of anyone"*). How exactly the second is to be understood is debatable. Without a doubt, however, "external political freedom" is not to be thought of. Rather, it is about the inner dignity that Israel knew how to maintain as the "firstborn son" of God (Exod 4:22; cf. Hos 11:1) even in times of external forces.[55] The knowledge of such inner dignity, called freedom, is linked here to the descent from the arch-father Abraham, which is quite remarkable. According to the study by S. Vollenweider, in early Judaism the speech of freedom is "incomparably more strongly linked to the *sonship of God,* which still shines through in John 8:41," whereas "for the *synagogue* . . . explicit evidence of *freedom* based on *Abraham* is very sparse."[56] It is therefore possible that the connection between verse 33b and c is based on a specific tradition, which is perhaps mediated via Scripture, but in any case understands the descent from Abraham as the basis for a consciousness of election of free people.[57] If Jesus's listeners therefore object to his implicit demand that they must first be liberated, then this should not be *morally* discredited as "pride and self-importance"[58] but should be seen as *the* expression of a *theological* conviction according to which Abrahamic filiation, participation in God's covenant, and faith in the Messiah Jesus go hand in hand. However, the evangelist could

---

54. In themselves, σπέρμα (vv. 33, 37) and τέκνα (v. 39) are synonyms, but σπέρμα may have been deliberately chosen here to emphasize the genealogical aspect.

55. Schnackenburg, *Johannesevangelium,* 2:262–263: "Despite all political oppression, they know themselves to be free sons of Abraham who have never bowed inwardly to foreign rule."

56. Vollenweider, *Freiheit,* 192–193. Jewish references for the connection between *freedom* and *sonship with God,* ibid. 130 with n. 122; 144 with n. 190–191; 152. Exod Rab 15:11 is characteristic of this: "By saying to Israel, 'You are sons of the Lord your God' (Deut 14:1), they were led out of bondage into freedom." For the connection with Abraham, see b. B. Qam. 8.6b: "R. Aqiba says that even the poorest in Israel are regarded as free, who have lost their wealth, for they are sons of Abraham, Isaac, and Jacob"; also Philo, *Sobr.* 56–57, about Abraham, but as the prototype of the wise man: "He alone is king, because he has received from the All-Ruler the indisputable power to rule over all; he alone is free, because he is freed from the most oppressive tyrant, the vain delusion."

57. Is such a specific formulation of the idea of Abraham's childhood not also an indication that a *certain* counterpart, namely contemporary "Jewish Christianity," is in mind here?

58. Thus Schnackenburg, *Johannesevangelium,* 2:263: "With their pride and self-importance, the Jews miss the very attitude that would make them receptive to Jesus's message of freedom."

not possibly accept this "*Jewish-Christian*" self-understanding from his Christological presuppositions, which he expresses unmistakably in Jesus's reply. This reply is formally an authoritative interpretation of the "core words" in 8:31b–32 spoken by Jesus himself.

In accordance with the opposition δοῦλος (servant)—ἐλεύθερος (free), which already subliminally determines the logion, Jesus's Amen-saying justifies the rejection of the "Jewish-Christian" position in two ways: (a) to what extent is the awareness of freedom expressed in verse 33 an illusion? Is there not a much deeper "bondage" lurking at its bottom that must first be uncovered and confronted? (b) Who else is able to free us from such bondage but the "Son"?

The answer is structured in such a way that, based on a central "social statement of experience" on the roles of servant and authorized son (v. 35a, b), it first interprets that of the servant (v. 34) and then, following the "statement of experience," that of the son (v. 36). The Christological-soteriological climax of the sequence may already have influenced the formulation of the preceding "statement of experience."[59]

Anthropology 34c	Statement of experience 35a 35b	Christology 36
Human = *Servant* of sin	SERVANT—SON	Jesus = *the Son,* who frees from sin

(a) Verse 34c declares[60] what human bondage profoundly means: bondage to the power of sin.[61] When the "sentence of experience" then says of the servant that he has no true home "in the house" because he has to leave it again, but the Son does, then the situation of man as a sinner becomes transparent: he is alienated from God and homeless. The Son is different. He remains in the house forever. The climax of verse 36 makes it clear that only Christ, the Son authorized by his Father, can be meant by him.

(b) Who else can liberate from the bondage of sin but the "Son" alone? From the logic of the social world of experience used to illustrate the facts, this assertion has its own plausibility: the υἱός is none other than "the Son with general authority, to whom the Father has given all things, all his possessions, into his

---

59. εἰς τὸν αἰῶνα can simply mean "forever," but it sounds more like "in eternity"; see 12:34: "we have heard from the law that *the Messiah remains forever.*" See also εἰς τὸν αἰῶνα in 8:51–52 referring to those who keep the word of Jesus as well as μένειν ("remain") in the given logion 8:31b!

60. Cf. Rom 6:16, 20; 2 Pet 2:19, but also Epictetus, *Diss* 4.1.3.

61. "It is the 'diabolical' cycle that the sinful deed constitutes the reign of sin and at the same time the reign of sin produces sinful deeds. It is uncovered by the revelatory work of the Son of God, who imparts the liberating knowledge of truth" (Metzner, *Verständnis*, 180).

power of disposal";[62] he also decides on the release of the slaves. Thus, Jesus gives freedom to all who are enslaved by sin (1:29) and grants them a home in the "dwellings" of his Father (14:2-3).[63]

At the same time, the evangelist makes it clear through his interpretative resumption of verse 32b (*"the truth* will make you free") in verse 36a ("if *the Son* therefore makes you free") that Jesus *in person* is the truth; in his words, this finds its linguistic expression, but connects itself first and foremost with himself as the Son of God (cf. 14:6). Outside of him, there is only appearance, or even more sharply, as the evangelist states in verses 44-47, "the lie." But it is the visible side of the work of the one who is called διάβολος, who is the "murderer of men from the beginning," "who does not stand in the truth," but is rather "a liar and the father of lies" (8:44). Even if his activity seems to reach its zenith in the death of Jesus, he has been up to mischief "from the beginning." In the light of the "truth" that Jesus is in person, this also becomes obvious.

7.2 "Do not taste death!" (John 8:51 par. 52)

The logion in John 8:51 is not only quoted again immediately after its first occurrence (8:52); it also has a parallel in the Gospel of Thomas.[64] Like our previous logion in John 8:31-32, John 8:51 par. 52 also forms the core of an associated dialogue scene in which the logion becomes an impetus to reflect on the unique dignity of Jesus.

7.2.1 The Context of the Saying

John 8:51 par. 52 belongs to the last dialogue scene of chapter 8, which brings the series of Jesus's confrontations with the "Jews" staged in the temple in Jerusalem to its final climax. The dialogue comprises six turns of speech and is concluded with a scenic note by the narrator: "So they picked up stones to throw at him,

---

62. Bühner, *Gesandte*, 206, on 3:35; 13:3 with reference to Jewish law, which recognizes the figure of a "general representative" with the "son of the house." See also John 15:15.

63. The fact that the release of the servants does not mean their deportation from the οἰκία but rather their remaining at home in it does not have to leave the world of experience of the parable behind: Being allowed to stay in the house of the *pater familias* meant social security for the *liberti* into old age.

64. Logion 1 immediately following the prologue: "These are the secret words which Jesus, who is alive, said and which Didymos Judas wrote down for Thomas. And he said: *Whoever finds the explanation of these words will not taste death*." On this, see Theobald, *Herrenworte*, 503-504.

Sayings of Promise and Consolation   301

but Jesus hid himself and went out of the temple" (8:59).[65] How does this (if one looks at the progress of the book) still provisional interruption of Jesus's communication with the "Jews" come about, which nevertheless—in view of the end—makes an inexorably final impression?

The scene begins with the accusation of demonic possession (v. 48), which "the Jews" have already raised against Jesus in 7:20 and will repeat again in 10:20. Jesus rejects it by bringing up his relationship with the Father (v. 49–50). The underlying logic is: "What Jesus is, he is not by virtue of a demon; he is through the Father. By insisting on what he is and what the Father has made him to be, he honors the Father."[66] This is followed by our logion, connected with the signal of the authoritative twofold Amen (v. 51). For "the Jews" it offers only one more reason to renew their accusation from the beginning: "Now we know that *you have a demon!*" (v. 52b). They repeat Jesus's slightly varied logion (v. 52d–f), bracketed by the reference to the fact that their father Abraham and the prophets had died (vv. 52c/53b, c). How does he want to make people believe that he can spare his followers death? A hybrid claim, nothing but an expression of his demonic possession! Jesus does not take up the keyword "Abraham" (which has dominated the scene since 8:33) in his reply for the time being in order to address his relationship to the Father once again in verses 54–55 (corresponding to his first statement in vv. 49–50), again using the terminology of mutual glorification. Only then (in v. 56) does he turn to Abraham, since the answer to the Jews' question "Are you greater than our father Abraham?" (v. 53a; cf. 4:12) is still outstanding. Jesus proves that this is the case, that he is indeed many times greater than Abraham, with his scriptural claim that Abraham rejoiced when he saw his day.[67] The objection of the "Jews," which reveals their total misunderstanding of this statement (Jesus, not yet fifty years old, claims to have seen

---

65. Note the underlying meaning of this statement: when the "Son of God" leaves the temple, God the Father leaves it; see also Matt 23:38–39 par. Luke 13:35 and 1 Kgs 9:7–8; Tob 14:4; Josephus, *J.W.* 6.299.

66. Dietzfelbinger, *Johannes*, 1:266.

67. Abraham's "rejoicing" probably refers to his "laughter" mentioned in Gen 17:17, with which he reacted to God's promise that he, the hundred-year-old, would receive another son from Sarah, the ninety-year-old. Insofar as the Jewish interpretation understood this "laughter" not as an expression of doubt but of joy, the text was also open to interpretations that linked this "joy" with the future of the promise (for details, see Schnackenburg, *Johannesevangelium*, 2:298). Philo, *Mut.* 130–131 understands God's word to Abraham: "I will give you a child from her" (Gen 17:16) as follows: "The one who gives something in the proper sense gives something entirely his own. But if this is true, then it is not Isaac the man who wants to be born, but the one who is synonymous with the best of high feelings, joy, inner laughter (= Isaac), a son of God, who (i.e., God) gives him (i.e., the son) for the delight and cheerfulness of completely peaceful souls."

Abraham!⁶⁸), then leads to the climax of the scene, in which Jesus sums up his complete superiority over Abraham based on his divine being: "Truly, truly, I say to you" (as in the opening logion in v. 51): "Before Abraham *was* (γενέσθαι), I *am* (εἰμί)" (v. 58). So Jesus does not belong to the order of "becoming," but to that of eternal "being," a statement that must inevitably provoke the reaction of the "Jews" of verse 59.⁶⁹ This concludes the scene, the *structure* of which is set out in the following diagram for better orientation.

A Jews (48)	Accusation of demonic possession
B JESUS (49–51)	┌── *relationship to God* (mutual glorification) └── Amen-saying
C Jews (52–53)	renewal of the allegation justification: claim and reality contradict each other. ┌── *reality*: "Abraham and the prophets have died." ├── Jesus' Amen-saying as an expression of his hybrid claim └── *reality*: "Abraham and the prophets have died."
D JESUS (54–56)	*relationship to God* (mutual glorification) subordination of the visionary Abraham to Jesus
E Jews (57)	objection
F JESUS (58)	Amen-saying The absolute *ego eimi* of Jesus as proof of his "essential superiority" over Abraham
G Scenic commentary (59)	

7.2.2 "Tradition Criticism"

The two versions of the logion are as follows:

8:51
Truly, truly, I say to you,
if anyone keeps my word,
he will not see death
   for eternity.

8:52

If anyone keeps my word,
he will not taste death
   for eternity.

---

68. There is also a deeper meaning in this, namely the expression of the irony of how one measures eternity with such a measurement of time (fifty years)!

69. According to Lev 24:11–16, the blasphemer is to be stoned to death; from the perspective of the synagogue, v. 58 is nothing other than "blasphemy" (cf. 10:33, 36)!

Two questions follow on from this: (1) Is there a tradition from the Johannine community here?[70] (2) If so, did the tradition exist in two versions or is the literary composition responsible for the differences between the two sayings?[71]

ad (1): The following observations can be made in favor of an affirmative answer to the first question:
(a) Unusual formulations in the Johannine tradition are: *taste* or *see* death.
(b) The logion contains a promise for those who keep the word of Jesus, but its resumption in verse 52 does not look at the *people* who allow themselves to be affected by Jesus's word, but directs the view to *Jesus with* Christological intent.[72] In other words, there is a slight discrepancy between the logion and its reception, a fugue, so to speak, which indicates that the evangelist has only used the *surplus meaning of* the saying in one particular respect, namely the Christological one, but leaves its actual point—the question of the life and death of believers—to rest here.
(c) According to B. Lindars (1972), the saying continues a synoptic logion that will be examined below.
(d) The evangelist treats the saying as a small unit that can be quoted, which rests in itself and is to be regarded as capable of being handed down.

ad (2): In themselves, stylistic-lexemic variations such as those between verses 51 and 52 offer nothing conspicuous, which is why they are hardly registered by the commentators. Nevertheless, it is worth asking whether there is a reason for the respective placement of the two phrases "to *see* death" and "to *taste*." A look at the content, use, and origin of the two metaphors could lead us further.

First of all, what do they contain? As the two verbs that appeal to the senses show, they refer to the *experience*[73] of death, specifically to its experience in the *process of* dying, to the experience of its *suffering*, which, paradoxically enough, for a reflected understanding of death is characterized precisely by the extinction of all experience. Whether the metaphor of "seeing" death, in Jewish terms, refers

---

70. Thus Lindars, *John*, 48; Lindars, "Use," 125–126; Becker, *Johannesevangelium*, 1:363–364; Koester, *Gospels*, 114; Frey, *Eschatologie*, 3:36.

71. So Becker, *Johannesevangelium*, 1:363–364; Lindars, *John*, 332–333, specifically claims v. 52 as a tradition.

72. Odeberg, *Gospel*, 305–306, correctly observes, "The problem is this: J[esus]'s claim is that his *followers* will escape death, whereas the Jews answer him, as if his claim had been simply that *He himself* was exempt from death."

73. J. Behm, "γεύομαι," *TDNT* 1: 675–677, here 676: γεύεσθαι = *to get to feel, to become intimate, to get to know through one's own experience*.

to the encounter with the angel of death[74] can hardly be said with certainty. Rather, the metaphor of "tasting" makes us think of the "bitterness of death" (1 Sam 15:32; cf. Sir 41:1) or, more precisely, of drinking the "cup of death"—a metaphor that is encountered in the targumim[75] and is perhaps also behind the phrase "tasting death."[76]

The metaphor of "seeing" death is biblical.[77] The findings are more differentiated for the metaphor of "tasting." There is no evidence for it in the Old Testament.[78] Instead, it is found sporadically in early Jewish literature[79] and often in rabbinic literature,[80] although—and this is remarkable!—mostly negated, for example with regard to the righteous (such as Enoch and Elijah), over whom the angel of death had no power, but who were rather raptured to God. Are these associations also linked to the negated use of the metaphor in John 8:52? In any case, it is noteworthy that in Mark 9:1 par., where the metaphor is also used in a negated way, a *real* sparing of certain people from the otherwise inevitable universal fate of death is meant.

It is therefore perhaps no coincidence that the phrase "*do not taste death*" is encountered in the mouths of "Jews" who believe that Jesus "spoke of a temporal prolongation of life,"[81] a *real* sparing of man from the fate of death. Such a "misunderstanding" could possibly be connected to this phrase, which lent itself to it from its other usage, rather than to the alternative "not seeing death." If one asks which formulation is to be claimed for the original

---

74. See, for example, the account of Abraham's encounter with the angel of death in T. Ab. A 16–20 and B 13–14, where the latter appears first in a deceptively bright and then in a cruel form to the patriarch who does not want to die: "Step away from me a little! For I say, I cannot bear to *look upon your form*" (A 20).

75. See R. Le Deaut, "Goûter le calice de la mort," *Bib* 43 (1962): 82–86. See T. Abr. A 16: "Then death said to him, 'Most righteous Abraham, behold, I tell you the truth, I am the bitter drink of death.'"

76. However, the phrase "to taste death" is also found in secular Greek sources (see below), without the metaphor of the "*cup* of death" necessarily being implied. Moreover, a figurative use of taste (γεύεσθαι) in both the positive and negative sense is relatively widespread in Greek literature (including the NT) (see the overview by Behm, "γεύομαι"). For the NT, see Heb 6:4–5.

77. See also Ps 16 (15):10; 89 (88):49; cf. Luke 2:26; Acts 2:27; Heb 11:5.

78. According to Behm, "γεύομαι," *TDNT* 1:675–676.

79. 4 Esdras 6:26: "Then [s.c. at that time] behold the men [s.c. like Enoch and Elijah] who were caught up and did not taste death from their birth"; LAB 48:1: "and you will taste what is death (*et gustabitis quod est mortis*)"; cf. also CH 10:8.

80. Str-B 1:751–752 (ET: 855–856); 2:525 (ET: 603). Also Greek, see Leonidas *Anthol Pal* 7.662: ἀδελφὸν ἀστόργου γευσάμενον θανάτου (Bauer-Aland 314).

81. Dietzfelbinger, *Johannes*, Vol. 1, 267.

Sayings of Promise and Consolation 305

logion, "to see death" or "to taste death," then everything speaks in favor of the second.[82] The striking metaphor of "tasting or savoring death" will have inspired the evangelist in the first place for his subsequent Christological staging, insofar as this profiles the superiority of Jesus over Abraham (and the prophets) against the background of the fact that they all "died," that is, had to taste death. If our logion is based on Mark 9:1*, then this would also speak for the originality of the οὐ μὴ γεύσηται θανάτου, to which, moreover, Gospel of Thomas 1 testifies. Consequently, the alternative "to see death" is due to the editing of the evangelist, who also has a particular preference for the semantic field of "seeing."[83] The original Johannine logion would have read as follows:

Truly, truly, I say to you,[84]
if someone keeps my word,
he will not taste death for eternity.

7.2.3 Form, Genre, and Message of the Saying

In terms of its genre, our logion is a genuine "Amen-saying."[85] With its sequence of affirmation, conditional clause, and promise, which makes use of the "oath-like assurance formula οὐ μή,"[86] it follows a saying pattern that is encountered several times in the synoptic tradition.[87] According to evidence from Mark 9:41, 10:15, or Matthew 18:3, among others, it probably goes back to Jesus himself.

All logia that follow this language pattern look to the future; they assure mercy of its reward (Mark 9:41), promise entry into the kingdom of God under certain conditions (Mark 10:15; Matt 18:3; Luke 18:17), or affirm that this

---

82. Analogous to 8:51/52, the original Johannine version of the logion is preserved in the second, subsequent place in 3:3/5.

83. Cf. 3:3; 3:36, etc.

84. The fact that the evangelist does not have the "Jews" repeat Jesus's authoritative Amen formula is no coincidence; in the Gospel it *only occurs* in Jesus's mouth (see XX above). It will belong to the original logion because it marks the authority of the one who alone is able to pronounce the subsequent promise.

85. See above at p. 27–30.

86. Οὐ μή = "by no means (taste death)." See above at ch. 1 n. 79.

87. See Mark 9:41; 10:15; Matt 18:3; Luke 18:17, always in connection with the Amen-formula. Apart from Matt 18:3, these sayings are formulated in the third person singular. A second pattern of sayings related to the first, which also contains the Amen introduction, combines the οὐ μή assurance with a temporal clause: Mark 9:1; 13:30; 14:25; Matt 5:18; 5:26; 10:23; the most prominent example, which probably goes back to Jesus himself, is Mark 14:25: "Truly, I say to you, I will not drink again of the fruit of the vine until that day when I drink it new in the kingdom of God."

generation will not pass away until all this happens (Mark 13:30; cf. 9:1). Because they announce the future as certain, the Amen-saying that precedes them makes sense; indeed, it is necessary in order to give due expression to the authority of the one who can thus anticipate the future. John 8:52* also looks to the future, but not to the future kingdom of God but of the individual believer. His question is about individual death, a question, it seems, that preoccupied the Johannine community as a whole.[88] Here it is answered by recourse to the life-giving power of Jesus's words: "If anyone keeps my word, he will not taste death for eternity." γεύεσθαι θανάτου: as we have seen above, this phrase is in itself a metaphor for *dying*, but does it really mean, as the "Jews" understand it, that whoever keeps the word of Jesus will be *spared from dying* forever? Obviously not! Far from suppressing death as an irrevocable reality (cf. John 11:25c), the decisive signal that reorients the metaphor is probably the concluding phrase εἰς τὸν αἰῶνα:[89] whoever keeps the word of Jesus will not savor the painful experience of death to *the end, not until eternity*. How his salvation from death is to be conceived is not stated but assumed;[90] it is in the interest of the logion to motivate the listeners to be faithful to the word of Jesus—a word that contains the promise of life.[91]

7.2.4 John 8:52*—A Continuation of Mark 9:1*?[92]

Mark 9:1	John 8:51*
1 Truly, I say to you,	Truly, truly, I say to you,
2 there are some standing here	if anyone keeps my word,
3 who will not taste death	he will not taste death
4 until they see the kingdom of God after it has come with power.	in eternity

---

88. Becker, *Johannes*, 1:173: "The question of eternal life is the fundamental existential question of the Johannine congregation in general."

89. The promise of our logion: "will not taste death *forever*" corresponds to that of *ego eimi* statement in 11:25–26: "I am the resurrection and the life. Whoever believes in me, *though he die, yet shall he live*; and everyone who lives and believes in me shall *never die*."

90. It is possible that the theologumenon of the resurrection of the dead at the end of time is not in mind, but rather of the individual-anthropological salvation of the soul from death; cf. p. 386–387 below.

91. This understanding of the word of Jesus was probably shaped by the early Jewish concept of wisdom; wisdom also holds life in store for those who receive and keep it.

92. On the significance of Mark 9:1* in the Johannine community see already at ch. 3.3.3!

Assuming that John 8:52* is based on Mark 9:1*,[93] the following two transformations can be recognized:

(1) *Line 2*: "If anyone keeps my word" stands for "there are some among those standing here." Thus, the Johannine logion specifies who is meant: They are the disciples of Jesus!

(2) *Line 4*: "For eternity" replaces the temporal clause "until they have seen the kingdom of God." "This is John's regular practice of making eternal life the equivalent of the kingdom of God in the tradition" (cf. 3:3, 5, 15).[94]

In addition, the following two observations were made:

(1) If Mark 9:1 in its traditional version represents a concrete promise for certain people ("some"), then John 8:52* is formulated in principle: "if *anyone*...."

(2) Mark 9:1 actually refers to the sparing of certain people from death due to the imminent full dawn of the kingdom of God. The logion in John 8:52*, however, looks deeper: According to it, the sparing from death, of which the old "saying of the Lord" spoke, does not refer to actual death, from which there is no escape, but to eternal death, from which God will save man. But what compels us to assume that John 8:52* actually represents a continuation of that old "saying of the Lord"?

According to B. Lindars, the finding that γεύεσθαι θανάτου does *not* occur *anywhere else* in the four Gospels outside these two references (Mark 9:1 par. John 8:52). This is indeed a strong argument for the reference of the Johannine logion to the "saying of the Lord" in Mark 9:1*, a reference that we can categorize as a critically continuing *metatext*. The third evidence for γεύεσθαι θανάτου in the Jesus tradition, which is not found in one of the canonical Gospels but in the apocryphal Gospel of Thomas, can also indirectly support this assumption (see note 64 above).

7.2.5 The Reception of the Logion of the Logion by the Evangelist

If the "saying of the Lord" with its epilogue has a *soteriological* point, the evangelist, as already indicated at the beginning, has interpreted the logion in terms of its *Christological* basis in the dialogue he stages between Jesus and the "Jews."

---

93. So Lindars, *John*, 332–333; but he does not ask the question whether the saying of Jesus preserved in the Synoptic Gospels did not undergo changes when it was included in the oldest Gospels, which cannot be ruled out, a question which is also important in so far as the "saying of the Lord" in John 8:52* probably does not presuppose any of the *written* Gospels.

94. Lindars, *John*, 48; since he considers John 8:52* to be a traditional saying, he would consequently have to assign this transformation to the Johannine tradition and not to the evangelist.

This reveals two trains of thought that appear to be in mutual tension but which nevertheless belong together internally:

(1) The "saying of the Lord" speaks of "*my* word," the word of *Jesus*, which contains the fullness of life. This sounds provocative enough in the Jewish mindset,[95] which the evangelist himself is aware of, as evidenced by the reaction of the "Jews" to this saying. All the more important are the traces in the text that show that the evangelist wanted to prevent any misunderstanding of the "saying of the Lord" as a signal toward a softening of biblical monotheism for the sake of clarity in his *own* understanding of God and Christ:

(a) He has Jesus take up the phrase λόγον τηρεῖν ("keep the word") from the "saying of the Lord" again in verse 55: τὸν λόγον αὐτοῦ τηρῶ. In other words, Jesus only proclaims the word that he has heard from the Father; if it holds life for those who keep it (just as he himself keeps it!), it is because it is the saving word of *God*, his *own* word.

(b) The phrase καὶ τὸν λόγον αὐτοῦ τηρῶ belongs to the sequence verses 54–55, in which—as in verses 49–50—the evangelist has Jesus address his *relationship with God* in the language of the *concept of the messenger*. According to this, the reliable messenger is characterized by the fact that he is not concerned with his own honor, but with that of his commissioner. Accordingly, Jesus says: "I honor my *Father*... I do not seek *my own* honor" (vv. 49–50). And in verse 54: "if I were to seek *my own* honor [which is what you accuse me of when you say, 'Who are you making yourself out to be?'], then my honor would be null and void." It is no coincidence that the evangelist has Jesus affirm this *twice*, in verses 49–50 and verses 54–55, and that these two sequences are placed like a frame around his *Amen-saying*. In this way, the evangelist makes it clear to the readers: *What* Jesus is, he *is through his Father* alone; it would be a gross misunderstanding to see his claim in competition with that of the only God, the μόνος θεός (5:44). Of course, this only describes *one* side of Jesus's unique relationship with God, which is also signaled by the continuation of the messenger passages just quoted. These passages formulate Jesus's δόξα-relationship with the Father in *both* directions and thus make it clear that the messenger model is "only" an analogy and that the greater dissimilarity between the image and reality of Jesus's unique relationship with God must not be obscured by this model: "There is he who seeks (my δόξα [honor/glory] and who judges."—"It is the Father who glorifies/honors me." Will an ordinary messenger be able to say this about his employer? The speech of the Father and his Son overlaps and deepens the messenger model.

(2) But the evangelist goes a little further in characterizing this other side of God's relationship to Jesus, as well as Jesus to God. It is again helpful to compare

---

95. In Jewish tradition, "keeping" (τηρεῖν) words refers to the observance of God's commandments and the traditions of the fathers.

this with the *ego-eimi saying* formed by the evangelist in John 11:25–26. His promise "and everyone who lives and believes in me will *never die*" corresponds exactly to our soteriological logion in 8:52*. In John 11:25–26, it is derived from the superordinate predication "*I am the resurrection and the life*," which denotes the *Christological* reason for the subsequent *soteriological* promise. In John 8:48–59, the evangelist takes the exact opposite approach: He begins with the *soteriological* promise handed down to him in order to trace it back to its *Christological* foundation by means of the subsequent dialogue. The goal of this train of thought is therefore the *ego-eimi saying* in 8:58, which makes it unmistakably clear that Jesus does not belong to the order of "becoming" (γίνεσθαι) and passing away, but to that of "being" (εἶναι), that is, that he is on the side of God. The most important stage on this path is the deliberate contrasting of Jesus with "Abraham and the prophets," who all had to "die" (vv. 52/53), that is, were subject to the power of death. *This is* precisely *not the case* for Jesus. His death[96] is, as the Gospel never tires of saying, *ascent, going* to the Father, *exaltation*, and *glorification*. And only as the one who is "the resurrection and the life" in person can he say of himself, "Whoever keeps my word will never taste death." The paradox of our scene is that the Christological claim behind this promise, as expressed in unsurpassable terms in 8:58, is not acceptable to Jesus's "interlocutors," who are therefore willing to get him out of the way: The bearer of true life is to be put to death!

7.3 The Dwellings in the House of the Father (John 14:2–3)

The promise of John 14:2–3 is one of the most controversial sayings of Jesus in the Fourth Gospel. While commentators for centuries considered it certain that the promise "*I will come again*" could only refer to the parousia of the Son of Man at the end of time, doubts crept into this seemingly unquestionable tradition of interpretation in the 20th century. While R. Bultmann pointed to the "coming of Jesus in the hour of death"[97] of the believer, R. Schnackenburg asserted the "present-tense eschatology of the evangelist": He wanted to "take into account the general early Christian expectation of the parousia but consciously reinterpret it in terms of the presence of Christ, his spiritual coming after the resurrection (vv. 18ff.)."[98] This model of interpretation has recently been called into question

---

96. The narrator does not speak too often of Jesus's "death" (cf. 12:33; 18:32; 19:33); otherwise it is true for him that this is only the *outside*, the *surface of* an infinitely deeper event that only faith is able to perceive and fathom.

97. Bultmann, *Johannes*, 465 n. 1.

98. Schnackenburg, *Johannesevangelium*, 3:70.

again.[99] However, one can only go further if one distinguishes between presuppositions and their creative reshaping by the evangelist, be it that one reckons with a real "saying of the Lord" of the Johannine community, which the evangelist does not interpret as a "saying of the Lord," the evangelist has taken up these words[100] or whether one reduces the guidelines to traditions—motifs and themes.[101] How is it to be decided here?

7.3.1 Text and Context
The Unit in the Johannine Farewell Discourse (14:1–4)

After the *prooemium* of the first Farewell Discourse (13:31–38),[102] its *corpus* begins with the declaration of confidence in 14:1a, which almost verbatim concludes it in 14:27.[103] The promise of trust in verse 1a is flanked by the exhortation to faith in verse 1b, c, which is echoed again toward the end of the first main part of the speech in verse 11.[104] The first speech unit, verses 1–4, leads into the "hinge verse" in verse 4, which in turn leads to Jesus's dialogue with Thomas in verses 5–7.[105] The text reads:

14:1   a   Do not let your heart be troubled.
       b   Believe in God
       c   believe also in me.
   2   a   In my Father's house are many rooms.
       b   *if it were not so,*

---

99. Schnelle, *Johannes*, 227–228 with 231–232.

100. Thus O. Michel, "οἶκος κτλ.," *TDNT* 5:119–159, here 132: "This saying [s.c. 14:2–3], which would seem to have lost its original form, is fairly isolated in the context, and is perhaps older than the sayings around it."; Becker, *Johannes*, 2:546–551; see also idem, "Abschiedsreden," 221–222 (there also references to older literature); Auferstehung 118–120; Dettwiler, *Gegenwart*, 120; Schnelle, *Johannes*, 227 ("claims of revelation of his school"); Frey, *Eschatologie*, 3:134–153.

101. See above all Dietzfelbinger, *Abschied*, 31–33.

102. See ch. 6.1.7 under (3)!

103. Verses 14:28–31 then form the *final part* of the speech.

104. Verse 11: "Believe me that I am in the Father, and the Father is in me, or else believe on account of the works themselves." The correspondence between 14:1b, c and 14:11 suggests that v. 1b, c should also be interpreted imperatively and not indicatively, which is still controversial today.

105. For this dialogue, see section 4.3.1 above!

Sayings of Promise and Consolation

> c *I would not have told you that*
> d *"I go*
> e *to prepare a place for you?*
>
> 3 a And if I go
>   b and prepare a place for you,
>   c I will come again
>   d and will take you to myself,
>   e that where I am
>   f you may be also.
> 4 a And where I am going,
>   b you know the way."

7.3.2 "Tradition-Criticism" Observations

The following observations can be made in favor of the "saying of the Lord" hypothesis:

(1) Verses 2–3 stand out from their context as a self-contained, independent piece.[106] The following paragraphs will show in more detail that the two verses are both formally rounded and consistent in content, which is why they are not dependent on the context in which the evangelist has embedded them in order to be understood.

(2) Verses 2–3 are *ambiguous*. With verse 2b–e (in italics in the text above), a meta-reflection is superimposed on the basic layer of the logion, which is syntactically only poorly linked to this basic layer. Apart from the various attempts at translation that this meta-reflection has always triggered, the connection of verse 3a–c to verse 2 seems to be particularly problematic: The second half of the logion added with a *coordinating* καί ("and"): "*and*, when I have gone and prepared a place for you, I will come again" does not actually fit a *question* in advance, but only what verse 3d, e itself also offers, namely a *promise* or *promise* that then finds its continuation in verse 3.[107] The stylistic figure of *concatenatio*, through which the two halves of the logion are interlocked, also arouses the expectation that what verse 3a, b refers to as a *fulfilled* condition for the continuation of the promise in verse 3c, d was originally articulated in advance *as a promise*. In other

---

106. The breaks at the edges of the logion become tangible in the terminological juxtaposition of "God (θεός)" (v. 1b) and "Father (πατήρ)" (v. 2a) as well as "go (πορεύεσθαι)" (v.2d.3a) and "go away (ὑπάγειν)" (v. 4a).

107. In other words, the coordination of vv. 2 and 3 requires a syntactical similarity of the two coordinated halves. See also 8:16; 12:32; 12:47, where there is a καὶ ἐάν ("and if") in each case.

words, the metareflexive remark in verse 2b–e is a comment of the evangelist, which he himself formed using two columns of the saying (v. 2d, e) and by means of an insertion of the "self-citation-formula" in verse 2b, c typical for him. What in the present text is Jesus's own quotation because of the citation-formula that has now preceded it (whose reference in the context remains admittedly unclear beforehand) was originally a statement of Jesus and as such a constitutive component of the presumed "saying of the Lord."

The prerequisite for this analysis is the assumption, substantiated in more detail above, that the phrase εἶπον ἂν ὑμῖν ὅτι ("had I told you") is actually an introductory (quotation) formula, that is, the ὅτι is not to be interpreted causally but as a ὅτι-*recitativum*. The fact that we are dealing here with a technique widely used in the Gospel, as shown above, leaves no doubt about the given explanation of verse 2c.

The required syntactic analysis should provide the answer to the question of whether in verses 2–3 the evangelist has only taken up traditional themes or motifs in order to subject them to his reinterpretation, or whether he is quoting a regular "saying of the Lord": the fact that the evangelist's commentary on verse 2b, c(–e) only fits into its new environment under tension clearly speaks in favor of the existence of a fixed oral tradition.

(3) "The 'many rooms,' the 'house' of the Father, the 'preparing' and the 'taking to oneself' as a concept of salvation are singular."[108] μονή does occur once again, in 14:23, but there with reference to the basic logion of verses 2–3.[109] The "house" (οἰκία / οἶκος) is often encountered as a social reality in the Gospel[110] and sometimes also serves metaphorical purposes: thus in 2:16, following Psalm 69:10 (= John 2:17), Jesus speaks of the Jerusalem temple as the "house of my Father," and in 8:35 the evangelist quotes a "sentence of social experience" according to which a servant does not remain in the estate, but the son does. Here, however, οἰκία does not become an image for the heavenly dwelling of the father, but the *tertium comparationis* consists in the legal figure of the "son of the house," who alone has the authority (granted to him by the *pater familias*) to dispose of the release of the house slaves. The image of the heavenly "house" in 14:2, although

---

108. Becker, *Johannes*, 2:549.

109. We can also recall the question that the two disciples of John ask Jesus at the beginning of the Gospel in 1:38: "Rabbi (which means Teacher), *where are you staying* (ποῦ μένεις)?" When it then says, "he said to them: 'Come and you will see.' So they came and saw where he was *staying* (ποῦ μένει), and they *stayed* (ἔμειναν) with him that day," then these discreet allusions can certainly be understood in the sense of 14:2–3: Jesus possesses his true abode as the Son of God in his Father's house; he opens it for his disciples, granting them a home as well. In this respect, it must be said that the evangelist has made 14:2–3 entirely his own, that the images of salvation used here, although "singular" in the Gospel, are closely interwoven with his other ideas.

110. See 4:53; 7:53; 11:20.31; 12:3.

Sayings of Promise and Consolation

compatible with 8:35, has its own history that leads into apocalyptic texts.[111] It cannot be derived from 8:35.[112] ἔρχεσθαι ("come") still occurs in the context of the first Farewell Discourse in 14:18, 23, but with clear reference to the basic logion in verses 2–3 and leaving aside the πάλιν ("again") of verse 3c, which indicates the reinterpretation of the logion. ἑτοιμάζειν ("prepare") is a Johannine *hapaxlegomenon*; παραλαμβάνειν is used in the sense of "take to oneself." This is the only time the word is used in this way within the work. In 1:11, it was used instead to mean "receive," "acknowledge," whereas in 19:16 "take into custody," "take over."

In contrast, the final climax of the saying in verse 3e, f ("so that where I am, there you may be also") sounds very Johannine. It is reminiscent of 12:26 ("and where I am, there will my servant be also") and 17:24 ("I desire that they also, whom you have given me, may be with me where I am, to see my glory"). If 17:24, as part of the "high priestly prayer" added by the editors at the very end of the Farewell Discourses in John 17, deliberately leads back to their beginning in 14:2–3, then 12:26 belongs to a group of sayings that have been handed down and also originate from the redactors. The Johannine sound of 14:3e, f does not argue against the hypothesis about the "saying of the Lord," since the traditions of the community (to which 12:26 also belongs!) are likely to have shaped the linguistic style of both the evangelist and the redactor. The decisive factor is whether verse 3e, f belongs constitutively to the logion in verses 2–3 as an eschatological climax or whether it remains comprehensible without the final clause. The former is the case.

(4) Verses 2–3 are in tension with their context. According to the parallels just mentioned with verses 3e, f ("so that *where I am, there you may be also*"), where both times the disciples' perfect fellowship with Jesus beyond the border of death is in view, it is also to be expected for 14:2–3 that Jesus's return refers to the eschaton, probably to his parousia at the end of days. But how can such a promise comfort the disciples in the hour of Jesus's departure?[113] Above all, there is no mention of Jesus's return in this sense anywhere in what follows: the purpose of Jesus's coming according to verse 18 is not to take the disciples *to himself* but to be *with them* here on earth; *they* are not to take up residence with the Father, but conversely he and his Father will take up residence *with them*

---

111. See 7.3.4!

112. But so Schnackenburg, *Johannesevangelium*, 3:69: "From 8:35, the expressions used in 14:2 are easily explained (also μοναί of the same root as μένειν); only there is no mention of a 'coming again' and 'fetching to oneself.'"

113. Brown, *John*, 1:625: "If the reference is thought to be to a coming at the end of time (which we now know to have been far from imminent), how was this to console the disciples who would never see it?"

(v. 23). This tension, which exists between verses 2–3 and verses 18–24 and points to profound processes of reinterpretation, should not be leveled.

(5) There are no inner- or extra-Johannine parallels to the saying in verses 2–3 that could confirm the assumption of its originally independent existence, unless one takes Irenaeus, *Haer.* 5.36.2 as such.[114] However, this is not advisable due to the uncertainty of the evidence. The conclusion from the arguments presented can only be that in 14:2–3 the evangelist makes use of a "saying of the Lord" tradition known to him from his congregation in order to subsequently subject it to reinterpretation. The objections raised against this assumption are not convincing.[115]

7.3.3 Form, Style, and Genre of the Saying

After excising the "self-citation formula" in verse 2b, c, the given "word of the Lord" may have read as follows:

```
A         "There are many rooms in my Father's house.
B  I  a  ┌ I'm going (πορεύομαι),
      b  └ to prepare a place for you.
   II a  ┌ And when I have gone
      b  └ and have prepared a place for you,
      c  ┌ I will be back (πάλιν ἔρχομαι)
      d  └ and I will bring you to myself (παραλήμψομαι),
      e  ┌ so that where I am,
      f  └ you are too."
```

The saying is comprised of two halves: a *main* or *leading sentence* in the form of a declaration (= A) and its *development* in the form of a detailed announcement (= B). This announcement consists of two interlinked sentences (I + II) in that

---

114. There, the church father refers to an interpretation of John 14:2 by "the presbyters," according to which the "many rooms" denote different degrees of blessedness ("therefore *the Lord said* [according to "the presbyters"] *that there are many rooms with the Father*. For all things belong to God, who gives everyone a suitable dwelling place..."), without noting that this word actually comes from the Gospel of John.

115. Schnackenburg, *Johannesevangelium*, 3:69–70: The evangelist had formed v. 2 from 8:35 and v. 3 independently on the basis of an admittedly reinterpreted *parousia* tradition (cf. 1 Thess 4:16–17). However, this *tradition-critical* differentiation (69: "But the figurative word of the dwellings ... must not be connected without further ado with the continuation in v. 3") cannot invalidate the *tradition criticism* observations that are based on the structural and content-related *unity* of vv. 2–3 (cf. section 7.3.3).

sentence II explicitly repeats sentence I as a precondition of itself.[116] The individual cola in part B are arranged in pairs. A main statement (πορεύομαι/ἔρχομαι) dominates both sentence I and sentence II; statements of purpose follow: Jesus's *departure* has the purpose of preparing the disciples' home at their destination; his return serves to bring them home there. Everything is outshone by the climax in II e, f, a final sentence that names the establishment of unlimited fellowship with the disciples as the actual goal of Jesus's actions. This climax is a constitutive part of the saying, it grows out of it and rounds it off. This is evident from the fact that it does not express the idea of fellowship personally, for example with the preposition σύν (being with), but locally, as being gathered together in the same place ("where I am also"), thus picking up on the earlier clause in the saying about the many dwellings of the Father and making it explicit in terms of content: these dwellings will not be empty in the future because they will be filled with life, with the fellowship of Jesus with his own, indeed these dwellings are themselves images of this fellowship.

In terms of its *genre*, this formally very sophisticated, well-rounded saying is a *promise* or a *consolation that is put* into the mouth of Jesus, who takes leave of his own in the face of death. The certainty that pulsates through this promise is expressed syntactically in the present tense forms of the verbs (πορεύομαι, ἔρχομαι) (just as the earlier clause is in the present tense): *The future can already be anticipated in the saying promising consolation*!

7.3.4 The Religious-Historical Horizon of the Saying

John 14:2-3 is one of the Gospel texts that has recently undergone the most thorough "history of religions" analysis.[117] According to Dettwiler[118] "a certain consensus" has emerged on three points: (1) the Old Testament, Qumran, and rabbinic literature are not suitable for comparison with 14:2-3;[119] (2) "the most

---

116. The stylistic figure of *concatenatio* used here is also found elsewhere in the Gospel, in given traditions (e.g., 1:1, 3, 4, 5) as well as in words coined by the evangelist himself (e.g. 13:31-32).

117. See S. Schulz, *Untersuchungen zur Menschensohn-Christologie im Johannesevangelium* (Göttingen: Vandenhoeck & Ruprecht, 1957), 162-164; G. Fischer, *Die himmlischen Wohnungen. Untersuchungen zu Joh 14,2f*, EHS 23/38 (Frankfurt: Peter Lang, 1975), 115-298; Dettwiler, *Gegenwart*, 149-154; Frey, *Eschatologie*, 3:138-145.

118. Dettwiler, *Gegenwart*, 149.

119. Dettwiler comments on Philo: This "is regularly used to elucidate the metaphor 'heavenly Father's house,' but the differences are unmistakable." This is correct, but in view of the evangelist's reinterpretation of the logion, the judgment should be more positive (cf. below). Philo, *Som*. 1.256 is quoted again and again: "For thus you [s.c. dear soul] will be able to return up to your father's house, escaped from the long and incessant storm in the foreign land." On Philo, see Fischer, *Wohnungen*, 189-192.

convincing parallels can be found within the two major streams of Jewish apocalypticism and Gnosticism"; (3) in recent years, "the overwhelming majority of exegetes" have rightly decided in favor of Jewish apocalypticism as the "most important parallel tradition" to 14:2–3.[120]

The first prerequisite for a comparison is to have as clear an idea as possible of the semantic contours of the saying. Is the coming of Jesus, of which verse 3c speaks, really his coming "at the hour of death" of *each individual* disciple, as R. Bultmann interprets the text in favor of his assumption that the "individualistic (eschatology) of the gnostic myth" is present here?[121] One argument against this is that πάλιν can in no way be rendered as "ever and ever,"[122] meaning that the return of Jesus is recorded as a unique and singular event. This finding is consistent with the fact that the logion does not take the perspective of the individual believers, but that of *Jesus*, whose actions are oriented toward the well-being of the *whole* congregation ("you"). The question is, however, whether the exclusion of a gnostic-individualizing interpretation leaves only the early Jewish-apocalyptic alternative or whether, in this case, specific transformations or intermediate stages should not also be expected. After all, N. Walter states that John's eschatology is "closer" to "Hellenistic eschatology" than to apocalyptic eschatology, since, for example, "the word of Jesus's entrance into the Father's house, in which he wants to prepare a place for his own (14:2–3), is conceived in a completely Hellenistic way."[123]

The decisive cornerstone of this debate is the observation that the *spatial* code decisively determines the thinking of our saying: The *otherworldliness* of the "Father's house," which Jesus alone is able to reach in the approach of his death in order to then open it for his disciples, consequently also shapes the idea of salvation; this is not conceived in this-worldly-earthly terms, does not mean the "becoming anew of the concrete, historical world" as in most early Jewish apocalyptic texts,[124] but obeys a *totaliter aliter*. The prerequisite for such

---

120. Dettwiler, *Gegenwart*.

121. Bultmann, *Johannes*, 465 n. 1.

122. Schulz, *Johannesevangelium*, 183.

123. N. Walter, "'Hellenistische Eschatologie' im Neuen Testament" (1985), in Walter, *Praeparatio Evangelica. Studien zur Umwelt, Exegese und Hermeneutik des Neuen Testaments*, WUNT 98 (Tübingen: Tübingen: 1997), 252–272, here 265, describes "Hellenistic eschatology" as "an 'above/below eschatology' . . . which is far more cosmologically oriented than apocalyptic eschatology from the outset. In contrast, apocalyptic eschatology focuses on temporal-futuristic statements of hope" (257).

124. Aune, *Revelation*, 2:439: "Yet it would be most unusual in Jewish apocalyptic to place the final consummation in heaven rather than on earth. Just two Jewish apocalypses, *2 Apoc. Bar.*

thinking is a specific experience of the world, which is possibly fed by the disillusionment of apocalyptic visions of the future, but above all is based on the insight that salvation as participation in "eternal life" *fundamentally* excludes an earthly realization.

In addition to the spatial component, however, there is now also a *temporal component* linked to the announcement of Jesus's coming that aims to lead the disciples home to their Father's house. This temporal component brings our logion back into the context of the early Jewish apocalyptic texts, insofar as they expect the appearance of an end-time savior figure, in particular the Son of Man emerging from the hiddenness of God, to bring about the final salvation of the elect.[125] Admittedly, the assignment of our saying to the world of these texts is probably only possible in a very *mediated way*. The *immediate* continuum of tradition in which it stands is rather determined (a) by the synoptic expectation of the eschatological coming of the Son of Man, although (b) this expectation is encountered in a (rather Hellenistic [?]) form that does not use the title of Son of Man itself, which also applies to the often rightly invoked parallel 1 Thessalonians 4:16–17, a "saying of the Lord" (λόγος κυρίου) quoted by Paul.

πάλιν ἔρχομαι ("I am coming again"):[126] on this, following Daniel 7:13, see especially Mark 8:38 ("... when he [s.c. the Son of Man] *comes* in the glory of his Father with the holy angels") par. Matthew 16:27; Luke 9:26; also Matthew 16:28.—In Mark 13:26–27, structurally comparable with John 14:3, both acts, the coming of the Son of Man and the gathering home of the elect through him into the kingdom of God, are linked together: "and then they will see the Son of Man *coming* in the clouds with great power and glory. And then he will send out the angels and will *gather* his elect from the four winds, from the ends of the earth to the ends of heaven."[127] The same applies to 1 Thessalonians 4:16–17, where, however, instead of the ἔρχεσθαι, the "descent" of the Lord is spoken of with a more "worldly" color that is accompanied by the descent of the still living into the air to meet the Lord. The "spatial" connotations of the whole process (the descent of the Lord "*from heaven*"; the rapture of the remnant "*into the air*") suggest that here, too, the salvation to be expected is not conceived in earthly

---

51:7–16 and 2 *Enoch*, reject the notion of a messianic kingdom on earth and situate the final eschatological state in the heavenly paradise."

125. In addition to Dan 7:13f., see above all the imagery discourses of 1 En. 45–57, 58–69, (70–71) and 4 Ezra 13.

126. See also 21:22–23, as well as Rev 1:7; 2:5, 16; 3:11; 22:7, 12.

127. Here, the unification is concretized imaginatively by the reference to the angels as agents of the Son of Man.

terms, but Christologically—as a completed "being with the Lord" (v. 17) though with a different, namely "heavenly" quality (cf. 1 Cor 15:47-49). This makes clear the bridge to John 14:2-3. The decisive point of the "saying of the Lord" in 1 Thessalonians 4:16-17 is, of course, that it announces the resurrection of the "dead in Christ" as the first event in the Lord's coming from heaven, because this contains the answer to the Thessalonians' question. The "word of the Lord" does not speak of judgment but in Mark 8:38 is linked with the coming of the Son of Man, who will take on the role of a *defender* for his own in the judgment—in contrast to Matthew 16:27, where it says of him that he will "repay each one according to his deeds."

παραλήμψομαι ὑμᾶς πρὸς ἐμαυτόν ("I will take you to myself"): At the end of the eschatological discourse in Luke 17 (= Q 17), which begins with the speech of the future "day of the Son of Man," that is, the "day" of his coming (Q 17:23-24), it says, "I tell you, there will be two at the dining table, one will be *taken* (παραλημφθήσεται) and one will be left behind. Two women will be grinding at the mill, one will be *taken* (παραλημφθήσεται) and one will be left behind" (Q 17:34-35).[128] The correspondence between John 14:3d and this Q-saying in the significant παραλαμβάνειν is remarkable!

In addition to the *structural* references of our logion to apocalypticism, it is also its individual motifs that can be traced into the early Jewish texts and thus support the religious-historical "localization" we have undertaken. In addition to the "Father's house" with its "many rooms,"[129] reference can be made to the eschatological term (τόπον) ἑτοιμάζειν ("[prepare a place]"),[130] but also, as already indicated, to the motif of the "coming," which in the Old Testament refers to YHWH, in Daniel 7:13 to the "Son of Man."[131] Of course, the decisive factor for John 14:2-3 is not the postulated "religious-historical" reference in general but specifically the *early Christian* (Synoptic and pre-Pauline) apocalypticism of the Son of Man, which, however, was "Hellenized" in John 14:2-3 according to the spatial dualism (below/above) present here and, moreover, stripped of any cosmological vividness. Our saying is not concerned with the *how* of a future

---

128. According to the Q-reconstruction: Hoffmann/Heil, Die Spruchquelle Q, 108f.

129. See esp. 1 En. 39:4-8; 41:2; 48:1; 71:5-9, 16; 2 En. 61:2f.; Apoc. Abr. 17:16; 29:15; 4 Ezra 7:121. See *Fischer, Wohnungen*, 137-178; Dettwiler, *Gegenwart*, 150-152.

130. The idea of a place of salvation already *prepared* by God, which then appears at the end of time, is widespread in early Jewish texts; see Apoc. Abr. 29:15: "Then [s.c. at the end of time] the righteous men ... will (hasten) to the place that has long been prepared for them"; see also Jos. Asen. 8:10fin. ("and they will enter into your rest, which you have prepared for your chosen ones"); 15:7. In the NT, see the use of ἑτοιμάζειν in Matt 20:23; 25:34, 41; 1 Cor 2:9; Heb 11:16; Rev 12:6.

131. See also Zech 9:9.

return to the Father's house[132] but with the promise of salvation as such, which consists in personal fellowship with the perfected Jesus.[133]

7.3.5 The "word of the Lord" and Its Interpretation by the Evangelist

If we compare John 14:2-3* with the Son of Man logia in Mark 8:38, Mark 13:26-27, and the pre-Pauline "word of the Lord" in 1 Thessalonians 4:16-17, then it is noticeable that the Johannine saying is special precisely because it does not testify to the expectation of Jesus's saving *coming*, his parousia, in isolation, but links it organically and consistently with a corresponding interpretation of his *death:* Jesus's going (in death) to his Father's house is the sufficient reason for expecting his "coming again" for the purpose of bringing home his own as well. The saying is therefore characterized by a kind of "way Christology." Of course, its emphasis is not on the interpretation of death as such but on it as the prerequisite for the promise of his *coming* that is based on it. Although Jesus's departure from his own in death dissolves his fellowship with his disciples on the surface, his promise of consolation holds out the well-founded prospect that this very fellowship will be restored after the parousia as the actual core of what "salvation" means, or rather, that it will only now take on its *perfect* form: "and I will gather you to myself, *so that where I am, there you may be also.*"

The evangelist's interpretation of the saying begins precisely at this point. First of all, the widely recognized observation that he chose the saying as the basis of the corpus of his farewell address or as its central theme shows the following: He must have shared the basic message of the saying, otherwise he would not have received it. His treatment of it cannot possibly have been merely polemical. This is also contradicted by its origin in his own (not a foreign) community tradition. On the other hand, one can and should also expect a critical or (better) more far-reaching reception. In this case, the evangelist would have picked up the bearers of the tradition where they stood, so to speak, to then lead them to a deeper understanding of the saying and its basic message by means of the subsequent Farewell Discourse. This seems to be the case, as we would like to demonstrate below.

---

132. In contrast, for example, to the "word of the Lord" in 1 Thess 4:16. Thus it is not clear from the metaphor of the "calling home" (cf. Matt 1:20, 24; Song 8:2 LXX) whether it presupposes the idea of resurrection, nor is it clear whether the "calling home" is still expected during the lifetime of the present generation and whether a "rapture" is then to be expected or not.

133. Dodd, *Tradition*, 417: "The theme, however, of journey-and-return is not entirely unknown to the Synoptics. . . . There are parables which speak of a master who goes away, leaving his servants behind, and subsequently returns" (see, e.g., Luke 19:12-15).

The message of the saying, as has become clear, is that Jesus's death as a departure may seem to definitively end his fellowship with his own, but in truth—and this alone is articulated by the saying—he actually lays the foundation for this fellowship by preparing the eternal dwellings in the "Father's house" in the only permanent quality appropriate to it. This intention of the statement corresponds exactly to the concern of the first Farewell Discourse, the aim of which is to promote insight into the *necessity of salvation* in the face of the experience of Jesus's permanent deprivation, which challenges faith. The critical deepening of the saying by the evangelist then takes place as follows: If the saying still quite traditionally ties the establishment of Jesus's salvation-granting fellowship with his own to the time of his parousia, the evangelist's entire endeavor in 14:4–31 is aimed at explaining why Jesus's "coming," which is still awaited by many, together with the disciples' subsequent return home, is already fulfilled post-Easter: "I will not leave you as orphans; *I will come to you.* Yet a little while and the world will see me no more, *but you will see me. Because I live, you also will live. In that day you will know that I am in my Father,* and *you in me, and I in you*" (14:18–20). These words cannot be understood in any other way than as a specific interpretation of John 14:2–3 by the evangelist: contrary to the faith-challenging experience of being orphaned as a disciple of Jesus in this world,[134] Jesus emphasizes that he "comes" to his own (cf. v. 3c), not only with the consequence that they can "see" him, that is, experience him in faith, but above all that they enter into his sphere of life in the same way that he sojourns in his Father's sphere of life. What the "word of the Lord" in John 14:2–3 says vividly and experientially with the metaphor of the journey, the preparation of the rooms, and the subsequent taking home of the disciples to the Father's house, the evangelist translates in verse 20 into the language of his very dense immanence formulas that, quite analogously to the imagery of 14:3d–f, also speak of Jesus's dwelling with the *Father* or the disciples *with Jesus* in the first place and of Jesus's dwelling in the *disciples* only in a subordinate second place. Verse 23 then offers the exact reversal of the imagery of the "word of the Lord" in a further course of conversation, also taking up the terminology from verse 2, when it says: "We will come *to him* [s.c. the one who keeps my word] and take up residence *with him*." The reason for this "paschal" reinterpretation of the idea of the "coming" of Jesus (and thus also of his Father) to his own is the conviction that Jesus meets the believing congregation after Easter in his *word* if they hold on to it and keep it (v. 21). This is because this word is a pledge and expression of the love of Jesus and his Father, and this love

---

134. Certainly, v. 18a is a refraction of congregational experience as a *challenge*, but the evangelist wants to see this *overcome* in Easter faith through the counterpoint of v. 18b.

has the character of an epiphany:[135] It is a pure presence and allows Jesus to be present in him in the form of his word, which the believer encloses in his heart, as the one who "lives" and who imparts life to those who hold on to him in faith, now and not only after their death (v. 19c).

Does such an interpretation destroy the basic message of John 14:2-3*? Probably not! It is true that John 14 leaves the idea of the parousia to one side when it interprets the coming of Jesus in terms of his "Easter" coming in faith and love, thereby stripping away any mythological remnants of the originally apocalyptic connotation of the parousia. *Do not wait for a future coming of Jesus from heaven*, the evangelist wants to say, *but realize that Jesus has already come to you now in his word! The present is not a waiting room of the future, but time fulfilled, filled with the coming of Jesus, who has taken up residence with you! A further coming of Jesus is not to be expected.* Does this mean that *any* expectation of the future is now obsolete because it has been absorbed by an extreme eschatology of the present? That would be contrary to the intention of the basic claim and also cannot be justified by the overall context of the speech. Admittedly, the future envisaged here—in terms of the history of faith—no longer allows us to expect a qualitative leap, a new salvation event that would somehow surpass the basic event of Jesus's "going" to the Father or his Easter "coming" to his own. *In John 14, the future is expressed in the mode of the "abiding"* (μένειν: v. 17) *of what is already present*, that is, it contains what is constant in the flow of time, or if we want to express it personally in view of 14:21 (". . . he will be *loved* by my Father, and I will *love* him"): The future here means the constancy of this love, its reliability, especially in view of the interruptions of time in death. Or as R. Schnackenburg writes in Johannine fashion on 14:3, "The 'I will bring you to myself' already *begins* after Easter, in the believing existence, insofar as it is a present experience of communion with Jesus, but is only *completed* after death (or after the parousia)."[136] One can agree with this, provided one deletes the addition in brackets: "or after the parousia." In his reinterpretation of John 14:2-3*, the evangelist has abandoned the idea of the parousia, and thus also any form of collective eschatology. Even if the textual basis for this in the Gospel is only very narrow, it nevertheless appears that he has tied the futuristic-eschatological

---

135. Verse 21b: "And whoever loves me will be loved by my Father, and I love him and *manifest myself to him*." On the connection between the paschal reinterpretation and the evangelist's theology of the Word, see M. Theobald, "Gott, Logos und Pneuma. 'Trinitarische' Rede von Gott im Johannesevangelium," in *Monotheismus und Christologie. Zur Gottesfrage im hellenistischen Judentum und im UrChristentum*, ed. H.-J. Klauck, QD 138 (Freiburg: Herder, 1992), 41-87, here 76-77.

136. Schnackenburg, *Johannesevangelium*, 3:71 (italics original).

perspective to a *theology of death* that he only hints at:[137] "Whoever believes in me, *even if he dies*, will live; and everyone who lives and believes in me *will not die forever*" (11:25–26). According to this text, which is extremely important for the evangelist, it is likely that individual death (and this is the only issue here) has become *insubstantial* for him, that is, he sees it only as a passage to life, expressed in the imagery of John 14:3: as a homecoming into the Father's house. The evangelist does not suggest any hypothesis about an intermediate state of the soul after death until the resurrection of the body "on the last day" (i.e., the day of the parousia).[138] It is therefore much closer to assume an *individual* eschatology, according to which the human soul is transferred to the heavenly rooms immediately after death.[139] This should not ultimately prove R. Bultmann right with his thesis that John 14:2–3 refers to the coming of Jesus at the hour of death of *each individual*,[140] but the aspect of death and its individual conquest should be included in the final climax of the evangelist's meaning in accordance with the original style of the "word of the Lord": "so that where I am, there you may be also." In the evangelist's opinion, this is only *completed* beyond and through the border of death.

John 12:32 offers a certain control over the meaning that the evangelist gives to the "word of the Lord" of John 14:2–3*, as the following synopsis of the two passages is able to show:

12:32	a	And I, when (ἐάν) I am lifted up from the earth,	14:3	a	And, when (ἐάν) I go
				b	and prepare a place for you,
				c	I will come again
	b	will draw all people to myself (πρὸς ἐμαυτόν).		d	and will take you to myself (πρὸς ἐμαυτόν).

---

137. Walter, "Eschatology," 258: "The 'Hellenistic eschatology,' in relation to human-historical existence, is by no means necessarily 'timeless'; on the contrary ... it also recognizes the temporal 'now/then' as an essential coordinate for man's earthly existence. But this temporal determination of human existence is also 'transient,' so to speak only of 'penultimate' relevance; it is insignificant compared to the decisive category of 'above/below'—it ends for the individual in death."

138. 5:28–29; 6:39c, 40c, 44c, 54b; 12:48 belong to editing!

139. See Theobald, "Futurische versus präsentische Eschatologie? Ein neuer Versuch zur Standortbestimmung der johanneischen Tradition" 534–573.

140. It remains the same: The "coming" of Jesus refers to his paschal coming here and now, to his presence in the faith of those who keep his word.

Structurally and in terms of the *vocabulary* used, the two statements are so closely *related* that one is almost tempted to say that the evangelist already had the "word of the Lord" of 14:2–3 in mind when he formulated 12:32. In the conditional antecedent clause, the deeper meaning of Jesus's death on the cross is stated, both times in a spatial-dualistic conceptual framework. If, according to 14:2–3, Jesus's death is his entrance into the *heavenly* house of the Father, i.e., anything but a death into nothingness, 12:32 understands Jesus's crucifixion (cf. v. 33) as an elevation *away from the earth*—that is, not to the crossbeam, but in truth *into heaven*, to the right hand of the Father. The respective epilogue then articulates (both times with a future verb) the salvific action of the exalted one, which is also presented in each case as a movement emanating from the exalted one, brought about by him and carried out through him toward himself, that is, into communion with him.

First of all, it is important that in 12:32 the ἑλκύειν ("drawing") of the apodosis is directly linked to the event of "exaltation" articulated in the conditional protasis, so that one must say that the "drawing to oneself" is a direct soteriological consequence of the event of exaltation. Analogously, for 14:3c, d it is true that the acts expressed here are also no longer parousia-related, but are to be thought of as the direct fruit of Jesus's departure to the Father. There is also no more room for the idea of parousia in 12:32.[141]

J. Blank understood ἑλκύειν as the "activity" of the exalted one, which brings about the post-Easter "coming to faith."[142] J. Becker writes, "Just as Jesus was exalted in his hour of death, so he draws the individual to himself in his hour of death into exaltation."[143] But then he adds, "But this drawing does not bypass the historical situation of the person. Thus the 'drawing' also has a decidedly historical-anthropological meaning as an offer of the possibility of faith (6:44)."[144] It is probably necessary to think of the two together: man's being "drawn" by the exalted one means his faith obtained through him, his "coming to Jesus"; however, this "being drawn," which already begins in faith, has such an inner dynamic that it only reaches its goal beyond and through the boundary of death.[145] In this way, 12:32 confirms the Johannine meaning of the "word of the Lord" in 14:2–3* presented here.

---

141. This is also completely far from the context because the latter sees the final judgment in the "casting out" of the "ruler of this world" as having already taken place; see v. 31.

142. Blank, *Krisis*, 291.

143. Becker, *Johannes*, 2:462.

144. Becker, *Johannes*, 2:395.

145. On this, see 6:44 ("the Father draws him, *and I will raise him up on the last day*"): Here the redactor has interpreted the eschatological dynamic of the "drawing" in *his* sense (= resurrection on the last day) through the epilogue, see Theobald, "Gezogen," 319.

7.4 The Sayings of Jesus as a Reason for Assurance in Faith

The three logia examined could probably be accompanied by others, but there is not enough space here for a comprehensive examination of all possible words of promise and consolation in the Gospel.[146] The result obtained is nevertheless informative enough and may be regarded as representative of a certain type of Johannine saying of the Lord.

(1) All three sayings are *not* Jesuanic.[147] They come from the Johannine community but have motivic and generic references to the synoptic tradition.[148] John 8:51/52 can even be considered a continuation of a certain synoptic logion beyond such general bridges, for which there are also traces in Gospel of Thomas 1.[149]

(2) We do not know much about the "place in life" of the logia. After all, the catechesis or initial instruction for converts could be named with good reason for John 8:31-32. The "Amen-saying" of John 8:51/52 was probably used in the liturgy of the congregation, according to its solemn opening formula.

(3) If we look at the *content* of the words of promise and consolation, three things stand out:

(a) John 8:31-32 and 8:51/52 make faithfulness to the word of Jesus *as* such the criterion for the fulfillment of the promise. It is therefore no longer just about this or that word of Jesus, but fundamentally about his saving, salvific word in general. Such a generalization can also be observed sporadically in the synoptic tradition, for example in Mark 8:38 par.[150] and, significantly, in the final parable of Jesus's programmatic discourse in Q, where the phrase "my words" (Matt 7:24 par. Luke 6:47) refers to the composition of the discourse there as a whole; in the two Johannine logia, however, the basic principle of "my words" (Matt 7:24 par. Luke 6:47) could also be used. In the two Johannine logia, however, the fundamental nature of the formulation could have a special reason beyond the requirements of the tradition, provided that the τηρεῖν of Jesus's word was in

---

146. Think also of 4:35-36; 5:24; 5:25; 9:4; 12:24-26, etc.

147. For 8:31-32 and 8:51/52 one can refer to the fundamental nature with which *the word of Jesus* is spoken there on a meta-level, for 14:2-3 to the specific eschatology.

148. *Concerning the motif*: 8:31-32 reproduces the idea of μαθητής, 14:2-3 follows on from the early Christian expectation of the Son of Man.—*Concerning genre*: 8:51/52 corresponds to the classical scheme of Amen-sayings, etc.

149. See above at n.64 and 7.2.4.

150. Mark 8:38: "For whoever is ashamed of me *and of my words* in this adulterous and sinful generation."

competition with the observance of *God's commandments*.[151] This would mean that Jesus's word would have succeeded the Torah as the actual soteriologically relevant factor in these logia. The fundamental nature with which the saving and liberating power of Jesus's word is ascribed here would be the result of the confrontation of the Johannine community with the question of the relationship between its Christology and the Jewish Torahology.[152]

(b) In order to avoid misunderstandings, it should be emphasized that when John 8:31–32 and 8:51/52 make lasting faithfulness to the word of Jesus the criterion for the fulfillment of the promise in a conditional sentence, then this is not a proclamation of "works righteousness"! Rather, for those addressed who are ready to follow Jesus or are in the process of doing so, these sayings are about *reassuring them of* their future, which is *given to* them as freedom from death.

(c) All three sayings address the *question of death*, which is what links them together. In 8:31–32, it is the Hellenistic signal word of freedom, which wants to be proven in death as the basic pathos of existence. In 8:51/52, the word of Jesus explicitly promises protection from death (not dying!) as a final savoring of its destructive power until the end. John 14:2–3 is particularly interesting with regard to the Johannine "line of development": On the one hand, the saying still adheres to the early Christian idea of the parousia of the Son of Man; on the other hand, however, it shows that salvation from disaster is conceived "spatially," that is, as being taken out of the world's house of the dead and moved into the dwellings of God. The driving force behind the saying that looks at the death of *Jesus in order to gain a* perspective from it for the question of the future of believers is the problem of dying where every person is indefensibly themselves. The sayings contain the beginnings of a present eschatology but does not yet develop it itself.

---

151. See p. 308 n. 95 above.

152. If Mark 13:31 asserts the unbreakable validity of Jesus's words (as Matt 5:18 par. Luke 16:17 asserts of the Torah with similar words), then here, too, there is probably a transfer of a statement originally referring to the Torah to the words of Jesus.

Part III

The Johannine "Line of Development"

In 1968, J. M. Robinson introduced the concept of early Christian "lines of development" as a theoretical model for describing and interpreting the early history of Christianity, based on a research-historical sketch of the Gospel of John.[1] In 1971, this concept found its first consistent form in the anthology "Trajectories through Early Christianity," for which he and his companion H. Koester were jointly responsible.[2] Although comprehensive in scope, the study

---

1. Robinson, "Die johanneische Entwicklungslinie," 216–250.

2. Here, in ch. 1 of the book ("Dismantling and Reconstructing the Categories of New Testament Scholarship"), Robinson reveals the theoretical model of the two authors ("From 'background' to 'lines of development,'" 8–20). The following moments are characteristic of this: (1) the opposition to positivism in historiography, for which historical developments "would themselves easily become an inadequate manifestation of reality, an empty space between the atoms of facts of which actual reality was composed" (9–10); (2) the overcoming of a religious-historical method that is interested in the "background" of the NT writings; this, however, is usually seen more as an "immovable backdrop" or "permanent stage construction" (31), but not in its own historical dynamics; (3) a development of the concept on two levels, "on the one hand on the level of the broadest and most comprehensive historical movements that affect the whole culture ..., on the other hand on the level of individual, special currents, e.g. the changes in religious understanding or the development of a specific religious tradition within the larger stream of the movement," e.g., the Johannine one (13); (4) the avoidance of the idea of a goal-oriented movement that should be "clearly determined from the beginning": "The future is open" (13–14). The latter should be held against those who see the Gospel of John and its tradition as leading with a certain inevitability into the gnosis of the second century.

of the Gospel of John plays a paradigmatic role from the outset.³ The reason for this is that both scholars, quite apart from the Gospel of John's turbulent reception history in the second century, already saw it in its own diachronic layering as a polyphonic work that unites different tendencies and lines in itself which needed to be drawn out. J. M. Robinson demonstrated this in his article on the path from the source of the signs to their in-depth interpretation by the evangelist to the "orthodox redactor" as the person responsible for the final form of the Gospel of John;[4] H. Koester has provided a corresponding model for the Johannine "revelatory discourses" in several individual studies up to his volume *Ancient Christian Gospels* (1990). On the one hand, in today's research, which is largely characterized by attempts to level out the jagged and not tension-free Johannine landscape into a plane synchrony, it does not seem to be useless to remind one of these attempts at a Johannine "line of development"; on the other hand, on the basis of the analyses presented, it will be necessary to subject them to examination. This will be done in chapters 8 and 9, even if only within the perspective limits imposed by the analyzed material.

---

3. This probably reflects the great legacy of R. Bultmann and his commentary on John, considering that both H. Koester and J. M. Robinson were students of the Marburg theologian.

4. Robinson, "Entwicklungslinien," 18: According to him, the evangelist uses the source of the signs in such a way that through their critical processing he expresses the higher level of truth and the deeper insight that he himself has attained. It could be that he is helped in this by a gnostic current within the cultural development of his environment. Finally, there is an orthodox editor whose merit is to have added sufficient "normal material" that was missing in the evangelist's work. In this way, he wanted to slow down a movement toward gnosis into which the Gospel had fallen. Apparently, Gnosticism had opened up a line of development in its own direction for the interpretation of the Gospel of John, through which it could be adapted to gnostic usage. In this way, the editor, although he could no longer fully agree with the evangelist in view of his changed situation, "saved" the Gospel for the canon and thus for posterity.

CHAPTER 8

Between an Origin in Jesus and Gnostic Dissolution?

The Tradition-Historical Location of the Johannine Saying

WE PROCEED IN two steps. The first step is to merge the contours of the Johannine sayings into an overall picture (8.1). Here we are guided by considerations of a more fundamental nature: What Christology lies behind the Johannine traditions? What can we say about their *Sitz im Leben*? Can we shed light on the origins of the Johannine "line of development"? Then (8.2), we confront this result with H. Koester's model, which is of interest to us insofar as he also traces the core of the evangelist's compositions of discourse and dialogue back to ancient sayings, but places them in a gnostic line. He does not, however, do this without interruption but recognizes an anti-gnostic reaction to a gnostic interpretation of the message of Jesus in the reception of the sayings in the Gospel, which according to him is to be found at a very early stage. Later this can then be clearly seen in the Gospel of Thomas, in the *Epistula Jacobi*, or in the *Dialogue of the Redeemer*. We will examine whether the Johannine sayings, even if in a broken way, can actually be drawn into such an early Christian gnostic "line of development."

8.1 Contours of the Johannine Tradition of Sayings

Not all the sayings known in the Johannine community must have found their way into the Fourth Gospel. If it only offers a selection, then we should be wary of generalizations. Nevertheless, the sayings actually received by the evangelist can be regarded as representative of the Johannine "line of development."

8.1.1 Formal Characteristics of the Johannine Tradition of Sayings

Certain linguistic patterns persist in the Johannine tradition, even across its genres, including those known from the synoptic Jesus-tradition. The following peculiarities of a generally very undemanding syntax are worth mentioning:

(1) A strong preference for conditional sentences with ἐάν (= if),[1] including the pattern ἐάν μή (= if not) + conjunctive and negated apodosis[2] (occasionally formulated with οὐ μή[3]), whereby the ἐάν-clause may also be inferior.

(2) Such double negation with οὐ μή (= by no means) is often found in sayings that do not have a conditional ἐάν; these are all affirmations or assurances of Jesus.[4]

According to H. Schürmann we can see here a linguistic peculiarity of *Jesus*: "In the sayings of the Lord, one speaks who is the 'Lord,' who has 'power' (Mark 1:22). The language of Christ is characterized by a special decisiveness and 'power,' which is particularly evident in the fact that emphases, especially intensifications and accentuations, are preferably found in Jesus's speech";[5] the emphatic οὐ μή with conjunctive aorist, rarely with indicative future, is a good example of this peculiarity. This also includes an ἀλλά (= but) following a negation (οὐ [μή], ἀλλά) found in the Gospels "quite predominantly in men's words." "Obviously we can still hear the *ipsissima vox* of Jesus in its so decisive manner from this very frequent contradictory formulation in the sayings of Jesus—although such a formulation is obvious in speeches."[6] For the previously mentioned sayings, one can refer to 5:24d, e; 8:12d, e; 10:5a, b.

(3) It corresponds to the simple syntax of sayings when their *protasis* often, like in the synoptic tradition, has participatory form;[7] relative clauses also occur.[8] The pattern πᾶς (= everyone) + participle occurs, too, in the Synoptics.[9]

---

1. See 3:5; 5:19c, d; 6:44; 8:31, 51–52; 10:9c, d.; 14:3, 14a, b. On the Synoptics, see Aune, "Tradition," 229–230 ("conditional sayings").

2. 3:5, 5:19c, d, 6:44, 14:6. See Matt 11:27 par. Luke 10:22. οὐδείς / εἰ μή or οὐδέ / εἰ μή corresponds to Aramaic, according to J. Jeremias, *Abba. Studien zur neutestamentlichen Theologie und Zeitgeschichte* (Göttingen: Vandenhoeck & Ruprecht, 1966), 48–49.

3. 8:51–52. The pattern is also found in sentences that clearly go back to the evangelist: 4:48; 20:25.

4. 6:35c, d; 6:37d; 8:12d; 10:5a. The evangelist also mentions this in 4:14, 48; 8:12, 51–52; 10:28; 11:26, 56; 13:8, 38; 16:7 (v.l.); 18:11; 20:25, i.e., a total of eighteen times.

5. Schürmann, "Sprache," 100–101. According to him, it occurs in all strata, ten times in the Markan tradition, in Q (Matt 5:26 par. Luke 12:59; Matt 23:29 par. Luke 13:35, etc.), in the Lukan and Matthean special material (Luke 1:15; 10:19; 18:7, etc.; Matt 5:18.20; 10:23; 25:9).

6. Schürmann, "Sprache," 102. Mark: twenty-five times; Matthew: thirty times; Luke: sixteen times; John: forty-six times; Acts: five times.

7. 5:24, 6:35c, d, 6:45c, 8:12c, 13:20b, 15:23.

8. 14:13, 15:16fin; see Aune, "Tradition," 228–229 ("'Whoever,' or 'the one who' sayings").

9. 3:15, 6:45; see also 6:37. Moreover, see Matt 7:21 par., etc.

(4) J. Schlosser observes: "What is perhaps most striking is the relative abundance of correlative comparison":[10] καθώς (ὥσπερ)—οὕτως (= like / so). However, this pattern only occurs twice in given traditions: in 3:17 (Moses—Son of Man) and 20:21 (Father—Jesus / Jesus—disciple). Otherwise, the evangelist (5:21, 26; 14:31) and the redactor (12:50) refer to the relationship between God and Jesus (Father—Son).

Phraseological characteristics of the saying tradition include: talk of "eternal life";[11] the image of "coming to Jesus"[12] or to the "Father,"[13] an alternative to the idea of discipleship[14] that is also proved[15] synoptically; the phrase "keep the word (of Jesus)";[16] the comprehensive characterization of people's response to Jesus's call by means of the verb "believe."[17] These linguistic peculiarities run through the Johannine sayings and also connect them, more or less closely, with the synoptic tradition.

8.1.2 The Wealth of the Johannine Genres and the Question of the *Sitz im Leben* of the Traditions

In part, the Johannine tradition of sayings moves along the paths of the synoptic genre and in part goes far beyond them. The fact that the boundaries are fluid is demonstrated by the vitality of the tradition beyond the exegetical classification of *Synoptic versus Johannine*, which is inherently artificial: On the one hand, we came across "synoptic" logia in the strict sense (in ch. 2). On the other hand, we observed the phenomenon of updates and "metatexts" (in ch. 3), which means that the Johannine community literally appropriated old logia and transformed them. It was then only a small step to the creative recreation of their own logia (chs. 4–7). Sayings of messengers, disciples, a saying about entering the kingdom of God, sayings of the Son of Man, parables as continuations of Jesuanic poetry (parables about shepherds), and wisdom sayings stand for continuity with the

---

10. J. Schlosser, "Les *logia* johanniques relatifs au Père," *RevSR* 69 (1995): 87–104, here 89, with reference to 5:21, 26; 6:57; 12:50; 14:31b; 15:9; 20:21.

11. 3:15; 4:36b; 5:24; 12:25; only ζωή: 6:35, 53; 8:12.

12. 5:40; 6:35c, 37b, c, 44a, 45d, 65c; 7:37d; see also 7:34d.

13. 14:6c.

14. ἀκολουθεῖν (= to follow) still in 8:12c; 10:5a; 12:16b.

15. See Luke 6:47; 14:26 (Q); Matt 14:28; Mark 10:14 par. Matt 19:14 / Luke 18:16.

16. 8:51b, 52–53; see also 5:24b; 8:31b; 14:21, 24.

17. 3:15; 5:24b; 6:35d.

oldest tradition.[18] The "I am" sayings in their concise and elaborate form and sayings of promise and consolation, on the other hand, document the expansion of the Johannine communities into new territory. But even these continuations already breathe the Johannine "spirit."

One characteristic of this is the *cognitive* trait of some logia, often observed above, which is why they are often called *sayings of revelation*. For example, the "I am" sayings unfold the soteriological depth of the person of Jesus as the epiphany of God in impressive images, thus appealing to the understanding of the person of Jesus. Or a word of wisdom such as that of the futile search (John 7:33–34) leads us to recognize the preexistent wisdom of God in Jesus. Understanding Jesus better, however, also means strengthening faith, and so the pragmatic aim of such sayings is probably to reassure the congregation of its faith, to build up its own Christologically based faith identity. Beyond such a rather general statement, can anything more precise be said about the *Sitz im Leben* of individual Johannine traditions?

First of all, a remark should be made on the ecclesiologically relevant problem of whether the Johannine writings reveal traces of congregational functions that were not present in the Johannine communities? In other words, does it contain references to persons or groups in the congregations who could be possible tradents of our traditions? H.-J. Klauck has collected evidence that shows that we should not think of the Johannine community as a charismatic fringe group, fraternity, sect, or conventicle, but that it certainly had organizational structures. Of course, we must not lose sight of what is special about the Johannine "line of development": This "certainly lies in the fact that tradition bearers and congregation never really diverge, but from beginning to end the *immediacy of Christ* and *spiritual giftedness of* each individual believer are scrupulously preserved."[19] But there were "bearers of tradition," more precisely "apostles, prophets, and teachers" (see 1 Cor 12:28): "apostles" in the sense of *"emissaries"* or *itinerant missionaries* (cf. John 13:16, 20);[20] "teachers": the author of the book,

---

18. In addition, there are phraseological elements from the synoptic logia that live on in the Johannine sayings, e.g., "come to me" (= ἔρχεσθαι πρός με): see above p. 249f. and p. 527 n. 17; or "cast out" (ἐκβάλλειν). See John 6:37; 15:6a but also 12:31; on the other hand, Matt 8:12; 9:34; 12:24, 27–28; 22:13; Luke 13:28, etc.

19. H.-J. Klauck, "Gemeinde ohne Amt? Erfahrungen mit der Kirche in den johanneischen Schriften," in *Gemeinde—Amt—Sakrament. Neutestamentliche Perspektiven* (Würzburg: Echter, 1989), 195–222, here 215, with reference in particular to 1 John 2:20 and 2:27b: "You have no need for anyone to teach you." A particularly telling detail: "In the feeding miracle in Mark, the disciples distribute bread and fish to the crowd (Mark 6:41). In the parallel in John, this mediating role is omitted. Jesus himself distributes the food directly to 5,000 (!) men in John 6:11" (216).

20. Of course, it is correct that John avoids the *title* apostle because it is not the Twelve or a differently defined circle of apostles who standardize the testimony of Jesus but the Paraclete

Between an Origin in Jesus and Gnostic Dissolution? 333

the editors, but also the author of 1 John and the two small letters, about whose relationship to the circle of editors of the Gospel it is, of course, hardly possible to say with certainty. "If we ... have spoken of a Johannine school and defined it more precisely as a class of theologians in the congregation, it is only natural to describe the members of this group as theological *teachers*."[21] Finally, according to Klauck, *prophets* come into question as the third "inner-congregational factor," whereby he cites indications in the Corpus Johanneum that point to a living prophetic spirit in the congregations themselves; "and it is (then) obvious that it makes itself heard in certain prophetic personalities."[22] "The main reason for the postulate of a prophetic status in the Johannine congregation," however, is "the fact that the Paraclete bears prophetic traits," as evidenced in particular by the task assigned to him in 16:8 of *convicting* the world and *exposing* its sin (ἐλέγχειν). "This ἐλέγχειν is (however) according to 1 Corinthians 14:24 the task of the early Christian prophecy."[23] If the "Spirit of truth" as "the other Paraclete" (John 14:16) continues the work of Jesus after his departure on earth, then "those who have taken on a prophetic-Paraclete ministry in the congregation" would consequently stand "in the extension of this handing over of the commission."[24]

---

who assures the disciples of the truth of Jesus's words or, according to secondary editing, the "beloved disciple" is the guarantor of the Johannine tradition.

21. Klauck, "Gemeinde," 207, with reference to the διδάσκειν of Jesus often mentioned in John (6:59; 7:14, 28; 8:20; 18:20) as well as his address as διδάσκαλος (1:38; 13:13–14; 20:16; see also 3:2; 11:28). "We may infer from this with all due caution the activity of *teaching* and *passing on traditions* that was practiced in the congregation and that could not be entrusted in principle, but *de facto* to certain 'functionaries.' The dialogical style of some of the discourses, the disputes, and discussions in some passages of the Gospel can be understood as a written reflection of the school system in the Johannine circle. The restless back and forth of Jesus's speech, the disciples' questions, self-quotations, and quotations from others in 16:16–19, for example, finds a plausible explanation in this way."

22. Klauck, "Gemeinde," 207, "The emissaries of the other party [i.e., the author of 1 John] are called 'pseudo-prophets' in 1 John 4:1. Did their own bear the name of prophets (cf. the itinerant prophets, whose task includes teaching in Did. 11)?" See also Roloff, in: *TRE* 2:517: It is possible that "the voice of a movement has been preserved in the Johannine congregations which, at the end of the first century, wanted to bring the spirit of prophecy to bear polemically against the institutional forms gaining ground on a broad front"; Dettwiler, *Gegenwart*, 303; Dietzfelbinger, *Johannes*, 2:169. Schnackenburg, "Gemeinde," 56–58, disagrees with the assumption that the Johannine congregation regarded "prophets" as special. Schnackenburg is rather cautious about the assumption that the Johannine community knew "prophets" as special bearers of the Spirit. He emphasizes the Johannine "teachers": "Their functions are teaching, passing on, and interpreting the tradition" (58).

23. Klauck, "Gemeinde," 208: "But if all speak prophetically, and an unbeliever comes in or one who is ignorant, he is *convicted* (ἐλέγχεται) by all, judged by all." See also John 4:19 with 4:25, 29.

24. On early Christian prophecy as a *Sitz im Leben* of the sayings of the exalted Jesus in the synoptic tradition, see M. E. Boring, *Sayings of the Risen Jesus: Christian Prophecy in the Synoptic*

It is likely that they also played a role in the Lord's Supper of the community. A link between presiding over the Lord's Supper and a specific ecclesiastical office, as with Ignatius of Antioch, is obviously unknown in the Johannine congregations. Instead, "the father of the family, who according to Jewish and sometimes also pagan meal customs spoke the words of blessing, could also have performed this task at the Lord's Supper. Visiting itinerant missionaries may have been treated as honored guests and offered the opportunity to perform the table blessing at the Lord's Supper as a distinction.... Prophets could also take the floor at the celebration of the Lord's Supper and say the prayer of blessing guided by the Spirit."[25]

Against this background, the above assignments of individual logia to typical situations of the congregation now also gain plausibility. John 7:37 ("Let anyone who is thirsty come to me") is, because of the parallel in Revelation 22:17, demonstrably a saying that belongs to the celebration of the Lord's Supper and was perhaps spoken here by the father of the house as an invitation to participate in the Eucharist. John 6:35 ("I am the bread of life") and 15:1-6* ("I am the true vine") also belong here because of their motifs, just as the "I am" sayings in the Lord's Supper are likely to have their *Sitz im Leben*.[26] The same can be said of 6:53 ("Very truly, I tell you, unless you eat the flesh of the Son of Man"), especially since the liturgical introductory formula ("Very truly, I tell you") also points in this direction. Above all, it allows us to locate 5:24; 8:51; 12:24-26; and 14:12-14 here. In contrast, 8:31b, 32 ("if you continue in my word, you are truly my disciples") or the sentences in 4:37b; 6:63a, b; 9:4; and 11:9-10 belong more in the *catechesis*. In 3:5, the saying on the subject of rebirth, one can consider whether it is not an element of a Johannine baptism.

8.1.3 Wisdom Christology

Before we take a closer look at the Christian titles used in the Johannine sayings, let us take a closer look at the Christological matrix of sayings, which, as we have seen in chapter 6, is *wisdom* in nature: Jesus is identified with preexistent Wisdom, which is shown by the fact that central motifs from the early Jewish theme of personified Wisdom are transferred to him: "Wisdom invites, but her invitation is not accepted, so she turns away and disappears."[27] If H. von Lips

---

Tradition, SNTS.MS 46 (Cambridge: Cambridge University Press, 1982); critically: Aune, "Tradition," 222-223.

25. Klauck, "Gemeinde," 210.

26. See chapter 4.4 under (6)!

27. H. von. Lips, *Weisheitliche Traditionen im Neuen Testament*, WMANT 64 (Neukirchen-Vluyn: Neukirchener Verlag, 1990); see above Chapter 6.1.3!

Between an Origin in Jesus and Gnostic Dissolution? 335

assigns the motif of "inviting wisdom" to John 7:37 (cf. Matt 11:28; Prov 9:5; Sir 24:19; 51:23-24), but also 6:35 (bread of life) and 15:1, 5,[28] he rightly sees the corresponding motif of "departing wisdom" realized in 7:33-34. If this saying is conceived in terms of its motivic structure as the word of the *earthly* Jesus, then the invitations in John 6:35 and 15:1, 5 go beyond this: in them, the exalted Christ, present in his community, speaks. With regard to John 16:16, where, following on from 7:33-34 and 14:19, there is also mention of Jesus's disappearance, i.e., more precisely, of his no longer being seen, von Lips notes, "If the motif of return is used here, then a tradition-historical connection with the word of Sophia in Matthew 23:29 par. would also be conceivable. It would then be based on the apocalyptic version of the motif of Sophia disappearing and returning at the beginning of the time of salvation."[29]

The wisdom-Christological matrix also becomes clear in the sayings that emphasize the *mediation of* Jesus in 10:9 and 14:6: just as wisdom, especially according to its Hellenistic-dualistic form in Philo, shows the way to God, indeed is this way itself (cf. *Deus* 142-143), so no one comes to the Father except through (διά) Christ.[30] There are further observations. The shepherd in the parable of John 10:2-5* is not a royal messianic figure who has his roots in the history of Israel's promise, rather he has the characteristics of a redeemer: he comes from God's world, as is also the case with personified *wisdom*, and with his call "from outside" he opens up a new, undreamed-of possibility of salvation for his own. Finally, the question arises as to whether the close, reciprocal relationship between Jesus and his "Father," as it is expressed several times in the Johannine sayings,[31] has its formative archetype in the corresponding relationship between wisdom and God. Here we should think in particular of 5:19-20, where it says: "The Father loves the Son and shows him all." The same applies to Wisdom: She not only receives comprehensive power from God, he also knows her[32] and she receives unique knowledge from him,[33] which is why she can act as a mediator

---

28. Von Lips, *Traditionen*, 315: "In 6:35, the promise not to hunger and thirst is added to the word 'I am'; in 15:5 it is the promise to bear much fruit. Both motifs are widespread in the wisdom literature: the motif of eating—drinking has already been mentioned [cf. Prov 9:5; Sir 24:21 (cf. 15:3); 51:24]. The motif of tree and fruit is explicated in Sir 24: 5:13ff. where it compares wisdom with various beautiful, large, and fragrant trees and plants, and in v. 17 explicitly with a vine that bears fruit; v. 19 brings the invitation to 'feast on the fruits of wisdom.'"

29. Von Lips, *Traditionen*, 316.

30. On the soteriological διά in Philo see above p. 127 n. 46 and p. 191 n.141 and below pp. 339-340.

31. See esp. 5:19-20c; 6:35b, c; 6:37; 11:9-10; 13:16!

32. Job 28:23-27; Sir 1:8; Bar 3:32; 1 En. 63:2; 84:3, etc.

33. Prov 8:12; Wis 7:25ff., 8:3-4, 8-9, 9:4, 9, 11.

of revelation.[34] At the same time, she maintains a special relationship with those who receive her or into whom she enters. Similarly, the relationship between, for example, Jesus the shepherd and his own sheep is a very special one: they know his voice and follow only him![35] If P. Hoffmann assumes for the "Johannine" logion in Q (Matt 11:27 par. Luke 10:22) that his absolute speech of Jesus as "the Son," who stands in a unique relationship with God the Father, is fed by the wisdom tradition,[36] then this also throws light on the sayings of the Gospel of John, in which the title "the Son" plays a prominent role beside that of the "Son of Man."

8.1.4 The Titles "Son" and "Son of Man," Used for Christ in the Sayings Material

As in the synoptic tradition, Jesus uses only two titles for himself in the Gospel of John: "Son (of God)" and "Son of Man." He always speaks of the Son (of God) or the Son of Man in the third person; only once, in 10:36, does he identify himself with the Son of God in the first person.

If the number of references to "Son of Man" in the Gospel of John declines in comparison with the findings in the Synoptics—which, however, says nothing about the significance of this title for Johannine Christology—the number of references to an absolute "Son" in John has increased to a quite astonishing degree. Christology, the evidence for an absolute "the Son" in John has increased to quite an astonishing degree compared to the Synoptics: the one reference each in Mark (13:32 par. Matt 24:36) and Q (Luke 10:22 par. Matt 11:27), which are increased in Matthew by one more occurrence in the baptismal formula at the end of his book, are contrasted in John with fifteen references to Jesus's sayings[37] and three references to the Baptist's sayings about Jesus.[38] In addition, there are

---

34. Wis 7:27: "And while remaining in herself, she renews all things; in every generation she passes into holy souls and makes them friends of God, and prophets; for God loves nothing so much as the person who lives with wisdom."

35. It is noteworthy that this relationship of the shepherd to his own is interpreted in 10:14b, c as a relationship of *mutual recognition* and, in a form reminiscent of Q 10:22b, c (cf. above pp. 350, 383!), is traced back to *the mutual recognition of Father and Son*. For the Johannine understanding of the reciprocity of mutual recognition is essential for the Johannine understanding of the Father-Son relationship.

36. Hoffmann, *Studien* 136; 138: "In the wisdom tradition there are statements about the relationship between God and wisdom that are similar in content to the Father-Son statement" (with supporting references).

37. 3:16 (+ τὸν μονογενῆ), 17; 5:19 (two times), 20, 21, 22, 23 (two times), 26; 6:40; 8:36; 14:13; 17:1 (two times).

38. 3:35, 36 (two times).

Between an Origin in Jesus and Gnostic Dissolution? 337

several references to "Son of God."[39] This finding expands considerably if we add the countless places in John where "my Father," an absolute "the Father" and "Father!" (in the vocative) occur.[40] If the absolute "the Father" corresponds to an absolute "the Son" in ten cases[41] and the "I" of Jesus in fifty cases,[42] then we can see how this increase in the use of the designation "Father" for God[43] in the Gospel of John can be explained by the strictly Christological perspective of this book. Contrary to the Johannine tendency to increase the number of references to the Father in the Synoptics, the reference to "your Father"[44] is reduced to just one occurrence in the Gospel of John: John 20:17, where the words of the resurrected Jesus to Mary Magdalene say, "Go to my brothers and say to them, 'I am ascending to my Father *and your Father*, to my God and to your God.'" The fact that this logion—"the climax of the Gospel's sayings of Jesus"—combines "the otherwise separate keywords 'my Father' and 'your Father,' whereby 'your Father' appears here for the first and only time" in the Gospel of John, is highly significant and means: "The fact that Jesus can refer to God as *their Father* in front of the disciples is the result of Easter faith."[45] Easter is for the disciples the event by which they are taken into the unique relationship of Jesus with God, his Father, as adoptive children, which consequently also now empowers them to call God their Father.

G. Schneider, following R. Schnackenburg, said that "the more prominent Johannine logia on Jesus's relationship to the Father 'will be attributed entirely to the evangelist, who in them unfolds his Christology of the Son of God sent

---

39. In Jesus's sayings in 3:18; 5:25; 10:36; 11:14, in the mouth of the Baptist in 1:34; in the mouth of a disciple in 1:49 and 11:27; in the mouth of the opposing Jews in 19:7. The narrator speaks of Jesus as the "Son (of God)" only twice (!), in 1:18 and 20:31.

40. According to the statistics of Schneider, "Gott," 1752: "mein Vater": Mark: 0; Luke: 4; Matt: 16; John: 25; absolute "der Vater": 1/4/4/74; "Vater!" (in the vocative): 1/5/2/9.

41. In 5:19 (two times), 20, 21, 23 (two times), 26; 6:40; 14:13. There is also 17:1 (two times), where the vocative πάτερ corresponds to the ὁ υἱός.

42. According to the census by Schlosser, "Logia," 91.

43. It is noteworthy that comparable tendencies can also be observed, for example, in the Gospel of Thomas: "In the theological terminology the most striking parallel between Thomas and John is the use of the term 'Father' for God. The term occurs in the *Gospel of Thomas* thirty times and is certainly part of the tradition of Thomas's sayings" (Koester, *Gospels*, 123). Jesus never names his Father in the Gospel of Thomas with a mere "θεός"! Remarkable: Gos. Thom. 3: ὁ πατὴρ ὁ ζῶν; John 6:57: ὁ ζῶν πατήρ.

44. Mark/Luke/Matt/John: 1/3/14/2; John 8:42 (Jesus to the Jews: "If God were *your Father*, you would love me.") can be disregarded.

45. Schneider, "Gott," 1777–1778.

into the world."[46] However, J. Schlosser has already cast doubt on this blanket assumption with his careful diachronic considerations and observations. For 6:37; 5:19; and 16:23, he paradigmatically shows the possibility of predetermined logia from the Johannine tradition.[47] This position could be confirmed on a broader basis by the analyses of the preceding chapters. In a total of six logia, which the fourth evangelist owes to the tradition of his community, he is given the absolute "the Son" together with the speech of the "Father": in 5:19–20; 6:37; 6:44–45; 14:2–3; 14:6; and 15:1–2/5–6. The correspondence "the Son"—"the Father" is found in 5:19–20 (here the explicit reference to "the Son" is necessary because of the deliberately used familial metaphor), whereas in the other references the mention of "my Father" (14:2; 15:1) or "the Father" (6:37, 44–45; 14:6) is contrasted with Jesus's "I." Three further traditional points of adhesion are: (1) the early Christian scheme of mission received in 3:17 ("God has sent the Son" + soteriological indication of purpose[48]), (2) the "Son of God" confession of the signs source (1:34, 49; 11:27; 20:31), and (3) Jesus's own testimony of the Sonship of God from the Passion narrative given to the evangelist, as it can be grasped indirectly in 10:36 and directly in 19:7. Otherwise, the abundant use of the designations "Son" and "Father" can be traced back to the literary activity of the evangelist or the editors, as can be seen in particular in the phraseological conventions of the book.[49]

If we look at the *content* of the traditional Father-Son logia, it is striking how concentratedly the *unity of action of Father and Son* is brought closer together. There is no doubt that the Father is entitled to unrestricted sovereignty: "the Son can do nothing on his own, but only what he sees the Father doing" (5:19); "the Father gives to the Son," that is, *he* chooses people and entrusts them to his Son (6:37), or in other words, "*he* draws" them to the Son (6:44). Reaching the "house" of the Father is the meaning and goal of human life (14:2–3, 6).

However, the Father has bound himself completely to the *mediation of* his Son in order to achieve his goals: *The latter* prepares a place for people in "his Father's house"; to be where he also has a home means salvation and life (14:2–3); just as the Father gives the chosen ones to the *Son,* so they also come *to him* (6:37, 45–46). The spatial metaphor of "coming" refers to the "Son" (6:37, 44–45; 7:37) as well as to the "Father" (14:6). The logia gain cognitive power from the

---

46. Schneider, "Gott," 1777, referring to Schnackenburg, "Tradition," 88.

47. Schlosser, "Logia," 94–96. See already Hunter, *John*, 95–96.

48. There is also Rom 8:3; Gal 4:4–5, 6; 1 John 4:9, 14. See E. Schweizer, "Zum religionsgeschichtlichen Hintergrund der 'Sendungsformel' Gal 4,4f., Röm 8,3f., Joh 3,16ff., 1Joh 4,9," *ZNW* 57 (1966): 199–210.

49. See the formula "the Father who sent me" (e.g., 8:18, 28/29) or the reference to the Father in the context of the unfolded concept of a messenger (e.g. 5:43; 8:38a).

familial metaphor that characterizes them (house, son, father), which brings its own plausibility; it is not only about Jesus's relationship to God, but also about the believers' relationship to God, who are "drawn into" (6:44) the space of love (5:20) that exists between Father and Son: ἕλκειν is metaphor of love![50]

The second title of Christ in the Gospel of John, which admittedly does not attain the meaning of the title of the Son for a long time, is that of the "*Son of Man.*" While it is found in 3:14–15 following the synoptic tradition, it has its own coloring in 6:53. Does this eucharistic saying see the title "Son of Man" as an expression of the *earthly-human* side of the Son of God, as did the church fathers later?[51] This is conceivable insofar as, according to 6:51c–58, the Eucharist as a whole is about the confession of Jesus's earthly-human life commitment ("flesh"!) for the life of the world. If, therefore, the reference to Jesus as the "Son of Man"—as far as can be seen—does not play a prominent role in the Johannine liturgy itself,[52] then it is only the evangelist who has assigned it a supporting function for the Christological conception of his book.[53]

8.1.5 Christological Exclusivity and Its Consequences

According to everything that can be discerned from the contours of the Johannine sayings, it was not only the evangelist who brought the belief in Christological exclusivity into the world; it was already alive in his community before he wrote it down in the Gospel and provided it with his interpretation: "*no one comes to the Father except through me*" (14:6). To properly assess this conviction of faith, it should be borne in mind that it made use of a Jewish-Hellenistic matrix that was ready for it to draw on and into which it could inscribe itself, regardless of the fact that it also underwent a change and intensification as a result which ultimately proved to be extremely conflict-laden. The matrix itself is the early Jewish conviction that, despite the experience of God's radical transcendence, he can still be encountered in the form of various mediators, wisdom, the Torah, and the temple—in his instructions for living, which the Torah contains, but also in the orderly cult in Jerusalem, in which he is there for Israel, making atonement and forgiving sins. If the earthly Jesus is *identified*

---

50. See the references in Theobald, "Gezogen," 323–334.

51. Thus C. Colpe, "ὁ υἱὸς τοῦ ἀνθρώπου," *TDNT* 8:400–477, (cf. Ignatius, *Eph.* 20:2). Lindars, "Use," 119, differs, with reference to 3:14: "The Son of Man title is derived from the passion predictions."

52. On 8:28, see below at p. 383.

53. See below at pp. 378–380.

with the preexistent wisdom of God in the Johannine tradition, then this matrix gains a hitherto unknown concreteness and clarity through the fact that it is a specific historical figure with a name, in whom the wisdom of God now becomes tangible, which is also accompanied by the transformation of the matrix itself. Although the idea of a *single* mediator was also comprehensible in the early Jewish horizon—think of the ultimately unrivaled uniqueness of the Jerusalem temple or a statement such as Philo's on the "wisdom that is tangible in the Torah, *through which alone* (δι' ἧς μόνης) the souls that ask are granted refuge in the uncreated (= God)" (*Deus* 160)—the conflict potential of the Christological idea of mediation is based on the one hand on its inherent oppositional structure where Christ moves to the *place where* the Torah, wisdom, and the Temple stand in Judaism and on the other hand on the fact that a *human being* is now granted what, according to Jewish understanding, is *God's* prerogative alone; because personified Wisdom belongs on *his* side, the Torah is *his* instruction for life and the Temple is the place of *his* presence. If the oppositional structure of the Christological idea of mediation is also expressed in the Johannine sayings, usually only implicitly,[54] but sometimes, as in 10:9 or 14:6, also directly, the further point of conflict—the claiming of *divine* prerogatives for a *human* figure in history—becomes tangible in scenes such as 5:18; 10:33, 36; and 19:7, that is, in disputes between the earthly Jesus and his Jewish opponents, into which is projected back what was actually first the subject of dispute between the Johannine circle and the synagogue. But the problem also (and perhaps primarily) becomes virulent in *Jesus's "I am" sayings* and can also be grasped in terms of tradition, insofar as here the (allegedly blasphemous) *"I am" sayings* of the Jewish opponents of the Johannine circle become the subject of dispute. The (allegedly blasphemous) claim of the divine ἐγώ εἰμι for the man Jesus had to become irrefutably manifest.[55]

Finally, the Johannine sayings are revealing from the following two points of view: (1) the fact that Christology in the Johannine sayings is drawn into a wisdom matrix means above all that the path to salvation, which was previously bound to a life according to wisdom, is now linked to faith in Jesus. ζωή (αἰώνιος)

---

54. This is due to the basic character of these sayings, which do not serve the polemical debate but rather the group's self-discovery and, moreover, have their *Sitz im Leben* primarily in the space of worship.

55. Therefore, the following judgment of J. Zumstein, "Zur Geschichte des johanneischen Christentums," in *Kreative Erinnerung. Relecture und Auslegung im Johannesevangelium* (Zurich: TVZ Theologischer Verlag, 1999), 1–14, here 13, seems to me to be correct: "As ... the oldest of the logia included in the Johannine revelatory discourses prove, the high Christology arose very early and is perhaps even to be placed at the beginning of the Johannine line of development. The achievement of the author of the Gospel does not consist in having conceived the high Christology, but in having closely connected it with the Passion kerygma."

Between an Origin in Jesus and Gnostic Dissolution? 341

as a term for salvation—no longer the epitome of successful *earthly* life but of "*eternal* life" in the hereafter, untouched by death—already pervades the Johannine sayings,[56] not only the theological conception of the evangelist. A tendency toward present eschatology was therefore inherent in the Johannine sayings, but was not yet fully developed. This is interesting to observe because, from a diachronic perspective, it becomes clear that it was not primarily the experience of disappointed expectation of the near future that led to the concept of life already present but the Christological conviction of encountering the "light of the world" or the "bread of life" in *Jesus himself*. (2) The Johannine "dualism" as a function of faith in Christ is likewise already present in the Johannine sayings. It can be grasped not only in the "I am" sayings but also, for example, in 14:2–3. To follow Jesus as the "light of the world" means to escape the darkness of this earth. This becomes impenetrable wherever Jesus's light does *not* shine. The "dualism," as the specifically Hellenistic variant of wisdom theology in Philo shows, may be "ideologically" predetermined and, as it were, in the air, but in the Johannine sayings it clearly functions as a framework for Christological exclusivism, according to which, where Christ is absent, no "door" (10:9) opens from this world of darkness to God's world of light. It is only in the Gospels that the eschatological implications of the Christological sayings are then clearly developed and reflected upon.

8.2 Comments on Helmut Koester's Hypothesis

In the identification of Johannine sayings, the above analysis coincides with that of Helmut Koester in a number of cases, making it attractive to us. We present the way in which Koester got his results (9.2.1) and add further comments (9.2.2).[57]

8.2.1 The Gnostic Milieu of the Johannine Sayings

In contrast to his teacher R. Bultmann's literary-critical model of a source of revelatory speeches, H. Koester recognizes correctly in principle that the basis of the tradition of the speeches and dialogue compositions of the Gospel consisted only in given sayings (already in dialogue form or not[58]), which the evangelist

---

56. See 3:14–15; 4:35–36; 5:24; 5:25; 6:35b, c; 6:53; 7:37–38; 8:12; 8:51, etc.!

57. On the *Epistula Jacobi* (NHC I/2), which is of exemplary importance for the question under discussion here, see Theobald, *Herrenworte*, 548–553 ("a gnostic token of Johannine reception history?").

58. Koester, *Gospels*, 257: "In many instances, the author of the Fourth Gospel did not compose these discourses *de novo*, but utilized and expanded older existing discourses." Thus, John

would then have interpreted in his own large-scale compositions and shielded against (gnostic) misinterpretations. Koester's sensitivity for the perception of such sayings arose on the one hand from his insight into the traditional grain of the Johannine composition itself. On the other hand, however, it is above all the result of his comparison with gnostic writings, in particular the Gospel of Thomas, the *Epistula Jacobi*, and the *Dialogue of the Redeemer*. Indeed, one gets the impression that it was only the intimate connoisseur of these writings who saw himself in a position to find the corresponding traditional material in the Gospel of John.

One of the most important prerequisites that allows Koester to establish a *fundamental comparability* of the Gospel of John not only with the Gospel of Thomas but also with the *Epistula Jacobi* and the *Dialogue of the Redeemer*, is the assumption that is also relevant to genre criticism: *Epistula Jacobi*, without its external (epistolary) and internal framework (appearance of the risen one + final departure of Jesus into the world of light), was originally a dialogue between the *earthly* Jesus and his disciples, which is therefore comparable with the dialogical passages of John 13–16, insofar as Jesus here takes leave of his disciples *before his death*.[59] Since the *Dialogue of the Redeemer* lacks a framework that could have placed Jesus's conversations with his disciples in the Easter period between the "resurrection" and the "ascension," Koester finds it easy to interpret this writing accordingly from the outset.[60] The Gospel of Thomas, for which a sequence of sayings without a *continuous* thread of dialogue is characteristic, does not offer

---

14:2–12 and *Dial*. 25–30 ran so parallel that one must assume "John 14:2–12 appears to be a deliberate Christological reinterpretation of the more traditional Gnostic dialogue, which the *Dialogue of the Savior* has preserved in its more original form" (180).

59. Koester, *Gospels*, 200, but J. Hartenstein, *Die zweite Lehre. Erscheinungen des Auferstandenen als Rahmenerzählungen frühchristlicher Dialoge*, TU 146 (Berlin: de Gruyter, 2000), 262, disagrees: "An understanding of the epistolary frame as a preface speaks ... against theories of a secondary framing." Similar to Schneemelcher, *Apokryphen*, 1:189–191, she also limits the genre of the "dialogue gospels" (the term comes from Koester) to literary texts that offer conversations between the *risen Christ* and disciples or a "revelation of Jesus framed by his appearance and disappearance" (Hartenstein, *Lehre*, 252).

60. B. Blatz, "Der Dialog des Erlösers," in *Neutestamentliche Apokryphen*, vol. 1: *Evangelien*. ed. W. Schneemelcher, 6th ed. (Tübingen: Mohr Siebeck, 1990), 245–253, here 247; on the other hand, see *Diaogue of the Redeemer* in the context of writings such as the Sophia of Jesus Christ, the Gospel of Mary, the Gospel of Thomas, the Book of Thomas: "In all cases, we are dealing with dialogues between the Risen Christ and his disciples. The comparison shows that only the dialogue of the Redeemer lacks the framework." Hartenstein, *Lehre*, 256, differs: "In my opinion, *Dial*, like in the Gospel of Thomas, avoids a temporal integration of the revelations—a post-resurrection setting is not clearly recognizable."

Between an Origin in Jesus and Gnostic Dissolution? 343

a commitment to a specific time period.[61] This view of things corresponds to Koester's genre-critical definition of the gnostic "dialogues," which can be characterized with Schneemelcher, "somewhat shortened and sharpened," as follows: "The 'dialogues,' which Rudolph sees as an independent gnostic further development of Greek literary genres, are understood by Koester as a further development of older collections of sayings, which is at the same time an interpretation."[62] Finally, when Koester, in his book *Ancient Christian Gospels*, uses the following criterion to determine whether a writing belongs to the corpus of gospel literature: "This corpus should include all those writings which are constituted by the transmission, use, and interpretation of materials and traditions from and about Jesus of Nazareth,"[63] then it seems only logical that he only uses the Gospel of Thomas, the *Epistula Jacobi*, and the *Dialogue of the Redeemer* from the extensive corpus of apocryphal gospel production for his study.

According to these basic conditions, Koester's textual observations then lead him to a model for determining the relationship between the Gospel of John and the gnostic "dialogue gospels," which can be presented as follows:

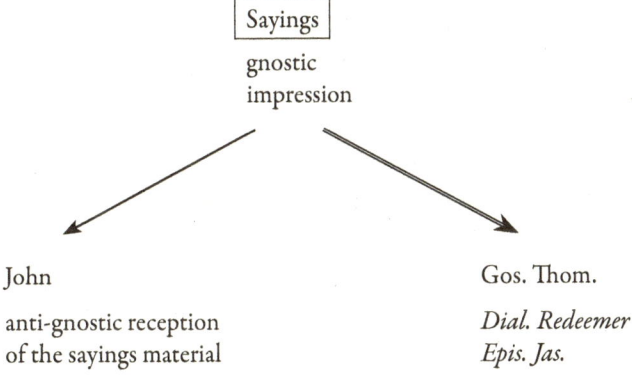

In his speeches, the evangelist then draws on old sayings that are gnostic in origin, and he does so critically by (1) editing the given sayings and partially reformulating them and (2) interpreting them through their positioning in the dialogue

---

61. Hartenstein, *Lehre*, 256: "Rather, the claim to timeless validity already seems to express itself in timelessness in Scripture. The 'living Jesus's' (Incipit) speaks supra-historically, independently of his death and resurrection." See also P. H. Sellew, "The Gospel of Thomas: Prospects for Future Research," in *The Nag Hammadi Library after Fifty Years: Proceedings of the 1995 Society of Biblical Literature Commemoration*, ed. J. D. Turner and A. McGuire, NHMS 44 (Leiden: Brill, 1997), 327–346.

62. Schneemelcher, *Apokryphen*, 1:191.

63. Koester, *Gospels*, 46. See also Hartenstein, *Lehre*, 28.

compositions and shielding them from misinterpretation. Koester achieves two things with this model: First, he is able (with the help of the later "dialogue gospels") to characterize the "milieu" from which the Gospel of John originated and for which it was written in more detail,[64] namely as "gnostic," and second, he succeeds (now with the help of the Gospel of John), the age of the collections of sayings processed in the "dialogue gospels" in order to be able to use *both* groups of writings, canonical and apocryphal gospels, on an equal footing for the reconstruction of the origins of the Jesus tradition of sayings and thus of the message of Jesus himself. The extent to which and whether this hermeneutical circle is valid at all depends, of course, on the specific textual data and their interpretation, for which a few examples from John 7–8 will be offered below:

(1) *John 7:33–34 with 8:21–22; 13:33*:
Parallels: Gospel of Thomas 38;[65] *Ep. Jas.* 2:23–27

Ep. Jas. 2:23–27:
We said to him,
"Have you (already) gone away
and have you distanced yourself from us (forever)?"
But Jesus said,
"No.
But I will go to the place (soon),
from which I came.von dem ich gekommen bin.
If you want to come with me,
then come!"

Koester[66] does not seem to assume that the evangelist made an editorial change to John 7:33–34 in this case; at least he does not comment on it.

(2) *John 7:37–38 and 4:14*:
Parallels: Gos. Thom. 13; 108

Log. 13:

Jesus said to his disciples,
"Compare me and tell me who I am like . . . ."
Thomas said to him,

---

64. Koester, *Gospels*, 113–114: "very little use has been made of parallels from the *Gospel of Thomas* for the interpretation of the Fourth Gospel and in the investigation of its religious milieu."

65. To Gospel of Thomas 38 see Theobald, *Herrenworte*, 445–448.

66. Koester, *Gospels*, 259–260.

"Master, my mouth will not bear it at all,
that I say whom you are like."
Jesus said,
"I am not your master, *since you have been drinking
(and) have become drunk from the bubbling spring.
this one that I have measured....*"⁶⁷

Log. 108:

Jesus said,
"*Whoever drinks from my mouth will become like me;
I myself will become him,
and the hidden things will be revealed to him.*"

There are only these four references (two from John, two from the Gospel of Thomas) to the metaphor of drinking in the tradition of Jesus's sayings, and these are all "variations of the same saying."⁶⁸ Older than the evidence of John are the two logia of the Gospel of Thomas to which they reacted: If, according to Gospel of Thomas 13, drinking from that well "immediately" inspires the one who drinks with the divine spirit, Jesus's conversation with the woman at the well shows "that the establishment of faith is a more complex process."⁶⁹ The assertion of a reciprocal identity with the Revelator, including the (resulting) communication of hidden knowledge in Log. 108 is responded to by "the complex reformulation of the saying" in John 7:37–38, "Scripture confirms that Jesus remains the source of living water. The believer does not achieve mystical identity with the revealer."⁷⁰

(3) *John 8:12, cf. 11:9–10; 12:35–36*:
Parallels: Gos. Thom. 24; 77⁷¹

Log. 24:

His disciples said,
"Teach us about the place where you are,

---

67. See also Odes 11:6–8a [Syr] ("and the speaking water drew near to my lips from the fountain of the Lord, who is without envy. And I drank and became drunk with the living water that does not die, and my drunkenness was not without gnosis" (*Lattke*, FC XIX 125).

68. Koester, *Gospel*, 116. He puts aside Rev 22:17 (but see above at pp, 268–273).

69. "[T]he Johannine reformulation of the saying is visible in the phrase '*unto eternal life*'" (Koester, *Gospel*, 116).

70. Koester, *Gospel*, 117.

71. Text above at p. 164 note 39.

because it is necessary for us to research it."
He said to them,
"He who has ears, let him hear.
There is light inside a person of light,[72]
and it shines for the whole world.
If it does not shine, there is darkness."

Beyond the synoptic sayings (Matt 5:14–16; 6:22f.; Luke 8:16; 11:33–35), the Gospel of Thomas and John have, according to Koester, further developed the light motif into a "mythological metaphor," which here stands for the revealer and denotes his "true nature." If the evangelist hesitated to call "the metaphysical identity" of the believer light,[73] he conversely identified Jesus with the "light" in 8:12 with the help of his own ἐγώ εἰμι formula in an exclusivity polemically directed against Gnosticism[74] in order to ensure that the believer only reaches the light of life by obediently following *Jesus* but not on the gnostic path inwards or the search for his own spark of light ("there is light within a man of light"). In contrast, the logia of the Gospel of John represented the more original tradition. Incidentally, the "I am" formula goes back to the evangelist not only in 8:12 but also in the other ἐγώ εἰμι sayings.[75]

(4) John 8:31–32:
    Parallels: Gos. Thom. 19

Jesus said,
(A) "Blessed is he who was before he became.[76]
(B) *If you become my disciples
    and hears my words,*
    these stones will serve you.

---

72. See John 11:10c.

73. Koester, *Gospels*, 117 (apart from the ἐγώ εἰμι predication, 8:12 is tradition).

74. Koester, *Gospels*, 117; Gos. Thom. 77 is not accepted as a parallel to John 8:12 because of thematic divergence and the different nature of the formula (self-predication instead of recognition formula). See Koester, *Gospels*, 263 n. 4.

75. Koester, *Gospels*, 118 n. 1: "'I am' sayings are relatively rare, or even completely absent, in such writings as the *Gospel of Thomas*, the *Dialogue of the Savior*, and the *Apocryphon of James*. This would tend to support the thesis that the Johannine 'I am' sayings were created by the author of the Fourth Gospel." Koester, *Gospels*, 263: The ἐγώ εἰμι formulas are "an important ingredient of John's anti-Gnostic Christology because they assert that it is only through belief in Jesus who is the life that salvation can be gained, not through the discovery of light in oneself."

76. See John 8:58.

(C) For you have five trees in paradise,
that do not move in summer (and) winter
and whose leaves do not fall off.[77]
Those who know them will *not taste death*."[78]

Hearing the words of Jesus—becoming his disciple: the sequence of these two motifs is the bridge between Gospel of Thomas 19 and John 8:31, whereby Koester even assumes: "a saying that Thomas seems to have preserved in a more original form."[79] The μένειν ἐν (= remain in) and the subsequent "Stoic maxim" of the liberating truth go back to the editing of the fourth evangelist.

(5) *John 8:51 par. 52; cf. 6:63, 68–69*:
Parallels: Gos. Thom. 1;[80] 18; 111

Jesus's words contain life! This basic idea links the sayings together, whereby the *"hermeneutics of Thomas" is obvious*: "Not Jesus' words themselves, but their interpretation gives life, that is, the finding of their hidden truth."[81] The "subtle correction" that the evangelist makes in the logion of John 8:51/52—τηρεῖν (= keep) goes back to him (cf. 14:13, 21; 15:10)—as well as the interpretation of 6:63 ("the words that I speak to you are spirit and life") and 6:68 ("you have words of eternal life") through their context, which is based on the theme of the *obedience of faith*, ensure the understanding of those words in an anti-gnostic sense.

In short, according to Koester, the Johannine reception of the sayings has its aim in the fact that it is to narrow down Christologically what the Gospel itself still treats quite openly. In the fourth evangelist, the way of Jesus, embedded in his transcendent "whence" and "whither," is no longer a model of human redemption by virtue of saving knowledge of *one's own* "whence" and "whither"; rather, Jesus now appears as the *exclusive* place where the truth of God begins in this world, with the consequence that only *his discipleship* brings salvation. In other words, Jesus, as the embodiment of God's wisdom, was no longer the

---

77. According to M. Fieger, *Das Thomasevangelium. Einleitung, Kommentar und Systematik*, NTA.NF 22 (Münster: Aschendorff, 1991), 89, these trees symbolize "the light, i.e., the unchanging life from which man originates (cf. Log 50) . . . The attempt to identify the five trees more precisely in the Gospel of Thomas fails."

78. See John 8:52!

79. Koester, *Gospels*, 115. But the middle (= B) of the three building blocks that are joined together in Log. 19 with its decisive motif ("these stones will serve you") has *no* parallel in John.

80. See Theobald, *Herrenworte*, 503–504.

81. Koester, *Gospels*, 115.

mirror in whose contemplation the called person could become aware of *their own* rootedness in transcendence, but the place where *the light of God* himself shone in this world. According to this conception, the path thus leads from a gnostic "inclusivism" (sayings) to a Christological "exclusivism" (John).[82]

It is interesting that Koester seeks to establish this thesis, apart from his analysis of the sayings in John 7-8, above all on the Farewell Discourses of Jesus in 13-14 and 16, that id, on dialogical passages in which Jesus is in conversation with *disciples*;[83] here the prominent position of the evangelist postulated for himself is indeed most likely to be expected, at any rate it is closer in such a conversational constellation than in Jesus's dialogues with his opponents (John 7-8). He claims of the Johannine Farewell Discourses that they "explicitly" reject the gnostic solution.[84] But does this also come up directly in the disciples' discussions? On the one hand, Koester refers to the popular theme of *seeking and finding* in gnostic texts, the implementation of which, prepared by John 1:38 (cf. also 20:15), 41, 45, and 18:4, would reach its apex in Log. 13:33 and its subsequent interpretation: If the gnostic answer to the question of *how* to follow Jesus was "those who are prepared spiritually can follow the redeemer to the heavenly realms,"[85] the Fourth Gospel counters this with a reference to brotherly love as the practical behavior demanded by Jesus for the time of his absence (13:34) as well as post-Easter faith. So how do we find Jesus after his departure in death?[86] The dialogue section in John 14:1-14 provides an answer to this question, which, with the sequence of its individual elements,[87] can be read as a rejection of the gnostic answer to the initial question, as offered by *Ep. Jas.* and *Dialogue of the Redeemer*: It is not the knowledge of one's own origin from the world of light that brings salvation but only the knowledge of the Father in the person of Jesus.

---

82. Is this intended to expose the Christological exclusivism of the Gospel of John as a secondary, derived phenomenon, in comparison to which the gnostic model would be closer to the historical Jesus?

83. Koester, *Gospels*, 179-181, 195, 264-267.

84. Koester, *Gospels*, 265.

85. Koester, *Gospels*, 265.

86. This was the central question of the Farewell Discourses, to which Gnosticism had already given its answer (see above): "For the disciples too, the question of being with Jesus after his departure, and reaching the place to which he is going, is central for continuing belief in him" (Koester, *Gospels*, 265).

87. Jesus *alone* makes it possible for the disciples to enter the heavenly dwelling place of God (14:2-6); Jesus rejects the search for visionary experiences as an alternative to faith (14:8-9); the knowledge of Jesus and his Father is opposed to the model of self-knowledge (14:7-11); it is Jesus himself who works in his disciples (14:12-14).

It will be conceded that this is a plausible conception in itself. Its strength lies in bringing the texts closer to understanding, but the question arises as to what extent is it plausible in view of the tradition-critical problems. The following objections arise from the perspective of the analyses presented above.

8.2.2 Additional Comments

(1) *Methodologically*, as explained at the beginning,[88] a distinction must be made between tradition and tradition criticism. Koester offers hardly any approaches to this, which is why he concludes that there is an underlying logion even when there is a common motif or an identical phraseological element, without having to secure this in terms of form and genre criticism. In this way, the criterion of parallel transmission, which can only be one among others, moves into a central position that it does not deserve. As a result, the postulate of sayings material in which John on the one hand and the Gospel of Thomas, *Dialogue of the Redeemer*, and *Epistula Jacobi* on the other should meet, and then above all in a form such as that offered by the Gospels of the dialogues, is anything but compelling.

(2) Koester has not provided any proof that the sayings received by John were already gnostic in character, nor conversely that John's reception was fundamentally anti-gnostic. In particular, his thesis that the ἐγώ εἰμι formula owes its existence to the editorial activity of the evangelist is not convincing in view of the (albeit more distant) parallels in Revelation and the relative prevalence of ἐγώ εἰμι in Hellenistic religiosity. Much more plausible is the assumption that (a) the common root of John and the "dialogue gospels" is to be found in the stream of wisdom-Christological sayings and (b) the Gnosticization of these sayings is rather secondary, as can be seen in the Gospel of Thomas, the *Dialogue of the Redeemer*, and *Epistula Jacobi*. In any case, the sayings received by the evangelist do not yet show any traces of Gnosticization, not even the four sayings units that he made the backbone of his first Farewell Discourse (13:33; 14:2–3; 14:6; 14:12–14).

Thus, if the Johannine sayings itself were anything but impregnated with Gnosticism, they do, on the other hand, have characteristics that could provide starting points for a later Gnosticization. One example is the *dualization of wisdom,* according to which it no longer merely refers to a happy *earthly* life but rather to "eternal life" *in the hereafter.* Linked to this is a further characteristic: The insight that the confession of Jesus as the embodiment of this wisdom implies that his actual home is heaven and that his journey in death to the Father must therefore be understood as a return there, from whence he has always come.

---

88. See above at pp. 10–11.

As soon as the assertion of such a correlation between "future" and "origin" was no longer limited to the person of Jesus, but was rather seen as an anthropological model according to which the recognition of one's own "whence" means salvation, insofar as it enables the return of the "self" to its own eternal home, the path was clear to a Gnosticization of the tradition, with a simultaneous dualization of anthropology. However, such a Gnosticization can only be clearly seen in the Gospel of Thomas and in the "dialogue gospels" of the *Dialogue of the Redeemer* and *Epistula Jacobi*. It follows from this that *the development ran from Sophia to Gnosis*, as research can also confirm in other respects.[89]

(a) As far as the Gospel of John is concerned, it is of course remarkable that it already recognizes the thought form of the correlation of "future" and "origin" in a derived form for the existence of believers.[90] John 3:1–15 is significant: Analogous to the "Son of Man," whose ascent to heaven can only be conceived on the condition of his prior descent from heaven (3:13), it also applies to believers that they will only find "entrance into the kingdom of God" if they are born "from above" (3:3), that is, "of water and the Spirit" (3:5). However, this "being born" does not refer to the prior descent of individual chosen ones from the world of God's light, which, in itself, would mean participation in salvation through *an* encounter with Jesus. Rather, it refers to the event of baptism, in which the believer in Jesus receives a new existence from the Spirit of God. After all, the aforementioned form of thought is present here, albeit in a non-gnostic form. Later on, the idea of a "birth from God" in the Johannine circle was given a strong place. According to 1 John, the idea of a "birth from God" later found a strong echo in the Johannine circle, especially among the opponents of this letter, whose dualistic baptismal Christology presupposes a corresponding baptismal theology.

(b) The *Johannine sayings material* also occasionally recognizes the thought form of the correlation of "future" and "origin" for the followers of Jesus (cf. 6:37; 6:44–45), here, however, also in a completely non-gnostic form, related to the election by the Father or the praise of his grace: only those to whom it is given by the Father or whom the Father draws come to Jesus.

(3) According to Koester, the Johannine *dialogues*, because they are impregnated with Gnosticism, are supposed to fix the given units of speech on the basis of an anti-gnostic reading.[91] He does not consider the reverse constellation, in

---

89. See H.-M. Schenke with the programmatic title: "Die Tendenz der Weisheit zur Gnosis," in *Gnosis*, FS H. Jonas (Göttingen: Vandenhoeck & Ruprecht, 1978), 351–372.

90. The origin of a person, his εἶναι ἐκ, also determines his nature! This axiom belongs to the basic stock of Johannine figures of thought.

91. The attempt to claim not only individual sayings but also entire dialogic units as pre-Johannine can be regarded as a failure. Similar attempts to those of Koester can also be found

which predetermined units of speech function as unquestionable authorities to which the dialogues orient themselves as their *core words* and from which they draw authoritative meaning. In such a constellation, however, it would be clear that the respective units of speech cannot have a disputed history of interpretation behind them.

According to Koester, the meaning of the Johannine dialogues can be derived from the postulated imaginary critical conversation between the given sayings and their reception by the evangelist, that is, between a Christian (= antignostic) voice and another Christian (= gnostic) voice. But how do the dialogues staged by the evangelist relate to this, which often enough, namely, in John 7–8, bring opposing conversational constellations onto the stage, that is, conversations between Jesus, the Jerusalem crowd, and the authorities of the holy city, the "Jews"? Such dialogues seem much more likely to help the Johannine community *find itself.* Such dialogues seem to serve the self-discovery of the Johannine community in the face of its questioning by the contemporary *synagogue* rather than the demarcation from Christian gnostic currents in its own house. The situation may be different in Jesus's dialogues with his own *disciples*, such as those in the context of the Farewell Discourses. However, here the relationship between the literary staging of the dialogue and the actual communication relationships would have to be reflected upon.

(4) The latter must be done by first agreeing on the central idea of a speech and dialogue composition, here the first Farewell Discourse in 13:31–14:31. If it is true that in its main part, in 14:1–29, it offers a present-eschatological reinterpretation of the originally more futuristic-eschatologically oriented logion of 14:2–3*,[92] then the determination of the central thrust of the discourse must be oriented toward the process of interpretation that takes place within it: the intention to go beyond early Christian expectations of the parousia and make the paschal presence itself comprehensible in faith as the place where the otherwise still expected return of the exalted Christ can already be believed to have happened. Or in other words, to make the time after Jesus's departure appear not as a time of emptiness, of waiting for his return, but as the time filled with his presence in the *Word* (14:10, 21, 23, 26). Does the author of the first Farewell Discourse therefore have representatives of early Christian eschatology in mind as his primary ideal interlocutor? How then can the other qualifications of the presence of faith that still follow be assigned to this presumed main line of

---

in Richter, Taufetext, 328–334 (the basic material of the Nicodemus dialogue comes from the so-called "Grundschrift"); Schnelle, Christologie, 226, 228 (John 6:30–35/41–51b = a given dialogue from the Johannine school) or Schenke, Vorgeschichte, 77–78; Richter, Dialog 573–603.

92. The Martha-Jesus conversation in 11:21–27 offers an impressive confirmation of this thesis (see below at p. 371–373).

thought in detail? Namely (a) that Jesus in his salvific death has an unassailable lead over the disciples' Easter discipleship (13:33, 36–38), (b) that the path to the heavenly home cannot be detached from the one who opened it in his approach to the Father (14:4–6), (c) that the knowledge of the Father cannot be expected apart from the knowledge of the Son (for example, in one's own mystical experiences or visionary experiences) (14:8f.)?

A limine exclusion does not seem to be the will to specify the message of Jesus in a Gnosticizing milieu, for example in the sense that the author wanted to see the unassailable soteriological *prae* of Jesus's death as opposed to the attempt of a gnostic emancipation of the knowledge of the salvation-historical uniqueness of the Jesus event. It is also possible that he wanted to know that the present practice of faith was based inseparably on the *words* of the *earthly* Jesus, as remembered by the Paraclete after Easter, because there were already tendencies in his environment to speculate about "secret teachings" of the *resurrected* one to select disciples. It is also conceivable that 14:9 opposes the assumption that (visionary or otherwise mediated) experiences of God outside of faith in Jesus could also lay claim to authenticity. However, such positions cannot be established with certainty either in the reception of allegedly *gnostic* sayings or in the text *as a whole* because the aforementioned positions that may be in the background (which do not necessarily have to be entirely of gnostic provenance) are not *explicitly* mentioned in the text itself. This is probably because the thrust of the speech goes in a different direction: the reinterpretation of a traditional futuristic eschatology. In this respect, we cannot go beyond conjecture regarding other contemporary components that the author of John 13–14 could have taken into account.

Part IV

The Reception of the "Words of the Lord" in the Gospel of John

THREE ASPECTS OF the reception of the sayings in the Fourth Gospel must be distinguished: the more *formal techniques* with the help of which the evangelist stages the "words of the Lord" that have come down to him (ch. 9), the *basic theological options* that guided him in the process (ch. 10), and his *hermeneutical framework*—the concept of the Paraclete.

CHAPTER 9

The Tradition of the Sayings and Their Transformation into Dialogue[1]

THE EVANGELIST'S MOST important means of staging "his" Jesus is undoubtedly the transformation of the *sayings* that have come down to him *into dialogue*. He leads us to interpret the "words of the Lord" by linking them back to situations in a specific time and place, confronting them with statements by followers and opponents, but also by undecided people, thus showing "his" Jesus in "dialogue" in the broadest sense. He never goes so far as to abandon his role as narrator in order to switch to the genre of "drama." The "dialogues" remain *narrated* dialogues, i.e., dialogues bound to a specific time and place, despite all the transparency of the present that they are given.

9.1 Processes of Transformation into Dialogue in the Synoptic Tradition

Processes of transformation into dialogue already exist in various forms in the synoptic tradition. One example is the so-called controversy dialogues of Jesus, which, according to W. Weiß, generally arose as concretizing and updating productions of a previously independent Jesus-logion. According to him, the situation is different with the so-called scholastic dialogues.[2] The scholastic

---

1. For information about the "dialogue" genre, see K. Berger, "Hellenistische Gattungen im Neuen Testament," in *ANRW* II 5/2 (1984), 1031–1432, here 1301–1316; *Formgeschichte*, 60–62, 249–256; as well as R. Hirzel, *Der Dialog. Ein literarhistorischer Versuch*, 2 vols. (Hildesheim: Olms, 1963 [ND = Leipzig: 1895]); K. Rudolph, "Der gnostische 'Dialog' als literarisches Genus," in *Probleme der koptischen Literatur*, ed. P. Nagel, Wissenschaftliche Beiträge der Martin-Luther-Universität. Halle Wittenberg 1 (Halle: Martin-Luther-Universität Halle-Wittenberg, 1968), 85–107; P. Perkins, *The Gnostic Dialogue. The Early Church and the Crisis of Gnosticism*, Theological Inquiries (New York: Paulist Press, 1980); U. Schoenborn, *Diverbium Salutis. Literarische Struktur und theologische Intention des gnostischen Dialogs am Beispiel der koptischen "Apokalypse des Petrus,"* StUNT 19 (Göttingen: Vandenhoeck & Ruprecht, 1995), 11–12, 99–101.

2. See Mark 10:2–12; 12:13–17; 12:18–27; 12:28–34, etc.

questions, which are addressed to the teacher in the expectation of receiving a decision from him, are functionally oriented toward instruction. Accordingly, the process of creating these texts is also unique: "With one exception (10:2, 9), the scholastic dialogues are uniformly conceived. In all the pieces, the answer depends on the question."[3] While the debates serve above all to *reassure* the Christian community, which is emancipating itself from the synagogue and Judaism, the scholastic dialogues take up factual questions that originate *from within the community*. While the debates are of an apologetic nature and are based on the premise that Jesus is the *only teacher* due to his messianic-divine authority, the scholastic dialogues deal with practical life orientation related to marriage, divorce, children, poverty and wealth, taxes (relationship with the Roman state), basic ethical norms ("highest commandment"), and related theological questions (resurrection).

The fourth evangelist is not familiar with arguments or scholastic dialogues.[4] The design of the dialogic compositions in the Gospel goes back entirely to the author, which explains the wealth of forms and literary possibilities from which he was free to choose.

In contrast to the consistently brief dialogue in the Synoptics, those in the Fourth Gospel are strikingly expansive. While a simple question-and-answer scheme is the usual model there, John's dialogues can involve multiple turns.[5] C. H. Dodd draws attention to another important difference: "Whereas in the Synoptics it is the exception for a dialogue to be initiated by Jesus, and the rule is for it to be initiated by an interlocutor, the reverse is true in the Fourth Gospel. *A dialogue commonly opens with an oracular utterance by Jesus.*"[6] This difference in the manner of "transformation into dialogue" is so remarkable because it makes us aware of the serious changes in form and history between John and the synoptic tradition: Now it is no longer a question-and-answer game in which both parties are on the same level (a disciple desires information or instruction from the teacher, for example), but *at the origin* is a word from the *heavenly* "Revelator" who establishes new truth *by himself.* The "Revelator" and his "dialogue partners" move on a fundamentally different level of reality. One

---

3. W. Weiss, *"Eine neue Lehre in Vollmacht". Die Streit- und Schulgespräche des Markusevangeliums*, BZNW 52 (Berlin: de Gruyter, 1988), 313.

4. Exemptions include John 4:31-38; 9:1-5; 11:7-11.

5. Jesus's conversation with the woman at the well (John 4:7-26) comprises thirteen utterances, though the conversation with Martha (John 11:21-27) is five.

6. Dodd, *Tradition*, 317-318 (emphasis mine).

wonders which non-Christian genre patterns have influenced the Johannine dialogues here.[7]

The *apologetic* interest in the confrontation with the contemporary synagogue not only lives on in the Gospel of John, it is of primary importance insofar as the Gospel seeks to theologically process the trauma of the community, its exclusion from the synagogue (John 9:22, 34; 12:42; 16:2), in large parts of the book. We do not know how long ago this exclusion took place. But the fundamental questions behind it run through the book, and above all a large part of Jesus's dialogues with the Jewish authorities (Pharisees, "the Jews") can be read as a reflection of this conflict. Rather, these dialogues, in which Jesus is the protagonist (and not his disciples), are an attempt not only to justify the Christological position of the Johannine circle with reference to Jesus's words but also to demonstrate the inevitability of the rupture between the Johannine Christians and the synagogue by projecting the later schism back into the life of Jesus himself. If Jesus's encounter with "the Jews" was already a story of conflict and his "dialogues" with them can only be told as failed ones,[8] then it was only a matter of time before the same fate would befall the believers in Jesus in the synagogue after Easter. In this respect, these "dialogues" of Jesus with his opponents also have a relieving, compensatory function. They do not simply depict current conflicts but offer their resolution by recourse to the words of Jesus himself.

The *practical* impulse of the synoptic school and teaching discussions has no echo in the Gospel of John. An *ethical* interest in shaping the areas of life of the congregation is not his primary interest. The tradition of the school and doctrinal discussions lives on in rudimentary form[9] but is now filled with new content, above all of a Christological-eschatological nature. One has the impression that the new wine is tearing the old skins!

It is possible that, in addition to an apology for and the doctrinal continuation of Christological-eschatological beliefs within the congregation, there is

---

7. See also below at pp. 373–374 and n. 52s.

8. "We may rightly ask whether we are allowed to speak of discussion or debates, if these terms presuppose at least some common ground. All along dialogues end as a monologue, and always Jesus' statements are the ones that really matter" (de Jonge, Christology, 224). Nevertheless, we are sticking to the term "*dialogue*" here for reasons of form-criticism, because the change of conversational utterances is constitutive for it, not the question of the success or failure of communication.

9. Dodd, *Tradition*, 321–329, discusses seven Johannine "dialogues," which he considers to be related to synoptic traditions according to their form: 3:1–3; 3:25–30; 4:31–34; 6:67–70; 7:3ff.; 9:2–5; 9:38–41.

a *third aspect*: the confrontation with a "Jewish Christianity" that remained in the synagogue and was unable to come to terms with the high Christology of the Johannine circle in order to remain at the level of a prophetic-messianic Christology *without the idea of pre-existence*. The study of the Nicodemus dialogue and John 8,[10] as well as other parts of the book, point in this direction.[11]

9.2 The Dialogues of the Gospel of John and Their Structural Principles

If we try to translate the above considerations into a *typology of Johannine forms of dialogue*, taking into account Jesus's respective "interlocutors" in the Gospel, then one arrives at a schema with the following four possible variations:

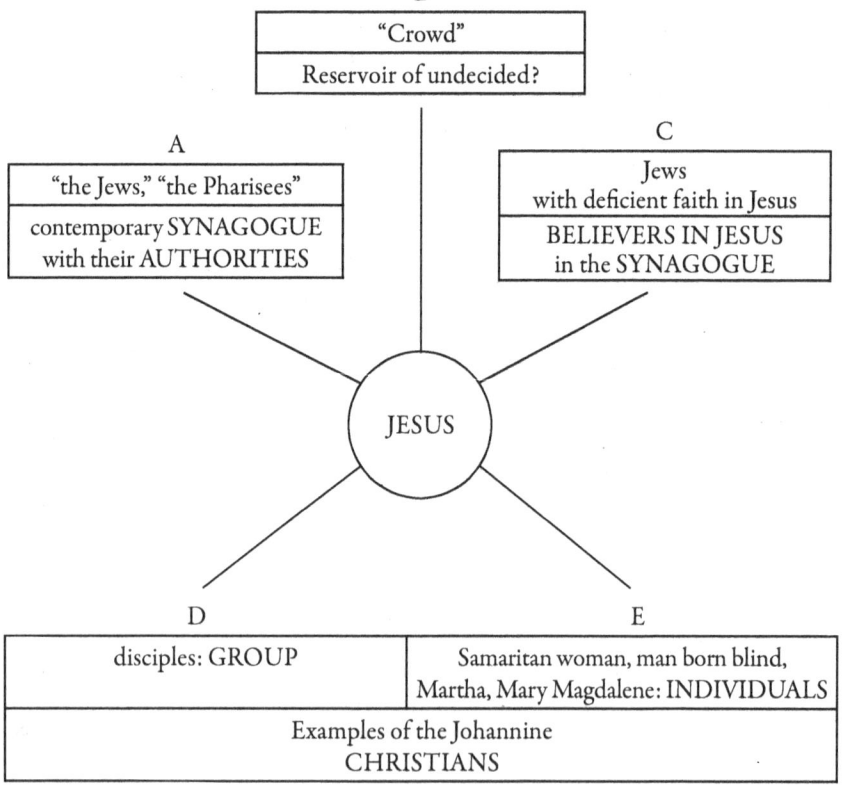

---

10. See above pp. 63–64 and 284–287.

11. Theobald, *Studien*, 204–255.

9.2.1 The Disputes with "the Jews" and "the Pharisees" (Type A)

Jesus's dialogues with the "Jews" or "Pharisees" only occur in the first half of the Gospel in chapters 1–12. John 1:19 already shows that the Ἰουδαῖοι must primarily be an authority that can send messengers[12] to conduct official interrogations or questionings, the subjects of which are of a religious-legal nature. Since the seat of this authority with jurisdiction is Jerusalem (1:19: "the Jews sent priests and Levites *from Jerusalem* to ask him [John] . . ."), it can be identified with the Sanhedrin, the highest Jewish authority.[13] However, this Sanhedrin—as with the Synoptics—is only explicitly mentioned once in the Gospel of John (11:47–53), on the occasion of the Jesus's condemnation to death. However, the authority is already present long before this, not only in 7:45–52, an episode that, in the climax of the sequence of scenes in John 7, indicates an official assembly of precisely those groups that (according to 11:47) belong to the Sanhedrin: the chief priests and Pharisees. According to 7:48 (cf. also 3:1; 7:26; 12:42), its members are also called οἱ ἄρχοντες, which refers to people in a leading position or with authority; elsewhere the term is also used for rulers of the synagogue.[14] It is possible that this indicates a *transparency* of that Jerusalem authority to bearers of *synagogue* jurisdiction from the time after 70 CE, which could have been intended by the evangelist in view of the trauma of his congregation, the exclusion from the synagogue they experienced.[15] It is also noteworthy that, according to 12:42, it is "the Pharisees" who are the driving forces behind the opposition to Jesus in that constellation,[16] although it is precisely here that the Gospel—think of the "Pharisee" Nicodemus, a ἄρχων Ἰουδαίων (3:1; cf. 7:50–51)—can also differentiate. The assumption of an opinion leadership of the Pharisees according to the presentation of the Gospel would plausibly explain the extent to which the text can often switch

---

12. See 1:19, 24, as well as 7:32 (cf. 45) and 18:3), 12–13, 22–23.

13. The "servants (sent) by the *chief priests and Pharisees*" (18:3), whom Judas commands, are called "the servants *of the Jews*" in 18:12. Consequently, they are identical with the Sanhedrin.

14. See Luke 8:41; Matt 9:18 (diff. Mark 5:22).—οἱ ἄρχοντες = the Jerusalem authorities: Acts 3:17; 13:27; see also 4:5, 8, 26.

15. See 6:41.52, the only place in the book where "the Jews" *outside* Jerusalem enter into a dialogue with Jesus, namely in a *synagogue* in Capernaum (6:59); 18:20 *generalizes* this case: "I have spoken openly to the world, I have always taught *in the synagogue* and in the temple, where *all Jews* come together."

16. See also 7:32; 12:19.

between the designation οἱ Ἰουδαῖοι and οἱ φαρισαῖοι.[17] *According to this, the image of the Jewish authority in the Gospel of John is strongly influenced by the dominance of the Pharisaic movement* (which actually played a leading role in the reorganization of Judaism after the catastrophe of the "Jewish war"), which is not the case for the time of Jesus.

However, these observations do not quite do justice to the multilayered use of the term οἱ Ἰουδαῖοι in the Fourth Gospel. As the apostrophizing of Nicodemus as "ἄρχων of the Jews" (3:1), but also the multiple references to the *feasts of the Jews* (2:13; 5:1; 6:4; 7:2; 11:55; cf. also 19:42) show, the term can also generally refer to the members of the religious community to which the Christians of the Johannine circle belong (although a considerable proportion of them were Christians). However, they do not suppress the fact that their own "Master," Jesus, was also a Jew [4:9], even if they then pit him *against* "the Jews" from *their* perspective). The term οἱ Ἰουδαῖοι can also occasionally be associated with the memory of the depth of Israel's salvation history (4:22: "salvation comes from the Jews"). A geographical aspect can also resonate,[18] such that the impression almost arises that "the Galileans" (4:45) and "the Judeans" (apart from the Samaritans, ch. 4, as a third group) are opposed to each other. The geographical aspect is related to the fact that "the Jews" are located in Jerusalem—as the highest authority of the religious community and thus as its representatives, sometimes even blurring lines with its members.

The following dialogues of Jesus with the "Jews" or "Pharisees" can be found in the Gospel:

(1) 2:18–22 (*Place*: Jerusalem—Temple; *Time:* Pesach)
(2) 5:(16). 17–18, 19–30, 31–47 (*Place*: Jerusalem; *Time:* "a festival of the Jews"[19])
(3) 6:41–51 (*Place:* Capernaum—Synagogue)
(4) 6:52–58 (*Place:* Capernaum—Synagogue)[20]

---

17. See 8:13, 22; 9:13–17, 18, 40; see also 4:1.

18. See 7:1: "After this Jesus went about in *Galilee*. He did not wish to go about in *Judea* because *the Jews* were looking for an opportunity to kill him."

19. In itself, this is not a "dialogue," but 5:18b, c functions as an indirect expression of opinion by the "Jews," to which Jesus then responds in 5:19–30.

20. In 6:52 "the Jews" only speak "among themselves," but everything that follows is a response to their objection.

(5) 7:15–24   (*Place:* Jerusalem)
(6) 7:14.25–36   (*Place:* Jerusalem—Temple; *Time:* Succot)
(7) 8:12–59   (*Place:* Jerusalem)[21]
(8) 9:39–41   (*Place:* Jerusalem)[22]
(9) 10:22–30, 31–39   (*Place:* Jerusalem—Temple [Hall of Solomon]; *Time:* Temple Dedication Festival)

The richness of these dialogues, all of which—with the exception of (3) and (4)—take place in Jerusalem, is remarkable. Number 1 (questioning of Jesus by the Jews following his sign in the temple) and number 9 (interrogation of Jesus by the Jews in the temple) are of an *official judicial nature*. They are also based on synoptic tradition. It is interesting to note that both passages are connected with the Johannine Passion tradition, 2:18–22 as a Johannine interpretation of the so-called cleansing of the temple, which was originally part of the Passover of Jesus's death, and 10:22–39 as a Johannine rewriting of essential elements from the story of the official interrogation of Jesus by the high council, which was then suppressed in 18:19-27. The framing of all of Jesus's dialogues with the Jews/Pharisees precisely through these two[23] confirms that "the Jews" refers to the highest Jewish judicial authority acting against Jesus from the beginning (cf. also 1:19).

The simplest dialogues comprise only two units of utterance, a *question* from the opponents and an *answer* from Jesus (as in 6:41–42/43–51; 6:52/53–58; 10:24/25–30. This scheme can be varied in different ways. In 2:18–22, following 2:18 (*question*)/19 (*answer*), it is extended by a *question* (2:20) that unmasks the Jews' misunderstanding; 7:15–24; 8:12–20; and 8:21–29 are multipart exchanges that can also involve different interlocutors of Jesus. In chs. 7 and 8, such conversations form *episodes* in very artfully designed *sequences of scenes*, as the following diagrams illustrate.[24]

---

21. Here the reference to the "Pharisees" in v. 13 changes from v. 22 to "the Jews."

22. The "Pharisees" of 9:40 must be identical with the "Jews" of 9:18, 22, the Jerusalem authorities.

23. 10:22–39 is Jesus's *last* dialogue with the opposing Ἰουδαῖοι. 12:29–36 reports an exchange of words between Jesus and the (Jerusalem) "*people.*"

24. If John 7 consists of *three* scenes (A—B—C) with two (A) or three episodes (so in B and C respectively), John 8 can be divided into five scenes (A—B—C—D—E).

	Sequence of Scenes in John 7 (At the Feast of Tabernacles)		
	A 7:2–13: Prelude	B 7:14/25–36: The middle of the feast	C 7:37–52: The last day of the feast
episodes	(1) 7:2–9: Before Jesus went to Jerusalem (2) 7:10–13: Jesus incognito at the festival; expectations and <u>popular opinions about Jesus</u>	(1) 7:14/25–29: The „where from" of Jesus (2) 7:30–32: <u>reactions</u> and <u>popular opinions about Jesus</u> (3) 7:33–36: The "where to" of Jesus	(1) 7:37–39: revelation saying about the "living water" (2) 7:40–44: <u>reactions</u> and <u>opinions of the people about Jesus</u> (3) 7:45–52: Questioning of the servants sent out after 7:32 by their employers (high priests and Pharisees)
core logia		(1) vv. 28–29 ("he cried out") (3) vv. 33–34	(1) vv. 37–38 ("he cried out")
scenic notes	(1) v. 2 (2) v. 10	(1) v. 14 (2) v. 30	(1) v. 37 (2) v. 40 (3) v. 45
dialogue participants	(1) brothers of Jesus	(1) Jerusalemites (2) the Jews	
themes	(1) revelation to the world	(1)–(3) the "<u>where from</u>" and "<u>where to</u>" of Jesus	(1) the Easter spirit (Jesus's future: his "where to")

	Sequence of Scenes in John 8 (in the Temple)				
	A 8:12–20	B 8:21–30	C 8:31–36	D 8:37–47	E 8:48–59
core logia	<u>v. 12</u>: light of the world	<u>v. 21</u>: you will die in your sins (v. 28)	<u>vv. 31–32</u>.: the truth sets free		<u>vv. 51/52</u>: not to taste death
I am	v. 12	vv. 24/28			v. 58

Sequence of Scenes in John 8 (in the Temple)					
	A 8:12–20	B 8:21–30	C 8:31–36	D 8:37–47	E 8:48–59
Amen-formula			v. 34		v. 51 v. 58
scenic notes	v. 20 (place)	v. 30			v. 59
dialogue participants	the Pharisees [audience: the crowd]	the Jews [audience: the crowd]	Jews who came to faith	(the Jews)	the Jews
themes	Jesus's self-testimony	to be out of this world = die below—above (dualism)	the truth sets free—also the descendants of Abraham	children of Abraham? children of the devil truth—lie (dualism)	Jesus: greater than Abraham

What are the main *literary techniques* that are used to interpret the (largely traditional) *core sayings* or words of revelation of Jesus in the corresponding dialogue compositions? Even if we will encounter some of the techniques again in the dialogue types to be discussed, it seems advisable to pay attention to their specific use in each dialogue type. The following elements should be mentioned:

(1) *Riddle and misunderstanding*: This is a "literary form" (to paraphrase H. Leroy),[25] which in the Fourth Gospel is a typical feature above all of the *disputes*, namely, Jesus's dialogues with the opposing Jews or Pharisees.[26] It has a relatively stable sequence of elements: *Jesus's saying* (= riddle)—*misunderstanding* (usually formulated as a question) of the Jews—*Jesus's answer*.[27] The misunderstanding works in such a way that the point of a (given) "word of the Lord" is taken as an

---

25. Differently in T. Thatcher, "The Riddles of Jesus in the Johannine Dialogues," in *Jesus in Johannine Tradition*, ed. R. T. Fortna and T. Thatcher (London et al.: WJK, 2001), 263–277.

26. See Leroy, *Rätsel*, 184 with n. 2, but of course not only! Leroy, *Rätsel*, 269–271, offers a tabular overview of *all* riddle-misunderstanding passages in the book, including those in Jesus's dialogues with his disciples.

27. If this contains the solution to the riddle, then not for the interlocutors involved *in the text*, but only for its reader. Thatcher, "Riddles," 277: "FE's [Fourth Evangelist's] own audience differs from Jesus' audience, whether Jews or disciples, in that they possess the hermeneutical key to the underlying logic of all of Jesus' riddles, his descent and ascent."—Jesus's *answer* can also be missing (as in 7:35–36) or contained in a commentary by the evangelist for the readers (as in 2:21).

element of a (Johannine) "special language," which is either known, and then one also understands the meaning of the "word of the Lord," or not known, and it eludes the audience and remains hidden. *Originally*, the (received) "word of the Lord" *did not have the* character of a riddle *dependent on interpretation*; rather, it was characterized (despite possible metaphors) by immediate comprehensibility. If now in the Johannine dialogues it loses its original character and mutates into a riddle, then this process has something artificial about it. It must, however, be seen that it is entirely in the service of the representation of that rupture which, according to the evangelist, was ultimately caused by Jesus himself: the incurable schism between the synagogue, which lacks a proper understanding of Jesus (cf. 12:39–40!), and the Johannine circle, which was given such an understanding. The linguistic means by which Jesus's sayings—which were originally directly understandable—are transformed into those of a "special language"[28] can be manifold in detail: be it that ambiguous expressions[29] or metaphors[30] are used, be it that a Johannine understanding of common terms is confronted with a Jewish one.[31]

The previously mentioned basic scheme of "literary form": *The words of Jesus—misunderstanding of the Jews—Jesus's answer* can be extended or varied. The following cases occur in the texts of dialogue-type A:

(riddle-)*saying* of Jesus	2:19	7:33–34	8:18	8:21	8:51	8:56
misunderstanding of the Jews (or rather Pharisees)	2:20	7:35–36	8:19a	8:22	8:52–53	8:57
Jesus's *answer*	(2:21)	–	8:19b	8:23–24	8:54–55	8:58

(2) The aim of dialogue-type A is also served by other signals that *interrupt communication*, such as the deliberate isolation of Jesus's words: The evangelist has "his" Jesus proclaim a word of revelation without him saying it directly to those involved in the conversation.[32]

(3) Jesus's words trigger *discussions* among the people or among the "Pharisees" or "Jews" about their meaning.[33] Such lists of *differing* opinions about Jesus

---

28. Leroy, *Rätsel*, 21–25: "A sociologically definable group is the tradent of the special language. The community of the group determines the community of the special language; conversely, the group is consolidated by the language community and shielded from the outside" (22).

29. E.g., 3:3 (ἄνωθεν); see also 7:34/35, 8:18.

30. E.g., 2:19 (ναός = ναὸς τοῦ σώματος).

31. E.g., 8:32–33 (ἐλευθερία): see above at pp. 293–295.

32. See above at pp. 26–27.

33. See 7:26–27, 31, 40–43.

The Tradition of the Sayings and Their Transformation   365

serve, among other things, to illustrate, as if it were in an echo, the weight of meaning of the preceding words of revelation.

(4) In the context of the narrated dialogues, the "words of the Lord" are *scenically tied back* to the life of Jesus, that is, they now stand in a sequence of events leading to his death. According to the evangelist, they must not be abstracted from this.[34]

(5) As far as the "words of the Lord" themselves are concerned, the evangelist uses the stylistic device of their *repetition* to lead us to their interpretation.[35] Even if they appear in the mouths of his opponents, this is an incentive for the listeners of the book to reflect on their deeper meaning themselves.

(6) The numerous *questions* in the book, which express a wide range of possible reactions to Jesus's words, are also of particular significance in this context: astonishment, incomprehension, and a genuine desire to know.[36]

(7) An important technique for interpreting the "words of the Lord" consists in the *exchange* of individual phrases in a saying,[37] but also in its *conciseness*,[38] which can serve to focus a particular thought.

9.2.2 Jesus's Dialogues with the "Crowd" (Type B)

There are only two independent dialogues of Jesus with a "crowd" (ὄχλος) in the Gospel: (1) 6:26–40 (the ὄχλος, witness of the miraculous spitting: 6:2, 5, 14, 22, 24–25);[39] (2) 12:29–36 (the ὄχλος in Jerusalem). Otherwise, Jesus's encounters with a "crowd" are only episodes in overarching dialogical sequences of scenes, as in chapter 7 (vv. 12–13, 20, 25–27,[40] 31, 40–44, 49[41]).

In terms of their character, the first two dialogues mentioned are very similar to Jesus's disputes with the *Jews*. Here too, for example, the "literary form" of *Jesus's* (enigmatic) *saying* and the (incomprehensible) *answer* of the participants in the conversation, without any kind of bridging of the conflict, plays an important

---

34. See below at p. 380.

35. See above at pp. 21, 22.

36. See 2:20; 3:4 (πῶς), 9 (πῶς); 7:35 (ποῦ); 8:19 (ποῦ), 22, 33 (πῶς), 53, etc.

37. See 3:3/5, 8:51/52, etc.

38. E.g., in 8:21 in contrast to 7:33–34 (see above at pp. 249–250).

39. However, from v. 41 onwards, this dialogue turns into one with "the Jews."

40. The τινὲς ἐκ τῶν Ἱεροσολυμιτῶν (v. 25) should probably be understood as people from the Jerusalem "crowd."

41. Verse 49: "But this crowd (ὄχλος), which does not know the law—they are accursed," is how the members of the high council judge the crowd, who had previously (in 7:42) argued with the Scriptures.

role (6:32–33 [= Jesus's Amen saying as a riddle]—6:34 [answer of the Galilean crowd]). Following their exchange with Jesus, the *Jerusalem* crowd is explicitly told: οὐκ ἐπίστευον εἰς αὐτόν (12:37), after the narrator had stated shortly before: "and Jesus departed and hid himself from them (ἐκρύβη ἀπ' αὐτῶν)." (12:36)[42]

On the other hand, the ὄχλος episodes, for example in chapter 7, with their elements of discussion, strongly convey the impression of an *undecided* crowd, without it being possible to say that the positive statements about Jesus expressed here lead to the full faith in Christ which the evangelist associates with the confession of Jesus as the preexistent Son of God and Son of Man. In this respect, the Jerusalem crowd appears not only as the breeding ground on which the *hostile* statements against Jesus arise (on the part of the *"Jews"*) but also as the reservoir from which *the movement of Jewish Christians with an inchoate faith* is recruited according to the evangelist's account. The texts stand *between* dialogue-types A and C.

9.2.3 Jesus's Dialogues with "Jews who have become believers" (Type C)

The participants in Jesus's conversation in 8:31–36 are a portrait of *Jews who believe in Jesus* and think they can remain *in the synagogue* with their messianic confession of Jesus. While these Jews appear as a *group* in 8:31–36, 3:1–15 offers a dialogue between Jesus and one of their high-ranking representatives, Nicodemus (ἄρχων τῶν Ἰουδαίων), a Pharisee. Here too, as the following diagram illustrates, the interpretation of "the words of the Lord"—core logia—takes the form of a dialogue:

	The Nicodemus-dialogue (John 3)	
	A 3:1–15 dialogue	B 3:16–21 monologue
core logia	vv. 3/5—vv. 14–15	(v. 17: scheme of sending—traditional nucleus)
Amen-sayings	vv. 3/5—v. 11 (opening of the last speech unit)	—
scenic notice	vv. 1–2b	—
dialogue participants	Nicodemus (Pharisee/an ἄρχων)	—
form	three contributions to dialogue each: Nicodemus—Jesus	kerygmatic teaching with two "strophes" (16–18/19–21)

---

42. This is the last of four similar notes, namely 8:58b ("But Jesus hid himself…"); 10:39; 11:54; 12:36, all of which reflect Jesus's reaction to the *Jews'* desire to kill him.

The Tradition of the Sayings and Their Transformation 367

The fact that the techniques of this interpretation—above all the "literary form" of (riddle) *saying*, subsequent *misunderstanding*, and Jesus's *answer*—serve exactly the same purpose in 3:3–15 and 8:31–37 as in the dialogues of type A, namely to show the rift between the revelator and his interlocutors, means that the Jesus of the Fourth Gospel treats both equally: the official phalanx of opposing "Jews" and the group of Jews *in the synagogue* who believe in Jesus. In John 8, the conversation with the latter is *embedded* in the overarching dialogue with "the Jews"—an expression of the fact that the evangelist (and with him the Johannine circle) was not willing to accept the movement of the messianic Jesus-Jews (in the synagogue) as an independent force *sui generis*. How important the confrontation with this movement was for the evangelist (even beyond the two dialogues mentioned) is shown by passages such as 2:23–25; 7:31, 40; 11:45, 48a, b; 12:11, 17–19 and 12:42. Above all, the fact that 2:23–25[43] is placed right at the beginning of the narrative of Jesus's ministry *alongside* his first official interrogation by the "Jews" on the occasion of his appearance in the temple (2:18–22) can be understood as a kind of clef to the whole of his life: the Johannine Jesus as an exponent of the Johannine circle is in conflict with *both* fronts, without one ("the Jews") being able to be reduced to the other (the so-called "Jewish Christians"), as is occasionally suggested. M. de Jonge may have hit the nail on the head here: "For sure, 8:30–47 remains a difficult passage, but maintaining . . . that the equation between 'believing Jews' and 'the Jews' in ch. 8 provides a decisive argument for the theory that the Gospel is only engaged in a polemic against Jewish Christians of inadequate faith, certainly goes beyond the evidence. . . . There is no reason to assume that whenever Jews are mentioned, either as sympathizers or as opponents, Christians of inadequate faith are envisaged."[44]

An *insertion* of "Jewish-Christian" ideas about the person of Jesus into a fictitious *dialogue between Jesus and "the Jews"* may be found in 6:41–42. If the typical "Jewish" attack against the high Johannine Christology refers to the alleged fact of a blasphemous violation of biblical *monotheism* through the confession of Jesus as the Son of God (cf. 5:18; 10:33, 36; 19:7), the objection of 6:41–42 takes the *human* reality of Jesus ("son of Joseph, whose father and mother we know") as its starting point in order to cast doubt on the Johannine preexistence Christology. Behind this could be the "Judeo-Christian" position, according to which Jesus is "the prophet" or "the Christ"; although this ascribes

---

43. "When he was in Jerusalem during the Passover festival, *many believed* (ἐπίστευσαν) *in his name* because they saw the signs he was doing. *But Jesus on his part would not entrust himself to them* (οὐκ ἐπίστευσεν αὐτὸν αὐτοῖς), because he knew all people."

44. De Jonge, Christology 228; the confrontation with "Jewish Christians" ("who do not espouse Johannine Christology [in the past and in the present]") need not necessarily reflect an acute conflict with them.

to him an outstanding role in the history of salvation, he remains *a human being* who is only elevated into the world of God at Easter.

9.2.4 Jesus's Dialogues with the "Disciples" (Type D)

If Jesus's dialogues with "the Jews" (or "Pharisees") are exclusively in the *first* half of the book, the situation is exactly the opposite for those that Jesus has with the group of "disciples": These characterize the appearance of the *second* half of the book, permeating Jesus's Farewell Discourses in John 13–16, which are given their peculiar floating character by them. They are neither solitary monologues nor strict lectures by Jesus nor dialogues, which would be determined from beginning to end by the even alternation of utterances. They lie, so to speak, in the middle, whereby the ratio between the two poles fluctuates conspicuously in the rambling speeches. In John 15:1–16:4c (= second Farewell Discourse) only monologue prevails, whereas the third Farewell Discourse (16:4d–33) also has two passages in which the μαθηταί have their say (16:16–22; 16:29–32), in each case in connection with a concise word of Jesus (16:16; 16:28). In contrast, the *first* Farewell Discourse is characterized by the fact that here Jesus speaks to the assembled group of μαθηταί as a whole but they never respond as such (as in the third Farewell Discourse), instead only named individuals take the floor: Peter, Thomas, Philip, and Judas. As each of them only speaks in one passage and Jesus's answers always apply to the *whole* group of people present, we can assume that they do not represent any particular opinions but rather the group of disciples as a whole. One gets the impression that this group represents, so to speak, the *archetype* of true discipleship or, to put it the other way round, that the readers of the book, specifically the Johannine circle, may see themselves *prefigured* in this group. They themselves are present in that hour of farewell, as Jesus shows them the inner necessity of his "going" to the Father.

However, there are already dialogues between Jesus and the group of μαθηταί in the *first* half of the book, but these are consistently brief and mostly inserted into given narrative contexts: 4:31–38; 6:60–65; 9:2–5; 11:7–10/11–16. Two things are remarkable about these texts:

(1) According to their *form*, these dialogues, apart from 6:60–65, still clearly show their origin in the genre of school and teaching discussions. It is therefore no coincidence that the disciples address their Master as ῥαββί in 4:31; 9:2; and 11:8. In the corresponding texts of the Gospel of Mark, the form of address is διδάσκαλε.[45] Moreover, 9:2–5 is revealing, for here the form of a student-teacher conversation is clearly evident: Following the situation mentioned in 9:1, the disciples ask a *question* of *general* interest (9:2), to which Jesus gives them his

---

45. See Mark 10:17, 35, 12:14, 19, 32.

The Tradition of the Sayings and Their Transformation 369

answer (9:3–5). This pattern also shines through in 4:31–38 and 11:7–10, but here the content of the conversation is even more strongly integrated into the overarching narrative than in 9:2–5; it deepens Jesus's journey and thus ultimately serves Christology. *While the synoptic school and teaching discussions deal with an astonishing breadth of practical life and ethical issues, the Johannine disciple-teacher dialogues focus on Christological issues.*

(2) Jesus's *answers* in these conversations are usually based on *given logia*: in 4:31–38 on the parable in 4:35–36; in 6:62–64 on the statement in 6:63a, b; in 9:3–5 on the rule of life 9:4; and in 11:9–10 finally on the wise saying in 11:9c, d, 10a, b. Here the laws of formation still seem to be at work, which were already to be observed behind the processes of dialogue in the synoptic line of tradition.

The first Farewell Discourse has the following structure:

	The First "Farewell Discourse" John 13:31–14:31		
	A	B	C
rhetorical macrostructure	13:31–33/36–38 prooemium	14:1–26 corpus (main part)	14:27–31 peroratio (end)
subdivisions	(1) 14:31–32 + 33: passion theological programmatic sayings (2) 14:36–38: following dialogue Peter—Jesus	(1) 14:1–14: Jesus's going away (2) 14:15–26: Jesus's return	(1) 14:27–29: recapitulatio of B (2) 14:30–31: transitio to the passion
core logia	13:33	to (1) 14:2–3 (= programmatic saying of the corpus) 14:6 ("I am" saying) 14:12–14 (Amen-saying)	14:28 (recapitulatio of 14:2–3)
dialogic passages	13:36–38 (Peter)	to (1) 14:5 (Thomas) 14:8 (Philip) to (2) 14:22 (Judas)	
Inclusios		14:1a ("do not let your heart be troubled") 14:2f. 14:16–14:26 (Paraclete)	14:27e ("Do not let your heart be troubled, or let it be afraid") 14:28

Here, too, it is noticeable that the *core logia* of the speech, which were given to the evangelist, are regularly reflected in the echo of dialogical interjections from individual disciples—questions and requests: Peter takes up the euphemism ὑπάγειν (= to go away) from the wisdom sayings in 13:33 (13:36), and Thomas expresses the common idea that a path must have a *goal* (so that when this is reached, it may fall into oblivion), thus providing the cue for 14:6 ("*I* am the way ..."). Finally, Philip provides the impetus for a deeper interpretation of this "I am" saying with his plea: "Lord, show us the Father, and we will be satisfied" (14:8). Jesus's answer then gives rise to the Amen-saying in verses 12–14, which concludes the first main part of the speech corpus and, as shown above, is also based on ancient tradition. It follows from these observations—and this applies to the evangelist's dialogue technique in general!—that *the interjections of the "interlocutors"* are anything but interjections from cue suppliers, which—perhaps for reasons of literary enticement—only allow Jesus to catch his breath, so to speak. Rather, they *have the important function of profiling his words*, not by adding complementary aspects—a Platonic "dialectic" would be absurd given the revelatory nature of Jesus's words—but by pointing out demarcations, expressing or suggesting positions that *cannot* be meant, in order to translate Jesus's intention into clarity for the readers step by step.[46] It is clear that this function of profiling Jesus's words is different in the individual types of dialogue. The following should be noted about the literary techniques, especially in the *dialogues with the disciples*:

(1) *Riddle and misunderstanding*: This "literary form" is also found in the dialogues with the disciples,[47] but here, in contrast to the dialogues of types A–C, it is embedded in a dynamic that is intended to lead to understanding, at least according to the strategy of the entire book. The reasons for its use, especially in the dialogues with the disciples, are as follows: First, according to the evangelist's

---

46. Dettwiler, *Gegenwart*, 112: "In terms of content, then, the interjections on the part of the disciples represent an important technical instrument of Johannine gradual hermeneutics. The reader/hearer is to be led from (his) average position to the genuinely Johannine position by the incomprehensible interjections and the corresponding answer of Jesus and thus participate in the Johannine revelation."

47. Corresponding to the riddles and misundersandings in the dialogues of type A (see above):

Saying of Jesus	4:10		4:32	6.5	11:11	13:36d, e	14:4	14:7	16:16
misunderstanding or lack of understanding of the disciples/ dialogue partners	4:11	4:15	4:33	6:7	11:12	13:37	14:5	14:8	16:17f.
Jesus's answer	4:13–14		4:34ff.		11:14	13:38	14:6	14:9	16:19ff.

Only 11:14 offers an explicit solution to the previous riddle!

conception, an understanding of Jesus's words is only possible *after Easter*, as a result of the *Paraclete*'s work of remembrance (14:26). It is therefore consistent that the disciples are portrayed as not yet understanding Jesus within a narrative of the life of the *earthly* Jesus; insofar as they are already given the gift of understanding Jesus's words, however, this means—with regard to the readers of the book—the anticipation of Easter knowledge. On the other hand, the "literary form" of misunderstanding in the dialogues with the disciples makes it clear that an understanding of Jesus's sayings, like faith itself, can *fundamentally* only be understood as a *gift*, as being introduced to all truth by the Paraclete (cf. 16:13).

(2) The first Farewell Discourse in particular reveals another technique for linking the core logia: The evangelist forms *bridging verses* that lead from one theme to another. For example, he adds the sentence "and wherever I go, you know the *way*" to the logion 14:2–3, thus preparing 14:6, 7c, d ("and you have seen him") leads to Philip's request: "Show us the Father . . . !" (14:8), and 14:21 ("and I will show myself to him") initiates Jude's question in 14:22.

(3) Another characteristic feature of the first Farewell Discourse is the technique of the *connecting keywords*.[48] It conveys the impression that one utterance follows from the other and thus emphasizes the inner unity of the entire composition. The evangelist also uses this device in Jesus's dialogues with individual persons, to which we must now turn briefly.

9.2.5 Martha and the Samaritan Woman
Jesus's Dialogues with Individuals (Type E)[49]

In addition to the actual *dialogues between the disciples*, the Gospel also contains conversations between Jesus and *individual* people that at first glance differ in length: While Jesus's conversation with the man born blind after he was thrown out of the synagogue only consists of a brief exchange (9:35–38), the reader witnesses an extended conversation in the scene of Jesus's encounter with a woman at Jacob's well. Throughout, these conversations were formed by the evangelist himself and fit into traditions that were given to him. Thus, he did not invent the characters in the conversation: the Samaritan woman, the man born blind, Martha, and Mary Magdalene. Instead, he invented what these characters now represent in the book. They are living figures with biographical features of a story of faith, and this is mainly due to the evangelist's manner of portrayal. It is perhaps no coincidence that he *did not*, as far as can be seen, make use of his community's tradition of sayings when composing the corresponding

---

48. See, e.g., 14:4, 5 (ὑπάγειν), 10, 11, 12 (ἔργα), etc.

49. On the dialogue with Nicodemus, see p. 366 above; the dialogue with Pilate (John 18), the core of which goes back to the Passion narrative, is a special case, since Jesus is talking to a *gentile* here.

dialogues. For these dialogues, in contrast to those with "the Jews," are impressive examples of a *mystagogy* in which Jesus's interlocutors (the term is not out of place here!) actually experience something like a development, a progression in the knowledge of faith. From this point of view, these texts required a consistent conversational approach, for the literary realization of which the model of interpreting given logia by means of dialogical staging did not lend itself, but rather the attempt, by means of keyword connections, that is, by taking up and recoding a phrase or a term from the respective preceding discourse, to illustrate the process of a Johannine deepening of faith in a scenic dialogical manner. This applies in particular to the Martha-Jesus conversation in John 11:20–27, which can be understood as a compact counterpart to the first Farewell Discourse insofar as it demonstrates the process of the reinterpretation of futuristic-eschatological ideas *behind* John 14 itself *directly* in dialogue. Here the reader witnesses how the author imagined the deepening of common Christian faith: Jesus picks Martha up from her Pharisaic-Jewish conviction of faith,[50] which had also been received by early Christians (man will be raised "on the last day" [11:23–24]) and leads her to the belief that with the one who is "the resurrection and the life" in person (11:25) that "last day" has already dawned: in the middle of history, *in the encounter with him*. Consequently, the conversation ends with Martha's confession of faith, which, according to 20:31, corresponds exactly to the purpose of the book as a whole: "Yes, Lord, I believe (πεπίστευκα) that you are the Messiah, the Son of God, the one coming into the world" (11:27). The encounter with the man born blind, whose eyes Jesus has opened, also leads to a confession about Jesus, the Son of Man (9:35–38). In Jesus's conversation with the woman at the well, the circumstances are more complex: The "literary form" of (riddle) *saying* and *misunderstanding* determines the first part of the dialogue (4:10/11–12; 4:13–14/15), without explicitly resolving the misunderstanding. Jesus also reveals himself to her as the Messiah with his ἐγώ εἰμι saying (4:25–26), without the woman (like the man born blind [9:38] or Martha [11:27] later) responding with her own confession of faith. However, this self-revelation of Jesus then triggers reactions in the woman that not only indicate that she has understood Jesus's saying about the "living water" he gives (4:28 says, "Then the woman left her water jar"). She hurries into the city, functions like a missionary among her fellow citizens until, after Jesus has stayed with them for two days, they finally confess from their own experience, "this is truly the Savior of the world" (4:42). The conversation between the resurrected Jesus and Mary

---

50. John 11:19 is interesting: "And many of the Jews had come to Martha and Mary to *console* them about their brother." What was the content of their comfort? The narrator does not tell us. Since those Jews belonged to the school of Pharisees, it was the belief in the resurrection of the dead "on the last day" that comforted the sisters and which Martha also professes according to 11:24.

Magdalene in 20:14-17 is similar. After initially not recognizing Jesus—"Supposing him to be the gardener" (20:15)—she recognizes him because Jesus calls her by name. She then receives from him the commission to hurry to the disciples to announce Jesus's "ascension" to the Father and thus enters into a dynamic that only reaches its goal in Thomas's confession of faith, "My Lord and my God!" (20:28). One gets the impression that all these conversations adhere to a literary strategy that works toward a deepened *understanding* of faith within its audience and aims to achieve an authentic expression in a conscious confession of faith.

9.2.6 The Johannine Dialogues
A Review

Even though we have distinguished five different types of dialogues according to the respective "interlocutors" of Jesus, this overview shows that it is not possible to make an absolute distinction between the texts of the individual groups. This became particularly clear from the fact that the "literary form" of (riddle) *saying* and *misunderstanding* is encountered in each of them, albeit with different purposes. The other techniques used in the dialogues are also never limited to *one* type. Nevertheless, the structuring of the overall field is helpful, as it not only provides an initial orientation, but also reveals, for example, the continuity with regard to the dialogical text forms of the synoptic tradition: on the one hand, connections with the tradition of the "*disputes*," on the other with that of the *scholastic and doctrinal discussions*. Accordingly, the field of text types in John is ultimately divided into two halves (A—B—C / D—E): Jesus's conversations with his opponents ("Jews," "Pharisees") and those with his confidants or chosen ones. *Tertium non datur!* This means that the conversations with the "Jews who had come to believe" (8:31) clearly belong to the first half of the field.

It is striking how important the "literary form" of riddle and misunderstanding is in *all* types of dialogue. This is reminiscent of the allegorizing tendencies in the parables of the synoptic tradition, for example in Mark 4,[51] with which the separation of outside and inside, of the circle of disciples and the people who do not understand is connected: Thus the "mystery of the kingdom of God" is "given" to some but withdrawn from others (cf. Mark 4:11). One can ask whether the Johannine dialogues, in which the *one* revelator who knows about the heavenly mysteries (3:13) is confronted by people who do not or do not yet know, also come from apocalyptic thought patterns like Mark 4. We can also think of the extended dialogues between the angels who know about God's end-time

---

51. On this see Klauck, *Allegorie*, 259; on the background see pp. 79-84.

plans and the scribe Ezra in the apocalypse of the same name.[52] Admittedly, the eschatological mysteries in John are "de-apocalyptized" and reduced to the *one* mystery of Christ, who says of himself that *he* is the "resurrection and the life." But if essential contents of John's Christology (like the speech about the "Son of Man," of the judgment entrusted to him or of the "resurrection") originate from apocalyptic traditions, then an influence of such contexts on the form of the revelatory dialogues of John cannot be excluded in principle.[53]

All this shows, however, that the Johannine dialogues, as much as they relate to real conflicts of communication that obviously have a traumatic effect on the Johannine community, do not depict them in a one-to-one manner but rather try to process them in many different ways. In the following chapter, we will consider what this looks like in terms of content.

---

52. See U. Schoenborn, *Dialog und Offenbarung. Zur Strategie literarischer Vergewisserung in Krisenzeiten*, Theologie 6 (Münster: LIT, 1996), 15–38, on the topic of "Dialogical interaction and revelation in 4 Ezra." His summary, 38, also sheds light on John: "The dialogue gathers the opponents and leads them on the path from non-recognition to recognition. This path is part of the mystery and therefore proves to be wonderfully irresistible. The special status of the theology of the 4 Ezra is expressed in the fact that revelation enters into dialogical interaction with earthly wisdom/foolishness and that it seeks to win over the reader through ironic disguise."

53. Dodd, *Tradition*, 319–321, rightly drew on individual "dialogues" from the *Corpus Hermeticum* from the perspective of genre history (CH IV 6; X 6f.; XII 15ff.; XIII 1), even though its beginnings lie in the second century at the earliest. Schoenborn, *Dialog*, 39–54 ("Lehrbare Offenbarung. Dialog und Mysterium im hermetischen Traktat 'Poimandes'") analyzes an instructive example. On the gnostic dialogues of revelation, see Schoenborn, *Diverbium*.

CHAPTER 10

The Evangelist's Interpretations of the Words of the Lord
Theological Principles

WHILE THE INDIVIDUAL examinations of the given sayings each led to the question of how the evangelist received and interpreted them, the following is concerned with outlining the theological *principles* that guided him. Much of this can already be found in the summaries of the previous chapters. We can therefore be content here with a few observations and theses on Christology (10.1), its relationship to theology (10.2), and eschatology (10.3).

10.1 Sophia and the Son of Man

(1) As the main author of our book, what would the evangelist be without the communities in which he lived and in which he grew up? When people today like to portray him as a brilliant theologian and outstanding head of a school (M. Hengel), it is all too easy to overlook on whose shoulders he stood. He owes the basic structures of "his" Christology to those who, in the Jewish-Hellenistic milieu, taught to see Jesus as the personified preexistent wisdom of God and also gave lasting expression to their faith in corresponding words of wisdom. The evangelist received these words and was inspired by them in various ways for his theological conception, which should by no means be separated from the form of their *literary* realization. It is precisely *in this*, that is, in the manner of their *narrative* realization, that the originality and greatness of our evangelist should be seen. Here is an example.

The "core logia" of the sequence of scenes in John 7 (*Feast of Tabernacles*)[1] are, as we have seen above in chapter 7, words of wisdom that have transferred the early Jewish myth of the hidden wisdom of God that appeared on earth to Jesus (7:33–34; 7:37–38). The evangelist does not leave it at the recitation of these words. He stages their myth in its entirety with the help of the sequence of scenes in John 7–8 and thus makes it clear that Jesus's claim *and* his appearance, his word *and* his story are *congruent*, indeed that his word is *authenticated* by his personal journey.

---

1. See pp. 261–262.

What is striking about the first scene of chapter 7 is that although the Feast of Tabernacles is just around the corner, Jesus does not want to go up to Jerusalem, contrary to his usual custom, and explains this to his brothers, only to change his mind later when they have gone to the feast. He goes up to Jerusalem "not publicly, but secretly" (v. 10). In the middle of the feast, he then suddenly appears in public—in the temple—to teach there (v. 14). It is obvious that this process—the emergence of Jesus from seclusion at a time determined not by him but by the Father[2]—has a profound meaning. The questions that his behavior triggers among the people of Jerusalem already show this: "Where (ποῦ) is he?" say "the Jews" when he is incognito among them (v. 11). After he has appeared in the temple, they say among the "Jerusalemites" (v. 25): "of this one we know where he is from (πόθεν ἐστίν); but the Messiah, when he comes, no one knows (γινώσκει) *where he is from* (πόθεν ἐστίν)" (v. 27). This objection to Jesus is probably based on a well-known view in Judaism, as Justin's *Dialogue with Trypho* later proves: "Even if the Messiah is born and is somewhere, he is still unknown (ἄγνωστος). Indeed, he himself does not know about himself, nor does he have any power, until Elijah comes and anoints him and makes him manifest to all."[3] A *transcendent* origin of the Messiah is not in view with this idea, nor would it be expected given the profile of Jesus's interlocutors sketched by the evangelist here. Rather, they contrast Jesus's known origin from Nazareth (1:45–46) or Galilee (7:41) with their conviction that the Messiah must be unknown from his birth until his public appearance, thus remaining caught up in an *earthly-human* way of thinking with their criticism of Jesus's claim. Nevertheless, by applying their "doctrine about the Messiah,"[4] they involuntarily confirm Jesus's claim, which of course only the listeners and readers of the book who witness this fictitious "dialogue" understand. For when, following the Jewish objection to Jesus, the evangelist has Jesus himself solemnly "proclaim": "You know me, and you where I am from (πόθεν εἰμί). I have not come on my own. But the one who sent me is true, and you do not know him" (7:28). This means: With your (unquestionable) knowledge of my *earthly* origin, you are only obstructing your view of my *true* mystery, my origin from the "true one." Thus, what the Jerusalemites themselves declared actually applies to this encounter with Jesus: "The Messiah, when he comes, no one recognizes (γινώσκει) where he is from." *They do not* recognize his actual πόθεν and thus confirm the truth of Jesus's claim to the readers and listeners of the book, measured against their own "doctrine about the Messiah." Beyond the question of his *earthly* origin, Jesus's secret lies elsewhere, in the *world of God, from whose concealment he emerges at the time given to him by the Father.*

---

2. John 7:6: "My time has not yet come, but your time is always here."

3. Justin, *Dial.* 8:4; see also 49:1; 110:1; cf. John 1:26; see de Jonge, Expectations 252–256.

4. Schnackenburg, *Johannesevangelium*, 2:203.

This, however, which is also the matrix of Jesus's words of wisdom received in chapter 7, is what the evangelist—according to the plausible explanation for Jesus's incognito journey to Jerusalem and his surprising emergence from obscurity in the middle of the feast—has literally staged in the corresponding sequence of events. Finally, this also includes the narrator's note at the very end of chapter 8, which is linked to John 7 not by the setting of the feast (Feast of Tabernacles) but by the location of Jesus's speeches ("the sanctuary"), which reads: *But Jesus hid himself and went out of the temple*" (8:59b).[5] *Just as the wisdom of God, which finds no acceptance among men, hides itself and returns to its true home, the same applies analogously to Jesus.*

There is also a second point: The Fourth Gospel differs significantly from the Synoptics in that Jesus does not only go up to Jerusalem once for the Passover feast on which he is crucified but goes up to the holy city four times,[6] with the consequence being that a large part of the Gospel narrative takes place in Jerusalem or in the temple. If Jesus repeatedly leaves Jerusalem of necessity in between and still returns to the holy city, then the reader gains the impression that Jesus belongs here as the revealer of God, his Father. Nowhere else is his mission fulfilled but here alone. If one asks why this must be so, then one can of course point to the inner reference of, for example, Davidic messianic expectations in connection with Jerusalem, the heart of Israel. However, closer to the evangelist's conception, which radically transcends such messianologies, is a reminder of the myth of the personified wisdom of God, which takes up residence in the temple: "Then the Creator of all things gave me a command, and my Creator chose the place for my tent. He said, 'Make your dwelling in Jacob, and in Israel receive your inheritance.' Before the ages, in the beginning, he created me, and for all the ages I shall not cease to be. *In the holy tent I ministered before him, and so I was established in Zion. Thus in the beloved city he gave me a resting place, and in Jerusalem was my domain.* I took root in an honored people, in the portion of the Lord, his heritage" (Sir 24:8–12). Is it therefore not obvious that Jesus, as the personified wisdom of God, repeatedly pushes his way into the holy city in order to teach here in the public sphere of the temple,[7] and ultimately also meets his death at its gates? In short, *the evangelist has also taken up the wisdom-theological matrix of the sayings he received*

---

5. Earlier, in 8:59a, it says, "So they picked up stones to throw at him." Compare with Matt 23:37–39; 24:1: "Jerusalem, Jerusalem, the city that kills the prophets and *stones those who are sent to it!* ... See, your house is left to you, desolate.... *As Jesus came out of the temple and was going away.*" See also above p. 366 n. 42.

6. See 2:13; 5:1; 7:10; 12:12.

7. *Teaching* in particular is also a primary task of wisdom (see the evidence in the list by Hunter, *John*, 33–35)!

in a positive way by staging them extensively in his book and thus making them narratively vivid.

(2) Alongside the conviction that Jesus is the *wisdom* of God *in person*, there is the other conviction in the Gospel that he is *the Son of Man*. Both convictions are interlinked in the way they are presented in the book, but each has retained its own profile. Apart from their respective origins in the history of tradition, there is an asymmetry between them in that the wisdom-Christological layer in the book has not received a titular fixation,[8] whereas the Son of Man sayings, some of which are very different, have their common denominator in the title ὁ υἱὸς τοῦ ἀνθρώπου.[9] The Son of Man sayings, which the fourth evangelist probably received from his community's tradition (namely 3:14–15 and 8:28, also bring the conceptual framework that is decisive for the Johannine wisdom sayings. The same applies to the traditional-historical points of adhesion of the Son of Man sayings formed by the evangelist, that is, to the themes "seeing the Son of Man at the end of time" (1:51), "glorification of the Son of Man" (13:31–32), or "judgment" (5:27). It was only the evangelist who fused these themes, which were linked to the end-time dimension of the Son of Man, as well as the Son of Man logia that had come down to him, with the wisdom-based conceptual framework of preexistence and incarnation, and thus made the wisdom-Christological matrix into the basis for other traditions and historical contexts.

In the case of the Son of Man logia and traditions, this was primarily done by linking the title to the descent-ascension scheme (κατάβασις—ἀνάβασις), which, according to E. Ruckstuhl, is based on *early Jewish wisdom* tradition. Ruckstuhl makes a particular case for this in 3:13.[10] And indeed, the *correspondence between* statements of ascent and descent is nowhere as concise as in early Jewish texts, primarily those of wisdom, but there consistently in the order of ascent-descent and in contexts in which, from a consciously adopted *earthly-human* perspective, the question is whether the qualitatively infinite distance between earth and heaven can be overcome by the creature at all. If there can only be a "no" to this question, then these texts focus on the revelation-theological answer (which they also want to promote through this "no") that it is *God alone* who, with the *gift of his wisdom* or his *Holy Spirit*, can overcome the infinite distance between himself and human beings, between earth and heaven, and is also willing to do

---

8. Apart from the prologue, in which the Christ is called ὁ λόγος.

9. This coresponds to the early Christian (synoptic) Jesus tradition as a whole, which does not recognize σοφία as a Christian title in Jesus's sayings but does recognize ὁ υἱὸς τοῦ ἀνθρώπου.

10. E. Ruckstuhl, "Abstieg und Erhöhung des johanneischen Menschensohns" (1975), *Jesus im Horizont der Evangelien*, ed. E. Ruckstuhl, SBA 3 (Stuttgart: Katholisches Bibelwerk, 1988, 277–311, here 290–291, 292.

The Evangelist's Interpretations of the Words of the Lord

so. However, nowhere is this answer brought into the ascent-descent terminology, the elements of which would then have to be *reversed*: Wisdom *descended* from heaven and (as far as the myth of her retreat is concerned) *ascended* to it again. In accordance with their theocentricity, the early Jewish texts prefer inspirational language models[11] or occasionally, as in 1 Enoch 42, speak of the "exit" and "return" of wisdom.

Thus, there is much to suggest that the New Testament discourse of the (Easter) "ascension" of Christ, which probably only in a second step from the point of view of tradition entailed the corresponding discourse of his prior "descent," that is, his incarnation, is a specifically early Christian linguistic model that transformed the original apocalyptic discourse of Jesus's resurrection from the dead into a phrase ("*he* ascended") with cosmic breadth ("he ascended *into heaven*") but also retains Jesus's indestructible subjecthood in death. Acts 2:34, Ephesians 4:8–10, and John 20:17 are witnesses to the independent point of adhesion of Jesus's *anabasis* in the Easter discourse. John 3:13; 6:33, 38, 41–42, 50–51/62 on the one hand and Ephesians 4:8–10 on the other also testify independently of each other to how obvious it was to conclude from Christ's Easter *anabasis* to his previous *katabasis* in his incarnation, that is, to his preexistence. As far as John 3:13 is concerned, the two lines of tradition mentioned previously obviously flow together here: The wisdom insight into the fundamental inability of man to "ascend into heaven," as well as the paschal discourse on *anabasis*, with its specific logic that an "ascent into heaven" necessarily presupposes a prior origin or descent from it. Thus 3:13, as explained above,[12] becomes the decisive omen for 3:14–15, insofar as verse 13 formulated by the evangelist provides the necessary interpretative framework or horizon for the subsequent Son of Man saying in verses 14–15: *The paschal justification of salvation stated in verses14–15 in the path of the Son of Man to the cross and exaltation can only be understood by those who, according to wisdom-based logic, also recognize the original coming of this Son of Man from heaven, that is, his divine nature. Wisdom Christology here becomes the necessity for proper discourse about the Son of Man.*

Furthermore, the reference to the "Son of Man" in the Fourth Gospel refers to the *earthly* Jesus. The background to this is probably the knowledge that in early Jewish tradition, the Son of Man was originally a *heavenly* figure who played a decisive role in the final judgment (Dan 7; 1 Enoch's figurative discourses; 4 Esdras 13). This explains, on the one hand, that *God's heaven opens* above Jesus as the *earthly* Son of Man and, on the other hand, that the evangelist associates

---

11. E.g., Wis 9:17: "Who has learned your counsel, unless you have *given wisdom* and sent your *holy spirit* from on high?"

12. See pp. 116.

his earthly appearance with the execution of the "last things": the execution of judgment on nonbelievers and the final imparting of life to believers.

(3) The Johannine Son of Man sayings (including those already received by the evangelist from his community tradition) are focused on the *interpretation of Jesus's death*, the decisive salvation event in which God commits himself to people and opens the way to life for them (3:14–15; 13:31–32, etc.). It is remarkable how the evangelist specifically interprets logia that have nothing to do with Jesus's death and uses logia that explicitly have him in mind as an opportunity to reflect on him in depth. Here is an example of each.

The saying received in John 7:37–38 originally read something like this: "If anyone is thirsty, let him come to me and drink [of the living water that I will give him . . .]." Jesus in person is the source of eternal life! For the evangelist, it is clear that he has become this through his death and his "glorification" (v. 39d), and so he editorially transforms the saying into a paschal *prophecy*[13] that is fulfilled on the cross (cf. John 19:34). Moreover, in his *commentary* on the saying in verse 39, he hints at how the truth of the "Trinitarian" God shines through in Jesus's death on the cross: Here, in the event of Jesus's glorification *by God*,[14] the *Spirit* is released, which (like the streams of water) gives life. From the body of *Jesus's* death (and nowhere else!) God lets this Spirit spring forth in abundance!

The evangelist offers the wisdom saying in 7:33–34 three times (like Mark's prophecy of suffering and resurrection in Mark 8:31; 9:31; 10:33–34). Each time, in the dialogues that follow, he emphasizes different aspects of the keyword ὑπάγειν and thus circles around the "death" of Jesus announced in the saying: For some it means "dying in one's own sins" (8:21), being lost in absolute remoteness from God; for others it contains a salvific advantage of Jesus before them, the believers, from which they can draw hope and confidence for their own path (13:33, 36, 38; 14:1–31). In this *one* word ὑπάγειν ("go" in 7:33; 8:21; 13:33, 36; 14:4–5) lies the truth of Jesus's death for the evangelist! Yes, it is not too much to say that this is the case: From the opening word of the prooemium (13:33) together with the programmatic sayings of the corpus of the speech (14:2–3), the evangelist developed the magnificent composition of his Farewell Discourse in John 13–14. The theological meditation of these two sayings was the soil from which it grew!

10.2 Christology and Theocentricity

(1) It became clear that a large part of the "words of the Lord" are characterized by a high Christology. In particular, the I-am words testify to the *divinity*

---

13. John 7:38c: "Out of his [Jesus's] body *will* flow rivers of living water."

14. John 7:39d: Ἰησοῦς οὐδέπω ἐδοξάσθη: a *passivum divinum*!

that was attributed to Jesus as the ultimate authentic revelation of God in person. These words themselves do not specify Jesus's relationship to God but leave it in limbo. Their entire emphasis rests on the majesty with which they surround the speaker as the mediator of "eternal life." Other sayings, on the other hand, with their reflections on the "Son" and the "Father," lay the foundation on which their relationship to each other can be understood.[15] However, these words are also consistently characterized by the intention of establishing Jesus's *unique* position in the event of God's revelation of salvation, as Jesus is not just any son for them, but *"the* Son" par excellence, without whom there is no access to the Father (14:6c: "no one comes to the Father except through me"). When the evangelist, in the three passages of his book where the original conflict between the synagogue and Johannine Christians flashes up (the accusation that the latter violated biblical monotheism with their high Christology), each time deals with Jesus's claim to be the Son,[16] then it must have been specifically the sayings about the *Son* they formed that went beyond the (traditional) syntagm *"Son of God"* (υἱὸς τοῦ θεοῦ) and spoke of *"the* Son" in an absolute way, which fueled the quarrel between them and the synagogue.

As far as the evangelist's *reception of* all these words is concerned, this testifies to a high sensitivity for the explosive nature of the topic of *monotheism and Christology.* It is not that Jesus's dialogues with the Jews composed by the evangelist are characterized by the intention of giving an answer to this problem to the *outside world,* to the synagogue. This has undoubtedly had the effect, however, that the evangelist now feels compelled to give an account of Jesus's relationship to his Father, which he does in the firm conviction that the accusation from the synagogue is *not* true. He also sees himself (like all witnesses of the New Testament) as bound to the biblical confession of the "one and only God" (5:44: ὁ μόνος θεός) but understands this (like hardly any other theologian of the New Testament before him) as *the great challenge* to determine Jesus's relationship to his Father more appropriately than before. When he unflinchingly rejects the accusation of the synagogue (especially in 5:19–30), it is primarily for two reasons:

First, he is firmly convinced that Jesus *did not* arrogate his soteriological dignity to *himself,* usurped a "God-like" status *for himself,* so to speak, which would presuppose (as the "Jewish Christians" who remained in the synagogue probably thought) that Jesus could be seen completely adequately as ἄνθρωπος (cf. 10:33: σὺ ἄνθρωπος ὢν ποιεῖς σεαυτὸν θεόν). The latter in particular reveals the basis from which the synagogue (whether on the part of the messianic followers

---

15. See esp. 5:19b–20c!

16. See 5:17–18, 10:33, 36, 19:7.

of Jesus or on the part of the Jews who were distant from Jesus) argued against the Johannine Christians. Second (and this is only the flip side of the reason given in the first place), he would not have accepted the accusation of blasphemy against the "one and only God" because he was firmly convinced that it was this "one and only God" *himself* who "*gave*" Jesus to the people as the "bread from heaven" (3:16; 6:32) and "sent" him into the world. However, if the responsibility for the mission of the "Son" lies with the "one and only God" himself,[17] then the one requires the other: Jesus's high dignity as a Son requires the unsurpassable commitment of the "one God" in his mission, just as, conversely, the commitment of the "one God" in the execution of this mission requires the dignity of the "one sent," his "Son" Jesus of Nazareth. It is precisely because the evangelist thinks radically *from above* in his Christology that he is able to hold together the unity of God and the unique Sonship of Jesus. But how can the evangelist's sensitivity to the problems of *monotheism and Christology* be established in the *reception* of the sayings in detail?

(2) An indicator of the sensitivity is the use of the idea of Jesus as the *messenger of God*, which is not fixed in titles for him, but is omnipresent in the Gospel. It is crucial to note that this idea (a) is consistently expressed verbally (usually in the form of a participle of πέμπω), and that this (b) always has *God* as its subject: "*He who sent me*" (cf. 4:34; 7:16, 28; 8:26, 29 and others) is considered a fully sufficient predication of God in terms of content. This observation is important for the reason that it confirms the observation just made that the evangelist, when he speaks of Jesus's role, is thinking strictly *from above*, that is, from the God who sent Jesus into the world and is therefore *entirely* responsible for him and the work of salvation that took place through him. The fact that the model of "sending into the world" is to be strictly distinguished from the apparently similar model of the sending of prophets is due to the fact that in the Gospel of John it is linked to the language about God "the Father" and Jesus "the Son." The use of the formula can vary semantically in the individual passages: Either it emphasizes Jesus's subordination to the *Father*, "who sent him," and then indicates that Jesus is *what he is* only *through the Father*,[18] or it emphasizes Jesus's majesty in polar opposition to this, which consists precisely in the fact that the "Father sent *him*." The accents can change from passage to passage and are by no means mutually exclusive.

The "omnipresence" of the formula in Jesus's speeches is now an unmistakable sign that it is one of the evangelist's *principles of construction*, with which he has expanded the logia that have come down to him from the tradition of sayings,

---

17. John 3:16: "For *God* (ὁ θεός) so loved the world that he gave (ἔδωκεν) his only Son."

18. E.g., in 5:30.

together with his own material, into the present dialogues and monologues. It is significant, however, that where the idea of Jesus's mission first appears in the Gospel, in 3:17, common Christian mission phraseology is present (cf. Gal 4:4; Rom 8:3; 1 John 4:10, 14). However, the use of the participial mission formula ("he who sent me") obviously goes beyond this and can be considered typical of the evangelist in every respect. In detail, he uses the formula in the reception of the saying as follows:

(a) He inserts them directly into the wording of the logia (e.g., in 5:24; 6:44; 7:33; 9:4). In 9:4, instead of "we must work . . . as long as it is day," it now says "we must *work the works of him who sent me* as long as it is day."

(b) The formula appears in commentary additions to logia, whether such an addition precedes (e.g., in 4:34 the parable 4:35–36) or whether it follows like 6:38 on 6:37: "All that the Father gives me will come to me, and he who comes to me I will not cast out, *for I have come down from heaven, not to do my will, but the will of him who sent me.*" The constellation in 8:28b, c + 28d–29 is similar: It looks as if the commentary addition in verses 28d–29 seems to want to put the divine ἐγώ εἰμι of the given Son of Man saying inspired here by Isaiah 43:10 LXX into the appropriate perspective: "When you lift up the Son of Man, then you will know that I am. *I do nothing on my own initiative, but as the Father has taught me, I speak. And he who sent me is with me. He has not left me alone, for I always do what pleases him.*"

(c) The sending formula or motifs connected with it are used in the wider context of a received logion—for example, in 5:23, 30 (in view of 5:19–20c; 5:24), or in 8:16, 18 (in view of 8:12), or in 8:54 (in view of 8:51/52). Here, as in 5:19–30, the sending formula can even become a macro-syntactic structuring signal, as for example in 14:24 at the end of the passage in 14:15–24 (= second main part in the corpus of the first "Farewell Discourse") before the second and last Paraclete saying in 14:25–26.

(d) Finally, it should be noted that the evangelist naturally also knows other means of theocentric reconnection of Christologically centered sayings beyond the sending formula. The *commentary* in 7:39 discussed above (with its *passivum divinum* ἐδοξάσθη) on the saying in 7:37–38 offers a good example of this.

In short, in his book, the evangelist consistently pursues the intention of placing Jesus's path and words in the authoritative theo-logical horizon. The consistent references to the time or the hour that has not yet come for Jesus, which the Father himself has determined in his sovereignty, are perhaps one of the most emphatic narrative devices he uses: God, the Lord over time, especially over Jesus's time! In this way, Jesus's death in particular, as the decisive vanishing point of the entire book, is placed in the theocentric perspective.

10.3 Christology and Eschatology

It became clear that the vast majority of the "Lord's words" in John's Gospel cannot yet be pinned down to the idea of an "eternal life" already *present* in faith, which is considered typical of the fourth evangelist. The "I am" sayings, for example, speak in the form of a promise of sharing in "life" and thus leave in limbo how the promised life is realized in faith. The promise still recognizes the tension between the "light of life" (8:12) that is already shining now and its holistic gain after death. There are also logia in the tradition of the community, such as the programmatic saying of the first Farewell Discourse in 14:2–3 which, despite the transformation of apocalyptic eschatology that can be observed in it, holds on to the expectation of Jesus's "return" (however conceived).

The situation is different with the saying in 5:24, which can therefore be attributed to the evangelist himself. Due to its formal coherence and conciseness of content,[19] it can be assumed that it already had a life of its own before it was included in the Gospel.[20] It does not originate from the community's treasure trove of traditions but was created by the evangelist as a corrective to it. The reasons for this lie in the way in which the traditional concept of ἔχειν ζωὴν αἰώνιον in verse 24c[21] is made *more precise* by the subsequent parts of the verse (24d, e) and is *defined* in its specific sense:

---

19. This depends in particular on the correlation of v. 24d (does not come into question) and 24e (motif of the *transitus*, the μετάβασις), whereby one wonders where this motif comes from. If we take the following texts for comparison: Jos. Asen. 8:10 ("who called from darkness into light... and *from death into life* [...]"); Ps. Philo, *De Jonah* 153; Luke 15:24, 32; Melito, *Passover* 68 ("it is he who snatched us... out of darkness into light, out of death into *life*."; Const. Ap. 7.39.3, then it follows that with the motif of *metabasis*, the saying ties in with the event of *conversion*, the calling into the *living space* of the congregation, which according to the above texts is understood as the raising of the dead, the transition from death into life. This assumption is confirmed by the fact that shortly before, in v. 21, the evangelist used the predication of God raising the dead and applied it to Jesus, a predication that can also be applied to the "raising" of people for the church: see Luke 3:8 par.; Rom 4:17; Jos. Asen. 20:7, etc.

20. 1 John 3:14 presupposes the saying: "*We know* [how?] that we have passed from death to life (μεταβεβήκαμεν ἐκ τοῦ θανάτου εἰς τὴν ζωήν)"; this knowledge is reinterpreted as follows in the immediately following explanatory sentence: "Because we love the brothers." It cannot be determined whether the author of 1 John took the saying from tradition or from the Gospel.

21. Apart from the occurrence of this phrase in Log. 3:14–15 and 8:12 (here varied to ἔχειν τὸ φῶς τῆς ζωῆς), both ζωὴ αἰώνιον and the phrase ἔχειν ζωὴν αἰώνιον may be regarded as elements of the Johannine sociolect. This is supported by the fact that the combination of ζωὴ αἰώνιον with the verb ἔχειν occurs in all layers of the Corpus Johanneum: see 3:16; 3:36; 5:26, 39, 40; 6:40, 47; 6:53, 54; 10:10; 20:31; 1 John 3:15; 5:12, 13.

The Evangelist's Interpretations of the Words of the Lord 385

24a	Very truly, I tell you	
24b	anyone who hears my word and believes …,	tradition
24c	has eternal life	
24d	and[22] does not come under judgment,	εβηκεν
24e	but has passed (μεταβέβηκεν) from death to life	

With verse 24e, the saying ties in with the ecclesiological experience that conversion and calling into the community are equivalent to a transfer into the space of life in God, a transition from death to life. By correlating this idea with verse 24d, the saying also makes it clear in advance that this *metabasis*, which has already happened for believers, is to be understood in a radically eschatological manner: For the individual, entering God's space of life means that he or she will *not* come into judgment, that is, will not fall prey to judgment. Thus, εἰς κρίσιν ἔρχεσθαι is to be translated here because of the mirror image relationship between verse 24d and e.[23] If θάνατος and κρίσις belong together, then κρίσις is the counterpart to μετάβασις ἐκ θανάτου εἰς τὴν ζωήν, insofar as it holds the person who does not listen to the life-creating word of Jesus in the reality of death and binds him to it eschatologically and definitively. κρίσις therefore does not mean the future last judgment, before whose incorruptible forum the believer need not appear, but which will inevitably arise for humanity at the end of time, but the negatively qualified judgment, which *hic et nunc* befalls those who do not listen to Jesus's word of life.

We *cannot* therefore conclude from the saying that the person who composed it explicitly left room for the early Christian expectation of a general judgment of the dead. If we add the corresponding "teaching" in 3:16–21, which also contains the negative flip side of 5:24 (3:18b: "but those who do not believe are condemned [κέκριται] already"), then we are much more likely to assume that the evangelist radically transformed the traditional idea of judgment by combining it with the ultimately all-decisive great alternative of *believing/not believing*. Here he saw the realization of the reality that is traditionally associated with the future judgment of God: The reality of damnation and death on the one hand and that of salvation and life on the other.

Logion 5:24 is of exemplary significance. It shows where and in what form the evangelist's typically *present* eschatology reveals itself: Wherever the mention

---

22. καί explicativum! Therefore, the phrase should be translated: "He has eternal life, that is: …"

23. What is *not* meant is: "The believer does not come before the *future judgment of God*, no longer has to answer to him (but this itself takes place in any case, as vv. 28–29 show!)." Such an exegetical harmonization of v. 24 and v. 28, which attempts to save vv. 28–29 for the evangelist, fails because of the wording of v. 24.

of "eternal life" is subjected to a critical interpretation, which includes specific eschatological terms such as κρίσις (3:16–21), ἀνάστασις (11:23–27), πάλιν ἔρχεσθαι (14:3), but also entire series of ideas such as that of 5:25 (eschatological hour in which the dead will hear the voice of the Son of God and then live) specify the given concept of life. Such clarifications are signals of a creative process of updating, and as certain as the "word of the Lord" tradition of the Johannine community is open to such a present-eschatological continuation and also accommodates it, it nevertheless represents a new stage.

It is still unclear what factors exactly led the evangelist to his present-eschatological continuation: the experience of disappointed expectations of the near future; the image of *Christuss praesens*, which led to the reorganization of traditional eschatology; "the attitude of the environment in which the Johannine community lived";[24] or perhaps a "paradigm shift" that announced itself in Judaism after the catastrophe of the destruction of Jerusalem. In the wake of that destruction, not only disappointed apocalyptic visions of the future were rejected (because they had indirectly contributed to the catastrophe) but also "salvation" was no longer conceived as the utopian completion of earthly human striving for happiness in a "new aeon." It was instead recognized in its own strictly otherworldly quality that overcomes death. Had a new "general weather situation" come into being, under the auspices of which not only the gnosis was heralded, but also the reorganization of eschatology in the post-Pauline era, for example in Ephesians, Colossians, or Hebrews?

As important as such overarching "spiritual-historical" factors undoubtedly are for the Fourth Gospel, the study of the "sayings" of the book has also shown the importance of the inner factual logic, especially Christology, for the formation of the evangelist's specific eschatological soteriology. In view of certain harmonizing tendencies in recent research, it is important not to blur the *specific* profile of the evangelist. He did not expect a last judgment according to works (5:28–29), and certainly not a judgment of believers. It was not a "last day" as the vanishing point of history that determined his theological thinking, but the Easter day, "that day" (14:20), which always dawns when people encounter the exalted one himself in the word of Jesus as the "resurrection and the life" (11:25). For this reason, he may also have rejected or reinterpreted the early Christian idea of a "return" of Jesus as a worldly event, as John 14 shows, namely as the coming of the exalted one to those who believe. To accuse him of betraying

---

24. According to Schnackenburg, *Johannesevangelium*, 2:543, this is to be brought "strongly into play": "Apart from the confrontation with orthodox Judaism . . . we also repeatedly come across questions that were alive in the Hellenistic world of that time, especially in Gnosticism. The people of that time were fascinated by the question of the meaning of human existence, the whence and whither of their lives, and were driven by the longing for an inner fulfillment of their human existence, an imperishable goal of their earthly path."

the longing of believers for a future full of salvation in favor of the eschatologically fulfilled present, the blissful moment of their encounter with Jesus, is probably an insinuation. Of course, the evangelist's "present" eschatological faith contains hope and confidence in the future, as 11:25–26 in particular shows, but this is not geared toward the expectation of a bodily resurrection of the dead "in Christ" on the "last day" but rather, according to the evangelist, proves itself in dealing with their own death (as the Lazarus narrative illustrates). In other words, for the evangelist, belief in the presence of "eternal life" necessarily includes the conviction that this "life" *does not* evaporate in the death of the individual but rather (in the words of 12:32) that the exalted one "draws believers to himself" from their death.[25] How exactly he imagined this anthropologically, whether he followed the Platonism widespread in early Jewish literature, according to which the soul of the pious returns to God in death, we ultimately do not know, but it is quite possible (if not probable).[26] Significantly, the final redaction of the book in the Johannine circle added an exclamation mark to the text with 6:39c, 40c, 43c, 54b ("and I will raise him up on the last day"), thus indirectly indicating that such a concept was not only in the cards but was also linked to the specific profile of the evangelist. In general, the intention of the redaction in 5:28–29 or 6:39c, et cetera, seems to be wrongly determined if it is said to have as its aim the addition of the *futuristic* dimension of salvation missing in the Gospel. This was and is anchored in the evangelist's conception! Rather, the redactor was concerned with *questions of theological anthropology*: What about the *ethical responsibility* of human beings (5:29: τὰ ἀγαθὰ ποεῖν / τὰ φαῦλα πράσσειν), if participation in "eternal life" is decided exclusively by faith in Jesus? What about the dignity of the *bodily* constituted human being if the hope of a resurrection of the dead on the "last day" is irrelevant? Is not salvation, "eternal life," then shortchanged by a decisive dimension? These are important exclamation marks that the redactors placed in the final text, more questions than answers, as they did not systematically compare their "additions" with the evangelist's conception, but more or less left them to stand on their own. In this way, however, they not only contributed to the acceptance of the book in the community, they also remain a thorn for all its recipients, not to suppress the theological-anthropological questions raised by them, for which the evangelist obviously had no eye, but to work through them "scripturally-theologically."

What is the decisive point that led the evangelist to understand ζωή αἰώνιον in the present-eschatological sense described? It seems to me—and this is already

---

25. 12:32: "And I, when I am lifted up from the earth, will draw all to myself (πάντας ἑλκύσω πρὸς ἐμαυτόν)."

26. See M. Theobald, "Futurische versus präsentische Eschatologie? 534–573.

confirmed by the traditional "saying"—that it is the "category of personal relation and participation" that structures the concept of ζωή in the Fourth Gospel.[27] In other words, the essence of ζωὴ αἰώνιον is the *communion of man with the Father and with the Son*. This can be formulated very differently in the Gospel, as ἔρχεσθαι πρὸς αὐτόν (6:37), ἕλκειν (6:44), πιστεύειν, γινώσκειν (17:3), et cetera. However, the most significant formulation offered by the evangelist himself is found in the first Farewell Discourse: "They who have my commandments and keep them are those who love me; and those who love me will be loved by my Father, and I will love them and reveal myself to them" (14:21).—"Those who love me will keep my word, and my Father will love them, and we will come to them and make our home with them" (14:23). *Fellowship of believers with the Father and the Son as an event of mutual love made possible and sustained by the Spirit of God!* Is this not the root of the experience of a *fulfilled* presence in faith? Is this not also the basis of an unshakeable confidence that such fellowship will endure and endure beyond my own death, indeed that this death loses its drama in view of the already given "communion" (v. 23) of man with the Father and the Son in faith, which is fulfilled as being loved and loved again? Of course, none of this is enthusiasm, but has its basis in a "mysticism" of the Word, the Word *of Jesus*, as we will have the opportunity to see in more detail in the following and final chapter of this book.

---

27. Schnackenburg, *Johnannesevangelium*, 2:438: "The life that a person receives through Christ is not a material endowment or magical power but a divine reality, participation in the life of God, the living Father and the source of all life (cf. 5:26; 1 John 1:2). The believer's possession of life, which is a gift of the Father through the Son (1 John 5:11), brings about *fellowship with the Father and the Son* (cf. 1 John 1:3; 2:23-24; 5:12)" (emphasis mine).

CHAPTER 11

Hermeneutics of "Remembrance"[1]

AFTER ANALYZING THE *formal techniques* used by the evangelist in incorporating the "words of the Lord" into his Gospel (ch. 9) and determining the *basic theological options* that guided him in doing so (ch. 10), we now enter the lowest floor of this building, as it were, with the question of the *hermeneutical framework* that underlies his reception of the "words of the Lord," which supports the other two. We start from the well-founded assumption that the evangelist has actually connected his two Paraclete sayings of 14:15-17 and 14:25-26 with something like a hermeneutical authorization for his handling of the Jesus tradition and that of his community. Before we turn to these two sayings (section 11.2), however, our attention should be drawn to the so-called formula of remembrance (John 2:22; 12:16; 15:20; 16:4; see section 11.1).[2] The aim of these two observations is to understand what the evangelist means by "remembrance."

11.1 The "Formula of Remebrance"

(1) *"Remember the word that I have said to you,* 'Servants are not greater than their master" (John 15:20; cf. 16:4). It is obvious that the author of the second Farewell Discourse has used a formula that contains the following elements: the request to "remember a word (of Jesus)," a subsequent citation formula ("that he spoke"), and the quotation of the "word of the Lord" itself. That it is indeed a

---

1. On this see especially N.A. Dahl, "Anamnesis," *StTh* 1 (1948): 69-95; Mußner, Sehweise, 38-42, 45-51; P. Bonnard, "L'anamnèse, structure fondamentale de la théologie du Nouveau Testament," in *Anamnesis. Recherches sur le Nouveau Testament*, CRThPh 3 (Genf et al.: Faculté de Théologie de Lausanne, 1980), 1-11, here 10-11; H. Weder, "Evangelische Erinnerung. Neutestamentliche Überlegungen zur Gegenwart des Vergangenen," in *Einblicke ins Evangelium* (Göttingen: Vandenhoeck & Ruprecht, 1992), 183-200, here 196-198; Zumstein, *Erinnerung*, 46-61; Dettwiler, *Gegenwart*; J. Schröter, *Erinnerung an Jesu Worte. Studien zur Rezeption der Logienüberlieferung in Markus, Q und Thomas*, WMANT 76 (Neukirchen et al: Neukirchner Verlag, 1997), 462-466.

2. On the texts to be discussed here, see also Cameron, *Traditions*, 91-124; Robinson, History, XXVI, attributes "the discovery of the formula of 'remembering' Jesus's λόγοι" to Rendel Harris (1897) and W. Lock (1897) (the bibliographical references are in XXII, XXIII).

formula is proven by its occurrence in very different literary corpora:[3] in Mark 14:72 par. Matthew 26:75 / Luke 22:61, in the Lukan *Doppelwerk*. In addition, there are texts that only offer the formula in an approximate form, but which presuppose it in its basic form: John 2:17, 22; 12:16; and 14:26 (= E), the two references from the Corpus Catholicum (Jude 17–18; 2 Pet 3:2–3) and Papias of Hierapolis Frg. 2 (Eusebius, *Hist eccl*. 3.39.3),[4] Gospel of Marcion p. 10.4–6,[5] and Epistula Jacobi p. 2.7–15.[6] The fact that several of these texts combine λόγος or ῥῆμα with the genitive κυρίου[7] suggests that the formula originally spoke of "the words of the Lord." This is noteworthy because the fourth evangelist does not use this term, as already observed above (in 2.2.2) and possibly does so deliberately. We will see why below in 11.2. Moreover, the formula seems to have originally taken the form of an imperative ("*remember . . . !*"), which served as a prelude to the tradition(s) subsequently quoted.[8]

The *Sitz im Leben* of the formula can be determined fairly precisely: Since it can no longer be grasped at some point during the second century, it is probably characteristic of that phase of early Christianity in which the tradition was still passed on *orally* despite the fact that the Jesus tradition was already being written down.[9] Passing on the tradition here means "remembering the words of the Lord," which we should certainly not simply imagine as a primordial process, but as a process of transmission in regulated catechetical channels.

---

3. In the following diagrams, the preceding numbers indicate the stable elements of the formula: 1 = terminology of remembrance; 2 = "word(s) of the Lord"; 3 = citation formula; 4 = quotation.

4. "Without hesitation, I will combine for you everything that I have ever learned from the elders and *memorized* (καλῶς ἐμνημόνευσεν) with the interpretations, vouching for its truth. For I did not delight, as most do, in those who speak many words, but in those who teach the truth, nor in those who *keep in memory* (τοῖς τὰς ἀλλοτρίας ἐντολὰς μνημονεύουσιν) *strange instructions*, but those (instructions) given *by the Lord* (παρὰ τοῦ κυρίου) to faith and springing from the truth itself."

5. "Tell us *the words of the Savior which you* [fem, sg.] *remember*—which you know [but] we do not, nor have we heard them" (Robinson, CGL III 461).

6. "[When] all the twelve disciples sat together at the same time and remembered the things which the Savior had said to each of them, whether in secret or in public, and arranged them in books." The theme of "remembrance" runs through the whole of work: see p. 3.12; 5.33; 12.35.

7. Luke 22:61; Acts 11:16; 20:35; 1 Clem 13:1–2; 46:7–8; Polycarp, *Phil*. 2:3; Papias Frg. 2.

8. Imperative are Luke 24:6; John 15:20; 16:4; Jude 17; 2 Pet 3:2; 1 Clem 13:1–2; 46:7–8; Polycarp., *Phil*. 2:3.

9. See Cameron, *Traditions*, 92, on Ep. Jas.: "This term (s.c. 'remembering') was employed in the early church to describe the process of creating, collecting, and transmitting sayings of Jesus."

If the formula in the Corpus Johanneum is used by both the evangelist and the redactor, then this is a further signal among many others that indicate the existence of a living "word of the Lord" tradition in the Johannine community.

(2) The Johannine use of the "formula of remembrance" shows its profile when seen against the background of its other uses, to which we must therefore briefly turn in the following.

	Luke 22:61	Luke 24:6–7	Luke 24:8
1	Then Peter remembered (ὑπεμνήσθη)	remember (μνήσθητε)	they remembered (ἐμνήσθησαν)
2	the word of the Lord,	how he told you …	his words
3	how he had said to him,	with the words	
4	"Before the cock crows …"	…	

Acts 11:16	Acts 20:35
he remembered (ἐμνήσθην)	remembering (μνημονεύειν)
the word of the Lord (τοῦ ῥήματος τοῦ κυρίου),	the words of the Lord Jesus (τῶν λόγων τοῦ κυρίου Ἰησοῦ),
how he said,	for he himself said,
John baptized …	It is more blessed …

In Lukan material, it is a specific event that triggers the disciples' memory of an earlier word spoken by the Lord because it is fulfilled or comes true in this new event. After Peter's threefold denial of Jesus, the cock crows. "The Lord turns and looks at Peter." He then remembers Jesus's words: "Before the cock crows today, you will deny me three times!" (Luke 22:60–61).—On Easter Sunday, it is the "men in brightly shining garments" who remind the women at the empty tomb of Jesus's promise of resurrection, which is now being fulfilled on the third day (Luke 22:6–7). It says, "And they remembered his words" (Luke 24:8). Remembrance here means becoming aware of the truth of the promise.—In the house of Cornelius, Peter told the Jerusalem community, he remembered the word of the Lord: "John baptized with water, but you will be baptized with the Holy Spirit" (Acts 11:16). Why did he remember this in the house of Cornelius? Because it was there that exactly what that word announced took place: When he began to proclaim the good news of Jesus, "the Holy Spirit fell on them (i.e., the gentiles) as on us (i.e., the Jews) at the beginning" (Acts 11:15). Accordingly, it is the progression of history guided by the Spirit of God that confirms the words of the Lord. Remembering them *does not* happen at human initiative but is triggered by events in which the Spirit of God is at work.—Acts 20:35 is a case in point. Just as *Peter* was able to remember a "word of the Lord" at a decisive fork in the road of the book (Acts 11:16), Luke also put a "word of the Lord" into the mouth of "his" *Paul* in an extremely important scene—his farewell to the "elders of the church" in Ephesus—at the very end of his speech to them: "It is more blessed to give than to receive." It is not without reason that the formula here is in the plural (λόγοι τοῦ κυρίου): "You know for yourselves that I worked with my own hands to support myself and my companions. In all this I have given you an example that by such work we must support the weak, remembering *the words of the Lord Jesus.*" (Acts 20:34–35). According to this, Paul himself is a living memorial of the memory of Jesus thanks to the way he lived his life, which brought to light the essence of Jesus's message: "to care for the weak."

	1 Clem 13:1–2	1 Clem 46:7–8	Poly. *Phil.* 2:3
1	most of all let us remember (μεμνημένοι)	remember (μνήσθητε)	remembering (μνημονεύοντες)
2	the words of the Lord Jesus (τῶν λόγων τοῦ κυρίου Ἰησοῦ), which he spoke as <u>he taught</u> [...]:	the words of Jesus our Lord (τῶν λόγων Ἰησοῦ κυρίου ἡμῶν),	
3	For he said this,	for he said,	what <u>the Lord</u> (ὁ κύριος) said as <u>he taught</u>,
4	"Show mercy, that you may receive mercy..."	"Woe to that man..."	"Do not judge..."

The formula is found in the Apostolic Fathers independently of any events as a trigger for remembrance, namely in a purely paraenetic sense. "Above all, *let us remember the words of the Lord Jesus* (μεμνημένοι), *which he spoke*, teaching meekness and longsuffering. *For he said*, 'Have mercy, that you may find mercy. Forgive, that you may be forgiven. As you do, so shall it be done to you. As you give, so shall it be given to you. As you judge, so shall kindness be shown to you. With the same measure with which you measure, so shall it be measured to you'" (1 Clem 13:1–2; see also 46:7–8; Polycarp, *Phil.* 2:3). According to this text, "remembrance" means having the words of Jesus, in particular the core of his message, the Sermon on the Mount, before our eyes every day as a guideline for our own lives, and in concrete terms this means living according to the words of Jesus.

	Jude 17–18	2 Peter 3:1–3
0	but you, beloved,	... beloved ...
0		in them I am trying to arouse your sincere intention by reminding you (ἐν ὑπομνήσει)
1	must remember (μνήσθητε)	that you should remember (μνησθῆναι)
2	the words (τῶν ῥημάτων)	the words (ῥημάτων) spoken in the past by the holy prophets, and the commandment of the Lord (τοῦ κυρίου) and Savior.
	of the apostles of our Lord (τοῦ κυρίου ἡμῶν) Jesus Christ;	
3	for they said to you,	First of all you must understand this,
4	"In the last time...."	that in the last days ...

The formula has a special application in Jude 17–18. Here, it does not introduce a "word of the Lord" but an early Christian prophecy, which (like the "words of the Lord") probably comes from oral tradition: "At the end of time there will be mockers who are guided by their ungodly desires; they will destroy the unity, for they are earthly-minded people who do not possess the Spirit."[10] This prophecy traces the preceding formula back to the apostles, who derive their authority from the fact that they are "apostles of *our Lord Jesus Christ*." It is not for nothing that the sovereign title κύριος appears here from the basic form of the formula. While in Jude 17–18 it still retains its original character as a sign of living oral tradition, in 2 Peter, which used Jude, it has been transformed into a "dogmatic" form (2 Pet 3:2–4). The subject of "remembrance" there is now: (a) the "words proclaimed in advance" of the "holy prophets," that is, the Old Testament interpreted in Christian terms (see also 2 Peter 1:19–21), and (b) the "instruction of the Lord" as handed down by the apostles. "Remembrance" (2 Pet 3:1: ὑπόμνησις) therefore means the conscious commitment of faith to the prophetic testimony of the Old Testament and the word of Jesus, which both agree with one another. Even if 2 Peter applies this specifically to the pending question of the delay of the parousia (v. 3: "recognizing this *first*"), the text already gives an outline of what will later make a career as a "scriptural argument." This introduces the most important applications of the "reminder formula." These are not unilinear but exhibit a certain breadth that is related to the individual interests of the authors who received them.

(3) What characterizes the use of the "reminder formula" in the Fourth Gospel?

---

10. See 2 Tim 3:1–5; also Acts 20:29–30; 1 Tim 4:1–2.; 1 John 2:18–19.

	John 2:17	John 2:22	John 12:16
0		After he was raised from the dead,	but when Jesus was glorified,
1	His disciples remembered (ἐμνήσθησαν)	his disciples remembered (ἐμνήσθησαν)	then they remembered (ἐμνήσθησαν)
2			
3	that it was written,	that he had said this	that these things had been written of him and had been done to him
4	"Zeal for your house will consume me."	(v. 19: temple word)	
2		and they believed the scripture and the word that	
3		Jesus (ὁ Ἰησοῦς) said.	

First, it is noteworthy that it is nowhere found in its presumed imperative basic form (*"remember . . ."*) but (as is usually the case in Luke[11]) as a note by the narrator: "Then his disciples remembered." The term λόγος κυρίου is also missing in the evangelist. Instead, the formula in John 2:22 and 12:16 is linked to a temporal clause that indicates *when* the disciples' memory was revived: "when Jesus was raised from the dead" (2:22) or "had been glorified" (12:16). As in Luke, the disciples' memory is therefore not the result of a process of reflection based on their own spiritual impulses but was rather triggered by an event—not just any event but the event itself: the raising of Jesus from the dead (as it says in 2:22 at the beginning of the Gospel in traditional early Christian terminology) or his "glorification" (as the evangelist says in his own language in 12:16 toward the end of the first large main part of his book [chs. 1–12]). In contrast to Luke, the evangelist's event structure of remembrance is *not* related to *various* events of salvation-historical significance (such as the announcement of the angels in the empty tomb or the "Pentecost" of the gentiles in Cornelius's house) but is exclusively related to the basic Easter event of Jesus's exaltation and glorification. The fact that 2:17/22 and 12:16 are indeed of fundamental importance for the concept of "remembrance" can be seen from the fact that these are not just two random passages but a deliberately composed *inclusio* with which the evangelist has linked the first half of his book (chs. 1–12). This is also confirmed by a survey of the content to which the memory extends here.

---

11. Only in Luke 24:6 does the third evangelist offer the basic imperative form.

In contrast to the other uses of the "formula of remembrance," the evangelist shows an astonishing expansion of its scope: It refers not only to Jesus's words (2:22) but (as in 2 Pet 3:2) also to Scripture (2:17 [Ps 69:10], 22; 12:16 [Zech 9:9]) and, third, to events in Jesus's life such as his so-called entry into Jerusalem (12:12–15). This expansion corresponds to the observation that 2:17/22 and 12:16 bracket the *entire* narrative context of Jesus's public activity: *Accordingly, the object of the Easter "remembrance" is Jesus's activity in word and deed as a whole, yet this is not seen in isolation, but read and interpreted in the light of "Scripture."*

According to the texts of the evangelist, remembering Jesus is only ever possible post-factum, namely *post-factum resurrectionis*. It means understanding facts—Jesus's words and events from his life—in the light of Scripture, which was still unthinkable before Easter. It is unclear why the following connection applies: ὅτε ἐδοξάσθη ὁ Ἰησοῦς τότε ἐμνήσθησαν. Is this merely the designation of a temporal connection (ὅτε—τότε) or is more meant? Are there also causal connections and what kind are they?

(4) Before we turn to this question, let us take a brief look at the two texts from the redaction: 15:20 and 16:4:

	John 15:20	John 16:4
0		But I have said these things to you so that when their hour comes
1	remember (μνημονεύετε)	you may remember (μνημονεύετε)
2	the word	
3	that I said to you,	that I told you about them.
4	"Servants are not greater than their master."	

Here, too, it is confirmed once again that the second (and third) Farewell Discourse follows a different theological concept than the first. First, the fact that the second discourse concludes with the "formula of remembrance" testifies to its significance: *"But I have said these things to you so that when their hour comes you may remember that I told you about them"* (16:4a, b). The hour whose coming will evoke the memory of Jesus's words is *not* the hour of Jesus's exaltation and glorification (cf. only 12:23) but the hour of those who will exclude Jesus's disciples from the synagogue.[12] "Remembrance" does not mean that Jesus's words are

---

12. 16:2: "Indeed, an hour is coming when those who kill you will think that by doing so they are offering worship to God."

only *now being understood*; rather, its purpose is to give comfort, to strengthen faith in the one who has already foreknown everything, and thus to release forces that allow us to resist challenge and doubt.

In 15:20, the "formula of remembrance" marks the beginning of the so-called traditions of persecution. This text also has its own character. It is remarkable that it is the only place in the Gospel where the formula appears in its *basic form*. Moreover, it only appears here (and in 16:4) in the New Testament in the mouth of Jesus. The post-Easter formula has therefore been projected back from the catechesis as its original *Sitz im Leben* into the life of the earthly Jesus. The fact that it is the departing Jesus (not the exalted one) who encourages the disciples in 15:20 to remember his word shows once again that, according to the conception of the second Farewell Discourse, "remembrance" is not specifically linked to the Easter event of Jesus's glorification—in complete contrast to the evangelist's view!

11.2 The Concept of the "Paraclete" as a Hermeneutic Framework for the Interpretation of the "Words of the Lord" by the Evangelist

We have saved the decisive text of the evangelist on the question of "remembrance" for the reason that we can only really understand it when we see that it is, so to speak, a "metatext" for the "formula of remembrance" and is also likely to have been its genetic origin. We are talking about the second Paraclete saying in 14:25–26 which reads as follows:

25 a   I have said these things to you
    b   while I am still with you.
26 a   But the Paraclete,
    b   the Holy Spirit,
    c   whom the Father will send in my name,
    d   will teach you *everything*,
    e   and remind (ὑπομνήσει) you of *all*
    f   that I have said to you."

The substance of the "formula of remembrance" can be grasped in verse 26e, f: "*He will remind you of all that I have said to you.*" However, at the end of Jesus's Farewell Discourse, as in the time of his earthly ministry, it is no longer just about a single saying that is to be remembered, but the memory of Jesus now begins to emerge as a whole. That is why it is also pointedly said twice: "He will teach you *everything*, and remind you of *all* that I have said to you."

But when Jesus becomes a fact of history and the memory of him begins to take shape as a whole from a distance, then at first glance this may appear to be an achievement of human memory. For the evangelist, however, it is not! So he has "his" Jesus announce a successor or representative for the time after his death, called a "paraclete" (= "counselor"), who is responsible for precisely this: to evoke in the disciples the memory of him, that is, everything *he* said, and to keep it alive among them. Therefore, when it says in the Easter "prologues" of 2:17, 22, and 12:16 that "the disciples *remembered*," this only scratches the surface of what actually happens after Easter. In truth, it is the Spirit of God, sent at Easter by the Father in the name of Jesus, who makes it possible for the disciples to remember in the first place, indeed who himself is the *subject* who reminds the disciples of everything Jesus has said.

The condition of possibility for this has already been articulated in the first Paraclete saying in 14:16–17. It provides the connecting centerpiece between the "outside" of the Easter "prolepses" (2:17, 22; 12:16) "*the disciples* remembered" and the deep vision of 14:26 "*the Paraclete*... will remind you of everything." This middle section reads: "He (s.c. the Paraclete) abides with you, and he will be *in you*" (14:17e, f). In other words: Because the Paraclete or the Holy Spirit *does not remain external to* the disciples but rather animates them *from within*—indeed "will be *in them*." It follows that the Easter experience, which reads "*the disciples* remembered," is nothing other than the realization of the prophecy of Jesus: "*The Paraclete* will remind you of everything"! So we can also say that the post-Easter "assistance," the Holy Spirit, is the "*power of* remembrance"[13] given by God himself in the name of the departing Jesus, who not only *makes* Jesus *present* to his own against all human forgetfulness but also brings him close to the *understanding* of his own in the act of making him present—as the Easter "prolepses" 2:17, 22 and 12:16 show. *The power of remembrance therefore also means the power of internalization, which includes becoming familiar with the words of Jesus.*

To what extent does this concept of the "Paraclete" also contain the hermeneutical framework for the evangelist's interpretation of the "words of the Lord"? The starting point is the observation that, in the opinion of the evangelist, there is *identity* and *non-identity* between the actions of the "Paraclete" and those of the earthly Jesus. The *non-identity* between the two is based on the fact that, alongside Jesus, the Holy Spirit is the "*other* Paraclete" (14:16), his successor, who will inaugurate a *new* way of διδάσκειν, a "teaching" *distinct* from Jesus's λαλεῖν: "*I* have said these things to you while I am still with you. But the Paraclete... will teach you everything, and remind you of all that I have said to you"

---

13. Weder, "Erinnerung," 196; on p. 197 he states that "the Paraclete is the paschal memory of the man Jesus made flesh."

(John 14:25–26). When Jesus has gone, the Paraclete has the floor. On the other hand, he appears like the "double" of Jesus:[14] Just as Jesus can be called "counselor" (14:16; 1 John 2:1), so can he; just as his activity was "teaching," so is his. However, the image of the "double" does not yet capture the whole truth. For the Paraclete will teach nothing other than what Jesus *himself* said. In terms of the content of the teaching, there is therefore *identity*. Formally speaking, the post-Easter teaching inaugurated by the Paraclete may be something *new* and *different from* what Jesus said, but in substance the *same thing is being said* in each case. Indeed, it must be said that the Paraclete gets to the heart of what Jesus said *and meant*, bringing its fullness of meaning to light, so that Jesus's teachings only come into their own in the teaching of the Paraclete.[15] The *identity* between them is therefore meant to be *historical and dynamic*, not static, which is ultimately due to the fact that Jesus's death stands between the two. While Jesus's teachings are *prospectively* oriented toward his death, his going to the Father is the *vanishing point* of all his teaching, the "Paraclete" comes from this event in the first place: It is the Paraclete's sense of salvation that is authentically unlocked and brought to expression in the memory of Jesus's words. Finally, if one asks how the second Paraclete's saying distributes its weight in the dialectic of identity and non-identity, then the answer can be found in verse 26f ("all that *I* [ἐγώ] have said to you") and can only be: his interest is the *preservation of Jesus's identity*. He opposes an emancipation of the post-Easter spirit from the *way of Jesus*, but thus also a spirit-led wisdom or gnosis that loses its ground underfoot: by relativizing the *basic* historical *event of Jesus's death and exaltation*.

An answer to the question as to why the "words of the *Lord*" are not mentioned anywhere in the Fourth Gospel has not been found before now. We can give an answer now. It should be noted in advance that the respectful and honorific form of address κύριε toward Jesus is quite common in the mouths of the disciples and also others in the Gospel;[16] the evangelist, however, *never* speaks of Jesus as the κύριος before Easter—only in 4:1, 6:23, and 11:2, where, however, there are very probably later additions by the redactor. The situation is different in John 20, that is, in the account of the Easter appearances of the exalted one. Here the evangelist suddenly says that the disciples have seen "the Lord" (20:20; cf. 20:2, 18), and above all the scene with Thomas leads to his

---

14. Zumstein, *Erinnerung*, 56–57.

15. The fact that in 14:26 the function of "remembering" is preceded by that of "teaching" means that "remembering" does not merely mean recalling the past, bringing it to mind, but bringing to understanding what was previously not understood. The καί between the two verb phrases can also be interpreted epexegetically: "He will teach you everything, *that is*, remind you of everything."

16. See, for example, 4:11, 15, 19, 49; 5:7; 6:34, 68; 9:36, 38; 11:3, 12, 21, 27, 32, etc.

confession: "My Lord and my God!" (20:28). According to this, it seems that ὁ κύριος had a special *paschal* resonance for the evangelist (as well as for Paul and the formation of early confessions in general). Is this the reason he avoided speaking of the "words of the *Lord*"? For he was firmly convinced—as we have seen—that the Paraclete recalls *nothing other* than the words of the *earthly* Jesus, in other words the "words *of Jesus*"! Therefore, speaking of "words of the *Lord*" or the phrase "*the Lord* spoke" would not have fit into his concept.

However, the above considerations now also make it clear to what extent 14:16–17 and 25–26 actually contain the *hermeneutical framework for the* evangelist's (and his congregation's) approach to the tradition of Jesus's words. This tradition is also characterized by the dialectic of identity and non-identity. *An antiquarian approach to the words of Jesus was alien to the Johannine community*. They would never have dreamed of merely repeating them in their original wording. If they, like no other early Christian community, had the courage to say the words of Jesus *anew*—using the whole range of possibilities available to them!—then it is on the contrary an expression of the fact that they were deeply convinced of their *lasting* relevance: *Jesus had not spoken his words to his contemporaries alone (and not primarily). Rather his words are actually* for *people here and now*! For the evangelist, faithfulness to the words of Jesus therefore also included the need to "translate" them and make them transparent to the questions and needs of his own congregation. However, he knew that he was legitimized to do this by the Paraclete, the guarantor that the exalted Jesus would also be present in his own time. If *he*, the Paraclete, says the words of Jesus anew—recalling them—then he also legitimizes the process of producing the words of Jesus, as analyzed here. All this required the development of a pneumatology, a challenge that the fourth evangelist (and with him the Johannine school) also recognized. He took up this challenge by not allowing the experience of the Spirit to slide into the nonbinding in a charismatic, rapturous way, but on the contrary, by linking it precisely with the performance of the presence of Jesus, his work and his words. Therefore, the Johannine tradition of the "words of the Lord" may have obtained its own and new character, but the evangelist knew that their *identity* with the intention of *Jesus* was founded *in the work of the Spirit*.

11.3 "Remembrance" as a Creative Process of Understanding in the Gospel of John
Summary and Outlook

We can spare ourselves a list of the results at the end of our study. In continuation of what has just been said, we will now only highlight a few points that reveal the significance of the Johannine conception for the church and for theology today.

11.3.1 The Precarious Situation of "Remembrance"

It is certainly no coincidence that the Lukan history and the Gospel of John, two "late works" from the second early Christian generation, show clear traces of reflection on the theological significance of "memory." In view of the profound ruptures in tradition that had already taken place and were still emerging—especially those associated with the painful process of the congregation's separation from the synagogue—it was important to maintain continuity with the origins of Jesus's life and with the apostolic generation and to reflect on the right way to "remember" the beginning. Different constellations could arise in the process.

In the Lukan *Doppelwerk*, one has the impression that its author wrote the work because he wanted to use a historical account of the process of the congregation's separation from the synagogue to establish the memory of its origins for his addressees—that with his account of how the church grew beyond Israel, he wanted to instill in the *gentile Christian* communities a lasting memory of its standard-setting origins: the *memory of the church's essential rootedness in Israel*. His concern was to write against gentile Christian forgetfulness!

The fourth evangelist did not have this problem. He was preoccupied with the exact opposite constellation: an oppressive, overpowering memory, the *trauma of the exclusion of his congregation from the synagogue*, which wanted to be "worked through" humanly but above all theologically.[17] As a means to this end, he wrote the Gospel of John in which he recounted Jesus's past in such a way that it became transparent in relation to his own present and its problems, specifically the separation of church and synagogue. He hoped that this would have a special effect on the readers of his book: that they would want to recognize in it the deeper meaning of their *own* path, which had not led them out of the synagogue without pain.

Everyone knows how precarious "memory" is. If the past is burdensome or tainted with guilt, it is repressed and consigned to oblivion. If we hope to gain something from it for the present, we glorify it and make it subservient to our own interests. The mechanisms of ideologizing and functionalizing the past tend to work so perfectly in all areas that we deeply distrust the human ability

---

17. The decisive reason for the synagogue committee—according to an important *result of* our study—lay in the high Christology, as represented not only by the evangelist but already by the "words of the Lord" of the Johannine tradition. The Johannine believers in Jesus probably still hoped to be able to convince their Jewish fellow citizens of their own way of faith, as did the messianic Jesus-believing Jews with their deficient Christology (cf. pp. 366–368 above); only the exclusion from the synagogue dashed these hopes. In contrast, the evangelist endeavors to demonstrate the inner necessity of his own faith in Christ and to defend it against false accusations and misunderstandings, not in an apology *to the outside world*, but to reassure his own congregation *internally*.

to "remember." It is also against this background that John 14:26 needs to be read, and then the Johannine point of the inclusion of the past begins. The point of the inclusion of the human phenomenon of "memory" in the Gospel begins to shine brightly.

The meaningful remembrance of the life of Jesus and especially of his death as an *approach to the Father* is *not* a human achievement but a profound *gift* of the Holy Spirit, a *gift* of the Paraclete. Man could not bring this past back into his memory on his own, let alone understand it. *Remembering* must be given to him. Otherwise, the living presence of Jesus's words is not possible.

11.3.2 Increase in Meaning *post factum resurrectionis—in infinitum*? The Transition of Prophecy into the Gospel as Scripture

Despite all the mistrust of human memory that has just been expressed, it is important to bear this in mind: As a rule, historical events only reveal their fullness of meaning post-factum, at a distance from the collective and individual memory, and even then their meaning cannot be unilaterally and definitively established or guaranteed, but remains dependent on interpretation: *The events of the past move along with the people who remember them, as it were, and, depending on the capacity of those who view them and the contexts in which this happens, the events reveal very different sides of themselves.* This also applies analogously to the process of "remembrance" as described by the evangelist and as documented in his book with the additions by the redactors, the literary reflection of the diverse processes of relecture in the Johannine community.

"The constitutive past" of Jesus's life reveals its meaning "not by itself." "It is the subject of an illuminating retrospective that crystallizes in the *turning point at Easter*." "The past only becomes faith-constituting in retrospect, its meaning lies before it, so to speak." This means that "remembering does not simply consist of holding immovable and accomplished facts in memory, but of placing them in a perspective that allows their true meaning to be discovered."[18]

It is from such a perspective that the "words of the Lord" in the Johannine tradition were initially formed. Then followed Jesus's great monologues and dialogues, to which the evangelist adds the "words of the Lord" as core sayings and points of crystallization. Finally, some of these have also been echoed, such as the "bread of life discourse" in John 6 in 6:51c–58, or the first Farewell Discourse in John 13:31–14:31, in the other Farewell Discourses in John 15–16, and in Jesus's "high priestly prayer" in John 17.

---

18. Zumstein, *Erinnerung*, 55. Mußner, Sehweise, rightly spoke of the Johannine "act of seeing" as a "creative process" (43).

J. Zumstein sums up these processes as follows: "Remembering expands the past, allows it to grow and deepens its meaning."[19] At the same time, he recognizes a "potential for crisis" in this "multiplication of memory," which, according to him, lies in the fact that the different interpretations to which the remembered past entitles us "compete" with each other, even compete against each other, thus triggering a "conflict of interpretation." In fact, the Gospel caused such a conflict "with the juxtaposition of different readings. Its ambiguity favored the emergence of different views within the Johannine congregations. Each of them could justifiably refer to the Gospel." Thus, the Johannine school was finally confronted with the necessity "to take a stand on the 'correct' interpretation of the testimony given by the evangelist about the past." According to Zumstein, "*This regulative interpretation of memory* is found in 1 John, a document that provides a kind of commentary on the Gospel and reveals the canon of its reading."[20] Or to put it another way, "Memory owes it to itself to specify what it remembers."[21]

As correct as the understanding of 1 John as a commentary on the Gospel is, one must not overlook the fact that its last redaction was already guided by the intention of transforming the theological openness of the book into unambiguity at important points.[22] The "conflict of interpretation" in the Johannine congregations rightly diagnosed by Zumstein was *not triggered* by the rereading of the redaction but *preceded* it. Thus, in truth it only provided the *basis for* the final redaction of the book.[23] In addition, the book as a whole, as it presents itself in its final form, claims to be *authoritative Scripture* (20:30–31; 21:24–25), which, according to its opening in John 1:1 ("In the beginning was the Logos..."), which surpasses Genesis 1:1 ("In the beginning God created..."), places itself alongside the Scriptures of Israel, indeed sees itself as superior to them as *the* scriptural document that unlocks the Torah. In this respect, it has *itself* already *broken off* the process of its redactional updating, definitively forbidding it in order to admit only listeners and readers who are open to encountering in it the word of Jesus authentically presented by the "Paraclete" and thus Jesus himself.

---

19. Zumstein, *Erinnerung*, 59.

20. Zumstein, *Erinnerung*, 59.

21. Zumstein, *Erinnerung*, 60.

22. E.g., in the theological anthropology, see above p. 386–387.

23. This was no longer about the traumatic relationship of the Johannine congregations to the synagogue or to the messianic Jews there. Theobald, *Fleischwerdung*, 298–300; M. Theobald, "Häresie von Anfang an? Strategien zur Bewältigung eines Skandals nach Joh 6,60–71," in *Ekklesiologie des Neuen Testaments*, FS K. Kertelge (Freiburg: Herder, 1996), 212–246, here 240–241.

The "words of the Lord" in the Johannine community, born of prophetic spirit, have thus become *Scripture* itself as the "core sayings" of Jesus's speeches in the Gospel.

11.3.3 Outlook

The Fourth Gospel should not be idealized. It obviously has its theological limitations, which should be taken into account unvarnished. In particular, its Christologically narrow understanding of the Holy Scriptures of Israel shows a onesidedness that can no longer be accepted in a biblical theology today.[24] Also, as we have seen, the depiction of the "Jews" in Jesus's dialogues is so shaped by the contemporary perspective and our own traumatic experiences that the corresponding statements of the Gospel (John 8!)—also in view of their disastrous reception history over the centuries—require a highly sensitive approach in our time. None of this needs to be discussed further here.[25] Instead, the actual heart of the book should be presented once again at the end. It is a fascinating project on Christ that possesses all its "shocking" greatness (Dietzfelbinger) in the simple and fundamental insight that this *Christus praesens* must speak *anew* in every age:

> This is the place of the Paraclete. As the continuator of Jesus in the post-Easter era, he brings Jesus to speak at a new level and in a new time. He leads us into the truth of Jesus in each new situation. This is a previously unknown truth (16:12); therefore it cannot be expressed with an earlier, traditional word of Jesus; it requires a new word that is valid and appropriate today. As decisively as the word of the Paraclete is the word of Jesus, so decisively must the Paraclete speak this word anew.[26]

In the Gospel of John, this program is implemented in an exemplary manner. Yes, one would say with a great deal of courage and not without provocation. At any rate, numerous generations of theologians since the Enlightenment have felt this way when they have repeatedly rubbed their eyes in amazement and asked

---

24. Walter, Problematik, 344: "not every form of scriptural use in the New Testament is theologically sufficiently legitimized simply by the fact that it exists, indeed that it is occasionally pursued with emphasis"; see also Theobald, "Schriftzitate," 361–366.

25. See the anthology by R. Bieringer, D. Pollefeyt, and E. Vandecasteele-Vanneuville, eds., *Anti-Judaism and the Fourth Gospel: Papers of the Leuven Colloquium 2000*, JCHS 1 (Leiden: Brill, 2001).

26. Dietzfelbinger, *Johannesevangelium*, 2:169 (emphasis original).

the question: Did the historical Jesus really speak the way the fourth evangelist portrays him, so completely different from what we read in Mark, Matthew, and Luke? Now this offense must not be reduced to the historical question, as is usually the case, but must also be taken seriously as a *theological* provocation. What does it mean and what consequences does it have for theology and the church that the fourth evangelist and his community *did not* maintain an antiquarian relationship to the words of Jesus, his message, but rather endeavored to find the "new word, the word that is valid and appropriate today" (Dietzfelbinger)?

As we have seen, the Johannine "words of the Lord" are anything but the result of *creato ex nihilo*, so to speak. Rather, they are based on synoptic sayings, take up leitmotifs of Jesus's message (discipleship), continue genres of the synoptic tradition (pastoral parables), understand themselves as metatexts to synoptic logia (the door saying) and strive to break new ground in all of this. In connection with this, however, important, even central themes of Jesus's message (such as the kingdom of God) are filtered out of the stream of tradition or transformed. Entirely new structures emerge. A world of "words of the Lord" grows up, allowing an image of Christ to emerge before the eyes of the observer that bears unmistakable features: the icon of the Son of God on the golden ground of the divine, which becomes epiphanic in him, radiant with light. What are the reasons for such "spiritual" creativity?

Of course, one can cite various factors here, for example the Jewish-Hellenistic milieu of the Johannine community, as we have seen above, especially through comparisons with the oeuvre of Philo of Alexandria. This is related to the specific discourse of the transcendent God who is at home there and who is dependent on mediation, above all on wisdom; or "ideological" factors such as the "dualistic" interpretation of reality, according to which the light of God is seen as radically different from the darkness of this world. This model has, of course, already become a function of the evangelist's image of Christ, insofar as its *exclusivity* to the claim of mediating the truly divine in this world inevitably entails the illusionless admission of otherwise impenetrable darkness. This is another, perhaps the decisive reason for the Johannine creativity in dealing with the Jesus tradition. The compulsion to develop the factual logic of Christology from within, starting from the confession of Jesus's Easter exaltation from death as the basic axiom of faith.[27] What is fascinating and groundbreaking about the Gospel of John is that this was done with great sensitivity to the signs of the times, with fundamental reference to the present. Its author narrates the

---

27. See in particular the reflections on the emergence of the Christological descent-ascension model above at p. 379.

life of Jesus in such a way that it becomes permeable to the questions and needs of his community. This enabled his work to have a meaningful effect on its addressees. But this means that *the experience of one's own presence is accorded a unique dignity*!

One of the most beautiful stories in the Gospels in which this is narratively realized and illustrated is that of *Jesus's encounter with the Samaritan woman at Jacob's well* (John 4).[28] There, in a dramatic conversation with him, this woman becomes aware of the truth of her own existence. It is his presence in which she becomes transparent to herself in her thirst for life, which runs through her biography like a trail (John 4:16–18). In this way, she encounters *his* truth, the truth of the Messiah. The woman sets off, leaves her water jug at the well, and hurries into the city where she becomes Christ's messenger: "Come and see a man who told me everything I have ever done! He cannot be the Messiah, can he?" (John 4:29). Even this question about Jesus, put so convincingly, awakens the faith of others: "Many Samaritans from that city believed in him because of the woman's testimony, 'He told me everything I have ever done'" (John 4:39). But the Samaritans hurried to Jesus, offered him hospitality, and hosted him in their midst for two days. And at the end they confess to the woman: "It is no longer *because of what you said* that we believe, for we have heard *for ourselves*, and we *know* that this is truly the Savior of the world" (John 4:42).

Faith based on *personal* experience! A faith that arises from the testimony of others, but does not rest on this word, which remains external to itself, but learns to go its own way on its own responsibility and to give an account of it! In this way, the practice of faith becomes authentically *one's own*, becomes mature and adult and attains spiritual presence.

The same applies to the continuation of the "words of the Lord" in the Johannine congregation and in the Gospel. It too has its deepest foundation in the "yes" to our own presence, in the "yes" to the Paraclete who speaks here and now. Of course—and the fourth evangelist knows this!—this speaking of the "Paraclete" takes place in no other way than as a reminder of what *Jesus* said, did, and attested to through his life and suffering. How can the two be combined, which often enough plunges theology and the church into painful trials today: unwavering faithfulness to the words of *Jesus* and a trusting yes to the *present*, the courage to *expose* oneself to their experiences in the certainty that, despite all doubts and irritations, one will ultimately encounter the "Paraclete"? But do theology and the church today have this belief that the "Paraclete" instills in

---

28. On the following, see in detail Theobald, "Ansätze einer biblischen Spiritualität. Impulse aus dem Johannesevangelium," *GuL* 75 (2002): 166–182, especially the section: "Ermutigung zu einem selbstverantworteten Glaubensweg" (pp. 173–179).

them the necessary and healing *memory of Jesus* and also keeps it alive, through the generations? Or are they both like the disciples at the end of the first Easter day, when they sat "filled with fear" behind "locked doors" (John 20:19)?

> Jesus came and stood among them and said:
> Peace be with you (John 20:19).
>
> Do not let your hearts be troubled.
> Believe in God,
> believe also in me (John 14:1).
>
> Remember the word
> that I said to you … (John 15:20).

BIBLIOGRAPHY

Not listed are the well-known aids (dictionaries, grammars, etc.) and source editions of early Christian and pagan antique writings.

Attridge, H. W. "'Seeking' and 'Asking' in Q, Thomas and John." Pages 294–302 in *From Quest to Q.* FS J. M. Robinson. BEThL 146. Leuven: Peeters, 2000.
Aune, D. "Oral Tradition and the Aphorisms of Jesus." Pages 211–265 in *Jesus and the Oral Gospel Tradition*, edited by H. Wansbrough. London: T&T Clark, 2004.
———*Revelation I–III.* WBC 52A–C. Dallas: Thomas Nelson, 1997–1998.
Ball, D. M., *"I Am" in John's Gospel: Literary Function, Background, and Theological Implications.* JSNT.S 124. Sheffield: Sheffield Academic Press, 1996.
Barrett, C. K. *Das Evangelium nach Johannes.* KEK.S. Göttingen: Vandenhoeck & Ruprecht, 1990.
Baur, F. C., "Ueber die Composition und den Charakter des johanneischen Evangeliums." ThJB [T] 3 (1844): 1-191.397-475.615-700.
Bauckham, R. "Rediscovering a Lost Parable of Jesus." *NTS* 33 (1987): 84–101.
Becker, J. "Die Abschiedsreden Jesu im Johannesevangelium." *ZNW* 61 (1970): 215–246.
———*Das Evangelium nach Johannes I–II.* 3rd ed. ÖTK 4/1-2 Gütersloh: Gütersloher Verlagshaus, 1991.
———"Die Herde des Hirten und die Reben am Weinstock. Ein Versuch zu Joh 10,1–18 und 15,1–17." Pages 149–178 in *Die Gleichnisreden Jesu 1899–1999. Beiträge zum Dialog mit Adolf Jülicher*, edited by U. Mell. BZNW 103. Berlin: de Gruyter, 1999.
Beierwaltes, W. *Lux Intelligibilis. Untersuchung zur Lichtmetaphysik der Griechen.* Munich: Uni-Druck, 1957.
Berger, K. *Die Amen-Worte Jesu. Eine Untersuchung zum Problem der Legitimation in apokalyptischer Rede.* BZNW 39. Berlin: de Gruyter, 1970.
———*Die Auferstehung des Propheten und die Erhöhung des Menschensohnes. Traditionsgeschichtliche Untersuchungen zur Deutung des Geschickes Jesu in frühchristlichen Texten.* StUNT 13. Göttingen: Vandenhoeck & Ruprecht, 1976.
———*Formgeschichte des Neuen Testaments.* Heidelberg: Quelle & Meyer, 1984.
———"Hellenistische Gattungen im Neuen Testament," in *ANRW* II 5/2 (1984), 1031-1432.
Becker, J., Die Auferstehung Jesu Christi nach dem Neuen Testament: Ostererfahrung und Osterverständnis im Urchristentum, Mohr Siebeck, Tübingen 2007.
Beutler, J. *Habt keine Angst. Die erste Abschiedsrede (Joh 14).* SBS 116. Stuttgart: Katholisches Bibelwerk, 1984.

Beyer, K., *Semitische Syntax im Neuen Testament I. Satzlehre*. StUNT 1. 2nd ed. Göttingen: Vandenhoeck & Ruprecht, 1968.

Bienaimé, G. "L'annonce des fleuves d'eau vive en Jean 7,37–39." *RTL* 21 (1990): 281–310, 417–454.

Bieringer, R., D. Pollefeyt, E. Vandecasteele-Vanneuville, eds. *Anti-Judaism and the Fourth Gospel: Papers of the Leuven Colloquium 2000*. JCHS 1. Leiden: Brill, 2001.

Bjerkelund, C. J. *Tauta Egeneto. Die Präzisierungssätze im Johannesevangelium*. WUNT II/40. Tübingen: Mohr Siebeck, 1987.

Blank, J. *Krisis. Untersuchungen zur johanneischen Christologie und Eschatologie*. Freiburg: Lambertus-Verlag, 1964.

———*Das Evangelium nach Johannes*. GSL.NT 4/1–2. Düsseldorf: Evangelische Verlagsanstalt, 1977 and 1981.

Blatz, B. "Der Dialog des Erlösers." Pages 245–253 in *Neutestamentliche Apokryphen*. Volume 1: *Evangelien*, edited by W. Schneemelcher. 6th ed. Tübingen: Mohr Siebeck, 1990.

Böcher, O. *Der johanneische Dualismus im Zusammenhang des nachbiblischen Judentums*. Gütersloh: Mohn, 1965.

Bonnard, P. "L'anamnèse, structure fondamentale de la théologie du Nouveau Testament." Pages 1–11 in *Anamnesis. Recherches sur le Nouveau Testament*. CRThPh 3. Geneva: Faculté de Théologie de Lausanne, 1980.

Borgen, P. *Bread from Heaven. An Exegetical Study of the Concept of Manna in the Gospel of John and the Writings of Philo*. NT.S 10. Leiden: Brill, 1965.

Boring, M. E. *Sayings of the Risen Jesus: Christian Prophecy in the Synoptic Tradition*, SNTS.MS 46. Cambridge: Cambridge University Press, 1982.

Bornkamm, G. "Das Anathema in der urchristlichen Abendmahlsliturgie." Pages 123–132 in *Das Ende des Gesetzes. Paulusstudien. Gesammelte Aufsätze I*. BevTh 16. 5th ed. Munich: Kaiser, 1966.

Bovon, F. *Luke 2: A Commentary on the Gospel of Luke 9:51–19:27*. Minneapolis, MN: Fortress Press, 2012.

Braun, H. "Das 'Stirb und Werde' in der Antike und im Neuen Testament." Pages 136–158 in *Gesammelte Studien zum Neuen Testament und seiner Umwelt*. 3rd ed. Tübingen: Mohr Siebeck, 1971.

Brown, R. E. *The Gospel According to John*. 2 vols. AncB 29–29A. New York: Doubleday, 1966–1970.

Büchsel, F. *Die Johannesbriefe*. ThHK 17. Leipzig: Evangelische Verlagsanstalt, 1933.

Bühner, J.-A. *Der Gesandte und sein Weg im 4. Evangelium. Die kultur- und religionsgeschichtlichen Grundlagen der johanneischen Sendungschristologie sowie ihre traditionsgeschichtliche Entwicklung*. WUNT II/2. Tübingen: Mohr Siebeck, 1977.

Bultmann, R. *Das Evangelium des Johannes*. 19th ed. Göttingen: Vandenhoeck & Ruprecht, 1968.

———"γινώσκω." *TDNT* 1:689–714.

———*Theologie des Neuen Testaments*. 7th ed. Edited by O. Merk. Tübingen: Mohr, 1977.

———*Die Geschichte der synoptischen Tradition*. FRLANT 29. 10th ed. Göttingen: Vandenhoeck & Ruprecht, 1995.

Burchard, C., "The Importance of Joseph and Aseneth for the Study of the New Testament," NTS 30 (1987) 102–134.

Burkert, W. *Antike Mysterien. Funktion und Gehalt*. 3rd ed. Munich: C. H. Beck, 1991.

——— *Homo Necans. Interpretationen altgriechischer Opferriten und Mythen*. 2nd ed. Berlin et al.: de Gruyter, 1997.

Cameron, R. *Sayings Traditions in the Apocryphon of James*. HThS 34. Philadelphia: Augsburg Fortress, 1984.

Catchpole, D. R. "Q and 'the Friend at Midnight' (Luke XI. 5–8/9)," *JThS.NS* 34 (1983): 407–424.

Claudel, G. "Jean 20,23 et ses parallèles matthéens," *RevSR* 69 (1995): 71–86.

Collins, R. F. "Proverbial Sayings in St. John's Gospel." Pages in 128–150 in *These Things Have Been Written: Studies on the Fourth Gospel*. LThPM 2. Leuven: Peeters, 1990.

Conzelmann, H. "Paulus und die Weisheit." *NTS* 12 (1965/66): 231–244.

Crossan, J. D. *In Fragments: The Aphorisms of Jesus*. San Francisco: Harper & Row, 1983.

——— "Aphorism in Discourse and Narrative." *Semeia* 43 (1988): 121–140.

Cullmann, O. *Das Gebet im Neuen Testament. Zugleich Versuch einer vom Neuen Testament aus zu erteilenden Antwort auf heutige Fragen*. 2nd ed. Tübingen: Mohr Siebeck, 1997.

Culpepper, R. A. *The Johannine School. An Evaluation of the Johannine-School Hypothesis Based on an Investigation of the Nature of Ancient Schools*. SBL.DS 26. Missoula: Society of Biblical Literature, 1975.

Dahl, N.A. "Anamnesis." *StTh* 1 (1948): 69–95.

Delff, H. *Geschichte des Rabbi Jesus von Nazareth. Kritisch begründet, dargestellt und erklärt*. Leipzig 1889.

——— *Das vierte Evangelium, ein authentischer Bericht über Jesus von Nazareth, wieder hergestellt, übersetzt und erklärt*. Husum 1890.

Dettwiler, A. *Die Gegenwart des Erhöhten. Eine exegetische Studie zu den johanneischen Abschiedsreden (Joh 13,31–16,33) unter besonderer Berücksichtigung ihres Relecture-Characters*. FRLANT 169. Göttingen: Vandenhoeck & Ruprecht, 1995.

Dibelius, M. "Die Mahl-Gebete der Didache." *ZNW* 37 (1938): 32–41.

——— "Joh 15,13. Eine Studie zum Traditionsproblem des Johannes-Evangeliums" (1927). Pages 204–220 in *Botschaft und Geschichte I*. Tübingen: Mohr, 1953.

——— *Geschichte der urchristlichen Literatur*. Edited by F. Hahn. ThB.NT 58. Munich: Kaiser, 1975.

Dietzfelbinger, C. *Der Abschied des Kommenden. Eine Auslegung der johanneischen Abschiedsreden Abschied*. WUNT 95. Tübingen: Mohr Siebeck, 1996.

——— *Das Evangelium nach Johannes I–II*. ZBK.NT 4/1-2. Zurich: Benzinger, 2001.

Dodd, C. H. *The Interpretation of the Fourth Gospel*. Cambridge: Cambridge University Press, 1953; reprint 1963.

——— *Historical Tradition in the Fourth Gospel*. Cambridge: Cambridge University Press, 1963.

——— "A Hidden Parable in the Fourth Gospel." Pages 30–40 in *More New Testament Studies*. Manchester: Manchester University Press, 1968.

———. "Behind a Johannine Dialogue." Pages 41–57 in *More New Testament Studies*. Manchester: Manchester University Press, 1968.

Dunn, J. D. G. *Jesus and the Spirit: A Study of the Religious and Charismatic Experience of Jesus and the First Christians as Reflected in the New Testament*. London: Eerdmans, 1975.

Edwards, R. A. "The Eschatological Correlative as a Gattung in the New Testament." *ZNW* 60 (1969): 9–20.

Emerton, J. A. "Binding and Losing—Forgiving and Retaining." *JThS.NS* 13 (1962): 325–331.

Ensor, P. W. *Jesus and His "Works": The Johannine Sayings in Historical Perspective*. WUNT 2/85. Tübingen: Mohr Siebeck, 1996.

Farina, V. *Die Leiblichkeit der Auferstandenen. Ein Beitrag zur Analyse des paulinischen Gedankenganges in 1Kor 15,35–58*. Würzburg: Fenske, 1971.

Fieger, M. *Das Thomasevangelium. Einleitung, Kommentar und Systematik*. NTA.NF 22. Münster: Aschendorff, 1991.

Fischer, G., *Die himmlischen Wohnungen. Untersuchungen zu Joh 14,2f*. EHS 23/38. Frankfurt: Peter Lang, 1975.

Fitzmyer, J. A. *The Gospel According to Luke: Introduction, Translation, and Notes I–II*. AncB 28/28A. New York: Doubleday, 1981 and 1985.

Frey, J. "'Wie Mose die Schlange in der Wüste erhöht hat . . .'. Zur frühjüdischen Deutung der 'ehernen Schlange' und ihrer christologischen Rezeption in Johannes 3,14f." Pages 153–205 in *Schriftauslegung im antiken Judentum und im Urchristentum*. Edited by M. Hengel and H. Löhr. WUNT 73. Tübingen: Mohr Siebeck, 1994.

———. "Heiden—Griechen—Gotteskinder." Pages 228–268 in *Die Heiden. Juden, Christen und das Problem des Fremden*. Edited by R. Feldmeier and U. Heckel. WUNT 70. Tübingen: Mohr Siebeck, 1994.

———. *Die johanneische Eschatologie II–III*. WUNT 110 and 117. Tübingen: Mohr Siebeck, 1998 and 2000.

Frey, J., R. Zimmermann, and J. G. van der Watt, eds., *Imagery in the Gospel of John: Terms, Forms, Themes, and Theology of Johannine Figurative Language*. WUNT 200. Tübingen: Mohr Siebeck, 2006.

Gaechter, P. "Zur Form von Joh 5,19–30." Pages 65–68 in *Neutestamentliche Aufsätze*. FS J. Schmid. Edited by J. Blinzler, O. Kuss, and F. Mußner. Regensburg: Pustet, 1963.

Gardner-Smith, P. *St. John and the Synoptic Gospels*. Cambridge: Cambridge University Press, 1938.

———. "St. John's Knowledge of Matthew (Mt 10,24–25; Joh 13,16; 15,20)." *JThS.NS* 4 (1953): 31–35.

Gärtner, B. E. "The Pauline and Johannine Idea of 'to Know God' Against the Hellenistic Background: The Greek Philosophical Principle 'Like by Like' in Paul and John." *NTS* 14 (1967/68): 209–231.

Gemünden, P. von. *Vegetationsmetaphorik im Neuen Testament und seiner Umwelt. Eine Bildfelduntersuchung*. NTOA 18. Freiburg et al.: Herder, 1993.

Giebel, M. *Das Geheimnis der Mysterien. Antike Kulte in Griechenland, Rom und Ägypten*. Zurich et al.: Patmos, 1990.

Gnilka, J. *Das Evangelium nach Markus*. EKK II/1-2. Zurich: Benzinger, 1979.

———*Das Matthäusevangelium I-II*. HThK.NT I/1-2. 2nd ed. Freiburg: Herder, 1988.

Goldsmith, D. "'Ask, and it will be Given...' Toward Writing the History of a Logion." *NTS* 35 (1989): 254–265.

Goodenough, E. R. *By Light, Light. The Mystic Gospel of Hellenistic Judaism*. New Haven, CT: Yale, 1935.

Grässer, E. *An die Hebräer III*. EKK XVII/3. Zurich: Benzinger, 1997.

Haenchen, E. "Das Johannesevangelium und sein Kommentar" (1964). Pages 208–234 in *Die Bibel und Wir. Gesammelte Aufsätze II*. Tübingen: Mohr Siebeck, 1968.

Hahn, F. "Die Worte vom lebendigen Wasser im Johannesevangelium. Eigenart und Vorgeschichte von Joh 4,10.13f.; 6,35; 7,37–39." Pages 51–70 in *God's Christ and His People*. FS N. A. Dahl. Edited by J. Jervell and W. A. Meeks. Oslo: Universitetsforlaget, 1977.

———"Die Hirtenrede in Joh 10." Pages 185–200 in *Theologia Crucis—signum crucis*. FS E. Dinkler. Tübingen: Mohr, 1979.

———*Christologische Hoheitstitel. Ihre Geschichte im frühen Christentum*. FRLANT 83. 5th ed. Göttingen: Vandenhoeck & Ruprect, 1995.

Harner, P. *The "I Am" of the Fourth Gospel: A Study in Johannine Usage and Thought*. Philadelphia: Fortress, 1970.

Hartenstein, J. *Die zweite Lehre. Erscheinungen des Auferstandenen als Rahmenerzählungen frühchristlicher Dialoge*. TU 146. Berlin: de Gruyter, 2000.

Heckel, T. K. *Vom Evangelium des Markus zum viergestaltigen Evangelium*. WUNT 120. Tübingen: Mohr Siebeck, 1999.

Hirzel, R. *Der Dialog. Ein literarhistorischer Versuch*. 2 vols. Hildesheim: Olms, 1963 (ND = Leipzig: 1895).

Hoffmann, P. "Mk 8,31. Zur Herkunft und markinischen Rezeption einer alten Überlieferung." Pages 170–204 in *Orientierung an Jesus. Zur Theologie der Synoptiker*. FS J. Schmid. Edited by P. Hoffmann, in collaboration with J. Schmid. Freiburg et al.: Herder, 1973.

———*Studien zur Theologie der Logienquelle*. NTA.NF 8. 3rd ed. Münster: Aschendorff, 1982.

———"QR und der Menschensohn. Eine vorläufige Skizze." Pages 243–278 in *Tradition und Situation*. Münster: Aschendorff, 1955.

Hoffmann, P. / Heil, C., Die Spruchquelle Q. Studienausgabe Griechisch und Deutsch, Darmstadt ³2029.

Hossfeld, F.-L. and E. Zenger. *Die Psalmen I. Psalm 1–50*. NEB 29. Würzburg: Echter, 1993.

Hübner, H., Die Weisheit Salomons (ATDA 4), Göttingen 1999.

Hunter, A. M. *The Gospel According to John*. London: Cambridge University, 1968.

Jeremias, J. "Kennzeichen der ipsissima vox Jesu." Pages 145–152 in *Abba. Studien zur neutestamentlichen Theologie und Zeitgeschichte*. Göttingen: Vandenhoeck & Ruprecht, 1966.

———"Das Vater Unser im Lichte der neueren Forschung." Pages 152–171 in *Abba. Studien zur neutestamentlichen Theologie und Zeitgeschichte.* Göttingen: Vandenhoeck & Ruprecht, 1966.

———*Die Gleichnisse Jesu.* 8th ed. Göttingen: Vandenhoeck & Ruprecht, 1970.

———*Neutestamentliche Theologie I. Die Verkündigung Jesu.* 3rd ed. Gütersloh: Gütersloher Verlag, 1973.

Jonge, M. de, Jewish Expectations About the 'Messiah' According to the Fourth Gospel, in: NTS 19 (1972/73) 246–270.

———"Nicodemus and Jesus. Some Observations on Misunderstanding and Understanding in the Fourth Gospel." Pages 29–47 in *Jesus, Stranger from Heaven and Son of God: Jesus Christ and the Christians in Johannine Perspective.* Missoula, MT: Scholars Press, 1977.

———*The Testaments of the Twelve Patriarchs: A Critical Edition of the Greek Text* (PVTG), Leiden 1978.

———"Christology, Controversy and Community in the Gospel of John." Pages 209–229 in *Christology, Controversy and Community*, edited by D. G. Horrell, C. M. Tuckett, and D. R. Catchpole. Leiden: Brill, 2000.

Joüon, P. "Notes philologiques sur les évanglies," RSR 18 (1928) 345–359.

Kaipuram, S. *Paroimiai in the Fourth Gospel and the Johannine Parables of Jesus' Self-Revelation.* Rome, 1993.

Kertelge, K. *Die Wunder Jesu im Markusevangelium.* StANT 23. Munich: Kösel, 1970.

Kirchner, D. "Brief des Jakobus." Pages 234–244 in *Neutestamentliche Apokryphen in deutscher Übersetzung.* Volume 1: *Evangelien.* Edited by W. Schneemelcher. Tübingen: Mohr Siebeck, 1999.

Klauck, H.-J. *Allegorie und Allegorese in synoptischen Gleichnistexten.* NTA.NF 13. Münster: Aschendorff, 1978.

———*Herrenmahl und hellenistischer Kult. Eine religionsgeschichtliche Untersuchung zum ersten Korintherbrief.* NTA.NF 15. Münster: Aschendorff, ²1986.

———"Gemeinde ohne Amt? Erfahrungen mit der Kirche in den johanneischen Schriften." Pages 195–222 in *Gemeinde—Amt—Sakrament. Neutestamentliche Perspektiven.* Würzburg: Echter, 1989.

———*Der erste Johannesbrief.* EKK 23/1. Zurich: Benziger, 1991.

———"'Christus, Gottes Kraft und Gottes Weisheit' (1 Kor 1,24). Jüdische Weisheitsüberlieferungen im Neuen Testament." Pages 251–275 in *Alte Welt und neuer Glaube. Beiträge zur Religionsgeschichte, Forschungsgeschichte und Theologie des Neuen Testaments*, edited by H.-J. Klauck. NTOA 29. Fribourg: Universitätsverlag, 1994.

———*Die religiöse Umwelt des Urchristentums I. Stadt- und Hausreligion, Mysterienkulte, Volksglaube.* Stuttgart: Kohlhammer, 1995.

Klein, H. "Vorgeschichte und Verständnis der johanneischen Ich-bin-Worte." *KuD* 33 (1987): 120–136.

Kloppenborg, J. S. *The Formation of Q. Trajectories in Ancient Wisdom Collections.* Philadelphia: Fortress, 1987.

Koester, H. "Gnostic Sayings and Controversy Traditions in John 8,12–59." Pages 97–110 in *Nag Hammadi, Gnosticism and Early Christianity*, edited by C. W. Hedrick and R. Hodgson. Peabody, MA: Hendrickson, 1986.

———*Ancient Christian Gospels. Their History and Development.* London: SCM Press, 1990.

Kollmann, B. *Ursprung und Gestalten der frühchristlichen Mahlfeier.* GTA 43. Göttingen: Vandenhoeck & Ruprecht, 1990.

Kundsin, K. *Charakter und Ursprung der johanneischen Reden.* Acta Universitatis Latoiensis I/4. Riga: Latvijas Universitate, 1939.

Le Deaut, R. "Goûter le calice de la mort." *Bib* 43 (1962): 82–86.

Léon-Dufour, X. *Lecture de l'Évangile selon Jean I–IV.* Paris: Seuil, 1987–1996.

Leroy, H. *Rätsel und Missverständnis. Ein Beitrag zur Formgeschichte des Johannesevangeliums.* BBB 30. Bonn: Hanstein, 1968.

Lietzmann, H. *Messe und Herrenmahl. Eine Studie zur Geschichte der Liturgie.* AKG 8. 3rd edition. Berlin: de Gruyter, 1955.

Limbeck, M. *Das Gesetz im Alten und Neuen Testament.* Darmstadt: WBG, 1997.

Lindars, B. *The Gospel of John.* NCeB. Grand Rapids, IL: Eerdmans, 1972.

———*Essays on John.* Edited by C. M. Tuckett. SNTA 17. Leuven: Peeters, 1992.

———"Traditions Behind the Fourth Gospel" (1977). Pages 87–104 in *Essays on John*, edited by C. M. Tuckett. SNTA 17. Leuven: Peeters, 1992.

———"Discourse and Tradition: The Use of the Sayings of Jesus in the Discourses of the Fourth Gospel" (1981). Pages 113–129 in *Essays on John.* Edited by C. M. Tuckett. SNTA 17. Leuven: Peeters, 1992.

———"Slave and Son in John 8:31–36" (1984). Pages 167–182 in *Essays on John*, edited by C. M. Tuckett. SNTA 17. Leuven: Peeters, 1992.

Lohmeyer, E. *Das Vater-unser.* 2nd ed. Göttingen: Vandehoeck & Ruprecht, 1947.

———*Das Evangelium des Markus.* KEK. 17th ed. Göttingen: Vandenhoeck & Ruprecht, 1967.

Lührmann, D. *Das Markusevangelium.* HNT 3. Tübingen: Mohr, 1987.

Luz, U. *Das Evangelium nach Matthäus I–IV.* EKK I/1–4. Zurich: Benziger, 1985–2002.

———*Die Jesusgeschichte des Matthäus.* Neukirchen: Neukirchener Verlag, 1993.

Mack, B. L. *Logos und Sophia. Untersuchungen zur Weisheitstheologie im hellenistischen Judentum.* StUNT 10. Göttingen: Vandenhoeck & Ruprecht, 1973.

MacRae, G. W. "The Meaning and Evolution of the Feast of Tabernacles." *CBQ* 22 (1960): 251–276.

Maneschg, H. *Die Erzählung von der ehernen Schlange (Num 21,4–9) in der Auslegung der frühen jüdischen Literatur. Eine traditionsgeschichtliche Studie.* EHS.T 23/157. Frankfurt: Peter Lang, 1981.

Menken, M. J. J. *Old Testament Quotations in the Fourth Gospel: Studies in Textual Form.* Kampen: Pharos, 1996.

Metzger, B. M. *A Textual Commentary on the Greek New Testament.* Stuttgart: Deutsche Bibelgesellschaft, 1994 (=London: United Bible Socities, [4]1994).

Metzner, R. *Das Verständnis der Sünde im Johannesevangelium.* WUNT 122. Tübingen: Mohr Seiebeck, 2000.

Minear, P. S. *Commands of Christ*. Nashville, TN: Abingdon Press, 1972.
Morgen, M. "Le fils de l'homme élève en vue de la vie eternelle (Jn 3,14–15 éclairé par diverses traditions juives)." *RevSR* 68 (1994): 5–17.
Mußner, F., Die johanneische Sehweise und die Frage nach dem historischen Jesus, Freiburg: Herder Verlag 1965.
———Der Jakobusbrief (HThK.NT 13/1). Freiburg, 1987.
Nagel, T. *Die Rezeption des Johannesevangeliums im 2. Jahrhundert. Studien zur vorirenäischen Aneignung und Auslegung des vierten Evangeliums in christlicher und christlich-gnostischer Literatur*. Arbeiten zur Bibel und ihrer Geschichte 2. Leipzig: Evangelische Verlagsanstalt, 2000.
Niemand, C., Spuren der Täuferpredigt in Joh 15,1–11, in Protokolle zur Bibel 4 (1995) 13–28.
Noack, B. *Zur johanneischen Tradition. Beiträge zur Kritik an der literarischen Analyse des vierten Evangeliums*. TheolSkr 3. Kopenhagen: I kommisjon hos Rosenkilde og Bagger, 1954.
Norden, E. *Agnostos Theos. Untersuchungen zur Formengeschichte religiöser Rede*. 4th ed. Stuttgart: WBG, 1956.
Obermann, A., Die christologische Erfüllung der Schrift im Johannesevangelium. WUNT 2/83, Tübingen: Mohr Siebeck, 1996.
Odeberg, H. *The Fourth Gospel: Interpreted in Its Relation to Contemporaneous Religious Currents in Palestine and the Hellenistic—Oriental World*. Amsterdam: Almquist & Wiksell, 1929 [ND 1974].
Painter, J., Tradition, History and Interpretation in John 10. Pages 53–74 in *The Shepherd Discourse of John 10 and Its Context* (SNTS.MS 67), edited by J. Beutler and R. T. Fortna. Cambridge 1991.
Perkins, P. *The Gnostic Dialogue: The Early Church and the Crisis of Gnosticism*. Theological Inquiries. New York: Paulist Press, 1980.
———Johannine Traditions in AP.JAS. (NHC I,2), in JBL 101 (1982) 403–414.
Pesch, R. *Das Markusevangelium II*. HThK.NT 2/2. Freiburg: Herder, 1977.
Piper, R. A. "Matthew 7,7–11 par. Luke 11,9–13. Evidence of Design and Argument in the Collection of Jesus' Sayings." Pages 411–418 in *Logia. Les paroles de Jésus*. FS J. Coppens. BETL 59. Leuven: Peeters, 1982.
———"Satan, Demons and the Absence of Exorcisms in the Fourth Gospel." Pages 253–278 in *Christology, Controversy and Community: New Testament Essays in Honour of David R. Catchpole*, edited by D. Horrell and C. M. Tuckett. SuppNovT. Leiden: Brill, 2000.
Potterie, I. de la. "Je suis la Voie, la Vérité et la Vie (Jn 14,6)." *NRTh* 88 (1966): 907–942.
Rengstorf, K. H. "Zu den Fresken in der jüdischen Katakombe der Villa Torlonia in Rom." *ZNW* 31 (1932): 33–60.
Richter, G., Zum sogenannten Taufetext Joh 3,5, in Studien zum Johannesevangelium (BU 13), Regensburg 1977, 327–345.
Riedweg, C. *Mysterienterminologie bei Platon, Philon und Klemens von Alexandrien*. UALG 26. Berlin: de Gruyter, 1987.
Riesner, R. *Jesus als Lehrer. Eine Untersuchung zum Ursprung der Evangelien-Überlieferung*. WUNT II/7. Tübingen: Mohr Siebeck, 1981; 2nd ed. 1984.

Bibliography

Robinson, J. M., "Die johanneische Entwicklungslinie." Pages 216–250 in *Entwicklungslinien durch die Welt des frühen Christentums*, edited by H. Koester and J. M. Robinson. Tübingen: Mohr Siebeck, 1971.
Robinson, J. M., Hoffmann, P. and Kloppenborg, J. S., *The Critical Edition of Q*. Leuven: Peeters, 2000.
Robinson, J. M., "History of Q Research." Pages XIX–LXXI in *The Critical Edition of Q*, edited by P. Hoffmann and J. S. Kloppenborg. Leuven: Peeters, 2000.
Roloff, J. *Die Apostelgeschichte*. NTD 5. Göttingen: Vandenhoeck & Ruprecht, 1981.
Ruckstuhl, E. *Jesus im Horizont der Evangelien*. SBA 3. Stuttgart: Katholisches Bibelwerk, 1988.
——— "Abstieg und Erhöhung des johanneischen Menschensohns" (1975). Pages 277–311 in *Jesus im Horizont der Evangelien*, edited by E. Ruckstuhl. SBA 3. Stuttgart: Katholisches Bibelwerk, 1988.
Ruckstuhl, E. and P. Dschulnigg. *Stilkritik und Verfasserfrage im Johannesevangelium. Die johanneischen Sprachmerkmale auf dem Hintergrund des Neuen Testaments und des zeitgenössischen hellenistischen Schrifttums*. NTOA 17. Göttingen: Vandenhoeck & Ruprecht, 1991.
Rudolph, K. "Der gnostische 'Dialog' als literarisches Genus." Page 85–107 in *Probleme der koptischen Literatur*, edited by P. Nagel. Wissenschaftliche Beiträge der Martin-Luther-Universität. Halle Wittenberg 1. Halle: Martin-Luther-Universität Halle-Wittenberg, 1968.
Sänger, D., Antikes Judentum und die Mysterien. Religionsgeschichtliche Untersuchungen zu Joseph und Aseneth (WUNT 2/5), Tübingen 1980.
Sato, M., *Q und Prophetie. Studien zur Gattungs- und Traditionsgeschichte der Quelle Q*. WUNT II/29. Tübingen: Mohr Siebeck, 1988.
Schenke, H.-M. "Die Tendenz der Weisheit zur Gnosis." Pages 351–372 in *Gnosis*. FS H. Jonas. Göttingen: Vandenhoeck & Ruprecht, 1978.
Schenke, L, Die literarische Vorgeschichte von Joh 6,26–58, BZ.NF 29 (1985) 68–89.
——— "Der 'Dialog Jesu mit den Juden' im Johannesevangelium." Ein Rekonstruktionsversuch, NTS 34 (1988) 573–603.
Schlatter, A. *Der Evangelist Johannes. Wie er spricht, denkt und glaubt. Ein Kommentar zum vierten Evangelium*. Stuttgart: Calwer, 1975.
Schlier, H. "ἐλεύθερος," *TDNT* 2:487—502.
Schlosser, J. "Les *logia* johanniques relatifs au Père." *RevSR* 69 (1995): 87–104.
Schnackenburg, R. *Das Johannesevangelium*. HThK.NT IV/1–4. Freiburg: Herder, 1965–1984.
——— "Tradition und Interpretation im Spruchgut des Johannesevangeliums (1980)." Pages 72–89 in *Das Johannesevangelium*. HThK.NT IV/4. Freiburg: Herder, 1984.
——— "Das Brot des Lebens (Joh 6)." Pages 119–131 in *Das Johannesevangelium*. HThK.NT IV/4. Freiburg: Herder, 1984.
——— "Die johanneische Gemeinde und ihre Geisterfahrung." Pages 33–58 in *Das Johannesevangelium*. HThK.NT IV/4. Freiburg: Herder, 1984.
Schneemelcher, W. *Neutestamentliche Apokryphen*. Vol. 1: *Evangelien*. 6th ed. Tübingen: Mohr Siebeck, 1990.

Schneider, G. "Auf Gott bezogenes 'mein Vater' und 'euer Vater' in den Jesus-Worten der Evangelien. Zugleich ein Beitrag zum Problem Johannes und die Synoptiker." Pages 1751–1781 in *The Four Gospels*, FS F. Neirynck, edited by C. M. Tuckett and A. Vanasegbroeck. BEThL 100. Vol. 3. Leuven: Peters 1992.

Schnelle, U., Antidoketische Christologie im Johannesevangelium. Eine Untersuchung zur Stellung des 4. Evangeliums in der johanneischen Schule (FRLANT 144), Göttingen 1987.

——"Die Abschiedsreden im Johannesevangelium," *ZNW* 80 (1989): 64–79.

——*Das Evangelium nach Johannes*. ThKNT 4. Leipzig: Evangelische Verlagsanstalt, 1998.

Schoenborn, U. *Diverbium Salutis. Literarische Struktur und theologische Intention des gnostischen Dialogs am Beispiel der koptischen "Apokalypse des Petrus."* StUNT 19 Göttingen: Vandenhoeck & Ruprecht, 1995.

——*Dialog und Offenbarung. Zur Strategie literarischer Vergewisserung in Krisenzeiten*. Theologie 6. Münster: LIT, 1996.

Scholtissek, K. *In ihm sein und bleiben. Die Sprache der Immanenz in den johanneischen Schriften* (HBS 21), Freiburg: Herder-Verlag, 2000.

Schröter, J. *Erinnerung an Jesu Worte. Studien zur Rezeption der Logienüberlieferung in Markus, Q und Thomas*. WMANT 76. Neukirchen et al: Neukirchner Verlag, 1997.

Schulz, S. *Untersuchungen zur Menschensohn-Christologie im Johannesevangelium*. Göttingen: Vandenhoeck & Ruprecht, 1957.

——*Q—Die Spruchquelle der Evangelisten*. Zurich: Theologischer Verlag, 1972.

Schürmann, H. *Das Lukasevangelium I–II*. HThK.NT III/1–2.1. Freiburg: Herder, 1969 and 1993.

——*Traditionsgeschichtliche Untersuchungen zu den synoptischen Evangelien. Beiträge*. KBANT. Düsseldorf: Patmos, 1968.

——"Die Sprache des Christus. Sprachliche Beobachtungen an den synoptischen Herrenworten." Pages 83–108 in *Traditionsgeschichtliche Untersuchungen zu den synoptischen Evangelien. Beiträge*. KBANT. Düsseldorf: Patmos, 1968.

Schüssler Fiorenza, E. "The Quest for the Johannine School. The Apocalypse and the Fourth Gospel." *NTS* 23 (1977): 402–427.

Schwankl, O. "Die Metaphorik von Licht und Finsternis im johanneischen Schrifttum." Pages 135–167 in *Metaphorik und Mythos im Neuen Testament*, edited by K. Kertelge. QD 126 Freiburg: Herder, 1990.

Schweizer, A., Das Evangelium Johannes nach seinem innerhen Wert und seiner Bedeutung für das Leben Jesu kritisch untersucht. Leipzig 1841.

Schweizer, E. *Ego Eimi. Die religionsgeschichtliche Herkunft und theologische Bedeutung der johanneischen Bildreden. Zugleich ein Beitrag zur Quellenfrage des vierten Evangeliums*. FRLANT 56. 2nd edition. Göttingen: Vandenhoeck & Ruprecht, 1965.

——"Zum religionsgeschichtlichen Hintergrund der 'Sendungsformel' Gal 4,4f., Röm 8,3f., Joh 3,16ff., 1Joh 4,9." *ZNW* 57 (1966): 199–210.

——*Das Evangelium nach Matthäus*. NTD 2. 13th ed. Göttingen: Vandenhoeck & Ruprecht, 1973.

Scott, M. *Sophia and the Johannine Jesus.* JSNTS 71. Sheffield: Sheffield Academic, 1992.
Segovia, F. F. "The Theology and Provenance of John 15:1–17." *JBL* 101 (1982): 115–128.
Sellew, P. H. "The Gospel of Thomas: Prospects for Future Research." Pages 327–346 in *The Nag Hammadi Library after Fifty Years. Proceedings of the 1995 Society of Biblical Literature Commemoration*, edited by J. D. Turner and A. McGuire. NHMS 44. Leiden: Brill, 1997.
Sellin, G. "Gotteserkenntnis und Gotteserfahrung bei Philo von Alexandrien." Pages 17–40 in *Monotheismus und Christologie. Zur Gottesfrage im hellenistischen Judentum und im Urchristentum*, edited by H.-J. Klauck. QD 138. Freiburg: Herder, 1992.
Smith, D. M. *John among the Gospels: The Relationship in Twentieth-Century Research.* Minneapolis, MN: Fortress, 1992.
Söding, T. "Wiedergeburt aus Wasser und Geist. Anmerkungen zur Symbolsprache des Johannesevangeliums am Beispiel des Nikodemusgesprächs." Pages 168–219 in *Metaphorik und Mythos.* Edited by K. Kertelge. QD 126. Freiburg: Herder, 1990.
Standaert, B. "Crying 'Abba' and Saying 'Our Father': An Intertextual Approach of the Dominical Prayer." Pages 141–158 in *Intertextuality in Biblical Writings*, edited by S. Draisma. Kampen: Peeters, 1989.
Stegemann, E. W., Urchristliche Sozialgeschichte. Die Anfänge im Judentum und die Christusgemeinden in der mediterranen Welt, Kohlhammer, Stuttgart 1995.
Telsner, D. *The Kaddish: Its History and Significance.* Jerusalem: Tal Orot Institute, 1995.
Thatcher, T. "The Riddles of Jesus in the Johannine Dialogues." Pages 263–277 in *Jesus in Johannine Tradition*, edited by R. T. Fortna and T. Thatcher. London: WJK, 2001.
Theissen, G. and A. Merz. *Der historische Jesus. Ein Lehrbuch.* Göttingen: Vandenhoeck & Ruprecht, 1996.
Theobald, M., *Die Fleischwerdung des Logos. Studien zum Verhältnis des Johannesprologs zum Corpus des Evangeliums und zu 1 Joh.* NtA NF 20. Münster: Aschaffendorf Verlag, 1988.
———"Gott, Logos und Pneuma. 'Trinitarische' Rede von Gott im Johannesevangelium." Pages 41–87 in *Monotheismus und Christologie. Zur Gottesfrage im hellenistischen Judentum und im Urchristentum*, edited by H.-J. Klauck. QD 138. Freiburg: Herder, 1992.
———"Sohn Gottes" als christologische Grundmetapher bei Paulus: ThQ 174 (1994) 185–207.
———"Häresie von Anfang an? Strategien zur Bewältigung eines Skandals nach Joh 6,60–71." Pages 212–246 in *Ekklesiologie des Neuen Testaments.* FS K. Kertelge. Freiburg: Herder, 1996.
———"Gezogen von Gottes Liebe (Joh 6,44f.). Beobachtungen zur Überlieferung eines johanneischen 'Herrenworts.'" Pages 315–341 in *Schrift und Tradition*, edited by K. Backhaus and F. G. Untergassmair. Paderborn: Schöningh, 1996.

———"Der Jünger, den Jesus liebte. Das narrative Konzept der johanneischen Redaktion." Pages 219–255 in *Geschichte—Tradition—Reflexion III*. FS M. Hengel. Tübingen: Mohr Siebeck, 1996.

———"Schriftzitate im 'Lebensbrot'-Dialog Jesu (Joh 6). Ein Paradigma für den Schriftgebrauch des vierten Evangelisten." Pages 327–366 in *The Scriptures in the Gospels*. Edited by C. M. Tuckett. BETL 131. Leuven: Peeters 1997.

———"'Spruchgut' im Johannesevangelium. Bestandsaufnahme und weiterführende Überlegungen zur Konzeption von J. Becker." Pages 335–367 in *Das Urchristentum in seiner literarischen Geschichte*. FS J. Becker. Edited by U. Mell and U. Müller. BZNW 100. Berlin: de Gruyter, 1999.

———Herrenworte im Johannesevangelium (HBS 34). Freiburg: Herder, 2002.

———Das Johannesevangelium—Zeugnis eines synagogalen "Judenchristentums"? in: Sänger D./Mell U. (Hgg.), Paulus und Johannes. Exegetische Studien zur paulinischen und theologischen Theologie und Literatur. Publikation der Referate (FS Becker), (WUNT 198), Tübingen 2006, 107–158.

———Die Ernte ist da! Überlieferungskritische Beobachtungen zu einer johanneischen Bildrede (Joh 4,31–38), in: K. Huber/B. Repschinski (Hgg.), Im Geist und in der Wahrheit. Studien zum Johannesevangelium und zur Offenbarung des Johannes sowie andere Beiträge (FS Martin Hasitschka zum 65. Geb.), Neutestamentliche Abhandlungen Bd. 52, Münster 2008, 81–108.

———"Futurische versus präsentische Eschatologie? Ein neuer Versuch zur Standortbestimmung der johanneischen Tradition." Pages 534–573 in *Studien zum Corpus Iohanneum*. WUNT 276. Tübingen: Mohr Siebeck, 2010.

———"Ansätze einer biblischen Spiritualität. Impulse aus dem Johannesevangelium." *GuL* 75 (2002): 166–182.

———*Das Evangelium nach Johannes Kapitel 1–12* (RNT), Regensburg 2009.

———*Studien zum Corpus Iohanneum* (WUNT 267), Tübingen: Mohr Siebeck 2010.

———"Zulassungsbedingungen zur Eucharistie. Erwägungen zu Did 10,6." Pages 111–39 in *Bau und Schrift: Studien zur Archäologie und Literatur des antiken Christentums*, edited by T. Khideselhi and N. Kavvadas. (FS H. R. Seeliger zum 65. Geb.) 2015, 111–139.

———*Das sog. "johanneische Logion" in der synoptischen Überlieferung (Mt 11,25–27; Lk 10,21f.) und das vierte Evangelium*. Erwägungen zum Ursprung der johanneischen Christologie, in Studien zum Corpus Iohanneum 165–189.

———"Johannine Dominical Sayings as Metatexts of Synoptic Sayings of Jesus: Reflections on a New Category within Reception History." In *John, Jesus, and History, Vol. 3: Glimpses of Jesus Through the Johannine Lens*, edited by P. N. Anderson, F. Justin S. J., and T. Thatcher. Atlanta, GA: SBL Press, 2016.

———"Das Johannesevangelium und Q. Wie groß ist ihre gemeinsame Schnittmenge und wie erklärt sie sich?" In *Built on Rock or Sand? Q Studies: Retrospects, Introspects and Prospects, Biblical Tools and Studies 34*, edited by D. A. Smith, G. Harb, and C. Heil. Leuven: Brill, 2018, 467–495.

———Ein Gott oder "zwei Götter im Himmel"? Zum Wandel der johanneischen "Parakletsprüche." in V. Burz-Tropper (Hg.), Studien zum Gottesbild im Johannesevangelium, WUNT 2/483), Tübingen 2019, 123–146.

Tuckett, C.M. "The Fourth Gospel and Q." Pages 281–290 in *Jesus in Johannine Tradition*, edited by R. T. Fortna and T. Thatcher. Louisville, KY: Westminster John Knox, 2001.

Untergaßmair, F. G. *Im Namen Jesu. Der Namensbegriff im Johannesevangelium. Eine exegetisch-religionsgeschichtliche Studie zu den johanneischen Namensaussagen.* FzB 13. Stuttgart et al.: Verlag Katholisches Bibelwerk, 1973.

Vermes, G. "The Targumic Versions of Genesis 4,3–16." Pages 92–126 in *Post-Biblical Jewish Studies*. SJLA 8. Leiden: Brill, 1975.

Vögtle, A. *Die "Gretchenfrage" des Menschensohnproblems. Bilanz und Perspektive.* QD 152. Freiburg: Herder, 1994.

Vollenweider, S., *Freiheit als neue Schöpfung. Eine Untersuchung zur Eleutheria bei Paulus und in seiner Umwelt.* FRLANT 147. Göttingen: Vandenhoeck & Ruprecht, 1989.

Waaijman, K. "Der Weg—Grundmotiv der Spiritualität." Pages 31–57 in *Arbeitsgemeinschaft Theologie der Spiritualität (AGTS), "Lasst euch vom Geist erfüllen!" (Eph 5,18). Beiträge zur Theologie der Spiritualität.* Theologie der Spiritualität 4. Münster: LIT, 2001.

Walker, W. M. O. "The Lord's Prayer in Matthew and in John." NTS 28 (1982): 237–257.

Walter, N., Zur theologischen Problematik des christologischen 'Schriftbeweises' im Neuen Testament, in: NTS 41 (1995) 328–357, 357.

———"'Hellenistische Eschatologie' im Neuen Testament" (1985). Pages 252–272 in *Praeparatio Evangelica. Studien zur Umwelt, Exegese und Hermeneutik des Neuen Testaments.* WUNT 98. Tübingen: Tübingen: 1997.

Watt, J. G. van der. "'Metaphorik' in Joh 15,1–8." BZ.NF 38 (1994): 67–80.

Weder, H. "Evangelische Erinnerung. Neutestamentliche Überlegungen zur Gegenwart des Vergangenen." Pages 183–200 in *Einblicke ins Evangelium*. Göttingen: Vandenhoeck & Ruprecht, 1992.

Weidemann, H.U., Nochmals Joh 20,23. Weitere philologische und exegetische Bemerkungen zu einer problematischen Bibelübersetzung, MThZ 52 (2001) 121–127.

Weiss, B., *Das Johannesevangelium als einheitliches Werk. Geschichtlich erklärt*, Berlin 1912.

Weiss, J. *Das Urchristentum*. Edited by R. Knopf. Göttingen: Vandenhoeck & Ruprecht, 1917.

Weiss, W. *"Eine neue Lehre in Vollmacht." Die Streit- und Schulgespräche des Markusevangeliums.* BZNW 52. Berlin: de Gruyter, 1988.

Weiße, C. H., Die Evangelische Geschichte kritisch und philosophisch bearbeitet, Leipzig 1838 (2 Vol.).

Wellhausen, J., Das Evangelium Johannis. Berlin: Georg Reimer 1908.

Wendt, H. H., Das Johannesevangelium. Eine Untersuchung seiner Entstehung und seines geschichtlichen Wertes. Göttingen 1900.

Wengst, K. *Das Johannesevangelium I–II.* ThK.NT 4.1–2. Stuttgart: Kohlhammer, 2000–2001.

Westermann, C. *Das Buch Jesaja. Kap. 40–66.* ATD 19. 2nd ed. Göttingen: Vandenhoeck & Ruprecht, 1970.

Wiefel, W. *Das Evangelium nach Matthäus.* ThHK 1. Leipzig: Evangelische Verlagsanstalt, 1998.

Wilckens, U. *Das Evangelium nach Johannes.* NTD 4. Göttingen: Vandenhoeck & Ruprecht, 1998.

Williams, C. H. *I Am He: The Interpretation of "Anî hû" in Jewish and Early Christian Literature.* WUNT 2/113. Tübingen: Mohr Siebeck, 2000.

Zehnder, M. P. *Wegmetaphorik im Alten Testament. Eine semantische Untersuchung der alttestamentlichen und altorientalischen Weg-Lexeme mit besonderer Berücksichtigung ihrer metaphorischen Verwendung.* BZNW 268. Berlin: de Gruyter, 1999.

Zeller, D. *Die weisheitlichen Mahnsprüche bei den Synoptikern.* FzB 17. Würzburg: Echter Verlag, 1977.

———*Charis bei Philon und Paulus.* SBS 142. Stuttgart: Katholisches Bibelwerk, 1990.

Zerwick, M. *Biblical Greek, Illustrated by Examples: English Edition Adapted from the Fourth Latin Edition by J. Smith.* SPIB 114. Rome: Gregorian & Biblical Press, 1994.

Zumstein, J. *Kreative Erinnerung. Relecture und Auslegung im Johannesevangelium.* Zurich: TVZ Theologischer Verlag, 1999.

———"Zur Geschichte des johanneischen Christentums." Pages 1–14 in idem, *Kreative Erinnerung. Relecture und Auslegung im Johannesevangelium.* Zurich: TVZ Theologischer Verlag, 1999.

———Das Johannesevangelium (KEK), Göttingen 2016.

INDEX OF ANCIENT SOURCES

Old Testament

Genesis

1	24
1:1	402
1:2	44
1:3	169
2:7	77, 95
2:10	171, 278
17:16	301
17:17	301
19:17	196
26:18	50
30:31	50

Exodus

4,22	298
7:15	52
12	126
12:24	24
16	162
16:31	157
17:6	271
17:11	126
20:7	132
23:20–21	194
24:16	59
33:4	24
33:13	178

Leviticus

10:3	132
14:3–4	167
14:4	173
24:11–16	302n69

Numbers

20:17	192
21:4–9	121, 123–127
24:17	175n80

Deuteronomy

4:29	255
24:4	51
25:4	24n64
28:14	192
30:1–10	57

1 Samuel

10:6	52
15:32	304

2. Kings

1:11	50
18:4	125
21:3	51

Tobit

8:5	132

1 Maccabees

2,49	

2 Maccabees

8:1	288n20

Job

28	190n131
28:23–27	335n32
33:30	172n68

Psalms

1	188
27:11	188
36:10	167
37:10	257
43:3	167
69:10	23
78:16	273
78:24	25, 152, 153, 155, 162, 271
85:7	51
104:9	51
105:41	271
118:22	122
119:105	167

Proverbs

1:20–33	253, 254
1:28	253
6:23	167, 168
8:17	256
8:35–36	256
9:5	155

Song of Songs

4:15	272

Wisdom of Solomon

9:17	379n11
16:6–7	127
18:4	173

Sirach

6:27	256
15:3	155
24:17	237
24:19–21	157
24:21	155, 157
36:4	132
41:1	304
51:24	155

Isaiah

2:5	167
5:16	132
6:10	50, 51, 54n50
8:23–9,1	175
10:24–25	257
26:20–21	257
29:17	257
40:3	185
42:6	168
43:6	58
42:7	172
43:10–11	263n37
43:10	383
48:21	272n60
49:6	168, 172
49:10	157, 278n84, 279
52:13	121, 123
54:9	120
55:1	269
55:1–3	155, 275, 276
55:6	255
65:24	86

Jeremiah

2:13	272, 278n86
2:21	236n123

12:15	51	*Zechariah*	
18:4	50	9:9	395
29:1–23	255	14:6	273
31:9	58	14:8	272
31:31–34	57		
34(41):15	49	**Early Jewish writings**	
51:33	257	**(Apocrypha/Old Testament)**	
		Apocalypse of Abraham	
Ezekiel		17:16	318n129
28:22	132	29:15	318n130
29:43	132		
36:24–28	57	*Aristobul*	
38:23	132	Fr. 5	169n54
47:1–12	272		
		2 Baruch	
Daniel		17:4	167n45
1:2	214	18:1–2	167n45
2:20	132n54	29:5–6	155
2:28	122n19	29:6	279n89
7:13	317, 318	29:8	153n11
		39:6	254n12
Hosea		39:7	237n129
1:4	257	48:33–36	254n12
5:6	253	59:2	167n45
5:15	253	77:16	167n45
10:1	236n123		
11:1	298	*1 Enoch*	
		39:4–8	318
Joel		41:2	318
4:18	272	42	254, 379
		42:1–3	190n136
Amos		45–57	317n125
8:11–12	253	48:1	318
		48:4	168
Haggai		58–69	317n125
2:6–7	257	63:2	335n32

69:27	215	*4 Maccabees*	
71:5–9	318	4:5	189n126
71:16	318n129		
84:3	335n32	*Pseudo-Philo*	
94:5	254n11	De Jonah 153	384n19
108:12	172n66		
108:14	172n66	Liber antiquitatum biblicarum	

2 Enoch

61:2–3	318	11:1	167n45
		12:8–9	236n127
		18:10–11	236n127
		19:6	167n45
4 Esdras		22:6	29n81
4:20	167n45	23:10	167n45
5:9–12	190n136, 253–254	23:12	236n127
6:6	120n14	26:5	29n81
6:26	304n79	28:4	236n127
7:121	318n129	30:4	236n127
13	379	39:7	236n127
13:52	120n14	48:1	304n79
13	317n125, 379		
14:16–17	254n10	*Testament of Abraham*	
14:20	172n67	16–20 (A)	304n74
		16 (A)	304n75
Joseph and Aseneth		13–14 (B)	304n74
8:3	77n116		
8:5	157n19, 158, 160n27	*Testaments of the Twelve Patriarchs*	
8:9	157n19, 158	Jos. 20:1–2	172
8:10	77n116, 318n130, 384n19	Levi 14:3–4	167
		Levi 18:3	168–169
15:5	157n19, 158	Levi 19:1	167, 171
16:16	157n19		
19:5	157n19, 158	**Qumran**	
20:7	384n19		
21:21	157n19, 158n20	1QS 1:9	172
		1QS 1:10	172
Jubilees		1QS 1:20	29n81
1:15	255n13	1QS 2:10,18	29n81
1:23–25	57–58	1QS 3:6–7	172n68

Index of Ancient Sources

1QS 3:3	168n48	Her. 70	194n149
1QS 3:9–10	195	Her. 241	193, 194
1QS 3:13	172	Her. 249–267	171
1QS 3:19,20	172	Her. 264	170
1QS 3:20	168n48, 172	Leg. 1.31–42	95n168
1QS 3:24–25	172	Leg. 2.81	127n46
1QS 4:2	168n48	Leg. 3.171	171n64
1QS 8,12–16	195n157	Leg. 3.100	58
1QS 9:9	195	Leg. 3.161	95n168
1QS 9:18–19	195	Migr. 143	189n128
1QS 11:3	168	Migr. 146	189n128, 192n143
1QS 11:5	168	Migr. 171	189n128
1QH 8:7	272n63	Migr. 173–174	189n128
1QH 8:16	272n63	Migr. 174	193
11Q18		Mos. 2.50–51	295n47
=11QNJ frg. 24	272n63	Mos. 2.71	59
CD 2:6	195	Mut. 130–131	301n67
CD 19:33–34	272n63	Opif. 31	169n56, 171n64
		Opif. 134f.	95n168
		Post. 102	192
Philo (Alexandrinus)		Praem. 45–46	170
Abr. 70	170	Prob. 45–47	294
Agr. 97.109	127n46	QE 46	59
Cher. 40–50	58	QG 4.46	193
Conf. 95	191n139	Sobr. 56–57	56
Conf. 61	169n56	Som. 1.34	95n168
Decal. 29	191n138	Som. 1.75	169n58
Decal. 114	191n138	Som. 1.118–119	171
Det. 80	95n168	Som. 1.164–165	58
Deus 142–143	191, 335	Som. 1.164	59
Deus 145	187	Som. 1.256	315
Deus 159–161	192	Spec. 1.40–42	178
Deus 160	340	Spec. 1.279	168n47
Ebr. 208	169n56	Spec. 1.319–323	58
Fug. 138	157n18	Spec. 1.339	170n59
Gig. 54.57	58	Spec. 4.123	95n168
Gig. 64	192n144	Virt. 178	59
Her. 56	95n168	Virt. 182	295

Josephus (Flavius)

J.W. 1.111	91
J.W. 6.299	301n65

Rabbinic texts

Mishna

RHSh 3:8	126
Suk 5:3	166n42
Suk 4:5	271n57

Babylonian Talmud

Yev 48b	58n59
BB 4a	168n48
Meg 16b	168n49
San 90b	222n86
MQ 16a	91

Jerusalem Talmud

RHSh 57b	212

Midrashim

Mek. Exod. 17:11	126
Mek. R. Sim. Exod. 17:11	126
Midrash Lamentations 1:3 (85A)	168n50
Midr. Ps. (= Midr. The.) 56:4	172n68

Neues Testament

Matthew

3:2	13
3:10	13
4:17	13
5:13	221
5:14–16	175
5:14	168, 176
5:16	173
5:17	295
5:29	13
5:32	13
5:33–37	29
6:8	73n104
6,9	130–131, 136
6:13	136
6:15	13
6:19	95
6:22–23	221
7:7–11	256
7:7–8	258
7:13–14	195
7:19	13
7:24	324
9:13	13
9:15	145
10:7–8	110
10:7	13
10:24–25	108
10:39	108
10:37–38	291
11:27	6, 212
11:28–30	247
11:27	6, 213, 214, 336
11:28	277, 335
12:6–7	13
12:40	119
16:17–19	108
16:18	90, 96, 97, 99, 108
16:19	88, 89, 91–93, 98, 99, 100, 107
16:27	318
16:28	142
18:3	41, 45, 39, 46, 48–56, 108, 109, 305

Index of Ancient Sources

18:8–9	13	8:14	160, 161
18:18	88–94, 96–98, 100, 105, 107–109	8:31	12, 39, 121–123, 143, 380
18:19	75, 79, 87	8:34	108
18:20	75, 87	8:38	317, 318, 319, 324
18:35	13	9:1	98, 138–139, 141–143, 305, 306, 307
19:9	13		
21:22	75n107	9:31	12, 123, 380
21:32	195	9:36–37	49
23:16–22	29	9:37	109
23:29	335	9:41	305
23:33	13	10:5	52
23:38–39	301n65	10:13–16	47
24:27	119	10:15	39, 41, 45, 46, 48, 54, 55, 56, 305
24,37–39	119		
26:21	123	10:33–34	12, 123, 380
24:36	214, 336	11:22–24	72–75, 85, 86, 108–110
25:1–12	145		
26:75	390	11:24	64, 70
28:18	214, 215	11:23	87
		12:10–12	122
Mark		13:10	176
1:15	146	13:26–27	317, 319
1:22	330	13:30	306
2:17	247	13:32	213, 217, 336
2:19–20	145	14	133
2:19	247	14:9	176
3:24	221	14:21	259, 260
4	373	14:25	28, 28
4:11	373	14:36	64
4:21	175		
4:22	176, 247	*Luke*	
6:7	110	5:4–11	108
6:13	110	6:47	324
6:35–41	161	7:35	247
8:1–9	161	8:16	346
8:34–35	109	9:22	123
8:14–21	161	9:26	317

9:27	139, 141	2:20	364
10:5-6 (Q)	106	2:22	23, 389, 390, 394–395
10:9	110	3	366
10:11	110	3:1	359, 360
10:22 (Q)	6, 213, 214, 330n2, 336	3:2–15	61–64
		3:3	14, 25, 39–46, 56, 60–64, 108, 109, 111, 128, 145, 147
11:2–4 (Q)	69		
11:2	130–131, 136		
11:9–13 (Q)	256	3:5	25, 39–46, 56, 60–64, 108, 109, 111, 128, 145, 147, 334
11:9–10 (Q)	64, 68, 69–71, 258		
11:20	146		
11:30	119	3:7	14
11:33–35	346	3:8	244
11:49	247	3:13	127–128, 378
13:24	199	3:14–15	114–119, 121–123, 127–130, 143, 146, 339, 378–379
14:26–27	291		
17:22	260		
17:23–24 (Q)	318	3:14	18
17:24	119	3:16–21	128–130
17:26–27	119	3:16	382
17:28–32	119	3:17	331, 338
18:17	39, 41, 45, 48, 56, 305	3:29	144, 244, 245
22:6–7	391	4	405
22:60–61	391	4:14	344
22:61	390–391	4:29	405
24:6–7	391	4:35–36	244, 245
24:8	391	4:37	244, 334
24:36–40	102	4:42	405
24:41–49	102	4:43–45	20–21
		4:44	20
John		5:17–18	16
1:1	402	5:17	217
1:19	359	5:18	198
1:45	198	5:19–30	204–206, 381
1:49	198	5:19–20	204–217, 244, 335, 338
1:51	26		
2:17	23, 390, 394–395	5:19	29
2:19	364	5:20	339

5:21–27	217–219	7:35–36	364
5:21	331	7:36	18
5:24	330, 334, 384–385	7:37–39	26, 265–277, 280–
5:26	331		281, 334, 380
5:27	147	7:37	335
5:28–29	386, 387	7:41–42	198
5:29	387	7:40	198
5:35	244, 245	7:52	198
5:44	217n71, 381	8	362, 363
5:45–47	23–24	8:12	25, 163–166, 173–
6	161–163		176, 199, 235, 330,
6:14	198		345, 384
6:20	161	8:13–20	176–179
6:26	16, 29	8:18	364
6:32	29, 137, 382	8:19	364
6:34	138	8:21–30	262–264
6:35	25, 151–156, 161–163,	8:21	14, 18, 247–251, 344,
	199, 235, 334, 335		364
6:36	16	8:22	18, 364
6:38	18, 20	8:24	14
6:39	20	8:28	146
6:41–42	198	8:31–36	283–288, 297–300
6:41	20	8:31–32	18, 25, 283–292,
6:42	18		324–325, 334, 346
6:44	14, 339	8:33	18
6:47	29	8:35	244
6:51–58	339, 401	8:48–59	300–302
6:53	29, 146, 334	8:51, 52	300, 302–309,
6:63	334, 347		324–325, 334, 347,
6:65	14		364
6, 68–69	347	8:56–58	364
7	362, 375–377	9:4–5	176
7:28–29	26	9:4	244, 245, 334
7:31	198	9:22	198, 357
7:33–36	261–262	9:34	198, 357
7:33–34	14, 18, 26, 198,	9:35–38	147
	247–256, 258–260,	9:39	147
	282, 335, 344, 364	10:1–6	29

10:1–5	144	13:31–14:31	369, 401
10:1	29	13:31–38	264–265
10:3–5	244, 335	13:31–32	146
10:5	330	13:33	14, 16, 17, 247–251, 344
10:7–18	30		
10:9	144, 199, 235, 335	13:36	16
10:11–12	144, 201, 244	14	196–198, 320–322
10:14–15	216	14:1	406
10:15	6	14:1–4	310–311
10:33	198, 217	14:2–3	16, 17, 26, 309–319, 384
10:36	16, 198, 217, 336, 338		
		14:6	179–187, 191, 194, 196–198, 199, 235, 335, 339
11:4	16		
11:9–10	176, 244, 245, 334, 345		
		14:6–7	184
11:25–26	16, 235, 387	14:12–14	64–67, 75–80, 334
11:40	16, 17	14:13–14	68, 71, 72, 109, 136, 259
12:13	198		
12:16	389, 394–395	14:15–17	149, 389
12:23	18, 131, 146	14:16–17	397–399
12:24–26	225–226, 334	14:21,23	388
12:24	109, 219–221, 244	14:25–26	149, 389, 396–399
12:25	108	14:26	390, 401
12:28	130, 131–135, 136, 144	14:28	16
12:32	18, 322–323	15–16	401
12:33	20	15:1–16:4	240–243
12:34	18, 19	15:1–8	226–240
12:35–36	176, 244, 345	15:1–6	334
12:38	22	15:1–2	201, 235, 244
12:42	198, 357	15:1	335
12:44–50	27	15:5–6	201, 235, 244
12:50	331	15:5	335
12:46	176	15:7–8	81–82
13:10	20	15:13	7
13:11	20	15:16	81–82, 136, 259
13:16	5, 14, 108–110, 332	15:20–21	108
13:18	22	15:20	5, 14, 389, 395–396, 406
13:20	108–110, 332		

Index of Ancient Sources

15:25–26	149	20:21	110, 331
15:25	22	20:23	88–91, 99–110
16:2	357	20:30–31	402
16:4	389, 390, 395–396	21	108
16:14	14	21:22–23	98, 138–142
16:15	14	21:22	20, 143–144
16:7–11	149	21:23	20
16:16–20	15	21:24–25	402
16:16	14, 18		
16:17	18	*Acts*	
16:19	14	2:33	123
16:21–22	244	2:34	379
16:23–24	82–84, 136, 259	4:25	137
16:26–27	82–84, 136	5:31	123
17	401	9:2	145, 195
17:1	131	11:16	391–392
17:2–3	136	16:17	196
17:6	136	20:34–35	392
17,11	136	20:35	391
17:12	22		
17:15	136	*Romans*	
17:26	136	2:17–19	168
18:4	20	5:2	195
18:5	14	8:9	292
18:6	20	8:14	296, 292n31
18:8	14	8:15–16	137
18:9	20, 22	8:26–27	137
18:32	20, 22, 32		
18:37	18	*1 Corinthians*	
19:7	198, 217, 338	7:10	31
19:21	18	10:4	272n62
19:24	22	12:28	332
19:36	22	14:24	333
20:17	337	15:28	217
20:19–23	100–102	15:36	220n76
20:19	406	15:47–49	318
20:21–23	76–77, 94–97, 99–105		

2 Corinthians

3:17	296
11:2	145

Galatians

3:28	296n51
4:4–5	338n48, 383
4:6	338n48

Ephesians

1:13	288
2:13	195
2:18	182, 195
3:12	195
3:20	64
4:9–10	220, 379
5	145
5:26	231n106

Colossians

1:5–6	288n20
1:15–20	282

1 Thessalonians

1:6	48n17
2:13	48n17
4:15	142n81
4:16–17	314n115, 317–319

1 Timothy

2:4	288n20
5:18	24n64

2 Timothy

2:15	288n20
2:25	288n20
3:7	288n20

Hebrews

2:10	128n48
7:25	195
7:26	123
10:19–21	195
10:20	196
13:20	128n48

James

1:5–8	64, 87
1:25	295
4:2–3	64, 88

1 Peter

1:23	231n106
2:4	195
3:18	195

2 Petrus

3:1–3	390, 393
3:2	395

1 John

2:18–19	242, 285
2:20.27	332n19
3:14	384n19
3:21–22	84–85
4:9	338n48
5:14–15	84–85

2 John

1	288n20

Jude

17–18	390, 393

Revelation

2:7	274

Index of Ancient Sources

2:17	275
3:20–21	275
7:16–17	278
21:6	273n64, 278–280
22:1	268, 278–279
22:6	275n73, 278–279
22:16–17	273–274
22:17	137, 268–270, 275, 277, 278–280, 334

Early Christian writings and church fathers

Barnabas

12:5–7	118n7
12:7	125n35

1 Clement

13:1–2	24n64, 390n7, 392
24:5	225n97
46:7–8	392

2 Clement

2:4	24n64
3:2	24n64
4:2	24n64
6:1	24n64
8:5	24n64
9:11	24n64

Clement of Alexandria

Paed. 2.10	31n87
Paed. 113.3	31n87
Quis div. 3.1	31n87

(Pseudo-)Clement

Hom. 11.26.2	53n43
Hom. 13.21.2–3	60
Recog. 1.69.5	53n43
Recog. 6.9.2	53n43

Dialogue of the Redeemer

342–343, 348–350

Didache

9:1–2	238–239
9:2	274
9:4	239
10:6	275, 280

Epistula Jacobi (NHC I/2)

	341n57, 342–343, 348–350
2:7–15	390
2:23–27	248n2, 344
8:16–23	225n97
10:32–34	64n71

Eusebius

Hist. Eccl.

3.39.1	31n87
3.39.3	390
3.39.15–16	31n87

Gospel of Thomas

1	347
2	64n71
13	344–345
18	347
19	346–347
24	345–346
38	260n28, 344
77	164n39
92	64n71
94	64n71

108	34, 345	30:1	272n63
111	347	33:11b,12	200n169

Hippolytus

Haer. 5.8	223n92
Haer. 8.10.8	53n43

Origen

Cels 7.8–9	200n169

Ignatius

Eph. 20:2	339n51
Magn. 9:1	288n20

Polycarp

Phil 2:3	390n7, 392
Phil 7:1	31n87

Irenaeus

Haer. 1 praef. 1	31n87
Haer. 1.8.1	31n87
Haer. 5.36.2	314

Shephard of Hermas

Sim. 6.3.6	64n71

Roman-Hellenistic literature

Chrysippus

(Arnim, SVF III 360)	294n45

Justin

1 Apol 60	118
1 Apol 61:3	43n4
1 Apol 61,4	41, 53n43
1 Apol 66:1	43n4
Dial. 8:4	376
Dial. 49:1	376n3
Dial. 91:4	118n7, 125n35
Dial. 94:1–5	118n7
Dial. 94:2–3	125n35
Dial. 110:1	376n3
Dial. 112:1–3	118n7, 125n35
Dial. 138:2	43n4

Cicero

Paradoxa Stoicorum 33	293n37

Epictet

diss. 1:28,20	256n16
diss. 2:1,22	293n37
diss. 2:17,29	82n130
diss. 4:1,3	299n60
diss. 4:1,51	256n16
diss. 4:8,35–40	222

Melito

Passover 68	384

Plutarch

Cato Minor 67.2	293n37
Is Os 13	223
Is Os 65–66	223
Is Os 69–70	223
Fragment 104	222

Odes of Solomon

11:6,7	272n63, 345n67
30	277

INDEX OF CONTEMPORARY NAMES

Attridge, H. W.   68n78, 260n25
Aune, D.   169n53, 272n63, 274, 281n81, 316n124, 330n1.8

Barrett, Ch. K.   1, 177n87
Becker, J.   1, 2, 10, 44, 61, 99n183, 103, 164, 176n86, 179n91.92, 180, 203, 205, 209, 226, 231, 232n112, 235–237, 248, 263n36, 288, 292n32.33, 306n88, 310n100, 312, 323
Behm, J.   303n73, 304n76.78
Berger, K.   27, 117, 258n19, 262, 355
Beutler, J.   185n109
Blank, J.   21n59, 129, 180, 207, 209, 323
Blatz, B.   342
Böcher, O.   168, 173n70
Borgen, P.   25n67, 151, 152n4
Boring, M. E.   333n24
Bornkamm, G.   274, 275
Braun, H.   222, 225n96
Brown, R. E.   7, 17n45, 95n166, 103n194, 106n204, 142n85, 187n119, 195n157, 196, 197, 207n17, 253n8.9, 260, 263, 313
Büchsel, F.   85, 90n150
Bultmann, R.   1, 4, 5, 7, 9, 10, 16n43, 17, 39, 43, 44, 47, 48n18, 79, 97n173, 99n183, 118n7, 135n64, 142, 155, 163, 173, 187n118, 207, 208, 209, 211n43, 220, 226n98.99, 231n107, 232, 233, 238, 256n17, 264, 265, 288n18.20, 289n23, 292, 293, 309, 316, 322, 328n3, 341
Burchard, C.   159, 160
Burkert, W.   58, 59n65, 223, 224n95

Cameron, R.   244, 390n9
Catchpole, D. R.   70n91
Claudel, G.   89, 90, 98, 99
Conzelmann, H.   169, 170, 175, 190
Crossan, J. D.   68, 85
Cullmann, O.   86
Culpepper, A.   8

Dahl, N.   25, 156, 389
Delff, H.   3
Dettwiler, A.   231, 310, 315, 316, 318, 333, 370, 389
Dibelius, M.   5, 7, 8, 26, 238, 239
Dietzfelbinger C.   76, 77, 80n126, 82, 151n2, 157n117, 180, 181n97, 183, 184, 185, 204, 219n72, 226n99, 230, 231, 232n131, 235, 267, 301, 304, 310n101, 403, 404
Dodd, Ch. H.   5, 6, 7, 25, 35, 37, 39, 41, 68, 89, 103, 108, 134, 136, 137, 198, 203, 204, 207, 211, 212, 213, 219, 221, 222, 244, 283, 285, 289, 290, 293, 319, 356, 357, 374

Edwards, R. A.   120
Ensor, P. W.   207, 210, 214

Fieger, M.   347
Fischer, K. M.   315, 318
Fitzmyer, J. A.   69n81
Frey, J.   8, 17, 82n131, 83n132, 124, 125, 126, 204, 262, 315

Gaechter, P.   207, 212, 213
Gardner-Smith, P.   5
Gärtner, B. E.   170n59
Gemünden, P. v.   220n78.81, 222n85, 225n96, 232n112, 236n121.128, 237n131
Giebel, M.   222n89, 223
Gnilka, J.   47, 52, 97, 259
Goldsmith, D.   70
Goodenough, E. R.   169n55.57
Grässer, E.   196n158

Hahn, F.   1, 8, 156n15, 265n44, 280
Hartenstein, J.   342n59.60, 343n61.63
Heckel, T. K.   108
Heil, C.   291n29.30, 318n128
Hoffmann, P.   22, 214, 215, 216n58.70, 291n29.30, 318n128, 336
Hossfeld, F. -L.   167
Hübner, H.   126
Hunter, A. M.   203n2

Jeremias, J.   27–29, 49, 50, 54, 55, 58n59, 213n51, 214n57, 289, 290, 330n2
Jonge, M. de   167, 357n8, 367
Joüon, P.   49, 50, 54

Kaipuram, S.   203, 224n94
Kertelge, K.   161n32

Kirchner, D.   226n97
Klauck, H. -J.   71n94, 85, 160, 176, 222, 247, 332, 333, 334
Klein, H.   160n29, 164n37
Koester, H.   4, 118n5, 248n2, 293n35, 327, 328, 329, 337n43, 341, 342, 343–351
Kollmann, B.   160n28, 279n89
Kundsin, K.   8, 9, 200

Leroy, H.   257, 288, 292n33, 363, 364n28
Lietzmann, H.   275n1
Limbeck, M.   90
Lindars, B.   1, 7, 11n32, 31, 48, 53n42, 61, 117n5, 179n92, 195, 214n56, 259n22, 260n24, 261n29, 289, 290, 303, 307, 339n51
Lohmeyer, E.   122n19, 130n53, 131
Lührmann, D.   161
Luz, U.   13n37, 49n20, 50n28, 86, 91n152.154, 93, 94, 138n73, 142n84, 173, 175n80.81, 214n54, 215, 216

Mack, B. L.   189, 190n137, 194n150
Menken, M. J. J.   267n49, 271n58, 272n61
Merz, A.   106n205
Metzner, R.   89n148, 299n61
Mußner, F.   295n48.49, 389, 401n18

Nagel, T.   33, 34
Niemand, C.   236n124
Noack, B.   9, 10, 13, 17, 29
Norden, E.   199, 200

Obermann, A.   24n65
Odeberg, H.   127n46, 303n72

Index of Contemporary Names

Pesch, R.   72, 86n141.143
Piper, R. A.   110n214

Rengstorf, K.-H.   168n49
Riedweg, C.   59n64
Riesner, R.   212, 213
Robinson, J. M.   31n88, 109, 214n57, 327, 328, 389n2, 390n5, 407
Roloff, J.   196n158, 333n22
Rudolph, K.   343, 355,

Sänger, D.   160n27
Sato, M.   120
Schenke, H.-M.   350n89
Schenke, L.   285, 286n11, 351
Schlatter, A.   24n65
Schlier, H.   293n39.40
Schlosser, J.   331, 337n42, 338
Schnackenburg, R.   16, 18, 29n82, 46, 83n132, 84, 94, 105, 113, 125n33, 134, 135, 141, 159n23, 160, 184n104, 187n119, 209, 210, 226n100, 231n106, 237, 238, 263, 264, 298n55.58, 309, 313n112, 314n115, 321, 333, 337, 376, 386n24, 388n27
Schneemelcher, W.   343, 408, 412
Schneider, G.   216n70, 337, 338
Schnelle, U.   83n132, 124n28, 164, 226n98.99, 234n115, 310n99.100
Schoenborn, U.   374n52
Schulz, S.   315n117, 316
Schürmann, H.   69, 70, 71, 289n20, 330
Schüssler Fiorenza, E.   280
Schweizer, A.   3

Schweizer, E.   46, 48, 54n52, 55, 132n56.57, 200n168, 338
Sellin, G.   194n152
Söding, T.   58
Standaert, B.   136n67
Stegemann, E. W.   212n45

Thatcher, T.   363
Theissen, G.   106n205

Untergaßmair, F. G.   134

Vermes, G.   89n147
Vögtle, A.   118, 119n9, 122
Vollenweider, S.   293, 294, 295, 298

Walker, W. M.   136n66
Walter, N.   316, 322n137, 403n24
Weder, H.   397n13
Weidemann, H.-U.   94n165, 96
Weiss, B.   3, 4n7
Weiss, H. F.   189
Weiße, C. H.   3
Wellhausen, J.   3, 44
Wendt, H. H.   3
Wengst, K.   177n87, 271n57, 284n4, 285n10
Westermann, C.   120n11.13
Wiefel, W.   93n160
Wilckens, U.   83, 124n28, 136, 137, 239

Zehnder, M. P.   187n117, 188
Zenger, E.   167
Zerwick, M.   95n166
Zumstein, J.   205n7, 340n55, 389, 398, 401, 402

INDEX OF SUBJECTS

Anthropology 350, 386–387

Baptism 43–46, 55, 56, 58–59, 62n69, 63, 66, 91, 94, 96, 111, 115, 147, 160n29, 231, 334, 336, 350

Christology 3, 29, 31, 62–63, 110, 128, 144–145, 127, 169, 174, 198–201, 282, 286, 319, 325, 334–336, 350, 358, 367, 374–375, 379, 380–388, 400n17, 404
- Descent-ascension 116–117, 146, 219, 378–379, 404n27
- Jesus's death 225, 319, 323, 352, 380, 383, 398
- Messiah 167–168, 169n53, 175n81, 198, 237, 250n6, 261n31, 266, 285–286, 298, 299n59, 372, 376, 405
- Preexistence 62–63, 128, 146n95, 162, 208–209, 217, 281, 286, 367, 378–379
- Son of God 40, 205–206, 210, 212, 215–218, 289–290, 299, 300, 336–339, 367, 381–383
- Son of Man 40, 116, 123, 127–128, 130, 143, 146, 168, 205–206, 214–215, 259, 309, 376–380, 383
- Way-Christology 128, 145, 319
- Wisdom-Christology 169, 189, 258, 260, 281–282, 334–336, 340, 347, 349, 375–380, 404

Death 307, 322, 325, 385, 387, 388

Eschatology 384–388
- apocalyptic 215, 279, 313, 316–317, 318, 321, 373, 374, 384, 386

Eucharist 120, 146, 147, 151, 155, 156, 160, 237–241, 274–277, 279–280, 334, 339

Exorcism 110, 287

Incarnation 4, 194, 263, 350, 378–379

Jews 359–365, 403
"Jews Christian" 283–285, 297n53, 366–367, 381

Kingdom of God 25, 39–44, 47–50, 52–53, 55, 52–60, 63, 70, 86–87, 92–93, 109–110, 136–137, 142, 145–146, 175, 245, 305–307, 317, 331, 373, 404

Life (eternal) 347, 380–381, 384–387
Lord's supper *see*: Eucharist
Logos 83, 167, 169, 171–172, 191–193, 197, 209, 297, 402

Love 129, 209–211, 241–243, 339, 348, 388

Monotheism 163, 198, 213, 217, 308, 367, 381, 382

Paraclete 149, 265n43, 272, 332n20, 333, 371, 352, 383, 389, 396–399, 401–403, 405

Remembrance 371, 374, 379, 389–396, 397, 399–401

Resurrection 23, 43n5, 121, 122, 143, 198, 206n14, 219, 222, 224, 285, 286n11, 306n89.90, 309, 318, 319n132, 322, 323n145, 356, 372, 379, 386, 387, 391

Rebirth 43, 44, 46, 54–56, 58–59, 60, 95, 111, 334

Redaction of the Gospel 5, 44, 143, 146, 227, 387, 395, 402

Salvation 96, 129–130, 135, 153, 172, 196, 200, 225, 280, 298, 306, 316–320, 325, 338, 341, 380, 386, 387

Sonship
 of God 58, 298
 of Abraham 296, 298–299

Soul 170–171, 192–193, 194n149, 294, 306n90, 322, 387